Children and Adol

Children and Adol

Children and Adolescents
a developmental perspective

John W. Santrock
University of Texas/Dallas

Steven R. Yussen
University of Wisconsin/Madison

ωcb

Wm. C. Brown Publishers
Dubuque, Iowa

Book Team

T. Greg Bell
Editor

Susan J. Soley
Associate Developmental Editor

Sandra E. Schmidt
Assistant Developmental Editor

Catherine Dinsmore
Designer

David A. Welsh
Production Editor

Shirley M. Charley
Visual Research Editor

Vicki Krug
Permissions Editor

wcb group

Wm. C. Brown
Chairman of the Board

Mark C. Falb
President and Chief Executive Officer

wcb
Wm. C. Brown Publishers, College Division

Lawrence E. Cremer
President

James L. Romig
Vice-President, Product Development

David Wm. Smith
Vice-President, Marketing

David A. Corona
Vice-President, Production and Design

E. F. Jogerst
Vice-President, Cost Analyst

Marcia H. Stout
Marketing Manager

Linda M. Galarowicz
Director of Marketing Research

Marilyn A. Phelps,
Manager of Design

William A. Moss
Production Editorial Manager

Mary M. Heller
Visual Research Manager

Copyright © 1984 by Wm. C. Brown Publishers. All rights reserved

Library of Congress Catalog Card Number: 83–071928

ISBN: 0–697–00081–8

2–00081–01

Printed in the United States of America

With special appreciation to our wives Mary Jo and Suzann, and to our children Jennifer and Tracy, and David and Elayna.

Brief Contents

Contents

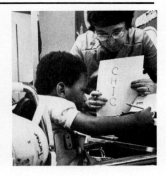

Preface

C*hildren and Adolescents* is designed as an introduction to child development. It tells the story of human development from conception through adolescence. The marvel of how we develop, of how we become who we are, is written and presented in a manner that you will find both informative and enjoyable. In particular, you will discover that there is a strong concern for applying our knowledge about childhood and adolescence to the real lives of children and adolescents.

To the Instructor

Child development is taught in one of two basic ways—either chronologically, the approach adopted in this book, or topically. We have already written a topical approach to child development called *Child Development*. Why write another book on the same subject, this time from a chronological perspective? Because we have received a number of requests from instructors who like *Child Development,* but who nonetheless teach child development from a chronological perspective. Also, the second edition of *Child Development* is much less applied and more research-oriented than the first edition. Still, a number of instructors prefer a more applied orientation.

We believe it is important to keep a sound research base in presenting information about children and adolescents to students. You will find, however, that when research is described in *Children and Adolescents* it is presented in a lively and interesting fashion. Further you will see that many of the research projects described are discussed in terms of their application to children's education, family life, and problems. Thus we believe you will find that this book presents a healthy balance between applied and research concerns.

Yet another decision to be made by an instructor teaching a class in child development is whether to select a book with a heavy emphasis on infancy and early childhood or a book that provides a more balanced coverage of infancy, early childhood, middle and late childhood, and adolescence. We believe that many child development texts have given too little attention to development during middle and late childhood and adolescence. Many students in your classes will never take a separate course in adolescence. For this reason, we present a balanced treatment of the infant, preschool, elementary school, and adolescent years in *Children and Adolescents*.

However, please notice that while middle and late childhood and adolescence have appropriately been given more attention here than in other child development texts, we have not sacrificed material about infancy and early childhood. To the contrary, we think you will find some of the discussions of infancy and early childhood more up-to-date, interesting, and comprehensive than those in other child development books.

For example, consider the topic of physical development in early childhood. In many child development texts this topic is given chapter treatment, but carefully note how short, bland, and somewhat superficial the discussion is. To remedy this problem, we have carefully selected a wealth of sound material for inclusion in our discussion of physical development in early childhood. For instance, you will read about the effects of nutrition not only on physical development but on cognitive development as well. And you will also find a thorough discussion of motor development, including an overview of training programs that promote physical development.

In addition you will find that *Children and Adolescents* is written at an easier reading level than *Child Development,* 2nd Edition. Each of the five sections of this book opens with a **Profile,** an easy-to-read description of the lives of infants, children, and adolescents. Each chapter opens with an **Imagine** section, such as "Imagine . . . what you were like as a newborn and what you were capable of doing" and "Imagine . . . what happens when parental and peer pressures are at odds." You will also find that *Children and Adolescents* contains more pedagogical aids than any other child development text (see Textual Learning Aids, page xxiii).

Our intention in writing *Children and Adolescents* was to provide an interesting, easy-to-read, informative, chronological book that contains a balanced treatment of infants, children, and adolescents and includes frequent applications to education, families, and problems. To this end, we hope you will find this book not only to be different from other chronological books but helpfully so.

Audience
This book is appropriate for students enrolled in an introductory course in child development. Depending upon the college or university, the course is likely to be titled child development, child psychology, or developmental psychology. The course is usually taught in the psychology, education, home economics, or human development department. The typical student in such a course is likely to be a sophomore, junior, or senior undergraduate who has had a general introduction to psychology. However, *Children and Adolescents* requires no previous knowledge of psychology and is written at a level that permits students to build a conceptual framework of the field from the ground up.

Instructor's Manual
Michael Walraven has prepared an instructor's manual for use with *Children and Adolescents* that will save you time in preparing for this course. Included in the manual for each chapter is an overview, a list of learning objectives, suggested lecture outlines and classroom activities, questions for review and discussion, multiple-choice questions (with answers provided), and essay questions, as well as an essay on how to use task groups in the classroom and a list of audiovisual aids.

To the Student
Children and Adolescents contains sixteen chapters, which in turn are organized into five sections, plus an epilogue.

Section 1: Introduction
In Section 1 you will be asked to think about your infant, preschool, elementary school, and adolescent years and what they were like. In chapter 1 you are asked to imagine what the main contemporary problems of children are. Then the historical background of how children have been studied and treated is charted for you. We ask and attempt to answer the question "What is development?" You will learn about the different methods and strategies we use to find information about children. Applications include information on how role-taking opportunities may be effective in reducing delinquency and an evaluation of the effects of the television show "Sesame Street" on children.

Chapter 2 emphasizes the major theories and perspectives of development—psychoanalytic, cognitive-developmental, social learning, humanistic, ethological, evolutionary, anthropological, and sociological. Applications focus on a behavior modification program and Parent Effectiveness Training.

Section 2: Foundations of Development in Infancy

Section 2 outlines the foundations of development and infancy. Chapters 3 through 6 emphasize biological, cognitive, and social, emotional, and personality themes of development. To open the section you will meet Steven and Cynthia Parke and follow them from the time Cynthia discovers she is pregnant, through the birth of their son Mark, and continuing on until the time Mark is two years old.

To begin chapter 3 you are asked to imagine what you were like as a newborn, particularly what you were capable of doing. There is continuing interest in understanding the foundations and origins of development. You will discover that we are making progress in unraveling some of the mystery that has existed between conception and birth, particularly in determining the point in prenatal development at which harmful agents, such as drugs, are likely to do their greatest damage. Stunning color photographs take you inside the mother's womb to see the world of the fetus. The interaction of heredity and environment is described as an important theme of human development. Applications focus on genetic counseling and test-tube babies.

In chapter 4 you are stimulated to think about whether we can teach math and foreign languages to infants and, just as importantly, whether we should. We explore what is known about the sensory and perceptual world of infants, their cognitive development, and how they learn. Applications emphasize how we measure the infant's intelligence and how classical conditioning can be used in toilet training.

At the beginning of chapter 5 you are asked to imagine that you are an infant looking at a picture book and you have just uttered your first word. You will learn that language is a remarkable phenomenon and that in the last twenty-five years we have changed the way we view the nature of language development. Applications evaluate strategies that adults use in verbal exchanges with children and whether the cries of babies are distinctive.

At the beginning of chapter 6 you are asked to imagine that you are faced with choosing a day-care center for your one-year-old infant. As we evaluate the role of early experience in development, you will discover how infants socialize their parents just as their parents socialize them, and how important it is for parents to develop a synchronous relationship with their infants. You also will learn how attachment, independence, and the development of the self are important themes of infant personality development. Applications stress how mothers deal with "easy" and "difficult" infants, the family systems approach to therapy, and personality disturbances in infancy.

Section 3: Early Childhood

Section 3 emphasizes development in early childhood and consists of three chapters—Physical Development, Cognitive Development, and Social, Emotional, and Personality Development. To begin the section, you will look at the life of Mark Parke as he grows from the age of two to the age of six. You also will meet Stacy Henson, who lives next door to Mark, to find out what her life in early childhood is like.

As you begin chapter 7 you are asked to imagine what it would be like to live in an impoverished area of the Philippines. Then you are told about the effects of nutrition on physical and cognitive development and about motor development, including training programs that promote physical development. Applications focus on scribbling and drawing—the art of early childhood—and the play spaces of young children.

In chapter 8 you are asked to imagine what you are likely to see if you visit a Montessori preschool. Piaget's theory of how the child's mind works in early childhood is portrayed, but attention also is given to another important perspective on young children's cognition—information processing theory. In addition you will find out how intelligence is defined and explore hereditary-environmental influences on intelligence. Changes in language, including prereading skills and writing, are also included. Our overview of early childhood education includes detailed information about Project Head Start and Project Follow Through. Applications include foster grandparents and institutionalized young children and "Sesame Street"—Education Through Television.

In chapter 9 you will be asked to imagine what it would be like to be an abused child. Information on how changes in family structure, particularly divorce and working mothers, influence young children is presented. The pervasive role of television in children's lives is examined. Parenting techniques, play, and changes in the self, sex roles, and moral development are highlighted. Applications deal with how preschool teachers can help reduce aggression among peers and how easy and how ethical it is to change the sex-typed behavior of children.

Section 4: Middle and Late Childhood

Section 4 focuses on development in middle and late childhood—the elementary school years. To begin the section we visit with Mark Parke and Stacy Henson again to see how they develop through the elementary school years. You will also meet two other children who live in their neighborhood—Chip Martin and Don Mitchell—to see what their lives are like between the ages of six and eleven.

Chapter 10 focuses on physical development and intelligence. To begin the chapter you are asked to imagine that you are a black parent and that your child is being placed in classes for mentally retarded children. The continuing slowdown in physical development is outlined. Major emphasis is given to handicapped children and their education, including information about learning disabled and hyperactive children. Different views on the concept of intelligence are presented, and you will gain an understanding of gifted and mentally retarded children. Applications focus on educational interventions for handicapped children, modifying impulsive learning, and the clinical use of the WISC intelligence test.

Chapter 11 emphasizes children's cognitive development. At the beginning of the chapter you will be stimulated to think about ways in which elementary school children can improve their memory. Piaget's ideas about cognitive development are presented but are discussed alongside recent developments in the field of information processing. You will read how memory and problem-solving skills develop during the middle and late childhood years. Applications focus on the use of Piaget's theory in elementary school education and learning mathematics the fun way.

Chapter 12 emphasizes social development in children. As you begin the chapter you are asked to imagine what it would be like to visit China and observe children there at home and at school. Information about families includes further ideas about the changing nature of families that children are now being exposed to, as well as the role of siblings. Substantial discussion of peers includes ideas about peer tutoring, peer sociotherapy, popularity, children's groups compared to adolescents' groups, and cultural variations in groups. Discussion of schools includes the nature of children's schooling and the organization of schools. Schools and social class and schools and ethnicity are given appropriate attention. Applications include a peer-oriented clinic for children with problems and sex roles in the school hierarchy.

Chapter 13 emphasizes emotional and personality development. At the beginning of the chapter you are motivated to think about what should go into a curriculum of moral education. How children think about themselves and others, self-esteem, sex role development, including sex differences and stereotypes, achievement, and moral development are the timely topics discussed, and information about the problems and disturbances of elementary school children is described. Applications focus on the recent change in Kohlberg's thinking about moral education and how to help children cope with anxiety.

Section 5: Adolescence

Section 5 portrays development in adolescence. We reenter the lives of Mark Parke, Stacy Henson, Chip Martin, and Don Mitchell to see how they are making the transition from childhood to adulthood.

Chapter 14 provides an overview of the historical background of adolescence and information about physical and cognitive development. The fascinating but controversial ideas of G. Stanley Hall are outlined, and adolescents at different points in history are described. Our discussion of physical development emphasizes various aspects of the pubertal process—changes in height and weight and sexual maturation, including contemporary sexual attitudes and behavior and the body images of early- and late-maturing adolescents. Cognitive development includes ideas about formal operational thought and individual variation in adolescent cognition, as well as how adolescents reason about social circumstances. Applications emphasize sex education in the schools and how Piaget's ideas have been applied to secondary education.

Chapter 15 focuses on social development in adolescence. At the beginning of the chapter you are motivated to think about what happens when parental and peer pressures are at odds during the junior high school years. Ideas about the family stress adolescent independence, the effects of divorce on adolescents, and what adolescents are like as parents themselves. Substantial information about peers and group behavior is provided, including friendship, cliques, and dating. Cross-cultural comparisons of adolescents include fascinating information about sexual practices and rites of passage. Our discussion of schools emphasizes the nature of secondary education, patterns of social interaction in schools, and positive characteristics of competent teachers. The description of work experiences in adolescence highlights both positive and negative aspects. Applications include suggestions as to how parents can cope more effectively with adolescents and teaching strategies with low- and high-ability students.

Chapter 16 outlines emotional and personality development in adolescence. The chapter begins by asking you to think about what the youths of Adolf Hitler, Martin Luther, and Mahatma Gandhi might have been like. Substantial attention is given to Erik Erikson's ideas about identity development, although the bulk of the chapter emphasizes a variety of problems and disturbances in adolescence—drugs, alcohol, juvenile delinquency, school-related problems, suicide, eating disorders, and schizophrenia. Applications focus on school policy and drug use, intervention programs designed to help delinquents, and the life of a sixteen-year-old anorexic girl.

Epilogue: The Transition from Adolescence to Adulthood

Our epilogue suggests that development does not end with adolescence. You will be stimulated to think about what the criteria for adulthood are, be reminded that there is constancy as well as change in our development, and note that there is substantial individual variation in our development.

Textual Learning Aids

Extensive learning aids are included in *Children and Adolescents*. Each section begins with a **Profile,** an easy-to-read description of the lives of infants, children, and adolescents that includes many important developmental themes. Then **In This Section You Will Learn About** alerts you to major topics to be discussed in the section. Each section ends with a discussion which I think you will find is very special. It is called "Know Yourself." You will be asked to think about your own childhood, be stimulated to talk with your parents about what you were like as a child, be motivated to ask your friends about their childhood years, and be encouraged to think about what you will be like as the parent of an infant, child, and adolescent. Each chapter begins with a topic outline followed by a section called **Imagine,** a stimulating set piece designed to get the student to think about his or her own development as a child and to encourage and motivate the student to read further into the chapter. Terms with special meanings are set in boldface type in the text, then listed as **key terms** at the end of each chapter, and subsequently defined in the Glossary. **Applications,** which deal with the education, family life, and problems of children, are set off in boxes that appear in each chapter. Photographs, illustrations, and cartoons give visual emphasis to important ideas and help to make learning about child and adolescent development enjoyable as well as informative. Each chapter ends with a summary, review questions, and an annotated reading list. Both subject and author indexes are provided at the end of the book.

Student Study Guide

A student study guide is available for use with *Children and Adolescents.* For each chapter in the text, the study guide includes a chapter preview, a list of learning objectives, a programmed review, a multiple-choice self-test, and a list of learning activities. Also included is an essay entitled "How to Be a Better Student."

Acknowledgments

Our very special thanks go to James Romig, Vice-President of Product Development at William C. Brown, for making this book possible. He has continued to share our enthusiasm for psychology, writing, and sports. We are indebted to him for removing any obstacles in publishing this book in the time frame requested. We also owe special thanks to Richard Owen, who served as an editorial consultant and to Susan Soley, Associate Developmental Editor and Sandy Schmidt, Assistant Developmental Editor. David Welsh, Senior Production Editor, has done a flawless job in making my words make more sense and in assisting in the production of the text. Catherine Dinsmore, the designer, has made Children and Adolescents, a book that is simply beautiful to look at. Shirley Charley deserves credit for her thorough visual research contributions. Vicki Krug also deserves credit for her expedient work in obtaining permissions.

We benefited considerably from the reviews of the text. The following individuals provided valuable feedback: David S. Berg, Community College of Philadelphia; Victor A. Christopherson, University of Arizona; Mark Grabe, University of North Dakota; Trinidad B. Litman, Northern Virginia Community College; Sherrill Richarz, Washington State University; and Diane Pollard, University of Wisconsin-Milwaukee.

With more than one thousand typed pages in the original manuscript, typing was not an easy task. Thanks go to Laurie Bura and Marsha Becker for sharing this task cheerfully.

Michael Walraven deserves our gratitude as well. You will find that he has prepared an instructor's manual and student study guide that will greatly enhance the use of this text.

Finally, thanks go to our families—Mary Jo, Tracy, and Jennifer Santrock, and Suzann, David, and Elayna Yussen, who continue their support and enthusiam.

John W. Santrock
Steven R. Yussen

Children and Adolescents

In This Section You Will Learn About

History, Description, and Methods

Contemporary aspects of child development

The child in historical perspective, including how children have been treated at different times in history

What development is, including the importance of maturation and experience

The methods we use to collect information about children and adolescents

The strategies we follow to determine how aspects of the child's development are determined by or related to certain phenomena

How role-taking opportunities may be effective in reducing delinquency

The time span of our inquiry about children

The effects of the television show "Sesame Street" on children

The ethical concerns of researchers who study children

Theories and Perspectives

The childhood of famous theorists

Why we need theories of childhood and adolescence

The psychoanalytic perspective of Sigmund Freud and Erik Erikson

The cognitive structural perspective of Jean Piaget

The behavioral view of B. F. Skinner, including behavioral contracts for children with problems

The application of a behavior modification program

The cognitive social learning theory

The humanistic perspective, including information about Parent Effectiveness Training

The ethological, evolutionary perspective

The anthropological, sociological perspective, including information about Margaret Mead's perception of the American culture

The importance of adopting an eclectic theoretical approach to the study of children and adolescents

Profile

It has been a long time since you were an infant . . . a preschooler . . . an elementary school child. However, for many of you it hasn't been very long since you were an adolescent. What were your infant, preschool, elementary school, and adolescent years like? How much of them can you remember?

Let's start off with your infant years, the first few years of your life. You probably won't be able to remember what went on in those years, yet you will see as you read this book that the first two years of life serve a very important foundation for child development. Even though you probably can't remember anything about your own infant years, it is likely that you have seen one or more babies in the last few years. What did they look like? How big were they? What could they do? That is, could they walk, talk, smile, frown, think? If you have not observed any infants, we encourage you to try to do so as soon as possible. The time you spend with a baby or two will help you a great deal in understanding our description and explanation of development during the early years of life. Indeed you will find that the best way to learn about infants or children of any age is to spend time observing and interacting with them. Try to think ahead; about a week before you are to start a section in this book—such as early childhood—try to find a child or two in that age range and spend some time with them.

What about your early childhood or preschool years? What were they like? If you are like the authors, you can remember a little bit about those early years. If you can find some old photographs of your early childhood years—say, when you were between two and six—get them out and study them. What were you like then and what was your life like? Were you a bundle of energy or were you more passive? Did you like to engage in masculine activities, feminine activities, or a little bit of both? What was your relationship with your parents like? Did you get in trouble with them a lot? How did they discipline you? Did you go to a preschool? If so, what was it like? Did your mother work, or was your father the single breadwinner? How much time did you spend in play? And what kinds of things did you like to play?

Let's go on to your elementary school years—what we call middle and late childhood in this book—approximately the years six to eleven. One of the first things likely to come into your mind will be related to school. Your teacher in the first grade—what was he or she like? Think about the building you went to school in. Was it big, small? Old, new? Was school fun then, or was it a pain? Did you have lots of friends? One best friend? Were the things you did after school the same as those you did in early childhood, or were they different? How did your parents treat you? Did they allow you more freedom toward the end of elementary school, or did they clamp down hard on you? How achievement oriented were you? Did you work hard in school and spend several hours a night doing homework, or did you spend more time fooling around and having a good time?

Chances are you can remember a good deal about the beginning of your adolescence, the time when your body began changing and you were not sure what was happening. To be sure you were excited about the changes that were taking place, but there were probably times when your image of yourself was a little shaky. Probably during your adolescent years you began to spend more time thinking about girls if you were a boy and about boys if you were a girl. Think about all of the times you spent with your peers. Think about conflicts with your parents. Were you pushing for independence, and were they putting some constraints on you that you didn't like? How about your first date? What was the other person like? Did you go steady? At some point during adolescence you probably worked at a job, at least part-time, and you may have begun thinking seriously about a career. Are you pursuing the same career now that you thought about when you were fourteen or fifteen years old? How are you different now from when you were in junior high school? In high school? Did you begin to think a lot about what you were like as a person and what other people were like

in adolescence? Did you and do you still alternate between feelings of being all powerful and feelings of insecurity? Do you make more mature decisions now than when you were in junior high and high school?

You have been the children and adolescents in this Profile. You are but one of the many individuals you will be introduced to at the beginning of each of the sections of this book. In some ways you are like all the people you will meet in the Profile sections, and yet in other ways you are different from every other person. Keep this point in mind—we share certain communalities with all other people, and yet we are different from all other people. For example, you and all other people were born with a genetic code inherited from two parents, each of us has a brain, parents and peers are important to all of us, and experiences during our childhood years help to shape the kind of people we become. But the particular genetic code, the particular brain, the nature of our relationships with our parents and peers, and the specific experiences we have as children often differ from one individual to the next. One of the goals of this book is to point to the common themes and individual variation in infancy, childhood, and adolescence and to help you understand more about your own childhood years as well as the development of other children.

1 History, Description, and Methods

Imagine . . . that you are faced with deciding on the main contemporary problems children encounter

What are the problems? Why even study child development? Perhaps you are a parent or teacher and face children each day. The more you learn about them, the better you can deal with them. Perhaps you are preparing for some other career in which you will serve future generations of children. Or you hope to gain some insight into your own recent history—the nature of your own childhood and how it shaped your adult makeup. Maybe you just stumbled into this course as we (your authors) did, some years ago, thinking that it sounded intriguing and that the topic of development just had to raise some provocative issues about the nature of our common human experiences. Whatever your reasons, you will surely find that children's growth and development *is* a provocative field of inquiry. This was the case fifteen years ago, as we started off in the field, and it is still true today.

Everywhere a person turns in contemporary society, children and their well-being capture public attention, the interest of scientists, and the concerns of policymakers. Consider some of the social topics you read about in newspapers and magazines every day: genetic research, child abuse, homosexuality, mental retardation, parenting, and children's intellectual capabilities. What the experts are discovering in each of these areas has direct and significant consequences for our understanding of children and our societal decisions about how they are to be treated.

Genetic researchers are discovering new techniques to diagnose potential problems in the unborn child, both prior to and after conception. They are learning how to predict genetically determined disturbances in development, various forms of deformities and retardation, and the likely sex of the future child. In addition, some remarkable breakthroughs have occurred in the ability to produce conception in the laboratory and to sustain growth of the unborn fetus outside of its natural mother. All of these techniques and capabilities are having profound consequences on genetic counseling for parents, arguments about when "life really begins," debates about the legal right of women to have abortions, and ethical dilemmas about tampering in the laboratory with the genetic makeup of unborn children.

Child abuse is a problem whose widespread occurrence has just become understood during the past decade. Although there are no sure data on just how many cases of abuse occur each year, we do know something about the profile of the people who abuse children, the emotional consequences for the children being abused, and the short-term remedies for offering help to both the abused and the abusers. Medical professionals and social service practitioners have formed child abuse teams throughout the country to spot cases of child abuse in their early stages and to offer help for the victims. Some progress is being made, but there are difficult hurdles to overcome. Chief among these is the complex historical and legal tradition in our country that places families in the "driver's seat" in any conflict over a child's welfare.

Homosexuals in our society are pressing vigorously for guarantees of economic, political, and social equality under the law. They feel that they have human rights like all other groups and should not be denied any job, office, or social privilege available to others in society. The thornier issues involve the rights of homosexuals to hold public school teaching positions, elective offices, and parent and adoptive parent privileges. Any rational decision about these matters must be formed by an understanding of what it means to be homosexual, how this atypical gender identification came about in the first place, and the childrearing conditions that do and do not influence its occurrence. Unfortunately, many people still cling to beliefs about homosexuality that have been scientifically refuted.

Parents and educators must face the challenging task of helping many mentally retarded children grow and adapt in a world that is beyond their easy comprehension and intellectual pace. How are they to do this most effectively? What experiences and social grouping arrangements will have the best payoff? Should the children be tracked separately in school or "mainstreamed"—that is, joined with their nonretarded age peers in school? The answers are not easy, but they surely depend upon the type of retardation, the knowledge we have acquired about the nature of children's learning and cognitive development, and practical attempts to train retarded children to master a number of intellectual and practical living skills.

This brief survey of contemporary social issues has purposefully been left sketchy. You will hear more about them in later chapters of the book. In the meantime, we hope your appetite has been whetted for the exciting field of study that you've just begun.

Introduction

In this first chapter, we introduce you to the field of child development. It is a lively and exciting enterprise, and we hope to infect you with our enthusiasm for it. We begin by looking at the child in historical perspective, discussing when the concept of childhood emerged, different philosophical views on the nature of the child, and how the child has been treated at different points in history. Then we ask the question "What is development?" In our attempt to answer this complex question, you will read about how maturation and experience interact to influence the child's development. You also will be introduced to the ways in which we will discuss different phases of the child's development—infancy, early childhood, middle and late childhood, and adolescence. Although the child should be viewed as an integrated human being, you will find out how it is sometimes helpful to study different strands or aspects of development—physical, cognitive, social, emotional, and personality, for example. Then you will focus on the study of child psychology as a scientific enterprise, looking at different scientific methods and developmental comparisons. Finally, you will learn about the ethical standards we abide by in our study of children.

A number of phrases have been used by different experts to describe the subject matter of this book. These include child psychology, child development, human development, life-span development, and developmental psychology. Do not be confused by these terms or by our somewhat arbitrary decision to title the book *Children and Adolescents*. All of these phrases refer to substantially the same area of interest but with slightly different focuses. All are concerned with growth and development and with the forces that shape change. However, the terms children and adolescents suggest a preoccupation with the period prior to adulthood, whereas *life span* suggests an interest in change from birth to death. The term *human* suggests a restriction to evidence about people, whereas *developmental* widens the domain of inquiry to include evidence about growth in lower animals and social systems. Finally, the term *psychology* implies a focus upon understanding change from the perspective of this single social science, whereas *development* implies that other social and natural science perspectives will be brought to bear on the inquiry. In our own treatment, we do not worry excessively about these distinctions, but they are useful to keep in mind. The fact that the book is entitled *Children and Adolescents* appropriately conveys a message that a very broad perspective will be used to help you better understand children and further that our discussion will not be confined only to infants and children but will include adolescents as well.

The Child in Historical Perspective

Our conception of childhood has changed dramatically in modern times from what it was in the not too distant past or in medieval and ancient societies. This historical change can be traced along several distinct lines. First is the concept of childhood itself. What is it? How long does it last? And what is its purpose? Next is the treatment of children in contrast to other members of society—their role in the family and the protections and rights offered them under law. Finally, for our coverage here, is how did knowledge about childhood come into being? Why did adults study childhood, and what were their conclusions? We will consider each of these in turn.

Concept of Childhood

Philip Aries' book *Centuries of Childhood* (1962) has become a classic source on the concept of childhood. He makes clear that our present concept is a very recent one. We have only to look at representative samples of art across the ages to convince ourselves of this. Notice the way the children are pictured in the photo on the facing page. They are dressed much like adults; they are in the company of adults; they are engaged in adultlike activities. It is hard to escape the impression that they *are* miniature adults. We have to go back very far—virtually to infancy—before seeing any signs of demarcation between young people and adults. It is not much of a simplification to state that writings about children—whether they were theological, pedagogical, or philosophical—also show this impoverished view of development; there were basically two stages—*infancy* (lasting from birth to anywhere from three to six years) and *adulthood* (beyond infancy). We might generously add a third period—*preadulthood,* a time in which children (as we call them today) learned the ways of the world of grown-ups and acquired the skills for a livelihood. For women, puberty, and the subsequent ability to bear children, probably marked the end of preadulthood. Absent from most of history is a clear vision of childhood that admits the presence of many distinct stages with attendant differences in physical skills, intellectual capabilities, and personality characteristics. Instead, life periods were defined according to whether work and the business of life could be handled (adulthood) or not (infancy or preadulthood). According to this viewpoint, the years from infancy to adulthood served simply to ready the person for work, reproduction, and adult responsibilities. Absent was any consistent theme that childhood was a special period, with unique needs and purposes, unique opportunities for such things as fantasy and play, and unique contributions to make to the life cycle.

In the past, children were viewed as miniature adults.

Children's Treatment by Society

Despite recent complaints from both political liberals (Bronfenbrenner, 1980) and conservatives (Laxalt, 1980) that government frequently ignores comprehensive programming for families and children, the fate of children today is a picnic in comparison to that of children of earlier times.

Consider that prior to the nineteenth century many infants were often sent away to be cared for by wet nurses or placed in public institutions until they were old enough to make an economic contribution to the family. These substitute care arrangements were so bad that many children were never seen again by their families, often dying of neglect and malnutrition. If we move further back in time to early medieval or ancient times, outright killing of infants—infanticide—was a common practice. Few societies had clearly stated and enforceable laws that protected children against this practice. Consider, for example, the practices of the Spartans in ancient times as documented in the passage taken from Plutarch's *The Lives of the Noble Grecians and Romans*.

Nor was it in the power of the father to dispose of the child as he thought fit; he was obliged to carry it before certain triers at a place called Lesche; these were some of the elders of the tribe to which the child belonged; their business it was carefully to view the infant, and, if they found it stout and well made, they gave order for its rearing, and allotted to it one of the nine thousand shares of land above mentioned for its maintenance, but if they found it puny and ill shaped, ordered it to be taken to what was called the Apothetae, a sort of chasm under Taygetus; as thinking it neither for the good of the child itself, nor for the public interest, that it should be brought up, if it did not, from the very outset, appear made to be healthy and vigorous. (1932, pp. 49–73)

What of the treatment of the child who managed to survive the period of infancy? The picture does not improve. Behavioral scientists and child advocates have sensitized us in recent years to the problem of *child abuse*—of parents who physically beat and sexually harass their children and, in rarer instances, actually murder them. There is no strong evidence that abuse is more widespread now than in the past, however; we are simply more aware of the problem. A recent government bulletin offers reliable figures on child abuse.

In 1977 over 512,000 reports of child abuse and neglect were submitted to the American Humane Association from 48 states, the District of Columbia, and 3 territories.
. . . It is generally recognized that the actual incidence of child abuse and neglect is greater than that reported because many incidents go unreported. The United States General Accounting Office estimates that about 1 million children are abused or neglected each year. Of these, 100,000 to 200,000 are physically abused, 60,000 to 100,000 are sexually abused, and the rest are neglected. The Center also estimates that 2,000 children die each year from abuse and neglect. (1980, U.S. Government Accounting Office report HRD–80–66)

In the past, by contrast, abuse was much more rampant, and there were no legal sanctions taken against it as there are today. For example, only since the 1960s have a number of states passed laws that give social workers the right to investigate conditions in the home and judges the right to intervene in the family and remove children from the home when it is for their welfare.

Society has been slow to take measures against the neglect and maltreatment of its children. Universal education was not widely supported and practiced until the nineteenth century. For example, Massachusetts passed the first compulsory elementary school law in the country in 1852. Within the next fifty years, thirty-two states had followed suit. Laws protecting children from excessive hours of work and harmful working conditions were not widespread in the United States until 1938. And not until recently have child-directed forms of social welfare—day care, foster care, and income maintenance for nonworking parents with dependent children, to name just a few—become commonplace.

Acquiring Knowledge about Children

For many years the study of children was dominated by philosophical debates that were difficult to settle or consisted of theological accounts (Senn, 1975; White, 1980). Techniques for examining the actual lives of children or the forces that impinged upon them were not developed. Two classic philosophical debates, for example, concerned the *origin of knowledge* and the child's *moral status*.

Two extreme alternatives about the origin of knowledge were debated by philosophers. According to the position of **innate knowledge,** the child is born with both knowledge about the world and strong propensities to learn. Plato argued that knowledge is innate. He wrote in *The Republic* (Plato, 1968), "But then, if I am right, certain professors of education must be wrong when they say that they can put a knowledge into the soul which was not then there before, like sight into blind eyes. . . . Whereas our argument shows that the power and capacity of learning exists in the soul already" (Book VII). By contrast, seventeenth-century British philosopher John Locke suggested that at birth the child's mind is a blank slate, a **tabula rasa.** All knowledge results from learned experiences.

The second subject for philosophical debate concerned the moral goodness of the child and the need for moral training. This is translated today into a concern for the child's social awareness and the need to teach the child acceptable social skills. Two early perspectives of the child's moral status were (1) the child is inherently bad, or sinful, at birth and must be led along the high road to piety in life; and (2) the child is inherently good at birth, and this good start must be supported and reinforced by society, which must help the child stay clear of its corrupting evils.

The "sinful" view of the child was espoused by the Catholic Church through most of the period in history that has come to be called the Dark Ages, from about the fifth to the fourteenth centuries (Aries, 1962). It has persisted beyond that time as well—in all theological preaching that actively applies the belief of **original sin** to everyday life. It can be seen today in a variety of mainstream Christian religions, the "moral majority" movement, and elsewhere. According to this view, the child's development must be carefully guided, with social instruction provided to correct antisocial tendencies.

Child Development in Contemporary Times

In the past century and a half, our view of children has changed dramatically. We now conceive of childhood as a highly eventful and unique period of life that lays an important foundation for adult years and is highly differentiated from them. In most approaches to childhood, a large number of distinct periods are identified in which special skills are being mastered and new life tasks are being confronted. Childhood is no longer seen as an inconvenient "waiting" period during which adults must suffer the incompetencies of the young. We now value it as a special time for growth and change, and we invest great resources in caring for and educating our children. We protect them from the excesses of the adult work world through tough child labor laws; we treat their crimes against society under a special system of juvenile justice; and we have governmental provisions for helping children when ordinary family support systems fail or when families seriously interfere with the children's well-being.

Most significant is that we now have a science of childhood. Future policies for and decisions about children can be based upon an accumulating body of knowledge of what children are like, based in turn on scientific evidence rather than philosophical speculation.

What is science? What, in particular, is the science of child development? To anticipate the answer briefly, the science of childhood is characterized by a systematic body of theories that can be verified or proved false on the basis of factual evidence collected about children. A highly sophisticated field has evolved in which collecting evidence is based on well-defined rules, exemplary practices, and mathematical concepts about handling the evidence and drawing inferences from it. But before we turn to scientific methods used to study children, let's first look at what we mean by development and an overview of the phases of development.

What Is Development?

You are a fascinating creature. There is no one else in the world quite like you. Your thoughts, feelings, and behaviors are unique. And yet you are a lot like other people your age. In school you have learned many of the same skills that other students have learned, and as a part of society you have learned to care about many of the same things that others care about.

How have you become simultaneously unique and yet similar to others of your generation? What processes and events have contributed to this outcome? These are the questions addressed by child psychology, which attempts to understand the processes and events that contribute to change throughout infancy and childhood and adolescence. Some of that change contributes to your uniqueness, while some of it moves you along common pathways with others. Some of the processes and events recur throughout childhood, making the task of seeing continuity in development easy. Others occur only during isolated periods of time; these help in gaining an understanding of the nature of age-related differences among people.

Maturation and Experience

The central concept of this textbook is **development.** What do we mean when we say that a child has "developed" in some respect? Psychologists use the term to refer to a pattern of forward movement or change that begins at conception and continues through the entire life span. The pattern of movement is complex because it is often the product of several processes—maturation, physical growth, and experiences, for example. However, if we looked at the entire life cycle, we might appropriately define development as a pattern that involves growth (as in infancy) and decay (as in death).

Maturation involves changes dictated by the genetic blueprint we each have. Our brain and central nervous system grow and become differentiated; our anatomy changes; and there are changes in our chemical and hormonal makeup as we move toward maturity. One example of maturation is the gradual specialization of the brain. Each of the hemispheres directs different psychological activities (such as spatial processing in the right hemisphere and language in the left). Prior to adolescence, these functions within the brain are flexible. So for example, an accident to a specific part of the brain during early childhood may temporarily disrupt one of these activities, but other parts of the brain will gradually take over, functioning as backup systems. As we approach adolescence and beyond, however, accidents are more likely to produce permanent damage because the specialized functions acquired have become more rigidly locked in to specific locations in the brain.

Children are interested in comparing their physical growth with each other.

Physical growth refers to the simple changes in a child's size and weight and to the gradual, quantitative changes that can be charted for other physical and anatomical features. Weight gain, overall height changes, growth of head and limbs, and the changing size of the brain, heart, and lungs are all part of this process. Patterns of growth are important; we have learned much about them and can use them as clinical instruments to determine whether a child is healthy and developing normally. For example, the weight of the average newborn baby doubles in a period of six months from birth. If a child deviates substantially from this figure, a pediatrician may want to examine the baby's diet and check for other growth anomalies. Conversely, we can use growth patterns to predict when a child is making normal transitions from period to period. As we will see in chapters 3 and 14, there are two periods of very rapid growth spurts in childhood—the first two years of life and the one- to two-year period that marks the transition into adolescence. A careful record of the child's growth serves as a particularly useful tool to determine when middle childhood has ended and puberty has begun.

Illustration by Bil Keane, from *I Lost Everything in the Post-Natal Depression,* by Erma Bombeck. Copyright © 1970, 1971, 1972, 1973 by Field Enterprises, Inc. Copyright © 1970, 1971, 1972 by the Hearst Corporation. Reprinted by permission of Doubleday & Company, Inc.

Experiences constitute the broadest and, in some sense, vaguest ingredient in the mix of development. Experiences run the gamut from the child's **biological environment**—which includes such things as nutrition, medical care and drugs, and physical accidents—to the **social environment**—family, school, community, peers, and the media. Experiences can be understood in microscopic terms when we look at specific vitamin intake or chart the specific interactions between a mother and child; alternatively, experiences can be reckoned macroscopically when we examine the overall medical care given a family or the mental health dynamics operating in a child's family (e.g., how the members generally get along with one another, the degree of family stress present, and the degree of family adaptation to the larger society). The level at which experiences are defined and studied very much depends upon the theoretical perspective of the expert involved. As we shall see in chapter 4, learning is often defined in very precise, detailed terms. Thus a learning psychologist might choose to examine the specific responses a child has learned—through imitation or reinforcement, for example—in stressful situations at home, to understand how the child handles stress and conflict with peers. By contrast, a sociologist would be more likely to study on a broader scale the social experiences in which a child

is involved by measuring changes in the social composition of the family's neighborhood or socioeconomic status over a period of time to see what impact this has on the child's opportunities and activities.

Whatever approach is taken, experiences are a key to development. Without them, maturation and growth would not occur, and we would have no field of development to be discussing. As an extreme example, consider that children must have some nourishment to grow and that they must have some stimulation of the five senses before being able to function—the absence of human contact has had the dramatic and documented effect of producing children who are mentally retarded and lack a spoken language. Less dramatically, contemporary students of development seek to understand what kinds of experiences shape maturation and growth and the processes by which this interaction among them takes place. For example, what kinds of interactions promote adaptive attachments between young children and their caregivers? What early experiences promote the rapid and advanced acquisition of spoken language? How does experience influence the development of thinking and moral reasoning skills? One type of answer given is that environments rich in stimulation generally produce the most favorable results. If you interact with a baby girl a lot and show her love, you will produce a healthily attached tyke. Talk a lot to the little boy, and he will learn language quickly. Prod the child to think and exercise moral judgment, and he or she will achieve intellectually and develop strong moral character. This type of answer would make life simple, but unfortunately it frequently does not prove to be right. As we probe the mysteries of change, we find that subtlety is necessary. More important than the amount of interaction, we find that timing is central in the development of healthy attachment; the caregiver must respond in synchrony with the infant's needs. More important than the amount of talk directed at the young child is the level at which the talk is structured; short phrases, clear pauses, and clear patterns of intonation are helpful. More important than the opportunities to think and exercise moral judgment is that the child be concerned with them at the appropriate stage of thinking development.

Briefly, the contemporary study of development is concerned with the pattern of movement or change in the child's life. Contemporary psychologists attempt to describe and predict this change and explain how maturation and growth are shaped by the child's experiences. You will see these themes appear repeatedly thoughout the text. The insights gained about them will frequently be surprising.

Phases of Development

In our overview of the history of childhood we have seen that philosophers and psychologists have different opinions of how the phases of development should be viewed. Next we look at how the phases will be presented in this book.

In the contemporary study of development there is by no means agreement on what the phases of development actually are and when they occur. There is also a great deal of disagreement about the nature of the processes that lead to change from one phase to the next. For the purposes of organization and understanding, development can be divided into the following phases: infancy, early childhood, middle and late childhood, and adolescence. Approximate age bands are placed on the periods to provide a general idea of the time in development when a period first appears and when it ends.

Infancy is usually recognized as extending from birth to eighteen or twenty-four months. (For the first few days after birth, an infant is referred to as a **neonate**.) Infancy is a time of extreme dependence upon adults, with many physiological and psychological activities just beginning (language, symbolic thought, sensorimotor coordination, social learning). This period usually ends when the child talks in short phrases and finds it easy to walk great distances from the caretaker.

Early childhood, which extends from the end of infancy to about five or six years, roughly corresponds to the period in which the child prepares for formal schooling. Sometimes this period of development is referred to as the preschool years. Among the tasks mastered are the ability to care for oneself (e.g., personal hygiene, dressing oneself), self-sufficiency (e.g., self-initiated play), and development of school-readiness skills (e.g., following instructions; using writing implements; identifying letters, numbers, and sounds). In addition, peer relations and play become more pronounced. First grade usually marks the end of this period.

Middle and **late childhood** extends from about six to eleven years of age, roughly corresponding to the elementary school years. Sometimes this period of development is called the elementary school years. Such fundamental skills as reading, writing, and arithmetic are mastered, and there is formal exposure to the larger world and its culture through the study of history, civics, business and government, art and music, and contemporary social problems. Thought processes usually are very concrete and less abstract than in the next period.

Adolescence is the period of transition from childhood to early adulthood, entered at approximately ten to thirteen years of age and ending at eighteen to twenty-two years of age. Adolescence begins with the onset of rapid physical change—dramatic gains in height and weight, change in body contour, and development of secondary sex characteristics (enlargement of the breasts, development of pubic hair and facial hair, deepening of the voice). It is a time for readying the development of mind and body for an independent, productive life in the adult world. The development of identity and abstract, logical thought also characterize adolescence. More and more time is spent outside the family during this period. There is an increasing tendency to talk about early and late periods of adolescence. Early adolescence generally corresponds to the junior high school years, roughly between the ages of ten to twelve and fourteen to fifteen. One teacher even referred to early adolescence as the "tweenage" years to reflect her belief that early adolescence is a transition *between* late childhood and late adolescence. Late adolescence, then, refers to the late teens and possibly early twenties, roughly between the ages of sixteen to seventeen and twenty to twenty-two.

Strands of Development

As you read about the different phases of development, you will soon see that the chapters have been organized around different strands of development. The five strands of development that will be emphasized in this book are physical, cognitive, emotional, social, and personality development. As we describe each of the phases of development, we will discuss at length each of these strands of development.

**"PJ drank the dribbles of coffee out of your cup!
Will that stump his growth?"**

The Family Circus. Reprinted courtesy the Register and Tribune
Syndicate, Inc.

Physical development refers to the simple changes in size and weight and the gradual, quantitative changes that can be charted for other physical and anatomical features. Weight gain, overall height changes, growth of head and limbs, and the changing size of the brain, heart, and lungs are all part of this process. Patterns of growth are important; we have learned much about them and can use them as clinical instruments to determine whether a child is healthy and developing normally. For example, the weight of the average newborn baby doubles from birth to six months. If a child deviates substantially from this average, a pediatrician may want to examine the baby's diet and check for other abnormalities in growth. On the other hand, we can use growth patterns to predict when a child is making normal transitions from period to period. As we will see in chapters 3 and 14, there are two periods of very rapid growth spurts—the first two years of life and the one- to two-year period that marks the early portion of adolescence. A careful record of the child's and adolescent's growth serves as a particularly useful tool to determine when late childhood has ended and adolescence has begun.

Cognitive development refers to the age-related series of changes that occur in mental activity—thought, memory, perception, attention, and language. As part of our study of cognitive development, you will probably be surprised to find out how precise we have become in discovering what infants know at different points in the first two years of their lives. You will learn how the child's memory develops. You also will learn how the infant develops perceptions of depth and space, as well as the remarkable feats of attention a baby displays in the first month of life. How children's language develops and whether it is a good idea to push the child into learning to read in the infant years will also be discussed.

Social development and **emotional development** are broad labels that encompass many different aspects of the child's world, aspects that often overlap. The word *social* refers to the child's interactions with other individuals in the environment. A mother hugging her daughter for a good report card, a father spanking his son for being sassy, siblings arguing with each other, and a teacher warmly greeting a boy at the door of her classroom are all aspects of the social world. Social development focuses on how these many different aspects unfold as the individual grows.

Emotional development often contains many of the same components as social development. However, emotional development places more emphasis on the child's feelings and affective responses (the words *affect, emotion,* and *feeling* can be used interchangeably). The attachment of an infant to the mother is an important topic discussed in chapter 6, as is the development of the self, which will be discussed throughout the text. The infant's cries and smiles are emotional responses that are important aspects of the attachment process. Feeling happy most of the time is an emotion that reflects a positive self-concept. Other emotions that will be discussed are anxiety, anger, and guilt.

As we discuss **personality development,** three aspects, in particular, will be emphasized: the self and self-perception, sex-typed behavior and sex-role development, and moral development. As a rule, the label *personality* has referred more to a property of the child than to social development. Yet you will see that it is impossible to meaningfully present the aspects of personality without frequently referring to the child's interactions with and thoughts about the social world. And when we discuss moral development, an important aspect of personality, you will discover that a prominent aspect of moral development is the child's feelings about or affective reactions to moral situations.

Although we will sometimes discuss the different strands of development in separate chapters, or parts of chapters, keep in mind while reading this text that the child is an integrated human being, with only one mind and one body. Physical, cognitive, social, emotional and personality development are inextricably woven together. In many chapters you will learn how social experiences shape cognitive development, how cognitive development restricts or promotes social development, and how cognitive development is tied to physical development.

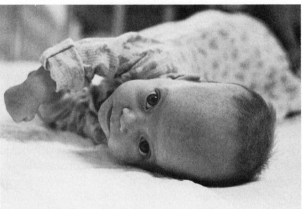

Infants develop physically, cognitively, and socially.

Child Psychology as a Scientific Enterprise

Urie Bronfenbrenner (1970), an expert on social development, has observed childrearing techniques in several different cultures. In the vignette that follows, he describes how Soviet youth discipline themselves for violating accepted rules of behavior.

Ivanov is a fifth-grade leader of his school's youth group, the Pioneers. He went swimming with some friends without adult supervision and after a reprimand from the school authorities, he must now face a disciplinary council composed of his own peers. Ivanov is asked to stand and tell the group what he has done. The answer is barely audible, "I went swimming."

As his answers are written down by the secretary, a girl asks, "You and who else?" He names seven others. Another girl comments, "Fine thing; you're the commander leading your men." A boy asks, "Do you realize that last year a child drowned in that very pond?"

The questions and accusations continued. The major effort is two-sided: first, to impress Ivanov with the fact that, in violating the rule, he had jeopardized the lives of his classmates as well as his own; second, that his act constituted a betrayal of the faith invested in him as a Pioneer commander. Ivanov is speechless, and trembles slightly and struggles to hold back the tears.

This vignette illustrates one of the ways that people have investigated processes of development—through scientific observation.

The study of child psychology has emerged today as a full-fledged scientific enterprise. Thousands of professionals are actively involved in scientific inquiry into the nature of children and how they develop. Well over one hundred new doctorates in child psychology are awarded each year by the nation's universities. Millions of dollars are spent each year by federal, state, and local governments to support basic research. By conservative estimate there are more than a dozen highly respected technical journals in this country that publish annually over a thousand reports of original research dealing with child development. In short, child psychology is an active scientific field.

But what exactly do we mean when we say that child psychology is a science? How are current efforts to understand children any different from those of the philosophers and historians already mentioned? Scientific inquiry differs from philosophical speculation and the casual observations of historians in a number of ways. For one, scientists propose formal theories that are subject to rigorous tests with actual children. For another, there are specific methods for conducting these tests and for uncovering additional facts about children. Together the theories and methods ensure that we do not delude ourselves with fanciful ideas or whimsy

in describing children, for a bad idea or theory can be quickly dismissed with several well-chosen empirical tests. In chapter 2 we highlight the major theories of development, and in the remainder of this chapter we describe a number of scientific methods.

Our discussion of scientific methods is organized into three parts. First, we outline a number of methods used to collect data about children; second, we evaluate the techniques that can be called on to determine whether there is a relationship between the phenomena we are studying; and third, we narrate the strategies available to make developmental comparisons.

Methods of Data Collection

If I want to find out something about children, what are the methods available to me? What kinds of measures can be used to accurately obtain the information I need? In this section, observation, interview and questionnaire, and standardized testing—the methods most frequently used by scientists who study children—will be evaluated.

Observation

Perhaps the most basic tool of any science is systematic observation. If you want to examine some characteristic of children's behavior, try to observe it in the children themselves. Observational studies of children can range from highly structured laboratory assessments to highly unstructured observations. In an unstructured situation, the child might be observed at school, at home, or in the neighborhood—in real life, natural contexts. Observations may focus on verbal behaviors, nonverbal behaviors, or both. They may be conducted by observers trained to code the behavior of the children in specified ways or be videotaped and/or audiotaped. The use of videotaped records has greatly expanded the precision of observational techniques. A videotape can provide a complete record of a child's behavior, allowing the investigator the luxury of poring over the record of behavior long after it has occurred.

Most observational studies involve at least a minimal amount of structure—often the observer is trained to look for certain behaviors. For instance, if the study is on coercive interaction between children and adults, the observers would be trained to watch for behaviors such as commanding, yelling, insulting, disobeying, and so on. In most instances, it is wise to have some type of focus rather than observing children with no particular goal in mind. During observation everything else must become secondary. This may seem like a simple point, but it is surprising how many college students become sidetracked by endless irrelevancies in a child's behavior during an observation. It is difficult to observe a child continuously even if the behavior of interest is narrowly defined; fatigue and the need to record observations often make this impossible. As a result, most

Trained observers focus their attention on specific aspects of the child's behavior.

observational studies use **time sampling**—a procedure in which the child is observed during only a portion of the time. For example, if you want to observe aggression during ten-minute recess periods at school, you can observe the child in alternating two-minute observe-record (on-off) cycles.

Preliminary unstructured observations, though, can be a rich source of ideas for future work. For example, it is not unusual for many researchers to generate ideas for research out of experiences they have had with their own children. Similarly, an ambitious exception to the belief that observation should entail some structure is represented in the **naturalistic observations** of Roger Barker (1968). With this technique, a child's behavior is monitored by teams of observers as the child goes about a typical day's activities. This technique differs from other observational techniques in the exhaustiveness with which the child's life is explored.

Finally, a key or essential factor in the observation is **reliability.** If one person is asked to observe the same events that another witnessed, the same observations should be reported by both. The observational records are reliable to the extent that independent observers have strong agreement on what occurred. If substantial agreement cannot be reached by the two observers, then the observational procedure is unreliable and, as a result, worthless.

As a rule, the more specific and concrete the observational category, the easier it is to achieve reliability. For example, it is easier to get two observers to agree that they have seen *physical* aggression occur than it is to get the observers to agree simply that aggression has occurred because physical aggression is a more precise, concrete category than general aggression (which also could include such behaviors as verbal and nonverbal teasing, commanding, and so forth). Also, it is easier to ensure observational reliability when categories are being observed.

However, observations, like other strategies for collecting information about adolescents, are not without their drawbacks. A major problem in observational research is the child's reaction to being observed: Does being observed change the way a child behaves in a situation? The problem is so acute that some investigators have suggested that observers dress and behave in a manner as consonant with the people they are observing as possible to reduce reactivity (Wahler, House, & Stambaugh, 1976). It also may be a cogent strategy to sample behavior periodically over a fairly long period of time (say, four to five times over a three-month period) in the hope that initial reactivity will wear off after the subjects have acclimated to the observer's presence (Jones, Reid, & Patterson, 1974).

Interview and Questionnaire

Many scientific inquiries into the nature of child development have been based on the techniques referred to as interview and questionnaire. An **interview** is a set of questions put to someone and the responses that person makes. The interview can range from very structured to very unstructured. For example, a very unstructured interview might include questions such as "Tell me about some of the things you do with your friends" or "Tell me about yourself," while a very structured interview might question whether the respondent highly approves, moderately approves, moderately disapproves, or highly disapproves of his friends' use of drugs. Highly unstructured interviews, while often yielding valuable clinical insights, usually do not yield information suitable for research purposes. Open-ended interview questions usually produce a wide variety of answers that make attempts to categorize and analyze the data difficult. However, open-ended interview questions can be helpful in developing more focused interview questions for future efforts.

Researchers are also able to question children through surveys or questionnaires. A **questionnaire** is similar to a highly structured interview, except that children read the questions and mark their answers on a sheet of paper rather than verbally responding to the interviewer. An example of research conducted by means of a questionnaire or survey is the work of Jerome Bachman and his colleagues at the University of Michigan (Bachman, 1982). They sampled the incidence of and attitudes toward drugs in 17,500 high school seniors from all parts of the United States.

One major advantage of surveys and questionnaires is that they can easily be given to a very large number of children. A sample of responses from five to ten thousand children is quite possible to obtain. However, surveys and questionnaires must be carefully constructed.

A number of experts who study development (for example, Ausubel, Sullivan, & Ives, 1980) have pointed out that surveys and questionnaires have been badly abused instruments of inquiry. Questions on surveys should be concrete, specific, and unambiguous, but often they are not. Some assessment of the authenticity of the replies should be provided, but often is not. (This assessment may involve a spot check against available records or the inclusion of built-in questions that reveal insincere and careless responses.)

Structured interviews conducted by an experienced researcher can produce more detailed responses than are possible in a questionnaire and can help eliminate careless responses as well. The interviewer has the opportunity to ensure that he or she understands the child's answers. A good interviewer can encourage a child to open up. But interviews are not without problems either. One problem is that in a face-to-face situation where anonymity is impossible, a child's responses may reflect **social desirability** rather than actual feelings or actions. In other words, a person may respond to gain the approval of others rather than say what he or she actually thinks. When asked about her sexual relationships with boys, for example, an adolescent female may not want to admit having had sexual intercourse. Skilled interviewing techniques and built-in questions to help eliminate such defenses are critical in getting accurate information in an interview.

Another problem with both interviews and surveys is that some questions may be retrospective in nature—they require the participant to recall events or feelings that occurred at some point in the past. It is not unusual, for example, to interview adults about experiences they had as children or adolescents. Unfortunately, retrospective interviews are seriously affected by distortions in memory. It is an exceedingly difficult task to glean accurate information about the past from verbal reports. However, because of the importance of understanding retrospective verbal reports, 1978 Nobel prizewinner Herbert Simon is seriously investigating better ways to gain more accurate verbal assessments of the past (Erickson & Simon, 1978). Simon's work focuses on short-term and long-term memory, as well as on information that is incomplete and/or inconsistent.

Standardized Testing

One question that frequently arises as scientists and educators attempt to understand child development is "How does one child compare to others in some social or cognitive characteristic—for example, IQ, independence, morality, or introversion-extroversion?" One research method that helps answer this question is the use of standardized tests specifically designed to assess such differences. Standardized tests are devices developed to identify an individual's relative performance in a large group of similar individuals. A good test usually has a reasonably large number of items, is given in an objective, standardized way, and can be scored easily. The **standardization** of tests refers to the establishment of a fixed or standard procedure for giving and scoring the tests, as well as the development of norms for age, grade, race, sex, and so on. Norms refer to a pattern or representative value for a group.

Standardized tests always should be reliable and valid. *Reliability* is the degree to which the test will yield the same results for a child on two or more occasions. If eight-year-old Jane is given an IQ test in January and the same test again in May of that year, her scores on the test should be similar if the test is reliable. **Validity** is the extent to which the test accurately evaluates what it is meant to evaluate, as indicated by some independent evidence about the child. The standardization process is complex and involves the sampling of large groups of individuals; a good test takes several years to develop. The final product contains detailed information that enables the tester to identify the child's relative standing in his or her peer group in regard to the characteristic being tested.

Standardized test information is helpful to those who want to evaluate the child's developmental progress, to clinicians and counselors who may be looking for problem areas in a child's life, and to researchers who hope to find out something about the characteristics of the children they are investigating in a research study.

Standardized tests, though, are not without problems either. Probably the most widely used standardized test is the familiar IQ test that most of us have taken at some point in our lives. Much more will be said about IQ tests in chapter 9, where we will provide more details about their strengths and weaknesses. Briefly, it has been argued that while IQ tests are carefully standardized measures, many developmental psychologists do not believe they are valid assessments of the child's cognition. Such critics argue that standardized IQ tests measure *how much* the child knows rather than the more important point of *how* the child thinks. Standardized tests have also been criticized for not being ecologically valid. By this, the critics are referring to the fact that the child's intelligence is assessed by the taking of a thirty- to sixty-minute test administered by a strange person in a strange room. The test does not assess the child in the natural context of his or her everyday world, as he or she interacts with parents, peers, and teacher, for example.

Multimethod Strategies
Too many studies of children rely on only one of the aforementioned methods. However, taken together the methods may provide complementary information. Properly conducted interviews or questionnaires can inform us about children's attitudes about themselves and others, but they often do not do a very good job of telling us how children actually behave (which ideally is obtained through detailed observations). Finally, standardized tests can provide information about how one child differs from most other children his or her age. Consequently, it often is a wise strategy to use more than one method when trying to find out information about children.

Along a similar line, it is often valuable to collect information from more than one source and in more than one setting. For example, we might be interested in finding out about the child's self-concept. With regard to different sources, we might ask the child about her self-perceptions, then we might also ask about her best friend's, her parents', and her teacher's perceptions of the child's self-concept. Further, it is often important in studying children to evaluate them in different settings or contexts. In this regard, rather than finding out how the child feels about herself in general,

we might want to know if she feels differently depending upon whether she is at school, at home, or in a neighborhood play situation with peers. Either by asking different people about the child or by observing her behavior in different settings, we likely will obtain a more complete, accurate picture of her self-perceptions than by relying on the child's self-report alone.

In addition to choosing a method or methods for collecting information about children, researchers must decide upon a strategy for trying to understand the relation between various factors they are studying, as we see next.

Experimental, Quasi-Experimental, and Correlational Strategies
We can choose to set up our study of children in one of three ways: experimental, quasi-experimental, or correlational.

Experimental Strategy
Ideally we would like for our research to be conducted in an experimental way because more than the other strategies, the experimental allows us more precisely to determine whether something is causing the child to act, think, or feel in a particular way. An **experiment** is a carefully controlled context in which the factors that are believed to influence the child are tested. The experimenter manipulates the "influential" factors, called **independent variables,** and measures the results, or **dependent variables.**

Fortunately, the concept of *variable* is not difficult, and it is just what its name implies. A variable is something that can vary, that is, take on different "values" or "levels." Age, for example, is a variable because it can take on values between 0 and 100 years or more. Other common variables are IQ, height, and years of education. The important thing to remember about variables is that they must take on at least two different values. Thus, although age is a variable, five years of age is not.

By taking great care in developing and controlling the experimental procedure, the experimenter can prevent extraneous factors (independent variables other than those that are the focus of the experiment) from interfering with the child's thoughts, feelings, and actions.

A concrete example may help to clarify what constitutes an experiment. Suppose it is believed that children learn to solve problems simply by observing other people solve them. This belief could be subjected to experimental test by means of the following procedure. Each child in one group is individually exposed to a person who repeatedly assembles a jigsaw puzzle that has fifteen pieces. Each child in a second group is individually exposed to the same person and the same jigsaw puzzle but does not see that person assemble it.

Children vary in their exposure to solving problems.

Each child in both groups is then asked individually to assemble the jigsaw puzzle, and a record is made of the time taken to do so.

The independent variable in this experiment would be the amount of exposure the child has to the person solving the problem. There are two degrees of this—some exposure to the person assembling the puzzle and no exposure. The dependent variable is the amount of time a child takes to assemble the puzzle.

If the group of children who had had some exposure assembled the puzzle more rapidly than the group who had had no exposure, the initial hypothesis would be confirmed: children learned something—rapid puzzle assembly—following an experience in which they saw someone else performing that action.

Other factors might explain the superior performance of the one group of children. Perhaps they were brighter or had more experience with jigsaw puzzles or had more experience watching people solve problems. How do we know that the independent variable selected was the influential one? One way is by matching the two experimental groups of children so that they are identical with respect to all other such potential factors. Another way would be by means of the technique known as **randomization.** With randomization

only some children are selected from a much larger group for the experiment. They are then assigned randomly to one or the other exposure condition. If the assignment is truly random, then there is only a slim chance that the two groups will differ from each other in some particular characteristic because any extraneous factor will have been randomly distributed in the groups. Generally, the technique of randomization is preferred over matching. Another example, this one an actual study of delinquent behavior, should help you to understand more fully the importance of experimental research in our study of children. See application 1.1 for a description of strategies to help delinquents.

Experiments are useful when carefully controlled information about children is desired because this technique permits the experimenter to make inferences about **cause-and-effect** relations.

Quasi-Experimental Strategy
Often a technique can be employed that resembles the experiment in all important respects except one—the degree of prior control exercised over the independent variable. In such a pseudo experiment, sometimes called a **quasi experiment,** we accept a practically imposed definition of the independent variable, acknowledging that it may be imperfect and partially confounded with

Application 1.1
An Experimental Study: Role Taking and Delinquency

Michael Chandler's (1973) study of role-taking skills and delinquent behavior is an example of an experimental approach to studying adolescents. In the study, an attempt was made to measure and remediate deficiencies in the role-taking skills of forty-five chronically delinquent eleven-to-thirteen-year-old boys. After measuring significant differences in role taking between the delinquent boys and a group of forty-five nondelinquents, the delinquent boys were randomly assigned to one of three experimental (also sometimes called treatment or intervention) conditions. One third of the delinquent boys were placed in an experimental program that involved drama and video filmmaking as a means of remedial help in role taking. The remaining boys were assigned to one of two control groups, one of which was called a *nontreatment* control group, the other labeled a *placebo* group. In the nontreatment control group, no contact with the research staff occurred until posttreatment assessment of role-taking skills was made. The remaining fifteen delinquent boys, those in the "placebo" group, went to the same place, interacted socially with the same research staff, and made the same films as the experimental treatment group. But in contrast to the members of the experimental treatment group, these fifteen boys did not participate in the special treatment activities directed toward increasing role-taking skills.

Comparison of the role-taking skills of the boys in the three groups indicated that only the boys in the role-taking treatment group increased their role-taking skills by the time the treatment ended. In this experiment, the independent variable was the type of treatment program the boys were exposed to, the dependent variable their posttreatment role-taking skills. Note that the experimenter carefully manipulated the treatment conditions, but that role-taking behaviors were free to vary. The investigator also tried to minimize some unwanted factors in the experiment; for example, by randomly assigning the boys to different groups, the experimenter decreased the possibility that any one group was simply smarter or more socially adept than the others.

others. (The word *quasi* means almost, so a quasi experiment means almost an experiment.) For example, we might evaluate the impact of day-care center care versus home care on children's social development by studying a group of children selected from each type of setting. Because families themselves determine where their child will be assigned, we do not know what other factors may be involved that could be confused with the one of interest here; parental education, work experience, childrearing philosophies, and other background characteristics could also be different in the two groups. Quasi experiments are useful in getting information about social matters that create tricky problems for exercising tight experimental control.

Correlational Strategy
Often it is of interest to know how one measured characteristic is associated with another—height with weight, intelligence with learning ability, parental discipline with child morality. One measure of association is the **correlation** index. Correlations are referred to in discussions of heritability (chapter 3) and intelligence (chapter 9).

The correlation index ranges from -1.00 to $+1.00$. A negative number indicates an inverse relation. For example, a student of ours recently found that children relatively high in ability to adopt the social perspective of other people were relatively low in impulsive behavior. A positive number indicates a positive relation. A frequent finding, for example, is that children with relatively high IQ scores are also relatively rapid learners. The higher the number in the index (whether positive or negative), the stronger the association between the variables. An index of "0" indicates that there is no association between the variables.

A correlation alone cannot be used to support the interpretation that one event causes another. We can't argue, for example, that because height and weight are positively correlated we grow tall because we gain weight (or vice versa). It is always possible that some unnoticed third factor is the causal agent, linking these two events with each other. However, correlations are useful because they suggest likely places to look for causal connections. If a correlation of a particular kind and value is repeatedly found when two characteristics are measured, then this is strong reason to test out a causal hypothesis by conducting a formal experiment.

One example of a correlational study is Rudolph and Bernice Moos's assessment of the relation between classroom social climate and student grades and absences from school (1978). Moos and Moos evaluated the relation between the social environments of nineteen high school classes and student absenteeism rates and the average final grades given by the teachers. Classes with high absenteeism rates were usually highly competitive and teacher controlled and low in teacher support. Classes in which the teachers gave above average grades were usually marked by high student involvement and low teacher control.

Note that no independent variable was manipulated in this study; as the authors pointed out, no causal implications can be drawn from their data. Classroom climate, grades, and absenteeism are probably interrelated in complex ways. Some teachers may create an authoritarian pattern early in the school year so that students quickly learn the rules of the classroom. Such teachers likely can be more supportive because they have little need to justify their control later in the year. On the other hand, when teachers point out to the students early in the year what their grading policies will be, the grading policies may affect the development of the classroom climate, and this may in turn influence the motivation of the students, absenteeism, and final grades. To make things even more complicated, such relationships may be affected by the backgrounds of the students and the subject matter of the class.

But even though cause-and-effect linkages cannot be ascertained in correlational studies, such studies often pave the way for experimental investigations. As Moos and Moos (1978) suggest, experimental treatment programs could be established in which high-risk classrooms are identified early in the school year through classroom environmental observations and feedback provided to the teachers about the characteristics of the setting. Then different experimental groups could be created for pre- and posttreatment evaluation, much in the same manner as was true in the experimental study by Michael Chandler (1973) described in application 1.1.

Suppose you have identified a significant question about children you wish to answer. Suppose the inquiry is to focus on changes in how children between four and eight years of age learn. The first decision to make is which method you will employ to study this question—that is, observation, interview-questionnaire, or standardized testing. Then you decide whether to use an experimental, quasi-experimental, or correlational strategy. One final decision still to be made is discussed next—the time span of your inquiry.

Time Span of Inquiry

In addition to the choice of the particular measures you use to study children (observation, interview, questionnaire, or standardized test) and the decision to adopt an experimental or correlational strategy, you must consider another factor: whether to study children from a cross-sectional or longitudinal perspective or a combination of the two.

Longitudinal Method

Repeated testing of an individual child, or many children, over a significant developmental span of time is referred to as a **longitudinal comparison.** In the example of a study to investigate changes in learning, the repeated testing would occur over the four-year period as children grow from four to eight years of age. It would be up to the investigator to determine just how many tests would be performed during this interval and over what periods of time. You might test each child once a year at the same time each year, for example. The longitudinal method is valued because it permits the observer to watch change unfold in individual children.

If you wanted to observe the stability of specific characteristics such as attachment or aggression over an extended period of time, you could do it only by the longitudinal method. In actual practice, however, this method has many drawbacks and is often impractical. It is difficult, for one thing, to complete a study adequately over a long period of time—like the four years of our hypothetical example. Children will drop out of the study as a result of school and residence changes; testing personnel may change; and the cost of the study in time and money may be excessive. Repeated testing is also a problem. The child's performance may improve at test sessions because of familiarity with the test rather than because of increased maturity. The shorter the span of time to be covered and the fewer the number of test repetitions planned, the easier a longitudinal study becomes.

Cross-Sectional Method

Longitudinal studies have been important in child psychology, but considerations of cost and efficiency have limited the number of large-scale, long-term longitudinal projects. By contrast, a greater number of cross-sectional investigations have occurred. The **cross-sectional method** refers to a comparison in which groups of children of different ages are studied at about the same time, and age changes in the way children learn are inferred from differences among the groups. In our hypothetical example, changes in learning can be studied by testing separate groups of four-, six-, and eight-year-olds. You might observe that most of the four-year-olds learn a problem best under one set of conditions, the six-year-olds under a second set, and the eight-year-olds under a third.

A cross-sectional study is valued because it permits the detection of a developmental change in a fairly short period of time. However, it has its drawbacks too. For one, it is difficult to be sure that the group differences reflect individual change. For another, we don't know, strictly speaking, that the difference in learning between the group of four-year-olds and the group of eight-year-olds is due to age. Maybe the eight-year-olds are different because they grew up under different circumstances—different educational environments, childrearing practices, and so forth.

The cross-sectional approach is valuable for obtaining answers to questions in which a quick first estimate about some change is required and resources are limited. This condition often exists in research on how children learn and remember, attend and perceive, and interact with peers.

Combined Longitudinal–Cross-Sectional Method

The cross-sectional comparison is suspect because it is not known whether apparent age changes really reflect individual changes. The longitudinal comparison is problematic because it is both time-consuming and expensive. The longitudinal comparison also has another potential flaw—how can it be known whether the individual change experienced by a child over a period of time is due to a general age change? This individual change could as well be due to some unique experiences common to children growing up at this particular time. They may have been exposed to an educational program on television or to a new curriculum in school. Would this age change be observed in another child who was born at a different time and did not have this unique experience? Using the **combined longitudinal–cross-sectional method** allows us to see whether both techniques yield the same pattern of developmental change. It can also allow us to see whether special experiences occurring in one period of time, rather than through maturation and generalized experience, are accounting for longitudinal change. If the longitudinal and cross-sectional comparisons yield different patterns, the cause of the discrepancy can sometimes be identified. This is illustrated in application 1.2.

In addition to selecting a method or methods, a strategy for determining relationships between variables, and the time span of inquiry, researchers who study children also need to be concerned about the ethical nature of their research. For example, to find out which kind of discipline technique may cause children to inhibit their behavior on both a short-term and a long-term basis, we might think about conducting an

experiment in which we randomly assign parents to different discipline strategies, one of which is spanking their child when he or she does something wrong. Don't think too long and hard about how to conduct such an experiment, however, because it is unethical, as we see next.

Ethical Standards in Working with Children

Child psychologists subscribe to the code of ethics of the American Psychological Association and the Society for Research in Child Development. Most training programs require their graduate students to learn these codes. To be licensed to practice psychology in most states, prospective psychologists must pass a formal test on ethical standards. Among the most important concepts in working with children are the following ethical imperatives:

1. Always obtain informed consent from parents or legal guardians if children are to be tested in any way or are to be the objects of research. Parents have the right to a complete and accurate description of what will be done with their children and may refuse to let their charges participate.

2. Children have rights, too. The psychologist is obliged to explain precisely what the child will experience. Children may refuse to participate, even after parental permission has been given. If so, the investigator must not test the child. Similarly, if a child becomes upset during some professional interaction, it is the psychologist's obligation to calm down the youngster. Failing to do so, the activity must be discontinued.

3. The psychologist must always weigh the potential for harming children against the prospects of contributing some clear benefits to them. If there is the chance of any harm—such as when drugs are to be used, social deception is to take place, or the child is to be treated aversively (e.g., punished or reprimanded)—the psychologist must be able to convince a group of impartial peers that the benefits of the experience for the child clearly outweigh any chance of harm.

4. The psychologist must always adhere to accepted standards of practice using techniques and procedures that treat children courteously and respectfully. Since children are in a vulnerable position and lack power and control when facing an adult, the psychologist should always strive to make the professional encounter a positive and supportive experience.

Application 1.2
Studying the Effects of "Sesame Street" on Children

We made up the following example to illustrate the value of the combined longitudinal–cross-sectional method. Suppose it is believed that children's prereading skills improve as children advance from three to five years of age. One of the indicators of this improvement is the number of letters of the alphabet that can be identified on sight. A study is conducted to test this idea. In 1968, three groups of children are tested: three-year-olds, four-year-olds, and five-year-olds. Each group is referred to as a **cohort** and we will call the groups cohorts A, B, and C. (A cohort refers to one's time of birth, say 1965, or to one's generation, such as the 1960s. Thus cohorts can differ with respect to the years of education they have experienced [your cohort has more education than your parents' cohorts, for example], childrearing practices, and health.)

In our example, individual children are presented with flash cards to see how many letters of the alphabet they can identify. The results show an apparent increase with age in letter identification. Children in the respective groups correctly identify an average of five, twelve, and nineteen letters. A longitudinal component is then added to the study, retesting cohort A (the original three-year-olds) in 1969 and 1970 and retesting cohort B (the original four-year-olds) in 1969. See inset table 1.1 for the results. Cohort A improves dramatically from 1968 to 1969—the children in this group advance from five to twenty-four correct identifications. The children in cohort B also improve, advancing from twelve to twenty-four correct. But notice what else has happened. Cohort A at four years of age is doing as well as cohort B at five years of age. Both get twenty-four items correct. And both are doing better than cohort C, who at five years of age has only nineteen items correct. So although the original cross-sectional comparison (row 1—cohorts A, B, and C tested in 1968) yields changes from ages three to four and from

ages four to five, the longitudinal sequences do not. The changes for cohort A occur between three and four years of age, but not between four and five years of age. For cohort B, change occurs between four and five years of age. And the level of performance of the oldest children in the original cross-sectional comparison does not match the performance of the children retested in the longitudinal sequences.

What might account for these differences? It appears that something might have happened between 1968 and 1969 to produce a dramatic change in alphabet identification skills. Well, that was the first season of the popular children's TV program "Sesame Street." One of the major programming goals of "Sesame Street" is to teach young children to identify letters of the alphabet. The results of our hypothetical example seem to suggest that the TV planners of "Sesame Street" have accomplished their goal.

Obviously, our hypothetical example was a loaded one. Cohorts and test dates were chosen so that an apparent age change turned out not to be an age change at all but the result of special educational experiences. But the phenomenon is real. For example, Hayne Reese (1974) observed cohort changes in young children's ability to use mental imagery in a learning problem. The change occurred during 1969. Again, the nationwide broadcasting of "Sesame Street" may have been the cause. There are other documented cases of cohort effects. John Nesselroade and Paul Baltes (1974), for example, found changes in adolescent personality during the 1970 to 1972 period. As measured by several personality tests, adolescents became more extroverted and independent over this period of time. Although the causes of this change have not been precisely determined, an increase in student activism and a decline in respect for public and educational leadership noted during this period may have been responsible.

Inset Table 1.1
Example of Cohort Change Effects

| | Cohort A (Born: 1965) | | | Cohort B (Born: 1964) | | | Cohort C (Born: 1963) | |
Test Date	Age	Mean Number of Letters Identified	Age	Mean Number of Letters Identified	Age	Mean Number of Letters Identified
1968	3	5	4	12	5	19
1969	4	24	5	24		
1970	5	24				

Big Bird helps preschoolers learn.

Summary

The last two centuries have been significant in terms of the history of child development in that childhood has been understood for the first time as differentiated and unique; children are treated well; and philosophical debates have been replaced by scientific study.

In the contemporary study of child development, there is still disagreement on what the phases of development are and when they occur. In this text, development will be presented according to these phases: infancy, early childhood, middle and late childhood, and adolescence. Development is defined as a pattern of movement or change that begins at conception and continues throughout the life cycle. The pattern of change involves growth (as in infancy) and decay (as in death). The pattern of movement is complex because it often involves different processes—maturation and experiences, for example. Five strands of development that are emphasized in this book are physical, cognitive, social, emotional, and personality development.

As a science, child development employs a number of different methods to collect data, consists of different strategies for determining the relations among various phenomena studied, and uses different time spans of inquiry. Three of the most widely used methods in studying children are observation, interview-questionnaire, and standardized testing. Because each of these methods often uncovers different information about children and also because each method has problems associated with its use, a wise strategy is to use a variety of methods. Similarly, a more complete, accurate picture of the child's development may be obtained by using different sources of information and studying the child in different settings. In order to determine the relation between the phenomena being studied researchers call on one of three strategies: experimental, quasi-experimental, or correlational. The experimental strategy allows us to determine the effect of an independent variable on a dependent variable and is the method most likely to allow us to pinpoint the factor(s) causing the child's behavior. However, in some cases we cannot obtain as much control over the independent variable as we would like, as in the case of day care. In this situation, we conduct a quasi experiment, sometimes called a pseudo experiment, in which we acknowledge incomplete control over the independent variable. A third strategy is the correlational method, which allows us to determine the relationship between two or more variables but does not provide an accurate picture of the cause-and-effect relationship between the variables.

Further, researchers have to choose a time span for their inquiry. The majority of studies of children are cross-sectional, being conducted over a very short period of time. For example, a cross-sectional study usually involves only one testing of children. However, when we repeatedly test children over a significant developmental span of time, say once each year for three years, the study is called longitudinal. Because of problems associated with both the cross-sectional and longitudinal strategies, some researchers have developed the combined longitudinal–cross-sectional approach. A final consideration by researchers who study children is the ethical nature of their research.

Key Terms

adolescence

biological environment

cause and effect

cognitive development

cohort

combined longitudinal–cross-sectional method

correlation

cross-sectional method

dependent variables

development

early childhood

emotional development

experiences

experiment

independent variables

infancy

innate knowledge

interview

late childhood

longitudinal comparison

maturation

middle childhood

naturalistic observation

neonate

original sin

personality development

physical development

quasi experiment

questionnaire

randomization

reliability

social desirability

social development

social environment

standardization

tabula rasa

time sampling

validity

Review Questions

1. Describe the child in historical perspective. How does our contemporary perspective on the child differ from the way the ancients viewed the child?
2. What do we mean by the term *development*? How do maturation and experience influence development?
3. Describe the different phases of development, as well as some different strands or aspects of development.
4. Discuss the issues involved in viewing development from a transition or crisis, stage or nonstage, and continuous or discontinuous perspective.
5. What are the basic methods for collecting information scientifically? Describe each and indicate when it is likely to be most useful.
6. What are the different strategies for determining relationships among variables?
7. How can we make age comparisons in our study of children? What are the advantages and disadvantages of each approach?
8. What are the ethical standards that guide our study of children?

Further Readings

Achenbach, T. *Research in developmental psychology: Concepts, strategies, methods.* New York: Free Press, 1978.
An easy-to-read introduction about the nature of how research is done in the field of development, with examples of different techniques and approaches.

American Psychologist, January 1983. *American Psychologist* is the journal of the American Psychological Association.
This particular issue is devoted to social policy and children, including a number of easy-to-read articles about ethical standards and the welfare of children.

Ariès, P. *Centuries of childhood.* (R. Baldick, Trans.). New York: Knopf, 1962.
A fascinating history of childrearing practices, beliefs about childhood, and the circumstances of children throughout history.

Brim, O. G., and Kagan, J. (eds.). *Constancy and change in human development.* Cambridge, Mass.: Harvard University Press, 1980.
This scholarly treatment of the issue of age-related change in development is written by a number of experts in the social and biological sciences. Reading level is medium to difficult.

Sears, R. R., and Feldman, S. S. (eds.). *The seven ages of man.* San Francisco: Kaufman, 1973.
An excellent, easy-to-read introduction to different phases of the life cycle written by a variety of authors.

2 Theories and Perspectives

magine . . . that you have developed a major theory of child development

What would influence someone like yourself to develop a theory about how children develop? The individual interested in developing such a theory usually goes through a long university training program that is likely to culminate in a doctoral degree. As part of the training, the individual is exposed to many ideas about a particular topic such as personality, child development, adolescence, or clinical psychology. But another factor that could explain why an individual develops a particular theory focuses on the kind of life experiences the theorist had during his or her childhood years. In this introduction to various theories that have been proposed to explain development, we describe the childhood of four prominent theorists who have helped to shape our views: Erik Erikson, Jean Piaget, B. F. Skinner, and Carl Rogers.

Erik Erikson. Erik Homberger Erikson was born June 15, 1902, near Frankfurt, Germany to Danish parents. Before Erik was born, his parents separated and his mother left Denmark to live in Germany, where she had some friends. At age three Erik became ill, and his mother took him to see a pediatrician named Homberger. Young Erik's mother fell in love with the pediatrician, married him, and gave Erik the middle name of his new stepfather.

Erik attended primary school between the ages of six and ten and then the gymnasium (high school) from age eleven to eighteen. He studied art and a number of languages rather than scientific courses like biology and chemistry. Erik did not like the formal atmosphere of his school, and this was reflected in his grades. At age eighteen, rather than going to college, the adolescent Erikson wandered through the continent, keeping notes about his experiences in a personal diary. After a year of travel through Europe, he returned to Germany and enrolled in an art school, became dissatisfied, and enrolled in another. Then he began to give up his sketching and eventually traveled to Florence, Italy. Robert Coles vividly describes Erikson at this time:

To the Italians he was not an unfamiliar sight: the young, tall, thin Nordic expatriate with long, blond hair. He wore a corduroy suit and was seen by his family and friends as not odd or "sick" but as a wandering artist who was trying to come to grips with himself, a not unnatural or unusual struggle—particularly in Germany. (Coles, 1970, p. 15)

Jean Piaget. Jean Piaget was born August 9, 1896, in Neuchâtel, Switzerland. Jean's father was an intellectual type who taught young Jean to think system-

Erik Erikson

Jean Piaget

atically. Jean's mother also was very bright, and strongly religious as well. His father seemed to maintain an air of detachment from his mother, who has been described by Piaget as prone to frequent outbursts of neurotic behavior.

In his autobiography, Piaget detailed why he chose to pursue the study of cognitive development rather than emotional development:

I started to forego playing for serious work very early. Indeed, I have always detested any departure from reality, an attitude which I relate to . . . my mother's poor mental health. It was this disturbing factor which at the beginning of my studies in psychology made me keenly interested in psychoanalytic and pathological psychology. Though this interest helped me to achieve independence and to widen my cultural background, I have never since felt any desire to involve myself deeper in that particular direction, always much preferring the study of normalcy and of the workings of the intellect to that of the tricks of the unconscious. (1952, p. 238)

While his studies had taken him in the direction of biology and other intellectual pursuits, the deteriorated health of Piaget's mother had an important impact on his first job after he completed his doctorate degree. In 1918 Piaget took a position at Bleuler's psychiatric clinic in Zurich, where he learned about clinical techniques for interviewing children. Then, still at the young age of twenty-two, he went to work in the psychology laboratory at the University of Zurich, where he was exposed to the insights of Alfred Binet, who developed the first intelligence test. By the time Piaget was twenty-five, his experience in varied disciplines had helped him see important linkages among philosophy, psychology, and biology.

B. F. Skinner. B. F. Skinner was born in 1904 in Susquehanna, Pennsylvania, where he lived until he went to college. Skinner describes his home environment as "warm and stable." His younger brother (by

2½ years) was much better at sports and more popular than B. F. was, and he frequently teased B. F. about his literary and artistic interests. When the younger brother died suddenly at the age of sixteen, Skinner felt guilty because his brother's death didn't bother him. B. F. Skinner says about his youth:

I was always building things. I built roller skates, scooters, steerable wagons, sleds, and rafts to be poled about on shallow ponds. I made seesaws, merry-go-rounds, and slides. I made slingshots, bows and arrows, blowguns and water pistols from lengths of bamboo, and from a discarded water boiler a steam cannon with which I could shoot plugs of potato and carrot over the houses of our neighbors. I made tops, diabolos, model airplanes driven by twisted rubber bands, box kites, and tin propellers which could be sent high into the air with a spool-and-string spinner. I tried again and again to make a glider in which I myself might fly. . . .

B. F. Skinner

I went through all twelve grades of school in a single building, and there were only eight students in my class when I graduated. *I liked school.* . . . An old maid school teacher, Mary Graves, was an important figure in my life. Her father was the village atheist and an amateur botanist who believed in evolution. . . . Miss Graves was a dedicated person with cultural interests far beyond the level of the town. . . . She was my teacher in many fields for many years. . . . Miss Graves was probably responsible for the fact that in college I majored in English literature and afterwards embarked upon a career as a writer.

B. F. was never physically punished by his father, and was punished only once by his mother—she washed his mouth out with soap and water because he said a bad word. However, B. F.'s father frequently informed B. F. of the punishment he would get if he turned out to be a delinquent. He took B. F. through the county jail, and once on a summer vacation took him to a color slide show of Sing Sing prison! His mother monitored his behavior closely. If B. F. deviated, she would say, "Tut-tut, what will people think?" (Skinner, 1967)

Carl Rogers. Carl Rogers was born in Oak Park, Illinois, a Chicago suburb, in 1902. He was the fourth of six children, five of whom were boys. His parents had grown up on farms and were down-to-earth individuals who shared strong religious convictions (particularly his mother). They believed very strongly in the work ethic and often expressed the value of hard work to Carl.

Rogers says that his parents devoted a considerable amount of energy to creating a family life that would "hold" the children and control the way their lives would go. He indicates that they were experts at the techniques of subtle and loving control. Carl never remembers being given a direct command, but he knew that he was never to dance, smoke, play cards, go to movies, or show any sexual interests. Swearing was not as great a taboo, probably because Carl's father often cursed to vent his anger.

Rogers mentions that he had virtually no social life outside of his family, although he doesn't remember this bothering him. When he was twelve, the family moved to a farm—apparently his parents, particularly his mother, wanted to shield their children from the evils of city life. Carl attended three different high schools and had to travel a long distance to get to them.

Rogers talks also about an experience that helped him develop independence from his family. While in Wisconsin, Carl lived at the YMCA with his brother. During his junior year, he was selected as one of ten students to go to Peking, China, for a World Student Christian Federation conference. The trip took six months and had a great impact on Carl's life. He struggled with his religious identity while he was away and thought frequently about his world views compared to those of his parents. At the end of the China trip, Carl had developed confidence in his own views and his own future (Rogers, 1967).

After you have read about each of the theorists' views in this chapter, come back to our descriptions of their infant, childhood, and adolescent years. Try to detect ways in which their experiences might have led them to develop their views of child development.

Carl Rogers

Introduction

In this chapter we survey the major developmental theories and perspectives: the psychoanalytic, represented by Sigmund Freud and Erik Erikson; the cognitive-developmental, the view of Jean Piaget; the behavioral social learning, reflected in the approaches of B. F. Skinner and Albert Bandura; the humanistic, influenced strongly by the thinking of Carl Rogers; the ethological, evolutionary; and the anthropological, sociological. The chapter concludes with an eclectic view of child development and applications that reveal how the theories can be applied to the real world of children by helping them cope with stress.

Why Theories?

If you are like a lot of students, you probably are thinking, "Why do I have to read this chapter on theories? I don't care about theories. What do they have to do with helping me to understand children's development?" At the beginning of this chapter we hope to make a convincing argument of why it is important to know about theories of development. And the applications we have chosen for this chapter show how the theories can be used to help boys and girls with problems.

A **scientific theory** is an organized and logical set of statements and laws. One of its functions is to describe carefully some observable event. Suppose we are interested in how a mother's style of interaction with her child affects the child's style of interaction with other children. The best way to begin is with a theory that describes different styles of interaction. The theory provides a framework for defining the study.

Another function of a theory is to explain some observable event. Consider the example just given. Suppose we observed that a mother punished and abused her child, who then responded in kind to peers. A common sense theory might explain this with the cliché like mother, like child. This form of explanation is not very satisfying because it fails to indicate why children are like their mothers or how this likeness occurs. Answers to such questions as why and how children become what they are are part of a theory's explanatory value.

A third function of a theory is to predict observable events. Suppose we observed the interactions of many groups of mothers and children. Suppose further that we identified three or four distinct styles of mother-child interaction. A theory should predict how each group of children will behave with peers; this prediction should follow naturally from the network of statements and laws that constitutes the theory; and the prediction should be correct a large percentage of the time.

The value of a scientific theory lies in how well it fulfills each of these three functions. A good theory should be *complete* and *terse;* yet it is important for the theory to describe and explain as much as possible. A theory is not complete or terse if it must be changed to handle every new observation that is encountered. A good theory should also be *precise,* making specific predictions about what can be expected in different situations so that the theory can be clearly proved wrong. If a theory is to survive, the number of times its predictions are confirmed should greatly exceed the number of times its predictions are disconfirmed.

Developmental psychologists propose new theories and revise old ones as significant new observations appear. A good theory offers a formal and public statement about matters that may have been unclear or unknown previously. It is important to understand facts in formal, logical ways, and because there is probably no such thing as an isolated fact—all facts have prior assumptions, whether we are conscious of them or not—a good theory helps us to understand the formal assumptions that underlie these facts.

In their concern for explaining age-related sequential themes of development, psychologists have debated whether it is appropriate to describe different phases of development as **stages.** For example, does the child's biological, cognitive, and social functioning undergo dramatic transformation at the onset of adolescence? Or, by contrast, is the child's progress void of abrupt transition?

In this chapter we look at four psychological perspectives of development and two from outside of psychology. The first two perspectives described—psychoanalytic and cognitive-structural—argue for the existence of stages in development. The next two perspectives presented—behavioral social learning, and humanistic—are nonstage theories. Age-related themes of development are not to be found in the behavioral and humanistic views. Rather, development is seen as continuous and void of any abrupt transitions. While the final perspectives discussed—ethological, evolutionary and anthropological, sociological—come from outside the discipline of psychology, they have strongly influenced our views of development.

Stage Theories

The two dominant stage theories in developmental psychology are the psychoanalytic and cognitive-structural perspectives. This section reveals the psychoanalytic views of Sigmund Freud and Erik Erikson and the cognitive-structural approach of Jean Piaget.

The Psychoanalytic Perspective

The **psychoanalytic perspective** refers to the set of assumptions shared by Sigmund Freud and many followers of his psychoanalytic theory of development (Erikson, 1968; Freud, 1949; Horney, 1950). Among the contemporary psychologists whose works draw heavily upon Freud's ideas and assumptions is Erik Erikson. There are many others whose basic framework is psychoanalytic, but Freud and Erikson have had the greatest impact on the contemporary science of developmental psychology.

Sigmund Freud

The psychoanalytic theory of Freud stresses the biological forces that shape human destiny, one of which is **instinct.** Freud believed that the human infant is born with a collection of unconscious instinctive drives that supply energy and direction for behavior. All of development may be seen as the result of changes in the way instinctual energy is channeled and organized. Instinctual energy often changes direction and intensity to maintain a balance in the child. Even when balance is reached, however, instinctual energy continues to fluctuate. Thus instinctual energy is dynamically organized—it is not static, but always changing.

Freud's theory is a structural one. It claims that the life of an individual can be divided into three different structures, or parts: the *id,* the *ego,* and the *superego.* The ego and the superego grow out of the id as the infant develops. As the different structures develop, the organization of instinctual energy shifts from a loose and uninhibited state to a structured and controlled one.

At birth the infant is dominated by instinctual impulses, the **id.** These impulses operate unconsciously and irrationally. The infant has both physical needs, such as hunger, and psychological needs, such as sensory stimulation. The instincts continually force the infant to find an object that will satisfy these needs as rapidly as possible. Because the infant is primitive in the way he or she perceives and thinks, he or she cannot evaluate between similar objects to satisfy a need. Thus an image of a bottle and an actual bottle of milk are both objects that the infant may actively seek out to satisfy thirst. This search for any object to satisfy a need, without regard for its reality or need-reducing value, is referred to as the **pleasure principle,** or primary process thinking.

The infant gradually learns to distinguish between objects that are truly satisfying and those that only appear to be satisfying. This learning constitutes the beginning of the development of the **ego.** The ego consists of rational thoughts, perceptions, and plans to help cope with reality. Much of its functioning is conscious and rational, and it attempts to channel instinctual energy toward objects that will realistically satisfy needs. This

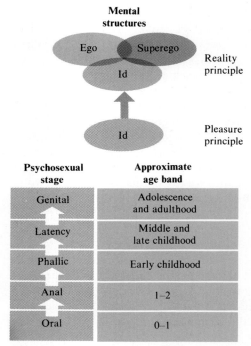

Figure 2.1 Freudian personality structures and stages of psychosexual development.

orientation toward reality and need-reducing value is referred to as the **reality principle,** or secondary process thinking.

The final mental system to develop is the **superego,** which consists of moral rules to guide the child's actions. The rules are internalized directives that develop from the various dos and don'ts the child learns while growing up.

All three mental systems, when fully developed, press for their demands to be met simultaneously. The id perpetually seeks to discharge instinctual energy immediately, the ego seeks to hold off acting until a realistic course of action can be found, and the superego continually directs the child to act in a good way or to refrain from acting in a bad way.

As the three mental systems evolve, the child experiences five clearly distinguishable developmental stages. Each one can be defined in terms of an overriding problem that guides the child's actions, thoughts, and feelings. The first three are closely tied to the satisfaction that is felt as the child stimulates or exercises particular parts of the body, the so-called **erogenous zones.** (See figure 2.1 for a representation of the mental structures and stages of personality from Freud's perspective.)

The first stage, known as the **oral stage,** centers on the child's pleasure from stimulation of the oral area—mouth, lips, tongue, gums. This stage lasts from birth to around one year. The activities of sucking, chewing,

The infant is motivated to seek oral gratification.

and biting provide the chief sources of pleasure. When the oral area is stimulated some instinctual energy is freed and tension is reduced.

The period called the **anal stage,** lasting from two to three years of age, centers on the child's pleasure with eliminative activity. The shift to the anal stage is brought about by maturation of the sphincter muscles and the child's ability to hold back or expel waste material at will. It is assumed that exercise of the anal muscles results in the freeing of instinctual energy and the reduction of tension. This period is not easily forgotten by parents, who typically experience great concern over their initially unsuccessful efforts to toilet train their child. When toilet training has been accomplished, the anal stage has reached its peak—the child has achieved well-regulated control over anal activity. Many debates have arisen about the proper method and time for toilet training (e.g., Anthony, 1957). However, few of the premises offered have much to do with the specific theoretical claims of Freud (e.g., Beloff, 1962).

During the **phallic stage,** which lasts from about four to five or six years of age, instinctual energy is focused on the genital area. Physical changes in the child cause this area to be a pleasurable one when stimulated. It is during this period, Freud thought, that boys

and girls become acutely aware of their sexual anatomy and the anatomical differences between the sexes. This awareness sets up a number of complex psychological events referred to as the **Oedipus complex** in boys and the **Electra complex** in girls. Each complex consists of the child's alternating feelings of love and hate for each parent as the child competes with one parent for the love and attention of the other parent. Working through these complexes, which are actually highly stressful conflicts about sexual affiliation and identity, takes from eight to ten years and forms the basis for the mature adult's personal and sexual identity.

The troublesome feelings and thoughts the child experiences while attempting to work out these conflicts are often repressed, driven from consciousness and locked away in the unconscious id. This repression marks the onset of the **latency stage,** the long period of middle childhood from about six to twelve years of age. During the latency stage the child concentrates on exploring the environment and mastering the vast number of intellectual skills and tricks needed for getting along in society. This activity channels much of the child's psychological energy into "emotionally safe" areas that help the child forget the highly stressful problems of the previous stage.

The **genital stage,** the last of Freud's stages of development, occurs from about thirteen to nineteen years of age. During this period the repression of Oedipal and Electra conflicts is lifted and teenagers experience a sudden surge of interest in sexual matters. After a number of groping attempts, the adolescent forms a stable sense of personal and sexual identity. The period is brought on by, among other things, the rapid physiological changes occurring in the adolescent at about twelve or thirteen years of age.

Several processes and mechanisms in Freud's theory, when taken collectively, help to explain developmental changes in behavior. In addition to those already mentioned is **tension reduction.** Freud believed that the goal of all activity is the reduction of tension, the release of pent-up psychological energy in some sphere. Tension reduction is inherently pleasurable and is the principal motivating force behind all behavior. Tension can arise from physical growth, preoccupation with an erogenous zone, conflict among id, ego, and superego, or the environment.

Another mechanism for change is **identification.** Freud used this term to refer to several different phenomena, the most important of which is the incorporation of behavior and attitudes of another person into one's own structure of thought and action. Many different people serve as figures for identification as the child develops—peers, siblings, teachers, television heroes—and the child tries many on for size to suit different needs at different times. The most important figures, however, are parents, with whom most children form a stable identification by the time they are in their mid-teens. In general, the process of identification allows the child to take on similarity with an individual who seems powerful or who possesses other desirable characteristics.

When the child is overwhelmed by anxiety, the ego can reduce the anxiety in a number of ways. Among these ways are the so-called **defense mechanisms.** Defense mechanisms work unconsciously; that is, the child is not aware of them. They also tend to distort the child's perception of his or her own feelings, thoughts, and sensations. Several of the more prominent defense mechanisms are *repression, projection, reaction formation, fixation,* and *regression.* **Repression** has already been discussed in one specific context (the Oedipal conflict). However, it is actually quite general and can be defined as an anxiety-provoking thought or feeling being forced out of consciousness into the unconscious. With **projection,** an anxiety-provoking thought or feeling is shifted from its actual source (the child) to an external object or person. The child comes to believe that someone else has the troublesome feeling or thought, with the result that the anxiety becomes externally rooted and is thereby easier to deal with. **Reaction formation** is a defense that consists in changing a troublesome thought or feeling into its opposite. This defense alters the conscious source of anxiety but does not remove it from the unconscious.

Finally, there are the related defenses of **fixation** and **regression.** As the child moves from one stage to the next, there are times when movement is difficult. The difficulty may stem from the child's extraordinary satisfaction with the way he or she is satisfying excess tension. (For example, in the oral stage the child may really enjoy sucking a bottle.) Or the difficulty may stem from a reluctance to try out new ways. Whatever the reason, the child may become temporarily stuck, or *fixated,* in this stage. Regression refers to a backsliding in development. If a child experiences undue anxiety in a particular stage, he or she may temporarily shift back to an earlier one that provided a great deal of pleasure. It is not uncommon, for example, to see four- or five-year-olds emulate infants by crawling on the ground and using infantile speech to draw attention from a parent in a frustrating situation. Some occurrence of fixation and regression is a normal part of development. These defense mechanisms become abnormal when they occur frequently or persist for long periods of time.

Few psychologists today accept all of Freud's major theoretical concepts. Freud's belief that virtually all behavior is motivated by unconscious desires seems overdrawn; for example, many of the things that bother people and motivate their behavior are quite well known

Sibling rivalry sometimes leads to regression.

to them. Freud's belief that the major impetus for development lies in the resolution of psychosexual conflicts also seems a bit overdrawn; children's affections for each parent do grow hot and cold, but such fluctuations are not limited to any one period of time. And children do show plenty of interest in sexual matters during the so-called latency period.

Erik Erikson
One serious misgiving of contemporary psychoanalytic thinkers arises from the fact that Freud shortchanged the importance of culture. He failed to see that each society handles children in very different ways. As a result, the stages of development only loosely describe the pattern of change for all children. That culture exerts a strong influence on the timing and dynamics of each stage is a theme reflected in the work of Erik Erikson.

Although Erikson accepts the basic outline of Freud's theory, he places more emphasis on the influence of culture and society as a shaper of the child's destiny. Much of his own professional work was with children and families in different cultures, which reflects his anthropological approach to the study of individual development. Erikson's theory is particularly important because it stresses rational, or *ego,* processes and because it casts a life-span frame of reference on development.

Phases of the life cycle	1	2	3	4	5	6	7	8
Late adulthood								Ego integrity vs. despair
Middle adulthood							Generativity vs. stagnation	
Young adulthood						Intimacy vs. isolation		
Adolescence					Identity vs. role confusion			
Middle and late childhood				Industry vs. inferiority				
Early childhood			Initiative vs. guilt					
Infancy		Autonomy vs. shame, doubt						
Infancy	Basic trust vs. mistrust							

Figure 2.2   Erik Erikson's eight stages of development.

Erikson postulates eight stages of development—sometimes called the **Eight Ages of Man.** Each one centers around a salient and distinct emotional concern stemming from biological pressures brought on by sociocultural expectations from outside the person. These concerns, or conflicts, may be resolved in a positive and healthy manner or in a pessimistic and unhealthy way. Each conflict has a unique time period during which it ascends and overshadows all the others. In order for later stages of development to proceed smoothly, each earlier stage conflict must be resolved satisfactorily. These stages of development are represented in figure 2.2. In the left-hand column are the major phases of life-span development. The eight conflicts are listed diagonally, in order of their ascendancy.

The first stage, **trust versus mistrust,** corresponds to the oral stage in Freudian theory. An infant is almost entirely dependent upon his or her mother for food, sustenance, and comfort. The mother is the primary representative of society to the child. If she discharges her infant-related duties with warmth, regularity, and affection, the infant will develop a feeling of trust toward the world. The infant's trust is a comfortable feeling that someone will always be around to care for his or her needs even though the mother occasionally disappears. Alternatively, a sense of mistrust or fearful uncertainty can develop if the mother fails to provide these needs in the caretaking setting. According to Erikson, she is setting up a distrusting attitude that will follow the child through life.

Autonomy versus shame and doubt is the second stage and corresponds to the anal stage in Freudian theory. The infant begins to gain control over the bowels and bladder. Parents begin imposing demands on the child to conform to socially acceptable forms and occasions for eliminating wastes. The child may develop the healthy attitude of being capable of independent or autonomous control of his or her own actions, or the child may develop the unhealthy attitude of shame or doubt because he or she is incapable of control.

Initiative versus guilt corresponds to the phallic period in Freudian theory. The child is caught in the midst of the Oedipal or Electra conflict, with its alternating love-hate feelings for the parent of the opposite sex and with fear of fulfilling the sexual fantasies that abound. The child may discover ways to overcome feelings of powerlessness by engaging in various activities. If this is done, then the basic healthy attitude of being the initiator of action will result. Alternatively, the child may fail to discover such outlets and feel guilty at being dominated by the environment.

Industry versus inferiority, coinciding with the Freudian period of latency, covers the years of middle childhood when the child is involved in expansive absorption of knowledge and the development of intellectual and physical skills. As the child is drawn into the social culture of peers, it is natural to evaluate accomplishments by comparing himself or herself with others. If the child views himself or herself as basically

Erik Erikson's view stresses that development is a life-long process.

competent in these activities, feelings of productive-ness and industriousness will result. On the other hand, if the child views himself or herself as incompetent, particularly in comparison with peers, then he or she will feel unproductive and inferior. This unhealthy at-titude may negatively color the child's whole approach to life and learning, producing a tendency to withdraw from new and challenging situations rather than meet them with confidence and enthusiasm.

Identity versus role confusion is roughly associated with Freud's genital stage, centering on the establish-ment of a stable personal identity. Whereas for Freud the important part of identity formation resides in the adolescent's resolution of sexual conflicts, for Erikson the central ingredient is the establishment of a clear path toward a vocation—selection of a job or an oc-cupational role to aspire to. This allows the adolescent an objective that he or she and other members of so-ciety simultaneously acknowledge. If the adolescent comes through this period with a clearly selected role and the knowledge that others in society can clearly identify this role, feelings of confidence and purpose-

fulness emerge. If not, the adolescent may feel con-fused and troubled.

Erikson introduced the first of the post-Freudian stages, **intimacy versus isolation.** Early adulthood brings with it a job and the opportunity to form an intimate relationship with a member of the opposite sex. If the young adult forms friendships with others and a sig-nificant, intimate relationship with one individual in particular, then a basic feeling of closeness with others will result. A feeling of isolation may result from an inability to form friendships and an intimate relation-ship.

A chief concern of adults is to assist the younger generation in developing and leading useful lives. **Gen-erativity versus stagnation** centers on successful rear-ing of children. Childless adults often need to find substitute young people through adoption, guardian-ship, or a close relationship with the children of friends and relatives. Generativity, or the feeling of helping to shape the next generation, is the positive outcome that may emerge. Stagnation, or the feeling of having done nothing for the next generation, is the unhealthy out-come.

In the later years adults enter the period of **ego integrity versus despair,** a time for looking back at what they have done with their lives. Through many differ-ent routes, the older person may have developed a pos-itive outlook in each of the preceding periods of emotional crises. If so, the retrospective glances will re-veal a picture of life well spent, and the person will be satisfied (ego integrity). However, the older person may have resolved one or more of the crises in a negative way. If so, the retrospective glances will yield doubt, gloom, and despair over the worth of one's life.

It should be noted that Erikson does not believe the proper solution to a stage crisis is always completely positive in nature. Some exposure and/or commitment to the negative end of the individual's bipolar conflict often is inevitable (for example, the individual cannot trust all people under all circumstances and survive). However, in a healthy solution to a stage crisis, the positive resolution of the conflict is dominant.

Psychoanalytic theorists stress that individuals go through a number of different stages in their life cycle and that these stages occur in a fixed sequence. They also believe that mental structures are an important part of development. From this perspective, psychoanalytic theory is no different from the next theory described, *cognitive-structural*. But the two theories differ radically in that cognitive-structural theory gives little or no attention to unconscious thought processes.

The Cognitive-Structural Perspective

The **cognitive-structural perspective** focuses on rational thinking processes in the child. In the psychoanalytic perspective, there is an interest in qualitative stages of change in children. These stages are seen as ordered in a uniform sequence for all children. The term *cognitive* in the cognitive-structural perspective underscores the interest in thought and rational mental process. The term *structural* highlights the concern with the way thought is organized at different stages. The leading contemporary figure who holds this point of view is Jean Piaget. Others include Lawrence Kohlberg, who has worked out an interesting theory of moral development that will be described in detail later in the text.

Jean Piaget

Piaget's ideas form one of the few complete theoretical statements about intelligence available in psychology. In common with others, Piaget believed that the core of intelligence is rationality—logical thinking—and that intelligence develops from the interplay of several hereditary and environmental forces. But there are many differences between Piaget's theory and other views of intelligence, particularly those with a psychometric (measurement) orientation. For one, Piaget was concerned with how children think rather than with what they think or how many facts they know. For example, it was important to Piaget whether a child can order the primary colors from lightest to darkest but quite unimportant whether the child knows the name of each color or can spell the names correctly. As a result, Piaget rarely looked at the content of thought but rather at its form.

For another, Piaget was interested in the general nature of children's thought rather than in how children at the same stage of thought differ. Finally, Piaget

had a tendency to examine the ideal form of a child's thought, that is, the way the child can reason, given no distractions, good concentration, and high motivation. Ordinary reasoning exercised in everyday situations often fails to reflect a child's ideal potential. With most standard intelligence tests, by contrast, psychologists study the content of thought, individual differences in intelligence and everyday thought.

A brief outline of Piaget's stages of thought follows. As is the case with all such theories, the time periods designated for various stages are only approximate. An individual child may move out of a stage sooner or remain in a stage longer than is indicated by the ages given. The more significant claim is that a child moves through the given stages in the established sequence and that no children violate this sequence.

The **sensorimotor stage** lasts from birth to about two years of age, corresponding to the period known as infancy. During this time the infant develops the ability to organize and coordinate sensations and perceptions with physical movements and actions. This coordination of sensation with action is the source of the term *sensorimotor*. The stage begins with the newborn, who has little more than reflexes to coordinate his or her senses with actions. The newborn sucks, turns his or her head, follows moving objects with his or her eyes, and performs other simple reflexes. The stage ends with the two-year-old, who has complex sensoriaction patterns and is beginning to operate with a primitive symbol system. For example, the two-year-old can imagine looking at a toy and manipulating it with his or her hands before actually doing so. The child can also use simple sentences—for example, "Mommy, jump!"—to represent a sensoriaction event that has just occurred.

The **preoperational stage** lasts from two to seven years of age, cutting across the preschool and early middle school years. During this time the child's symbolic system expands. The use of language and perceptual images moves well beyond the capabilities at the end of the sensorimotor period. Despite these advances, however, a number of limitations cause the child's thought to fall far short of what is seen in the later middle school years. Piaget perceives these limitations as "flaws" in the soon-to-develop "operational" structure of thought. Among the major flaws are the child's egocentrism, an inability to conserve, and a failure to order objects in a series and classify them. The child tends to see things from his or her own perspective and to confuse this perspective with that of others. He or she has difficulty manipulating the images and representations of events and is therefore likely to get stuck (centered) in static states and fail to reverse situations mentally. For example, if liquid is poured from a short, fat container into a tall, thin one, the child may notice only that the height of the water has changed (centering). If asked to imagine what would happen if the water were returned to the original container, the child would have a tough time visualizing the reversal (irreversibility).

The **concrete operational stage** lasts from seven to eleven years of age, cutting across the major portion of the middle school years. During this time the child's thinking crystallizes into more of a system, and the flaws of the preoperational stage completely disappear. The shift to a more perfect system of thinking is brought about by several changes. One of these is the shift from

egocentrism to relativism. Relativism is the ability to think from different perspectives and to think simultaneously about two or more aspects of a problem. Another change is the child's ability to pose and operate on a series of actions mentally. Performing mental arithmetic, imagining a game of table tennis, and thinking about how to tie a knot are all examples of this change. Children in the sensorimotor and preoperational stages, by contrast, are unable to perform these mental operations.

One limitation of concrete thinking is that the child has to rely on concrete events in order to think in this way. The child needs to be able to perceive objects and events that he or she will think about. An interesting shortcoming of the child in this period is that he or she often fails to distinguish between representations of events and the events themselves, because the representations are closely tied to the concrete events. For example, a child may maintain a hypothesis about what a friend can be expected to do in a certain situation (e.g., Karen fights with people when she is angry) even if the friend seldom does what the child expects. The child treats the hypothesis as a fact rather than as the possibility of a fact.

The last stage of development is the **formal operational stage,** which emerges between eleven and fourteen years of age. By the time adolescence is reached, Piaget presumed, the child has reached this most advanced level of thinking. The most important single feature of this stage is the adolescent's ability to move beyond the world of actual, concrete experiences. He or she can think logically, using abstract propositions (e.g., suppose one country has as much democracy as another does tyranny; further suppose a third country. . . .). The adolescent also can use make-believe events or statements that are contrary to reality (e.g., suppose you are looking at your hand, and it is invisible. What do you see in front of you?). Finally, the adolescent is able to conjure up many hypotheses to account for some event and then test these out in a deductive fashion, just as a scientist might. In figure 2.3 the Piagetian cognitive-structural stages are compared with the Freudian psychosexual and Eriksonian psychosocial stages. Note how both Piaget and Freud only presented one stage for adolescence and adulthood, while Erikson developed four.

Piaget used several interrelated processes to illustrate how change occurs in children's thought. Three are discussed here: adaptation, organization, and equilibration. If children are to develop normally, they have to interact effectively with the environment. Effective interaction is called **adaptation.** For Piaget the interaction is a cognitive one. It involves the child's use of sensorimotor, preoperational, or operational thinking skills. Adaptation is subdivided into **assimilation** and **accommodation,** which usually occur together. In assimilation, the child tries to incorporate features of the

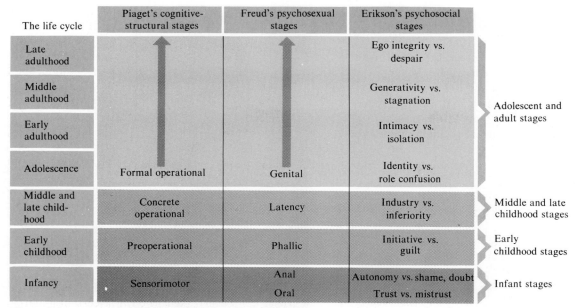

The life cycle	Piaget's cognitive-structural stages	Freud's psychosexual stages	Erikson's psychosocial stages	
Late adulthood			Ego integrity vs. despair	
Middle adulthood			Generativity vs. stagnation	Adolescent and adult stages
Early adulthood			Intimacy vs. isolation	
Adolescence	Formal operational	Genital	Identity vs. role confusion	
Middle and late childhood	Concrete operational	Latency	Industry vs. inferiority	Middle and late childhood stages
Early childhood	Preoperational	Phallic	Initiative vs. guilt	Early childhood stages
Infancy	Sensorimotor	Anal / Oral	Autonomy vs. shame, doubt / Trust vs. mistrust	Infant stages

Figure 2.3 A comparison of Freud, Erikson, and Piaget's stages of development.

environment into already existing ways of thinking about them. In accommodation, the child tries to incorporate new features of the environment into thinking by slightly modifying existing modes of thought. An example may help to clarify these terms.

A young girl is presented with a hammer and nails to use in hanging a picture on her bedroom wall. She has never used a hammer before. From experience and observation, however, she realizes that a hammer is an object to be held, that it is swung by the handle to strike the nail, and that it is swung repeatedly. Realizing each of these things, she incorporates her behavior into a conceptual framework that already exists (assimilation). But the hammer is heavy, so she must hold it near the top. As she swings too hard, the nail bends, so she must adjust the pressure of her taps. These adjustments show her sensitivity to the need to alter the concept slightly (accommodation).

A second mechanism of change is **organization.** Every level of thought, from sensorimotor to formal, is organized in some fashion. Continual refinement of this organization is an inherent part of development. The girl who has only a vague idea about how to use a hammer may also have a vague idea about how to use other tools. After learning how to use each one, she must interrelate these uses and organize her knowledge if she is to become skilled in using tools. In the same way, the child continually integrates and coordinates the many other branches of knowledge that often develop independently. Organization occurs within stages of development as well as across them.

Equilibration explains how a child shifts from one stage to the next. The goal of better organization is to reach a more lasting state of balance in thought. This goal is achieved as thought becomes more logical and abstract. But before a new stage of thought can be reached, the child must face the inadequacy of the current one. He or she must experience cognitive conflict, or uncertainty. If a child believes that the amount of liquid is changed simply because it was poured into a container with a different shape, he or she might be puzzled by such issues as where the extra liquid came from and where there is actually more liquid to drink. These puzzles will eventually be resolved as thought becomes concrete. In the everyday world the child is constantly faced with such counterexamples and inconsistencies.

Piaget's theory has guided European and North American scholars for over thirty years. It has offered a rich description of thought processes in children, a large number of hunches and ideas about how development takes place, and some dramatic claims about the structure of thought. As we move through the 1980s Piaget's influence will continue to remain strong. As John Flavell (1980) put it in a brief eulogy on Piaget's death in 1980, "We owe him nothing short of the whole field of cognitive development."

However, there are already signs that Piaget's style of theorizing has given way to a more modest approach, sometimes referred to as information processing (Flavell, 1980; Siegler, 1978). New-wave scholars remain skeptical about the validity of tightly knit stages of thought. As they survey the research evidence, it seems to them that children's thinking is more influenced by the specific form in which a problem is presented than in some global stage capacities. And in place of Piaget's loose concepts about change (i.e., adaptation and organization), they offer precise processes that account for change, such as computer models of the mind, models of attention and memory, and specification of concrete strategies for solving problems.

Nonstage Theories

The behavioral social learning perspective and the humanistic perspective stress that human development is void of abrupt transitions. While the two perspectives share the belief that development does not occur in discrete phases, you will discover that they disagree about a number of other aspects of development.

The Behavioral Social Learning Perspective

Behaviorists and social learning theorists believe that overt, directly observable behavior is more important in understanding development than the covert feelings studied by psychoanalytic theorists or the private thoughts investigated by cognitive-structural theorists. Social learning theorists also emphasize the importance of environmental influences; they believe that the greatest changes in development come about through social experiences. Such changes in behavior are regulated by three basic laws and principles: reinforcement, punishment, and imitation, or modeling. These basic principles apply to all people in all cultures.

Two major variations of the behavioral social learning perspective will be discussed in this chapter: the stimulus-response behaviorist approach of B. F. Skinner and the cognitive social learning theory of Albert Bandura.

The Stimulus-Response Theory of B. F. Skinner

Few theories of human development have created as much controversy as the one proposed by B. F. Skinner. While much of his research work has involved rats and pigeons, Skinner has made numerous applications of his views to human development as well (see, for example, *Walden Two,* 1948; and *About Behaviorism,* 1974). The book that has created the greatest controversy in recent years, however, is *Beyond Freedom and Dignity* (1971). The main theme of this book is that individuals are controlled by their external environments. Skinner argues that we are ruled and regulated by the consequences of our actions. He designs a futuristic culture that fosters individual dignity.

Skinner believes that if we are to understand the nature of development, we must examine the behavior—not the thoughts and feelings—of individuals. He believes that looking for internal determinants inhibits

The mother's nurturance is a powerful reinforcer.

the search for the true determinants of behavior, which reside in the external environment. Some psychologists would argue that Skinner is saying that individuals are empty organisms. However, Skinner (1953) has stated that he objects to looking for internal determinants of behavior not because they do not exist but because they are irrelevant to the relationships between stimuli and responses. (**Stimuli** may be defined as the observable characteristics of the environment that affect the individual and responses as the overt behaviors of the individual. A simple example: a child's mother tells her to clean her room [stimulus] and the child actually does clean the room [response].)

According to Skinner, one of the major ways stimuli and responses are linked together is through the principle of **operant conditioning** (sometimes referred to as **instrumental conditioning**). In this type of learning, the individual operates on the environment; that is, the individual does something, and, in turn, something happens to him or her. Another way of saying this is that the individual's behavior is instrumental in causing some effect in the environment. The lives of individuals are full of operant conditioning situations. For example, consider the following conversation:

John Hey, where did you get that new notebook?

Bob My mother bought it for me.

John Oh, yeah? Why?

Bob Because I got mad about something and started yelling at her.

John You mean if you get mad and throw a fit, your mom buys you a notebook?

Bob I guess that's the way it works!

At the heart of such occurrences is this principle: Behavior is determined by its consequences. According to this principle, behavior followed by a positive stimulus is likely to recur, while behavior followed by a negative stimulus is not as likely to recur. The positive experience is referred to as **reinforcement,** and the negative experience is labeled **punishment.**

Think for a moment about the last two weeks in your life, focusing on the positive and negative consequences of your actions. Perhaps a man frowned at you when you smiled at him, or a friend told you what a nice person you were for buying her a book. Perhaps a teacher wrote a note on the bottom of your term paper complimenting your writing skills, or your basketball coach made you run fifty extra laps around the gym for being late to practice. At any rate, the lives of infants, children, adolescents, and adults are full of situations in which behavior is followed by positive or negative consequences. These consequences have significant effects on the future behavior of the individuals involved.

One area of development in which the principle of operant conditioning has been applied liberally is **behavior modification.** This approach to changing behavior is widely practiced by clinicians, counselors, and teachers in an effort to resolve problems. Sometimes even parents are trained to more effectively manage problems by following the principles of operant conditioning (e.g., Patterson, in press). Basically, the procedure of behavior modification involves substituting acceptable patterns of behavior for unacceptable ones. Contingencies are established to ensure that acceptable responses will be acquired or learned; this learning is facilitated by reinforcement. Behavior modification experts argue that most emotional problems occur because their environment is arranged with the wrong set of contingencies—meaning that unacceptable behaviors are inadvertently reinforced. Hence the adolescent who frequently engages in delinquent behavior may be doing so because he or she is rewarded for such behavior, either through the material rewards of the objects stolen or the social attention received from peers. For a look at one way in which behavior modification is used to control problem behavior, see application 2.1.

Skinner's ideas have been used extensively in restructuring the learning environments of individuals. Many psychologists, though, reject Skinner's notion that the cognitive determinants of behavior cannot be studied and are not important to understanding the linkage between stimuli and responses. Even some of Skinner's fellow behaviorists feel this way; while they

We influence the behavior of others rather than completely controlling it.

give ball-park approval to Skinner's ideas about reinforcement contingencies, observable behavior, and careful experimental methodology, they nonetheless believe he is wrong to ignore the cognitive determinants of behavior.

The Cognitive Social Learning Theory

Cognitive social learning theory is a label that best describes the behavioral views of Albert Bandura (1977). From Bandura's perspective, the statement that behavior is determined by its consequences refers to the self-produced consequences of one's own actions as well as to consequences of the actions of others. In other words, self-reinforcement is often just as important as reinforcement from others.

Consider the achievement behavior of a woman who is required to perform certain duties on her job. Although she cannot ignore her desire for a salary increase, her own need for excellence will just as likely motivate her to improve and do a better job on her work assignment. Substandard performance, on the other hand, might lead her to self-criticism. In this sense, the woman's achievement behavior is as much a function of her reaction to herself as to the reactions of others. This concept differs from Skinner's theory, which argues that behavior is determined only by external consequences.

Application 2.1
A Behavioral Contract for Sam

Sam is a ten-year-old who is a nuisance in his classroom. He fights with other children, he steals things, and he seldom attends to his classwork. Not surprisingly, he is doing very poorly in school. Gerald Patterson and his colleagues (Patterson, Cobb, & Ray, 1972) have developed a program to help children like Sam. They attempt to substitute acceptable behaviors in place of unacceptable ones by identifying acceptable behaviors, reinforcing them with pleasurable outcomes (for example, being allowed to watch TV), and removing the child from the classroom ("time-out") when his behavior gets out of hand. An effort is made to involve all of the people who normally interact with the child—teacher, parents, and peers. The procedure is more effective if the child is treated in the same way by everyone. This approach is one example of **behavior modification.** It is based on the principles of association and reinforcement. In the particular brand of behavior modification practiced by Patterson, the procedure is formally agreed to by all parties in the form of a contract. Here is a contract developed for Sam. It spells out the details of what everyone must do to help Sam change his behavior. Patterson and others have had remarkable success with it (Homme et al., 1970; Patterson et al., 1972).

Sam's Contract
The following is a contract between Sam and his teacher, his principal, and his counselor, in order for Sam to learn ways to behave during school. Sam will earn points during school hours so that he can do some of the things he enjoys at home. The total number of points that he can earn each day is 50. The behaviors are the following:

Talking in a normal tone of voice (e.g., not yelling)

Cooperating with his teacher (e.g., not arguing) and doing as he is asked on the playground and in the halls

Minding other teachers

Remaining in his chair unless schoolwork requires moving in the classroom (e.g., not roaming around the room)

Talking to other children at proper times (e.g., not disturbing other children when they work)

Following his teacher's directions for work (e.g., doing the work assigned)

Sam will start with a total of fifty points each day and will lose a point for each time he does not follow the terms of his contract. Each time he loses a point, he is to be placed in time-out for five minutes. At the end of each schoolday, his teacher will call his mother with the total points Sam earned for that day. Sam will be allowed five minutes of TV for each point earned.

For the following behaviors Sam is to be sent home from school for the day:

1. Destroying property
2. Fighting with other children to the point of hurting them
3. Taking property belonging to someone else
4. Swearing
5. Refusing to go into time-out

When Sam is sent home, his principal will call Sam's father to tell him what Sam has done. The principal will then call Sam's mother so she will know that Sam is being sent home. When Sam arrives home, he is to do some task around the house or yard until school is out, at which time he can follow the normal routine of the household—except that he will not watch TV that night.

When Sam does not follow the rules of the lunchroom, he is to be sent from the lunchroom to the principal's office without finishing his meal.

His mother will keep the number of points earned each day in order to assess Sam's progress. His mother will also continue to teach Sam reading skills until he is able to read the reading material in the classroom. The therapist will continue to supervise Sam's mother until the reading program is completed.

To be signed by all parties:

_____

Sam

_____

Mother

_____

Father

_____

Teacher

_____

Principal

_____

Date

The existence of self-produced consequences and personal performance standards suggests that using reinforcement to control someone else's behavior will not always be successful. As Bandura (1977) has pointed out, if external reinforcement were always effective, we would behave like weather vanes—in the presence of a John Bircher we would act like a John Bircher, while in the presence of a Communist we would behave like a Communist. Instead, behavior develops through the process of reciprocal control. Consider the following conversation between a seventeen-year-old boy and girl:

Bob Oh, come on, Nancy, let's go to the drive-in tonight.

Nancy (looks away as if she doesn't hear him)

Bob Look, Nancy, I'm talking to you! Don't ignore me.

Nancy What, Bob?

Bob I said, let's go to the drive-in tonight.

Nancy Bob, I know what you want to do—you just want to make out.

Bob (Yelling) Don't make me look like a fool! You make me feel so stupid when you embarrass me like that.

Nancy Well, maybe we can go in a couple of weeks.

Bob Well, all right.

What has been learned in this interchange? Nancy has learned that she can control Bob's advances with vague promises. Bob has learned that if he gets upset and amplifies his feelings, he can at least get Nancy to make some kind of promise. This type of interchange occurs all the time in relationships throughout the life span. It is a coercive process in which two people attempt to control each other's behavior. Indeed, whenever one person is trying to control another, the second person is usually resisting control or attempting to control in return. In this sense, Bandura (1971) asserts that the manipulation and control of people suggested by Skinner in *Walden Two* could never evolve.

Bandura (1977) refers to this concept of behavior as **reciprocal determinism.** The individual is not completely driven by inner forces or manipulated helplessly by environmental factors; rather, the person's psychological makeup is best understood by analyzing the continuous reciprocal interaction between behavior and its controlling conditions. In other words, behavior partly constructs the environment, and the resulting environment, in turn, affects behavior.

Bandura (1971, 1977) also believes that individuals learn extensively by example. Much of what we learn involves observing the behavior of parents, peers, teachers, and others. This form of social learning is called **imitation, modeling,** or **vicarious learning.** For example, the ten-year-old who watches the teacher smile at her friend for turning in her work on time may be motivated to do likewise.

Bandura believes that if learning proceeded in the trial-and-error fashion advocated by Skinner, it would be very laborious and even hazardous. For example, to put a fifteen-year-old girl in an automobile, have her drive down the road, and reward the positive responses she makes would be senseless. Instead, many of the complex educational and cultural practices of individuals are learned through their exposure to competent models who display appropriate ways to solve problems and cope with the world.

Sometimes it is said that social learning theorists take a mechanical view of development. Jonas Langer (1969), a cognitive-structuralist, has even labeled the social learning view as a **mechanical mirror theory.** The label suggests that individuals do not control their own destiny but instead are controlled and manipulated by environmental influences until they mirror their environments in mechanical fashion. On the other hand, the cognitive-structural and psychoanalytic views of development emphasize the internal forces that control the individual's growth. In the psychoanalytic view, the forces are the relationships of the three personality structures to each other, while in the cognitive-structural view, they reside in the organization of rational thought.

Certainly it is valid to say that social learning adherents believe behavior is influenced by the individual's response to the environment. To this extent, the social learning model indicates that an individual's behavior is controlled by the external environment. However, as we have just seen, many social learning thinkers, such as Bandura, stress that the individual controls and even constructs his or her own environment. Recall the example of the boy trying to get his date to go to the drive-in movie. Not only was he controlling her behavior, but she was controlling his as well. Many contemporary social learning theorists stress just this type of bidirectional stimulus control (e.g., Bijou, 1976).

But probably the strongest criticism of behaviorism has come not from psychoanalytic and cognitive-structural theorists but from a group of psychologists referred to as humanists. The greatest area of controversy between humanistic and behavioristic theorists involves their views of the individual and his or her relationship to the environment. Specifically, humanists and behaviorists differ on whether the individual is an active creator of environment or a passive recipient of it, whether he or she is free to determine his or her own fate, and the nature of the construct referred to as the "self." Humanistic theorists believe that behaviorists like Skinner take the "person" out of personality and view the individual as a passive organism incapable of determining his or her own course of action. And while humanistic theorists see the self as a fundamental unity of personality around which all aspects of the individual are organized, most behaviorists believe the construct of self as a mental structure is so global and broad in nature that it is meaningless as a predictor of an individual's behavior.

The Humanistic Perspective

The **humanistic perspective** includes a number of ideas to explain the nature of an individual's personality and techniques that can be used to change personality. Just as there is no single social learning theory, there is no single humanistic theory. However, humanistic theorists as a group all agree that human psychology should be studied with a human model, not an animal model, and that human psychology should not be viewed in a mechanical manner. What should be studied, say the humanists, are conscious feelings, ideals, and intentions.

This view of human development has produced an orientation that focuses on human growth, personal fulfillment, and self-actualization. Humanistic therapy attempts to enable the individual to reach his or her full potential through exploration of individual emotional dynamics (Poppen, Wandersman, & Wandersman, 1976). Humanistic theory is much farther away from the theory of development advocated by Skinner than from that proposed by Bandura. Remember that Skinner clearly does not believe that internal or cognitive processes control behavior; behavior is controlled by external, environmental events only. Most humanists are at the opposite end of the control continuum— they focus on the internal determinants of personality. They emphasize the subjective experience of the individual or how the individual interprets the world, rather than on actual behavior. And many humanists focus on uniquely human aspects of experience, such as creativity and intentionality, that do not exist in subhuman species.

From the perspective of the humanist, the individual has an internal, dynamic personality structure that organizes conduct, emotions, and thoughts. Although Freud also believed that individuals have an internal personality structure, he believed that subconscious forces controlled the person, while humanists believe that control is held by conscious mental processes.

The humanistic approach is less scientific than the other five approaches covered in this chapter. Many humanistic approaches represent a cluster of attitudes about how to view children rather than a rigorous set of formal propositions and axioms. Nonetheless, despite the empirical insufficiency of many humanistic views, the theories themselves seem to have considerable clinical value and provide rich insight into the lives of individuals. One theorist, Carl Rogers, has been a dominant figure in the humanistic movement.

Carl Rogers

Carl Rogers' theory defines the personality of the individual in terms of subjective experiences. Rogers (1974) believes that subjective experience should be studied by focusing on the whole person rather than just parts of the person. He points out that every individual has a tremendous potential for self-understanding that usually is not brought out in everyday exchanges with people. Rogers feels that by providing the right psychological climate, this potential can emerge.

Such thinking has implications for therapists who work with individuals as well as for people who need to communicate more effectively with one another. According to Rogers, the therapist must have an open mind to really hear what the individual is saying. Such careful listening benefits the individual and provides the therapist with the clearest possible perception of the workings of the individual's mind. The therapist must lay aside all preconceptions about the individual and strive to discover the true nature of the person's feelings and thoughts. And the therapist should role play often, trying to experience the world just as the individual does. Rogers' ideas about therapy have served as the basis for the widespread approach to dealing with problems called **Parent Effectiveness Training (P.E.T.).** This program was developed by Thomas Gordon (1970) to help parents communicate more effectively with their children. P.E.T. stresses open and honest two-way communication between the child and parents, problem-solving skills, positive ways to deal

Application 2.2
Parent Effectiveness Training

Parent Effectiveness Training, or P.E.T. as it is often referred to, has attracted a number of parents looking for ways to deal more effectively with their children. The movement has become so widespread that there are about ten thousand individuals who have received training at P.E.T. institutes so that they can in turn teach P.E.T. courses in their communities.

P.E.T. stresses open and honest two-way communication between child and parent, problem-solving skills, positive ways to deal with conflict, and cooperative goal setting.

P.E.T. emphasizes a humanistic and democratic approach to parent-adolescent relationships. Perhaps the most important contribution that Thomas Gordon, the architect of P.E.T., has made to helping parents and adolescents is the detail in which he analyzes communication patterns. Also, the training sessions seem to be on target with the actual "goings on" in families. Many parents respond to sessions by saying, "Gee, that's exactly what is happening in our family . . . so this must be the way I should deal with it."

The program's simplicity may be another attractive feature to parents. But the simplicity of P.E.T. and the stereotyped ways in which parents in the program are taught to deal with children has been criticized by many empirically minded psychologists. The critics believe that the child and her parents are much more complex than Gordon makes them out to be and that sometimes it is wiser to have many parenting strategies available for parents, because some strategies work better with some children than others.

However, the parent-training strategies advocated by Gordon do have some very important messages for parents. One communication pattern that P.E.T. tries to change is referred to as the "you-message." Many parents fall into the trap of frequently barraging their child with criticism, blame, ridicule, and so forth. They may tell the child, "You are inconsiderate"; "You just want everybody to watch you"; "If you were a good person, you wouldn't do things like that"; "You are just no good"; and so on. Such communication patterns put the child down and lead to feelings of inadequacy. They all place the blame on the child. In P.E.T. sessions, parents learn to replace "you-messages" with "I-messages." For example, "I don't feel like doing that with you now because I have worked hard all day, and I need rest" might replace "You are always bugging me—will you please leave me alone!"

Why are "I-messages" more effective than "you-messages"? "I-messages" focus the communication on the feelings of the parent rather than the culpability of the child. "I-messages" may be more effective because they arouse the child less than "you-messages." Furthermore "I-messages" place responsibility on the child for modifying her behavior. In this way, Gordon believes such communication patterns help the child achieve a sense of self-responsibility.

with conflict, and cooperative goal setting. To learn more about Parent Effectiveness Training, see application 2.2.

The **self** is an important construct in Rogers' theory. Calvin Hall and Gardner Lindzey (1978) describe the individual's need to find congruence between the self and real-world experiences. When the individual finds this congruence, he or she is considered well adjusted; but when there is a considerable degree of incongruence, the individual might be categorized as maladjusted. Congruence between the self and experience produces realistic thinking, whereas incongruence leads to anxiety, defensiveness, and distorted thinking.

In addition to emphasizing the relationship between the self and real-world experiences, Rogers (1959) also discusses the relationship between the individual's ideal self and real self. The real self, or self-structure, is the self as it really is, whereas the ideal self is the self the person would like to be. The greater the discrepancy between the ideal and real selves, the greater the likelihood that the individual will become maladjusted.

Unlike psychoanalytic and cognitive-structural theorists, but like social learning theorists, humanists do not view maturation of the self on a timetable or as a series of developmental stages. Rogers does, however, describe how childhood experiences with significant adults affect the individual's self-perception in later life. If the child's experiences with parents, siblings, peers, and teachers are characterized by what Rogers calls unconditional positive regard, significant adjustment problems are less likely to surface when the child reaches adulthood. However, if significant people often evaluate the individual in a negative way, the individual learns that many of his or her actions gain disapproval. The more negative feedback received, the more distorted the self-perception in an effort to be insulated from negative evaluations. The discrepancy between experiences and self-perception produces feelings of anxiety that can lead to maladjustment.

The gap between the perceived self and real experiences with others affects the individual's interaction with others. The anxiety and defensiveness that result from this type of discrepancy often lead the individual to act in hostile ways toward others. Rogers feels that these problems should be resolved through a nonthreatening relationship with a person who completely accepts everything the individual says. This unconditional positive regard encourages the individual to express true feelings and makes the person feel better about himself or herself.

Not everyone, however, agrees with Rogers' approach to helping children and adolescents mature into more competent adults. Calvin Hall and Gardner Lindzey (1978) provide a summary of problems that are inherent in Rogers' humanistic theory. One criticism of Rogers is that his theory is based on a naive view of individual perceptions. For instance, many factors unavailable to conscious experience motivate the individual to act in particular ways. Also, no concern for the biological basis of development is evident in the humanistic perspective.

Perspectives from Outside of Psychology: Ethological, Evolutionary and Anthropological, Sociological Theories

Trying to explain development is an awesome, complex undertaking. Although this text is primarily a psychological approach to child development, psychology, by no means, has exclusive rights to child development. Explanations of development are housed in biology, anthropology, and sociology as well. In this section we look at some of the most important perspectives of development from outside of psychology—ethological, evolutionary and anthropological, sociological.

The Ethological, Evolutionary Perspective

Freud and Piaget's theories are biologically oriented, but one biological perspective that has influenced the study of development originated outside of psychology. Two European zoologists, Konrad Lorenz (1965) and Niko Tinbergen (1951, 1969), believed that behaviorism had led scientists to an unfortunate neglect of the innate nature of many behaviors. Their work formed the basis for a biological theory of behavior known as **ethology.** Some of their studies are now classic. Lorenz revealed the speed and totality with which young ducklings form rapid attachments to a variety of objects in their environment. He is also known for his work on the mating behavior of the stickleback fish. In these animal behaviors, we readily see stereotyped patterns of social behavior that are difficult to explain with traditional processes of learning, such as reinforcement.

Working mostly with graylag geese, Lorenz studied a behavior pattern that was considered to be programmed within the genes of the animals. A newly hatched gosling seemed to be born with an instinct for following its mother. Observations showed that the gosling was capable of such behavior as soon as it hatched from the egg. Lorenz proved that it was incorrect to assume that such behavior was programmed in the animal.

In a remarkable series of experiments, Lorenz separated the eggs laid by one female goose into two groups. One group he returned to the female goose to be hatched by her; the other group was hatched in an incubator. The first group performed as predicted; they followed their mother as soon as they were hatched. But the second group, which saw Lorenz when they were first hatched, followed him everywhere, just as though he were their mother. Lorenz marked the goslings and then placed both groups under a box. Mother goose and "mother Lorenz" stood aside as the box was lifted. Without error, each group of goslings went directly to its adopted "mother."

Lorenz used the word **imprinting** to describe this early modification of behavior. A number of interesting facts have resulted from imprinting experiments. In every case in which imprinting is observed, there is a **critical period** of time when the individual will respond to an imprinting experience. For chicks and ducklings this critical period lasts from the time of hatching for about thirty-six hours. Peak sensitivity occurs at thirteen and sixteen hours. After the critical period for imprinting, young animals can still be taught to follow another object, but the nature of the learning experience is distinctly different from the imprinting experience. Experiments with the young of rodents, dogs, and monkeys show that imprinting also takes place in mammals. In chapter 6 under the topic of early experiences, there will be extensive discussion of how biological predispositions may lead to a critical period, a time in the life cycle when development is most rapid and vulnerable to environmental experience.

Ethology is now receiving attention from many developmental psychologists who are searching for ways to understand how the individual's biological heritage influences the course of social development (Seay & Gottfried, 1978). The two areas of social development most influenced by ethological theory are attachment and aggression. As we will see in chapter 6, prominent theorists and researchers such as John Bowlby and

Konrad Lorenz, a pioneering student of animal behavior, is followed by imprinted graylag geese.

Mary Ainsworth argue that newborn infants are biologically predisposed to orient toward people, an evolutionary fact that shapes the way we view the attachment process. The ethological perspective on attachment contrasts with the behavioral view that the infant learns through reinforcement to be dependent upon the mother. Ethologists also believe that aggression has evolutionary roots and that the child is pre-programmed with aggressive tendencies. Ethologists stress that there is continuity between the aggressive actions of lower animals and young children and that these aggressive actions can be unlearned (Suomi, 1977).

A basic point in the ethological approach to development that requires more attention than can be given in this introductory chapter on perspectives of development is the belief that every individual carries a genetic code inherited from his or her parents. In chapter 3 you will read extensively about the basic ideas of behavior genetics, including the role of genetics in such characteristics as intelligence, physical traits, and mental retardation. To more fully understand the importance of the ethological approach to studying development we focus now, in a more detailed way, on the ethologist's emphasis on evolution.

The Role of Evolution in Development

The key to ethology is **evolution.** Ethologists believe that we can only fully appreciate the origin of behavior if we recognize that many patterns of behavior are transmitted through evolution. Biological evolution concerns the manner in which inherited genes predispose individuals to function in ways that are adaptively similar to their biological ancestors. Significant genetic change leading to an observable change in a characteristic (e.g., the disposition to be helpful) can typically take thousands of years. On the other hand, **cultural,** or **social, evolution** is much more rapid. It refers to the manner in which new behaviors are acquired and innate tendencies are modified through cultural transmission, for example, modeling, language, customs, and practices of a group. Thus some ethologists believe that the child's tendency to be helpful and to empathize with others results from a biological predisposition, but the tendency to express these prosocial actions can be dramatically and rapidly shaped by a culture. Thus history shows us that some societies teach children to be very helpful and humane, while other societies encourage callousness and inhumanity. What is unique about this perspective is the care taken to explain the subtle and intricate manner by which instinctual and environmental pressures combine to shape social destiny (Atkinson & Low, 1983; Hinde, 1983).

In evolutionary terms, humans are relative newcomers to earth, but in a short time they have established themselves as the most successful and dominant species. As our earliest ancestors left the forests to feed in the savannas and finally to form hunting societies on the open plains, they changed physically, mentally, and socially. A basic point in the evolutionary theory is that the organism is closely adapted to the environment in which it lives because natural selection favors the survival and reproduction of those physical, mental, and behavioral characteristics that are advantageous. Over the course of many generations humans have modified themselves to take advantage of the environment so they could survive. And although every human being is physically, mentally, emotionally, and socially unique, there are communalities among all individuals because

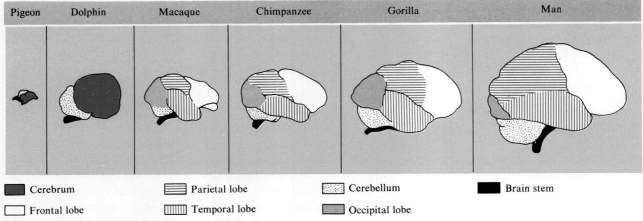

| Pigeon | Dolphin | Macaque | Chimpanzee | Gorilla | Man |

Cerebrum   Parietal lobe   Cerebellum   Brain stem

Frontal lobe   Temporal lobe   Occipital lobe

Figure 2.4 Brain evolution.

of their evolutionary heritage. For example, every living person is made up of cells, bones, muscle, blood vessels, and a brain (see figure 2.4 for a view of the evolutionary development of the brain). Thus the evolutionary perspective stresses not only the adaptiveness of the child to the environment but communalities with all other children as well. An extended discussion of the role of evolution in language development will appear in chapter 5.

The evolutionary process proceeds in an undetectable, slow manner. The better we adapt to our environment from generation to generation, the better we will survive and the more successful we will become as human beings. In our description of the ethological perspective, we indicated that children's attachment and aggression are two aspects of social development that likely can be traced to evolutionary beginnings.

The Anthropological, Sociological Perspective

Anthropologists and sociologists look for explanations of children's behavior in cultural values, social structures, and roles. Ideas about the nature of development and the techniques used to raise children differ from culture to culture and within the same culture over time. The label **culture** refers to the existing cluster of behaviors, attitudes, values, and products of a particular group of people. We can refer to the culture of the United States, the culture of Russia, the culture of China, and so forth. Of course, the culture of any of these nations is made up of many different subcultures that have their own sets of behaviors and values. The way in which cultures and subcultures impart behaviors, attitudes, and values to their children is often referred to as **enculturation** (LeVine, 1973).

In every culture there are defined goals that reflect what individuals are expected to do and become and represent what the members of the culture value and feel is worth working for (Merton, 1957). For example, the United States is a culture that places a premium on work and achievement; it is also a culture that requires all children to go to an institution called school. Achievement of these social tasks would reflect similar cultural expectations in many other cultures as well, but some behaviors may not be comparable for certain cultures. For example, sexual modesty is not expected in the Mangaian culture in the South Pacific, where sexual promiscuity is standard fare for youth (Hyde, 1979).

Cultures may vary considerably in the rate at which individuals achieve patterns of behavior, and individual development of a set of values is determined by the particular values of the culture. Masculinity and femininity often do not have the same referents from culture to culture; in one culture it may be considered masculine to wear plaid kilts while in another it may be thought masculine to play football. Next we present anthropologist Margaret Mead's perception of the culture American children experience.

Margaret Mead's Perception of the American Culture
Margaret Mead's well-known investigations as an anthropologist have shown that the culture we experience in the United States is different from the cultures of the South Sea islands. Just before her death in 1978 she wrote about our culture.

Mead's main points focus on the American family. She indicates that in times of upheaval in a nation, such as war, famine, or mass emigration, family life has always suffered. However, the changes that are occurring in the American family today are the results of more subtle changes in the American way of life.

One change is the increased longevity of people's lives. Fifty years ago, the older people who survived were generally hearty and were still linked closely to the family, often helping to maintain its existence. The elderly no longer maintain such a strong socializing role in the family.

A second change in our culture, Mead points out, is the move away from farms and small towns to the cities and suburbs. In the small towns and farms, individuals were surrounded by lifelong neighbors, relatives, and friends. Today, neighborhood and extended-family support systems are rare. Moreover, the American family is much more mobile than in the past—families move all over the country, often uprooting the child from a school and peer groups he or she has known for a number of years. And for many families, this type of move occurs every year or two, as one or both parents are transferred from job to job.

Related to the migration from rural to urban life is the growth of suburbs. Suburbs developed rapidly after World War II. Essentially comprised of relatively young middle-class people, the growth of suburbs caused increasing numbers of young parents to be isolated from their own parents and families. The loneliness and boredom of many surburban housewives led them to make greater efforts to find employment outside of the home, not just as a means of economic support for the family, but as a means of self-development as well.

According to Mead, coinciding with the development of the affluent suburbs has been the deterioration of the inner cities of our nation. Many people in the inner city, as a result, have grown up in families whose economic support is provided by the government. Inner city youth not only feel financial strains within their families but within their schools as well. Consequently, the inner city child generally receives an inferior education compared to that of the child who grows up in the suburbs.

Mead goes on to say that television has played a major role in the changing American way of life. Many children and adolescents who often watch television find that their parents are too busy working to share this experience with them. The youth increasingly experience a world their parents are not a part of. Furthermore, instead of participating in neighborhood peer groups, many boys and girls come home after school and plop down in front of the television set. Television also allows different groups of people to see new ways of life. Lower-class individuals can look into the lives of other individuals more closely, particularly the lives of middle-class families.

Another change Mead points out is a general dissatisfaction and restlessness. Women have become increasingly dissatisfied with their way of life, placing a

Margaret Mead, the famous anthropologist.

great strain on many marriages. With no elders to help and advise young people during the initial difficult years of marriage and childbearing, marriages begin to fracture at the first signs of disagreement. For those who marry, the cost of housing and other commodities places great strains on the marriage. Divorce has become an epidemic in this culture, for both middle-aged and young people. Many people who marry often divorce within a few years, and many children witness their own parents' divorce proceedings. Men become restless and look for stimulation and satisfaction outside of family life. The result of this restlessness and the tendency to divorce and remarry is a hodgepodge of family structures, with far greater numbers of single parent and stepparent families than ever before in history.

Mead believed that America is in great need of revised national policies regarding families. Who is responsible for the youth of divorced parents and the child whom nobody wants? Badly needed are better social services, revised welfare policies, and schools that are more responsive to the cultural diversity that now exists in the population. Mead also suggested that television became a positive force by portraying adult responsibility for children, revealing the needs of inner cities and suggesting ways for ruptured families to cope with the problems in their lives.

Culture, Subcultures, Values, and Roles

Cultures and subcultures can be described in terms of their **social structures.** The noted sociologist Alex Inkeles (1969) believes the following categorization of social structures provides a helpful system for understanding how culture influences development.

Ecological structure involves the size, density, physical distribution, and social composition of the population. These factors all determine the amount of control needed over individuals and groups.

Economic structure entails the type and amount of material resources in a society. Patterns of occupational recruitment in industrialized societies have

Development is influenced by the culture in which you live.

had strong influences on development. When farming and crafts were the primary occupations in our society, the child was socialized into an occupational role by serving an apprenticeship. This system has been replaced by instruction in specialized schools, a system that is more formalized and impersonal.

Political structure involves the importance of power structures and their subsystems in a society. Inkeles (1969) suggests that when youth are allowed to participate in politics and government—through their own efforts or through youth groups—the nature of socialization will be different than when adolescents are politically subordinate. The Little Red Soldiers and the Red Guard in China are examples of this type of socialization technique.

Value structure comes closest to the usual meaning of the label **culture.** Cultural ethics and morals, standards of right and wrong, and rules and regulations reflect the value structure of a culture. Moral education helps to transmit the value structure of a culture to the child.

In addition to analyzing the social structures of a culture, sociologists stress that within those roles it is not the individual who should be studied but rather the *roles* of the individual (Neugarten & Datan, 1973). A **role** is both a range of actions and a set of functions. Thus a child performs in roles such as student, son or daughter, peer, leader, athlete, musician, and so on. Development, for many sociologists, is defined in terms of the sum total of roles the individual plays and the changes that occur in the succession of these roles. Next we look at one particular perspective of development that has a strong sociological flavor.

Bernice Neugarten's Multiple Time, Changing Life-Cycle Perspective
Bernice Neugarten and Nancy Datan (1973) have described how studies of the life cycle have been more biological than social. They believe that it may be helpful to think of the life cycle in terms of three dimensions of time: life time, or chronological age; historical time; and social time, or the system of age grading and expectations that shape the life cycle.

Life time is based heavily on the biological timetable that governs the sequence of changes in the process of growing; Erikson's stages, described earlier in this chapter, are regulated strongly by this biological timetable. However, chronological age is at best only a rough indicator of an individual's position on any one of numerous physical or psychological dimensions, because from early in infancy individual differences are a known fact of development. Neugarten and Datan (1973) also argue that age is often not a very good index of many forms of social and psychological behavior, unless there is accompanying knowledge of the particular society as a frame of reference. They give an obvious example of a girl in the United States who will be a schoolgirl, but the same-aged girl in a rural village in the Near East who may be the mother of two children. It is argued that the significance of a given chronological age, or a given marker of life time, when viewed from a sociological or anthropological perspective, is directly a function of the social definition of age, or social time.

Social time refers to the dimension that underlies the age-grade system of a particular society. It has been characteristic of preliterate societies to have rites of passage marking the transition from one age status to the next, such as the passage from youth to maturity and to marriage (Van Gennep, 1960). According to Neugarten and Datan (1973), however, only a rough parallel exists between social time and life time in most societies. There are different sets of age expectations and age statuses in different societies.

Historical time controls the social system, and the social system, in turn, creates a changing set of age norms and a changing age-grade system that shapes the individual life cycle. For example, childhood as a distinct phase of life did not emerge until the seventeenth and eighteenth centuries, and the concept of adolescence did not emerge until the twentieth century. Changes in industrialization, urbanization, and our educational institutions account for these changing concepts. Scientists in this area also recognize the importance of the timing of major historical events in the life of an individual. Wars and depressions often act as historical watersheds, that is, major turning points in the social system. Significant historical events often affect levels of education, fertility patterns, sexual mores, labor participation patterns, and so forth.

The Developmental Perspective: An Eclectic Approach

There is no single, indomitable theory in explaining development. Each of the theories discussed in this chapter has made a contribution to our understanding, but none provides a complete description and explanation of development. Cognitive-structural theory provides the best explanation of the child's conscious mind and intellectual development, but it provides much less information on social development and the unconscious

Table 2.1
Perspectives of Development

Theory	Organizing Principles
Psychoanalytic	Biological instincts, psychosexual stages, and family processes
Cognitive-Structural	Cognitive processes and stages
Behavioral Social Learning	Learning processes
Humanistic	The self and self-concept
Ethological, Evolutionary	Genes, evolution, and adaptation
Anthropological, Sociological	Culture, social structure, and roles

aspects of the mind. Psychoanalytic theory best describes how the subconscious mind affects development, but it tells us much less about the effects of the social environment on the child. The behavioral social learning perspective provides the most detailed account of how the child learns and the influence of environment on learning, but it does not give us much insight into the child's thinking processes or emotions. Humanistic theory contains an abundance of information about the child's self-structure and self-concept and suggests specific ways to work through problems, but it lacks a scientific base and provides little information about phases of development. The ethological, evolutionary perspective has reawakened our interest in the biological underpinnings of development, but it too provides little information about different phases in development. And the anthropological, sociological perspective gives the best view of the importance of social structures and roles in development, but it has not been very beneficial in revealing knowledge about individual development. To help you remember the major organizing principles of each perspective, they are presented in table 2.1.

Development is much too complex to be explained by a single theory. It is important to realize that although theories are often helpful guides in understanding development, relying on a single theory to explain development is probably a mistake.

An attempt was made in this chapter to present six major perspectives objectively. The same **eclectic orientation** will be found in the remainder of the text. In this way, you can view the study of development as it actually exists—with different theorists making different assumptions about development, stressing different empirical problems, and using different strategies to discover more about individuals. In the next section we begin our long and exciting journey through the life cycle, starting with the first phase, infancy.

Summary

Six perspectives of development have received prominent attention:—psychoanalytic; cognitive-structural; behavioral social learning; humanistic; ethological, evolutionary; and anthropological, sociological. The first two perspectives—psychoanalytic and cognitive–structural—are stage theories; the second set of perspectives—behavioral social learning and humanistic—are nonstage theories; and the third set of views—ethological, evolutionary and anthropological, sociological—come from outside of psychology.

The psychoanalytic perspective is dominated by the theory of Sigmund Freud. Freud believed that individuals are driven by subconscious, instinctual forces. Conflict characterizes the life of the individual because the demands of reality (ego) and moral standards (superego) are never entirely freed from biological drives (id). Children pass through a series of psychosexual stages before they enter the genital stage, which begins with the onset of puberty and lasts throughout adulthood. The defense mechanisms of the ego help the individual conform to the pressures of reality and reduce tension. In Erikson's modification of Freud's theory, a greater emphasis is placed on conscious ego processes and on personality changes beyond adolescence. Erikson identified eight stages that cut across the entire life span. In each, the individual resolves a conflict between two emotional alternatives.

The cognitive-structural perspective, represented by the theory of Jean Piaget, holds that children are motivated by the intrinsic need to constantly adapt to their environments and reorganize their structures of thought. Piaget believed that children and adolescents progress through stages of sensorimotor, preoperational, concrete operational, and formal operational thought.

The behavioral social learning perspective views development as the result of learning from environmental experiences. B. F. Skinner, the behaviorist, argues that the child's behavior is determined solely by the external consequences of actions. The cognitive social learning theory of Albert Bandura still stresses the importance of studying behavior and the effects of the environment on it. However, Bandura believes that much of behavior is mediated by cognitive processes.

The humanistic perspective stresses that the core of development lies in conscious feelings, ideas, and intentions. Humanists focus on personal fulfillment and the sense of self-awareness. Humanistic therapy extends the humanistic perspective to help children reach their potential through the exploration of emotional dynamics. Carl Rogers has been one of the guiding forces behind the humanistic perspective, emphasizing a client-centered approach to understanding development.

From outside the discipline of psychology, ethological, evolutionary and anthropological, sociological perspectives provide additional valuable information about development. The ethological, evolutionary perspective emphasizes the importance of the child's biological heritage and adaptation to the environment. The anthropological, sociological perspective stresses that development can best be understood by analyzing the culture in which the child lives. In particular, the way in which the culture transmits values, roles, and social structures to children is important. One particular view of development that includes many sociological referents is Bernice Neugarten's belief that life time, social time, and historical time interact to produce changing rhythms in development.

Finally, it must be stressed that no single theory can explain the rich and awesome complexity of development. Each of the theories presented has made a different contribution, and it is probably wise to adopt an eclectic view as we continue to study development.

Key Terms

accommodation

adaptation

anal stage

anthropological, sociological perspective

assimilation

autonomy versus shame and doubt

behavioral social learning perspective

behavior modification

cognitive social learning theory

cognitive-structural perspective

concrete operational stage

critical period

cultural, or social, evolution

culture

defense mechanisms

eclectic orientation

ecological structure

economic structure

ego

ego integrity versus despair

Eight Ages of Man

Electra complex

enculturation

equilibration

erogenous zones

ethological, evolutionary perspective

ethology

evolution

fixation

formal operational stage

generativity versus stagnation

genital stage

historical time

humanistic perspective

id

identification

identity versus role confusion

imitation

imprinting

industry versus inferiority

initiative versus guilt

instinct

instrumental conditioning

intimacy versus isolation

latency stage

life time mechanical mirror theory

modeling

Oedipus complex

operant conditioning

oral stage

organization

Parent Effectiveness Training (P.E.T.)

phallic stage

pleasure principle

political structure

preoperational stage

projection

psychoanalytic perspective

punishment

reaction formation

reality principle

reciprocal determinism

regression

reinforcement

repression

roles

scientific theory

self

sensorimotor stage

social structure

social time

stages

stimuli

superego

tension reduction

trust versus mistrust

value structure

vicarious learning

Review Questions

1. What are some of the formal requirements of a theory of development?
2. What makes a theory of development a stage theory? Give examples of stage theories and nonstage theories.
3. Describe the main points in the psychoanalytic perspective. Distinguish between the psychoanalytic perspective of Freud and Erikson.
4. Describe the main themes of the cognitive-structural perspective.
5. What are the most important aspects of the behavioral social learning perspective? What are some differences between Skinner's view and Bandura's view?
6. Outline the major ideas in the humanistic perspective.
7. Describe how evolutionary theory is important for the study of development. What is ethological theory?
8. What are the main points of the anthropological, sociological perspective? Discuss Bernice Neugarten's multiple time, changing life cycle perspective.

Further Readings

Cowan, P. A. *Piaget with feeling: Cognitive, social, and emotional, dimensions.* New York: Holt, Rinehart & Winston, 1978.
Philip Cowan is head of the clinical psychology program at the University of California at Berkeley. He, like many clinicians, believe Piaget has more to tell us about social and emotional development than Piaget himself thought. Reading level is moderately difficult.

Erikson, E. H. *Identity: Youth and crisis.* New York: Norton, 1968.
This book represents Erikson's most detailed work on adolescents and includes a full description of his eight stages of the life cycle. Exciting reading with many insights into the nature of lives, which you should be able to adapt to an understanding of your own life. Easy reading.

Neugarten, B. L., and Datan, N. Sociological perspectives on the life cycle. In P. B. Baltes and K. W. Schaie (eds.), *Life-span developmental psychology.* New York: Academic Press, pp. 53–71.
Neugarten, a leading figure in the study of life-span development, describes her views of multiple time perspectives and the changing rhythm of the life cycle. This article stimulates thinking about the nature of development and is reasonably easy to read.

Patterson, G. R. *Families.* Champaign, Ill: Research Press, 1971.
An extremely easy-to-read, intelligent discussion of behavioral ideas designed to help family members cope with conflict. Patterson is director of the Oregon Research Institute, one of the leading behavioral research and treatment centers in the United States.

Shostrum, E. V. *Man, the manipulator: The inner journey from manipulation to actualization.* New York: Bantam, 1972.
In a very easy-to-read style, Shostrum tells us how to grow from a manipulative to a self-actualized individual. He gives hundreds of examples that suggest specific ways to improve our communication with others so that we can develop psychologically healthier relationships. In particular, valuable advice informs parents how to stop manipulating their children. Shostrum is a former president of the division of humanistic psychology in the American Psychological Association.

Know Yourself

An important goal of this course you are taking and this textbook you are reading is to help you learn more about infants, children, and adolescents. But an equally important goal of any psychology course and any textbook on psychology should be to help you better understand yourself as well.

What are *you* really like as a person? Have you thought about this question lately? Before going on to the next paragraph, stop for about ten minutes and reflect on yourself as a person. Think about your mind, the way you think, your feelings and emotions, your behavior, what you are like when you are by yourself and when you are with other people, your relationships with other people, what motivates you, and what your attitudes are. Also, think about how you became this way. In other words, how did you develop into the person you are today? You probably could take a lot longer than ten minutes for this task, but for now, limit your thoughts and insights to about ten minutes.

Many years ago, the famous Greek philosopher Socrates admonished the people of Greece to "know thyself." Socrates used this phrase broadly, in the sense that he felt people should try to understand the entire nature of their being—not just their inner mind and their origin but their feelings and behavior and the minds, feelings, and behavior of others as well. To Socrates, such knowledge and social awareness was the key to self-improvement. By suggesting the importance of self-knowledge and knowledge of others, he was emphasizing the study of a more complete person than had been accomplished in the past. Just as Socrates emphasized to the Greeks in the fifth century B.C. that intellectual insight into the nature of their being as people was the key to understanding life, so too will you be encouraged to look at yourself and other people you know, particularly at how you have developed into the unique individual you are. This process should help you to better understand the nature of development and to better understand yourself and the people you know.

To learn more about the nature of himself and others, Socrates not only spent considerable time contemplating what he was like as a person, but he went out among the people of Greece, conversing, watching, and analyzing as he went. So, too, do we believe that to truly understand the nature of how children and adolescents develop we need to study them in many settings and contexts. In your effort to get to know yourself better and to understand what children and adolescents are all about, we encourage you not only to think about yourself but to learn about children and adolescents by talking to other students about their experiences as they grew up and by observing and talking with infants, children, and adolescents.

Each section of this book will end with this type of think piece. In this first piece you have thought broadly about what you are like as a person and how you developed into the person you are. You have read about our debt to Socrates, who first stimulated people to know themselves and others. As we proceed through the various sections of this book, you will be motivated to think more deeply and in more detailed ways about the different phases of your development—your infant years, your early childhood, your middle and late childhood, and your adolescence. In this manner, we hope that you will come to understand the nature of development in children and adolescents and that you will also gain intellectual insight into yourself and others.

In This Section You Will Learn About

Biological Foundations and Physical Development

Test-tube babies

The basic building blocks of heredity

Genetic counseling

The importance of hereditary-environmental interaction

Prenatal development, including hazards that influence the embryo and fetus

The birth process and the newborn's capabilities

Physical development in the first year

Physical development in the second year, including gross and fine motor skills

Cognitive Foundations and Development

Whether we can teach math and foreign language to infants and whether we should

The development of hearing, touch, taste, smell, and vision

Visual perception, including attention

The theory of Jean Piaget

The importance of object permanence

Intelligence tests for infants

How infants learn, including the importance of imitation

Language Foundations and Development

How most children are bathed in an environment of language from a very early age

What language is

The old and new views of language

The role of biology in language development

Strategies adults use in verbal communication with children

The child as a language processor

The developmental course of language development, including speech sounds, syntax, and semantics

Whether the cries of babies are distinctive

The functions of language—perception, memory, thinking, and communication

Social, Emotional, and Personality Foundations and Development

The nature of infant day care

The importance of early experience in development

The link between nutrition in infancy and later emotional development

Mothers in and out of tune with their infants

The family as a system of interacting individuals

The family systems approach to therapy

What attachment is and how it develops

The role of the father in attachment

The development of independence and the self

Problems that develop in the area of attachment-independence

Profile

Meet Steven and Cynthia Parke. Cynthia is four months pregnant. The fetus that is to become her first child is approximately six inches long and weighs four ounces. Just this week Cynthia has felt movements of the fetus for the first time. Steven has been very supportive of Cynthia, being a sensitive companion when she hasn't felt well and taking her out to dinner more often. Their dinner conversation eventually gets around to what they think their baby is going to be like when it arrives. Cynthia thinks it will be a boy; Steven thinks it will be a girl. Steven has a martini before dinner, but Cynthia has chosen not to drink while she is pregnant. In addition, she has tried to maintain a regular exercise schedule and has eaten more nutritious meals since she has been pregnant.

Five months later, Cynthia anxiously calls Steven at his office. She tells him that she is starting to feel labor contractions and that they are getting closer together. Steven comes home immediately and takes her to the hospital. Some four hours later, they discover that Cynthia was right—their baby is a boy, weighing seven pounds, eight ounces. The baby is given an Apgar Test to check his heart rate, respiratory effort, muscle tone, body color, and reflex irritability. Mark Parke is healthy on all counts.

Although Mark is not yet a physical and mental whiz, he is not completely incompetent either. Many of his competencies involve motor reflexes. By the time he is two months old, he can hold his head and chin up, and by four months he can reach for objects in sight, although not with much success.

Between the ages of four and eight months, Mark becomes more oriented to objects in his world. For example, at seven months he shows a marked attachment to his mother and some indication of attachment toward his father. Both of his parents have been highly involved with Mark. They spend a lot of time talking to him and playing with him. Although they are a bit afraid they might spoil him, nonetheless they pick him up and cuddle him when he cries.

By the age of one year, Mark can say, "Mama" and "Dada." His father is very proud that Dada was the first word he spoke last month. Mark can also respond to simple commands or requests. When he is asked by his mother to take a drink, he does, unless he is in a bad mood. When anyone laughs at him, he often repeats the action he has just completed in order to get the person to laugh again.

At fourteen months Mark is expanding his world—he can now walk alone. As we follow him for several months, we find that he still bumps into a lot of things, but over the last few weeks he is beginning to run without falling down. As his mother says, "He now gets into everything and wants to go everywhere." His fine hand-eye coordination has improved as well. He now can stack two blocks, and when we look at him at sixteen months, he can put three on top of one another.

Mark is developing a sense of self, of independence, of competence as a human being. He no longer shows as much proximity-seeking of his mother, although he still likes to have her nearby in case something goes wrong or he needs something. Toward the end of his second year of life, we find that Mark's language has become more sophisticated. He no longer just says, "Dada," but "Daddy bye-bye."

Mark's mother stayed home with him until he was one year old. She and Steven spent considerable time exploring day care centers to find the best one so that she could go back to work. They never found one they liked, so instead they hired a woman who is sixty-four years old. Mark calls her Nanna, and really enjoys her, although Nanna may enjoy him even more. Her husband died two years ago, and Mark has brought a great

deal of joy to her life. Nanna lives only a mile from the Parkes' house, so Steven picks her up and takes her home every week day. She is also usually available on weekends and evenings if Steven and Cynthia have to or want to go somewhere. Steven and Cynthia are very thankful for Nanna; they both have successful careers, yet they are very concerned about who cares for their child. Nanna often reads to Mark and also is very nurturant toward him. If Mark has any noticeable problem, it is that he sometimes has difficulty handling control when it is placed on him. He is a bundle of energy, and sometimes it takes his mother, father, and Nanna to keep him on track.

3 Biological Foundations and Physical Development

I magine . . . what you were like as a newborn and what you were capable of
doing

As a newborn you were not as helpless as you looked.
First of all, the activities needed to sustain your life
were present at birth. You could breathe, suck, swal-
low, and get rid of wastes. You could look, hear, taste,
smell, feel, turn your head, and signal for help from the
first minute. Right from the start, your attention could
be captured by sharply contoured or circular shapes.
This indicates your mental curiosity was not entirely
swamped by your needs for food and comfort.

Physically, you were tiny. From head to heels, you
were about twenty-one inches long and weighed about
seven and one-half pounds. Your head, about five inches
long, was almost one quarter of your height, so you un-
derstandably were awkward. Just try to imagine yourself in this shape. Even with your present maturity and
skill, you would have a hard time getting around if your
head were twice as big and your arms and legs half
their size. You were bound by where you were put, and
you were at the mercy of your bodily needs. Your heart
beat twice as fast as a grown-up's, 120 beats a minute,
and you breathed twice as fast as an adult, about thirty-
three times a minute. You urinated as many as eighteen times and moved your bowels from four to seven
times every twenty-four hours. You slept fourteen to
eighteen hours a day. On the average, you were alert
and comfortable for only thirty minutes in a four-hour
period.

Reflexes governed your movements, which were
automatic and beyond your control. For example, if the
top or back of your hand or foot was stroked, your whole
arm or leg withdrew slightly and the hand or foot flexed
and then returned so that your fingers or toes could
grasp the stroker's finger. This withdrawal reflex only

existed until you began to use your limbs in a different
way—legs for standing and stepping, arms for reaching.

You showed many other reflexes. If you were held
in a standing position and someone gently pressed the
sole of one foot and then the other to the bed, you would
draw up each leg successively as if walking. Without
helping it, you actually could "walk" across a bed. Almost a year after your walk reflex vanished, it appeared as the voluntary, complex art of walking.

One of your most frequent and dramatic reflexes
as a newborn was the Moro reflex, a vestige from our
ape ancestry. If you were handled roughly, heard a very
loud noise, saw a bright light, or felt a sudden change
in position, you were startled, arched your back, and
threw your head back. At the same time you flung out
your arms and legs, then rapidly closed them to the
center of your body, and flexed your body as if you were
falling.

If an adult cried, then you cried because you were
startled. This reflex, normal in all newborns, tends to
disappear at three to four months of age. Steady pressure on any part of your body calmed you.

As noted earlier, if someone stroked the palm of
your hand or the sole of your foot at the base of the
toes, you grasped the person's finger. The more premature you were, the more tenacious your grasp was.
By using your toe grasp, an adult could lift your leg off
a mattress. With your hand grasp, an adult could gently
pull you to a sitting position or even suspend you in the
air hanging onto the adult's fingers for dear life, as if
to a tree branch (better leave this to the experts,
though). If someone stroked the outside of your sole an
opposite reflex, called the Babinski, was set off. Your
toes spread and your big toe shot up in the air.

Your mother learned as soon as she started feeding
you that stroking your cheek or the area around your
mouth made you root or turn toward the stroking object. This rooting reflex helped you to find the breast,

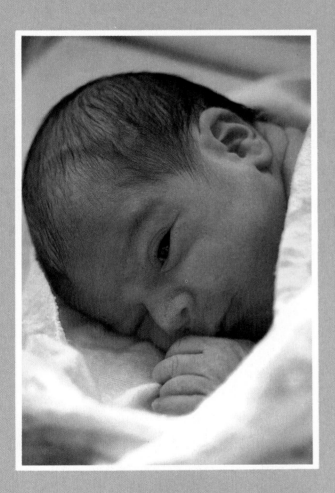

If You	Then the Baby's
Tap bridge of the nose, or shine a bright light suddenly into the eyes, clap hands about eighteen inches from infant's head, or touch white of eye with cotton	Eyes close tightly.
Make sudden contact or noise	Head drops backward, neck extends, arms and legs fling outward and back sharply (Moro reflex).
Extend forearms at elbow	Arms flex briskly.
Lightly prick soles of feet	Knee and foot flex.
Stand infant; press foot to bed	Feet step.
Pull baby to sit	Eyes snap open, shoulders tense. Baby tries unsuccessfully to right head (China doll reflex).
Pull baby on tummy on flat surface	Head turns to side and lifts. Baby crawls, lifts self with arms.
Support chest on water surface	Arms and legs "swim."

and the sucking reflex followed. If the inside of your mouth, which is more sensitive than the surrounding areas, was touched, this stimulated the rooting reflex even more. Thus it was easier for you to suck a bottle than the breast because the bottle touches this area. The following table summarizes what a newborn's reflexes are like.

If You	Then the Baby's	If You	Then the Baby's
Place on back and turn head to side	Body arches away from face side; arm on face side extends, leg draws up; other arm flexes (tonic neck reflex).	Place object over nose and mouth	Mouth works vigorously; head twists, arms fling across face.
Stroke top of foot or hand	Limb withdraws, arches, returns to grasp.	Stroke leg, upper part of body	Opposite leg or hand crosses to push your hand away; withdraws.
Stroke palm or sole at base of digits	Limb grasps.	Rotate baby to side	Head turns, eyes precede direction of rotation.
Stroke outside of sole	Toes spread, large toe sticks up.	Suspend by legs	Body curls to upside down ball, legs extend, arms drop into straight line; neck arches backwards.
Tap upper lips sharply	Lips protrude.		
Stroke cheek or mouth	Mouth roots, head turns and tongue moves toward stroking object; mouth sucks.		
Stroke cheek or palm	Mouth roots; arm flexes; hand goes to open mouth.		

Source: Caplan, 1981, pp. 7, 9, 21.

Introduction

The story of human development begins at conception. Here a single male sperm cell fertilizes a female ovum and a biological process is begun that will lead to the development of a fully formed infant. The course of development during this prebirth span—called the **prenatal period**—is awesome. From a single fertilized egg a complex human develops, intact with an intricate anatomy, organs, nervous system, and response capabilities. And each human newborn is unique. A major task of this chapter will be to describe the manner in which this prenatal development takes place and to highlight the landmarks along its path. A second major task will be to describe the course of physical development during infancy. Before beginning, however, we must first understand some biological principles that are responsible for the process of prenatal development and for shaping the course of further human development—the principles of heredity.

Heredity

Each of us has inherited a general biological code from our parents. Physically, this code is carried by biochemical agents referred to as **chromosomes** and **genes.** The chromosomes and genes guarantee that we are alike in one important respect: we are all human. A fertilized human egg cannot develop into a dog, a cat, or an aardvark. The general heredity code that all humans share is important. Aside from the obvious physical similarities such as our anatomies, brain structures, and organs, this hereditary code accounts for many of the psychological samenesses (universals) among us.

The particular kind of brain we have inherited, for example, is largely responsible for how our thought processes develop (explored extensively in chapters 4, 7, 8, 10, 11 and 14), how we acquire language (chapters 5, 8, and 11), and how we learn (chapters 4, 8, and 11).

Most of us, however, think more about the *specific* hereditary code that we have. The particular way in which genes are organized in the chromosomes varies from person to person. This variation is why some people are tall and others are short. Some have blue eyes, others brown. Some are male, others female. Some have dazzling intellects, others are dull. Some are vivacious and outgoing, others quiet and introverted. These differences are caused by differences in our genetic makeup.

Basic Building Blocks

Conception occurs when a sperm cell from the male unites with the egg, or ovum, of the female. Once the fertilized egg begins to divide, the process of development is in motion. This process is directed by genetic material contained in the nucleus of each original cell—the sperm and the egg. The nucleus of each of these cells contains twenty-three chromosomes, each of which is a long and complex chainlike structure containing many thousands of genes. These two cells, sometimes called reproductive cells, or germ cells, are the only ones we possess that contain precisely twenty-three chromosomes. All other body cells contain forty-six chromosomes arranged in twenty-three complementary pairs—one in each pair contributed by each biological parent. In the fertilized egg, the two sets of chromosomes pair off physically, producing forty-six chromosomes. As the fertilized egg divides and redivides

Your hereditary code not only produces individual variation, but psychological sameness as well.

"MY MOM SAYS I COME FROM HEAVEN. MY DAD SAYS HE CAN'T REMEMBER AN' MR. WILSON IS POSITIVE I CAME FROM MARS!"

DENNIS THE MENACE® used by permission of Hank Ketcham. Copyright © by Field Enterprises, Inc.

over the next several weeks—a process called **mitosis**—each new cell will have a replica of the same forty-six chromosomes arranged in the same way.

In each chromosome of a cell, there are thousands of smaller particles known as genes. A gene, once thought to be the smallest building block in the process of hereditary transmission, actually is a complex molecule. James Watson and Francis Crick (1953), two British scientists, astounded the world by describing the structure of this molecule, which is known as **DNA (deoxyribonucleic acid)**. Their discovery is reported in *The Double Helix* (Watson, 1968), a book with all the fascination of a mystery story. The discovery was the result of years of patient and compulsive work—trying out a chemical model, rejecting it, trying out another, rejecting it, and so on.

In unraveling this mystery, it was discovered that the very structure of the DNA molecule suggested how the phenomenon of chromosomal splitting occurs. This splitting is perhaps the most important part of the hereditary cycle. It guarantees duplication and the equal chromosomal partnership of the male and female parent cells. DNA consists of molecules arranged as if in a spiral staircase—the **double helix.** Two long strands (analogous to handrails or sides of a staircase) are connected by several short strands (analogous to steps on the staircase). The structure divides, or "unzips," with the two strands coming apart. (See figure 3.1 for a diagram of the DNA molecule and its structure.)

Genetic Transmission

The arrangement and characteristics of the chromosomes and genes inherited make each person different. The total constellation of chromosomes and genes and their unique configuration in an individual is referred to as the person's **genotype.** All of the observed and measurable characteristics of an individual are referred to as the person's **phenotype.** Phenotypical characteristics may be physical, as in height, weight, eye color, and skin pigment, or they may be psychological, as in intelligence, creativity, memory, extroversion, self-identity, and moral character.

What is the relation between an individual's genotype and phenotype? How does heredity determine what each person becomes in life? The answer is complex; this complexity will be shown in our discussions of the different mechanisms and possibilities for hereditary transmission. By way of anticipation, however, consider the following assertions.

Identical phenotypical characteristics may be produced by different genotypes. For example, three unrelated individuals may each have a measured IQ of 110 but vastly different genes for intelligence. And the converse is also true; differences in a phenotypical characteristic may be produced by the same genotype. For example, identical twins have been known to have different IQs (a not uncommon finding). So different IQs were produced by identical genetic makeups.

How are characteristics transmitted by the genes? How is it that one person develops blue eyes and another brown; one grows tall and another short? Many people believe that the child grows up to be the genetic average of the parents. According to this view, if one parent is tall and the other short, the child will attain a height that is intermediate between the two; if one parent is exceedingly bright and the other dull, the child will develop an average intellect. This view is patently false. Experience and careful observation indicate that children do not acquire the so-called average of their parents' characteristics.

It is true, however, that each parent contributes half of the chromosomes for the child. What does happen, then, when genes from the two parents are combined in their offspring? Some significant experimentation in the field of genetics, discussed in the next section, provides us with answers to this question. Increasingly, marital partners who want to have a child are turning to genetic counselors if they suspect some genetic problem may influence the health of the offspring—see application 3.1 for a description of what genetic counseling is like.

Mendel's Laws

Some human characteristics seem to be determined by the combination of one gene from the father with a corresponding gene from the mother. The color of the eyes

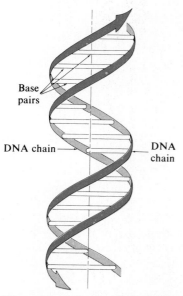

Base pairs

DNA chain

DNA chain

Figure 3.1 The double helix: the DNA molecule.

and straight hair or curly hair are determined in this way. Such abnormal conditions as lack of skin pigment (**albinism**), sickle-cell anemia, and **phenylketonuria,** sometimes called **PKU,** a form of mental retardation linked to an enzyme problem, are also determined by the combination of one gene from the father and a corresponding gene from the mother.

In the nineteenth century, Gregor Mendel uncovered some basic principles, now known as Mendel's laws, that explain what happens when genes are combined. Mendel conducted experiments in cross-fertilization of different kinds of garden peas, and these experiments have significant application to humans.

For each human characteristic there are two genes (one from each parent), which may carry identical codes or different codes. A person may have two genes carrying a code to signal the formation of brown eye pigmentation, or one gene bearing a code for brown and the other bearing a code for the blue eye pigmentation, or two genes carrying the code for blue. Some gene codes are **dominant** and others **recessive.** If both combining genes have a dominant code, or if one has the dominant and the other the recessive code, the offspring will have the dominant feature. The recessive feature will appear only if two recessive genes—one from each parent—combine. In determining eye color, brown is dominant and blue is recessive. So a child who inherits a brown-brown or a brown-blue gene combination will have brown eyes. Blue eyes will appear only when a blue-blue combination is inherited.

Geneticists frequently attempt to trace the probability of transmitting a dominant or a recessive gene across several generations in a family, based upon knowledge of how the resulting characteristic has been distributed on the family tree. Such research is especially helpful for parents in cases where there is a history of a genetically linked disorders, such as PKU.

It is common practice for geneticists to refer to all the genes in a population as the population's gene pool. This idea is useful in studies to determine the number and kinds of **harmful genes** within a population. Examples are genes that cause certain kinds of muscular dystrophy, feeblemindedness, diabetes, heart disease, and nervous system disorders. Many of these are rare recessive genes that are distributed throughout the population. Therefore, most individuals who carry them are not aware of it. It is only when two of the recessive genes come together that the undesirable trait appears.

Sex Linkage
Some characteristics depend on genes carried in the twenty-third chromosome pair—the pair that also determines the sex of the offspring—with the result that these characteristics are more or less likely to occur in members of one sex. Which way this sex linkage goes depends upon whether the gene is dominant or recessive and whether it occurs on the X (female) or the Y (male) chromosome.

A popular example of a sex-linked characteristic is color blindness. Many people are unable to distinguish red from green, an inability caused by a recessive gene that appears only on the X chromosome in the pair. (Some X chromosomes have a dominant gene bearing a normal code for the trait.) The Y chromosome does not have a gene that influences the outcome in any way. The odds are much greater for a male offspring to inherit color blindness (50 percent) than for a female (25 percent). However, statistics show even more disproportion; something like seven or eight times as many cases of color blindness are observed in men as in women.

Other Genetic Mechanisms
Genetic determination is often more complicated than you might think from the preceding discussion. For one thing, dominance and recessiveness are not absolute; they are relative for some characteristics, resulting in qualitative mixtures. For example, some red and white parent flowers produce pinkish offspring rather than pure red and pure white flowers. For another, few characteristics are determined by the action of single gene pairs; most are actually determined by the interaction of many different genes in the chromosomes. These traits are described as **polygenically** determined. Most important, children develop very few psychological characteristics that are solely the result of a particular genetic code. Virtually all psychological characteristics are the result of an interaction between the child's inherited code and environmental influences. Neither heredity nor the environment acts alone.

Application 3.1
Genetic Counseling

Bob and Mary Sims have been married for several years. They would like to start a family, but they are frightened. The newspapers and popular magazines are full of stories about infants born prematurely who don't survive, infants with debilitating physical defects, and cases of congenital mental retardation. The Simses feel that to have such a child would create a social, economic, and psychological strain on them and on society in general.

Accordingly, the Simses turn to a genetic counselor for help. Genetic counselors are usually physicians or biologists who are well versed in the field of medical genetics. They are familiar with the kinds of problems that can be inherited, the odds for encountering them, and helpful measures for offsetting some effects. The Simses tell their counselor that there has been a history of mental retardation in Bob's family. Bob's younger sister was born with Down's syndrome, a form of mental retardation. Mary's older brother has hemophilia, a condition in which bleeding is difficult to stop. They wonder what the chances are that a child of theirs might also be retarded or have hemophilia and what measures they can take to reduce their chances of having a mentally or physically defective child.

The counselor probes more deeply, because she understands that these facts in isolation do not give her a complete picture of the possibilities. She learns that no other relatives in Bob's family are retarded and that Bob's mother was in her late forties when his younger sister was born. She concludes that the retardation was due to the age of Bob's mother and not to some general tendency for members of his family to inherit retardation. It is well known that women over forty have a much higher probability of giving birth to retarded children that younger women have. Apparently the ova (egg cells) are not as healthy in older women as in women under forty.

In Mary's case the counselor determines that there is a small but clear possibility that Mary may be a carrier of hemophilia and transmit that condition to a son. Otherwise, the counselor can find no evidence from the family history to indicate genetic problems.

The decision is then up to the Simses. In this case the genetic problem will probably not occur, so the choice is

Genetic counseling is increasingly being sought by prospective parents.

fairly easy. But what should parents do if they face the strong probability of having a child with a major birth defect, as did pregnant women who were treated with the drug thalidomide? Ultimately, the decision depends upon the couple's ethical and religious beliefs. They must decide how to balance these against the quality of their child's life.

The moral dilemma is even more acute, of course, once a pregnancy has begun. **Amniocentesis,** a test that can detect Down's syndrome and more than one hundred other birth defects, can be performed about the fourteenth or fifteenth week of pregnancy. This test has been helpful to many older mothers. A long, thin needle is inserted into the abdomen to extract a sample of amniotic fluid, the liquid that cushions the fetus. Fetal cells in the fluid are then grown in a laboratory for two to four weeks and can then be studied for chromosomal and some metabolic disorders. The later amniocentesis is performed, the better the diagnostic potential. However, the earlier it is performed, the more useful it can be in deciding if the pregnancy will be terminated.

Table 3.1
Continuum of Indirectness of Genetic Influence

	Characteristics
Direct	Some forms of retardation (e.g., Tay-Sachs disease)
	↓
	Congenital defects
	↓
	Inherited susceptibility to disease
	↓
Indirect	Social stereotypes

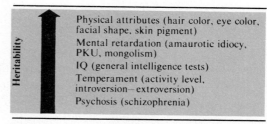

Figure 3.2 Comparative influence of heritability on aspects of development.

The Heredity-Environment Interaction

We can be more precise about the nature of the interaction of genetic codes and environment than about genetic determination alone. Anne Anastasi (1958) developed the notion of a continuum of influence of heredity on development, which she referred to as the **continuum of indirectness.** The most direct influence of heredity can be seen in inherited characteristics that cannot be changed by the environment. Various genetic forms of mental retardation, such as Tay-Sachs disease, fall in this category. No matter what educational or environmental intervention is tried, children born with Tay-Sachs will have progressive neurological deterioration, with the resulting impairment of mobility, sight, and speech.

A less direct influence of heredity can be seen in inherited characteristics that can be modified by society. For example, many congenital physical defects can be remedied through modern medicine; certain bone malformations or facial disfigurations can often be modified through surgery; and some forms of congenital blindness and deafness can also be corrected.

The influence of heredity is less direct in cases in which a child inherits susceptibility to disease. There are some individuals, for example, whose blood develops no antibodies to fight ordinary colds, influenza, or bacterial infection. Life for these individuals must be maintained in a sterile environment, safe from germs. Others are born with weak lungs or hearts or with allergies to pollens or foods. Each of these can influence the patterns of children's lives—the amount of protectiveness in parents, the people with whom they associate, as well as the limits of their activities and achievements. But it is relatively easy to ameliorate these susceptibilities through fairly simple physical regimens and medical treatment. Children with weak lungs may limit their physical activity, children prone to infection can be treated with drugs, and children with allergies to pollens or specific foods can simply avoid these irritants or be treated to develop immunity to them.

Perhaps the least direct effect of heredity is found in social stereotypes. Skin color, ethnic features, or other distinctive physical characteristics may make individuals vulnerable to stereotyping. This stereotyping can shape the way people respond to an individual. It may place the individual in a position of privilege; in the United States, for example, the white Anglo-Saxon male historically has held an economic and educational advantage over others. Or it may place the individual in a position of inferior status and ostracism; in the United States members of virtually every ethnic minority have had to struggle to overcome the disadvantages placed in their way because of stereotyping. See table 3.1 for an indication of the indirectness of genetic influences on various characteristics.

Genetic Influences on Development

What facets of development are influenced by inheritance? From our earlier discussion, one answer should pop out at you; namely, they all are. A better question is, What amount of variation in a characteristic among different people is accounted for by genetic difference? For a summary of this discussion see figure 3.2. If we know the tested intelligence of a group of children and we know something about their genetic similarity or dissimilarity, we should be able to conclude something about the correlation between the two (that is, intellectual similarity, genetic similarity). Unfortunately, most of the answers to this type of question are imprecise. Our ability to control other important variables, such as the similarity of the environments in which the children are reared, is often weak, and we sometimes don't have precise enough measures of genetic similarity. Estimates often vary widely as to the heritability of a particular characteristic. **Heritability** is a mathematical estimate, often computed with a standard heritability quotient. For example, estimating how much more alike identical twins are than nonidentical twins would be expressed as a heritability quotient.

Although heritability quotient values may vary considerably from one study to the next, it is often possible to zero in on the average magnitude of the quotient for a particular characteristic. For some kinds of physical attributes and mental retardation, the heritability quotient approaches 1.00. That is, the environment makes virtually no contribution to variation in the characteristic. This is not the same as saying that the environment has *no* influence; the characteristic could

Down's Syndrome is genetically transmitted.

not be expressed without it. For intelligence and temperament, evidence puts the heritability quotient in the neighborhood of .50 (Henderson, 1982; Scarr-Salapatek, 1975). For some forms of psychosis—particularly for certain forms of schizophrenia—the heritability quotient is in the neighborhood of .30 to .50. Later in the text, we will consider the specific evidence for the heritability of intelligence. However one problem of development deserves special attention at this juncture—mental retardation.

Mental Retardation: A Genetic Anomaly
There are a number of genetic disorders that create the condition commonly called mental retardation. Retardation is easily assessed by extremely poor performance on any of several standardized intelligence tests. However, not every child who is diagnosed as retarded has inherited this problem. In cases where a hereditary link cannot be identified clearly, it is difficult to pinpoint the precise cause or causes of retardation. Genetic transmission may easily be traced to the secondary features of retardation, such as the shape of the head or the appearance of the nose and mouth. In one form of retardation, amaurotic idiocy, blindness and physical paralysis result from impairments to the brain and nervous system. The syndrome seems to be due to the inheritance of a recessive gene from both the child's mother and father.

The PKU syndrome (phenylketonuria) is another type of retardation. Here the problem resides in a genetic code that fails to produce an enzyme necessary for metabolism. In the absence of this enzyme, the cells fail to break down an amino acid, phenylalanine, interfering with metabolic processes and generating a poisonous substance that enters the nervous system. Mental functioning deteriorates rapidly if the enzyme deficiency is not treated shortly after birth. Fortunately, the absence of this enzyme can be detected early and treated by diet to keep phenylalanine at a very low level so that normal metabolism can proceed and the poisonous substance will not be generated. Again, a recessive gene is responsible for this disorder.

Perhaps the most common genetically transmitted form of retardation is **Down's syndrome.** The Down's child has a flattened skull, an extra fold of skin over the eyelid, and a protruding tongue. Among other characteristics are a short, thin body frame and extreme retardation of motor abilities. The cause of Down's syndrome is an extra chromosome—Down's children have forty-seven chromosomes instead of the usual forty-six. It is not known why the extra chromosome occurs, but it may be related to the health of the female ovum or the male sperm. Women over forty years of age are many times more likely to produce a Down's child than younger women, ostensibly because the ovum is less healthy.

We have seen that heredity plays an important part in virtually every aspect of development through interaction with environmental experiences. And while we know that such **genetic-environment interaction** is very important in development, we still know very little about the precise nature of how this interaction works. We turn now to a consideration of the physical changes and patterns of maturation that are observable in infant development. We consider first the important changes prior to birth; second, we look at the birth process itself; and third, we provide a broad overview of the physical changes that follow during infancy.

Prenatal Development
Prenatal development can be divided into a number of discrete periods: conception, the germinal period, the embryonic period, and the fetal period.

Conception
The life processes begin when a single sperm cell from the male unites with the ovum (egg) in the female's fallopian tube in a process called fertilization, or **conception.** The ovum is produced in the ovaries at about midpoint in the female's menstrual cycle. Fertilization takes place within several days after the ovum begins its descent from the ovaries and through the fallopian tubes into the uterus. If the ovum travels to the uterus without being fertilized, it disintegrates within several days, rendering conception impossible until the next cycle. But some women are infertile—see application 3.2 to find out how these women can have test-tube babies.

Application 3.2
Test-Tube Babies

Perhaps the most dazzling occurrence in the past decade is the birth of several babies who were conceived outside of their mothers' bodies. The first documented case was of Louise Brown in England in 1978. Since then, a number of other births have occurred. The event signals the advances that have been made in genetics, the understanding of prenatal development, and the environment needed to sustain development after conception. It brings hope to millions of people worldwide who are infertile or would otherwise have little chance of bearing their own children. In each case, the procedure is to remove the mother's ovum surgically, fertilize it in a laboratory medium with live sperm cells obtained from a male donor, store the fertilized egg in a laboratory solution that substitutes for the uterine environment, and finally implant the egg in the mother's uterus.

Ruth Hubbard (1980), a professor of biology at Harvard University, has described this procedure in detail:

> The woman who is a candidate for **in vitro fertilization** has her hormone levels monitored to determine when she is about to ovulate. She is then admitted to the hospital and the egg is collected in the following way: a small cut is made in her abdomen; a metal tube containing an optical arrangement that allows the surgeon to see the ovaries and a narrow-bore tube (called a micropipette) are inserted through the cut; and the egg is removed shortly before it would normally be shed from the ovary. The woman is ready to go home within a day, at most.
>
> . . . After the egg has been isolated, it is put into a solution that keeps it alive and nourishes it, and is mixed with sperm. Once fertilized, it is allowed to go through a few cell divisions and so begin its embryonic development—the still mysterious process by which a fertilized egg becomes a baby. The embryo is then picked up with another fine tube, inserted through the woman's cervix, and flushed into the uterus. . . .
>
> If the uterus is not at the proper stage to allow for implantation (approximately seventeen to twenty-three days after the onset of each menstruation) when the embryo is ready to be implanted, the embryo must be frozen and stored until the time is right in a subsequent menstrual cycle. (pp. 10–12)

As with other remarkable breakthroughs in modern biology and medicine, this one is not without its ethical dilemmas. Ruth Hubbard, for example, wonders whether it is better to focus on giving each woman the opportunity to have her own "biological child" or to attend to the many children already born in the world who need parents (e.g., foster care and adoption). Others have wondered about

Louise Brown, the first test-tube baby.

the criteria to be used in matching donor sperm with eggs and about the subsequent legal rights of the male donor. Finally, we don't yet have enough information to know what kinds of risks may be involved for the mothers and the children in these remarkable experiments. We won't really know until many years have passed and enough data have been collected.

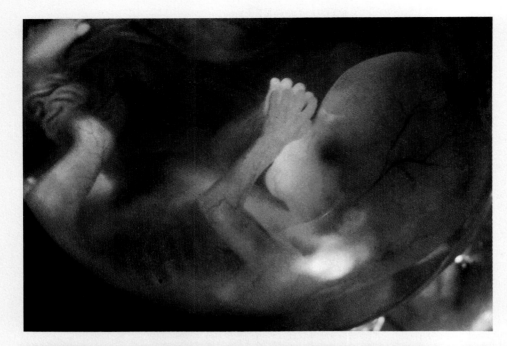

Fetus at nine weeks.

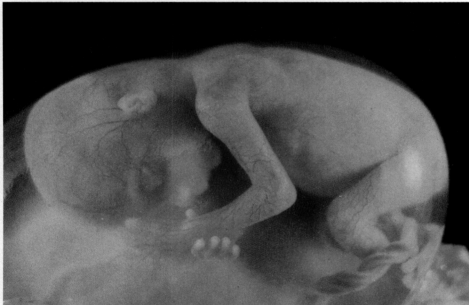

Fetus at twelve weeks.

Germinal Period

The **germinal period** lasts for two weeks after conception. Almost immediately, twenty-three chromosomes from the sperm cell and twenty-three from the ovum cell pair off, producing twenty-three pairs, or forty-six chromosomes. Within a day, chromosome pairs double and split, with half of them gravitating to each side of the cell. Then the fertilized ovum divides into two cells. Because the chromosome pairs in the original cell doubled, each new cell has exactly the same number of chromosomes as the original cell, that is, twenty-three pairs or forty-six chromosomes.

During the next ten to fourteen days two major developments occur. One is continued cell division. Prior to each division the chromosome pairs first double, with each new cell retaining a replica of the original twenty-three pairs of chromosomes. The second major development is the firm attachment of the ovum to the wall of the uterus within a week or ten days after fertilization. During this time the divided cells gradually form a spherical mass, which separates into an inner and outer part. The outer part becomes connected to the uterine wall and eventually forms part of the mother-fetus barrier that develops later. The inner mass becomes the fetus.

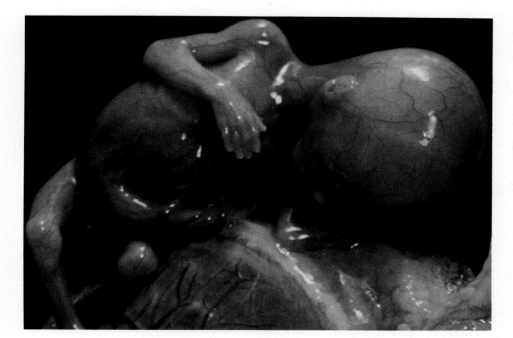

Embryonic Period

The **embryonic period** lasts from about two to eight weeks after conception. It is during this period that a primitive human form takes shape. The basic parts of the body—head, trunk, arms, legs—can be identified. Some finer features, such as eyes and ears, fingers and toes, are also discernible. Internal organs have begun to develop, some of which are functioning, at least to some degree. A primitive heartbeat, circulatory activity, liver and kidney function, and some nervous system action can be distinguished.

It is also during this period that the life-support system for the embryo is formed. The part of the embryo attached to the uterine wall becomes the placenta, the meeting ground for the circulatory systems of both embryo and mother. Semipermeable membranes keep their bloodstreams separate but allow such substances as oxygen, drugs, vitamins, and some nutrients (sugar and protein) to pass through to nourish the embryo. The umbilical cord transports waste substances from the embryo to the placental barrier; the cord also has membranes that allow for the passage of only certain substances. Blood cells are too large to pass through these membranes, so there is no direct link between the circulatory system of the mother and that of the embryo. By the end of this period the embryo is about one inch (2.5 cm) long and weighs about half an ounce (14 g).

Fetal Period

The **fetal period** lasts from about eight weeks until birth—a total of about seven months in full-term babies. By twelve weeks of age the fetus is about three inches (7.5 cm) long and weighs approximately one ounce (28 g). It has become active, moving its arms and legs vigorously, opening and closing its mouth, and moving its head. A number of physical and anatomical features become well differentiated. On the face, for example, forehead, eyelids, nose, and chin can be distinguished; the upper arms, lower arms, and hands are clearly distinguishable, as are the lower limbs. The genitals can be identified as male or female. Further progress is noted on a month-by-month basis.

By the end of the fourth month, the fetus is about six inches (15 cm) long and weighs about four ounces (110 g). Whereas a great deal of growth has already occurred in the head and facial structures, there is now an increased growth spurt in the lower parts of the body. A number of prenatal reflexes (automatic response involving one part of the body), such as arm and leg movements, become stronger and can be felt by the mother for the first time.

By the end of the fifth month, the fetus is about twelve inches (30 cm) long and weighs about a pound (450 g). Structures of the skin have formed; there are fingernails and toenails; and the fetus is more active, exhibiting a preference for a particular position in the womb.

By the end of the sixth month, the fetus is about fourteen inches (36 cm) long and weighs about two pounds (900 g). The eyes and eyelids are completely formed; there is a fine layer of hair on the head of the fetus; it exhibits a grasping reflex; and there is evidence of what appears to be irregular breathing movements.

WE HAVE THAT OUTSIDE TOO

PROMISE

the baby it can go back where it came from. (They never do.)

By the end of the seventh month, the fetus is about sixteen inches (40 cm) long and weighs about three pounds (1.4 kg). It is at this time that the chances of survival are good if the child is born prematurely. For this reason it is sometimes called the age of viability. If prematurely born, however, the infant is very sensitive to infection and must be cared for in a well-regulated environment provided by an incubator.

During the eighth and ninth months, the fetus grows longer, and there is a substantial weight gain—about four pounds (1.8 kg). At birth, the average American baby is twenty inches (50 cm) long and weighs seven pounds (3.2 kg). During these months the fatty tissues develop and the functioning of various organ systems (such as the heart and kidneys) is stepped up.

Environmental Influences on Prenatal Development

Some expectant mothers tiptoe about in the belief that everything they do and feel has a direct effect on their unborn child. Others behave more casually, assuming that their experiences have little impact on the unborn child. The truth lies somewhere between these extremes. Although living in a comfortable, well-protected environment, the fetus is not totally immune to the larger environment surrounding the mother. There are some well-documented ways in which this environment can affect the child. Thousands of babies every year are born deformed, mentally retarded, or suffer from other congenital defects as a result of events as early as two months prior to conception.

Geneticists and specialists in fetal life are finding that the mother's physical and mental health are critical factors in the development of a healthy infant. Some researchers believe that the months before a woman gets pregnant determine the health of the fetus and newborn infant (Witherspoon, 1980). Emotional upset and poor diet of a woman before pregnancy are implicated as possible problems that may alter the course of her infant's health. Environmental factors, such as the time of year the baby is born, also are associated with birth characteristics. For example, children conceived in the summer are about 20 percent heavier than those conceived in the winter, and about 10 percent heavier than those conceived in spring and fall. The rate of fetal malformations is one-third higher among children conceived in spring and fall than those conceived in the summer. Why this is so remains to be explained.

Hazards to Prenatal Development

For many years, scientists believed that almost all birth defects were genetically triggered. Now we know that many such abnormalities are also due to such factors as maternal diseases and blood disorders, diet, irradiation, drugs, temperature, and oxygen level. Maternal characteristics such as age and emotional well-being can influence the health of the newborn as well.

Scientists now label any agent that causes birth defects a **teratogen,** which comes from the Greek word *tera*, meaning monster, and the field of study that focuses on birth defects is called **teratology.** Some general conclusions from research in this embryonic field of research follow. Rarely is there a consistent link between specific teratogens (e.g., drugs) and specific birth defects (e.g., malformation of the legs). There are so many different teratogens that virtually every fetus is exposed to at least several of them. Consequently, it often is difficult to determine which teratogen causes a particular birth defect. And sometimes it takes a long time for the effects of some teratogens to show up—only about half are present at birth.

Despite these uncertainties about teratology, scientists have been able to discover the identity of some teratogens and the particular point of fetal development at which they do their greatest damage. Figure 3.3 reveals the particular point in prenatal development at which teratogens do the most harm. The most damaging effects occur in the first eight weeks of prenatal development, but damage to the brain can occur in the last months of pregnancy as well. Because the various organ systems begin and end their prenatal development at different times, their sensitivity to teratogens varies over time. Vulnerability to damage from teratogens for the brain is highest at fifteen to twenty-five days into prenatal development, for the eye from

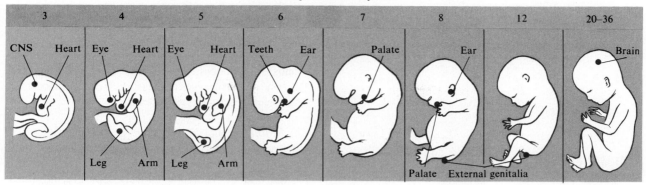

● Part of fetus where damage is greatest

Figure 3.3   The effects of teratogens at specific points in prenatal development.

twenty-four to forty days, for the heart from twenty to forty days, and for the legs from twenty-four to thirty-six days (Tuchmann-Duplessis, 1975).

Now that you have been introduced to the general way in which problems may surface in prenatal development, let's look at three aspects of teratology that have been given particular attention in recent years—maternal diet, drugs and other chemicals, and the mother's emotional state.

Maternal Diet
Because the fetus receives all of its nutrients from its mother's blood, the mother must have a good diet if the fetus is to develop normally. Pregnant women whose diets do not provide adequate nutrients have more premature deliveries, more infants with low birth weights, more complications such as anemia and toxemia, and more prolonged labor (Drillien, 1964). Adequate protein seems to be particularly important for the development of the infant's nervous system (Rosenbaum et al., 1969).

Research also has revealed that too much of certain vitamins may cause problems for the developing fetus. Clinical studies have suggested that high doses of vitamin A during pregnancy produce growth retardation and birth defects. The mechanism is unknown, but it seems to slow down the process by which cells are generated. High doses of vitamin D also have been implicated in dissolving calcium in the bone (Witherspoon, 1980).

Drugs and Other Chemicals
Many pregnant women take drugs, smoke, and drink alcohol without thinking about the possible effects on the fetus. Occasionally, a number of deformed babies are born, bringing to light the damage certain drugs ingested by the mother may have on her offspring. This happened in 1961 when many pregnant women had

been taking a popular mild tranquilizer, thalidomide. Thalidomide was a mild tranquilizer to the mother, but to a fetus, it was devastating. Not all infants were affected in the same way by the thalidomide. Each of the fetal organs or bodily parts appears at a particular point in development, often within a specified set of hours. Consider an arm—on the twenty-sixth day after conception, an arm is formed; and by the thirty-seventh day, the beginnings of hands appear. If the mother took thalidomide on day twenty-six (she probably didn't even know she was pregnant then), the arm probably wouldn't grow. If she took the drug two days later, the arm might not grow past the elbow. The thalidomide tragedy shocked the medical community and parents into the stark realization that a woman does not have to be a chronic drug abuser to damage the fetus—taking the wrong drug at the wrong time is enough to physically handicap the offspring for life.

Fetuses are also adversely affected when their mothers smoke or drink heavily. Women who smoke heavily during pregnancy have offspring who weigh less than normal for a number of months, which may make them more susceptible to a number of health problems. In one recent investigation (Landesman-Dwyer & Sackett, 1983), 271 infant-mother pairs were studied during the infants' eighth, twelfth, and sixteenth weeks of life by having the mothers keep diaries of their infants' and their own activity patterns. Previously, information had been collected about each mother's smoking patterns during her pregnancy. Mothers who smoked spent less time feeding their babies, by an average of twenty to thirty minutes per day, and their infants were awake on a more consistent basis than the infants whose mothers did not smoke during pregnancy.

YOU MAY LISTEN

to Beethoven for 9 months hoping to have a musician, and still have a tone deaf baby boy who wants to be a cocktail waitress.

Infants whose mothers are heroin addicts are born addicted to heroin. These infants may suffer from withdrawal when they are born, a circumstance that may prove fatal.

Infants who are born to alcoholic mothers tend to have more problems adapting to sights, sounds, temperature changes, and other demands of the environment than those born to mothers who drink moderately or not at all during pregnancy (Willemsen, 1979). Even moderate alcohol use during pregnancy may have significant long-term effects on the offspring. In one recent investigation (Streissguth et al., 1983), for example, maternal alcohol use just before and during early pregnancy was related to attentional deficits in children at four years of age. The average amount of alcohol consumed by the drinking mothers was only one drink per day! Such recent findings have led some women to forego all alcohol just before and during pregnancy.

Not only do many women consume alcohol just before and during pregnancy, but many prospective mothers also ingest large quantities of caffeine. Recently, the possibility that caffeine use during early pregnancy may have harmful effects on the newborn has been documented (Jacobson, 1983). Just prior to pregnancy more than 300 prospective mothers were queried about their use of coffee, tea, and cola. Caffeine consumption prior to pregnancy was associated with greater arousal and irritability and poorer self-quieting ability in the newborn. The possibility exists, then, that the mother's caffeine intake during early pregnancy may have effects on the infant's behavior.

At this time, there is no clear consensus on how much caffeine, alcohol, or cigarette smoking during or just prior to pregnancy is safe. Some pediatricians suggest that several glasses of wine daily will not harm the fetus, while others recommend total abstention several months before pregnancy is anticipated as well as during pregnancy. Some women who smoke heavily switch to filtered cigarettes when they become pregnant to lessen their tar and nicotine intake. But the smoke that comes through a filtered cigarette has more carbon monoxide than does smoke from a nonfiltered one, and the resulting decrease in the oxygen in the blood may impair fetal brain development.

The Mother's Emotional State

How can emotional stress in the mother influence fetal development? Because the nervous systems of the mother and the fetus are entirely separate, the reactions that occur in the mother's nervous system are not directly transmitted to the fetus. However, there are several ways her emotional state can influence the fetus. First, when the mother is under stress, gland secretions—adrenalin for example—increase. These secretions increase hormone levels in the blood stream. As the mother's blood circulates through the fetus, the same physical changes that have been stimulated in the mother can appear in the fetus—changes in heart rate, respiration, and blood pressure.

The mother's emotional state during pregnancy can influence the birth process. An emotionally distraught mother may have irregular contractions and a more difficult labor. This may produce irregularities in the baby's oxygen supply, or it may lead to irregularities after the birth. Babies born after extended labor may adjust more slowly to their world and show more irritability. One investigation revealed a clear connection between the mother's anxiety during pregnancy and the condition of the newborn infant (Ottinger & Simmons, 1964). Mothers answered a questionnaire about their anxiety every three months while they were pregnant. When their babies were born, their weights, activity, and crying were evaluated. The babies of the highly anxious mothers cried more before feedings and were more active than the babies born to less anxious mothers.

Birth and the Importance of Infancy in Life-Span Development

The past twenty years have witnessed an explosion of knowledge about the period of development from the moment of birth to about two years old. Experts in many fields are rapidly producing information about the life of the newborn, physical growth and change, perceptual and intellectual capabilities, nutrition and health, and many other topics. The standard reference handbook in the field of child psychology, *Carmichael's Manual of Child Psychology,* has reflected the explosion as well (Mussen, 1970, 1983). In 1970, three of the book's two dozen research essays dealt explicitly with the period of infancy. The new handbook (in four volumes) devotes a whole volume (and a dozen essays) to infancy.

Many overlapping and complementary reasons explain this interest and explosion of knowledge. One is the continuing intellectual interest in the origins of psychological development. Psychologists want to know what the newborn is capable of doing, how advanced these early competencies are, and how they develop further during the next two years. Psychologists have provided some unique insights about what the newborn knows and about how the newborn processes information. Doubtless, philosophers will continue to debate the innate knowledge versus acquired knowledge controversy on logical grounds, but they must now incorporate new empirical insights into their arguments.

Second, new techniques are available to the experts. It is now possible to record an infant's eye movements with precise photographic records; to measure brain activity while an infant is experiencing some event; to measure rather precisely an infant's physiological state of arousal; to measure changes in the infant's apprehension of events; and to manage the detailed information with high-speed computers.

Third, most classic theories of development (e.g., Freud, 1959; Piaget, 1952) make broad claims about the importance of events during infancy in laying a foundation for later development. If we believe Freud, then the parents' handling of the infant's oral and anal conflicts may fix later development. In his example, an individual's attachments to people, personal identity, gender attitudes, and emotional outlook all heavily depend upon how the parents interacted with the individual as an infant. And for intellectual development (e.g., Piaget, 1970), successful negotiation of the sensorimotor stages of thought is critical for mastering later stages of cognitive competency. If for some reason this early sequence is disrupted or retarded, later cognitive progress will be difficult. As these claims about the critical importance of early experiences have been taken more and more seriously, scholars have felt compelled to obtain evidence to test them. Some of the explosive growth in infant studies has been spawned by our newfound techniques for the very precise testing of such claims.

Fourth, there has been a renewed interest in clinical and medical diagnosis and in the prevention of birth and neonatal problems. Much has been learned about birth defects and their causes, and scientists can better identify serious problems in infants, for example, retardation and sensory and physical handicaps. The search for techniques and means of spotting such problems (and correcting them when possible) has increased our clinical knowledge as well as our knowledge about infants.

Let us turn our attention first, then, to the transition from fetus to newborn. This transition is an exciting one for parents as well as psychologists, and the process by which it occurs is truly awesome. Prior to birth, the fetus is a completely dependent organism; afterward, the child sustains many life-supporting activities independently. This section will consider both the birth process and the characteristics of the newborn baby.

The Birth Process
A few days or weeks before the child is born, the fetus becomes positioned head downward, with legs and feet extended upward. Labor, the activity by which the infant is pushed out of the mother's womb, is signaled by the onset of contractions in the uterus (see figure 3.4). A contraction is an involuntary narrowing and lengthening of the uterine cavity, followed by a period of relaxation. At the beginning of labor, a contraction lasts for a few seconds; near the end of labor, it may last for a few minutes. The mother's later-borns usually require a shorter delivery time than the firstborn because the birth canal has usually been enlarged during the first delivery. It can take from four to twenty-four hours for the birth canal to widen sufficiently for delivery of the child, and delivery may be as difficult for the baby as for the mother. The new arrival to our world appears splattered with the mother's blood and a thick, oily material called vernix, which allows the child to slip through the birth canal.

In many births the attending physician may need to guide the infant through the birth canal with forceps. Sometimes a normal birth cannot take place because the fetus is positioned incorrectly or the mother's birth canal is too small or there is some medical complication. In these cases a caesarian birth takes place; this is a surgical procedure in which the baby is delivered through the mother's abdomen. (This procedure was named after Julius Caesar, who supposedly was delivered in this manner.)

Birth marks a dramatic transition for the fetus. In the womb the fetus was in a dark, free-floating, low-gravity environment with a relatively warm, constant temperature. At birth the newborn must quickly adjust to light, gravity, cold, and a buzzing array of changing stimuli. In addition, the very process of being pushed out of the womb is strenuous and exhausting. A French physician, Frederic Leboyer (1975), proposed an alternative to the conventional method of delivery employed in most modern hospitals. The **Leboyer method** seeks to minimize the birth shock for the newborn by offering a postdelivery environment that is calm and peaceful, like the womb. During the delivery itself everyone speaks in hushed tones, extraneous noise is kept to a minimum, and the room is dimly lit. Immediately after the birth the newborn is placed on the mother's abdomen, with the umbilical cord still intact. The mother's body recreates the soft, warm feeling of the womb and the accustomed heartbeat. The baby is

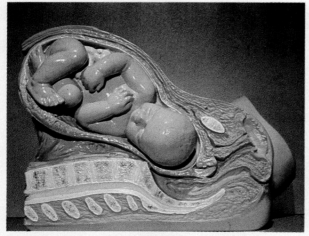

a. *The uterus at term; cervix not dilated.*

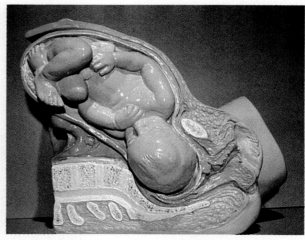

b. *Cervix dilates as the uterus contracts.*

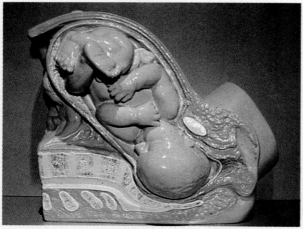

c. *Progress of the head to pelvic floor.*

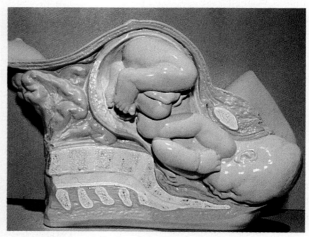

d. *Emergence of the head as it rotates.*

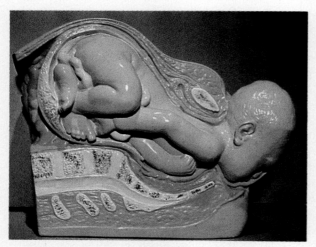

e. *Further extension of the head.*

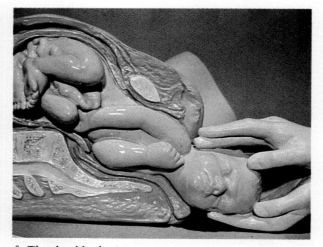

f. *The shoulder begins to emerge.*

Figure 3.4   Six stages of childbirth.

not spanked to start the breathing process, which begins by itself. The traditional practice of holding the baby upside down by its feet to straighten the spine is abandoned. Leboyer feels that this sudden straightening may be traumatic and prefers to let it occur more gradually. Thousands of newborns have been delivered in this fashion around the world. Their doctors and parents report that these infants seem to adjust calmly and happily to the world.

Birth Date and Weight

A full-term infant is one who has grown in the womb for the full thirty-seven to forty weeks from conception to delivery. Not all babies are born on schedule, however. Some are born *prematurely*. In a **premature birth** an infant is born after fewer than thirty-seven weeks in the womb. Most premature infants are smaller and lighter in weight than full-term babies, but there are also small babies born after a full term. Generally speaking, a baby weighing four pounds (1.8 kg) or less is considered premature if born after fewer than thirty-seven weeks in the womb, or if born at four pounds or less at full term, is labelled a **high-risk infant.**

Premature and high-risk infants are placed in a protective environment until they have matured enough to brave the world on their own. The protective environment is an incubator, a small, transparent shell of plastic and metal that is a self-contained living space in which the atmosphere and temperature are carefully regulated, the infant's vital signs are closely monitored, and pleasant stimulation (e.g., soft music and rocking) is provided. Because premature and high-risk infants often have difficulty breathing, sleeping regularly, and warding off simple germs and infections, the incubator environment is critical to their survival. Each year the intensive-care procedures for premature and high-risk newborns improve, and these infants have better odds for survival (Lipsitt, 1979).

There has been a great deal of interest in the development of premature babies stemming from the suspicion that they somehow grow up differently from normal children. The general finding is that children born at full-term and children born prematurely do differ somewhat in their development during infancy. For about six months after birth, premature infants sleep less regularly than full-term babies, cry more while awake, exhibit less interest in novel events, and develop social responses, such as smiling, more slowly (Parmalee, 1976). But these differences generally disappear in later infancy. Nonetheless, some studies have shown differences between full-term and premature babies during early childhood and adolescence. Full-term children may display higher intelligence and school achievement (Wiener, 1968) than do the prematurely born, but the differences are usually exhibited by only the very smallest of the prematurely born children, those with birth weights as low as three pounds

YOU SHOULD DEFINITELY
know by now where babies come from.

(.13 kg). It is likely that these children suffered from some neural or physical impairment that was not completely corrected. Premature birth itself, then, may not be the cause of later differences; a complication associated with the birth may be the culprit.

However, recent evidence suggests that a combination of low birth weight, premature birth, and social class may have harmful effects on cognitive development at four years of age (Millham et al., 1983). In one study children were assessed at least once per year through the first four years of life. The most severe cognitive deficits appeared when the premature, low-birth-weight infants came from an impoverished rather than a middle-class family.

The majority of infants, both full-term and premature, do not show serious impairments at birth—less than 10 percent have any abnormality, and most of these disappear during later development. One method that is frequently used to assess the health of the newborn is the **Apgar Scale,** shown in table 3.2. One minute and five minutes after birth the obstetrician or nurse gives the newborn a rating of zero, one, or two on each of five signs—heart rate, respiratory effort, muscle tone, body color, and reflex irritability. A high total score is favorable—seven to ten suggests the newborn's condition is good, five indicates there may be developmental difficulties, and three or below signals an emergency and that survival may be in doubt.

The Newborn's Capabilities

Because the newborn is capable of very few responses, for a long time it was difficult to assess what the infant sensed, perceived, or learned. In the past two decades scientists have developed sophisticated techniques to make inferences about these matters. The prevailing view used to be that the newborn is a passive, empty-headed organism that perceives nothing, does nothing,

Table 3.2
The Apgar Scale

	Score		
	0	*1*	*2*
Heart Rate	Absent	Slow—less than 100 beats per minute	Fast—100–140 beats per minute
Respiratory Effort	No breathing for more than one minute	Irregular and slow	Good breathing with normal crying
Muscle Tone	Limp and flaccid	Weak, inactive, but some flexion of extremities	Strong, active motion
Body Color	Blue and pale	Body pink, but extremities blue	Entire body pink
Reflex Irritability	No response	Grimace	Coughing, sneezing, and crying

Source: Adapted from Apgar, 1953, pp. 260–67.

and learns nothing. From the new evidence, however, this notion has been reversed. The newborn is now regarded as an active individual exploring the environment and picking up information through primitive, but nonetheless effective, perceptual apparatus, that is, the eyes, ears, nose, mouth, and skin. Remember our description of the newborn's body power in the Imagine section at the beginning of the chapter.

Infant Physical Development

The infant's pattern of physical development through the first year is exciting. At birth, the infant had a gigantic head (with dangerous soft spots) that flopped around in an uncontrollable fashion, reflexes were dominated by evolutionary movements, and the skin was wrinkled and blue. In a span of twelve months, however, the infant will be capable of sitting anywhere, standing, stooping, climbing, and probably walking.

The First Year

During the child's first year there are periods of relative quiet in growth and development and periods bursting with rapid change. One pattern of growth and development is particularly important for our discussion of the first year of the infant's life—the **cephalo-caudal pattern.** The cephalo-caudal pattern suggests that the greatest growth always occurs at the top of the person—the head—with physical growth in size, weight, and feature differentiation gradually working its way down from top to bottom (e.g., neck, shoulders, middle trunk, etc.). This same pattern is manifested within the head area, because the top parts of the head—the eyes and brain, for example—grow faster than the lower portions—such as the jaw. An illustration of this type of growth pattern can be seen in figure 3.5, indicating the prominence of the head area. Notice that an extraordinary proportion of the total body is

occupied by the head at birth but that by the time the individual reaches maturity, this body proportion is almost cut in half. Do you recall the artists' conceptions of children in ancient and medieval art (shown in chapter 1) with their childlike, but adult proportioned heads? The distortion of their perceptions of infants and children can now be seen.

What little motor maturity exists at birth is in the area of the head, reflecting the cephalo-caudal pattern. At birth, babies are able to move their heads a little from side to side—a performance that is easier when they are lying on their backs than on their stomachs. The adaptive nature of this ability becomes evident when we consider that infants would have trouble breathing if they could not turn their mouth and nose away in a face-down position. Breathing problems reflect one of the most puzzling issues in infant development. **Sudden infant death syndrome** (SIDS) refers to the unexplained death of a child during the first year of life because of breathing failure. Autopsies and reviews of the infants' pediatric histories offer no explanation of why children simply quit breathing—usually at night. There are approximately two deaths of this kind—also referred to as crib death—for every one thousand births each year. After the first ten days of life, sudden infant death syndrome is responsible for more deaths in the first year of life than any other cause.

Control of Trunk and Arms

At birth, the infant has no appreciable coordination of the chest or arms. By three or four months, however, two striking accomplishments occur in turn. The first is the infant's ability to hold the chest up while in a face-down position. The other is the ability to reach for objects placed within the infant's direct line of vision, without, of course, making any consistent contact with the objects (because the two hands don't work together and the coordination of vision and grasping is not yet possible). A little later, we see further progress in motor

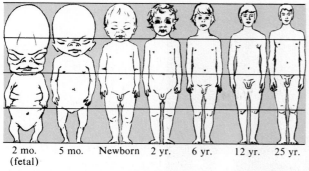

2 mo. 5 mo. Newborn 2 yr. 6 yr. 12 yr. 25 yr.
(fetal)

Figure 3.5 Changes in body form and proportion during prenatal and postnatal growth.
From *Human Embryology* by Patten. Copyright 1933.
Used with the permission of McGraw-Hill Book Company.

control; by five months the infant can sit up with some support and grasp objects, and by six months the child can roll over when lying in a prone position.

Use and Support of Legs

At birth, the newborn is capable of supporting some weight with the legs. This is proven by formal tests of muscular strength. These tests use a specially constructed apparatus to measure the infant's leg resistance as the foot is pulled with a calibrated spring device. This ability is also evidenced by the infant's partial support of its own weight when held upright by an adult. If the child is given enough support by the adult, some forward movement can actually be seen in a built-in stepping reflex, which disappears in a few months. Each leg is lifted, moved forward, and placed down, as if the infant were taking a series of steps. However, the sequence lasts only two or three steps and, of course, the infant does not have sufficient balance or strength to execute the movement independently.

It is not until eight or nine months that the infant can walk with limited help from an adult. Sometime later (perhaps ten or eleven months), the infant can support himself or herself standing alone, pull up into a standing position, and finally (perhaps by thirteen or fourteen months) walk. The actual month at which some milestone occurs may vary by as much as two to four months, particularly among older infants. What remains fairly uniform, however, is the sequence of accomplishments.

Fine Motor Control and Coordination

In addition to the cephalo-caudal pattern of development, there is a second principle called the **proximodistal** pattern of development. Simply put, this refers to the pattern of growth starting at the center of the body and moving toward the extremities. A concrete example is the early maturation of muscular control of the trunk and arms as compared with that of the hands and fingers.

The motor pathways to the brain mature sooner for areas in the center of the body than for areas at the extremities. However, coordination also progresses on the basis of sensorimotor linkages in the central nervous system. The sensory and motor control centers in the brain develop faster than the brain's ability to coordinate them. Environmental information picked up through the five senses (and registered in the **sensory cortex**) must be coordinated with an action stimulated by the **motor cortex.** When the infant reaches for an object, for example, the brain center that directs the movement must be in touch with the center that detects where the object is (perhaps the visual cortex). But that communication is governed by the **association areas of the cortex,** which develop later than the sensory and motor areas.

Some specific landmarks in the development of motor control and sensorimotor coordination follow. The focus on "eye and hand" is dictated by the importance placed on this system in many theories of development (e.g., Piaget, 1954; Bruner, 1973) and by our greater knowledge of this as opposed to other sensorimotor systems. Sensorimotor coordination will be considered again in the next chapter, where we explore Piaget's theory of cognitive development in greater detail.

From birth to one month, the infant shows little coordination of any sort but will briefly follow a slowly moving object, such as a hand or a light, until the object is out of the immediate perceptual field. In the next two or three months, visual pursuit becomes more intricate; the infant may follow the object in different directions and planes and will persist in viewing it for longer periods of time.

Manipulation of objects lags somewhat behind visual pursuit and exploration of objects. For example, depending upon the author consulted (e.g., Helms & Turner, 1981; Wood, 1974), the child does not systematically grasp and hold onto objects until four or five months. Prior to this, the child might make brief contact with objects, reach for them, or hold them briefly if they are placed in the hands by someone. Toward the end of the first year (nine to twelve months), the child becomes able to grasp, finger, and manipulate objects with more subtle use of the thumb, palm, and forefinger. The child may also hold an object in each hand, alternately inspect each, and bang the objects together.

After one year, progress is often noted by the precision of physical movements and the concrete "products" a child is capable of making. Two favorite measures, for example, are the number of blocks a child can stack (Bayley, 1965; Brazelton, 1974; Cattell, 1947; Denver Developmental Assessment, 1973) or the strokes the child can make with a pencil (Wood, 1974). Thus, on the average, at eighteen months children can stack three blocks, and at twenty-four months they can

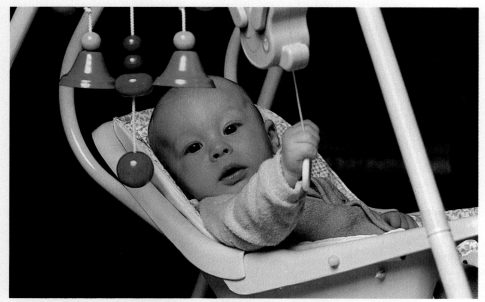

By five months the infant can sit up and grasp objects.

At about eighteen months, the infant can climb stairs.

stack five blocks. Not until about twenty-four months are children able to faithfully copy a horizontal or vertical line drawn on a piece of paper. Each activity, block stacking and writing, is viewed as an activity demanding precise coordinated use of the hands and eyes. Although adults take such coordination for granted, infants undergo a fairly lengthy course in mastering them. An outline of the milestones just listed is offered in table 3.3.

The Second Year

There is a deceleration in growth during the second year of the infant's life. The average infant gains approximately five inches in height and five to six pounds in weight. Somewhere around the last few months of the first year of life, and extending well into the second year, the infant begins to eat less. The plump infant gradually changes into a leaner, more muscular child during the second year. The brain also grows more slowly now. Head circumference, which increased by approximately four inches during the first year, increases only by about two inches this year. By the end of the first year, the brain has attained approximately two-thirds of its adult size, and by the end of the second year, about four-fifths of its adult size. During the second year, eight more teeth erupt to go along with the six to eight that appeared during the first year. By their first birthday, many infants have moved from an awkward, upright standing position to walking without support. Refinements of **gross motor skills,** such as walking, make significant strides during the second year.

Table 3.3
Milestones in Selective Sensorimotor Coordinations

Age in Months	Coordinations		
	Visual Pursuit	*Use of Hands*	*Fine Hand-Eye Control*
1	Follow slowly moving object		
2			
3	Sustain viewing of objects		
4	Follow object in different	Systematically grasp and hold	
5	directions and planes	objects	
6			
7			
8			
9		Finger objects	
10			
11		Hold objects in each hand and	
12		inspect them	
13			
14			
15			Stack two blocks
16			
17			
18			Stack three blocks
.			
.			
.			
24			Copy horizontal or vertical line; stack five blocks

Gross Motor Skills

Several months into the second year, the infant may be able to run and can sit down on a chair unassisted if the chair is short (when the seat is about ten inches off the floor). At about eighteen months, the infant can climb stairs, by twenty months walk downstairs with one hand held, and by twenty-four months run efficiently without falling very often. Between eighteen and twenty-four months, the toddler (the name often given to the infant who is in the second year of life) enters the "runabout age"—scurrying from place to place, throwing caution to the wind, and evidencing no concern for the danger of his or her ventures.

The development of walking and running skills is important for the infant's emotional as well as physical development. They provide infants with a sense of mastery of their world. Initially, the infant performs very poorly at walking and running, but during the course of the second year will pick himself or herself up time and time again to face the world and test reality.

Fine Motor Skills

What is the development of fine motor skills during the second year of life like? Frank and Teresa Caplan (1981) describe it this way:

The way she handles objects that go together is a good illustration of the halfway state the baby has reached. She puts her doll's sock next to its foot, for example, but cannot carry the operation further. She does the same thing with her own shoe, indicating that she knows where it belongs by holding it against her foot. She recognizes that her action is incomplete, gestures to any nearby adult for help, and gives a grunt of satisfaction when the task is performed for her. Her intentions clearly outrace her abilities at this point, a most frustrating state of affairs.

From the baby's point of view, unfamiliar objects are expressly made to be investigated, usually by being pulled apart. Doors that open and shut and drawers that pull out are much more interesting than his own small toys. If he can reach nothing else, his clothing will do. A period of silence in the playpen can often mean that he is busily pulling his garments off. Mothers who do not look on this particular activity with favor may come to tolerate it more easily if they regard it as an important prelude to their child's learning to dress himself. (p. 7)

Table 3.4
Gross and Fine Motor Development during the
Second Year

Gross Motor

Visually monitors walking, watching placement of feet in
 order to be able to deal with obstacles in path by avoiding
 them.
Runs, but generally lacks ability to start efficiently or stop
 quickly
Jumps crudely with two-foot takeoff
Walking rhythm stabilizes and becomes even
Goes up and down stairs alone without alternating feet
Can walk approximately on line
Likes to walk on low walls with one hand held
Can walk a few steps on tiptoe
Can be trusted alone on stairs
Can walk backwards ten feet
Can quickly alternate between sitting and standing
Tries to balance self on either foot, not yet successfully
Is sturdy on feet; less likely to fall
Still geared to gross-motor activity

Fine Motor

Turns pages of a book, one at a time
Manipulates more freely with one hand; alternates from
 one hand to the other
Has fully developed right- or left-handedness
Increased smoothness of coordination in fine-motor
 movements

Source: Caplan & Caplan, 1977.

Year-and-a-half-olds begin to show preference for one hand,
either right or left. This tendency shows up in their play,
holding of spoon or cup, handling of a crayon or pencil in
scribbling. Fine-motor improvement is reflected, too, in the
child's ability to dump raisins from a bottle (a test used by
child psychologists to appraise the manual dexterity and
thinking ability of very young children). (p. 219)

The Two-Year-Old's Physical Capabilities
By two years of age, the toddler has many of the physical skills we take for granted as adults. But even though
the two-year-old can climb and run actively, there still
are some gross motor movements he or she cannot perform, hopping being one example. The two-year-old's
vision is as sharp as it ever will be, and hearing is equally
competent. A summary of the gross and fine motor developments during the second year are shown in table
3.4.

In the next chapter we will discuss an important
aspect of physical development in infancy, that of *sensation*. Sensory development, reflected in seeing, hearing, touching, tasting, and smelling, is discussed in
conjunction with perception. We will see how sensorimotor development serves as a foundation for the infant's acquisition of knowledge about the world.

Summary
Human development begins at conception, when a single sperm cell from the male unites with the ovum from
the female to produce a fertilized egg. The hereditary
code transmitted by this fertilized ovum determines to
a large degree what the child becomes. The basic
building blocks that transmit this code are chromosomes and genes. There are twenty-three pairs of chromosomes formed in the original fertilized egg and
replicated in later cell divisions. One member of each
pair comes from each parent. The twenty-third pair of
chromosomes determines the sex of the infant. Within
a chromosome there are thousands of genes, which are
complex molecules composed of deoxyribonucleic acid
(DNA). Gregor Mendel established the principles of
dominant and recessive gene combination, sex linkage,
and polygenic action, which explain how characteristics can be transmitted. Every characteristic is determined jointly by the interaction of the environment and
hereditary background.

Conception takes place about midway through the
woman's menstrual cycle, with fertilization occurring
in the fallopian tubes. The fertilized egg becomes implanted in the uterus and undergoes a series of cell divisions (mitosis), forming a spherical mass (germinal
period) from which a human form and life-support system differentiate during the next six weeks (embryonic
period). During the final seven months (fetal period)
there is enormous physical growth, weight gain, and
completion of organ systems. During this prenatal period growth may be impeded by the poor health, diet,
and emotional temperament of the mother and by excessive use of any of several different drugs.

The birth process marks a dramatic transition for
the fetus from the dark, quiet chamber of the mother's
womb to the bright light and stimuli of our world. Procedures that have been used to deliver infants include
the caesarian method and the Leboyer method. Premature birth may lead to complications for the infant.
Because of such complications, many premature babies are exposed to protective environments that help
buffer their entry into the world.

The newborn is an unusual sight with a tiny body, large head, wrinkled skin, and mass of uncoordinated movement. Nonetheless, all senses operate at birth and the newborn brings a wide array of reflexes into the world. During the first year, patterns of physical development appear that do not change throughout the life cycle. One such pattern is labeled cephalo-caudal, suggesting that the greatest growth always occurs at the top of the person. A second pattern is called proximo-distal, which suggests that growth starts at the center of the body and later moves to the extremities.

From the time of birth to the end of the first year, dramatic physical transformations occur in the control of the head, trunk and arms, use and support of legs, and fine motor skills. However, there is a deceleration of growth during the second year of the infant's life. During the second year, the refinement of walking skills matures and by the second birthday most toddlers can run and climb efficiently.

Key Terms

albinism
amniocentesis
Apgar Scale
association areas of the cortex
cephalo-caudal pattern
chromosomes
conception
continuum of indirectness
DNA (deoxyribonucleic acid)
dominant gene
double helix
Down's syndrome (mongolism)
embryonic period
fetal period
fine motor skills
gene
genetic-environmental interaction
genotype
germinal period

gross motor skills
harmful genes
heritability
high-risk infant
in vitro fertilization
Leboyer method
mitosis
motor cortex
phenotype
phenylketonuria (PKU)
polygenically
premature birth
prenatal period
proximo-distal development
recessive gene
reflexes
sensory cortex
sudden infant death syndrome
teratogen
teratology

Review Questions

1. Define and explain the terms *chromosome, gene,* and *DNA.*
2. Explain and give examples of Mendel's law, dominant and recessive genes, sex linkage, polygenic action, the continuum of indirectness, and the heritability quotient.
3. What are the major developments during the germinal, embryonic, and fetal periods in prenatal development?
4. Describe the major events surrounding labor and delivery. What are the consequences of premature birth?
5. Why is infancy a popular topic today with scholars?
6. What does the newborn look like and what is he or she capable of doing?
7. Describe the milestones in infant motor development. Specifically consider control of the head, trunk, and arms; leg support; and fine manipulation skills.

Further Readings

Brazelton, T. B. *Infants and mothers: Differences in development.* New York: Delacorte, 1969.
An easy-to-read description of several infants developing during the first two years of life, with special focus on individual differences in temperamental style and parental practices.

Caplan, F. *The first twelve months of life.* New York: Bantam, 1981.
An easy-to-read, well-written account of each of the first twelve months of life.

Falkner, F., & Macy, C. *Pregnancy and birth.* New York: Harper & Row, 1980.
An easy-to-read description of experiences during pregnancy and the nature of childbearing.

Leboyer, F. *Birth without violence.* New York: Knopf, 1975.
The French physician describes his highly influential practice of delivery and his opinions about its value. Written in easy-to-read language and accompanied by illustrative photographs.

Watson, J. D. *The double helix.* New York: New American Library, 1968.
A personalized account of the research leading up to one of the most important discoveries of the twentieth century—the discovery of the structure of the DNA molecule. Reading like a mystery story, it illustrates the exciting, serendipitous side of science.

4 Cognitive Foundations and Development

I
magine . . . that your friend tells you her baby is learning math and a foreign language

To date, Billie Rash has made somewhere between 8,000 and 10,000 eleven-inch-square cards with pictures of shells, flowers, insects, flags, countries, words— you name it—on them. Billie has religiously followed the regimen recommended by Glenn Doman, the director of the Philadelphia Institute for the Achievement of Human Potential and author of the book *How to Teach Your Baby to Read*. Using his methods, learned through a $400 week-long "How to Multiply Your Baby's Intelligence" course she attended in Philadelphia, Billie has taught her children to read and is teaching them Japanese, geography, natural science, engineering, fine arts, and a little math. The children are now four and five years old and are enrolled in a language academy where they are taking courses in French and Spanish, while a private tutor coaches them in Persian. Both boys are learning violin at music school, and during the past summer they took swimming and tap dancing lessons.

Parents using the card approach print one word on each card, using a bright red felt-tipped pen. The parent repeatedly shows the card to the infant while saying the word. The first word usually is "mommy," then comes "daddy," the baby's name, parts of the body, and all things the infant can touch. The infant is lavishly praised when he or she can recognize the word. The idea is to imprint the large red words in the infant's memory, so that in time he or she accumulates an impressive vocabulary and begins to read. Subsequently, the parent continues to feed the infant and young child with all manner of data in small, assimilable bits, just as Billie Rash has done with her two boys (Benson, 1981). With this method, the child will be reading by two years old, and by four or five, will have begun mastering some math and be able to play the violin, not to mention the vast knowledge of the world he or she will

BABIES

make a great captive audience with whom to share those brilliant ideas no one else appreciates.

be able to display because of a monumental vocabulary. Maybe the SAT test you labored through on your way to college might have been knocked dead at six if your parents had only been enrolled in the "How to Multiply Your Baby's Intelligence" courses and had made 10,000 flash cards for you.

It is too soon to tell whether programs like the Doman method will be successful or have a substantial impact on children's later development. Some developmental psychologists believe Doman's so-called "better baby" institute is a money-making scheme and is not based on sound scientific information. Before we invest such extensive effort in trying to teach such skills to infants, we must first determine what their basic capacities are. What evidence do we have, for example, that infants can work with numerical concepts?

A rather dramatic demonstration of one important competency has been offered by Mark Strauss (Strauss & Curtis, 1982). He demonstrated that infants as young

as ten to twelve months are able to tell the difference between a complex stimulus containing three items and one containing either two or four items. One possible conclusion from this rather startling discovery is that one-year-old infants can count up to three or four items but no higher. Such a conclusion, however, is probably false. More likely, infants are able to notice in a single perceptual act up to five variations in the number of objects.

Not only is it important to ask the question of whether we can teach the concept of number to infants and conduct research that addresses this question, but it also is important to consider whether we should be trying to accelerate the child's development by trying

to get him or her to a more advanced cognitive level during infancy. Jean Piaget, the famous Swiss psychologist whose cognitive-developmental theory was introduced in chapter 2, called the question, What should we do to foster cognitive development? the American question, because it was so frequently asked of him when he lectured to American audiences. Piaget, as well as other cognitive-structural psychologists, believes there is something fundamentally wrong with the intense tutorial practicing that characterizes such methods as Doman. As you read this chapter, you will see that Piaget stresses the importance of letting infants actively organize their experiences themselves and spontaneously explore their environment.

Introduction

We have just seen that there is controversy about how much an individual can learn at a particular point in development. Can we, by providing an infant with an optimally enriched environment, get him or her to reason at very advanced levels? In the last chapter this question was discussed under the topic of heredity. In this chapter we will devote an entire section to the topic of learning. We will see the issue appear, and reappear, throughout this text. For example, in chapter 6 it will reappear in our discussion of the role of early experience in life-span development. At the heart of the issue are the roles of heredity-maturation and environment-experience in the individual's development. In this chapter we will look at whether the infant's perceptual and cognitive development is influenced more by heredity and maturation or by environment and experience. What do you think? Before you jump to a conclusion, don't forget our earlier discussion of hereditary-environmental interaction. As the chapter proceeds, you will be exposed to what developmental psychologists know about sensory and perceptual development, cognitive development, and learning in infancy.

Sensory and Perceptual Development

We make contact with the world around us through our five primary senses—hearing, touch, taste, smell, and sight. Psychologists distinguish between *sensation* and *perception*. **Sensation** is the pickup of information by our sensory receptors, for example, the ears, skin, tongue, nostrils, and eyes. The sensation of hearing occurs when waves of pulsating air are collected by the outer ear and transmitted through the bones of the middle ear to the cochlear nerve. The visual sensation occurs as rays of light are collected by the two eyes and focused on the retina. **Perception** is the interpretation of what is sensed. The physical events picked up by the ear may be interpreted as musical sounds, a human voice, noise, and so forth. The physical energy transmitted to the retina may be interpreted as a particular color, pattern, or shape.

The Senses

What are the basic sensory capabilities of the newborn? How do these change during infancy and early childhood? In this section we will consider the development of sensory processes and in the next section we will discuss categories of visual perception, including how the infant perceives depth and size and recognizes patterns and forms.

Hearing

Are infants able to hear when they are born? Evidence suggests that they are. One procedure proves that even the fetus responds to sound (MacFarlane, 1978). Just before the fetus is born and after the mother's membranes are broken, a very small microphone can be inserted in the uterus and placed near the fetus's ear. After a loud noise is made near the mother's abdomen (which can be recorded on the inside through an attachment to the microphone), the fetus's heart rate (recorded by fetal monitoring) speeds up, a sure sign that the sound has been detected. Just after birth, babies tune in most notably to patterned, rhythmic sound (like a human voice), to high frequencies more than to low frequencies, and develop early preferences for one voice (e.g., the mother's). They are also able to localize sounds and can crudely distinguish sounds coming from left and right (Bower, 1974).

One important aspect of auditory perception in infancy is **speech perception.** The human voice is an important stimulus for the infant (Rheingold & Adams, 1980). How much of it does the infant understand? The very young infant is able to perceive speech and distinguish speech sounds. For example, an infant as young as three months of age notices when taped recordings of his mother's speech are distorted in various ways. By nine months of age infants are able to distinguish their mother's voice from that of a stranger (Turnure, 1969). And by twelve months of age children show a preference for specific voice inflections and for speech redundancy in taped recordings (Friedlander, 1970).

Touch

Newborns are sensitive to touch. If they were not, then few of the reflexive responses mentioned in the preceding chapter (Babinski, Moro, rooting) would appear. Infants are also responsive to mild electric shock (Lipsitt & Levy, 1959). And females seem to be more sensitive than males to gentle touch, although this observation has not been consistently supported (Bell & Costello, 1964). Further, tactile sensations are thought to be an important aspect of the attachment process between the infant and his or her caretaker (Cairns, 1979).

Taste

The sense of taste is one of the more difficult senses to study because it is intimately involved with the sense of smell. However, a few observations can be made. Of the many different ways to categorize taste, the following is generally used as a basis for experimentation and discussion: sweet, sour, salty, or bitter.

The taste buds of infants are more widely distributed on the tongue than are those of older children or adults. Newborns are sensitive to strong tastes and can distinguish sugar, lemon, salt, and quinine (Pick, 1961, citing Neminova). Because newborns enjoy the taste of sugar, many experimenters have given them bottles of sugar water as a reward or to orient them to a situation (e.g., Lipsitt, 1969).

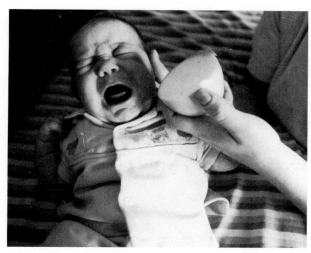

Newborns are sensitive to strong odors, like that of an onion.

Smell

Newborns are sensitive to very strong odors, such as those produced by ammonia and onion, and quickly turn away from these pungent stimuli. Newborns seem to adapt to odors that are presented repeatedly. Much as they adapt to other kinds of stimuli, infants pay less attention to odors that have been presented several times (Engen et al., 1963). Babies also learn the unique odor of their mother's breasts by six to ten days of age (MacFarlane, 1978).

Vision

What is the newborn able to see? How does this ability change? The infant can see a number of things; however, what the newborn sees is much more limited.

Visual acuity is a measure of the degree to which a person can see detail clearly. Normal vision for adults, according to the Snellen scale, is 20/20. For the newborn, visual acuity is poor, in the neighborhood of 20/150 or perhaps slightly better.

We now know that infants can detect variations in movement, color, and brightness. Robert Fantz (Fantz, Fagan, & Miranda, 1975) has developed a technique to study these abilities. He presents the infant with a pair of drawings in which the objects differ from each other in some important respect. He then observes whether the infant looks longer at one drawing than at the other. If so, it can be inferred that the infant can tell the difference between the two objects. In one study it was shown that two-week-old infants preferred to watch a moving point of light rather than a stationary form next to it (Fantz & Nevis, 1967).

The two eyes of a child are not well coordinated at birth (Banks & Salapatek, 1981; Salapatek, 1975). In children and adults both eyes work together to focus on objects and to perceive depth; in the newborn each

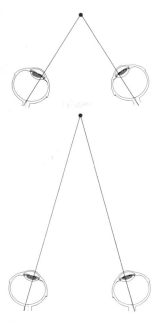

Figure 4.1 Convergence and divergence.

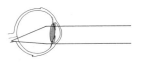

Figure 4.2 Accommodation; in focusing, the lens changes shape to adjust for the distance of the object.

eye functions as a semi-independent receptor of information. Hence, the newborn's perception of the world is very distorted as compared with the perception of older infants and children. Normally, in focusing on objects the two eyes may converge or diverge, as illustrated in figure 4.1. **Convergence** is the turning inward of the eyes to view an object close at hand. **Divergence** is the turning outward of the eyes to view an object far away. These **vergence** movements are important for depth perception, which we will discuss in a later section.

To focus on an object, the lens of each eye must also make adjustments for the distance between the eye and the object. It may foreshorten, creating a thick convex appearance, if an object is close to the eye. It will lengthen or stretch out, creating a flatter appearance, if an object is far away. These adjustments of the lens, illustrated in figure 4.2, are referred to as **accommodation.** (Piaget also uses the term *accommodation* but with a different meaning. Be sure to keep the two

One-month-old
Finish

Two-month-old

Start

Finish

Start

Figure 4.3 How one- and two-month-old infants scan the human face.
(*Source:* P. Salapetek, "Pattern Perception in Early Infancy," *Infant Perception: From Sensation to Cognition,* Vol. 1, ed, L. B. Cohen and P. Salapetek, Academic Press, 1975.)

meanings straight.) The newborn's eyes do not accommodate. Each eye seems to have a fixed lens adjustment set for objects about eight to twelve inches away. Thus objects that are very close or very far away are not in sharp focus.

Vergence movements and accommodation improve dramatically during the first three or four months of infancy (Salapatek, 1975). By this time the infant's focusing power is virtually as flexible as that of adults.

Visual Perception

Child psychologists are very interested in infants' attention, perception of space, and perception of the human face and in how infants perceptually learn about their world.

Attention

What do infants look at? What features of their environment draw their attention? And how do they scan their environments? A technique has been developed whereby eye movements can be recorded photographically as the infant looks at simple geometric forms (Banks & Salapatek, 1981). This allows inferences to be made about how the infant scans the form. A number of interesting results have been obtained with this method. For example, even the newborn is interested in geometric forms, such as circles and triangles, and will look at them for long periods of time! Additionally, the newborn selects a small portion of the figure for examination; there is very little broad scanning to inspect the whole figure. The newborn is preoccupied with detecting individual features of an object rather than the object as a whole. The older infant takes in more of the drawing and scans the contour more completely.

But, what about meaningful patterns, like human faces? In one study human faces were shown to one- and two-month-old infants (Maurer & Salapatek, 1976). The faces were those of their mothers or of a stranger. By a special mirror arrangement, the faces were projected as images in front of the children's eyes so that the infant's eye movements could be photographed. Figure 4.3 reproduces the plotting of the eye fixations and movements of a one-month-old child and a two-month-old child.

Notice that the one-month-old scanned only a few portions of the entire face, a narrow segment of the chin, and two spots on the head. The two-month-old scanned a wider area of the figure—the mouth, the eye, and a large portion of the head. The older infant spent more time examining the internal detail of the face, while the younger infant concentrated on areas on the outer contour of the face.

How Infants Perceive Space

When you were an infant and a young child, to effectively navigate in your environment, you had to rely on a number of useful perceptions, many of which concerned the space around you. For example, it was helpful to perceive that certain objects were nearby and others were far away, that certain objects were in front of things and others behind. And it was also helpful to perceive the actual size of an object, even though it may have been seen in a variety of different circumstances.

One technique for investigating space perception is the **visual cliff technique,** first developed by Richard Walk and Eleanor Gibson (1961). Children and adults tend to draw back from a sharp precipice. A visual situation was created that gave the impression of a sharp

The visual cliff experiment suggests that infants perceive depth.

drop, or cliff, and hence the term *visual cliff*. The "cliff" consists of a clear glass surface with a runway across the middle. On one side of the runway, a pattern several feet below the glass simulates a steep cliff; the other side appears to be either solid or with a modest drop. When an infant is placed on the platform and someone attempts to coax the child to either side, the infant readily moves to the "shallow" side but hesitates to move to the "deep" side. This reaction is taken as evidence of depth perception, with the infant's hesitation resulting from fear of the apparent cliff.

In the original study this reaction in children as young as six months of age was observed. In a later investigation it was discovered that infants could be coaxed across the deep side under certain conditions (Walk, 1966). When the pattern used under the deep side was solidly gray, for example, the infants were more likely to cross than when the checkerboard design was used. And when the distance between the glass and the apparent supporting surface beneath the deep side was several inches rather than several feet, the infants were also more easily coaxed to venture out.

This work, of course, is limited to infants who are able to crawl. Younger infants might also display a response to depth if there were some other way of measuring their reactions. In more recent work, in fact, other measures have been employed for this very purpose, including some that relied on changes in heart rate. One researcher, for example, found that infants as young as two months of age showed a change in heart

rate when lowered face-down on the deep side and no change in heart rate when lowered onto the shallow side. We may conclude, then, that even young infants are sensitive to a steep drop.

For young infants incapable of moving about, another technique for gauging sensitivity to depth has been developed; this is called **looming.** The visual impression of an object being hurled at the infant is created by rapidly expanding the image of something (for example, a colored circle) on a screen placed in front of the infant (Bower, 1974; Yonas, 1975). When something approaches us rapidly, its visual size increases rapidly. Young infants show slight distress—their heart rate and breathing will change—indicating that they have interpreted this common visual information as evidence of something moving toward them.

How Infants Perceive the Human Face

The human face is perhaps the most important visual pattern for the newborn to perceive. Eleanor Gibson (1969) reviewed several studies about infants' perceptions of the human face and concluded that the infant masters a sequence of steps in progressing toward full perceptual appreciation of the face. At about three and one-half weeks of age the child first becomes fascinated with the eyes in a face, perhaps because the child is capable of noticing simple perceptual features, such as dots, angles, and circles. At between one and two months of age, the child notices and perceives contour. At two months of age and older, the child begins to differentiate facial features: the eyes are distinguished from other parts of the face, the mouth is noticed, and movements of the mouth draw the infant's attention to it. By about five months of age, the infant has distinguished several other features of the face—its plasticity; its solid, three-dimensional surface; the oval shape of the head; the orientation of the eyes; and the mouth. Beyond six months of age, the infant is able to distinguish familiar faces from unfamiliar faces—mother from stranger, masks from real faces, and so on.

There has been a great deal of controversy about how perceptual learning in infancy occurs. Next we see that two schools of thought dominate this controversy—the *Gestalt view* and Eleanor Gibson's *distinctive features theory*.

Two Views of How Infants Perceive Their World

Perceptual learning focuses on changes in the way infants interpret and represent stimuli. Historically, there have been two very different ideas about how perception changes during infancy and childhood. One is the **Gestalt view,** and the other is the **distinctive features theory** of Eleanor Gibson (1969, 1979).

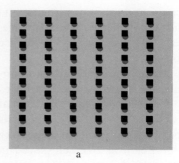

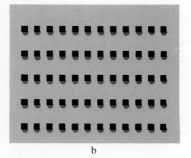

Figure 4.4 Similarity.

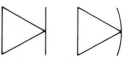

Figure 4.5 These figures depict the distinctive feature line-to-curve.

The Gestalt view of perception dominated thinking in psychology from about 1925 to 1960. The work of three German psychologists—Kurt Koffka (1935), Wolfgang Kohler (1959), and Max Wertheimer (1945)—formed this view. Most of the early work involved adults and lower animals, but not children. In the 1960s and 1970s psychologists began to examine some aspects of the Gestalt view in their work with children.

The basic idea of the Gestalt approach is that perception is organized and dictated by several properties of the perceptual field. The perceptual field is the actual total sensory field, or scene, taken in at any moment by one of the senses (e.g., vision). A major property of the perceptual field is that perception of it is a holistic event. That is, the whole is something different from the sum of its parts—hence the term *Gestalt.*

A number of forces determine how the field is perceived. These are sometimes called the laws of organization, or good form. The German term for this is **pragnanz.** One of these laws is the principle of similarity. For example, in looking at the patterns shown in figure 4.4, you would tend to see the direction of the surface as vertical in part *a* and as horizontal in part *b.* You would tend to group elements of the field that are similar.

A criticism of Gestalt theory (e.g., Gibson & Levin, 1975; Hebb, 1949) is that it is generally vague in describing how perceptual change comes about. What causes the sudden change, for example, as a person is

examining a figure-ground display? The answer is not really clear in Gestalt writings. However, Gestalt ideas have been stimulating because they have led to the demonstration of unique perceptual phenomena such as the one presented in figure 4.4.

In contrast to the Gestalt perspective, Eleanor Gibson (1969, 1979) views perceptual change as a gradual process. The infant and child become aware of features of the environment that have gone unnoticed. Another difference is that, in Gibson's view, the infant takes an active part in perception. The infant constructs perceptions; the field does not pop out at him or her with its organizing forces. Here is Gibson's theory in her own words:

Perception is selective by nature. Selectivity can even be demonstrated at birth in some species, as studies of innate releasing stimuli have shown. But the extent of selectivity at birth varies with species. In man a rather gross selectivity at birth becomes progressively refined with development and experience.

Perceptual learning then refers to an increase in the ability to extract information from the environment as a result of experience and practice with stimulation coming from it. That the change should be in the direction of getting better information is a reasonable expectation, since man has evolved in the world and constantly interacts with it. Adaptive modification of perception should result in better correlation with the events and objects that are the sources of stimulation as well as an increase in the capacity to utilize potential stimulation. (pp. 3–4)

It's not a passive absorption but an active process, in the sense of exploring and searching for perception itself is active. . . . Perceptual learning is self-regulating, in the sense that modification occurs without the necessity of external reinforcement. It is stimulus-oriented, with the goal of extracting and reducing the information in stimulation. Discovery of distinctive features and structure in the world is fundamental in the achievement of this goal. (p. 14)

. . . The criterion of perceptual learning is thus an increase in specificity. What is learned can be described as detection of properties, patterns, and distinctive features. (p. 77)

But what is a distinctive feature? This concept is at the heart of Gibson's theory. She defines it as a simple dimension of difference between two forms. For example, look at the forms shown in figure 4.5 taken from a study by Anne Pick (1965). What is different about the triangle and the line on the left from the triangle

The infant's perception is selective by nature.

and the line on the right? One has a curved line, the other has a straight line; the two forms are otherwise the same. The figures differ from each other, then, on the basis of a single feature—call it line-to-curve. This feature is distinctive. Other features may be the number of lines present, orientation or slant, the degree of rotation, and so on. In distinctive feature learning, then, the infant and child gradually learn more and more basic dimensions of differences among objects and events as they explore the world. Through repeated exploration of and exposure to the same stimuli, the infant and child perceive more and more differences and so have a richer basis for responding to and distinguishing events.

Keep in mind the information you have read in this section, for next you will see that sensorimotor activities form the basis of the most important theory of infant cognitive development, that of Jean Piaget.

Cognitive Development

The contemporary study of cognitive development is dominated by the ideas and research of one man—Jean Piaget—and his colleagues. Because of the importance

and dominance of his theory, the major portion of our material on cognitive development is devoted to it. You were introduced to Piaget and his theory in chapter 2; here we will focus on his ideas about the development of thought in infancy, and in later chapters describe his views of childhood (chapter 9), middle and late childhood (chapter 11), and adolescence (chapter 14). As an indication of how highly respected Piaget's view is, read the following eulogy, which appeared in the newsletter of the Society for Research in Child Development.

Jean Piaget died in Geneva, Switzerland, on September 16, 1980. He was eighty-four years old. It is hard to think of anything important to say about this great scientist that is not already well known to readers of this Newsletter—so truly outstanding and widely recognized were his contributions to our field. A long and detailed obituary for such a figure would certainly be richly deserved, but it would hardly be needed in present company. So let us, instead, honor his memory by briefly reminding ourselves of some of the many things child developmentalists owe him.

First, we owe him a host of insightful concepts of enduring power and fascination. . . . My favorites include the childhood concepts of object permanence, perspective, conservation, and measurement. . . .

We owe him a vast conceptual framework which has highlighted key issues and problems in human cognitive development and has informed and guided the efforts of nearly a generation of researchers in this area. This framework is now familiar vision of the developing child, who, through its own active and creative commerce with its environment, builds an orderly succession of cognitive structures enroute to intellectual maturity. . . .

We owe him the present field of cognitive development—that is, we owe him a wide field of scientific inquiry. What would exist in its place today had Piaget never lived is anyone's guess, of course, but there are those of us who remember well what it was—and especially wasn't—before his influence was felt. Our task is now to extend and go beyond what he began so well. (Fall,1980, p. 1)

Piaget's Theory

Piaget believed that the child passes through a series of stages of thought from infancy to adolescence. Passage through the stages is the result of biological pressures to *adapt* to the environment (assimilation and accommodation) and to organize structures of thinking. These stages of thought are described as *qualitatively* different from one another, which means that the way a child reasons at one stage is very different from the way a child reasons at another. This contrasts with the *quantitative* assessments of intellect made in standard intelligence tests where the focus is on how much the child knows or how many questions the child answers correctly. Thought development is landmarked by the following major stages: sensorimotor, preoperational, concrete operations, and formal operations (see table 4.1 for a brief account of each stage). In this chapter we will focus extensively on the stage of sensorimotor development, a stage that Piaget believed best describes the cognitive development of infants.

The Sensorimotor Stage

The sensorimotor stage lasts from birth to about two years of age, corresponding to the period that most psychologists identify as infancy. During this time mental development consists of the infant's progressing ability to organize and coordinate sensations and perceptions with his physical movements and actions, hence the term **sensorimotor** (Piaget, 1970). This stage begins with the newborn, who has little more than reflexive patterns with which to work and ends with the two-year-old, who has complex sensoriaction patterns and is beginning to operate with a primitive symbolic system. Unlike other stages, the sensorimotor stage is subdivided into six substages, which demarcate qualitative changes in the nature of sensorimotor organization. The term **scheme,** or **schema,** is used to refer to the basic unit for an organized pattern of sensorimotor functioning. Within a given substage, there may be many different schemes—for example, sucking, rooting, and blinking in substage 1—but all have the same organization. In substage 1 they are basically reflexive in nature. From substage to substage, the schemes change in organization. This change in organization is at the heart of Piaget's descriptions of the substages.

Substage 1: Simple Reflexes (Birth to One Month of Age)

The basic means of coordinating sensation and action is through reflexive behaviors, such as sucking and rooting, that the newborn has brought into the world. During substage 1 the infant exercises these reflexes. More importantly, he or she develops an ability and penchant for producing behaviors that resemble reflexes in the absence of obvious reflex stimuli. For example, the newborn may suck when a bottle or nipple is only nearby. At birth, the bottle or nipple would have produced the sucking pattern only when placed directly in the newborn's mouth or touched to the newborn's lips. This reflexlike action in the absence of a triggering stimulus is evidence that the infant is initiating action and actively structuring experiences, even shortly after birth.

Substage 2: First Habits and Primary Circular Reactions (One to Four Months of Age)

The infant learns to coordinate sensation and types of schemes or structures during substage 2, that is, habits and primary circular reactions. A *habit* is a scheme

Table 4.1
Piaget's Stages of Cognitive Development

Stage	General Description	Age Level
Sensorimotor Period	The child progresses from instinctual reflexive action at birth to symbolic activities, to the ability to separate self from object in the environment. He [or she] develops limited capabilities for anticipating the consequences of actions.	0 ½ 1 1½ 2
Preoperational Period	The child's ability to think becomes refined during this period. First, he [or she] develops what Piaget calls preconceptual thinking, in which he [or she] deals with each thing individually but is not able to group objects. The child is able to use symbols, such as words, to deal with problems. During the latter half of this period, the child develops better reasoning abilities but is still bound to the here-and-now.	2½ 3 3½ 4 4½ 5 5½ 6 6½ 7
Concrete Operations	At this stage, the child develops the ability to perform intellectual operations—such as reversibility, conservation, ordering of things by number, size, or class, etc. His [or her] ability to relate time and space is also matured during this period.	7½ 8 8½ 9 9½ 10 10½
Period of Formal Operations	This is the period in which the person learns hypothetical reasoning. He [or she] is able to function purely on a symbolic, abstract level. His [or her] conceptualization capacities are matured.	11 11½ 12 12½ 13 13½ 14 14½ 15

Source: Belkin & Gray, 1977.

based upon simple reflexes, such as sucking, which has become completely divorced from its eliciting stimulus. For example, an infant in the first substage might suck when orally stimulated by a bottle or when visually shown it, but an infant in the second substage may exercise the sucking scheme even when no bottle is present.

A **primary circular reaction** is a scheme based upon the infant's attempt to reproduce an interesting or pleasurable event that initially occurred by chance. In a popular Piagetian example, a child accidentally sucks his fingers when they are placed near his mouth; later he searches for the fingers to suck them again, but the fingers do not cooperate in the search because he cannot coordinate visual and manual actions.

Habits and circular reactions are stereotyped; that is, the infant repeats them the same way each time. The infant's own body remains the center of attention; there is no outward pull by environmental events.

Substage 3: Secondary Circular Reactions (Four to Eight Months of Age)

The infant becomes more object-oriented, or focused on the world, in substage 3 and moves beyond preoccupation with the self in sense-action interactions. The chance shaking of a rattle, for example, may produce a fascination in the child, and the child repeats this action for the sake of again experiencing fascination. The infant imitates some simple actions of others, such as the baby talk or burbling of adults, and some physical gestures. However, these imitations are limited to actions the infant is already able to produce. Although directed toward objects in the world, the infant's schemes lack an intentional, goal-directed quality.

Substage 4: Coordination of Secondary Reactions (Eight to Twelve Months of Age)

Several significant changes take place in substage 4. The infant readily combines and recombines previously learned schemes in a *coordinated* fashion. He or she may look at an object and grasp it simultaneously or visually inspect a toy, such as a rattle, and finger it simultaneously in obvious tactual exploration. Actions are even more outward-directed than before.

Related to this coordination is the second achievement—the presence of **intentionality,** the separation of means and goals in accomplishing simple feats. For example, the infant may manipulate a stick (the means) to bring a desired toy within reach (the goal). He or she may knock over one block to reach and play with another one.

As will be seen later, this substage has generated a great deal of interest on the part of investigators who wish to examine the logic and validity of the infant stages (Gratch, 1977).

Substage 5: Tertiary Circular Reactions, Novelty, and Curiosity (Twelve to Eighteen Months of Age)

In substage 5, the infant becomes intrigued by the variety of properties that objects possess and by the multiplicity of things he or she can make happen to objects. A block can be made to fall, spin, hit another object, slide across the ground, and so on. **Tertiary circular reactions** are schemes in which the infant purposefully explores new possibilities with objects, continuously changing what is done to them and explores the results. Piaget speaks of this period as marking the developmental starting point for human curiosity and interest in novelty. Previous circular reactions have been devoted exclusively to reproducing former events with the expectation of imitation of novel acts, which occurs as early as substage 4. The tertiary reaction is the first to be concerned with novelty. As such, it is the mechanism par excellence for trial-and-error learning.

Substage 6: Internalization of Schemes (Eighteen Months to Two Years of Age)

The infant's mental functioning shifts from a purely sensorimotor plane to a symbolic plane in substage 6, and the infant develops the ability to use primitive symbols. For Piaget, a **symbol** is an internalized sensory image or word that represents an event. Primitive symbols permit the child to think about concrete events without directly acting or perceiving. Moreover, symbols allow the child to manipulate and transform the represented events in simple ways. In a favorite Piagetian example, Piaget's young daughter saw a matchbox being opened and closed and sometime later mimicked the event by opening and closing her mouth. This was an obvious expression of her image of the event. In another example, a child opened a door slowly to avoid disturbing a piece of paper lying on the floor on the other side. Clearly, the child had an image of the unseen paper and what would happen to it if the door were opened quickly. However, recently it has been questioned whether two-year-olds really have such representations of action sequences at their command (Corrigan, 1981; Fischer & Jennings, 1981).

Object Permanence

One of the infant's most significant sensorimotor accomplishments is the understanding of **object permanence** (Flavell, 1977). In order to think logically about themselves and the world around them, children must grasp some simple ideas. One is that the self is physically separate, or distinct, from surrounding objects and events—a self-world differentiation. Another is that objects and events continue to exist even though the child is not in direct perceptual contact with them.

Imagine what thought would be like if people could not distinguish between themselves and other events in the world, or if events were believed to last only as long as the person has direct contact with them—highly chaotic, disorderly, and unpredictable, no doubt. This is what the mental life of the newborn infant is like; there is no self-world differentiation and no sense of object permanence (Piaget, 1952). By the end of the sensorimotor period, however, both are clearly understood. The transition between these extreme states is not abrupt; rather, it is marked by qualitative changes that reflect movement through each of the substages of sensorimotor thought.

Tertiary circular reactions reflect purposeful exploration.

The principal way object permanence is studied is by watching the infant's reaction when an attractive object or event disappears. If the infant shows no reaction, it is assumed that he or she has no belief in its continued existence. On the other hand, if the infant is surprised at the disappearance and searches for the object, it is assumed that he or she has a belief in its continued existence. According to Piaget, the following distinct stages exist in the development of object permanence:

Sensorimotor 1: There is no apparent object permanence. When a spot of light moves across the visual field, the infant follows it but quickly ignores its disappearance.

Sensorimotor 2: A primitive form of object permanence develops. Given the same experience, the infant looks briefly at the spot where the light disappeared, with an expression of passive expectancy.

Sensorimotor 3: The infant's sense of object permanence undergoes further development. With the newfound ability to coordinate simple schemes, the infant shows clear patterns of searching for a missing object, with sustained visual and manual examination of the spot where the object apparently disappeared.

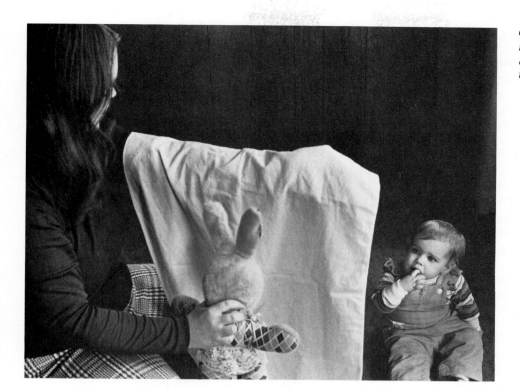

Sensorimotor 4: The infant actively searches for a missing object in the spot where it disappeared, with new actions to achieve the goal of searching effectively. For example, if an attractive toy has been hidden behind a screen, the child may look at the screen and try to push it away with a hand. If the screen is too heavy to move or is permanently fixed, the child readily substitutes a secondary scheme— for example, crawling around it or kicking it. These new actions signal that the infant's belief in the continued existence of the missing object is strengthening.

Sensorimotor 5: The infant now is able to track an object that disappears and reappears in several locations in rapid succession. For example, a toy may be hidden under different boxes in succession in front of the infant, who succeeds in finding it. The infant is apparently able to hold an image of the missing object in mind longer than before.

Sensorimotor 6: The infant can search for a missing object that disappeared and reappeared in several locations in succession, as before. In addition, the infant searches in the appropriate place even when the object has been hidden from view as it is being moved. This activity indicates that the infant is able to "imagine" the missing object and to follow the image from one location to the next.

Some Disagreements with Piaget about Object Permanence

Although Piaget's stage sequence is a neat summary of what might happen as the infant comes to fathom the permanence of things in the world, some experts believe the development of object permanence does not unfold the way Piaget thought. Let's look more closely at one of the criticisms of Piaget's ideas on object permanence.

Sometimes Piaget described infant *competencies* incorrectly. According to him, for example, the infant in substage 6 is able to mentally conceive of a series of actions and operate with this mental conception over time. Thus, if an object is made invisible by placing it inside a covered container, and then the object is moved from one hiding place to another so the infant cannot see it directly, the infant should be able to follow the unseen object's movement, since he or she supposedly has the object in mind. A close look at such tasks (Corrigan, 1981) reveals that at sensorimotor stage 6 the infant may succeed at finding objects without using specific image or memory of the object. Instead, he or she may rely on understanding what the person hiding the objects is doing and simply look in those locations where that adult has been. Such performances, then, depend, on learning "how to search," not on where the invisible thing is. Some critics go so far as to argue that two-year-olds probably do not readily utilize mental images of absent events at all (Fischer & Jennings, 1981).

Developmental Function and Individual Differences

The Piagetian perspective on infant cognitive development is a perspective with a strong hereditary-maturation orientation. The nature-nurture (heredity-environment) controversy is one of the most persistent issues in development. Robert McCall (1981) believes that the debates often fail to distinguish between what he calls developmental function and individual differences. **Developmental functions** are what scientists interested in the nature of the species study—for example, Piaget's attempt to describe in general the stages of mental development all members of the human species go through. By contrast, **individual differences** in the way infants proceed through the Piagetian stages do occur. The disagreement about Piaget's stages of object permanence reflects that there is a great deal of variation in the way one infant acquires and displays object permanence compared with how another goes through the process. Statements about developmental functions are general statements about the behavior, mental phenomena, or developmental changes being discussed. The general statements summarize what is typical of the largest number of subjects or for the "average" members of the species—in our case here infants' mental development. However, we know that the results obtained for most infants may not apply to all infants—the concept of individual differences.

It is advantageous to know whether an infant is advancing at a slow, normal, or fast rate of cognitive development. If the infant is advancing at a particularly slow rate of cognitive development, for example, environmental enrichment may be called for. And if an infant is progressing at an advanced rate of cognitive development, parents may be advised to provide toys that are designed to stimulate cognitive development in slightly older infants. To assess cognitive development in infancy, intelligence tests, usually referred to as **developmental scales,** have been devised. See application 4.1 to learn how child psychologists assess the infant's intelligence.

In chapter 10 we will look in greater detail at other approaches to assessing intelligence. Next we will look at infant development from a learning perspective, and we will find that it is far less cognitive than any perspective we have described so far. Indeed, in Skinner's view of operant conditioning, cognitive development is given no importance. In Bandura's social learning perspective the cognitive representations of a model's actions, however, are important. As you read the section on the learning theory perspective of infant development, keep in mind how it stands in stark contrast to the cognitive structural perspective of Piaget.

Application 4.1
Measuring the Infant's Intelligence

One of the most widely used developmental scales is the Bayley Mental and Motor Scales, consisting of a series of items to measure mental skills and to evaluate motor skills. The components of the Bayley Mental Scale were designed to measure the infant's adaptive responses to the environment. They include attention to visual and auditory stimuli; grasping, manipulating, and combining objects; shaking a rattle; and ringing a bell. Items that measure the infant's social and cognitive skills also are included: smiling, cooing, babbling, imitating, and following directions. Showing memory and being aware of object constancy (looking for a hidden toy) are part of the Bayley Mental Scale, as is beginning to understand language. The language items include following directions that involve the use of object names, prepositions, and the concept of "one." The Bayley Motor Scale tests the infant's ability to hold up his or her head, turn over, sit, creep, stand, walk, and go up and down stairs. It also tests manual skills, such as grasping small objects and throwing a

YOU'LL BE AMAZED
by baby's creativity. It's a sure sign of intelligence.

Reprinted by permission of Perigree Books from *Expectations: A Completely Unexpected Guide to Planned and Unplanned Parenthood,* by Andre Sala and Margot Duxler. Copyright © 1981 by Andre Sala and Margot Duxler.

ball (Bayley, 1970). According to the Bayley Scales, at approximately six months of age the average baby should be able to (Kessen et al., 1970)—

1. accept a second cube—baby holds first cube, while examiner takes second cube and places it within easy reach of the infant;
2. grasp the edge of a piece of paper when it is presented;
3. vocalize pleasure and displeasure;
4. persistently reach for objects placed just out of immediate reach;
5. turn his or her head after a spoon the experimenter suddenly drops on the floor; and
6. approach a mirror when the examiner places it in front of the infant.

At approximately twelve months of age the average baby should be able to

1. inhibit behavior when commanded to do so; for example, when the infant puts a block in his or her mouth and the examiner says, "no, no," then the infant should cease the activity;
2. repeat an action if he or she is laughed at;
3. imitate words the experimenter says, like "mama," and "dada";
4. imitate actions of the experimenter: for example, if the experimenter rattles a spoon in a cup, then the infant should imitate this action;
5. respond to simple requests, such as "take a drink."

Administering the Bayley Mental and Motor Scales.

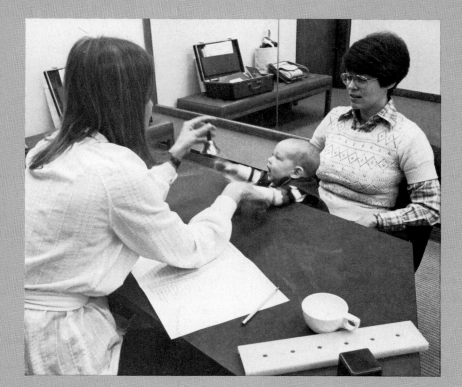

Learning

The study of child development has been significantly influenced by principles and techniques drawn from the dominant American perspective in psychology for most of the twentieth century—the psychology of **learning.** In chapter 2 you were introduced to some of the basic concepts in the learning perspective, a perspective referred to as behavioral social learning. This section presents an overview of the concept of learning and an analysis of the major kinds of learning that occur in infancy.

Definition of Learning

What is meant by learning? When the term *learning* is used by psychologists, it refers to a change in behavior that occurs as a result of experience. From the discussion in chapter 2, recall that learning refers to behavior that can be observed. Private thoughts, feelings, and emotions are beyond the scope of study unless they can be translated into directly observable responses. However, these translations are often possible (Mischel, 1977). A person who is angry, for example, may reveal this emotion in both facial expression and aggressive behavior. The thoughts of a child who is trying to solve a problem may be displayed in what the child says aloud or writes in a workbook. The behavior change should be relatively permanent, lasting for more than a few seconds or minutes. However, learning may last for several hours, days, or months; the particular time period is not important. **Practice** is the repetition of behavior that is being learned. Recall from the Imagine section that practice is an important component of Doman's perspective.

Some behaviors are not the result of learning. For example, all babies blink when a light is shone in their eyes at birth; and all babies cry or make an abrupt, involuntary movement when they hear a sudden, loud noise. These are examples of **reflexes,** behaviors that are wired into a person's nervous system. They occur without any practice.

There are also behaviors that are influenced by experience but depend on physical maturation and growth processes. For example, virtually all normal children eventually walk regardless of the amount of practice at this activity. Practice may speed up the process a bit but not by more than a month or two. And regardless of how little experience children have had, virtually all will be walking by the time they are eighteen or nineteen months old. Such behaviors are *maturational* rather than *learned.*

Some behavior changes occur very slowly and have a profound impact on many areas of children's psychological life. The logical skills required to understand the laws of physics and principles of higher mathematics are good examples of such changes. Although some psychologists believe these skills are learned behaviors (e.g., Gagné, 1977), they are viewed here as structures of thought or cognition. These structures develop more slowly than learned behaviors, they are mental in nature, and they underlie a broad array of observed behavior.

Kinds of Learning

Psychologists attempt to simplify their explanation of behavioral change by describing several different kinds of learning. Three are presented here—classical conditioning, operant conditioning, and imitation. They are sometimes referred to as basic mechanisms or laws of learning. They are very general; they apply equally to children of all ages and occur in diverse circumstances. A fourth form of learning, perceptual learning, described earlier in the chapter differs from the three being discussed here in that it does not involve an observable behavior.

Classical Conditioning

The theory of **classical conditioning,** first described by the Russian psychologist Ivan Pavlov (1927), was originally demonstrated by some simple behaviors of dogs. In classical conditioning it is assumed that learning occurs through a stimulus-response association. A stimulus (any event in the environment) initially causes some response to be made by the organism. For example, the presentation of food powder to a hungry dog causes the dog to salivate. The response occurs spontaneously without practice. The food powder is an **unconditioned stimulus (UCS);** the act of salivation is an **unconditioned response (UCR).**

Suppose another stimulus—a buzzer—is presented at the same time as the food (UCS). At the outset of the procedure, the buzzer does not cause the dog to salivate; it is a neutral stimulus. However, if the buzzer is repeatedly presented along with the food, the dog eventually salivates when the buzzer is presented alone. The buzzer is then referred to as a **conditioned stimulus (CS).** When the dog salivates to the sound of the buzzer alone, the salivation is a **conditioned response (CR). Conditioning,** or learning, has occurred as the result of the repeated association of a stimulus (buzzer) with a response (salivation)—hence, learning is based upon a stimulus-response association. See figure 4.6 for a simple diagram to help you remember classical conditioning.

John B. Watson (1924) was responsible for popularizing the concept of classical conditioning in the United States. In the 1920s he wrote extensively about its occurrence in everyday situations. Some of his writings were intended to give parents clues on how best to train their young children, and others to describe for

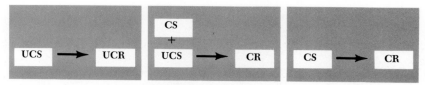

Figure 4.6 Steps in the classical conditioning of a response.

educators how environments can be set up to ensure efficient learning. To contemporary psychologists some of Watson's statements seem fanatical. He claimed that a child can be manipulated to become virtually anything the adult desires. In a famous statement he said:

Give me a dozen healthy infants well formed and my own specified world to bring them up in and I'll guarantee to take any one at random and train him to become any kind of specialist I might select—doctor, lawyer, merchant, chief, yes, even beggerman and thief, regardless of his talents, penchants, tendencies, abilities, vocations, and race of his ancestors. (p. 10)

This statement indicates the degree to which Watson believed conditioning can shape a person's life. His most famous experimental work is his demonstration of conditioning in a one-year-old child named Albert (Watson & Rayner, 1920). Albert had no observable fears when Watson first began the experiment. However, it could be shown that when a loud sound was made next to his crib, Albert was startled and tried to escape from the situation. The loud sound served as an unconditioned stimulus, and Albert's startled response and attempt to escape were unconditioned responses of fear.

Watson demonstrated that Albert could learn to fear other objects through conditioning. He paired a neutral object (a little white rat) with the loud noise, and after several presentations of this object Albert showed a startled response and an avoidance pattern to the neutral object as well as to the loud noise. Albert had previously shown no fear of white rats. Watson later demonstrated that the fear became generalized to include other small, white objects resembling the rat.

Since Watson's time psychologists have demonstrated that many fears in young children may arise from such a classical conditioning procedure (e.g., Jones, 1924). Some clinical psychologists today believe that the many fears adults harbor but cannot explain are due to early conditioning (e.g., Ringness, 1975). Thus many smells, sounds, and sights elicit anxiety in older children and adults, even though the smells, sounds, and sights themselves seem harmless. These may be conditioned stimuli that have been associated with fearful events in childhood (Lamb & Sherrod, 1981).

Although there is some debate about classical conditioning, it seems that a number of responses are learned in this manner during infancy—for example, crying, head turning, sucking, and visual attention (Lipsitt, 1967). See application 4.2 to learn how classical conditioning can be used in toilet training.

Operant Conditioning

Operant conditioning is a form of learning made famous by B. F. Skinner (1971), an American psychologist. In classical conditioning the initial unconditioned response is reflexive, or spontaneous, to a specific stimulus at the outset of conditioning. In operant conditioning the response initially occurs freely—that is, not in reaction to a specific stimulus.

In everyday life many responses that begin with a random event later bear regularly associated consequences. For example, a young infant turns to look at her father, and he cradles her affectionately. In school a child raises her hand, and the teacher praises her initiative. An adolescent babysitter smiles at his young ward, and the child gives him a hug. In each example the behavior led to a consequence that increased the likelihood of that behavior's occurring again. In Skinner's terminology, this effect on the response is called reinforcement. By contrast, many behaviors may result in consequences that decrease their likelihood of occurrence. A child may be scolded for seeking a parent's attention, or a bright student who raises her hand may be told not to ask so many questions. In Skinner's terminology, this effect is called punishment. Skinner is concerned with the functional value of an event rather than with whether the event is pleasant or unpleasant. Therefore, if an event follows a response and the response is repeated, the event is a *reinforcer,* whether pleasant or unpleasant. If an event follows a response and decreases the likelihood that the response will recur, the event is a *punisher.* See figure 4.7 for a representation of how the operant conditioning of a response works.

Application 4.2
Classical Conditioning, Affective Behavior, and Toilet Training

Once upon a time a young psychologist wanted to train his small son to the potty. Since children don't ordinarily find the seat too comfortable or stimulating, he decided to change its image by introducing an element of pleasure. He obtained a circus poster of a clown—colorful, smiling, with a big nose. He then placed a red light bulb on the nose and switched it on while the child was on the potty. The child was entranced and often wanted to go to the bathroom. Later, it wasn't difficult to rig an electrical circuit so that when the child urinated, a connection was made, and there was the lighted red nose.

But conditioning processes often produce *stimulus generalization,* which means that stimuli like the original, specific stimulus can evoke a similar response.

As you might anticipate, father and son went for a car ride one day and were stopped by a big red traffic light. Guess what happened!

But some conditioning isn't funny. Most teachers have experienced one or more of the following:

Four-year-old Mary comes to nursery school with her mother, but when Mother leaves, Mary cries and carries on, with strong emotional behavior. Only when Mother promises to stay does Mary quiet down again! She continues to watch fearfully lest Mother show some signs of abandoning her.

Peter becomes slightly nauseated whenever a test is announced. Sometimes he becomes actively sick and has to go home.

And Monday depresses us—that's why it's "Blue Monday." But we enjoy Friday—it is T.G.I.F. (Thank God It's Friday).

If you asked Mary, Peter, or yourself why these feelings occurred, you would probably get an answer, but it might well be a rationalization rather than the truth. That is because we frequently don't know enough about our real reasons for feeling as we do, although we can call upon our intellect for an explanation that may satisfy us. The behaviors described at left can be considered examples of *classical conditioning,* in which form of learning we are frequently unaware that we are learning, and are certainly not motivated to try.

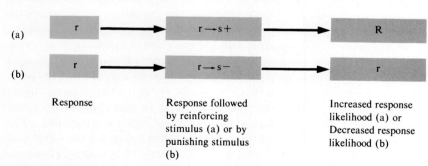

(a) r → r → s+ → R

(b) r → r → s− → r

Response   Response followed by reinforcing stimulus (a) or by punishing stimulus (b)   Increased response likelihood (a) or Decreased response likelihood (b)

Figure 4.7 Steps in the operant conditioning of a response.

Most practitioners of operant conditioning emphasize the superiority of reinforcement over punishment for changing behavior (e.g., Bijou, 1976; Skinner, 1980). Punishment has some undesirable side effects in addition to reducing the likelihood that a behavior will recur. It may arouse the child unnecessarily, illustrate that aggression (by the punisher) is acceptable, and interfere with learning the acceptable behavior in the situation.

Punishment and **negative reinforcement** are frequently confused. In negative reinforcement the removal of a stimulus event causes a response to recur. This reinforcement is termed *negative* because the consequence of the child's response is that a particular event is removed from the situation rather than added to it. Consider a simple example. A student has a teacher who constantly glares at her and scolds her because she is often looking around the room when she is supposed to be reading. The child buries her head in her reader, and the teacher stops berating her. If removal of the teacher's scolding occurs each time the child hides her head in a book, the child's response has been negatively reinforced.

A frequent criticism of operant learning is that it fails to give a very good account of how complex behavior (such as language, thought, and problem solving) is learned (e.g., Chomsky, 1965). Skinner himself (1980) has acknowledged this criticism but thinks his critics are either wrong (Skinner's account of language, 1957) or prematurely demand too much from psychology, still in its youth as a science (Skinner, 1980). Despite these arguments, however, there are good demonstrations of highly complex behaviors that are undeniably acquired under the well-described contingencies of reinforcement. For example, nursery school children have been taught to produce highly creative block constructions through reinforcement (Baer et al., 1975).

Imitation

In chapter 2, as part of our discussion of social learning theory, we saw that imitation is an important form of learning. Albert Bandura (1977) believes that imitation—sometimes called modeling—requires the coordination of motor activity with a mental picture of the act that is being imitated. Because very young infants do not imitate others, it seems likely that they either cannot form a mental picture of the act of another individual or cannot coordinate their motor actions with that picture.

Earlier in this chapter, we saw that Piaget studied imitation in infancy. According to Piaget, infants cannot imagine objects until approximately nine months of age. Before then, it is possible to get a baby to imitate such responses as opening and closing the hands,

Albert Bandura (1925–   )

which babies master early in life and can see themselves doing, although Piaget calls this action psuedo-imitation.

Once the infant has reached the point in development when he or she can represent an action with a mental picture or words, Bandura believes that the processes involved in imitation are basically the same regardless of the age of the individual. In other words, the imitation process is no different for a two-year-old than a thirty-five-year-old.

Attention is the first cognitive process that must be activated before the observer can reproduce the model's actions. The child may not hear the teacher present an idea in class if his or her attention is on the person in the next chair. The child's attention to a model is influenced by characteristics of the models themselves. Warm, powerful, atypical individuals command more attention than cold, weak, typical individuals. The child pays closer attention when informed that he or she will be required to reproduce what the model does at a later time than when no such information is given.

Imitation also involves the child's **retention.** To reproduce a model's actions at a later time, the child must code and store the information in his or her memory to be recalled later. A vivid image of what the model did assists retention.

A third concept involved in modeling is **motoric reproduction.** The child may attend to the model and adequately code what was seen, but because of limitations in motor development the child may not be able to reproduce what the model has done. For example, catching a ball may involve motor coordination beyond that of a child, who is thus unable to reproduce the modeled behavior. Reproducing the letters a teacher has drawn may be difficult for some first graders because their hand-eye coordination may not have developed adequately. Therefore, having first graders spend long periods of time trying to print letters that exactly match

"WHEN YOU'RE IN, YOU WANT OUT...WHEN YOU'RE OUT, YOU WANT **IN** !"

" I'M GETTIN' TO SOUND JUST LIKE **YOU**. "

DENNIS THE MENACE® used by permission of Hank Ketcham. Copyright © by Field Enterprises, Inc.

Children often imitate their parents.

the teacher's is not a wise strategy. This is not to say that children should not engage in activities, such as printing, that call for hand-eye coordination, but they should not be expected to reproduce all written symbols exactly at such an early age. Failure to recognize the role of motor development in imitation may lead to emotional problems and difficulty in social interactions for the child.

A final consideration in Bandura's conception of modeling involves reinforcement, or **incentive conditions.** There are many situations in which a person can easily do what a model has done but may not be motivated to do so. A child who watches a teacher demonstrate lunchroom etiquette may not be motivated to imitate the teacher's actions unless appropriate incentives are provided—perhaps in the form of a special luncheon treat. The appropriateness of the incentives, of course, will vary for individual children. In the next chapter, you will discover that concepts of learning, cognition, sensation, and perception are important in our effort to understand the foundations and development of language.

Summary

Among several important aspects of infant development are sensation, perception, cognition, and learning. Sensation is the pickup of information by sensory receptors. Perception is the interpretation of what is sensed. At birth or shortly thereafter, each of the five senses is operating—hearing, touch, taste, smell, and vision. Except for vision, however, little is known about the senses. With vision, marked changes have been observed in acuity, accommodation, and vergence during the first few months of infancy. Infants attend to isolated features of objects and, as they grow older, scan them more completely.

Perception of space is necessary to negotiate effectively in the environment. Distance is perceived through several binocular and monocular cues. That infants can perceive depth has been demonstrated by Gibson's visual cliff procedure. Among the patterns and forms preferred by infants are those with facial features. Patterns of change are noted particularly in the perception of facial features.

In perceptual learning, there is a change in the way stimuli are perceived. There is either a radical change in the field organization (Gestalt view) or a change in the distinctive features of events that are noticed.

Piaget is the leading contemporary figure in cognitive development. He proposed a broad theory of development based upon his experiences with philosophy, biology, and psychology. His theory proposes a series of stages of development from infancy through adolescence. In the sensorimotor period the infant moves through a series of six substages. In the first substage the infant reacts to events with simple reflexes. Through the next several substages, simple sensoriaction patterns become increasingly differentiated and coordinated until by the last substage, the child can represent these patterns with mental images. A special acquisition during infancy is object permanence, the understanding that objects continue to exist beyond their immediately perceived presence. Another aspect of infant cognition is the measurement of infant intelligence—one such widely used instrument is the Bayley Development Scales.

Learning is a change in behavior that occurs as the result of practice. Several different kinds of learning are important in infancy: (1) in classical conditioning, a neutral stimulus is paired with an unconditioned stimulus (UCS) and, after several trials, becomes a conditioned stimulus (CS), which elicits a conditioned response (CR); (2) in operant conditioning, behavior may change through reinforcement or punishment. A stimulus that follows a response and increases the likelihood of its occurrence is reinforcing; one that decreases the likelihood of occurrence is punishing; (3) in imitation, responses are acquired through observing the behaviors of others.

Key Terms

accommodation	operant conditioning
attention	perception
classical conditioning	practice
conditioned response (CR)	pragnanz
conditioned stimulus (CS)	primary circular reactions
conditioning	reflexes
convergence	retention
developmental functions	scheme (schema)
developmental scales	secondary circular reactions
distinctive features theory	sensation
divergence	speech perception
Gestalt view	symbol
incentive conditions	tertiary circular reactions
individual differences	unconditioned response (UCR)
intentionality	unconditioned stimulus (UCS)
learning	vergence
looming	visual acuity
motoric reproduction	visual cliff technique
negative reinforcement	
object permanence	

Review Questions

1. Distinguish between sensation and perception.
2. What are the newborn's basic hearing, feeling, tasting, and smelling capacities?
3. What are the newborn's basic capacities for vision at birth? How do these change?
4. What features of the environment attract the infant's attention? How does this change during infancy?
5. Describe the visual cliff experiment, especially with regard to infants' reactions.
6. How does the infant's perception of the human face change during the first half-year of life?
7. What are the major changes during the period of sensorimotor development?
8. What is object permanence? What are the substages of object permanence during infancy?
9. Define learning.
10. Describe classical conditioning.
11. Describe operant conditioning.
12. Explain imitative learning.

Further Readings

Bower, T. G. R. *The perceptual world of the child.* Cambridge, Mass.: Harvard U. Press, 1977.
A scholarly introduction to the study of infant perception, including the topics of space perception, distance perception, and size constancy. Technical in places but fascinating and easy to read.

Piaget, J. *The origins of intelligence in children.* New York: Norton, 1963.
This book focuses exclusively on Piaget's concept of the six stages of infant cognitive development. Examples of Piaget's theory reflected in his own three children should be focused on. Not easy to read, but worthwhile.

Becker, W. C. *Parents are teachers.* Champaign, Ill.: Research Press, 1971.
An extremely easy-to-read paperback with step-by-step instructions of how to apply basic learning principles to everyday situations with infants and children.

5 Language Foundations and Development

Imagine . . . that you are an infant looking at a picture book and you just uttered your first word

Imagine . . . *that you are an infant look-ing at a picture book and you just ut-tered your first word*

Young children are forever being asked to identify objects. This has been called the "great word game" and is motivated by adult pressure on children to identify the words associated with objects.

Anat Ninio and Jerome Bruner (1978) took a close look at the subtle interplay between a mother and her infant son as the two performed the great word game in two settings—reading picture books and playing with objects. The mother and child were part of a longitudinal study that covered the period from eight months to one year, six months in the child's life. The child was firstborn and his parents were white, English, and middle class. Labeling was part of the filmed play activity captured in the videotape records made every two to three weeks in the infant's home.

The investigators uncovered some remarkable findings. Chief among these was the ritualized nature of mother-child labeling activity. It seemed as though labeling of pictures was a highly structured activity that obeyed clear rules and had the texture of a dialogue. A number of scholars have described conversations as having fairly tight patterns in ascribing roles, turn-taking, imitating, and responding (e.g., Bruner, 1973; Snow, 1977; Cherry-Wilkinson et al., 1981). The labeling activity also had tight patterns. Each time mother and child interacted over a picture name, for example, they took about the same number of turns, lasting about the same length of time. And the linguistic forms of the mother's utterances in book reading were very limited. She made repeated use of four key types of statements, (1) "Look!" (to get the child's attention), (2) "What's that?" (3) "It's an X!" (labeling the picture for the child), and (4) "Yes!" (giving the child feedback on his utterance). These types of statements accounted for virtually all of the language the mother directed toward the child while reading books during the entire period of the study and obeyed some simple rules of occurrence. For example, the attention getter "Look!" always preceded the query, "What's that?" or the labeling phrase, "It's an X!" Similarly, the query always preceded the labeling phrase.

At the outset of the study, few of the child's verbal responses to the mother's queries were distinguishable words, of course. At best, the child produced consistent babble. By the end of the period, however, words were present. Associated with this change, the mother dropped reliance on one of her four statement types— "What's that?" Because the child now could produce a word for the picture, this part of the ritual could be dropped.

To summarize the authors state that the book reading dialogue seems . . . to be a format well suited to the teaching of labeling. It has few elements and strict ordering rules between them. It is flexible in the sense of accepting a great variety of responses by the child. It is highly repetitive. Not only do the fixed elements ("Look," "What's that" and "It's a (label)") appear over and over again, with minimal changes in the wording, but the variable elements, the labels themselves, appear repeatedly as well. (Ninio & Bruner, 1978, p. 12)

Introduction

Language is a remarkable phenomenon. It enables us to do a variety of things rapidly and efficiently. We use it to communicate with each other, with ourselves, and with others not present by way of the printed word. It is helpful in thinking, problem solving, remembering, learning, and perceiving the world. Without it today's modern civilization probably would not exist, for without language, how could society's complex social, technical, and political structures be maintained? Imagine maintaining friendships with people who live far away without being able to talk or write to them. Imagine constructing or operating a computer without verbal instructions to smooth the way. And imagine the members of a government body responding to their constituencies without the various language media.

No animal species other than humans can be credited with such an achievement as language. To be sure, other animals "talk" and even communicate with each other, but none do so with a language system quite like ours. Biological evolution and cultural evolution have conspired to make humans unique in this respect. Perhaps even more remarkable is the speed with which humans learn language. The newborn infant has a few distinguishable crying sounds; the twelve-month-old is uttering a few words; the four-year-old is producing adult sentences. What an incredible change in just a few short years!

The study of language development is one of the most exciting areas in child psychology today. Most of the insights into the nature of children's language development have come very recently—in the past twenty-five years or so—despite the interest taken in language by writers and philosophers for many centuries and by psychologists for as long as there has been a discipline of psychology. The insights stem from a basic change in the way language is defined, a change stimulated by developments in the field of linguistics, particularly the ideas of Noam Chomsky (1957, 1972). The study of language development is often referred to as developmental **psycholinguistics** to underscore how the two disciplines of psychology and linguistics now work hand in hand to further our understanding of language development.

The decade of the 1970s witnessed the impact of several other social science disciplines on the study of children's language acquisition—most notably sociology and anthropology. From these disciplines has come the insight that the social structure of the setting in which children learn to talk has an important influence on what they say, the language rules they learn, and the language rules they apply. This perspective has been referred to as **sociolinguistics.** In this chapter we will look at the basic building blocks of language development and describe its course of development through the infant years. In later chapters we will describe its developmental course in early childhood (chapter 8) and middle and late childhood (chapter 11).

Language: What Is It?

Language is a well-ordered system of rules that adults comprehend in speaking, listening, and writing. We do not necessarily have to know these rules in the sense that we can state them, any more than a bicyclist needs to describe the regular (ruleful) motion of pedaling with the aid of differential calculus in order to be able to pedal. We and the cyclist know the rules in the sense that we conform to them.

This system of rules is a precise way of describing language. To understand the nature of these rules, we must first understand the fundamental units employed to study language. Keeping all of these fundamental units straight may be difficult at first. However, if you take the time to learn their definitions now, your understanding of language development will be much easier in the long run.

Language is made up of basic sounds, or **phonemes.** English employs about thirty-six phonemes; other languages employ as few as twenty-five and as many as fifty.

Noam Chomsky (1928–   )

The English alphabet was originally constructed so that a given letter of the alphabet might correspond to a given sound. In actual practice, however, many letters have several alternative phonemes associated with them. This is particularly true of the vowels. The multiple sounds associated with letters is one of the stumbling blocks in learning to read and write English. Some other languages, like Spanish, have a simpler system of correspondence between phonemes and letters.

The study of the sound system, **phonology,** is principally concerned with the rules used to combine sounds with each other. Phonological rules guarantee that certain sequences occur (e.g., *ax, kl, apr, br*) and that others do not (e.g., *mx, kz, pq, bc*). The phonological rules differ from one language to the next, but all languages employ such rules.

At the next level is the **morpheme,** a string of sounds that conveys meaning. **Morphology** is the study of the rules used to combine morphemes. All words in the language consist of one or more morphemes tied together. However, not all morphemes are words. Some morphemes are what we ordinarily think of as word fragments; prefixes (e.g., *pre-, re-, ex-, con-*), suffixes (e.g., *-tion, -est, -icy*), verb tense markers (e.g., *-ing, -ed*), and singular-plural markers (*-s, -es*). Some languages, such as Latin, Greek and Russian, use morphemes to mark the case for each noun in the sentence. As with phonology, morphological rules guarantee that certain sequences occur in the language (e.g., *caption, happiest, contrary*) and that others do not (e.g., *sadtion, princeest, conhappy*). Again, specific rules differ for different languages.

At another level is **syntax,** the rules for combining words to produce acceptable phrases and sentences. More work has been done in the area of syntax than in either phonology or morphology. It is perhaps most evident in the realm of syntax that the rules young children use as they first learn a language are very different from those of older children and adults.

A **grammar** is a formal description of a speaker's syntactic rules. In school most of us learned rules that were also referred to as grammar. These were principally rules of thumb that taught us how to construct acceptable sentences and how to avoid unacceptable ones. Some of us also learned how to diagram sentences, that is, how to identify the units and parts of speech. The rules we learned in school did not explain how a sentence is produced; they typically taught us what *not* to do in constructing a sentence (and some of today's educational critics claim that even this has been done poorly). Moreover, these grammatical rules did not explain some other important facts about sentences.

Some sentences have very different meanings and logical organization, yet are very similar in appearance. For example,

Robert is ready to come.
Robert is readied to come.

In the first sentence Robert is in a specific frame of mind. In the second sentence Robert is the implied object of an activity—someone got him ready.

Some sentences mean the same thing and have the same logical organization but are expressed in slightly different ways. For example,

The boy hit the dog.
The dog was hit by the boy.

In the first sentence the idea is expressed in an active form. In the second sentence the idea is expressed in a passive form.

These and other facts about the differences and similarities among sentences are captured in modern linguistic grammars that distinguish between the **deep structure** and the **surface structure** of sentences. The basic underlying idea and organization of a sentence is its deep structure. The deep structure may be expressed in alternative surface forms. What is actually spoken or heard is the surface structure. Because a sentence has one underlying structure and many possible surface structures, syntactic rules—called **transformations**—explain the different surface forms for a single sentence. Thus there are transformations that explain passive and active forms of sentences, declarative and question forms, affirmative and negative statements, and others.

At the same time, the distinction between deep structure and surface structure can be used to explain why some sentences seem alike even though they express different ideas and logical organization. They have similar surface structures but different deep structures. Different transformational rules were applied to the different deep structures and produced the similar surface forms. They can be likened to two children with different genetic backgrounds and different environmental experiences who grow up to have the same IQ.

In addition to phonology, morphology, and syntax, there are other kinds of rules that are integral to language (figure 5.1). One concerns **semantics,** or the expressed meanings of words and sentences (e.g., Chapman, 1981; Dale, 1976; Nelson, 1978). Semantics has at least two components—the appropriate use of words in social contexts and the appropriate use of words in sentences. The child's appropriate use of words

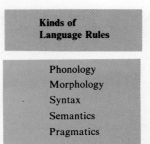

Kinds of Language Rules
Phonology
Morphology
Syntax
Semantics
Pragmatics

Figure 5.1 Kinds of language rules.

He said TRUCK, didn't you, darling. He said truck!

Taken from *Do They Ever Grow Up?* Copyright © 1978 by Lynn Johnston with permission of Meadowbrook Press, Deephaven, MN.

in social contexts develops partly as the result of expanding vocabulary. The more words in the child's vocabulary, the easier his or her task when asked to name an object or event. But knowledge also develops as the child gains a better understanding of the attributes that define the category to which a word refers. For example, a child may learn that "dog" refers to an animal that has four legs, barks, has a tail that wags, and so on.

The appropriate use of words in sentences is more complex. It is a process to which a growing number of language experts are turning their attention. They believe that a major mystery about language will be solved when semantic development is better understood (Chapman, 1981).

Let's consider for a moment just what the problem is. Look at the following string of words: "The happy nose threw the river at the movie." Would you say that this collection of words forms a grammatical sentence? It certainly seems as though the right kinds of words appear at the right places. Would you say that it is meaningful? In our ordinary use of language, noses do not possess emotions and are not capable of throwing things. Rivers cannot be hurled at objects, but even if they could, it makes no sense to say that a movie is the target. In other words, this "sentence" violates the ordinary rules of semantic relations. The problem is that children obviously produce many sentences they have never heard before. A sizable number of these are both grammatical and sensible. What are the rules they have learned that ensure the sense of the sentences? When and in what order does understanding of these rules appear in a child's development?

Finally, there are pragmatic rules in every language. **Pragmatics** concerns the appropriate use of language, with all of its social and physical requirements. Certain pragmatic rules guarantee that a specific sentence is uttered in one situation and not another. For example, it is appropriate to say "You look very nice" to someone who has obviously made an effort to present a pleasing appearance, but it is inappropriate to greet someone who is dirty and disheveled in this way. Other pragmatic rules specify that certain kinds of utterances are more appropriate in given situations than others. For example, it is more polite to request some milk with "May I have some milk please?" than with "Give me some milk." Pragmatic rules help us to get along smoothly in the world and assure that language is well integrated with other facets of psychological functioning.

One final distinction is in order. A child may know a linguistic rule but be unable to express it in actual speech. He or she may have *linguistic competence* but fail to evidence it with the appropriate *linguistic performance*. Adults often forget this and underestimate children's competence by relying on linguistic performance, with its qualities that seem different from adult language. Psychologists have had to find alternative ways to measure the child's language knowledge to avoid the trap of using any one performance measure as indicative of what the child knows.

Now that you have been through our explanation of language terms once, it may be helpful to go through and study them once more. Remember that keeping them straight in your head will help you as you proceed through the chapter.

How Is Language Learned?

For many years, some psychologists thought of language as just another collection of behaviors, much like walking, sitting, touching, eating, swimming, and laughing. And like other behaviors, its development was explained by the now-familiar principles of learning—stimulus-response, association, reinforcement, and imitation (Skinner, 1980). But learning theory leaves altogether too much unexplained. In this section we examine both old and new theories of how language is learned, including the roles of biology and the environment in language development.

The Old View

The father of American behaviorism, John B. Watson, in his classic work *Behaviorism* (1924), argued that language is complex behavior—complex because its most important representative, the fully formed sentence, consists of a series of stimulus-response associations. Each word itself is a series of stimuli and responses chained together, with the basic sounds being both responses and eliciting stimuli. (An eliciting stimulus is the sound that also activates the next response, another sound.) When a word becomes well learned, it becomes unitized, now serving as a single stimulus or response unit. The sentence in turn is a series of stimulus-response associations, with the word now serving as the basic unit (the stimulus and the response) in the chain. The means by which chaining occurs, according to Watson, is classical conditioning.

The stimulus-response view of language learning fails to explain the child's generativity satisfactorily. The child can utter hundreds and thousands of sentences; if Watson's intuition was correct, consider how many such chains the child would have to learn. Quite an extraordinary number. Some researchers have argued that the number actually exceeds the brain's capacity to store and retrieve information (e.g., Halwes & Jenkins, 1971). This view of language as chains of stimuli and responses lasted a surprisingly long time in American psychology. A number of prominent behaviorists supported it.

Of the many sentences the child produces, a large percentage are novel. A novel utterance is one that the child neither heard nor spoke previously. How can the mechanisms of learning account for this novelty? Suppose a child learned the following sentence by being reinforced or by imitating what someone else said:

My truck fell into the wagon.

How would he or she then be able to produce the following sentence, which was never heard before?

The mirror dropped on the chair.

The mechanisms of learning cannot explain this.

There are still other problems for learning theory. Suppose the child produced only a small number of utterances, had a brain that could handle the processing requirements of numerous stimulus-response chains, and did not generate novel sentences. Is there any evidence that the mechanisms of learning can account for significant changes in children's language competence? Do imitation and reinforcement, for example, change the child's manner of speaking? Is the child likely to produce a more grammatical complex sentence if such sentences are repeatedly modeled by a

Children generate an infinite number of words.

parent? Is a child more likely to utter sentences of a specific grammatical or sematic form if he or she has been previously reinforced for producing them?

The answers are all no. For example, a child is no more likely to utter a more complex sentence if the sentence is modeled repeatedly than if it is not (Dale, 1976). We sympathize with the mother who stubbornly tried to lengthen the form of her two-year-old child's two-word sentence, only to fail miserably.

Sandy Want milk!
Mother Oh, you mean "*I* want milk."
Sandy Want milk!
Mother Can you say "*I* want milk"?
Sandy Want milk!
Mother Sandy, please say "*I* want milk"!
Sandy Want milk!

Roger Brown (1973) has searched for evidence of naturalistic reinforcement in the language exchanges of mothers and their young children. There is evidence that parents do try to influence their children's speech with naturalistic rewards. They smile and praise their children for producing certain sentences that they like. But from the way parents choose to dispense rewards, it is amazing that children ever learn more mature speech. Some of the time parents reward children for uttering sentences that test grammatical limits without regard for their truth value or sensibleness. Thus a toddler, picking up a bar of white soap, was praised for his

Infants have a built-in motivation to acquire language.

statement "Mommy, soap black" because it was a three-word utterance while most of his speech was at the two-word stage. But what he said was actually incorrect.

Sometimes parents reward children for truthful or accurate statements that are phrased in a grammatically immature way. For example, the same toddler uttered the single word *white* and also was praised, this time for knowing the correct color. Brown's records indicate that parents are about equally likely to reward speech on each basis. If this is true, then children are being exposed to conflicting schedules of reinforcement. How do they ever learn anything? Perhaps a more compelling criticism is Brown's finding that the particular way a parent reinforces a child has little influence on the child's later speech.

A final criticism of learning theory is that it fails to explain the obvious orderliness, structure, and ever-present rules in children's speech. Strict learning theory predicts that there should be vast individual differences in the patterns of speech development for different children, because each child is exposed to a unique learning history. But a compelling fact is that there are certain sequences in each child's development that appear to be universal. For example, children emit cooing sounds before babbling sounds in infancy. They produce one-word utterances before two-word utterances. They master active forms of sentences before passive ones.

Children also struggle to uncover general rules for producing correct speech. We see them making similar "mistakes" ("The boy goed home." "The mouses runned.") at about the same time that they overgeneralize some of the early rules. Learning theory cannot account for these important facts about language development.

It seems obvious, then, that learning theory provides an inadequate explanation for language development. It cannot reasonably explain children's generativity or the novel statements they utter. Imitation and reinforcement do not seem to advance language rules. And the theory fails to explain the orderliness, structure, and ever-present rules in children's speech.

The New View

Psychologists now believe that learning takes a different form from that described by behaviorists. The exact nature of the learning remains illusive. Psycholinguists

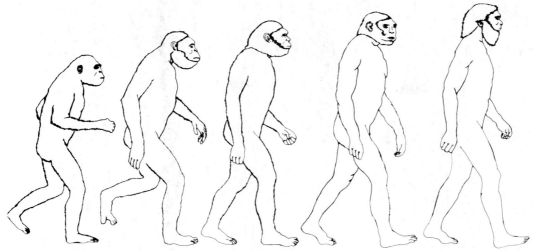

Our brain, nervous system, and vocal apparatus changed over hundreds of thousands of years as we evolved.

have not provided a precise account of the process in the way that behaviorists have precisely described how other behaviors are learned. There is general agreement, however, that language is learned as the result of the child's active attempts to induce rule systems from everyday speech. These systems are abstract from the very beginning of language learning, but the child is aided in several ways. First, the human brain seems especially sensitive to the structure and rules of language—the child has an innate propensity for learning language rules. Second, the everyday speech the child hears contains abundant information, redundancy, and feedback about language rules. And finally, the child has a strong, built-in motivation to learn language. He or she is continually exposed to people who have mastered it and cannot escape the need to communicate effectively with them (Brown, 1973).

We turn now to some specific components of the language learning process as it is conceived of in the new view.

The Role of Biology
It is clear that our biological heritage is a necessary foundation upon which language, more than other human acquisitions, is built. Without it, we would never have learned to talk.

Evolution   Language is a skill that evolved in two phases. The first was physical evolution, which took quite a long time. The brain, nervous system, and vocal apparatus changed over hundreds of thousands of years as we evolved from *Homo erectus* (about a million years ago) to *Homo sapiens* (about one hundred thousand years ago). The change ensured the development of the requisite physical equipment for the natural form of

language as we know it (speech) to develop. Prior to these changes the physical equipment to produce speech was inadequate.

Then came the important second phase, social evolution, which occurred more rapidly. Humans, with their newly evolved language equipment, had to create a system for communicating. More important, they had to have a compelling social need to motivate its development. There is evidence about how long it took to develop a speech system that moved beyond the expressive grunts, groans, and cries of *Homo erectus* to the highly abstract speech of modern humans. Conservative estimates put this achievement in the neighborhood of tens of thousands of years ago. Another estimate is that a modern speech system was developed about 70,000 years ago. Language, then, is a relatively recent acquisition for humans in the evolutionary scheme of things.

There is also only speculation about the social forces that led to the creation of language. Some anthropologists believe that social changes forced humans to use abstract reasoning powers more and to develop an economical system for reflecting upon and communicating reasonings to others (Crick, 1977). Among the social changes credited to this are the development of complex plans and strategies to provide food, shelter, and physical comfort for the individual and the family. But there may very well have been an individual motivational pressure that was as important as the social one. Just as the young infant in modern times seeks to master and create new skills for the sheer pleasure of feeling competent, so the humans of so long ago may have felt the need to develop a new, abstract skill to gain a sense of competence.

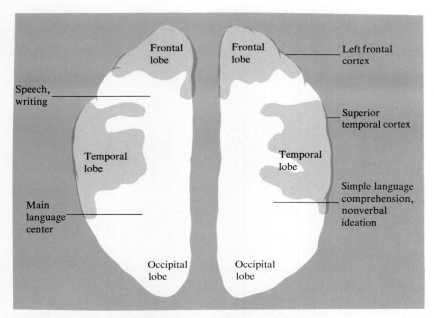

Frontal lobe

Frontal lobe

Left frontal cortex

Speech, writing

Superior temporal cortex

Temporal lobe

Temporal lobe

Main language center

Simple language comprehension, nonverbal ideation

Occipital lobe

Occipital lobe

Figure 5.2 Parts of the brain associated with language-related activities.

Adapted from *The Neurosciences: Third Study Program,* edited by Schmitt and Worden, by permission of MIT Press, Cambridge, Mass. Copyright 1974 by the MIT Press, Cambridge, Mass.

The Brain and Physical Maturation   Of the physical equipment involved in language, the brain is the most important (Lenneberg, 1967, Nelson, 1978). Without a *Homo sapien's* brain, language as we know it would not have developed. In figure 5.2 you see a diagram of the areas of the brain and the principal psychological functions they govern. As you can see, the main language center is located in the left half of the brain, in the area of the superior temporal cortex. If the brain is damaged in this area, as in a lesion, language functioning is often disrupted. Aphasia is one of the frequent results. Aphasics have a variety of symptoms; they may be unable to name objects, to call forth words to produce a sentence, or to produce words at all. One of the first to notice these problems and the area of the brain associated with them was Pierre-Paul Broca (1861). Accordingly, the main language center is often referred to as Broca's area.

As figure 5.2 indicates, other areas of the brain are also implicated as centers for language activity. For example, the brain center for speech and writing is in the left frontal cortex. Simple language comprehension seems to be governed by an area in the right hemisphere that corresponds to the left hemisphere's main language center.

Scientists who study brain functions realize that these language centers do not tell the whole story of the brain's role in language activity. For one thing, not everyone who has a lesion in Broca's area suffers speech impairment. For another, language functioning may be disturbed if other areas of the brain are damaged, areas not specifically designated as language areas. The brain works as a system, and in any system each part plays some role in many activities (Pribram, 1971).

As the child matures, two things happen to the brain that are significant for language. One is that identifiable language centers become localized. At birth each of the speech areas is not well differentiated from other areas of the brain in its functional operation, but by the end of middle childhood there is marked localization of brain function and by adolescence localization is complete. A second change is that language activity becomes increasingly dominated by the left half of the brain. The earlier in life that a brain injury occurs, the more likely it is that the child will recover without language problems. Experts believe that the less localization and specialization, the greater the brain's adaptability after injury.

A study by Patricia Day (1979) is a representative example of this phenomenon. She analyzed the ability of two children who had undergone brain surgery to perform a number of perceptual motor, cognitive, and linguistic tasks. One twelve-year-old girl experienced damage to areas in the right hemisphere, while the second child, a six-year-old girl, experienced damage to areas in her left hemisphere. Language disruption was more pronounced for the second child than for the first one.

There is also interest in the relation between the increasing dominance of language activity in the left hemisphere and reading ability. For example, one argument is that the degree of dominance (or asymmetry between the two halves of the brain) predicts reading comprehension ability. By contrast, the association between dominance and reading ability may be different for children at different levels of reading ability.

Animal Language   Humans are not the only members of the animal kingdom who communicate. Nonhuman primates gesture and shriek at each other, dogs bark and whine, bees have an elaborate dance ritual or indicate the location of nectar, and parrots and other birds mimic human speech. Do these communications qualify as language? Probably not. One list included more than one hundred characteristics of natural human language that no other communication system shares (Hockett, 1960).

Human language is *learned* and *learnable,* not instinctive. It is *spoken* (vocal) and *heard* (auditory). It consists of a finite number of sounds, which are combined in a multitude of complex ways. The sounds are perfectly *arbitrary;* that is, there is no obvious relation, a priori, between the sounds and the things they refer to. Human language is *reflexive;* that is, it can be used to discuss language. It is *prevaricative;* that is, it can assert things that are false. It includes both *referential* and *nonreferential* terms (in the sentence "It is a boy" the word *boy* refers to a discrete thing, while the word *it* has no referent). And finally, language is filled with dualistic *symmetry*—singular and plural forms, passive and active forms, positive and negative statements. A summary of some of the features of human language is provided in figure 5.3.

Several attempts have been made to teach primates an abstract language. In the 1930s the Kelloggs (1933) tried to raise a chimpanzee (Gua) with their infant son, talking and responding to the animal as they did to their own son. A similar experiment was tried in the 1950s by the Hayeses (1951). Both tries were failures in the sense that the chimpanzees learned very little language. They learned to produce a handful of single-word utterances and to communicate simple desires; in the latter case, they even produced some two-word utterances. Perhaps the problem is that animals do not have the vocal equipment to produce much human speech.

Because primates are adept at using their arms and hands in complex fashion, it seemed possible that they could be taught a kind of sign language. Allen and Beatrice Gardner (1971) taught a chimpanzee to produce manual signs adapted from the system of International Sign Lanaguage learned by the deaf. David Premack (1976) taught a chimpanzee to communicate by using physical forms as symbols of words. In both cases some remarkable results were obtained. The chimpanzees mastered a vocabulary of well over several hundred "words" and produced sentences of three and four words, and sometimes more. Some of their sentences were novel creations—that is, not first modeled by the

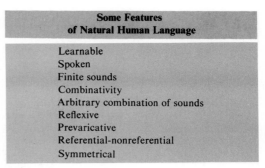

Figure 5.3

Some Features of Natural Human Language
Learnable
Spoken
Finite sounds
Combinativity
Arbitrary combination of sounds
Reflexive
Prevaricative
Referential-nonreferential
Symmetrical

experimenter. The chimpanzees engaged in play with their newly acquired languages; for example, they tried out new word sequences without any obvious intention to communicate, and they played jokes on the experimenter. This activity is similar to the word play of young children.

Have these animals, then, learned a language? The animals have learned to understand that signs represent specific objects and events, but there still is considerable controversy about whether these accomplishments qualify them for the distinction of being "language users." For example, language scientists argue that some chimps can produce sequences of three or four signs in order to get something they want (Premack, 1976), but the skeptics suggest that the animals have only memorized specific sequences and are not applying general rules. Even pigeons can be trained to peck at four keys in a specific sequence in order to obtain food, but no one argues that they are using "language" to get the food. Thus, while researchers agree that the chimps can use signs, usually to get something they want, the skeptics do not believe the chimps can use language, a rule-governed system of symbols in which new sentences are generated (Terrace, 1979). So the great ape language debate goes on.

The Role of the Environment
Just as the child's biological heritage is an important factor in language acquisition, so also is the environment. The child does not learn language in a social vacuum; he or she needs exposure to the speech of others. Speech complexity differs for children of different ages, so speech input must be geared to the child's level of development. It must be within a range of cognitive complexity that is not too far beyond the child's productive abilities but not too simple either.

Psychologists have studied how mothers address children at different stages of language maturity (Cross, 1978; Furrow, Nelson, & Benedict, 1979; Snow, 1972), both in natural settings and in controlled laboratory situations. Mothers employ several simplifying devices

Application 5.1
Strategies Adults Use in Verbal Exchanges with Children

Three adult strategies have been identifed in verbal interchanges with children (Cazden, 1972). One strategy is **prompting.** In a typical exhange the adult asks a question, the child fails to respond, and the adult follows with a variation of the same question. For example:

Adult Where is your toy?
Child (Silence)
Adult Your toy is where?

Another strategy is **echoing.** The child says something that is only partially understood, and the adult repeats the understandable portion and calls for more information. For example:

Child The car is in . . . (unintelligible speech)
Adult The car is where?

A third strategy is **expansion.** The child utters a short phrase, using a primitive language system, and the adult follows it with an expanded version designed to express a more complete thought. The adult seldom knows whether the expansion correctly captures what the child had in mind. For example:

Child Daddy car.
Adult Yes! Daddy has a car.

Each of these strategies can help the child to better understand the rules of grammar. More important, perhaps, they are valuable ways to provide feedback to the child about the success of his or her communicative effort. Parents of children who acquire language earlier may be engaging in these strategies more frequently than the parents of slower language learners (Brown, 1973) The parents who use these strategies, however, are probably doing other things differently with their children as well. Therefore, although the strategies are valuable, it is not clear just how valuable they are.

In their work on the development of competence in infants, Burton White and Jean Watts (1973) conducted home observations of infants and mothers, finding that the amount of time most mothers spent directly teaching their infants was surprisingly small. Instead of plain instruction, they tended to use various "low-keyed facilitative techniques" that generally were designed to encourage the child's activity. Indeed, the most effective mothers were those who excelled at performing the functions of "designer and consultant."

These mothers very rarely spend five, ten, or twenty minutes teaching their one- or two-year-olds, but they get an enormous amount (in terms of frequency) of teaching in "on the fly," and usually at the child's instigation. Although they do volunteer comments opportunistically, they react mostly to overtures by the child.

According to Rudolph Schaeffer (1977), the mother follows in order to lead: she lets her child in the first place indicate his interest at the moment and then proceeds, within the child's own context, to elaborate on that interest. In this way she lets him select his own topic and then begins to comment, demonstrate, and explain.

It is no coincidence that these facilitative mothers are effective in fostering competent language development. Katherine Nelson (1973), an expert on language development, emphasizes that a nondirecting parent who accepts a child's behavior—both verbal and nonverbal—facilitates the child's progress in language acquisition. But in those cases where the parent takes a highly active role and directs the child, the parent's behavior has an "interference effect" that delays the acquisition of new verbal skills.

Adults are not the only source of language stimulation for children. Children stimulate each other too. Children as young as four years of age can cater their language

when addressing infants and young children as compared with older children and adults. Sentences are shorter; vocabulary is simpler; grammatical structure is less complex; pauses between sentence boundaries are more definite and last longer; and key words and phrases are emphasized by volume and stress changes.

By contrast, mothers' speech addressed to older children and adults is complex and "messy." Sentences are very long. Often it is difficult to determine where one statement ends and another begins because of sentence fragments and lack of pauses. Grammatical structure is often very complex.

Aside from selecting different levels of complexity of speech to address children, are there other means by which adults influence development? As you will see in application 5.1, there are.

The Child as a Language Processor
In addition to biological programming and environmental input, the child also contributes to his or her own learning of language. Psychologist David McNeill (1970) has offered an intriguing explanation of how this is done, an explanation that has influenced the thinking of many experts. He draws an analogy of the child as an imaginary machine, a **Language Acquisition Device**

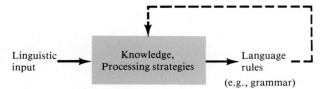

Figure 5.4 An imaginary language acquisition device. (*Source:* After McNeill, 1970.)

"You can't read this, PJ! It's an ADULT book — it has WORDS in it."

The Family Circus. Reprinted courtesy The Register and Tribune Syndicate, Inc.

to the speech maturity of the listener (Shatz & Gelman, 1973).

Young children can fine tune their speech fairly well. Not only can they determine the speech appropriate for children of different age levels, they can also cater their speech to individual differences in children of about the same age.

(LAD). Figure 5.4 depicts how such a machine works. Linguistic input is fed into the machine. In analyzing the input, the machine is aided by some already existing information about language *(knowledge)* and by some built-in techniques for language analysis *(processing strategies)*. The result of this analysis is a set of rules (the *output*) that describe how the input was generated. The rules are then incorporated into the knowledge component of the LAD. The output continually changes as additional information is fed into the device and as the device itself becomes reprogrammed *(new knowledge)*. In this way new rule systems are continually learned. McNeill intended the model primarily as a description of how syntactic rules are learned,

but it seems applicable to other domains of learning rules as well (e.g., phonology and semantics).

At birth all children bring the same *knowledge* and *processing strategies* to bear on the analysis of speech. Children begin life with the same capacity to process speech, regardless of which language their parents speak. This capacity, then, is universal and innate (inborn).

Just what does the child know at birth about language? This question deals with a controversial issue. Some claim that so-called innate knowledge is no more than a tendency to learn language. Others, like McNeill, take a stronger position. They argue that there are several specific language categories that the brain is "prewired" to detect.

These **language universals** are phonological (consonants, vowels, syllables, distinctive features), syntactic (sentences, noun phrases, verb phrases, subject-object relations), and semantic (certain knowable concepts). A child can also detect the difference between deep structure and surface structure. This "prewiring" corresponds to the knowledge component of the child, or LAD.

But there are also processing strategies. Which of these are universal and innate? Again, this question touches on an area of controversy. Among those who represent the position of **nativism,** proposals have included innate analysis of (a) segments, the tendency to notice where words begin and end; (b) stress and pitch, the ability to distinguish stressed from unstressed syllables and high from low pitches; and (c) distribution frequency, the tendency to notice which speech units (words, sounds) occur in which contexts.

As the child develops language, the structure of the language processor (the LAD) also changes. More knowledge about the structure and nature of language is acquired, and processing strategies gain new efficiency and precision. A precise specification of these changes is difficult, because they are intimately bound up in the child's new output; that is, the rules that are learned.

In the next section we will refer to many of the language terms that were defined earlier in this chapter—terms like *phonemes, morphemes, semantics,* and so forth. If these are not clear to you, go back and reread the section "Language: What Is It?"

Children as young as four years of age can cater their speed to the age of the listener.

The Course of Language Development

What is language like in infancy? What major changes can be observed? What are the major milestones—that is, when is the infant capable of various language feats?

For convenience, the discussion is divided into two parts dealing, respectively, with phonology and with syntax and semantics. Although it is easier to talk about these separately, the two are inseparable. Every speech act has a phonological, syntactical, and a semantic component that exist simultaneously and interdependently. Meaning and grammatical structure cannot be conveyed without sounds.

Phonology

Phonology is the study of rules used to produce sounds. An understanding of language almost naturally begins with the basic sounds used to express linguistic ideas. In this section the basic sounds of the English language are described, along with some ideas about how infants and children learn to combine them to produce meaningful speech.

Basic Sounds

It has been estimated that an adult speaking standard English employs thirty-six basic sounds. Each of these basic sounds is called a *phoneme* and is perceived as

identical by speakers of the language. A good example of an English phoneme is /k/, the sound represented by the letter *k* in the words key and ski and by the letter *c* in cat (Dale, 1976). Although the /k/ sound is somewhat different in each of these words, these variations are not distinguished and the /k/ sound is treated as a single phoneme. In the Arabic and Hindu languages, however, these variations would be distinguished and treated as phonemes. Therefore, it is apparent that sounds recognized as a single phoneme in one language do not constitute the same phonemic class for all languages. A convenient way to describe a sound is to indicate how it is produced. What parts of the vocal system are employed, and how? The major phoneme classes in English are of two types, **vowels** and **consonants.** Basically, a vowel sound is produced by the vibration of the vocal cords (voicing) as air is passed over them. The air then flows through the mouth without being interrupted. Consonant sounds are produced by interrupting the flow of air somewhere in the mouth cavity and then releasing it. Some consonants are voiced, and some are not.

Early Speech Sounds

When an infant is born, the only sounds he or she utters that are related to speech are cries. For an interesting dicussion of whether parents can detect their own baby's cries from those of other infants, see application 5.2. For the next few months the infant makes sounds we call **cooing,** which are vowellike sounds in which the /u/ phoneme appears frequently. Often this sound is preceded by a single consonant, as in coo, moo, woo, roo, soo. Other vowels are also heard, but the sounds are typically limited to a single syllable at a time.

At around six or seven months of age the infant begins babbling. Babbling is marked by strings of consonants and vowel phonemes put together. More phonemes are used, and there is a playful, experimental quality to their production.

Finally, near the child's first birthday, there are single-word utterances. Some are identifiable words in the language *(milk, want, see)*; others are childish approximations to adult words *(mama, dada, dollie)*. The child typically uses only a few phonemes in speech at this stage—fewer than during the babbling stage.

Syntax and Semantics

Syntax and semantics have been the most productive areas of language study in recent years. More is known about their development than about any other facet of language.

The place to begin is the child's first distinguishable utterances, his or her one-word statements, which appear at about one year of age. Up to this point, very little can reasonably be inferred about the child's knowledge of syntax and semantics.

Application 5.2
Are Babies' Cries Distinctive?

Crying is one of the first ways babies communicate. It is a form of primitive language. Can parents distinguish the cries of their own baby from those of others? And if parents can distinguish cries, can they interpret the meaning or cause of the crying?

Young infants don't tell us why they are crying, so it is hard to validate claims about differences in the origins of cries. However, it is possible to investigate parents' abilities to distinguish among the cries of different infants. Gisela Morsbach and Mary Murphy (1979) tape recorded the cries of five different babies between two and four days of age. Each of the babies was a healthy, full-term infant. Crying was elicited by an adult flicking the sole of the infant's foot with a finger, approximately three hous after the infant had eaten. By splicing fifteen-second taped segments of crying from different portions of their records, the experimenters were able to create a discrimination test with twenty pairs of crying segments. Some of the pairs contained crying segments for the same infants, while other pairs contained segments for different infants.

A total of 210 adult subjects were tested. The adults varied in their degree of experience with babies. For scientific purposes, each subject was considered to be responding knowledgeably to the test if he or she were able to identify at least fifteen of the twenty pairs correctly. The following table, adapted from the researchers' article (pp. 175–79), shows the percentage of people who were "correct."

Category	Percent
Midwives (twenty females)	57
Parents with children below one year (eleven females, eleven males)	27
Parents with children above one year (nineteen females, twelve males)	26
Nonparents who "sometimes" have contact (seventy-eight females, thirty-three males)	32
Nonparents who have "no contact" (fourteen females, twelve males)	34

A formal analysis of these results showed that the midwives, who, of course, had considerable experience with many newborns, did much better at discriminating the newborn cries than did all four of the other groups. However, the fact that from 25 to 35 percent of the remaining adults were able to perform the discrimination test correctly is a significant finding. Interestingly, it made little difference whether the remaining adults were parents or not. And the male adults did about as well as the females.

One-Word Phrase

The child's first words appear one at a time—"mommy," "sock," "haveit," "wanna," "byebye." The term **holophrase** was coined to indicate that the child's single word may actually be a whole phrase or sentence. Single words might seem poor substitutes for whole sentences, but those who keep frequent company with holophrastic speakers seem to divine the child's meaning quite well. This can be attributed to several factors. For one, these first words are often rich in informational value. The child has a knack for selecting the single word, from some longer adult speech form, that is the most important part of the thought (e.g., "Mommy" for "Mommy is here," "fell" for "the box fell," "hurt" for "I hurt").

In addition, the child uses variations in stress and pitch to distinguish between several possible meanings of the holophrase. Think how you might say "mommy" (a) to name a person who has just appeared in the room and (b) to implore a parent to help with a frustrating problem.

Finally, the child employs contextual cues to convey meaning with a single world. He or she may gesture at an object or mimic an action while producing the utterance or may depend upon the listener to understand the immediate events surrounding the statement so an appropriate inference can be drawn.

There seems to be some disagreement about what *syntactic* knowledge the child has. Some claim that it is absurd to speculate about whether the child grasps rules for combining words when the child never combines words. Others argue that the child must have an understanding of some rules, because he or she comprehends much of the complex speech that surrounds him or her. The argument is difficult to resolve because there is no direct means to test the child's sense of the grammatical content of a specific sentence or phrase.

What *semantic* knowledge does the child have? Here a more satisfying answer can be offered. The semantic rules are the means by which the child separates the different functions that may be served by the same word. The single utterance "byebye" may be (a) a greeting (as in "good-bye"), (b) a description of an action ("She went away"), (c) a statement of location ("He is in the other room"), or (d) a depiction of a psychological state ("Brother is asleep").

Early Language Stages

Beyond the one-word stage several important new developments occur in just a few short years. The changes are so rapid and so significant that psychologist Roger Brown (1973) has chosen to examine them at several arbitrary points in time. The result is a series of stages that describe different rule systems, but the stages are not tight systems of the Freudian or Piagetian variety.

In all, Brown has identified five early stages, two of which are described in detail here. A stage is identified by estimating the average number of words per sentence a child produces in a sample of from fifty to one hundred sentences recorded at about the same time. The average or **mean length of utterance (MLU)** for each stage is as follows:

Stage	MLU
1	1 + → 2.0
2	2.5
3	3.0
4	3.5
5	4.0

The first stage begins when the child produces sentences that consist of more than one word. The 1+ indicates that the average number of words in each utterance is greater than 1 but not yet 2, since some utterances are still holophrases. It continues until the child averages two words per utterance. Successive stages 2 to 5 are marked by increments of 0.5 in the MLU. This scheme is valuable for at least two reasons. For one, Brown has found that children may vary by as much as one-half to three-quarters of a year in chronological age and yet have similar speech patterns. Children with a similar MLU index seem to have acquired very similar rule systems. So MLU is a better index of language development than chronological age would be. It is also convenient to group children who are at the same level of development.

Stage 1 At the beginning of stage 1, the child produces a few two-word utterances. For example, he or she may say "allgone truck," "Daddy byebye," "Mommy book," or "me soap." These are intermingled with single-word utterances, for example, "I want book," "Mommy give candy," and "Dada went home." As MLU approaches 2.0, some children even produce four-word utterances; for example, "Mommy give toy here" and "I eat cookie kitchen." We can see that although MLU is 2.0 there is quite a spread in the complexity of speech, ranging from one to four words.

Children seem to be constructing abbreviated sentences, retaining the most informative words and dropping less informative words. Brown dubbed the speech *telegraphic,* noting its similarity in *brevity* and information yield to a telegram.

Stage 2 In stage 2 the length of the child's sentences increases, and it is not unusual to observe sentences that include four or five words. The principal accomplishment, however, is the mastery of several inflections. The child learns how to pluralize nouns, specify verb tense, include prepositions like *in* and *on,* insert articles like *a* and *the* in appropriate places, include pronomial forms, and so on. In other words, the child masters a number of rules for morphemes in the language.

Some of the morphemes that are mastered during this period are the present-progressive verb form (e.g., hitting); the prepositions *in* or *on;* plural forms; past-irregular verb forms (e.g., ran, bit, chose); the possessive (e.g., man's, sky's); articles (a, an, the); the past-regular verb form (e.g., walked, climbed); and the third-person singular in its regular form (e.g., "it smokes," "it bites").

Several interesting facts emerge about the development of these morphemes. One concerns their frequency of occurrence. Once the correct form begins to appear in the child's speech, he or she uses it in appropriate places virtually all the time; acquisition is very rapid, once begun. Another is that the order in which the morphemes are mastered is fairly uniform. The order of the list just given reflects that order. The present progressive is the first form mastered, the prepositions *in* and *on* appear next, and so forth. The order is constant, that is, for learning English; obviously, other languages that contain different rules for the use of morphemes cannot be directly compared.

The Functions of Language

Language is more than just an interesting phenomenon to examine and describe. It is also a system that is used for many purposes. No explanation of language would be complete without an account of the functions of language.

Perception

Language influences the way events are perceived. When a word or a sentence is uttered, the accompanying stimulus events are thereby made more distinctive. In sentences like "See the dent in the car's bumper" and "Look at the pinkish color the artist used to paint the man's foot," a responsive listener can perceive something about the event that would not have been perceived without language. Language helps to segment and call attention to certain facets of experience.

Each person acquires slightly different language habits. Each person uses different words, speaks and writes with different grammatical forms, and has favorite expressions and phrases. These differences in turn foster differences in perceptions of the world. Each person notices different things, segments experiences in different ways, and attaches unique meanings to events.

These differences are most pronounced in comparisons of people who speak different languages. Each language has unique connotative meanings associated with utterances; any translation will have a nuance different from that of the original. Such differences between languages lead native speakers to have very different perceptions of the world (Whorf, 1956; Sapir,

1958). In the realm of color perception, for example, the English language has many words to describe differences in hues (e.g., red, green, blue, orange, turquoise, magenta, and so on), while languages of some primitive societies have very few. In some Eskimo tongues there are about a dozen words to describe various colors, textures, and physical states of snow while English has just a few (e.g., snow, ice, sleet, hail). In each case the **Whorf/Sapir hypothesis** is that a language with more vocabulary or lexical categories produces perceptions that are more differentiated. So the speaker of English actually sees more shadings of color than the speaker of some primitive language does. Likewise, the Eskimo perceives many more kinds of snow than the speaker of English does.

Other interpretations are possible, however. The speakers of the two languages may have the same perceptions but be less able to code or work with them. And color categories may actually be universal and independent of language. For these reasons few contemporary psychologists accept the Whorf/Sapir hypothesis in its original version.

Memory

Numerous studies have shown that memory for nonlinguistic events is enhanced when language is associated with them. For example, if we see a series of pictures, our recollection of them is better if we are also provided names for the pictures (Brown, 1975). The same is true for recollections of physical behaviors. Much of what is learned and remembered is the physical behavior of other people. If language is attached to these behaviors, they are more easily remembered.

Clearly, language does not influence memory in exactly the same way throughout childhood. Preschoolers do not think to use linguistic devices to help themselves remember (Brown, 1975), which is sometimes referred to as a linguistic production deficiency. Although elementary school children do think to use such linguistic devices, the language techniques they employ are very simple (e.g., naming an object). During the latter elementary school years and beyond, children's language techniques become more sophisticated in the service of memory. They generate words, sentences, and stories to recall events. They repeat or rehearse these. And as they progress, they monitor the effects of this language activity on their memory. Thus we see that language techniques become more useful.

Thinking

Language also helps us to think and to solve problems. It provides us with a tool to represent ideas and arguments and to deal with the representations. Language seems so important in the process of thinking that many

Viewing the water, these people from different cultures have different words to describe what they see and therefore may think differently about water.

people believe it is impossible to think without language. This belief has led to some of the most heated debates in developmental psychology. At the center of the arguments is the relationship between thought and language. Is one dependent on the other, is each dependent on the other, or is this a relationship of some other sort? There are almost as many answers to this question as there are people who have attempted to answer it. One writer (Jenkins, 1969) even suggested facetiously that the answer is "all of the above!" That is, language is dependent upon thought, thought is dependent upon language, each is dependent on the other,

and (in some circumstances) the two are unrelated. It is instructive to understand some of the different points of view that have been expressed on the topic.

Some experts (e.g., Bruner, 1964; Vygotsky, 1962) believe that higher forms of human intelligence and thought are achieved because language is developed. Language is the vehicle that makes it possible to acquire concrete and formal operational thought, for example, because language develops early and becomes a rich and complete symbolic system soon after it is acquired. It provides remarkable power for representational systems (e.g., imagery) lag behind it in their

Table 5.1
A Developmental Sequence of Early Communicative Intents

Stage and Age	Intentions	Form	
Intentional communication (approximately eight to fifteen months)	Requesting objects or activity Refusing Commenting Action games	Early: Mid: or Late:	Gesture Vocalization plus Gesture Word plus Gesture Word only
Discourse functions (approximately sixteen to twenty-three months)	Requesting information Answering Acknowledging Repeating		
Symbolic functions (approximately twenty-four months on)	Symbolic play Evoking absent objects and events Misrepresenting reality		

development. For example, consider the abstract rules and classes the young child operates with by Brown's stage 2 of language development. Yet this same child is barely beyond the sensorimotor stage of thought in the nonlinguistic, cognitive realm. Language rules are clearly more sophisticated and abstract than early thought is.

As further evidence of the view that language leads to thought, some psychologists remind us of the importance of language in various cognitive tasks. There is evidence, for example, that children who solve concrete operational problems use more appropriate language than do children who fail to solve them (Sinclair DeZwart, 1969).

Jean Piaget (1968) has been the most prominent advocate of the position that thought is primarily independent of language. In his view, language is merely one symbolic vehicle for the expression of thought. There are also others, such as perception and imagery. Although language may become the best system humans possess for expressing thought, language is not the original vehicle for the development of thought; sensorimotor activity is.

As evidence for this position, psychologists point to a number of diverse facts about cognitive development. For one, children do not produce sentences—even two-word utterances—until they have progressed to sensorimotor stage 5 or 6. Perhaps some of the conceptual developments during this period actually serve as a foundation for language development rather than the other way around. Some candidates are object permanence, the deferred internal image, and the tendency to experiment actively, all of which occur by sensorimotor stage 5 or 6. In order to use words in referring to things, the child must first be able to conceive of things as permanent and to image the ones that are not present. To form word classes or grammatical

categories, the child continually juggles primitive, tentative rules, a process helped by a cognitive tendency to experiment actively (Chapman, 1981).

Another source of evidence is the cognitive development of deaf children. Hans Furth (1971) has shown that on a variety of thinking and problem-solving tasks, these children perform at the same level as children of the same age who have no hearing problem. If by language we mean spoken language, then this evidence argues against the primacy of language for the development of thought. However, some of the deaf children also had no command of written or sign language and performed at the same level as their hearing counterparts. So language, even in a broader sense, was not necessary for them to develop normal cognitive skills.

Communication

Finally, and perhaps most important, language helps people to communicate with each other. We describe objects and events to each other. We share our feelings. We construct complex chains of reasoning and argumentation with each other.

Roger Brown (1973) has noted that humans have a compelling need for communication from earliest infancy onward; it seems to be a built-in motivation. Animals give no evidence of such motivation for communication. In language experiments with animals, the chimpanzees had to be coaxed into communicative exchanges with the experimenter. The absence of a strong motivation to communicate is one of the most serious shortcomings of artificially taught languages.

The way children communicate and the different purposes communication serves have received extensive attention among sociolinguists interested in pragmatics. One developmental sequence proposed by Robin Chapman (1981) is shown in table 5.1. In the earliest

The function of language is to communicate.

stage (intentional communication), infants do not use language at all. They gesture and vocalize to express their interest in requesting an object, refusing to do something, commenting (naming, pointing to a feature) on an event, or initiating some activity. Toward the end of this stage, individual words are linked up with the actions to communicate the purpose. In the next stage (discourse functions), children use individual words and short phrases to serve a variety of purposes—to request information, answer a question, acknowledge someone's presence or verbal statement, and repeat (perhaps for clarification or pleasure) something they've heard.

Finally, in the last stage (symbolic functions), children use words to play, talk about objects and events that are not present, and to purposefully misrepresent reality (joke, tease, deny, or lie).

As children develop, their ability to communicate improves along several dimensions. They become able to speak more precisely as their linguistic rule systems mature. They become less dependent upon contextual cues and nonverbal gestures to get their points across. They move out of their egocentric shells, learning to take the perspective of both speaker and listener in formulating messages (Glucksberg & Krauss, 1967).

Summary

Language is unique to humans. In the contemporary view, that of psycholinguistics, it is defined as a well-ordered system of rules that each adult member of the language community comprehends. The rules deal with phonology, morphology, syntax, semantics and pragmatics. A child's understanding of rules (linguistic competence) is often ahead of his or her use of them (linguistic performance).

In the old view, language is learned through traditional mechanisms of learning, including stimulus-response association, reinforcement, and imitation. For a number of reasons this view no longer seems tenable. The new psycholinguistic perspective conceives of language as a system that develops as the result of the child's active attempts to induce rules from the speech around him or her. This learning is made possible by our biological heritage (the brain, nervous system, and vocal apparatus that each person has), by some regularities in the environment (the catering of language complexity by the community to the language maturity of the child), by the processing activities of the child (likened to a Language Acquisition Device—LAD), and by basic underlying cognitive skills.

The course of language development can be discussed from the standpoint of phonological landmarks and syntactic and semantic landmarks. Phonologically, standard English employs about thirty-six basic sounds, or phonemes. In infancy, the first sound are cries. For the next several months, cooing sounds are heard (vowellike noises in which the /u/ phoneme appears frequently). At about six or seven months of age the infant begins to babble, making sounds that include a string of consonant and vowel phonemes. When the child is one year old, he or she begins to make single-word utterances, employing only a few phonemes to produce them. Within a year or two later, the child has mastered virtually all of the basic sounds, although pronunciation quirks are evident for much longer.

In the realm of syntax and semantics, several stages have been identified. At first, there is the one-word utterance (the holophrase), appearing when the child is about one year of age. Children can express many ideas with a single-word utterance, although it strains credulity to claim that they are employing syntactic rules. Brown has identified five subsequent stages, each defined in terms of the child's average mean length of utterances (MLU). In stage 1 the MLU is $1 + \rightarrow 2.0$, with each succeeding stage having a 0.5 increment in MLU (hence stage 5 = 4.0). Stage 1 is characterized by two-word utterances, which have been variously described as telegraphic, obeying pivot-open rules of syntax, and fulfilling many semantic functions. In stage 2 the length of the child's utterances increases; more important, however, the child masters a number of inflections. The mastery of these inflections is very rapid, once begun, and occurs in a specific sequence.

Language is more than an interesting phenomenon to examine and describe; it is also a system that has many functions. Language influences the way we perceive events in the world; it helps us to notice events and to make events distinctive. Language enhances our memory for nonlinguistic events, making them meaningful and providing codes that help us to rehearse them. Language also helps us to think and to solve problems, although it is not clear whether thinking is a necessary by-product of language, or vice versa. Finally, language is used to communicate—to describe objects and events to others, to share feelings, and to reason with others.

Key Terms

consonants

cooing

deep structure

echoing

expansion

grammar

holophrase

language

Language Acquisition
  Device (LAD)

language universals

mean length of
  utterances (MLU)

morpheme

morphology

nativism

phoneme

phonology

pragmatics

prompting

psycholinguistics

semantics

sociolinguistics

surface structure

syntax

transformation

vowels

Whorf/Sapir hypothesis

Review Questions

1. What is language?
2. Briefly describe the old view of how language is acquired. What are its inadequacies?
3. How does biology enter the picture of language learning?
4. How does the environment contribute to language learning?
5. What is meant by LAD? What is its significance?
6. What are the major categories of sound in the English language? How are they produced?
7. Briefly describe the significant changes in phonological development.
8. How does Roger Brown define the major periods, or stages, in the early acquisition of syntactic and semantic rules?
9. What are the functions or uses of language?

Further Readings

Brown, H. D. Principles of language learning and teaching. Englewood Cliffs, N.J.: Prentice-Hall, 1980.
A good, elementary text on language acquisition and techniques for enhancing language development in instructional settings. Up to date and easy to read.

Dale, P. S. *Language development: structure and function* (2d ed.) New York: Holt, Rinehart & Winston, 1976.
An authoritative introduction to the study of language development. Each topic covered in this chapter is treated in greater depth here. Technical, but well written and readable.

Slobin, S. I. *Psycholinguistics* (2d ed.). Glenview, Ill.: Scott, Foresman, and Co., 1979.
An excellent, comprehensive treatment of the field of the psychology of language. It covers both language acquisition and development and language in mature individuals.

6 Social, Emotional, and Personality Foundations and Development

Imagine . . . that you are faced with choosing a day-care center for your one-year-old

Each weekday at 8 A.M., Ellen Smith takes her one-year-old daughter, Tanya, to the day-care center at Brookhaven college in Dallas. Then Mrs. Smith goes off to work and returns in the afternoon to take Tanya home. Tanya has excelled in day care, according to Mrs. Smith. Now, after three years at the center, Mrs. Smith reports that her daughter is very adventuresome and interacts confidently with peers and adults. Mrs. Smith believes that day care has been a wonderful way to raise Tanya.

In Los Angeles, however, day care has been a series of "horror stories" for Barbara Jones. After two years of unpleasant experiences with sitters, day-care centers, and day-care homes, Mrs. Jones has quit her job as a successful real estate agent to stay home and take care of her two-and-a-half-year-old daughter, Gretchen. "I didn't want to sacrifice my baby for my job," says Mrs. Jones, who was unable to find good substitute care in day-care homes. And, when she put Gretchen in a day-care center, she said that she felt like her daughter was being treated like a piece of merchandise—dropped off and picked up.

Many mothers worry whether day care will adversely affect their children. They fear that day-care centers may lessen the emotional attachment of the infant to the mother; retard the infant's cognitive development; fail to teach the child how to control his or her anger; and allow the child to be unduly influenced by other children.

Traditionally, it has been argued that effective socialization of the child into a mature individual depends on the development of a strong attachment bond between the infant and his or her mother or primary caretaker. If this relationship is severed for a lengthy period of time on a daily basis, the child's attachment to the caretaker may be weakened. Selma Fraiberg (1977), in her book, *Every Child's Birthright: In Defense of Mothering,* supports this traditional belief. Fraiberg says that she worries about babies and small children who are delivered like packages to neighbors, strangers, and storage houses. Fraiberg is not against all day care, though. She says that children between the ages of three and six can benefit from half-day nursery school programs that entail small groups and qualified teachers. The problem, according to Fraiberg, is that children in most day-care centers are there nine to eleven hours a day and are being cared for by poorly educated, unqualified personnel.

In many of the day-care/home-rearing comparisons, the day-care centers are university based or staffed. Such centers serve many different types of families, and while the programs differ, they do have some features in common. Babies are taken care of in small groups, and a caretaker is assigned to each infant who is younger than two years of age. The caretaker changes the baby's diapers and feeds the infant and is trained to enrich such routines by communicating with the infant. Periodically during the day, the caretaker seeks out the infant and engages him or her in some form of lively social interaction. The general conclusion from the comparisons of the high-quality university-staffed day care and home-reared children is that there are few if any differences in the attachment behavior of the children growing up under two different circumstances (Belsky & Steinberg, 1978).

The day care that most babies receive, however, does not approach the quality of the university-based day-care programs. Demonstration programs, such as Jerome Kagan's (Kagan, Kearsley, & Zelazo, 1978), do show that it is possible to provide group care for infants that will not harm them, and in some cases, actually aid their social development. Kagan's day-care

center included a pediatrician, a nonteaching director, and an infant-teacher ratio of three to one. And teachers' aids assisted at the center. The teachers and aides were trained to become competent caretakers of infants—to smile frequently, talk with the infants, and provide them with a safe environment that included many stimulating toys. However, United States government figures indicate that approximately 1.3 million babies are cared for by relatives in relatives' homes; 938,000 by relatives in the child's home; 1.2 million by nonrelatives in "family" day-care homes; and 620,000 by unrelated babysitters in the child's own home.

Recently, Brian Vaughn, Fredrick Gove, and Byron Egeland (1980) studied the effects of routine daily separations involved in day care on the formation and maintenance of infant-mother attachment in economically disadvantaged families. The out-of-home care arrangements were varied, and changes in the routine of care were common. Many of the infants were cared

for by an adult female in the nonrelative's home. Significant disruption in the infant-mother attachment relationship was found in the day-care group. Many day-care situations, then, fail to meet the psychological needs of infants.

Many more centers that are run by professionally trained, committed staff are needed. Opinions differ, however, on who should be responsible for developing the competent baby centers. Many individuals oppose public support for the care of the babies because they feel that it would lead to too much government control over families. Many middle-class families would prefer privately developed, self-supporting day-care centers that would incorporate the features of the superior university-based centers, but poorer working class families would not be able to afford to place their infants in such centers. This dilemma remains unsolved, and for the most part, a high quality of day care is not available in most communities.

Introduction

In this chapter we take a detailed look at the concept discussed in Imagine—that of **attachment.** You will learn its course of development, read evaluations of different theories of attachment, and discover individual differences in infant attachment. A second major focus will be the infant's development of independence—you will see that attachment and independence are not just opposites. A third major emphasis is the development of the self in infancy.

But before discussing these three important aspects of the infant's social, emotional, and personality development, the social agents that contribute the most to the infant's development—parents—will be discussed in greater detail. To back up even further, the initial topic of discussion will be the role of early experience in development. In Imagine, you saw how many parents are concerned about the kind of child care their infants experience. Just how important are such early experiences for life-span development?

The Importance of Early Experience

We have learned a good deal about infant development. We know about infants' physical growth, their motor capabilities, and their early sensory and perceptual competencies. But why study infants at all? Why is this period so important?

In many theories of development, experts push the idea that there are periods for the acquisition of some qualities or abilities. In Erik Erikson's theory, for example, infancy is the time for acquiring a basic sense of *trust,* while in Jean Piaget's theory, infancy is the time for acquiring *sensorimotor thought.* If these do not develop during infancy, claim the theorists, progress through the later stages of development will be more difficult.

To claim the existence of a critical period is actually to argue several different points: (1) particular accomplishment is most likely to occur in one period of the life span rather than in others; (2) the development or nondevelopment of the quality in the specified period should have consequences for later acquisition; and (3) if the quality does not develop during the specified period, it is unlikely to develop thereafter.

Of these three claims, the first is the easiest to prove. We simply amass evidence to demonstrate how likely a particular phenomenon is to occur in a particular period. If the likelihood is much greater for one period than for another, the case is proven. Thus for the following we can feel confident that infancy is indeed a critical period in this respect: (a) *object permanence,* wherein the child between four and eight months old will search for a hidden object in the last place it was seen (Uzgiris & Hunt, 1975); (b) *language,* in which the child begins producing two-word sentences between eighteen and twenty-four months of age (Brown, 1973); and (c) *attachment,* which the child evidences between six and eight months by proximity-seeking behavior to one or more caregivers and not to others (Schaeffer & Emerson, 1964).

The second claim, that there is a link between the critical acquisition and the child's later development, is perhaps the hardest to prove or disprove. The difficulty is that the most critical acquisitions are quite general and virtually all infants acquire them. This is true for object permanence and language, but as we will see later in this chapter, it is not true for attachment. A small minority of infants in most attachment studies fail to exhibit proximity-seeking behavior. How, then, can this claim be tested?

Finally, we consider the remaining claim about critical periods (recall our introductory discussion of critical periods under the ethological, evolutionary perspective in chapter 2), that if a quality does not develop during a specified period, it never will (irreversibility). With respect to infancy, this is the claim of the three most likely to be proven false. Many children are very late in producing object permanence and other sensorimotor milestones long after infancy. Human infancy is remarkably elastic; the human brain still has many degrees of freedom left for reprogramming long after age two, and most psychological acquisitions can still be taught with appropriate techniques if they have not yet been acquired during infancy.

What is true, however, is that society is fairly rigid in programming environments for infants and children. The rare child who has not learned to walk or talk or who is very slow in acquiring some other skill normally mastered in infancy is not likely to be placed in an environment that supports its emergence. Once infants have moved into childhood, adults and society place new demands upon them and "forget" how to provide experiences appropriate to an earlier stage of development. As a concrete example, consider the topic of attachment, a major focus of this chapter. Suppose an infant has not formed a close bond with one or more caregivers. The caregiver would most likely treat the nonattached youngster much as any other toddler, encouraging separation, fostering independent activity, and encouraging the independent exploration of the environment. But these may be inappropriate for what the child needs.

One aspect of early experiences that only recently has been studied is the role of infant nutrition in social and emotional development. Next, we see that even mild caloric deficiencies in the diets of infants may be linked with social and emotional characteristics in middle childhood.

The Link Between Nutrition in Infancy and Social and Emotional Development in Middle Childhood

David Barrett and Marian Radke-Yarrow (1983) have conducted investigations that suggest the infant's diet may be linked with emotional characteristics at the time the child enters elementary school. The first investigation, an eight-year longitudinal study, focused on 138 boys and girls in three rural Guatemalan villages. The second study was a survey of 65 six- to eight-year-old children from low-income families in San Diego.

In the Guatemalan research, children who had received supplemental high-calorie drinks in addition to their regular diets from birth to age four, and whose mothers had received supplements during pregnancy, were studied. The average child in the villages studied was not grossly underfed; for example, a typical four-year-old weighing thirty-five pounds was estimated to be living on about 1,300 calories a day, while standards established by the World Health Organization call for such a child to receive about 1,600 calories. To study the effects of the increased nutrition on emotional characteristics of the children, a battery of psychological tests was administered and the children were observed during various play, competitive, and problem-solving situations.

The results: Children who had better nutritional supplements prenatally and for the first two years after birth were consistently more active, involved, and helpful than their peers and less anxious; they also were more likely to express happy or sad emotions than were others in the group, who often appeared withdrawn or uninterested. Whether a child received food supplements from two to four years, however, did not seem to influence the six- to eight-year-old children's behavior.

More recently, the Central American children's behavior in novel, frustrating, and competitive situations has been reported (Barrett & Radke-Yarrow, 1983). The children who had received the high supplementation diet during their mothers' pregnancy and their own early childhood showed more competent social behavior in the face of frustration, novel environmental experiences, and competitive encounters. For example, these children were more likely to involve themselves with toys in a novel situation, used more strategies when presented a frustrating task, and approached competitive games in a more spirited manner.

In the second investigation, conducted with low-income families in San Diego, children whose mothers were undernourished during pregnancy and whose weight was low at birth were compared with children whose mothers had better diets. The undernourished

Nutrition in infancy is linked to emotional development in the early elementary school years.

group interacted less with their school-age peers, were more dependent on adults, and appeared as sadder and more unfriendly.

According to Barrett and Radke-Yarrow, these results suggest a cycle in which subtle alterations of the central nervous system and lack of energy often combine with a poor home environment to stunt the child's emotional growth. The result may be withdrawal on the part of the child and neglect or rejection on the part of the caregiver. It seems that the child attempts to adapt to the physiological stress of nutritional deficit by developing behaviors that remove him or her from the environment and inhibit the later development of appropriate patterns of social interaction. They believe that nutrition may be critical in the first few years of life because it is during the period of infancy that the child is beginning to develop patterns of dealing with the world and responding to others.

The Need for Stimulation

Without an environment that encourages exploration and offers variety, growth and development are likely to be hampered. A number of important ideas have been advanced to describe the nature of optimal stimulation and its key dimensions.

Psychoanalytic theory emphasizes the need for *predictability* and *comfort* in infant stimulation (e.g., Erikson, 1968). The infant should be subjected to routines and experiences that are orderly, come at expected times, and satisfy basic needs. Some novelty and variation is important, but it would not be introduced at the expense of predictability and comfort.

A recent effort to train parents to be more predictable (or in their social learning framework, *contingent*) is a good example of this idea (Dirkie & Gerber, 1980). A group of parents attended a class lasting eight weeks (sixteen hours) to learn how to care for their four- to twelve-month infants. The class included lecture, discussion, and demonstrations of general principles of child development; individual infant variation; discussion of how to read an individual infant's temperament; and explanations of reciprocal interactions between infant and parent. Mothers and fathers learned their lessons well. In comparison to a control group of parents, the trained parents subsequently were more responsive, predictable, and likely to anticipate infant needs, and they offered more contingent verbal and nonverbal responses to the babies in several follow-up measures. As a concrete example, a mother might nurse her infant in different rooms of a house with or without other people present. But the calm, quiet closeness she establishes and the regularity of the feeding schedule will foster the infant's trust and need gratification.

Cognitive-structural theory emphasizes the need for events in the infant's environment to strike an *optional mismatch* between the infant's current level of cognitive functioning and the level (i.e., substage) toward which the infant is developing. This is part of the theory of *equilibration* (e.g., Piaget, 1970; Kohlberg, 1976). An optimal mismatch means that stimulation should sometimes challenge and provoke the infant's already acquired schemes, either by revealing some insufficiency or contradiction present when an established scheme is applied or by introducing an event that cannot readily be handled with a current scheme. For example, Jerome Kagan (1976) believes infants need to be stimulated with *moderately novel events* some of the time. According to Kagan, infants accumulate a number of expectancies for events in the environment, for example, the appearance of the mother's face. If a new experience is introduced to be slightly dissimilar from the expected one, the infant will be motivated to explore it. For example, infants find cartoonlike representations of faces displayed on slides and photographs to be highly interesting (cf., Kagan, 1971). They may similarly find it exciting to explore the faces of people they have never seen before. What is novel for one infant may, of course, be passé for another. Novelty and its relative degree are intimately bound in the unique experiences each infant has had.

What is novel for one infant may be passé for another.

A final notion to consider is the *ethological* view that an infant must be stimulated in ways destined to trigger biologically built-in responses. The ethologist believes that the exercise of such innate responses is necessary for survival and, from the perspective of socialization, that this is what helps the infant to *affiliate* with and learn from other people. Among the responses that have been claimed to be under instinctive control are smiling, touching, and movement.

We see, then, that the early experiences parents provide for their infants are a very important part of development. Next, we focus even more extensively on parent-child relationships and the roles of families in infancy.

Parent-Infant Relationships and Families

The infant's interaction and experiences with his or her mother, father, and siblings provide the beginning of the life-long process of **socialization**, defined as the process whereby the individual acquires the attitudes and behaviors considered important and appropriate by the society in which the individual lives. In this section the importance of reciprocal socialization and synchrony in parent-infant interaction is explored and the family as a system is discussed.

Reciprocal Socialization and Synchrony in Parent-Infant Relationships

Richard Bell (1968, 1979) reviewed a number of studies related to caretaker effects on children and suggested that the effects may be due to the child's behaviors as much as to the caretaker's. For example, a relation between authoritarian discipline and the child's aggression often appears. However, aggression on the part of the child may elicit the parent's authoritarian discipline to begin with, perhaps just as easily as the parent's discipline can increase aggression.

There are rather strong individual differences in children's activity levels. Compare the child who is always squirming or who frequently gets into the kitchen cabinets to the child who works alone quietly without bothering others. Might these children evoke different responses from parents, teachers, and other social agents? In a very real sense, the child socializes parents and teachers just as they socialize him or her. This is referred to as **reciprocal socialization.**

Temperamental differences may contribute to differences in the way adults respond to infants. Joy Osofsky (1975) observed 134 mothers and their newborn infants to determine the relation between neonatal temperament and mother-infant interaction. Two observations were made, one during feeding and the other in a semistructured situation in which the mother stimulated the infant just after he or she had awakened. There was a consistent relation between the behavior of the infant and the behavior of the mother. Mothers of alert and responsive infants were responsive and sensitive.

What was the direction of the effect? Did responsive, alert infants cause their mothers to be responsive and sensitive, or was the reverse true? This question is virtually impossible to answer from correlational data. However, an additional assessment of the infant's behavior that may provide some clues was included. The infant's temperament was assessed when the mother was absent. The more responsive the infant in the independent assessment, the more likely it was that the mother presented stimuli effectively. Although these mothers may have been especially sensitive and had superior teaching skills, it also is probable that the temperament of the infants had some influence on the way they were treated by their mothers.

Mothers in and out of Tune with Their Infants
The fact that parents differ widely in sensing the needs of their infants is one of the remarkable discoveries of the past decade. Some quickly note their child's moods and periods of distress and act to comfort the infant. This is called **synchrony.** Others may not notice the need for action or may be slow to respond. This is called **asynchrony.** In the psychoanalytic perspective, synchrony will generate a sense of trust in the infant; asynchrony will breed distrust. Learning theory stresses the presence or absence of clear reward contingencies. Synchrony marks the presence of clear rewards; asynchrony denotes the absence of contingent rewards. Clear contingencies make learning easier. In application 6.1 you can read about the ability of mothers to respond differently to "difficult" and "easy" infants.

Some infants are "difficult."

As we have seen, the nature of parent-child relationships is very complex. Too often we have assumed that one parent's behavior causes the child's social behavior. Not only should the reciprocal nature of parent-child relationships be considered when explaining the child's social behavior, but as we see next, the entire system of interacting individuals in the family should be considered when we evaluate the child's development.

The Family as a System
As a social system, the family can be thought of as a constellation of subsystems defined in terms of generation, gender, and role (Feiring & Lewis, 1978). Divisions of labor among family members define particular subunits, and attachments define others, each family member being a participant in several subsystems, some dyadic, some polyadic.

As fathers become recognized as important socialization agents, it has become obvious that we should be studying more than two-party social interactions (Lamb, 1976). Children interact with more than one parent or adult most days of their lives, yet we know very little about how parents serve each other as sources of support as well as sources of dissatisfaction. One attempt to understand the link between spouse relationships and parent-infant relationships was conducted by Frank Pederson and his colleagues (Pederson, Anderson, & Cain, 1977). They believe that the three dyadic units of interaction, mother-father, mother-child, and father-child are interrelated. Using the husband-wife relationship as a point of reference, they set out to investigate the connections among family members. Forty-one families were observed on three separate occasions at home, with separate observations of husband-wife and parent-infant dyads. The infants were firstborn, five-month-old middle-class boys and girls.

Mothers and Their "Easy" and "Difficult" Infants

Did your mother describe you as an "easy" baby to bring up or a "difficult" one? In other words, what was your **temperament** like as an infant? Did your mother say you never fussed much, were easy to feed, slept on a regular schedule and at reasonable hours, and were content to play by yourself? Or did she describe you as a baby who cried at the drop of a pin, had picky eating habits, had trouble sleeping, and didn't play well?

In a recent investigation (Donovon, Leavitt, & Balling, 1978), the mothers of thirty-two infants were given a questionnaire that asked them to characterize their three-month-old infants' temperaments. They also were shown short videotape sequences of an unknown infant (also three months old) alternately smiling and crying. As mothers viewed the scenes, the experimenters measured the women's heart rate and skin conductance, both good indicators of attention and level of arousal. The mothers who described their infants as "difficult" responded less sensitively to the infants in the videotapes.

So, either the mother may learn very quickly (within three months in this case) to respond differently to a "difficult" or an "easy" infant, or the infant's temperament may partially stem from the way the mother handles him or her. It is likely that these findings evidence a little of both effects.

The importance of reciprocity and synchrony in parent-infant relationships is underscored in the following conclusions drawn by Rudolph Schaeffer (1977):

> Maternal techniques . . . can roughly be arranged along a continuum from passivity to activity . . . yet even at the active end of the continuum we see that the mother can hardly

be described as a dictator who arbitrarily imposes and directs. Her relationship with the child is rather that of a partner, though a senior partner by virtue of being more experienced, more powerful, and more likely to have consciously formulated ideas about the purpose and direction of the interaction. She rarely does anything without being aware of her child's precise requirements or without adapting her behavior in that light. The younger the child, the greater her need to adapt in this way and it is one of the wonders of nature that mothers (or almost any adult confronted by a small baby) can make these changes so naturally and spontaneously that they may not even be fully aware of what they are doing. This results in the fine degree of interpersonal synchrony that is so particularly evident when we study interactions microscopically. Whether we observe a baby feeding, playing, being bathed, changed, and put to bed, or merely being bounced on his mother's knee, we find a highly intricate pattern of interaction—a pattern that is based on the intrinsic organization of social behavior but that subsequently develops through the sheer experience of mutual contact.

> This takes us a long way from the traditional view of socialization, which saw this process as a quite straightforward matter of indoctrination: of telling small children about the use of spoons and potties, about the importance of saying thank you and not killing the new baby. The child had to fit into his social group, so one had to shape his behavior accordingly. We can now see that one cannot change a child unless one begins within the context of his own behavior. Change cannot be imposed from outside; it can only start from within the relationship between parents and child and thus becomes a matter of mutual adjustment. The two modify each other continually; they grow with each other. Socialization is a two-way and not a one-way business: like education, it is essentially a joint venture. (p. 77)

The first idea investigated was that positive interaction between husband and wife, such as smiling and affection, would be positively linked with the expression of positive affection toward the infant by each parent. The results: There was little relationship between measures of positive husband-wife interaction and their positive interaction with the infant. However, when negative interaction between husband and wife was observed (e.g., verbal criticism, blame), it was strongly linked to the negative affection shown by the father toward the infant. These findings suggest that the family is a network of interacting individuals functioning as a system.

One subsystem of the family that merits special attention is the husband-wife support system. Because many mothers now work, skills, as well as self-esteem,

may emanate from this system and may later be elaborated in other contexts. But a major function of family relations, from early childhood through adolescence, seems to be the provision of a basis for environmental exploration. Exploratory activity then brings the child into contact with many different social objects, among which are other children. Through interaction with these associates, the child extends his or her own competencies in communication and role taking. These associations also result in the direct acquisition of a constellation of unique attitudes and affections—each essential to social adaptation.

Jay Belsky (1981) recently developed an organization scheme of the family system that highlights the possible reciprocal influences that marital relations, parenting, and infant behavior/development may have

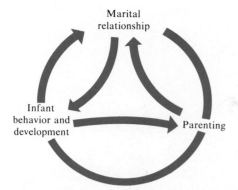

Figure 6.1 A scheme for integrating the disciplines of family sociology and developmental psychology during the infancy years.

on each other. As can be seen by following the arrows in figure 6.1, these three aspects of the family system may have both direct and indirect effects on each other. An example of a direct effect is the influence of the parent's behavior on the child, while an example of an indirect effect is how the relationship between spouses mediates the way a parent acts toward the child.

The idea of viewing the family as a system has also been emphasized by many clinical psychologists. Read application 6.2 for information about the family systems approach to therapy.

Attachment

We have seen that infancy is a period of special importance in social and emotional development and in our contemporary childrearing practices. We have learned that the infant is an active learner and processor of information, not a passive receptacle. The explosion of information on infants (e.g., Cohen, 1979) has provided scientific justification that infants are highly active participants in social exchanges from a very early time. Perhaps we should not be surprised, then, that our contemporary culture idolizes infants, treats the period as an extraordinarily important one, and views a good early start as a sine qua non for optimal development. Much of the interest in the period of infancy on the part of child psychologists has focused on the concept of attachment.

Attachment: What Is It?

In everyday language, an *attachment* refers to a relation between two individuals where each person feels strongly about the other and does a number of things to ensure the continuation of the relation. Many pairs of people could be attached: relatives, lovers, or a teacher and student. In the language of psychology, however, attachment is often restricted to a particular developmental period, to a relation between particular social figures, and to particular phenomena thought to

reflect unique characteristics of the relationship. The developmental period is infancy (roughly birth to two years), the social figures are the infant and one or more adult caregivers, and the phenomena in question are described in the following paragraphs.

The Bond Between the Infant and the Caregiver

The most comprehensive account of attachment to date has been put forth by British psychiatrist John Bowlby (1958, 1969). His view is ethological in the sense that the infant and the mother are said to *instinctively* trigger an attachment bond. The newborn is biologically equipped with signals to produce behavior on the part of the mother. The baby cries, clings, smiles, and coos. Later the infant crawls, walks, and follows the mother. Some of these behaviors are triggered by the mother, as when she leaves the room or puts the infant down. The goal for the infant is to keep the mother nearby.

Bowlby believes the development of attachment occurs in four phases during the first year of life. During the first phase, extending from birth to two or three months, the infant directs his or her attachment to human figures on the basis of an unlearned bias. Strangers, siblings, mothers, and fathers are equally likely to cause smiling or crying; the infant is not discriminating. In phase 2, from three to six months, attachment becomes focused on one figure—typically the primary caregiver (e.g., mother). Phase 3 extends from six to nine months and consists of an increase in the intensity of attachment to the mother. Because of increased locomotor skills, the infant now more readily seeks proximity to her. Finally, in the fourth phase (which extends from nine months to a year), the elements of attachment—maintaining contact and closeness to the caregiver, protesting when the caregiver leaves, and a fear of strangers—become integrated into a mutual system of attachment to which the infant and the caregiver both contribute.

Application 6.2
The Family Systems Approach to Therapy

Psychoanalytic theories of development spawned some unusually creative forms of treatment for children with a range of emotional disturbances such as depression, schizophrenia, and phobias. The brilliant insight of this perspective was that disturbed behavior is the product of unconscious conflicts that the child cannot release. Even with the shift in focus to culture, however, as in Erikson's theory, one principle of therapy remained constant—the definition of who "owned" the psychological problem. *The child did!* The child was typically treated alone, and, although others were known to have contributed to the disturbance (e.g., perhaps an overbearing father), the others did not get a chance to undo their harm directly in therapy. It was left for the child to work through the problem alone.

Now a new era of therapists has arrived. Some of them take Freud's notion about the role of the family more seriously, perhaps, than he did. In their view, the family is often the origin of the child's problems. But the child doesn't own the problems. The whole family does. If the child is disturbed, it is likely the result of other problems in the family. And whatever their origin, the child's problems must interfere with the lives and interactions of other members of the family. The solution, then, is to treat the whole family, as a unit, during the course of therapy. This perspective, known as the family systems approach, has received critical praise as an important new breakthrough in therapy (e.g., Minuchin, 1974; Napier & Whitaker, 1980).

In a warmly presented narrative account of how one "composite" family weathered this treatment approach, *The Family Crucible,* written by Augustus Napier and Carl Whitaker, offers important insights into this new theory and treatment approach. Briefly, here are some of the salient points.

The family is a system. Each member is related to every other member. When one person changes or develops, the whole system changes. Although we may think of one person having a problem in the family, such a perception necessarily oversimplifies what is really going on. Since any change in the system affects the whole system, any problem in it must be viewed as a problem in the way the whole system is working.

There are many levels on which to analyze the family system. There may be dyadic relations (e.g., mother-father, mother-daughter, father-daughter, brother-sister), triadic relations (e.g., mother-father-daughter, mother-father-son), or a relation among parts of the whole (e.g., mother-father-daughter-son). And each family learns from

The family system involves a complex set of interactions.

and evolves from earlier families—e.g., each set of grandparents. Thus mothers learn how to "mother" by modeling what their own mothers did; likewise, fathers learn to "father" by modeling what their own fathers did. (For simplicity, we are considering the case of a nuclear family that repeats itself over generations. It is easy to generalize the analysis to other family structures as well.)

The process of therapy, then, teaches the members of the family how to analyze their patterns of interaction with one another; how to spot roles they each play, such as "scapegoat"; and how to alter the way they feel about each other when the need to change is great.

The Role of the Father in Attachment

So far much of what we have said about attachment has emphasized the role of the mother in the attachment bond with the infant. But what about the fathers—do infants develop an attachment to fathers, and is it the same as the bond between mothers and infants?

It appears that under relaxed, comfortable circumstances infants do not show a preference for the mother over the father. For example, if we went to a home and watched an infant, mother, and father for an hour, we would be just as likely to see the ingredients of an attachment bond between the father and the infant as between the mother and the infant. To study this possibility, Michael Lamb (1977) observed seven- and thirteen-month-olds at home to see how they reacted to naturally occurring separations from their fathers and mothers. The babies touched, fussed to, asked to be held by, and went closer to their fathers just as much as they did to their mothers.

However, there is some suggestion that under stressful circumstances babies prefer to be closer to their mothers than to their fathers. When infant-parent attachment is observed in the laboratory—a strange environment for an infant and possibly one that produces more fear in the infant than does his or her home—we sometimes find that the infant shows a stronger preference for the mother than for the father.

Mothers and fathers seem to play different roles in the infant's life. Mothers are more likely to be the primary caregivers, and babies who are wet, hungry, tired, or sick are more likely to seek out their mothers than their fathers for this reason. By contrast, the father is more likely to be sought out by an infant for play. Thus both the mother and the father are important attachment figures for the infant, but the circumstances that lead an infant to show a preference for the mother or father seem to differ.

If we encounter a child during the preschool years or even later who has not developed an attachment to a caretaker during the infant years, should we in some way try to get the child to "relive" the infant-attachment process, or should we focus more on restructuring his or her current social relationships and attachments that are more relevant to life as a preschooler? At least one attachment expert, Eleanor Maccoby (1983), believes it would not be a wise idea to have the child return to a more "babyish" orientation—that is, one directed toward a single caregiver—but rather to focus on the development of an attachment process that is more appropriate for the preschool child, one that is likely to involve peers and a widening set of attachments in the social world.

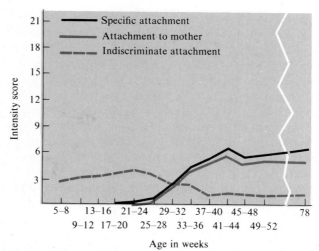

Figure 6.2 The course of infant attachment behavior.

Course of Attachment

How does attachment develop? The theories reviewed earlier offer some suggestions. In this section, the empirical sources of evidence about attachment will be reviewed.

In perhaps the most widely cited longitudinal study of attachment, investigators followed sixty Scottish infants who were from five to twenty-three weeks old at the outset of the study until they were eighteen months old (Schaeffer & Emerson, 1964). The investigators periodically interviewed the mothers about the infants' responses to separation episodes and observed the infants' responses to several standardized situations in which the interviewer (a stranger) slowly approached the infant. As with the interviews, the observations were made repeatedly throughout the period of the study. Figure 6.2 depicts the course of the infants' attachment behavior over time. It indicates that the infants protested being separated from anyone (indiscriminate attachment) during the first months of life. Beginning at about six months (twenty-five to twenty-eight weeks) attachment to the mother became more focused and remained strong from ten months through the remaining portion of the eighteen-month period. Attachments to other specific caregivers were at about the same level of intensity as attachment to the mother. And there were some additional findings that are not shown in the figure: for example, from seven months until almost the end of the first year, the specific attachment to the mother became more intense, and fear of strangers generally occurred at about eight months, approximately one to two months after the onset of attachment to the mother.

In another well-known study of infant attachment, Mary Ainsworth (1967) observed twenty-nine infant-mother pairs in Uganda, Africa, for a period of nine months. The children ranged in age from two to fourteen months during the investigation. Ainsworth's observations included smiling, crying, vocalization, separation protest, following, touching, greeting gestures, and using the mother as a base of exploration as indicators of attachment. As in the Schaeffer and Emerson study, the Ugandan infants began to show the most intense signs of attachment to their mothers at around seven months. However, there was evidence that the specific attachments began to develop earlier than in the Schaeffer and Emerson sample. For example, there were indications of attachment to the mother by four months in the Uganda infants. And interestingly, there was also a difference in the time of onset of fear of strangers. This fear emerged later in the Uganda infants, so the time lag between attachment and fear of strangers was much greater in this study.

Individual Differences in Attachment

To speak of attachment as a monolithic phenomenon experienced in the same way or in the same degree by all infant-caregiver pairs is, of course, a convenient fiction. There are striking individual differences among infants. For example, in the Schaeffer and Emerson (1964) investigation, one-fourth of the infants showed fear of strangers before specific attachment to the mother. This is quite a striking and nontrivial variation in the normative pattern of development. And in Ainsworth's (1967) early inquiry, five of the twenty-eight infants never did evidence positive affiliation with their mothers (e.g., clinging, proximity/seeking, visual contact).

Ainsworth (1979) stresses that one of the most important aspects of attachment is evaluating individual differences in attachment. Chiefly on the basis of infants' behaviors toward their mothers in reunion episodes, she makes a distinction between infants who seem to be securely attached versus those who are not. Among those who are designated as nonsecurely attached, a further distinction is made. One subgroup exhibits insecurity by avoiding the mother—ignoring her, averting her gaze, and failing to seek proximity. The other subgroup exhibits insecurity by resisting the mother—they may seek her proximity and cling to her, but at the same time fight against the closeness by, for example, kicking and pushing away. Finer subdivisions of

these three categories are possible as shown in table 6.1. In most groups of infants, it is assumed that the majority will be securely attached (two-thirds of Ainsworth's first sample of twenty-three babies were). It is the minority who evidence some maladaptive attachment.

What Is the Source of Individual Differences?
Where do such individual differences come from? This question has been the source of widespread speculation and much research. In terms of those infants who eventually achieve some degree of attachment, one widely held belief is that differences in the rate of achieving attachment reflect corresponding differences in the rate of cognitive development. In order to achieve a strong emotional bond with significant caretakers, goes the argument, the infant must first attain *object permanence* with respect to those people. That is, he or she must first divine that the people are permanent fixtures in the world who exist beyond the momentary time and place where they are experienced. Some research suggests that an infant's general level of cognitive development does correlate with the degrees of attachment (Clarke-Stewart, 1973).

Individual differences in the temperament of mother and child may also contribute to differences in the way attachment develops. Infants may be born with relatively enduring and different styles of responding to the world around them, for example, easy, difficult, and slow to warm up (Chess & Thomas, 1977). If caregivers are unable to synchronize their own behavior toward the infant because of a clash in temperaments or a simple inability to respond effectively to infant signals, attachment problems may arise.

Just as there are striking individual differences in the way infants express attachment, so are there powerful effects of the circumstances (situation) on the expression of attachment, as will be seen next.

Situational Variables

Alison Clarke-Stewart (1978) has offered a penetrating analysis of the importance of **situational variability** when studying infant behavior. She focused on "fear of the stranger" and analyzed the factors that determine how much fear or wariness will surface in the stranger's presence. The title of her paper, "Recasting the Lone Stranger," reflects her opinion that we may have oversimplified the stranger and treated him or her as a static variable, when the stranger is actually much more complex.

Clark-Stewart then proceeded to examine the influence of the stranger's *behavior* in a longitudinal investigation of fourteen middle-class infants over a one-and-a-half-year period (from one- to two-and-a-half

Table 6.1
Ainsworth's Classification of Attachment: Individual Differences

	Characteristics
Securely Attached	
group 1	Seeks interaction on reunion but not proximity. Does not resist when held. Little or no distress during separation episodes.
group 2	Seeks interaction and more proximity on reunion. Does not resist when held. Little or no distress during separation episodes.
group 3	Approaches mother on reunion. May also cry. Clutches when held, resists release. May or may not be distressed. Very active in seeking contact and resisting release.
group 4	Greatest desire for proximity, interaction, and being held throughout. Distress evident in separation episodes.
Insecurely Attached— Avoidant	
group 1	Fails to greet mother upon return. Fails to approach mother or attempt is aborted if picked up; likely to squirm to get down and does not cling.
group 2	Greets mother with mixed response, both approaching and turning and looking away. If picked up, always shows mixed response, momentarily clinging, but also slipping away.
Insecurely Attached— Resistant	
group 1	May reach or approach mother upon reunion and seek contact. But great ambivalence shown, with hitting, kicking, and pushing.
group 2	Fails to even contact mother. If approached or held, ambivalence shown.

Source: Ainsworth, 1979.

There are striking individual differences in the way infants respond to strangers.

years of age). A brief summary of her major findings follows.

In interactions lasting several minutes, strangers behaved in a hostile manner toward the mother by stomping into the room and launching into an angry and insulting dialogue with her, or in a happy manner by bouncing into the room full of joyous talk and animated conversation. Infants maintained less physical contact with their mothers during and after *hostile* interactions as compared with *happy* ones. Interestingly, the child's behavior toward the stranger was not influenced by the tone of the interaction between the stranger and the mother. By contrast, when strangers were either *nice* or *nasty* to the child directly, there were clear effects on the child's interaction with the stranger, but not with the mother. *Nice* strangers played with the child in a positive, pleasant, and friendly way with toys the child liked. *Nasty* strangers acted unpleasantly, unfriendly, and belligerently while playing with the child. The infants were more positive to the nice strangers (approaching, smiling, and touching) and more negative to the nasty ones (avoiding, crying, and aggressing).

Other situational variables have also been observed. For example, the one-year-old infant does not show as much distress to a stranger when sitting on the mother's lap as when sitting on a table (Morgan & Ricciuti, 1969). Infants fuss less and explore their environment more when a novel toy is present than when it is absent (Rheingold & Samuels, 1969). The readiness of infants to explore an unfamiliar object depends in part on how closely the mother is positioned to the infant (Schwartz, 1978). Eye contact may also be important. Adults who maintain visual attention to the infant may give him or her a sense of security. For example, five-month-old infants smiled and vocalized more and cried less when their mothers or a female stranger maintained eye contact with them as compared with visual orientation slightly farther away (Lasky & Klein, 1979).

In virtually every domain of social and emotional development, whether it be the study of attachment, self-concept, aggression, moral development, sex-role development, or achievement, we will find both individual differences and situational influences on the social and emotional characteristics being studied. In the next section, we consider the relation between attachment and the child's development of independence and exploratory tendencies.

Independence and the Development of the Self in Infancy

The initial discussion of the infant's development of independence focuses on how he or she performs the balancing act between attachment and independence. Two theories of how infants become independent will be discussed, developmental changes in independence will be described, and some fascinating ideas about how the infant's sense of self emerges will be covered. When the infant can detect that he or she has a self that is distinct from other people and objects in the world will also be examined.

Attachment and Independence-Exploration

Infants are highly active explorers of their environments. Soon after birth they reveal evidence of their systematic visual exploration, of their object manipulation, and of their general interest in moderately novel experiences. Exploration is one important source of learning about the properties of the environment.

In a classic study (Ainsworth, Bell, & Stayton, 1971), individual differences in the way one-year-old infants exhibited exploration and attachment in a home setting were examined. Those children judged as **securely attached** seemed to alternate between exploring their environments and seeking their mothers in a smooth, unstressed manner. However, infants in each of the **insecurely attached** groups had trouble exploring. Their activity was full of uncertainty and stress. The securely attached infants, for example, took pleasure in grasping and manipulating objects, while the others did not (Main, 1973).

To be securely attached to the mother, then, does not mean that the infant is less independent. Next, two ideas about the development of independence, each of which emphasizes the bond between the caretaker and the infant as an important part of the child's striving for independence, are discussed.

Theories of Independence

Margaret Mahler and Erik Erikson have focused considerable attention on the child's push for independence from parents. First, Mahler's ideas about separation-individuation are described; second, Erikson's comments about the stage of autonomy versus shame and doubt are presented.

Separation-Individuation

Margaret Mahler (1979) is a well-known psychoanalyst who has conducted very detailed clinical observations of infants and their mothers with the goal of finding out how infants and toddlers develop independence. Mahler believes that the child acquires a sense of separateness along with a sense of relatedness to the world through the process of **separation-individuation.** The process is characterized by the child's emergence from the symbiotic relationship with the mother (separation) and the child's acquisition of individual characteristics in the first three years of life. At the end of three years, the child has an independent, autonomous self. On the basis of these clinical observations, Mahler described subphases of the individuation process.

The newborn child is in an autistic stage, a time at which contact with the outside world is about to begin. The first change, called **differentiation,** begins at about four to five months and lasts for the next four to five months. There is a decrease in bodily dependence that coincides with significant increases in locomotor skills such as creeping, climbing, and standing up. The infant also begins to look beyond the immediate visual field, explores objects, and takes an active interest in the outside world. All of these activities emerge and are expressed in close proximity to the mother.

The next subphase of the development of individuation, referred to as **practicing,** lasts from about eight months to fifteen months. There is a steadily increasing interest in practicing motor skills and exploring and expanding the environment. The main characteristic of this subphase, though, is the infant's narcissistic interest in his or her own functions and body and in the objects that are involved in reality testing. While the infant in this period may be absorbed in his or her own activities for long periods of time, it may seem that he or she is oblivious to the mother. However, the infant returns to the mother periodically, as if he or she needs her physical proximity—a phenomenon referred to as emotional refueling.

The next subphase, called **rapprochement,** lasts approximately from fifteen to twenty-four months and roughly coincides with the period of development we sometimes refer to as toddlerhood. By the middle of the second year of life, the child has become more and more aware of his or her physical separateness. But as the child realizes his or her power and ability to move away from the mother physically, he or she now seems to have an increased need and a wish for the mother to share in every new acquisition of skill and experience. Thus active approach behavior toward the mother and a seemingly constant concern for the mother's whereabouts characterize this period much more than was the case during the practicing subphase.

The final subphase of individuation is called **consolidation of individuality.** This subphase should occur at about twenty-four to thirty months of age, and as the phase proceeds, the child is able gradually to accept once again separation from the mother (as during the practicing period). In fact, the child seems to prefer staying in a familiar playroom without the mother to going out of this room with her. During this phase, active resistance to the demands of adults and a strong desire for autonomy are apparent.

An example of how maternal-child interaction can interfere with the development of individuation was described by Mahler (1979). Anna's mother's marked emotional unavailability made Anna's practicing and exploratory period brief and subdued. Never certain of her mother's availability, and therefore always preoccupied with it, Anna found it difficult to explore her

The separation-individuation process focuses on the development of independence.

surroundings. After a brief spurt of practicing, she would return to her mother and try to interact with her in an intense manner. From such relatively direct expressions of need for her mother as bringing a book to read to her or hitting the mother's ever-present book in which she was engrossed, Anna turned to more desperate measures, such as falling or spilling cookies on the floor and stomping on them, always with an eye to gaining her mother's attention, if not involvement. Anna's mother was absorbed in her own interests, which were anything but child-centered. Along with her inability to let her mother out of her sight, Anna's activities were very low keyed: they lacked the vivacity and luster that characterized other children at her age.

Anna was observed during the preschool years at the nursery school she attended. When her mother would leave after dropping her off at school, Anna often threw a temper tantrum and would cling to her teacher. But the clinging frequently turned to hitting and yelling. In Mahler's view, Anna wanted only one thing to happen: her mother to return through the door. But when the mother did return, Anna did not show even a flicker of radiance or happiness. Her very first words

Symbiotic Infantile Psychosis and Infantile Autism

A psychosis is a severe abnormality that involves personality disorganization and loss of contact with reality. Two types of psychosis that may appear are symbiotic infantile psychosis and infantile autism.

Symbiotic Infantile Psychosis

Barbara is a four-year-old child who clings desperately to her mother, in a manner that forces her mother to attend to her needs on a moment-to-moment basis. When her mother leaves the house, Barbara reacts with paniclike screaming. Such children as Barbara have been described by Margaret Mahler (1979) as having **symbiotic infantile psychosis.** Think again about our description of Mahler's separation-individuation process in which the child develops a sense of separateness and independence from the mother. In rare cases, this process goes completely awry and produces a child like Barbara, who has intense anxiety and panic about being separated from her mother. It usually is manifested between the ages of two and a half and five years of age and often is preceded by normal development. In contrast to the autistic child who wants to be alone, the symbiotic child cannot tolerate even a brief separation from the mother. If the psychosis persists, the child becomes withdrawn and seclusive, staying close to the mother most of his or her life.

Infantile Autism

Infantile autism, often diagnosed during infancy, may persist well into childhood. Probably the most distinguishing characteristic of autistic children is their inability to relate to other people (Wing, 1977). As babies, they require very little from their parents; they do not demand much attention, and they do not reach out (literally or figuratively) for their parents. They rarely smile. When someone attempts to hold them, they often try to withdraw by arching their backs and pushing away from the person. In their cribs or playpens they appear oblivious to what is going on around them, often sitting and staring into space for long periods of time.

In addition to deficits in attachment to others, autistic children often have speech problems. As many as one out of every two autistic children never learn to speak. Those who do learn to speak may engage in a type of speech called **echolalia**—the child echos rather than responds to what he or she hears. Thus, if you ask "How are you, Chuck?" Chuck will respond with "How are you, Chuck?" Autistic children also tend to confuse pronouns, inappropriately substituting *you* for *I*, for example.

A third major characteristic of autistic children is the degree to which they become upset over a change in their daily routine or their physical environment. Rearrangement of a sequence of events or even furniture in the course of their "normal" day causes them to become extremely upset. Thus autistic children are not flexible in adapting to new routines and changes in their daily life.

were "What did you bring me?" and the whining and discontent started all over again. As can be seen in Anna's case, a very unsatisfactory mother-infant relationship led to problems in her development of independence. More information about problems in separation-individuation is given in application 6.3, along with a discussion of another severe psychological problem that develops in infancy—autism.

While Mahler's account of the separation-individuation process has stimulated thought about the development of independence in infancy and early childhood and given us a vivid picture of mother-infant interaction, it is not without problems. Susan Harter (1983) summarized some of the problems that surface in Mahler's perspective. Mahler's goal, at first glance, appears to be similar to that of cognitive-structural theorists, who are interested in how the infant develops a sense of self as an active, independent individual. From the cognitive-structural perspective, we discover the infant is an inquisitive young scientist who is preoccupied with the serious business of locating objects and people in space and coordinating sensorimotor schemes. As Susan Harter (1983) evaluated Mahler's perspective:

The budding terrible two as described by Mahler is faced with different developmental hurdles, and tends to evoke more sympathy. The infant is wrenched from the blissful stage of need gratification, must endure separation distress, struggle to create a soothing image of mother, tolerate the fickleness of an environment which initially seemed to yield to the infant's every whim only to frustrate the infant in a subsequent developmental hour of need; and finally, to make matters

The impact an autistic child can have on parents is described in the following excerpts from the popular book, *A Child Called Noah,* written in 1972 by Josh Greenfield about his autistic son Noah.

8–70: I also must note how very few people can actually understand our situation as a family, how they assume we are aloof when we tend not to accept or extend the usual social invitations. Nor have I mentioned the extra expenses a child like Noah entails—those expenses I keep in another book.

8–71: Even more heartbreaking has been the three-year period it has taken us to pierce the organized-medicine, institutionalized-mental-health gauze curtain. Most doctors, if they were unable to prescribe any form of curative aid, did their best to deter us from seeking it. Freudian-oriented psychiatrists and psychologists, if ill-equipped to deal with the problems of those not verbal, tried to inflict great feelings of guilt upon us as all-too-vulnerable parents. Neurologists and pediatricians, if not having the foggiest notions about the effects of diet and nutrition, vitamins and enzymes and their biochemical workings would always suggest such forms of therapy as practiced only by quacks. And county mental-health boards, we discovered, who have charge of the moneys that might be spent helping children like Noah, usually tossed their skimpy fundings away through existing channels that do not offer proper treatment for children like Noah.

4–16–67: We've decided to stop worrying about Noah. He isn't retarded, he's just pushing the clock hands about at his own slow speed. Yet . . .

8–16–67: We took Noah to a pediatrician in the next town, who specializes in neurology. He said that since Noah is talking now there was little cause to worry; that Noah seemed "Hypertonic," a floppy baby, a slow developer, but that time would be the maturing agent. We came away relieved. But I also have to admit that lately I haven't worried that much.

6–6–69: Noah is two. He still doesn't walk, but I do think he's trying to teach himself how to stand up. We're still concerned. And I guess we'll remain concerned until he stands up and walks like a boy.

7–14–69: Our fears about Noah continue to undergo dramatic ups and downs. Because of his increased opacity, the fact that he doesn't respond when we call his name and fails to relate completely to his immediate environment—pattern of retardation or autism—we took him to a nearby hospital. . . . I guess we both fear that what we dread is so, that Noah is not a normal child, that he is a freak, and his condition is getting worse.

2–19–70: I'm a lousy father. I anger too easily. I get hot with Karl and take on a four-year-old kid. I shout at Noah and further upset an already disturbed one. Perhaps I am responsible for Noah's problems. (pp. 91–92)

The specific cause of autistic behavior still is the focus of extensive speculation. Some experts stress the importance of underlying hereditary and biological mechanisms, while other experts believe social experiences are at fault.

worse, the toddler is greeted with social approbation for throwing him/herself, red-faced and screaming on the supermarket floor. (p. 23)

Harter feels that Mahler puts too much singular emphasis on the mother. Also, she feels that Mahler does not discuss individual differences in the rate of development through her subphases. Harter feels that many of Mahler's observations of mother-infant relationships have not been systematically documented.

Autonomy Versus Shame and Doubt
Another theorist, Erik Erikson (1968), also believes that the relationship between the mother and the infant is important in determining the extent to which the toddler will develop a sense of antonomy. Autonomy versus shame and doubt represents the second stage in Erikson's theory of development. The major significance of this stage in the life cycle lies in rapid gains in muscular maturation, verbalization, and the coordination of a number of conflicting action patterns characterized by tendencies to hold on and let go. Through such changes the highly dependent child begins to experience autonomous will. Mutual regulation between adult and child faces a severe test. This stage becomes decisive in whether the child will feel comfortable in self-expression or feel anxious and show extensive self-restraint. Erikson believes that if the child does not develop a sense of self-control and free will at this point in development, he or she may become saddled with a lasting propensity for doubt and shame.

For the toddler to develop independence, a firmly developed early trust is necessary. The sense of autonomy parents are able to grant their small children depends on the dignity and sense of personal independence they derive from their own lives. In other words, the toddler's sense of autonomy is a reflection of the parents' dignity as autonomous beings. Erikson believes that much of the lasting sense of doubt developed in the toddler is a consequence of the parents' frustrations in marriage, work, and citizenship.

Erikson goes on to describe how the struggles and triumphs of this stage of development contribute to the identity crisis all adolescents undergo, either by supporting the formation of a healthy identity or by contributing to estrangement and confusion. The most important contribution to the development of a sense of autonomy during the toddler years for the development of identity during adolescence is the courage to be an independent individual who can choose and guide his or her own future. The residue from successful resolutions of the autonomy-shame stage that influences the development of identity is reflected in one adolescent's statement, "I am what I can will freely."

Next we review the research that has been conducted on the topic of independence in the infant and toddler years.

Independence in Young Children

Research on independence in infancy and childhood has received far less attention than attachment. Harriet Rheingold (1973) describes how, in reflecting on her earliest work on infants, it was only after a number of years she began to recognize how independent many of the youngsters' behaviors were.

Some eight years ago I began a series of studies designed to measure the effect of a strange environment on the behavior of infants at ten months of age. Only after the last sentence of the discussion of the study was written did I realize that it was not so much the strange environment that caused the distress of the children placed in it without their mothers, nor even the absence of their mothers, as it was being *placed* and *left alone* (Rheingold, 1969). That this was so was demonstrated in a later study in which infants the same age were given the opportunity to leave their mothers and enter that same strange environment by themselves (Rheingold & Eckerman, 1969). All the children did enter on their own initiative, even when the environment contained no toy. Not only did they enter, but they crept to places in the room from which they could not see the mother. They returned to the mother's room, left again, and returned again—some infants many times—but on a third of the returns they did not contact the mother. (pp. 182–83)

Rheingold (1973) indicated that in the process of investigating the influence of different environments, it was becoming clear that she was seeing infants move away from their mothers. A review of the nonhuman primate research on independence (Rheingold & Eckerman, 1970) provided support for the belief that the infant detaches himself or herself from the mother. As the nonhuman primate grows older, it leaves the mother more frequently, goes farther, and stays away longer. To find out how far from the mother a human child would stray, Rheingold and Eckerman (1970) placed a mother and her child in a backyard—the mother was seated and the child was left free. They found a positive relationship between the age of the children (from one to five years) and the distance they traveled from their mothers. However, the continuing relationship to the mother was evidenced in the observations by older children bringing small items to their mothers—pebbles and leaves for example. These observations are similar to the concept of emotional refueling described earlier by Mahler (1979).

So far in this chapter we have described both the attachment process and the development of independence. In our discussion of independence in the infant and toddler years, comments were made about the process of individuation proposed by Margaret Mahler. In the next section we see that some of the same ideas developed by Mahler are incorporated in developmental psychologists' descriptions of the infant's sense of self, or sense of being, that is different from the mother or other humans in the environment.

The Development of the Self in Infancy

Individuals carry within them a sense of who they are and what makes them different from everyone else. They cling to this identity and begin to feel secure in the knowledge that this identity is becoming more stable. Real or imagined, the individual's developing sense of identity and uniqueness is a strong motivating force in life. But what about earlier in development—when does the individual begin to sense a separate existence from others?

Children begin the process of developing a sense of self by learning to distinguish themselves from others. To determine whether, in fact, infants are able to recognize themselves, psychologists have traditionally relied on mirrors. In the animal kingdom only the great apes can learn to recognize their reflection in a mirror, but human infants can accomplish this feat by approximately eighteen months of age. The ability of the toddler to recognize a mirrored reflection seems to be linked to the ability to form a mental image of his or her own face. This development of a sense of self does not occur in a single step but is rather the product of a complex understanding that develops very gradually.

Table 6.2

Development of Self-Knowledge, Emotional Experience, and Cognitive Growth

Age	Self-Knowledge	Emotional Experience	Cognitive Growth
0–3	Interest in social objects; emergence of self-other distinction	Unconditioned responses to stimulus events (loud noise, hunger, etc.)	Reflexive period; primary circular reactions
3–8	Consolidation of self-other distinction, recognition of self through contingency	Conditioned responses (strangers, incongruity)	Primary and secondary circular reactions
8–12	Emergence of self-permanence and self categories; recognition of self through contingency and onset of feature recognition	Specific emotional experiences (fear, happiness, love, attachment)	Object permanence, means-ends, imitation
12–24	Consolidation of basic self categories (age, gender, emergency of efficacy); feature recognition without contingency	Development of empathy, guilt, embarrassment	Language growth; more complex means-ends; symbolic representations

Source: Lewis & Brooks-Gunn, 1979, p. 227.

Michael Lewis and Jeanne Brook-Gunn (1979) have conducted a number of studies of the development of the infant's ability to recognize the self. Lewis and his colleagues (e.g., Lewis & Cherry, 1977) believe that the process of self-development parallels the development of the more traditional cognitive and emotional aspects of development. In table 6.2 the parallel development of self-knowledge, emotional experience, and cognitive growth is shown.

The mirror technique, initially used with animals (e.g., Gallup, 1977), was modified for use with human infants (e.g., Bertenthal & Fischer, 1978; Lewis & Brooks-Gunn, 1979). The mother puts a dot of rouge on her child's nose. During a pretest, an observer watches to see how frequently the infant touches his or her nose. Next, the infant is placed in front of a mirror, and observers detect whether nose touching increases. In both sets of research, at about eighteen months of age children significantly increased their nose touching, suggesting that they recognized their own image and coordinated the image they saw in the mirror with the actions of touching their own body.

In the investigation of Bertenthal and Fischer (1978), the developmental aspects of a growing awareness of a sense of self were studied. They revealed that by six months of age, infants reached out and touched some part of their image in the mirror. By the time they were ten months of age, the infants had successfully passed what was called the hat test. In the hat test the mother dresses the infant in a special vest. Attached to the back of the vest is a wooden rod with a hat on top.

This 18-month-old shows a sense of self.

Table 6.3
Summary of Stage Models Related to the Infant's Development of Self

Approximate Ages	Visual Recognition Studies	Mahler's Phases of Separation-Individuation	Ainsworth's Phases of Attachment
0–5	(1) No self-other differentiation	(1) Normal, autistic, and symbiotic phase	(1) Preattachment phase
5–10	(2) Awareness of bodily self as cause of movement	(1) Differentiation	(2) Attachment in the making
10–15	(3) Differentiation of self as active agent from others	(2) Practicing	(3) Clear-cut attachment
15–20	(4) Featural recognition of self	(3) Rapprochement	
18+	(5) Verbal labeling of the self	(4) Resolution and consolidation	(4) Goal-corrected partnership

Source: After Harter, 1983.

When the infant moves, the hat moves. Without a mirror the infant cannot see the hat. With a mirror, ten-month-old infants usually look up at the real hat, suggesting that the infant understands that the movement of the hat is in some way connected to the movement of his or her own body and that he or she must use the mirror to locate the hat.

So if the ten-month-old infant can locate the hat, why can't the child find the red dot of rouge? Bertenthal and Fischer (1978) argue that toddlers must build up an image, or a schema, of how their own face is likely to look in the mirror before they can detect the discrepancy created by the red dot. By eighteen months of age, then, toddlers do have sense of self and the development of this self-concept is related to cognitive development.

A summary of three views of the development of the self are presented in table 6.3. They include the cognitive-structural, visual recognition studies; Margaret Mahler's phases of separation-individuation; and Mary Ainsworth's phases of attachment.

Summary

How critical are early experiences in development? Experts do not all agree on the answer to this question, although the weight of theories and research suggests that early experience plays an important role. Empirically demonstrating that infancy is a critical period for later development is a difficult task. There is agreement, however, that the infant needs rich stimulation—recent research, for example, suggests that even moderately low caloric intake during infancy affects the social behavior and emotional characteristics of school-age children.

The infant's interaction and experiences with parents provide the beginning of the life-long process of socialization. The birth of a child creates a disequilibrium in the family system that requires a great deal of adaptation on the part of the parents. The infant socializes parents just as they socialize the infant, a process called reciprocal socialization. As parents adapt to the presence of an infant in their lives, it is important that synchrony in parent-infant relationships develops. It has also been recognized that it is important to study the family as a system of interacting individuals.

Attachment is defined as a relation between an infant and one or more adult caregivers. Each individual has a strong emotional feeling toward the other, which may be exhibited by the infant in behaviors aimed at maintaining proximity, protesting separation from the caregiver, and being anxious in the presence of strangers.

The ethological view of attachment represented in the writings of John Bowlby and Mary Ainsworth stresses the emergence of attachment as a natural biological result of certain instinctual response systems elicited by and directed toward the caregiver. The caregiver, in turn, may have some of his or her own biological needs met in the exchanges.

Several steps can be traced in the development of attachment. During the first four months, most infants have indiscriminate preferences for various adults. Between six and eight months, strong proximity-seeking behaviors are exhibited toward particular caregivers, and these may persist for as much as a year (attachment). Somewhat later infants protest and become anxious when separated from a caregiver (separation anxiety) and finally evidence anxiety when approached by strangers (stranger anxiety).

There are individual differences in attachment, and situational variables may influence its expression. It is possible to observe moderately stable differences in attachment behaviors among infants over short periods of time (e.g., four to eight months); variety of situational variables can moderate its appearance; and recent research evidence suggests some connection between the security of infant attachment and social and cognitive competence one to two years later.

Infants not only seek the company of their caregiver but also spend a good deal of time out of the immediate reaches of the caregiver. An interesting question focuses on how infants perform the balancing act between attachment and independence. There is evidence that infants who are securely attached to the mother show more exploratory tendencies than those who are anxiously attached. Two theories of independence—Mahler's individuation-separation and Erikson's autonomy versus shame and doubt—stress the importance of the symbiotic relationship between the infant and mother.

The push for independence seems to become most intense during the second year of life. There has not been nearly as much research on the early developmental aspects of independence as there has been in the area of attachment. Rheingold's work represents the most thorough attempt to study independence in infancy and young childhood. She found that from the ages of one to five children increasingly move away from their mothers to explore their environment. By eighteen months of age infants can recognize themselves, indicating the rudimentary beginning of the self-concept.

Key Terms

asynchrony

attachment

consolidation of
  individuality

differentiation

echolalia

family system

infantile autism

insecurely attached—
  avoidance

insecurely attached—
  resistant

practicing

psychosis

rapprochement

reciprocal socialization

securely attached

separation-individuation

situational variability

socialization

symbiotic infantile
  psychosis

synchrony

temperament

Review Questions

1. Discuss theory and research about the role of early experience in development.
2. How important is nutrition during infancy for the development of later social behavior and emotional characteristics?
3. What do we mean by socialization, synchrony in parent-infant relationships, and family system? Give examples of each.
4. What is attachment and how does it develop?
5. Describe individual differences and contextual effects on attachment.
6. What are the effects of day care on attachment?
7. What is the relationship between attachment and independence?
8. Describe the theories of independence of Mahler and Erikson.
9. Discuss the development of the self in infancy.
10. Compare Ainsworth's and Mahler's approaches to understanding the development of the self in infancy.

Further Readings

Emde, R., & Harmon, R. (Eds.). *Attachment and affiliative systems: neurobiological and psychobiological aspects.* New York: Plenum, 1981.
  A volume of papers by outstanding researchers in the field of attachment, including considerable information about the biological basis of attachment. Moderately difficult reading.

Lewis, M., & Brooks-Gunn, J. *Social cognition and the acquisition of the self.* New York: Plenum, 1979.
  An extensive overview of Lewis's work on the development of the self in infancy. Chapters explore the origin of the self, how to study the self in infancy, and ideas about a unified theory of the self. Medium reading difficulty.

Mahler, M. S. *The selected papers of Margaret Mahler, vol. 2: separation-individuation.* New York: Jason Aronson, 1979.
  A presentation of Margaret Mahler's insightful writing about the separation-individuation process in the first three years of life. Considerable information, including case studies, of aberrant mother-child relationships that restrict the development of independence. Medium reading difficulty.

Parke, R. D. *Fathers.* Cambridge, Mass.: Harvard University Press, 1981; and Schaeffer, R. *Mothering.* Cambridge, Mass.: Harvard University Press, 1977.
  These two books are part of the Harvard University Press series edited by Jerome Bruner, Michael Cole, and Barbara Lloyd on the developing child. Each of these books provides well-written accounts of the parent's role in infancy. Medium reading difficulty.

Know Yourself

In the Profile that introduced this section, you read, "It has been a long time since you were an infant. What were your infant years like? How much of them can you remember?" Recall that we said you probably wouldn't be able to remember what went on in those early years of your life. However, we have discovered that the first several years of life provide a very important foundation for development throughout the life cycle.

We also asked you to go out and observe some babies. Because you have read the four chapters in this section that focus on infant development, now is an excellent time to spend some more time with infants. See if your understanding of infants has increased now that you have read extensively about infant development. When you look at a seven-month-old now, you may be thinking, "Does she show an understanding of object permanence?" In watching a nine-month-old, you may be looking to see the extent to which the infant is securely attached to the mother or at how much the father is involved in taking care of the infant. When you observe an eighteen-month-old, you may be thinking about whether evidence of a developing sense of self is present, as well as the degree of independence being shown. The time spent with a baby or two now will help you a great deal in truly understanding our description and explanation of development during the first two years of life. It should also stimulate you to think about the nature of your own development as an infant.

To learn more about your infant years, talk to your mother, father, or other caregiver about what you were like as a baby. Try to find some old pictures of yourself and your parents when you were just born and when you were one and two years old. Were you a "difficult" or an "easy" baby? How did your parents deal with your crying—did they pick you up in an instant, or did they let you lie there and cry a long time? How much did your father participate in taking care of you as a baby? Ask your mother if she had any difficulties when she was pregnant with you and how the birth process itself went. When you began exploring your world, did your mother restrict you a lot or did she allow you to spontaneously investigate things? How much did she encourage your independence and the development of your self during the second year of your life?

Let's not forget that there are probably some important genetic foundations of your development. Although it is very difficult to pin down such effects, it may be helpful to think about what your close relatives are or were like—your mother, your father, your grandparents on each side of your family, your uncles and aunts, and your cousins. Which of these people do you resemble the most? By thinking hard about what you are like and what your close relatives are like, you probably can come up with some traits that characterize not only yourself but also people with close genetic ties to you.

After you have explored your own infant years, talk to a classmate or friend about what his or her infant years were like. Did your friend or classmate's parents treat him or her the same way your parents treated you? Was the attachment process the same for him or her as it was for you? Were you and your friend or classmate taken care of almost continuously by your mothers or were other caregivers involved?

Now that you have spent some time observing infants, exploring your own infant years, and conversing with someone else about the nature of his or her infant experiences, let's think about your ideas on infant development. If you were to become a parent yourself, what would you be like? If you are a female, would you be careful about your diet and the use of drugs during pregnancy? How would you interact with your baby? Would you put the baby in a day-care center and continue your career as soon as possible after its birth, or would you try to stay at home during the first two years of its life? Would you be more likely to let your baby spontaneously explore the world or to be more restrictive and tutor the baby in structured situations? Would you want your baby to develop a strong, secure attachment to a single caregiver, or do you believe it is more important for the baby to develop a widening set of ties

early in development? And how important do you think the first two years of life are in life-span development? Can experiences later in development possibly compensate for missed opportunities early in development?

By reading our description of infant development in this section, by observing infants, by talking to your parents or other caregivers about your own infant years, by conversing with someone else about his or her infancy, and by thinking about what kind of parent you would be with your own baby, you should know yourself better.

In This Section You Will Learn About

Physical Development

Changes in height, weight, fat, muscle, and other body parts

The slowdown in physical growth during early childhood

How gross motor (large muscle) skills develop more rapidly than fine motor skills

Individual variation in physical development and extremes such as drawfism and giantism

The importance of children's scribbling and drawing

Handedness

How motor development is assessed

Training programs that promote physical development

The play spaces of young children

Nutrition and its role in physical and cognitive development

Cognitive Development

A variety of preschool, early childhood models of education

Maria Montessori's ideas about training the senses of young children

Piaget's stage of preoperational thought

An alternative to Piaget's theory, the information processing perspective

The development of attention

How intelligence is defined and the psychometric approach to cognition

Genetic and environmental influences on intelligence

Foster grandparents and institutionalized young children

The role of families in intellectual development

The continuation of language development

Self-taught and prereading skills programs

What writing is

"Genie," who was isolated from the world, and her language development

Project Head Start and Project Follow-Through and their impact on impoverished children

"Sesame Street": education through television

Social, Emotional, and Personality Development

The parent's adaptation to the developing child

Changes in the American family and its effects on young children

The effects of working mothers on children

The effects of father absence and divorce on children

Dimensions of parenting techniques, including control and autonomy, warmth and hostility

The important childrearing strategy of authoritative parenting

Child abuse

The functions of the peer group

How the preschool teacher can control peer aggression

The role of play in children's lives

The coordinated world of parents and peers

The role of television in children's development

The development of the self in the preschool years

Sex-typed behavior and how difficult and ethical it is to change children's sex-typed behavior

The role of various biological and environmental factors in sex-role development

Profile

Profile

The last time we saw Mark Parke he was a two-year-old bundle of energy. Let's follow him through the early childhood years and see what his life is like. Although his parents are very satisfied with the care Nanna has provided Mark, when he reaches two and a half they decide it would be a good idea to place him in a preschool for part of the day. They are interested in a school that is much more than a "warehouse" for young children—they want a preschool in which Mark can learn as well. After visiting a number of preschools in their vicinity, Mark's parents settle on a privately owned early childhood center that they feel provides a good balance between play and learning.

During his early childhood years, Mark's physical growth begins to slow down from its rapid pace in the first two years of his life. Mark still shows a high level of energy, and on a number of occasions his preschool teacher has tried to slow him down a little when she thinks it is necessary. For example, at the age of 4, Mark decided one day that he would act like an airplane and dive bomb into three girls who were painting together. Needless to say, Mark got a lot of attention for his imitation of an airplane—the girls yelled at him as they wiped the paint off of their faces, and his teacher decided it was necessary to put him in a "time-out" area, away from everyone else in an effort to modify some of his boisterous behavior.

Mark's cognitive abilities have expanded during the preschool years. He is able to use images and symbols to represent his world better than he did when he was two, but there are still a lot of limitations in the way he thinks. He still is what is called "egocentric," in the sense that he doesn't do a very good job of distinguishing between his perspective and anyone else's. His attention to tasks is not as good as that of many other children at the preschool he attends, and his teacher already has had a conference with Mark's parents to discuss this matter. In an effort to improve his attentional skills, several evenings a week Mark's mother sits him down at the kitchen table and tries to help him increase his concentration on different tasks—like coloring, sorting objects, and so forth—without letting him just get up and run into the other room to watch television. Mark is far beyond saying, "Dada bye-bye." At age three, he said, "What Daddy read?" At age four, he was able to ask, "What Daddy is reading?" And at age five, he questioned, "What is Daddy reading?" Mark is also beginning to read; at preschool his teacher gradually developed Mark's prereading skills to the point at which, by the age of four, he was beginning to read some words. Now that Mark is five, he is much further along on the way to becoming a competent reader.

Next door to Mark lives Stacy Henson. Occasionally she and Mark play together, but most of the time Mark prefers the company of another boy down the street. Stacy has a girl friend who also lives down the street, a friend that she thinks is a lot nicer than Mark. Stacy's mother has told Mark's mother that every time their two children are together it seems like Stacy comes home crying because Mark has done something to her. Mark, at age five, tells his mom, "Boy, that Stacy; she sure is a big baby." Stacy, who is the same age as Mark, tells her mom, "I hate that Mark."

While Mark's mother has continued to work at her job as a computer analyst during Mark's early childhood years, Stacy's mother has preferred to remain a homemaker and has not pursued a career. Stacy's mother also waited until Stacy was five before she sent her to preschool. Stacy's mother is very nurturant toward her; Stacy's father spends very little time with her, having a job that requires him to travel away from home frequently. Mark's parents think Stacy is spoiled, but Stacy's mother feels that Stacy is developing maturely as a feminine young girl.

At the age of five, Stacy is just starting to be trained in some prereading skills at the preschool she attends, in a program that is part of the public school system. Nonetheless, she is making rapid progress, and after six months, we find that she is almost as far along as Mark in her reading skills. Her attention to tasks is certainly far superior to Mark's. Stacy still likes to engage in a lot of pretend play, and she and her girl friend sometimes dress up like women, putting on their mothers' clothes. One day Mark and his buddy Chip saw them prancing around outside of Stacy's house, and before Stacy and her friend could run inside, Mark and Chip tackled them and got their mothers' dresses muddy—another conversation between Mark's mother and Stacy's mother tonight?

When Mark, Stacy, and Chip were four years old, a boy named Don Mitchell, who is black, moved into their neighborhood. Don's father works as an officer at a bank and his mother is a teacher. His parents have worked hard to provide a good life for themselves and Don. The Mitchells moved to the predominantly white, middle-class neighborhood in the suburbs because they believe their children will receive a better education there than in the inner city area they moved from. The Mitchells—along with the Hensons and Parkes—could be characterized as achievement-oriented, serious parents.

During the first year Don lived in the new neighborhood, Mark and Chip did not play with him. But recently all three boys have been playing games together, and Don has become a good friend to Mark and Chip. Don's parents have placed him in the same private preschool Mark attends. He is the only black child there, and all of the teachers and teacher's aides are white as well. Don is a very polite, intelligent, and considerate child. It didn't take long for other children at the preschool to get to like him.

7 Physical Development

I magine . . . that you are five years old and live in the Bayambang area of the Philippines

Your parents are very poor. They do not get enough food to eat, and what they are able to afford does not constitute a well-balanced diet. There is a limited amount of protein in the Philippines; only the wealthy people get enough. Even if protein were plentiful, the price would probably be too high for your parents.

Compare yourself to a five-year-old growing up in Des Moines, Iowa. The five-year-old in Des Moines lives in a land where protein is plentiful. It is so plentiful that the five-year-old in Iowa has no worry about protein intake. Even if he comes from a lower-class family in the United States, he will get far more protein than the average five-year-old in the Philippines. Indeed, one of the major problems the five-year-old in Iowa may be facing is that he is getting too much fat in his diet—more about this appears later in the chapter.

Table 7.A presents a comparison of the malnutrition in the Bayambang area of the Philippines with nutrition in Iowa. Note that at all ages of childhood malnutrition in the Philippines is apparent.

Socioeconomic status within a culture is also linked with the nutrition and physical development of young children. The curves of body weight shown in figure 7.A reveal the average weights of young children from three different social classes in Manila (upper income, middle income, and lower income) along with young children living in Bayambang and Iowa (Bailey, 1970).

Table 7.A
Malnutrition Scores in Bayambang Area, Philippines, 1964 (Based on Two-thirds of Iowa Standard)

Age Group	% Below Malnutrition Line
Infants 0–5 months	5.7
Infants 6–11 months	17.8
Toddlers 1–3 years	24.0
Preschool 4–6 years	13.4
School age 7–9 years	16.7
School age 10–12 years	18.7

Source: Bailey, 1970 p. 45.

Note that the upper-income children from Manila approach their counterparts from Iowa while those from middle and lower income families have much lower body weights. Also note the average weight of young children from the Bayambang area of the Philippines, an impoverished area.

Where growth retardation is apparent, there is generally some inadequacy of many nutrients in the common diet, and caloric deficiency may also occur. It appears that protein, vitamin A, and iron deficiencies are the most common problems. These deficiencies seem to be particularly acute in impoverished areas when children are under the age of five.

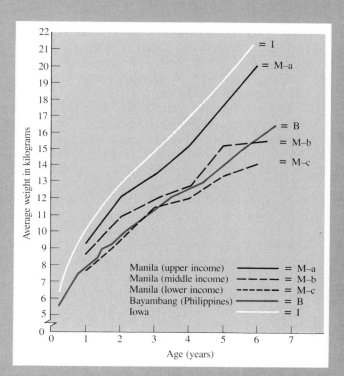

Figure 7.A Average weight of infants and toddlers of different socioeconomic groups (males and females combined).
(*Source:* Bailey, 1970, p. 43.)

Introduction

In this chapter we look at how physical growth continues to increase as children make the transition from infancy to middle childhood. Fortunately, the growth rate begins to slow down in early childhood, or we would be a species of giants. We evaluate continued growth in height, weight, fat, muscle, and other body parts. Individual variation in physical development is stressed, and some problems in growth, such as dwarfism and giantism, are outlined. Considerable attention is given to motor development, as we discover that gross motor skills develop more rapidly than fine motor skills during early childhood. Further discussion of motor development focuses on handedness and how motor development can be assessed. Our discussion then turns to training programs that promote physical development—physical education, perceptual motor, and movement. Further description of the importance of nutrition in early childhood emphasizes its effects on intellectual as well as physical development.

Height, Weight, Fat, Muscle, and Other Body Parts

The average child grows two and one-half inches in height and gains between five and seven pounds a year during early childhood. As the preschool child grows older, the percentage increase in height and weight is less with each additional year of age. Table 7.1 shows the average height and weight of children as they age from three to six years. Girls are only slightly smaller and lighter than boys during this age frame, a difference that continues until puberty. During the preschool years both boys and girls slim down as the trunk of their bodies becomes longer. Although their heads are still somewhat large for their bodies, by the end of the preschool years most children have lost the look that makes them seem top-heavy. Body fat also shows a slow, steady decline during the preschool years, sometimes allowing the chubby baby to look much leaner by the end of early childhood. As you might expect, girls have more fatty tissue than do boys, and boys have more muscle tissue.

Some body systems show signs of maturing—for instance, the child's heart rate slows down and becomes more stable (Eichorn, 1970). Nonetheless, there still are signs of immaturity in many body systems, including bones, joints, and muscles, which are much more susceptible to injury than those of children in middle and late childhood (Lundsteen & Bernstein-Tarrow, 1981).

Individual Variation

Clearly, there is a great deal of individual variation in our growth patterns. Think back to your preschool years. Although it is not easy to remember that far

Table 7.1
Physical Growth, Ages Three to Six (Fiftieth Percentile)

Age	Height (inches) Boys	Girls	Weight (pounds) Boys	Girls
3	38	37¾	32¼	31¾
3½	39¼	39¼	34¼	34
4	40¾	40½	36½	36¼
4½	42	42	38½	38½
5	43¼	43	41½	41
5½	45	44½	45½	44
6	46	46	48	47

Source: From *Growth and development of children,* 5th edition, by Ernest H. Watson and George H. Lowrey. Copyright © 1967, Year Book Medical Publishers, Inc., Chicago. Used by permission of Year Book Medical Publishers.

back, you may recall that the preschool years were the first time you started noticing that some children were taller than you, others were shorter, some were fatter, some thinner, some were stronger, some weaker.

Much of the variation in height is due to genetic factors, but there is evidence that environmental experiences contribute as well. In reviewing more than 200 studies of the heights of preschool children around the world, it was concluded that the two most important contributors to height differences are ethnic origin and nutrition (Meredith, 1978). Urban, middle-class, and first-born children were taller than rural, lower-class, and later-born children, possibly because the former experience better health care and nutrition. It also was noted that children at the age of five were approximately one-half inch shorter if their mother smoked during pregnancy. In the United States height differences among preschool children are mainly due to genetic inheritance because most children receive enough food for their bodies to grow appropriately. On the average, black children are taller than white children in the United States (Krogman, 1970).

Growth Problems

Children who experience growth problems, being unusually short or unusually tall (which is less frequent) usually do so for one of three reasons: a congenital reason, a physical problem that develops during childhood, or an emotional difficulty. In many instances individuals with congenital growth problems (those due to genetic conditions or prenatal difficulties) can be treated with hormones. Usually such treatment is directed at a master gland, the pituitary, located at the base of the brain. This gland secretes hormones that control growth. With regard to physical problems that develop during childhood malnutrition and chronic infections can stunt growth although if they are properly treated, normal growth usually is achieved (Lowrey,

Much of the variation in height is due to genetic factors.

1978). Finally, some psychologists believe that emotional problems can produce growth abnormalities. For instance, Lita Gardner (1972) argues that children who are deprived of affection may experience alterations in the release of hormones by the pituitary gland. This type of growth retardation is called **deprivation dwarfism.** Some children who are small and weak, but not dwarfs, also may show the effects of an impoverished emotional environment—although most parents of such children generally say they are small and weak because they have a poor body structure or constitution.

Next we see that motor development is also a prominent part of the growth pattern of early childhood.

Motor Development

Building towers with blocks . . . running as fast you could, falling down, getting right back up, and running just as fast again . . . scribbling, scribbling, and then scribbling some more on lots of pieces of paper . . . cutting paper with scissors—during your preschool years, you probably developed the ability to perform all of these motor activities. A summary of the manner in which a number of gross and fine motor skills change during the course of early childhood is outlined in table 7.2. One fine motor skill that is particularly important for children to practice is scribbling and drawing—the art of children—which is discussed in application 7.1.

Three- to five-year-olds often experience considerable large-muscle development, particularly in the arms and legs. Thus daily forms of exercise are recommended because of this considerable increase in gross motor skills during early childhood. It is also important that sedentary periods be kept brief and few. Although fine motor skills also are increasing during this period, they seem to show more growth during the beginning of middle childhood than during early childhood (Robinson, 1977).

Another important aspect of motor skills is called **handedness,** which hand we prefer to use.

Taken from *Do They Ever Grow Up?* Copyright © 1978 by Lynn Johnston with permission of Meadowbrook Press, Deephaven, MN.

Handedness

In most instances, hand preference appears in a noticeable way between the ages of two and five. About one in every ten children is left-handed (Hardyck & Petrinovich, 1977). For some years many parents tried to change their children's left-handed tendencies into right-handed ones. Fortunately, in recent years left-handedness has become more accepted, and we do not see as many parents trying to retrain their "southpaws" to become right-handed. Most psychologists believe that genetic inheritance and/or the prenatal environment are responsible for handedness. For the most part, left-handed children are as competent as their right-handed peers, and in some cases they may have an advantage. The youngest daughter of one of the authors is a thirteen-year-old nationally ranked tennis player, and being left-handed is a definite advantage. Right-handed players are not as accustomed to playing left-handed players, and the ball often spins a different way when a left-handed player hits it.

Table 7.2
Perceptual-Motor Behaviors Check List

The following tasks are reasonable to expect in 75 to 80 percent of the children of the indicated ages. Children should be tested individually.

The data upon which this is based has been collected from children in white middle-class neighborhoods.

A child failing to master four to six of the tasks for his or her age probably needs (a) a more thorough evaluation and (b) some kind of remedial help.

Various sex differences are indicated.

Two to Three Years	YES	NO
1. Displays a variety of scribbling behavior.	_____	_____
2. Can walk rhythmically at an even pace.	_____	_____
3. Can step off low object, one foot ahead of the other.	_____	_____
4. Can name hands, feet, head, and some face parts.	_____	_____
5. Opposes thumb to fingers when grasping objects and releases objects smoothly from finger-thumb grasp.	_____	_____
6. Can walk a two-inch wide line placed on ground, for ten feet.	_____	_____

Four to Four and a Half	YES	NO
1. Forward broad jump, both feet together and clear of ground at the same time.	_____	_____
2. Can hop two or three times on one foot without precision or rhythm.	_____	_____
3. Walks and runs with arm action coordinated with leg action.	_____	_____
4. Can walk a circular line a short distance.	_____	_____
5. Can draw a crude circle.	_____	_____
6. Can imitate a simple line cross using a vertical and horizontal line.	_____	_____

Five to Five and a Half	YES	NO
1. Runs thirty yards in just over eight seconds or less.	_____	_____
2. Balances on one foot (girls 6–8 seconds) (boys 4–6 seconds).	_____	_____
3. Child catches large playground ball bounced to him chest-high from fifteen feet away; four to five times out of five.	_____	_____
4. Rectangle and square drawn differently (one side at a time).	_____	_____
5. Can high jump eight inches or higher over bar with simultaneous two-foot takeoff.	_____	_____
6. Bounces playground ball, using one or two hands, a distance of three to four feet.	_____	_____

Six to Six and a Half	YES	NO
1. Can block print first name in letters 1½ to 2 inches high.	_____	_____
2. Can gallop, if it is demonstrated.	_____	_____
3. Can exert six pounds or more of pressure in grip strength measure.	_____	_____
4. Can walk balance beam 2 inches wide, 6 inches high, and 10 to 12 inches long.	_____	_____
5. Can run sixty feet in about five seconds.	_____	_____
6. Can arise from ground from back lying position, when asked to do so as fast as he can, in two seconds or under.	_____	_____

Source: Cratty, J. *Psychomotor behavior in education and sport.* Springfield, Ill.: Charles C. Thomas, 1974, pp. 61–63.

One aspect of development in which left-handed children sometimes do encounter difficulties, is handwriting. It is hard for children to write languages, such as English, that read from left to right without smearing what they have just written. It is therefore important for parents and teachers to be patient and provide encouragement to left-handed preschoolers and elementary school children who are learning to write.

Next we see that a number of tests have been devised to assess the motor development of young children.

Assessing Motor Development

The Bayley Motor Scale can be used for children through the age of two and a half; the Gesell Developmental Schedules and the Denver Developmental Screening Test can be used for those through the age of six. The Bayley test was designed primarily for very young children, mainly infants, so it is not surprising that postural control, locomotion, and prehensile activity are emphasized and that there is an absence of attention to such important aspects of movement as striking, catching, throwing, jumping, running, and kicking behaviors, which are included on the Gesell and Denver tests.

Application 7.1
Scribbling and Drawing: The Art of Early Childhood

Children's art is a fascinating topic. There are dramatic changes in how children depict what they see. Art provides unique insights into children's perceptual worlds—what they are attending to, how space and distance are viewed, how they experience patterns and forms.

Rhoda Kellogg is a creative teacher who has been watching and guiding young children's artistic endeavors for over thirty years. She has assembled an impressive collection of tens of thousands of drawings produced by more than two thousand preschoolers ranging from two to five years of age.

Adults who are familiar with children's art often view the productions of this age group as meaningless scribbling. Kellogg (1970) has tried to destroy this idea by showing children's productions to be orderly, meaningful, and structured.

A number of different levels of organization are evident in children's drawings. At the earliest ages, children produce *scribbles*. These scribbles are anything but simple or meaningless. There are about twenty kinds of scribbles, and the scribbles tend to be located in specific positions on the page. This position is referred to as a *placement pattern*, and there are about seventeen of them.

At the next level of organization are *emergent diagrams*, followed at subsequent levels by *diagrams, combines*, and *aggregates*. Each adds a level of sophistication and organization superior to the previous one, so that a hierarchy of productions can be seen. Children's attempts to draw such commonplace objects as humans, buildings, trees, flowers, cars, and boats can be related to the hierarchical learning that occurs. Kellogg believes that this hierarchical organization may be universal—that is, observable in all cultures. And she illustrates that this organization of visual forms provides a good description of how art became transformed from its simplistic level to a more mature one in the history of adult art.

In Kellogg's view,

As each child proceeds in self-taught art, he gradually accumulates a visually logical system of line formations. The system is logical in the sense that one sort of line formation leads to another. Whenever he uses art materials without the constraint of adult direction, the child remembers and employs as much of the system as he has taught himself. (p. 51)

. . . What accounts for the prevalence of shapes in spontaneous child art? Why do the various line formations tend to be made in a certain sequence? My analysis supports the belief that the human eye and brain are predisposed to see overall shapes, that this predisposition operates during the interplay of hand and eye in scribbling, that the child makes shapes with increasing purpose and clarity as he grows, and that he favors shapes that are balanced. In addition, the child's early pictorial work is strongly influenced by his previous scribbling, so that his drawing of Humans, Animals, Buildings, Vegetation, and Transportation items reflect the diagrams, combines, aggregates . . . that he has made before. (p. 248)

Scribble 1	Dot
Scribble 2	Single vertical line
Scribble 3	Single horizontal line
Scribble 4	Single diagonal line
Scribble 5	Single curved line
Scribble 6	Multiple vertical line
Scribble 7	Multiple horizontal line
Scribble 8	Multiple diagonal line
Scribble 9	Multiple curved line
Scribble 10	Roving open line
Scribble 11	Roving enclosing line
Scribble 12	Zigzag or waving line
Scribble 13	Single loop line
Scribble 14	Multiple loop line
Scribble 15	Spiral line
Scribble 16	Multiple-line overlaid circle
Scribble 17	Multiple-line circumference circle
Scribble 18	Circular line spread out
Scribble 19	Single crossed circle
Scribble 20	Imperfect circle

Twenty basic scribbles used by young children in drawing; an early stage of art.

. . . Children seem to thrive by making movements which to the adult appear to have no purpose other than pleasure. The movements of the child's body which produce an art work certainly are not made merely for the joy of movement. In fact, these movements aid in the coordination of moving and seeing. (p. 250)

. . . Perhaps scribbling gives the child a sense of body movement that he can enjoy fully because it is "safe" in comparison with the images that he must absorb to move with safety. That is, the child can scribble directional movement with a satisfying vigor far more safely than he can move his whole body. (p. 253)

 Vertical half. The scribblings are confined to one vertical half of the paper.

 Horizontal half. The scribblings are confined to one horizontal half of the paper.

 Two-sided balance. The scribblings are placed on one vertical or horizontal section of the paper to balance scribbles on the other side, with space between.

 Diagonal axis. The scribblings are evenly distributed on a diagonal axis so that two corners are filled and two are left empty.

 Quarter page. The scribblings are confined to a quarter of the paper.

 Two-corner pyramid. The scribblings cover one of the narrow edges of the paper and converge toward the center of the edge opposite, leaving two corners empty and making a pyramidal shape.

 Base-line fan. The scribblings flare up from one edge and move toward one or both of the adjoining edges.

Placement patterns representative of those produced by young children.

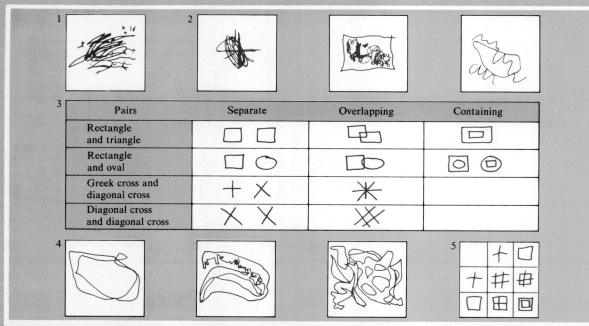

Later stages of children's art: (1) emergent diagram; (2) diagrams and scribbles; (3) combines; (4) aggregates; (5) combines.

The Denver Developmental Screening Test deserves further mention because it was created as a simple, inexpensive, and fast way to diagnose delayed development in children from birth through six years of age. The test is individually administered and includes an evaluation of language and personal-social ability in addition to separate assessments of gross and fine motor skills. Gross motor skills that are evaluated include the child's ability to sit, walk, broad jump, pedal a tricycle, throw a ball overhand, catch a bounced ball, hop on one foot, and balance on one foot. Fine motor-adaptive skills that are evaluated include the child's ability to stack cubes, reach for objects, and draw a man.

One promising test that provides a more detailed assessment of gross motor skills is the DeOreo Fundamental Motor Skills Inventory (DeOreo, 1976). Performance is evaluated in eleven categories: striking, balancing, skipping, jumping, galloping, hopping, catching, running, climbing, throwing, and kicking. Items are divided into product components, such as "Can the child run thirty-five yards in less than ten seconds?" and process components, such as "While running does the child keep his body erect or inclined backwards?"

Training Programs That Promote Physical Development

In the late 1940s a syndrome of characteristics was developed to describe the underachieving child; it included motor clumsiness (Strauss & Lehtinen, 1947), hyperactivity, and perceptual disturbances, as well as reading and writing difficulties. In the 1950s a number of other views followed, including the basic idea that "movement" was the basis for the development of intelligence. It was argued that sound intellectual and perceptual functioning depend on good motor functioning. Further, it was stressed that if the child is clumsy, perceptual difficulties—including incompetence in a variety of academic skills—are inevitable. It was also argued that to improve perceptual functioning and other academic skills, it is necessary for the young child to participate in a number of sensorimotor (or perceptual-motor) tasks (Getman, 1952; Kephart, 1971).

Practices based on these ideas began to proliferate in the United States during the 1950s and continued in the 1960s and 1970s. Young children spent endless hours walking balance beams, touching balls suspended from strings, and making angels in the snow. The programs evidenced some desirable outcomes but some undesirable ones as well. Among the desirable outcomes were that educators began to focus on the more clumsy children in their schools, and at times the movement programs to which these clumsy children

Motor skills tests assess fine motor skills such as manual dexterity.

were exposed actually helped them to improve their motor coordination. Children who at one time were often ignored now were being given extra attention. Other children who had perhaps been exposed too much to the printed page were given breaks in their school-day by being encouraged for example, to jump on trampolines, a sort of break that spaced the practice of reading in beneficial ways.

Unfortunately, many parents came to believe with almost hysterical adherence that simple motor activities and skills training would improve the academic skills of their children. When improvement was not forthcoming it was frustrating for both parent and child. In too many instances a less than helpful motor program was substituted for sound academic tutoring in such subjects as reading, and clumsy children were exposed to too narrow a range of motor activities. Such strategies are not likely to improve reading competencies, and they are not as good as other programs at improving motor skills. Furthermore, many children who are free of motor problems are still being placed in stilted and overly structured programs of perceptual-motor training when they would better be left alone to play in normal ways that would tax and improve their perceptual and motor abilities to a far greater extent.

Although many aspects of physical and motor development are the result of maturational processes, it is important that children experience an environment that allows them to practice their physical and motor skills. Training programs designed to promote healthy physical development can be divided into three types: physical education, perceptual-motor, and movement.

The Play Spaces of Young Children

Most preschool teachers are hard pressed to provide equipment that can accommodate the wide individual variation in skillfulness and readiness in their children. Commercial equipment usually is suited to a narrow and often highly skilled range of children. Rackets, bats, and paddles often are so long and heavy that young children quickly abandon them. In one investigation (Halverson, 1966), lightweight striking, throwing, and kicking equipment was shown to encourage more mature and efficient gross motor activity and to foster faster gross motor learning than when young children were exposed to traditional equipment.

Three guidelines may help to provide for a wide range of skillfulness and physical readiness on the part of young children. First, pieces of equipment that have the same form but vary in size can be grouped together. Second, equipment that children can adjust to accommodate their own development levels—for example, a batting-*t* fitted with a length of rubber tubing so the child can raise or lower the height of a supported ball—can be selected. Third, children can be provided with single pieces of equipment that accommodate wide ranges of developmental levels—for example, a walking board that is very wide at one end and is increasingly narrow at the other end.

At present, most movement environments stress climbing, hanging, and swinging. Little attention is devoted to other types of gross and fine motor behavior such as striking, catching, throwing, kicking, balancing, rolling objects, rolling oneself, zipping, lacing, buttoning, cutting, locking, latching, snapping, buckling, stacking, fitting, pushing and pulling, dancing, and swimming. Many experts on children's physical development believe more attention needs to be given to incorporating the means for greater varieties of movement into the play spaces of young children (Herkowitz, 1978).

Physical Education Programs
For young children, most programs strive to balance free play with teacher-directed activities targeted at specific skills. In elementary school, children spend more time in competitive games, individual activities designed to promote body and motor development, and dance activities. Calisthentics and exercise routines are also common.

Perceptual-Motor Training Programs
Perceptual-motor training programs focus on input or reception, and how it influences the child's performance, in contrast to physical education programs, which emphasize performance alone. A majority of the perceptual—motor programs have been designed by experts in special education who hoped that such programs would remedy children's learning difficulties (e.g., Cruikshank, 1967; Kephart, 1971). Physical skills stressed in such programs include eye-hand and eye-foot coordination and locomotor skills. Activities designed to enhance hand-eye coordination include tossing, catching, rolling, and bouncing. Eye-foot coordination exercises include kicking, leaping, and climbing. Locomotor activities focus on walking, running, jumping, hopping, sliding, skipping, and leaping.

The educators who designed the perceptual-motor programs made grandiose claims that they would increase the academic success of children with learning problems. The available empirical data (Lahey, 1975) suggest that such claims are false. Most children, however, can benefit from the systematic practice of perceptual-motor skills. Perceptual-motor coordination is a significant aspect of development in itself—consequently, it is important that we be sensitive to any child's perceptual-motor development, not just a child with learning problems.

Movement Programs
The third type of training program to promote children's physical development involves movement. Two aspects of movement that such programs attempt to improve are **expressive movement**—in which the body is seen as a medium for the expression of ideas and feelings (e.g., dance and drama)—and **objective movement**—in which the goal is to develop the body's power (e.g., gymnastics and athletics). Activities are designed to teach children skillful use of their body through combinations of movements rooted in principles of time, strength, space, and flow (Lundsteen & Bernstein-Tarrow, 1981).

Much of the development of play spaces for children has been based on intuition and hunches rather than any sound research evidence. In application 7.2

Balance is an important aspect of perceptual-motor development in children.

Most movement programs stress climbing, hanging, and swinging.

Eating habits are ingrained very early in life.

Nutrition and Physical Development

It is widely recognized that what we eat affects our skeletal growth, body shape, and susceptibility to disease. Recognizing that nutrition is important for the child's growth and development, the federal government provides money for school lunch programs. On the average, the preschool child requires approximately 1,400 to 1,800 calories a day. Children with unbalanced or malnourished diets show below average physical development by the third year of life. Some evidence suggests that when the appropriate nutrients are introduced into the diet of the malnourished child, physical development will improve. For instance, when provided milk supplements over a twenty-month period, deprived children between the ages of four and fifteen showed gains of 3.6 percent in height and 29 percent in weight.

What is an appropriate diet for a preschool child? Clearly there is individual variation and experts may disagree on detail, but in general the diet should include fats, carbohydrates, protein, vitamins, and minerals.

A particular concern in our culture is the amount of fat in our diet, and as we emphasized earlier, eating habits get ingrained very early in life. In table 7.3 you will find the number of calories and the percent of fat in the offerings of a number of fast-food restaurants. Most fast-food meals are high in protein, especially the meat and dairy products. But the average American has no need to be concerned about obtaining protein. What must be of concern is the vast number of young children who are being weaned on fast foods that not only are high in protein but also have a high fat content. (It is during the preschool years that many individuals get their first taste of fast foods.) The American Heart Association recommends that the daily limit for calories from fat should be approximately 35 percent. Compare this figure with the higher figures in table 7.3. Clearly, many fast-food meals contribute to excessive fat intake by young children.

Cultural Factors

Cultures in which children are fed lovingly and in which food is a source of great pleasure later become highly resistant to change. A major obstacle in relieving protein-calorie malnutrition is the resistance of cultures to the introduction of extra foods, and particularly protein foods, during the early years of the child's life. Strong resistance often centers around different types of foods: (1) Foods generally avoided at all ages, such as milk in Thailand; (2) foods thought unsuitable for infants and toddlers, such as meat in Guatemala; (3) foods linked to physiological processes, permitted only after certain traditional ceremonies, such as puberty rites; (4) overvalued foods, such as plantain in

we explore the world of play spaces for young children in an attempt to provide some guidelines for the exposure of children to an environment that promotes healthy physical development.

So far we have seen that there are important changes in physical and motor development during the preschool years. Another important aspect of physical development in early childhood is nutrition, as we see next.

Nutrition

Early feeding and eating habits are important aspects of development. We saw in chapter 6 that nutritional deprivation in the first several years of life has important implications for emotional development in middle childhood. Here we look further at the role of nutrition in physical development and intelligence. In particular, cultural factors in nutrition are highlighted.

Table 7.3
Fat and Calorie Intake of Selected Fast-Food Meals

Selected Meal	Calories	Percent of Calories from Fat
Burger King Whopper, fries, vanilla shake	1250	43
Big Mac, fries, chocolate shake	1100	41
McDonald's Quarter-Pounder with cheese	418	52
McDonald's Filet O'Fish sandwich	402	56
Pizza Hut ten-inch pizza with sausage, mushrooms, pepperoni, and green pepper	1035	35
Arby's roast beef plate (roast beef sandwich, two potato patties and cole slaw), chocolate shake	1200	30
Kentucky Fried Chicken dinner (three pieces chicken, mashed potatoes and gravy, cole slaw, roll)	830	50
Arthur Treacher's fish and chips (two pieces breaded, fried fish, french fries, cola drink)	900	42
Typical restaurant "diet plate" (hamburger patty, cottage cheese, etc.)	638	63

Source: Used with permission. Virginia Demoss, "Good, the Bad and the Edible." *Runner's World*, June 1980, p. 45.

Uganda and rice in Thailand; (5) disease-associated foods, such as mangoes in India, which are thought to produce jaundice. The style of living of the entire community and culture is often a decisive factor in how the young child is fed and how often.

Certain other cultural factors work against sound nutritional habits and are a source of conflict when health-interested outsiders suggest changes. In Malaysia, for instance, fish is among the best sources of animal protein, and yet fish is seen as unsuitable for young children because of its alleged capacity for producing intestinal worms.

Although it is widely known that what we eat affects our skeletal growth, body shape, and susceptibility to disease, we often fail to recognize that it also might affect our level of intellectual functioning. Next we look at this possibility.

Nutrition and Intellectual Development

The child who consistently does not eat breakfast and does not make up for this deficiency during the course of the day may not attend well to what is being taught because he feels weak and weary. When a difficult problem is given to him, he may lack the energy to sustain effort needed for solving it.

Perhaps the most direct evidence of the effects of nutrition is provided by animal studies, which have shown that the development of the brain is related to protein intake. In the following study (Zamenhof, van Marthens, & Margolis, 1968), one month before impregnation one group of female rats was placed on a high-protein diet, and a similar group was placed on a low-protein diet. When the brain and body weights of the offspring were measured, the weights of the offspring of mothers on the high-protein diet were greater than those of the offspring of mothers on the low-protein diet. The brains of the mothers themselves were subsequently analyzed: the brains of the mothers on the high-protein diet had more cells than did those of the mothers on the low-protein diet. Thus we may conclude that the nutrition of the mother may affect not only the development of her own brain but the development of her offspring's brain as well.

In another study, two groups of black South African infants, all one year old, were extremely malnourished. The children in one group were given adequate nourishment during the next six years; there was no intervention in the poor nutrition of the other group. After the seventh year, the poorly nourished group of children had significantly lower IQs than the adequately nourished group did (Stoch & Smythe, in Bayley, 1970).

Summary

Physical development slows markedly in early childhood as compared to infancy. Nonetheless, gross motor skills develop at a much faster pace than fine motor skills during the preschool years. Advances in height and weight occur, although the preschool child appears slimmer than during infancy. Locomotion and manipulative skills improve markedly during the preschool years. Many attempts at developing early childhood programs have focused on the importance of movement. Unfortunately, such programs have produced some undesirable as well as desirable effects. Among the desirable effects is that a number of heretofore overlooked clumsy children have been given attention, although the nature of the physical development program to which they have been exposed too often has been narrow. Furthermore, a number of children who could have profitably spent more time in the development of appropriate reading and academic skills have been made to spend too much time in simple movement exercises. The source of the problem has been the misfounded belief that through relatively simple movement programs the intellectual development of young children can be advanced almost infinitely. Unfortunately, many young children with no motor problems at all also were placed in such simplistic programs.

Physical development programs are an important aspect of early childhood development. Three such programs that have merit are: physical education, perceptual-motor, and movement.

More attention needs to be given to the play spaces of children, particularly because large muscle development is such an important aspect of physical development in early childhood. To this end, more effort should be expended in the development of equipment that provides for individual variation in physical skills and readiness.

Nutrition is another important aspect of the physical development of young children. Nutrition can influence not only physical development but intellectual and emotional development as well. Cultural factors are important in understanding children's nutrition, and within a culture socioeconomic standards are also significant. A lack of adequate protein particularly plagues many young children in the developing nations. In the United States most children receive adequate protein, but they often receive too much fat.

Key Terms

deprivation dwarfism   objective movement

expressive movement   perceptual-motor

handedness   training program

Review Questions

1. Discuss the changes in height, weight, fat, and muscle that characterize most children during early childhood. Point out individual differences and some growth deviations.
2. Outline the growth of motor development during early childhood.
3. What is the course of the development of handedness?
4. How can we better assess motor development?
5. Discuss the historical development of movement programs.
6. Outline three types of physical development programs now available for early childhood.
7. What aspects of children's play spaces need to be improved?

Further Readings

Cratty, B. *Psychomotor behavior in education and sport.* Springfield, Ill.: Charles C. Thomas, 1974.
Bryan Cratty is Director of the Perceptual-Motor Learning Laboratory at UCLA. He has spent considerable time in researching and conceptualizing better ways to enhance the physical development of children. This book presents a number of his selected articles, including information about the clumsy child, movement abilities in early childhood, and the role of physical development in early childhood education. Reasonably easy reading.

Ridenour, M. C. (Ed.), *Motor development.* Princeton, N.J.: Princeton Book Company, 1978.
A number of experts on the motor development of young children present their ideas on how to optimize such development. The book includes information on improving play spaces, movement experiences, evaluating motor development, and a list of annotated references. Reasonably easy reading.

8 Cognitive Development

Imagine . . . that you are visiting a Montessori preschool. What are you likely to see?

Introduction
Preoperational Thought
The Information Processing Perspective
The Roots of Information Processing Theory
Attention

Intelligence
Definition of Intelligence
Genetic-Environmental Factors
Genetic Influences on Intelligence
Environmental Influences on Intelligence
Intelligence: The Complex Influence of Genetic,
Biological, and Environmental Experiences

Application 8.1 Foster Grandparents and Institutionalized Young Children

Language Development
Later Speech Sounds
The Later Stages of Roger Brown's Theory of
Language Development
Egocentrism and Communication

Self-Taught Reading and Prereading Skills
Programs
Writing: What Is It?
"Genie" and Childhood as a Critical Period in
Language Development

Early Childhood Education
Compensatory Education
Head Start Children in Adulthood
Project Follow Through

Application 8.2 "Sesame Street" — Education Through Television

Summary

Key Terms

Review Questions

Further Readings

I magine . . . that you are visiting a Montessori preschool. What are you likely to see?

Maria Montessori was an Italian physician-turned-educator who developed a revolutionary approach to the education of young children at the beginning of the twentieth century. She began her work with a group of mentally retarded children in Rome. She was highly successful in teaching them to read, write, and pass exams meant for normal children. Some time later she turned her attention to poor children in the slums of Rome and had similar success in teaching them. Her approach has since been adopted extensively in private nursery schools, making its greatest impact on preschool education.

Montessori's approach is simultaneously a philosophy of education, a psychology of the child, and practical educational exercises that can be employed to teach children. Children are allowed a great deal of freedom and spontaneity to choose classwork, and they may move freely from one activity to another. Each child is encouraged to work independently, to complete tasks once they have been undertaken, and to put materials away in assigned places. The teacher serves as a facilitator rather than as the controller of learning, pointing out interesting ways to explore the various curriculum materials and offering help to any child who asks.

Montessori identifies four different sensitive periods, each concerning a different facet of development: the development of sensory abilities, the development of an awareness of order, the development of a sensitivity to language; and the development of a sensitivity toward movement.

A brief description is given of several different exercises used in the Montessori classroom to promote sensory and perceptual growth. The examples indicate the creative materials Montessori used to provide children with perceptual experiences as well as the unique way the Montessori program makes use of them.

Montessori (1967) here describes the materials to be used for teaching the young child tactile discrimination—that is, discrimination of different textures by touch:

a. a long rectangle plank divided into two equal rectangles, one covered with very smooth, the other with rough, paper
b. another board of the same shape as the first, but covered with alternating strips of smooth and rough paper
c. another board like the former, having strips of emery and sandpaper in decreasing grades of coarseness
d. a board on which are placed pieces of paper of the same size, but of different grades of smoothness, varying from parchment to the very smooth paper of the first plank

These boards, which keep the various objects to be touched in a fixed position, serve to prepare a child's hand for touching things lightly, and they also teach him how to make a systematic distinction. (p. 121)

The child is encouraged to stroke different areas of the board, to name the textures that are felt, and gradually to learn to discriminate differences between rough and smooth surfaces and to arrange them in order from roughest to smoothest.

Montessori also describes the exercises employed to teach the child about taste and smell:

Our second attempt was . . . to organize games for the senses which the children could repeat by themselves. We had a child smell fresh violets and jasmine; or, late in May, we used the roses gathered for the flower vases. We then blindfolded a child, saying to him: "Now we are going to give you something—some flowers." Another child would bring a bunch of violets close to his nose and he would have to recognize them. Then, as a test of the strength of an odor, he was offered a single flower, or a quantity of them.

Then we decided it would be easier to let the environment do much of this educational work. . . . We decided to sprinkle perfumes systematically about with the idea of making them progressively more delicate. . . .

The children become quite interested in distinguishing different tastes and coming to recognize the four basic flavors. Sweet and salt are both pleasant, but even bitter is tried as an experiment, and sour, especially in various fruits, is distinguished in various degrees.

Once interest has been aroused in tastes and their definite limitations, the world of fragrances is more clearly distinguished in its countless varieties of mixed sensations of taste and smell experienced in eating and drinking, as for example in milk, fresh or dried bread, soup, fruit, and so forth. And the tactile sensations of the tongue, which arise from contact with sticky, oily, and other types of substances, are distinguished from the sensations of taste and smell through an effort of the mind which is a real exploration of oneself and one's environment. (pp. 128–29)

Finally, Montessori describes exercises devoted to the perception of sound.

For the studying of noises, we have in our present system some rather simple and elementary material. This consists in boxes of wood (or cardboard). These boxes are made in pairs and are so constructed that a series of them will produce graduated noises. Just as with the other sense materials, the boxes are jumbled together and then paired off according to the noise they produce when struck. Then by judging the differences among the boxes in one series a child attempts to put them in a graduated order.

For the training of the musical sense, we have adopted a series of bells. . . . Each one of the bells is mounted on a separate stand. They constitute a group of objects which seem to be identical but which, when struck with a little hammer, reproduce [different] notes. Thus the only perceptible difference is one of sound.

The individual bells, which come in a double series, can be moved about. They can therefore be mixed up just as are the other objects used in the training of the senses. (p. 148)

These, then, are some of the exercises employed in the Montessori curriculum to teach children about the senses of touch, smell and taste, and hearing. They constitute a unique approach to the education of children's

senses and perception. Many of these techniques have been employed in contemporary preschool education and continue to be used in present-day Montessori schools.

While the Montessori approach to preschool education is favored by some psychologists and educators, others believe that the social development of children is neglected. For example, Montessori attempts to foster independence and the development of cognitive skills. However, verbal interaction between the teacher and child and extensive peer interaction are deemphasized. The critics of Montessori also argue that imaginative play is restricted. Later in this chapter, various types of preschool programs other than Montessori's will be described. Keep the Montessori approach in mind so you can compare its focus with these programs.

Introduction

In this chapter we continue our discussion of the child's cognitive development. Our discussion of cognitive development begins with an overview of Piaget's ideas about the stage of cognitive development he calls preoperational thought. We also take our first look at a very important perspective of cognitive development that is getting increased attention from developmental psychologists—information processing. Attention, perception, memory, thinking, and problem solving are among the important cognitive processes involved in the information processing perspective. We will describe the main points of the information processing perspective and pay particular attention to how it can be used to explain cognitive development in early childhood.

Another important aspect of cognition is the concept of intelligence. We attempt to define it and explore its genetic and environmental origins. Our discussion of language development continues, as we look further at the development of speech sounds, provide more information about Roger Brown's stages of language development, describe important aspects of prereading skills, including a description of what writing is, and evaluate whether childhood is a critical period in language development.

We also explore the nature of early childhood education. Various forms of preschool education are described, including efforts to evaluate the effectiveness of various compensatory education programs for impoverished children.

Preoperational Thought

Piaget's preoperational stage lasts from about two to seven years of age, cutting across the preschool and early elementary school years. During this time the child's symbolic system expands and use of language and perceptual images moves well beyond the abilities at the end of the sensorimotor period. Despite these advances, however, a number of limitations in the child's thought cause it to fall far short of adult thought, or even of thought characteristics of a child in the late middle school years.

At this stage the child's thought is not yet governed by full-fledged operations. **Operations** are internalized sets of actions that allow the child to do mentally what before was done physically. They are highly organized and conform to certain rules and principles of logic. The operations appear in one form in the concrete-operations period and in a more advanced form in the formal-operations period.

The preoperational stage is sometimes divided into an earlier phase (two to four years of age) and a later phase (five to seven years of age), with the limitations in operational thought appearing in full bloom during the earlier phase and withering away in the later phase. This development has prompted some people to call the later phase a transition period from the operational stage to the next stage of development, concrete operations (Flavell, 1972). Many children in the so-called transitional phase of the preoperational stage may give the appearance of concrete thinking in many situations, and progress toward concrete thinking about a problem may be speeded up with concentrated training efforts.

The most salient feature of preoperational thought is the child's **egocentrism,** that is, the inability to distinguish easily between his or her own perspective and that of someone else. The following telephone conversation between four-year-old Mary, who is at home, and her father, who is at work, is an example.
Father Mary, is Mommy there?
 Mary (Silence; nods.)
Father Mary, may I speak to Mommy?
 Mary (Again, silence; nods.)
Mary's response is egocentric in the sense that she fails to consider her father's perspective before formulating a reply. A nonegocentric thinker would have responded verbally. There are various other perspective deficits in the child's attempts to reconstruct how other people feel and think and to communicate with others (Shantz, 1983).

Another facet of preoperational thought is animism, the belief that inanimate objects have human qualities and are capable of human action. Remarks like "That tree pushed the leaf off and it fell down" or "The sidewalk was angry with me. It made me fall down" reveal this notion. Animism is a failure to distinguish the appropriate occasion for employing the human and the nonhuman perspectives.

Yet another characteristic of preoperational thought is the child's failure to *conserve* properties of objects in the face of superficial changes in their appearance. Consider the child confronted by two identical glass beakers, A and B, filled with milk to the same height. Beside them is an unfilled beaker, C. Beaker C is tall and narrow, beakers A and B are shorter and have a larger diameter (see figure 8.1). The milk is poured from B into C, and the child is asked whether the amounts of milk in A and C are the same or different. The nonconserver will say the amounts are different, tending to judge sameness or difference in terms of the relative heights or widths of the two containers. The child fails to understand that both containers hold the same amount of milk, even though they look different.

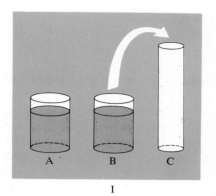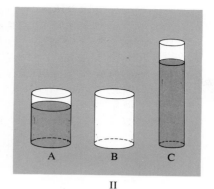

Figure 8.1 Liquid conservation.

The thoughts of a child in the preoperational stage involve increased symbolism.

The **conservation** concept is probably the most well-researched problem in Piaget's theory. In a recent year, for example, well over 100 articles appeared in scientific journals on this topic alone, and, cumulatively there are probably more than 1,000 studies involving the conservation construct. Investigators have examined conservation of a dozen or more attributes of objects—for example, number, weight, volume, area, and discontinuous quantity (Flavell, 1977). Experts have also related conservation ability to a host of other skills such as early reading ability, early arithmetic skills, reflection-impulsivity, gender concepts, and moral reasoning, to name just a few.

Conservation also may be important in thinking about people as well. The child is often faced with physical changes in the appearance of significant social figures. For example, Mom has her hair cut in a new way, Dad grows a moustache, or the teacher comes to school with a broken arm. To what extent do these physical changes foster the child's belief that the adult

has changed in some physical way or in some psychological way (the adult is happier, sadder, warmer, more hostile)? Perhaps more important, to what extent do these physical changes foster a belief that the adult's attitude has changed toward the child? Unfortunately there is little evidence to show how extensive such beliefs might be for children in the preoperational stage. The one exception is the development of gender, or sex-role conservation (Emmerich, Goldman, & Sharabany, in press; Kohlberg, 1969). The young child at this stage fails to realize "once a boy, always a boy; once a girl, always a girl." The child believes that the "sex" of a doll changes if such characteristics as hair, dress, and size are changed.

Another important limitation of the child's structure of thought in the preoperational stage is the inability to form and reason with hierarchical classification. Faced with a random collection of objects that can be grouped on the basis of two or more properties,

Cognitive Development 185

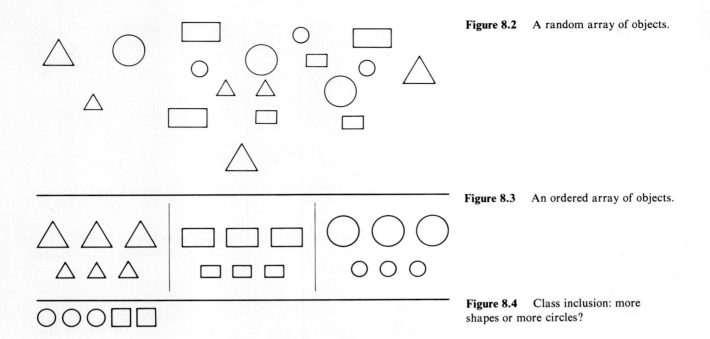

Figure 8.2   A random array of objects.

Figure 8.3   An ordered array of objects.

Figure 8.4   Class inclusion: more shapes or more circles?

the child is seldom able to use these properties consistently to sort the objects into what an adult would refer to as a good classification.

For example, look at the collection of objects shown in figure 8.2. An adult would respond to the direction "Put the things together that you believe belong together" with a sorting based on the characteristics of size and shape taken together. The adult's sorting might look something like that shown in figure 8.3. This kind of problem is often referred to as free classification.

The child's inability to reason with simple hierarchy is evident in a widely studied class inclusion problem (Winer, 1980). Suppose a child is shown a picture of objects as in figure 8.4 and asked, Are there more shapes in front of you or more circles? The child in this stage would probably be puzzled by the question but in any event would answer that there are more circles. He or she has a hard time thinking about the whole set of forms taken collectively while simultaneously thinking about the subset, the three circles. The child tends to focus on the various subsets (in this case there are two, circles and squares) for purposes of the comparison, despite what the question calls for.

An important social consequence of these deficits in the young child's thinking with classes is that he or she fails to understand (a) the various ways people can be cross-classified with regard to social characteristics and (b) the different ways people can be compared with a group that includes them. Consider the cross-classification problem first. Suppose a little girl is given a list of her peers to divide into groups according to whether

they are friends or enemies and whether they are boys or girls. She would rarely be able to arrive at a sorting arrangement with the following distinct clusters: friendly boys, unfriendly boys, friendly girls, unfriendly girls. Now consider class inclusion. Suppose a little boy lived on a street where five adults and six other children lived. The teacher asks: Are there more children or more people living on your block? The little boy would probably say that more children live there. The important point about these social classification and inclusion examples is that the child's thoughts about people are constrained in many important ways by preoperational limitations.

David Elkind (1978) illustrated one of these shortcomings in a series of studies to determine children's understanding of religious concepts such as God, denomination (Catholic, Protestant, or Jew), and religious rules. When asked the question, Can you be a Protestant and an American at the same time? the young six- and seven-year-olds frequently said no, whereas the older children (nine-, eleven-, and fourteen-year-olds) increasingly understood the possibility for simultaneous cross-classification.

Another feature of preoperational thought is that the child is incapable of serialization, that is, ordering a set of objects from least to greatest along some clearly quantifiable dimension. The approach to early childhood education described in the Imagine section of this chapter—the Montessori method—includes tasks that are likely to enhance the young child's ability to order objects in a serial fashion.

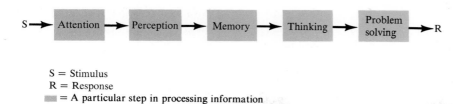

Figure 8.5 General stages of information processing.

S = Stimulus
R = Response
▨ = A particular step in processing information
▨➔▨ = Consecutive steps in processing information

Two organizing forces in preoperational thought are **centration** and **irreversibility.** Many of the limitations of this stage are caused by these two forces. Centration is a narrow concentration on one feature of the situation to the exclusion of others. In the liquid conservation problem, for example, the child may focus on the liquid as being higher in its new container but not on the fact that it is simultaneously narrower than before.

Irreversibility can also be illustrated by reference to the conservation problem. One way for the child to see that the amount of liquid has remained unchanged is by mentally reversing the action—pouring the milk from beaker C into beaker B—and imagining the result. The child in the preoperational stage cannot do this (Piaget, 1977).

Piaget's theory focuses on how the child *thinks* and *represents* the world and how these capabilities change with development. There is another perspective, however, from which to view cognitive development. It is called the **information processing approach** (Klahr & Wallace, 1975; Siegler, 1983).

The Information Processing Perspective

The information processing perspective, in which mental activity is synonymous with the processing of information, is concerned with the nature of information children are capable of picking up from the flow of environmental stimulation around them. The various stages involved in this pickup—attention, perception, memory, thinking, and problem solving—are presented in figure 8.5. Cognitive psychologists who study how the child processes information also are interested in the mechanism by which information is absorbed and transformed. The example given in figure 8.5 is a necessarily oversimplified one. For example, each hypothetical stage (e.g., perception) may overlap with other stages (e.g., memory) or be composed of several substages. Or, the child may generate an idea (thinking) that is placed back in memory for awhile for further reflection. The thoughts and memories may in this fashion flow back and forth.

The Roots of Information Processing Theory

In the context of recent history, information processing has three clear influential sources (Siegler, 1983). The first is the field of **communications.** Beginning over a quarter of a century ago, communication scientists sought to develop a general model of how someone sends a message over a particular **channel** of communication to a specific **receiver** (e.g., Broadbent, 1958). In doing so, scientists developed ideas about how to define the information contained in a message, the capacity of different channels to transmit information, and the processes by which receivers pick up information. The theory was developed along physical science lines, drawing upon physics and electronics and treating radio and television transmissions as prototypical cases of communication phenomena. However, the human was quickly added as a special case to explain the same phenomena, with the different human sensory systems treated as the sources for information pickup (e.g., seeing, hearing, feeling).

A second, closely related development was the growth of computer sciences and the interest in using the computer to model theories of artificial intelligence (e.g., Newell & Simon, 1972). Computers are essentially high-speed information systems that can be constructed and programmed. It was reasoned that computers offered a logical and concrete simplification of how information might be processed in the human mind. For example, both the computer and the mind employ *logic* and *rules*. Both have *limits* imposed on their capabilities to handle information and on what types of information can be processed. Some of these limitations have to do with the physical **hardware**—for the computer, the physical machinery; for the human, the limits of the brain and sensory systems. Other limitations are imposed by the **software**—for the computer, the programming; for the human, presumably, learning and development. Many experts believe that as progress is made in understanding computers, we will gain an increased understanding of how the human mind works. Some go so far as to claim that unless we have a working computer program that enumerates the steps needed to complete human cognitive activity, we really don't understand how the human mind might solve it (e.g., Simon, 1980). Thus much (but not all) of contemporary work on information processing is devoted to using the computer to model the steps involved in solving a variety of logical problems confronted by people in the everyday contexts of school (e.g., reading and mathematics), work (e.g., decision making), and leisure activities (e.g., playing chess).

The third development that has influenced the information processing field focuses on advances in the field of modern linguistics (discussed earlier in chapter 5). From such scholars as Noam Chomsky (1965) have come brilliant models of how to describe the structure of language and the rules underlying linguistic productions. Because language is among the highest achievements of humans, it is a good candidate for building models of cognition. Information processing psychologists have used models of language to understand how rules are organized in people's minds, how natural events are structured, and how people use rules to interpret events (Schank & Abelson, 1977).

We turn now to the first cognitive process described in the information processing paradigm displayed in figure 8.5—attention. Later, in chapter 10, we will look more closely at other cognitive processes in the information processing perspective—memory, thinking, and problem solving.

Attention

Simply described, **attention** consists of noticing an event (stimulus) in the environment. Our world consists of a bewildering array of stimuli, and it is impossible to process all or even a significant portion of the stimuli at any one time. William James (1898) described this overwhelming environment as a "blooming, buzzing" confusion over which the person must exercise some selectivity and choice. Remember that attention also is considered to be an important cognitive process in children's imitation (e.g., Bandura's view, chapters 2 and 4).

There seem to be great changes in a child's ability to pay attention during the early childhood years. The toddler, for example, wanders around a good deal, shifts attention from one activity to another, and generally seems to spend very little time focused on any one object or event. The preschooler, by comparison, is often seen playing a game or watching a television program for a half hour. The changes in ability to pay attention continue beyond the preschool years into the first or second year of school. In the classroom children are able to observe the teacher for extended periods of time, and they can pore over their books in long periods of independent study. These demands on attention exceed what was required of the preschooler, who is generally free to move about in various play activities. These apparent changes in attention have a dramatic influence on the child's learning (Stevenson, 1972).

The young preschool child who spends long periods of time at play or watching television does not have the same extended attention span for learning problems presented by psychologists, however. Researchers feel fortunate when they can sustain a three-year-old's attention for ten minutes and a two-year-old's for even two minutes (Perlmutter, 1980; Wellman, Ritter, & Flavell, 1975).

Because of this difficulty in working with very young children, there is little scientific information available about the changes in attention that occur in children from one to three years of age. However, a number of people researching the impact of educational television on young children have combined an interest in measuring the child's television viewing behavior with an interest in measuring the child's learning of television material.

In one study the attention of children from two to four years of age to an episode of "Sesame Street" was examined (Anderson & Levin, 1976). The children watched the program with their mothers in a setting resembling a living room. The youngest children often got up to play with toys or turned and talked to other people in the room. These patterns of distraction declined among the older children.

So far we have surveyed two major perspectives that focus on children's cognition—the cognitive developmental view and the information processing view. The third major perspective on cognition is called the psychometric approach—**psychometric** because the view invariably involves the use of measurement-based tests to assess cognition. Most often when cognitive activity is discussed from the psychometric perspective, it is referred to as **intelligence.**

Intelligence

In everyday conversation we often equate *intelligence* with IQ. When asked what IQ and intelligence are, most children and adults respond, "That's how smart you are." Intelligence must be more than just IQ (an abbreviation for the intelligence quotient that is derived from performance on intelligence tests).

Although most of us have an idea of what intelligence is, not everybody defines it in the same way. Psychologists and educators have been trying to pin down a definition of intelligence for many years.

Definition of Intelligence

One definition of intelligence emphasizes its global nature: intelligence is "the global capacity of the individual to act purposefully, to think rationally, and to deal effectively with the environment" (Wechsler, 1958, p. 7). Another definition stresses the global nature of intelligence as well as its genetic heritage: intelligence is "innate, general cognitive ability" (Burt, 1955, p. 162). Other definitions give specific abilities of the individual and learning more prominent roles. And, finally, the simplest—perhaps too simplistic—definition of intelligence has existed for many years: "Intelligence is what the tests measure" (Boring, 1923, p. 35).

The origins of interest in intelligence testing can be traced to general psychology and its concern for measurement. In particular, the work of Sir Francis Galton in the latter part of the nineteenth century served as the background for the development of interest in intelligence and intelligence testing. Galton was intrigued by the possibility that intelligence might be genetically determined and could be measured empirically. His overall interest was in individual differences, and his work on intelligence was part of this interest.

Individual differences simply refer to the consistent, stable ways individuals differ from one another. The entire psychological testing movement was (and still is) concerned with how individuals think, act, and feel in a consistent manner and in relation to how other individuals think, act, and feel. Because measurement has played such a prominent role in the history of inquiry about intelligence, various measures of intelligence will be presented in considerable detail. A discussion of specific tests of intelligence appears in chapter 10 on physical development and intelligence, because it is during the elementary school years that many children are given IQ tests. But there are many other aspects of intelligence that deserve attention during the early childhood years as well, among them the role of genetic-environmental factors in determining intelligence.

Genetic-Environmental Factors

Is intelligence due mainly to heredity or mainly to environment? The answer, of course, is that neither heredity nor environment acts alone; they interact to affect intelligence. The nature of this interaction is complex, and experts point out that unfortunately little is known about the specific input of genetics to intelligence (Scarr-Salapatek, 1975). What is known, however, does suggest that heredity cannot be ignored as an important influence on intelligence.

Genetic Influences on Intelligence
What is the influence of heredity in the broad range of normal and superior intelligence? Arthur Jensen (1969) examined the research literature that addresses this question. The most compelling information concerns the similarity of IQ for individuals who vary on a dimension of genetic similarity. If hereditary variation

As children grow through the preschool years, their attention improves.

among people contributes to differences in IQ, then individuals who have very similar genetic endowments should have very similar IQs, whereas individuals with very different endowments should have very different IQs. Identical twins have identical genetic endowments, so their IQs should be very similar. Nonidentical (fraternal) twins and ordinary siblings are less similar genetically and so should have less similar IQs. Children from different parents are the least similar genetically and should have the least similar IQs. If relevant groups existed in each of these categories, the correlation based on pairs of children should be high for identical twins, lower for fraternal twins and ordinary siblings, and lowest for unrelated children. The graph in figure 8.6 illustrates these correlations.

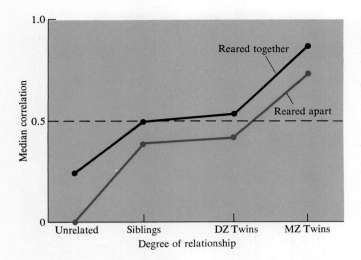

Figure 8.6 The influence of environmental similarity and biological relatedness on the similarity of IQ. From Jensen, Arthur R. "How Much Can We Boost IQ and Scholastic Achievement?" *Harvard Educational Review* 39— 1969:50. Copyright © 1969 by President and Fellows of Harvard College. Reprinted by permission.

On the basis of this kind of thinking and some complex calculations, Jensen places the heritability quotient at about .80 for intelligence. However, it must be noted that many scholars criticize Jensen's work, and few accept his estimate without qualification.

Perhaps most important is the very definition of intelligence. Standard IQ tests tap a very narrow range of intellectual functioning, most of it based on specific things learned at school and at home. There are many facets of mental life related to everyday problem solving, work performance, and social adaptability that are not covered in IQ tests; at best, the genetic arguments apply only to a limited part of mental life (Kamin, 1974).

Second, there are substantive disagreements on just how much variation can be fairly attributed to the environment. Some critics claim that most heritability studies have not included environments that differ from one another in radical ways, so it is not surprising that results support the interpretation that environment contributes little to variation. If studies were to include environments that differ significantly from one another, then greater variation would be attributable to the environment (Bronfenbrenner, 1972; Scarr & Weinberg, 1976).

Although there is indeed strong evidence for the heritability of IQ, there are also strong doubts that the actual figure is as high as Jensen claims. In a recent review of the heritability of intelligence, behavior-genetics expert Norman Henderson (1982) argued that a figure of about .50 seems more reasonable. And in keeping with a recent trend of providing a range rather than a point estimate of heritability for intelligence, .30 to .60 is given.

Because heritability is an incomplete explanation of IQ, we have to look at environmental factors that can have influence on intelligence. In the next section we will explore in detail some of the most important environmental influences that interact with heredity to affect the child's intelligence.

Environmental Influences on Intelligence

The important environmental influences on intelligence include experiences at home, the effects of being institutionalized, school experiences, culture, race, social class, and nutritional and biological factors.

Home   Families influence their children's intellectual development both genetically and environmentally; untangling these two sources of influence is a formidable task. While we do not know how much of the variance in intellectual development is due to enriched surroundings provided by parents, family structure, and other environmental factors, we do know that these factors are significant. Recent efforts have focused on intervention with parents of children with low IQs to see whether working with the parents as well as the child can advance the child's intelligence. Other work has evaluated the influence of the size of the family and sibling order on the child's intelligence.

A project that demonstrates the importance of the family in the development of intelligence is Rick Heber's Milwaukee Project. The children in this program were from the worst slum area of Milwaukee. Prior to the beginning of his project, Heber found that most mothers of children who had IQs below 80 also scored below 80 on the tests. He speculated that the children's intelligence might be helped by working with the mothers as well as with the children.

Heber began his experiment by selecting forty newborn babies and their mothers (whose IQs were below 75). They were placed in an experimental group or a control group. An extensive intervention program was set in motion with the mother-infant pairs in the experimental group. For example, the mother was given help in vocational training and caretaking skills with infants, and a teacher came to the home and worked with the infant. The enrichment program was continued in a child development center until the child was six years old.

Periodically during the six years the experimental children (who received the enrichment) and the control children (who did not) were given IQ tests. The IQ results for the children when they were six years old indicate impressive gains by the experimental group (average IQ of 121 versus average IQ of 87 for the control group). Later, at the age of nine, children in the experimental group were still outperforming children in the control group by about 20 points.

Recently there has been some skepticism about the details of the Milwaukee Project investigation. For example, some experts wonder if there is an error in the initial assessment of children's IQ, or some omission in reporting other characteristics of the intervention program. However, converging evidence supports the general conclusions of the study, and most experts believe that enriching the child's environment and developing the mother's competency skills are important influences on intelligence.

Institutionalization   In one widely quoted study, Harold Skeels (1966) removed children from an unstimulating orphanage and placed them in an institution where they received individual attention. The change in institutions significantly raised their level of intellectual functioning. In the Skeels study children were assigned an "adoptive mother"— an older, mentally retarded girl—who was given the responsibility of caring for them. At the end of two and one-half years, the children with the mentally retarded "mother" showed an average gain of 32 points in IQ; the children who remained in the inferior institution dropped an average of 21 points in IQ.

Many studies of **institutionalization** have been criticized heavily on methodological grounds. For example, some of the early studies (e.g., Spitz, 1945) interpreted the negative effects of institutionalization in terms of the lack of mother love. Studies of institutionalization, however, do not provide accurate tests of the intrinsic importance of the mother or the family in the child's development. Multiple mothering in the institution, separation from the mother, and such distortions in mothering as rejection and overprotection are possible explanations for the observed effects of institutionalization (Yarrow, 1964).

Descriptions of several institutions in the Soviet Union by Yvonne Brackbill (1962) and Urie Bronfenbrenner (1970) further support the belief that qualitative aspects of institutional care are important in determining whether the child will show intellectual deficits. Where nurses give considerable individual attention to the infants and provide them with many visual-motor opportunities, where toddlers are trained to become self-reliant and to engage in appropriate peer interaction, institutionalized children show normal intellectual and personality patterns. Application 8.1 relates how foster grandparents can also be of considerable benefit to institutionalized young children.

Education and Social Class   Education and social class are other important environmental factors that influence intelligence. In one recent investigation (Breitmayer & Ramey, 1983), sixty-three disadvantaged black children were followed for six and one-half years after birth. They were selected for study on the basis of low maternal IQ and family income. Half of them were assigned to an educational day-care program designed to prevent socially induced mental retardation, and the other half were assigned to a control group that received day care only. It was found that poor Apgar scores at birth as well as relatively low birth weight had a negative influence on intelligence at both five and six and one-half years only in the group of children who received day care only. The children with low Apgar scores who received enriched educational day care did not show depressed intelligence. Further assessment revealed that IQ deficits were influenced by the impoverished conditions in which the children were growing up but that enriched educational day-care experiences often were successful in remediating the effects of poverty on intelligence.

Intelligence: The Complex Influence of Genetic, Biological, and Environmental Experiences
In our discussion of environmental influences on intelligence we have been concerned primarily with the role of the family, institutionalization, and sociocultural factors. It is becoming clearer that there are many psychological and biological factors that influence children's intelligence. Intelligence, like all other aspects of the child's life, is multiply determined. For example, maternal deprivation alone does not cause a child to have a low IQ. Nor does father absence. Nor does attending a poor quality school alone cause the child to show a poor quality of intellectual functioning. Children's intelligence is influenced by a complex interaction of genetic, biological, psychological, and social factors. We have seen that the child's experiences at home do influence his intelligence. So, too, do school

experiences, nutrition, a healthy birth process, a childhood free of traumatic head injury, and the inheritance of "bright" genes.

Now we turn our attention to another important aspect of cognitive development in early childhood—language. Indeed, language is a very important aspect of intelligence, so important that virtually every intelligence test includes an extensive effort to get at such capabilities as the child's knowledge of vocabulary and similarities and dissimilarities among words. Further, in a later chapter we will see that a widely used intelligence test for children provides both a verbal IQ and a performance IQ in the assessment process.

In addition recall that recent advances in the field of modern linguistics served as one important base for the emergence of the information processing perspective. Also remember that in our consideration of the various functions of language, Piaget has argued that cognitive development serves as an important foundation for the development of language. Thus from all three cognitive perspectives on childhood—cognitive developmental, information processing, and psychometric, the role of language in development is a central focus.

Language Development

You may want to review some of the basic foundations of language development described in chapter 5 before going on.

In chapter 5 we described the major aspects of language development during infancy, among them early speech sounds, Roger Brown's first two stages of language development, and the relation of cognition to language. In this section we explore later speech sounds, the final three stages of Brown's theory, and whether childhood is a critical period in language development. We also discuss what writing is and the development of prereading skills.

Later Speech Sounds

Within a year or two after the first words appear, most of the basic sounds of standard English are heard in the child's speech, even though pronunciation quirks may be evident with some children for several more years. The /r/ and /l/ sounds may be confused, as in "rady," and "rightbulb." The /s/ and /sh/ sounds may be incorrectly substituted for one another, as in "shorry" "sore" (for *sure*), and "shertainly." And the /p/ and /t/ sounds may be juxtaposed, as in "tut" (for *put*), "tat" (for *pat*) and "perrible" (for *terrible*), to name but a few. Such quirks reflect the child's inability to discriminate phonemes that require very similar production (vocal) mechanics.

Copyright © 1960 United Feature Syndicate

Perhaps the final hurdle the child must overcome, lasting well into the elementary school years, is the mastery of deep structure and surface structure properties of phonological rules. Learning these properties converges with the learning of morphological and syntactic rules. A good example is the child's mastery of the sounds used to make singular nouns plural.

There are three sounds used to pluralize words in adult English: /s/ as in *cats,* /z/ as in *dogs,* and /ez/ as in *glasses.* One way to indicate when each form is to be used is to list the final consonants in words that take each form. But this method overlooks the deep structural relation present. The type of plural sound that is added is determined by the manner in which the final consonant is produced by the vocal apparatus. If the final consonant is a **voiced consonant** *(m, n, g),* then the plural form is voiced: /a/. If the final consonant is a **voiceless consonant** *(k, f, t, b),* then the plural form is also voiceless: /s/. However, whenever the final consonant and the plural sound are similar with respect to the location of articulation and the type of consonant, the schwa sound (/ə/) is inserted between them.

Children continue to make mistakes in plurals and tense markers into the early elementary school years because they have not mastered the rules that relate the underlying phonological structure to the surface sounds of speech.

The Later Stages of Roger Brown's Theory of Language Development

In stages 3, 4, and 5 of Brown's theory, the length of speech expands, but the major type of change that occurs involves the use of **transformational rules.** These are rules that relate a common deep structure to many alternative surface structures in speech. The rules that are mastered include rules that produce negative forms of sentences. ("The boy did not come"), questions ("Who came to the store?"), imperatives ("Come to the store"), relative clauses ("The boy who is here came home"), and compound phrases ("The boy came home and washed the dishes"). In each case the child must master several rules that transform a simple, structural sentence like "The boy came home" into one of the forms indicated.

Space limitations prohibit discussion of how each transformational system is learned, but there are some interesting parallels in the way each system is mastered.

At the earliest point in stage 3, children are able to add an element to a fixed location of the sentence to signal a transformational type. But they confuse word order, inflection changes, and verb-noun agreement. Here are some examples:

No eat cake.
What mommy read?
Do play?

In stage 4 inflections and some auxiliary verbs appear, but word order is still a problem. Some examples are

What mommy is reading?
No do eat the cake?
What want you to read?

In stage 5, most of the rules are mastered. Admittedly, this is a simplified account of what transpires in stages 3, 4, and 5, but is essentially accurate.

In chapter 5 we saw that cognitive and language development can interact in different ways. Next we explore the possibility that one aspect of cognitive development, *egocentrism,* may constrain or enhance communication.

Egocentrism and Communication

The problem of egocentrism has been central in the study of children's communication. We have all experienced situations in which children talk with total disregard for the listener. They babble on about some experience and show no interest in whether the listener *is* listening, much less comprehending.

A more commonplace problem is that children do not recognize how different the listener's perspective is from their own and fail to cater to it accordingly, even though they want to. The speaker may know something that the listener does not, and vice versa. The speaker may be privy to some experiences (e.g., perceptions, internal feelings) that the listener is not, and vice versa. To sustain an effective conversation, the speaker must bridge these two perspectives. He or she must be aware of the listener's perspective, discover how it is different from his or her own, and be sensitive to feedback from the listener as the conversation proceeds.

The young child's world is full of meaningful images.

Learning to read involves learning about sounds.

It takes two to communicate—a listener as well as a speaker. Listening skills are a part of communication. Interestingly, very little is known about the development of children's abilities to be effective listeners (e.g., Dickson, 1981). What is an effective listener? For one, he or she is attentive to the speaker, maintains an expression of interest, and has frequent eye contact with the speaker. For another, an effective listener provides feedback to indicate whether the message is coming across; this may be in the form of facial expressions, nods, or verbal comments. It may be that the development of listening skills closely parallels the development of speaking skills, because each person is both speaker and listener in many communicative settings.

Self-Taught Reading and Prereading Skills Programs

If learning to read is like learning to talk, the contemporary view of psycholinguists would say that children do much of this on their own. Frank Smith (1976), a leading expert on language development and reading, demonstrated this. He observed a young child "on the threshold of learning to read" in a supermarket and a department store. He found the world of children to be full of meaningful print and that children not only know how to learn words by their context, but that they will always turn to something new to learn if they have exhausted the possibilities of the situation they are in.

This is not to say, however, that reading instruction should be abandoned. Quite the contrary it should build on what the child already knows. Principles of individually guided instruction developed by educational experts at the University of Wisconsin are embedded in a program for teaching reading in early childhood. The program is referred to as the *Prereading Skills Program* (Venezky & Pittelman, 1977).

Three separate visual skills are central to the prereading skills program: attending to letter order, letter orientation, and word detail. A child must learn to recognize words by the left-to-right order in which the letters appear. Many kindergarten children, especially those who have not played with letters and words before entering school, have trouble attending to word order. The child must also pay attention to letter orientation. For example, to decide whether a letter is a *u* or an *n*, the child must pay attention to the relative positions of the line and the circle. A common mistake of children learning to read is to identify a written word by its first letter. This strategy may work with the limited vocabulary of a beginner, but as the reading vocabulary increases, the child must pay attention to all letters in a word to identify it.

In addition to exercises in the prereading skills program built around these visual skills, the program also concentrates on two basic sound skills, sound matching and sound blending. To associate sounds with letters a child must be able first to recognize individual speech sounds. Because isolating and matching individual sounds that occur in words is extremely difficult for many children, most children need special instruction to become familiar with speech sounds and to learn to identify them in words. Children who have learned to associate letters with sounds have acquired an important tool for beginning reading. Before they can

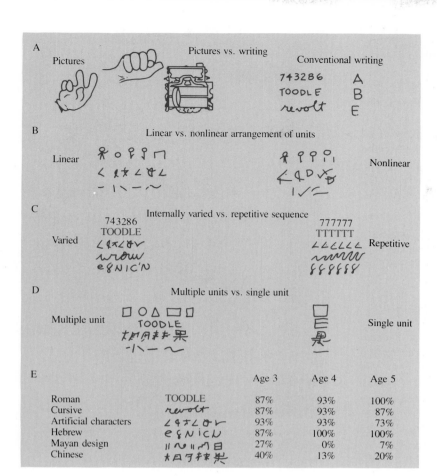

Figure 8.7 Displays contrasting features and nonfeatures of writing as characterized by Lavine.

		Age 3	Age 4	Age 5
Roman	TOODLE	87%	93%	100%
Cursive	*revolt*	87%	93%	87%
Artificial characters	∠ ⊄ᐁ∠ ⴱⵁ	93%	93%	73%
Hebrew	e ξ N ic ⋃	87%	100%	100%
Mayan design	‖ ∿ ‖ ⧀ 日	27%	0%	7%
Chinese	大日夛扗杲	40%	13%	20%

make use of this tool, however, they must understand that sounds can be put together—blended—to form words. For some children the ability to blend sounds into words develops naturally. Other children require extensive practice before they acquire this skill.

Writing: What Is It?

One of the earliest steps in learning to read is to discriminate between visual forms that are letters and words—writing—and those that are not. How early is this perceptual distinction mastered? And on what basis? Put another way, what do young children think writing is?

Some interesting answers to these questions appear in an unpublished study by Lavine (1972), reported by Gibson and Levin (1975). Lavine presented three-, four-, and five-year-old children in Ithaca, New York, with a series of simple problems. They were to distinguish between visual arrays that are writing (that "go in a mailbox") and those that are nonwriting (that "go in a different receptacle"). In one display, pictures and conventional writing were contrasted, as shown in figure 8.7, part A. Virtually all of the children, even the three-year-olds, discriminated correctly between

these pairs. In other displays contrasts were struck between linear and nonlinear arrangements (B), between internal sequences with varied items and internal sequences with repeated items, (C), and between multiple units and a single unit (D).

These features, of course, are useful. Writing often consists of *multiple, varied* forms in a *linear arrangement. Linearity* did not serve as a consistent cue of writing for the children, but *variety* and *multiplicity* did. This trend became more pronounced as the age of the children increased.

What other features might be used? Recall Gibson's set of distinctive features for the alphabet. Might children use these?

For children who cannot yet distinguish among the letters that have features in common, could the features nevertheless help them to distinguish between writing and nonwriting? Lavine's work also provides evidence to support an affirmative answer to this question. In another part of the same study, children were presented with a series of characters from several different languages. They were asked to identify each series as writing or nonwriting. In part E of figure 8.7, the different series are presented along with the percentage of children at each age who identified them as writing. As can be seen, a very high percentage of children identified all but two of the series as writing. The two exceptions are Chinese and the Mayan design. The basis for this result seems to be the set of features that Gibson has described. The set is very descriptive of all the language character systems except for Chinese and the Mayan design. Somehow most of the children sensed this fact, although a sizable minority of the three-year-olds did not. Gibson and Levin explain it this way:

The case is one of pure perceptual learning. Children seem to develop tremendous sensitivity to differences in graphic materials simply by having plenty of graphic displays around to look at. (1975, p. 239)

"Genie" and Childhood as a Critical Period in Language Development

Maya Pines (1981) vividly described the life of "Genie" and information about childhood as a critical period in language development. "Genie" is a pseudonym for a thirteen-year-old girl who had been isolated in a small room and had not been spoken to by her parents since infancy. She was found in 1970 in California.

The case came to light when Genie's fifty-year-old mother took her and ran away from her seventy-year-old husband after a violent argument. The mother was partially blind and applied for public assistance. The social worker in the welfare office took one look at Genie and called her supervisor, who called the police. At the time, Genie could not stand erect. She was unable to speak and could only whimper.

Authorities sent the girl to the Los Angeles Children's Hospital for tests. Charges of willful abuse were filed against both parents. On the day Genie's father was due to appear in court, he committed suicide. Charges against the mother were dismissed after her lawyer argued that she "was, herself, the victim of the same psychotic individual." Nevertheless, for many years the court assigned a guardian for Genie.

The discovery of Genie aroused intense curiosity among professionals who study brain development. They were eager to know what Genie's mental level was at the time she was found and whether she would be capable of developing her faculties.

Genie is now twenty-four years old. During her years of rehabilitation and special training she was observed and repeatedly tested. Hundreds of videotapes recorded her progress, and she has been the subject of several journal articles and a book. Although her case has failed to settle any scientific controversies, she has provided fresh ammunition for arguments on both sides of a major issue: If language learning isn't stimulated during a critical period in a child's development, will language be impaired or not emerge at all?

Genie inspired Susan Curtiss, an assistant professor of linguistics at UCLA, to develop a hypothesis about how language-learning affects the hemispheres of the brain.

Genie inspired Susan Curtiss, an assistant professor of linguistics at UCLA, to develop a controversial hypothesis about how language learning affects the two hemispheres of the brain. As described in Curtiss's book, *Genie: A Psycholinguistic Study of a Modern-Day "Wild Child,"* Genie is proof of human resilience. From the age of twenty months, and until she was thirteen and a half, Genie lived in almost total isolation. Naked and restrained by a harness that her father had fashioned, she was left to sit on her potty seat day after day. She could move only her hands and feet and had nothing to do. At night, when she was not forgotten, she was put into a sort of straitjacket and caged in a crib that had wire mesh sides and an overhead cover. She often was hungry. If she made any noise, her father beat her. "He never spoke to her," Curtiss wrote. "He made barking sounds [and] he growled at her."

When Genie arrived at Children's Hospital in November 1970, she was malformed, unsocialized, and severely malnourished. Although she was beginning to show signs of pubescence, she weighed only fifty-nine pounds. She could not straighten her arms or legs. She did not know how to chew and salivated a great deal and spent much of her time spitting. And she was eerily silent.

During those first months, various physicians, psychologists, and therapists examined her. Shortly after Genie was admitted as a patient, she was given the Vineland Social Maturity Scale and the Preschool Attainment Record; she scored as low as normal one-year-olds. At first, she seemed to recognize only her own name and the word "sorry."

Psychologists at the hospital eventually asked Victoria Fromkin, a UCLA psycholinguist, to study Genie's language abilities. Fromkin brought along Susan Curtiss. A graduate student at the time, Curtiss became so fascinated by Genie that she spent much of the next seven years researching the girl's linguistic development.

During her first seven months at Children's Hospital, Genie learned to walk with a jerky motion and became more or less toilet trained. She also learned to recognize many new words—probably hundreds by the time Curtiss started investigating her knowledge of language systematically in June 1971. And she had begun to speak. At first Genie spoke only in one-word utterances, as toddlers do when they start to talk. Then in July 1971, she began to string two words together on her own, not just while imitating what somebody else had said. She said "big teeth," "little marble," "two hand." A little later she produced some verbs. "Curtiss come," "want milk." In November of the same year she progressed to occasional three-word strings—"small two cup," "white clear box."

Unlike normal children, though, Genie never learned how to ask questions and didn't understand much grammar. A few weeks after normal children reach the two-word stage, their speech generally develops explosively. No such explosion occurred for Genie. Four years after she began to put words together, her speech remained like a somewhat garbled telegram.

Still, Genie's limited language development contradicted one aspect of a theory put forth in 1967 by Eric Lenneberg, a Harvard psychologist. Lenneberg asserted that language can be learned only between age two and puberty. The brain of a child before age two is not sufficiently mature for the acquisition of language, Lenneberg said, while after puberty, the brain has lost its flexibility and no longer can acquire a first language. Genie proved this wrong in one sense, Fromkin says, because the child "showed that a certain amount of language can be learned after the critical period."

On the other hand, Genie failed to learn the kind of grammatical principles that distinguish the language of human beings from that of animals. For example, she could not grasp the difference between various pronouns or between active and passive verbs. In that sense, she appeared to suffer from having passed the critical period.

Genie's language deficiencies could not be attributed to a lack of teachers. Within a few months after she arrived at Children's Hospital, she began going to nursery classes for normal children. She soon transferred to a special elementary school for handicapped children. Next she spent several years in a city high school for the mentally retarded. Outside school, speech therapists worked with her consistently. And one of the therapists and his wife took Genie into their own home to live with their three teenage children.

Genie's deficiencies never appeared to be inborn. Although Genie's mother has given contradictory accounts of her early history, Genie seems to have been a normal baby. During her first year of life, before she was isolated from the rest of her family, she may have been on the road to language. Her mother reported that she heard Genie saying words right after she was locked up.

Linguist Noam Chomsky believes human beings are born with a unique competence for language. But he says this competence must be activated by exposure to language at the proper time—before puberty, Chomsky speculates. Is this what had happened to Genie's brain? Curtiss raised that possibility. Genie is right-handed, but unlike 99 percent of right-handed people, she seemed to use the right hemisphere of her brain for language. That could account for some of the strange features of Genie's language development.

In her studies, Curtiss attempted to explain Genie's dependence on her right hemisphere. Possibly, language learning triggers the normal pattern of hemispheric specialization. So if language is not acquired at the appropriate time, the tissues normally committed to language atrophy. That would mean there are critical periods for the development of the left hemisphere. If such development fails, later learning may be limited to the right hemisphere.

Researchers who have studied deaf children report results that correlate with Curtiss's theory. In tests performed at the Salk Institute in La Jolla, California, right-handed children acquired either speech or sign language through the use of the left hemisphere. Researcher Helen Neville hypothesized that the nature of the language system learned determines, in part, what else goes to the same hemisphere. Together, these two hypotheses present a new view of the development of the brain's hemispheres.

In 1978 Genie's mother became her legal guardian. During all the years of Genie's rehabilitation, her mother also received help. An eye operation restored her sight, and a social worker tried to improve her behavior toward her daughter. Shortly after Genie's mother was named guardian, she astounded the therapists and researchers who had worked with Genie by filing a suit against Curtiss and the Children's Hospital among others—on behalf of herself and her daughter. She charged they had disclosed private and confidential information concerning Genie and her mother for "prestige and profit." She also accused them of subjecting Genie to "unreasonable and outrageous" tests to exploit the girl for personal and economic benefits. According to the *Los Angeles Times,* the lawyer representing Genie's mother estimated the actual damages at $500,000.

The case has not come to trial yet, but since 1978 Genie has been cut off from the professionals at Children's Hospital and UCLA. All research on Genie's language and intellectual development has come to a halt. However, the research that Genie stimulated continues. Much of it concerns the relationship between linguistic ability and brain development, a subject to which Genie has made a significant contribution.

In the Imagine section of this chapter some of the basic ideas involved in the Montessori approach to education were outlined. Next some of the forms preschool education can take, particularly compensatory education programs, will be explored.

Early Childhood Education

Throughout the twentieth century the most popular form of education for children before the first grade has been the child-centered nursery school program. A typical program lasts for two or three hours a day and from three to five days a week. Until the last ten or twenty years, children who attended these schools were primarily from middle-class families. The number of such programs has multiplied dramatically in recent years; and with changes in cost and in attitudes about the importance of early childhood education, children from a much broader range of backgrounds now attend these programs.

The list of basic differences in these **child-centered** schools is almost endless. For example, some focus on enhancing the social development of the child, while others seek to accelerate cognitive growth. Some emphasize daily, structured activities, while others let the child do whatever he or she wants to do. Some stress group activities; others stress individual activities.

Many experts argue that some of the best educational environments have existed for many years in the child-centered nursery schools. With their emphasis on the individual child, providing that child with a variety of experiences outside the nursery school and making education a fun-filled adventure in exploration, they put many public schools to shame. It is not surprising, then, that many of the so-called liberal reforms of public education loudly called for in the 1960s (e.g., Silberman, 1970) looked remarkably like the programs already in operation in child-centered nursery schools.

Changes in cost and in attitudes about the importance of early childhood education have opened programs to children from a much broader range of backgrounds.

Free schools, open schools, and alternative education—educational proposals to remedy the problems of public schools—have existed for some time and work fairly well for the younger child.

Compensatory Education

For many years children from low-income families did not receive any education before they entered first grade. In the 1960s an effort was made to try to break the poverty/poor education cycle for young children in the United States through **compensatory education.** As part of this effort, **Project Head Start** was initiated in the summer of 1965, funded by the Economic Opportunity Act. The program was designed to provide children from low-income families an opportunity to experience an enriched early environment. It was hoped that early intervention might counteract the disadvantages these children had already experienced and place them on an equal level with other children when they entered the first grade.

At first it seemed that Head Start was going to be successful; at the end of the preschool period, children who had been in the Head Start program demonstrated recognizable intellectual and social gains over comparable children who had not been in Head Start. However as these children went through the first grade, no longer experiencing the enriched educational program they had in preschool, their gains began to diminish and ultimately disappeared. Congress established **Project Follow Through** in 1967 when it had become apparent that a program comparable to Head Start was needed for the early elementary school years.

Project Head Start consisted of many different types of preschool programs in different parts of the country. Little effort was made initially to find out whether some types of programs worked better than others; however, it soon became obvious that some programs and some centers were doing a better job with low-income children than others. A significant aspect of Project Follow Through, then, was *planned variation,* in which different kinds of educational programs for children were devised to see whether specific programs are effective with all children or only with certain groups of children. For instance, one program may be more effective with the rural poor of Appalachia, and another may be more beneficial with ghetto children in New York City. By the 1972/1973 school year, twenty-two different Follow Through programs were being implemented in the United States, each in different areas. The results of these programs are still being evaluated.

Next we see that recent longitudinal data have been collected on young adults who were enrolled in Project Head Start.

The Head Start Program provides children from low-income families with an opportunity to experience an enriched early environment.

Head Start Children in Adulthood
Children who experienced Project Head Start many years ago are now young adults. How are they faring—better, the same as, or worse than their peers who did not go to Head Start programs? Robert Trotter (1981) describes the following recent findings about the Head Start children as adults:

Project Head Start continues to yield impressive results and remains a favorite of lawmakers and money givers, so its future looks bright—except for two potential problems. One has to do with sex, the other with funding.

First the sex problem. It appears that boys and girls don't derive equal benefits from the types of intervention provided by preschool programs. All children who have had preschool training tend to do better in school than those who did not get a head start. But by the time they reach young adulthood, any advantage the females may have had seems to have disappeared, leaving them no better off than girls who did not attend a preschool program.

This is among the most recent findings to emerge from ongoing study of a large group of poor, black children who took part in an experimental program in Harlem in the early 1960s. The research is being conducted by psychologists Cynthia Deutsch, Martin Deutsch, Theresa Jordan, and Richard Grallo, all of the Institute for Developmental Studies at New York University. The researchers described the program (which was as a forerunner of Project Head Start) and discussed their findings at the APA annual meeting in Los Angeles.

More than 150 young adults currently are involved in the study. Half of them entered an experimental preschool program when they were four years old. The others did not get this early training and are serving as a comparison group. All have been interviewed by the four psychologists every two or three years since the experiment started, and now, for the first time, sex differences are beginning to emerge.

In general, the males have been successful in school and in the job market: 32 percent are attending college, compared with 20 percent of those who did not get preschool training; 57 percent are employed full or part time, compared with 44 percent of the control group. The same positive benefits are not seen among the females. At this stage of their lives, they are no better off than those who started school at the usual age.

The researchers aren't quite sure why the young women aren't doing as well as the young men, but they suggest that the school system may have to take part of the blame. The preschool program emphasized verbal skills, inquisitiveness, and self-confidence. In elementary school, the boys were rewarded for displaying these qualities, but in many cases the girls were punished for the same behaviors. Some teachers, for instance, even complained that the girls were too assertive and asked too many questions.

These results, however, may not be the final word. The researchers are continuing to follow the progress of the young men and women, and already there are indications that the women may yet benefit from their early training. Many, for instance, had to leave school because they got pregnant, but there are preliminary indications that those who had been in the preschool program are more likely than the others to return to school and continue their education. If this proves to be the case, the girls, like the boys, may, as the researchers say, "have all of what it takes to make it."

And because many of them (at least the boys) are making it, Project Head Start will probably make it. The program, which provides a wide range of educational, nutritional, health and social services to economically disadvantaged children between three and five years of age, expired on September 30, but Congress is likely to vote to continue at least three and perhaps five years. In fact, Head Start is one of the few social programs that the Reagan administration stands behind. A funding level of $950 million for the program has been proposed by the administration. This is the same as the Carter administration's request and $130 million above the fiscal 1981 level. The increase would be enough to maintain Head Start at its current level of participation (339,700 children) and upgrade some programs.

The bad news is that other proposed cutbacks in social services may harm Head Start—to the tune of $36 million. The expected reductions in Comprehensive Employment and Training Act (CETA) programs, for instance, are likely to adversely affect Head Start programs because approximately one half of them use CETA workers for jobs such as bus drivers and clerical workers. The administration's proposed elimination of federal subsidies for snacks served to children through the child care food program would also affect Head Start. More than 10 percent of the funding for meals and snacks would be lost.

But despite these potential problems, it appears that Head Start, like many of its participants, is going to make it. (pp. 15, 37)

Project Follow Through

In all of the Follow Through programs parents are included both in and out of the classroom. Parents work as paid teachers' aids, as volunteers in the classroom, and as social-service staff assistants. In many of the programs, educational workshops have been developed to inform parents about the Follow Through program in their area and to instruct them in the ways they can help their children. Thus an important part of Project Follow Through is parent and community involvement.

All Follow Through programs must be comprehensive; that is, they cannot focus on a narrow aspect of the child's learning or development. Thus Follow Through programs include instruction, medical services, nutrition, psychological services, social services, and staff development.

Following are five different Follow Through models, reflecting the diversity that exists in early childhood education.

The *University of Oregon Engelmann/Becker Model for Direct Instruction* emphasizes that children fail in school because they have not been instructed properly. Disadvantaged children lag behind other children in developing appropriate skills. It is a highly structured program, with sequentially programmed lessons. Teachers systematically reward children for success and monitor them closely so that learning failures do not build up. This program is based on learning theory and behavior modification.

The *High/Scope: Cognitively Oriented Curriculum Model,* developed by Dave Weikart, is based on Piaget's theory of cognitive development. The child is seen as an active learner who discovers things about the world. He or she should not be "taught," in the sense of being told information; rather, he or she should "learn" by planning, doing, experimenting, exploring,

and talking about what he or she is doing. Communication and thinking skills are nurtured, and emphasis is placed on self-direction, not reliance on external reinforcement from others. Each child's level of development is continuously monitored so that appropriate materials can be used.

The *Florida Parent-Education Program* places more direct importance on the role of parents than the first two models mentioned. This program was developed by Ira Gordon to involve parents in the emotional and intellectual growth of their children. It assumes that the child's learning habits and personality are formed primarily through experiences in the early home environment; thus parents are trained to supervise the child's learning at home. Parent educators work in the classroom and visit parents on a weekly basis.

The *Far West Laboratory Responsive Educational Program* emphasizes the development of a healthy self-concept in the child and the freedom to decide his or her own course of learning. Teachers try to build up the child's confidence in ability to succeed and provide many different alternatives in the classroom so he or she can choose and direct activities. This program has much in common with a humanistic view of child development.

The *Bank Street College of Education Approach* is an eclectic approach in which academic skills are seen as acquired within a broader context of planned activities. The program focuses on the child's interests at school, at home, and in the community, and views the child as an active learner seeking to become independent and to understand the world. To help the child in these efforts, he or she is encouraged to select from different alternatives, to make decisions, and to cope with the world. The individual nature of the child also is taken into account; learning experiences are constantly restructured to meet the needs of each child.

In an effort to find out whether Project Follow Through is effective, a national evaluation is being conducted by Stanford Research Institute. Follow Through pupils are compared with pupils of similar social and intellectual backgrounds who have not participated in the project.

Means used to evaluate the success of Project Follow Through include observation to determine whether teachers are fulfilling their planned-variation goals, national standardized tests of achievement that measure children's math and reading skills, survey questionnaires and interviews with parents.

Because a new wave of children enters Project Follow Through each year, a large amount of information about Follow Through is accumulating. A recent national comparison of Follow Through and non-Follow Through programs supported the belief that educational intervention can have a positive effect on the child's social and intellectual development. Jane Stallings (1975) reviewed seven of the twenty-two variations in a national evaluation of Follow Through programs. In all, over two hundred first- and third-grade classrooms were involved in the evaluation. In Stallings' own words, here are some of the major findings pertaining to Project Follow Through's social impact on children:

In our study, *independence* is defined as a child or children engaged in a task without an adult. This type of independent behavior is more likely to be found in classrooms where teachers allow children to select their own seating and groups part of the time, where a wide variety of activities is available, and where an assortment of audiovisual and exploratory materials is available. The adults provide individual attention and make friendly comments to the children. . . . children in the classrooms of EDC (a humanistic, child centered approach) and Far West Laboratory evidence more independence than do the children in non-Follow Through and other sponsor's classrooms. (p. 103)

For this study, *cooperation* is defined as two or more children working together on a joint task. This kind of cooperation is more likely to be found in classrooms where a wide variety of activities occurs throughout the day, where exploratory materials are available, and where children can choose their own groupings. If the adults interact with two children, asking questions and making comments about the task, the children seem to be encouraged to join each other in cooperative tasks.

The children in the Bank Street College, High/Scope Foundation, and EDC programs more often joined each other in a cooperative task than did children in other models and non-Follow Through children. (p. 104)

Thus there is evidence that Project Follow Through enhances social development. The results even point to specific programs that have been the most effective in enhancing specific social behaviors. Not surprisingly, not all programs were shown to have facilitated all social behaviors equally.

Application 8.2
"Sesame Street" — Education Through Television

One of television's major programming attempts to educate children is "Sesame Street," which is designed to teach both cognitive and social skills. The program began in 1969 and is still going strong. Aimee Leiffer (1973) showed that "Sesame Street" can influence the child's social development in such areas as cooperation. But the major evaluation of "Sesame Street" has focused on its impact on the child's cognitive development. A national study of "Sesame Street," conducted by Sam Ball and Gerry Bogatz (1970), evaluated such major cognitive outcomes as symbolic representation (e.g., letters, numbers, and geometric forms), problem solving, and reasoning. The results are impressive. Children who frequently watch "Sesame Street" scored higher on these measures of cognitive development than did children who watch infrequently. Children from both low-income and middle-income families who watched the show often made gains on the cognitive measures; children from low-income families who did not watch the show often did not make such gains.

What are the educational goals of "Sesame Street"? The following discussion of these goals is based on an article in the *Harvard Educational Review* by Gerald Lesser (1972), who served as chairman of the National Board of Advisors to the Children's Television Workshop, which produces "Sesame Street." He discusses many different teaching techniques that are reflected in the actual production of "Sesame Street."

A fundamental message from "Sesame Street," Lesser asserts, is that education and entertainment can work well together. In the past, education and entertainment have been viewed as separate activities. Education is supposed to be work, not fun; with "Sesame Street," however, learning is exciting and entertaining.

A second point brought out in "Sesame Street" is that teaching can be done in both direct and indirect ways. Using the direct way, a teacher would tell the child exactly what it is he or she is going to be taught and then actually teach it. This method is often used on the program in teaching cognitive skills. But social skills are usually communicated in indirect ways. Thus rather than merely telling children "You should cooperate with people," a sequence of events is shown so that the child can figure out what it means to be cooperative and what the advantages are.

Should the world be shown to children as it is or as it ought to be? The advisory board of educators and psychologists decided that the real world should be shown, but with the emphasis on what the world would be like if everyone treated one another with decency and kindness. To show the real world as it really is, the program might show an adult doing something unjustifiably inconsiderate to another adult, with alternative ways of coping with this stress then acted out. Finally, the program would portray the happy outcomes when people stop acting inconsiderately.

Gerald Lesser also offered several suggestions for implementing the production techniques of "Sesame Street" in classroom teaching situations. Most of these suggestions emphasize the importance of attention in children's learning. For instance, in order to learn the social skills being shown in a "Sesame Street" episode on being a friendly person, the child has to attend to the television screen. If you, as a teacher or a parent, are trying to explain the value of cooperation, the child has to attend to what you are saying and doing in order for your commentary to be effective.

"Sesame Street" demonstrates that education may be best when it is entertaining. Using both direct and indirect methods, this TV program helps to develop children's cognitive and social skills.

Many experts now believe, and we think you would agree, that education may be best when it is enjoyable as well as informative. In application 8.2 one effort that has taken this idea seriously is presented as we evaluate the impact of the television show "Sesame Street" on young children.

Few developments in society over the last twenty-five years have had greater impact on children than television. Many children spend more time in front of the television set than they do with their parents. Although only one of the vehicles of the mass media that affects children's behavior—books, comic books, movies, and newspapers also have some impact—television is the most influential.

In the next chapter, in the discussion of social, emotional, and personality development in early childhood, you will read further evaluations of the influence of television on children.

Summary

From Piaget's cognitive developmental perspective, the preschool child thinks in a preoperational manner. The period of preoperational thought is marked by further advances in symbolic activity and the appearance of a number of differences between the child's thinking and full-fledged adult reasoning and logic. The child's thought is frequently egocentric, that is, lacking in self-other perspective discriminations, and is filled with animism, the belief that inanimate objects have human qualities. In addition, the child fails to conserve properties of objects and often does not serialize items correctly.

In the information processing view, cognition, or mental activity, is synonymous with the processing of information. The series of stages of processing include attention, perception, memory and retrieval, inferring, and problem solving. Historically, the information processing tradition can be traced to interest in the development of communication theory, computer modeling—particularly of artificial intelligence—and advances in modern linguistics.

Attention is the *noticing* of specific features of the environment. There are striking changes in the ability of children to sustain interest in activities from the toddler years to middle childhood, and younger children take longer to notice relevant features of events for learning.

The definition of intelligence is often closely tied to how it is measured. Nonetheless, we believe that intelligence is something more than what IQ tests measure. Definitions range from descriptions of global abilities and genetic heritage to specific abilities and environmental learning orientations. Intelligence is influenced by the interaction of heredity and environment. Genetic estimates of the heritability of intelligence are now put at a range of .30 to .60, which allows for a great deal of environmental variation. Among the most important environments that influence the young child's intellectual development are family experiences. Studies of institutionalization are inconclusive in regard to their effects on intelligence, although evidence of enriched stimulation in institutional settings has led to increased intellectual development in young children. One fruitful approach is the use of foster grandparents in helping to improve the intelligence of young children.

Our discussion of language development focused on later speech sounds, Roger Brown's stages of language development, the role of egocentrism in communication, the child's beginning reading skills, and the possibility of childhood as a critical period in language development. Possibly the final hurdle in understanding speech sounds lasts well into the elementary school years—mastering deep as well as surface properties of phonological rules. In stages 3, 4, and 5 of Brown's theory, the length of speech expands, but the major change involves the use of transformational rules. Young children are constrained by their egocentrism and thus don't listen very effectively. Consideration of children's beginning reading skills focuses on self-teaching as well as training them to focus their attention on letter order, letter orientation, and word detail. While the answer to the debate about whether childhood is a critical period in language development is still open, there is every reason to believe that in the development of language, early childhood is an important phase of the life cycle.

During early childhood the principal agencies for education are day-care centers, child-centered nursery schools, and special programs. Child-centered nursery schools have been the major educational force for middle-class children, offering a form of progressive education since the turn of the century. Projects Head Start and Follow Through are two well-funded programs started by the federal government to provide an enriched educational experience for children from lower-class families during preschool and early elementary school years. In the 1960s Head Start programs had a positive effect on children's cognitive development, but gains were generally lost after a year or two of regular public school. A recent study of Follow Through, which tries to maintain the enriched environment through the early elementary school years, suggests that such gains can be maintained. And the long-term effects of Head Start seem to benefit males more than females.

In terms of early childhood education, the television show "Sesame Street," has been shown to have a positive effect on children's cognitive development.

Key Terms

animism

attention

centration

channel

child-centered

communications

compensatory education

conservation

egocentrism

hardware

information processing
 approach

institutionalization

intelligence

irreversibility

operations

Project Follow Through

Project Head Start

psychometric

receiver

software

transformational rules

voiced consonant

voiceless consonant

Review Questions

1. Describe Maria Montessori's approach to early childhood education.
2. Discuss Piaget's stage of preoperational thought.
3. What is the information processing view of development?
4. Historically, what seems responsible for the evolution of the information processing perspective?
5. What are the major characteristics of attention, and how does it develop in young children?
6. How can intelligence be defined?
7. Describe genetic influences on children's intelligence.
8. Discuss environmental influences on children's intelligence, including family and institutionalization effects.
9. Describe some of the important changes that take place in language during early childhood.
10. Describe the young child's role as an active participant in learning to read and how this fits in with prereading skills programs.
11. Outline the language development of "Genie," and evaluate whether the childhood years represent a critical period in language development.
12. Describe the results of the evaluation of projects Head Start and Follow Through.

Further Readings

Curtiss, S. *Genie: A psycholinguistic study of a modern-day 'wild child'.* New York: Academic Press, 1981.
Susan Curtiss's vivid, exciting account of "Genie's" language development, her abuse, and attempts at rehabilitation. Easy reading.

Montessori, M. *Discovery of the child.* (M. J. Costelloe, S.J., Trans.). Notre Dame, Ind.: Fides, 1967.
An exciting account of Maria Montessori's sensory approach to early childhood education. Reasonably easy reading.

Siegler, R. S. Information-processing approaches to development. (W. Kessen, Volume Editor). *Carmichael's manual of child psychology,* vol. 1. New York: John Wiley, 1983.
A description of the information processing perspective of development that includes many new insights about this approach. Moderately difficult reading level.

9 Social, Emotional, and Personality Development

I *magine . . . what it would be like to be an abused child*

Unfortunately, parental hostility toward children in some families reaches the point where one or both parents abuse the child. Child abuse is an increasing problem in the United States (Parke & Lewis, 1980; Starr, 1979). Estimates of its incidence vary, but some authorities say that as many as 500,000 children are physically abused in the United States each year. Laws in many states now require doctors and even teachers to report suspected cases of child abuse. Yet many cases go unreported, particularly those of "battered" infants.

The government, psychologists, and educators have shown more interest in child abuse in recent years. In 1974 the federal government gave $85 million to local communities for programs dealing with child abuse, and research efforts to understand the causes of child abuse and ways to help its offenders have increased.

For several years it was believed that parents who committed child abuse were severely disturbed, "sick" individuals. However, parents who abuse their children are rarely psychotic (Blumberg, 1974). Ross Parke (Parke & Collmer, 1976) has developed a model for understanding child abuse that shifts the focus from the personality traits of the parents to an analysis of three aspects of the social environment—cultural, familial, and community influences.

The extensive violence in the American culture is reflected in the occurrence of violence in the family. Violence occurs regularly on television, and parents frequently resort to power assertion as a disciplinary technique. Cross-cultural studies indicate that American television contains more violence than British television (Geis & Monahan, 1976) and that in China, where physical punishment is rarely used to discipline children, the incidence of child abuse is very low (Stevenson, 1974).

To understand child abuse in the family, the interaction of all family members should be considered, regardless of who actually performs the violent acts against the child. Even though the father, for example, may be the person who has physically abused the child, contributions of the mother, the father, and the child should be evaluated.

Many parents who abuse their children come from families in which physical punishment was used. They may view physical punishment as a legitimate way of controlling the child's behavior, and physical abuse may be a part of this sanctioning. Many aspects of the ongoing interaction among immediate family members also affect the incidence of child abuse. The child may have some effect—for example, an unattractive child experiences more physical punishment than an attractive child (Dion, 1974), and a child from an unwanted pregnancy may be especially vulnerable to abuse (Birrell & Birrell, 1968).

The interaction of the parents with each other may lead to child abuse as well. Dominant-submissive husband-wife pairs have been linked with child abuse (Terr, 1970). Husband-wife violence or such stressful family situations as those caused by financial problems, for example, may erupt in the form of aggression directed against the defenseless child. Such displaced aggression, whereby a person shifts an aggressive reaction from the original target person or situation to some other person or situation, is a common cause of child abuse.

Community-based support systems are extremely important in alleviating stressful family situations and thereby preventing child abuse. A study of the support systems in fifty-eight counties in New York state revealed a relationship between the incidence of child abuse and the presence of support systems available to the family. Both family resources—relatives and friends, for example—and such formal support systems of the community as crisis centers and child-abuse counseling were associated with a reduction in child abuse (Garbarino, 1976). In sum, the family should not be viewed as an independent social unit but as embedded in a broader social network of informal and formal community-based support systems.

Introduction

We begin this chapter with information about the role of families, peers, and television in the young child's development. Then we continue our description of the development of the self, discussed earlier in chapters 2 and 6, and conclude with a discussion of sex-type behavior.

Family

Developmental psychologists no longer rely exclusively upon socialization experiences within the family to explain children's social development. Biological and genetic factors, cognitive factors, peers, and other aspects of the culture in which the child grows up have received increased attention. However, it is important that we not go too far in the direction of thinking that the family is but one of many influences on the child's social and emotional development, because the family still is the most important influence.

Parenting Behavior, Maturation, and the Social Behavior of Children

For years heated debates have dominated the discussion of how parents ought to rear their children. Some child development authorities have argued that it is best to allow the child considerable freedom and not to interfere with his or her decision making. Other authorities believe that more control in parenting is warranted, particularly in combination with a nurturant orientation toward the child. Such control should not be punitive but should involve setting firm rules and regulations by the parent. These rules and regulations should follow discussion sessions with the child; but once the child and parents agree on the rules, the parents should consistently enforce them. Some parents believe a more authoritarian approach to rearing the child is called for; they believe that many parents are too "easy" on their children. These parents may interact in seemingly "cold" ways with their children and physically discipline them when they do something wrong.

There are many other parenting strategies in addition to the three just described. Many parents are inconsistent in the way they deal with their children; the mother might nurture and act permissively toward the child while the father acts in an authoritarian and distant manner. There is also inconsistency on the part of one parent; for example, the mother might spank the child one day for losing a book and one month later reason with him or her about what happened.

One factor that should not be overlooked in considering the parent's behavior toward the child is the child's maturation. Mothers obviously do not treat a thirteen-year-old in the same way as a two-year-old.

The two-year-old and the thirteen-year-old have different needs and abilities, and the mother has different expectancies for the two children. According to Eleanor Maccoby (1980, pp. 395–96):

During the first year of a child's life, the parent-child interaction moves from a heavy focus on routine caretaking—feeding, changing, bathing, and soothing—and comes to include more noncaretaking activities like play and visual-vocal exchanges. During children's second and third years, parents often handle disciplinary issues by physical manipulation: They carry the child away from a mischievous activity to the place they want the child to go; they put fragile and dangerous objects out of reach; they sometimes spank. But as the child grows older, parents turn increasingly to reasoning, moral exhortation, and giving or withholding special privileges. As children move from infancy to middle childhood, parents show them less physical affection, become less protective, and spend less time with them (Baldwin, 1946; Lasko, 1954).

Maccoby (1980) believes that these changes in parental behavior seem clearly linked to the child's physical and mental growth—to changes in motor skill, language, judgment, and perspective-taking ability. As the child grows larger and heavier, parents seem less likely to resort to physical manipulation. Parents seem unlikely to reason with a child who doesn't yet talk and who seems to have a limited understanding of other people's speech.

Children's understanding of the nature of authority can influence parent-child relationships. William Damon (1977) has shown that children progress through a series of stages in their ability to understand authority. Preschool children do not detect that authority is an issue. On occasion, they even express the wrong assumption that their wants and desires do not conflict with their parents' demands. Soon, though, children become aware of such conflicts, recognizing that parental authority means parental power. At this point, children think they have to obey their parents because of their parents' strength and size. However, they also believe that they can disobey, provided their parents do not catch them. As they enter elementary school, children begin to recognize the reciprocal nature of parent-child relationships—they think that they should be obedient because their parents have done so much for them. Parental authority is now legitimate, not because of power but because of kindness. During preadolescence, parental authority is viewed as more differentiated; that is, authority is more legitimate in areas where parents are competent and knowledgeable. Parental authority now becomes more of a mutual relationship between the parent and the child, with both having to agree upon the rules and regulations. Thus it may be that parenting is somewhat easier during the child's pre-adolescent years in that parents may not need to use as much harsh discipline to get the child to comply. At this point in development the child should be more receptive to attribution statements, such as "My, what a nice boy you are" (Maccoby, 1983).

Another important factor that often goes unnoticed in parent-child relationships is that the child's parents are often maturing and changing at the same time their son or daughter is. Unfortunately, we have little information on how different levels of maturation in parents affect children. Parents may undergo significant maturational changes as they go from age twenty to thirty and forty. In his book *The Season's of a Man's Life,* Daniel Levinson (1978) writes about these changes, distinguishing between the experiences of very young parents in their late teens and early twenties and those in midlife in their thirties and forties. The novice adult phase is a time of reasonably free experimentation and of testing one's dreams in the real world. Midlife brings an awareness of mortality and worrisome thoughts about gaps between parents' occupational aspirations and their actual accomplishments. Think about other families with children whom you know or have known; you probably can recall a number of situations in which changes in adulthood affected parent-child relationships. Two such situations involve the divorce of parents and the increase in the number of working mothers, which will be discussed next.

Changes in Family Structure

The child's interactions and experiences with his or her mother, father, and siblings provide the beginnings of the lifelong process of socialization. However, fathers, siblings, other relatives, peers, and teachers generally have not been given the credit that mothers have for influencing the child's social development. Thus, if a son grows up to become a homosexual, it is often argued that the mother was overprotective, robbing him of his virility. If he develops schizophrenia, she probably did not give him enough love. If he fails in school, it is because she did not provide him with enough achievement-oriented experiences. In particular, the attachment bond between the mother and the infant is viewed as the basis for the development of a healthy personality later in life. Jerome Kagan (1979) believes this idea is one of the few sacred, transcendental themes in American ideology that remains unsullied.

Kagan predicts that the major result of an emotionally close parent-child bond is that it directs the child toward acceptance of the family's values. If these values coincide with those of the popular culture, all is well. If not, a close mother-infant bond may not be an advantage. As Kagan points out, the mother who establishes a deep mutual attachment with her infant

More children than ever before in history have working mothers.

daughter, but who promotes the once traditional female values of passivity, inhibition of intellectual curiosity, and anxiety over competence, may be preparing her daughter for serious conflict in adolescence and young adulthood.

Today more young children than ever before in the United States are spending less time with their mothers; more than one out of every three mothers with a child under the age of three is employed, and almost 42 percent of the mothers of preschoolers work outside the home (U.S. Department of Commerce, 1979). Is this change good for children? A recent opinion poll indicates that a majority of the public thinks it harms the family, but research evidence suggests a different conclusion.

Working Mothers

Because household operations have become more efficient and family size has decreased in America, it is not certain that children of working mothers actually receive less attention than children in the past whose mothers were not employed. Outside employment, at least for mothers with school-aged children, may simply be filling time previously taken up by added household burdens and more children. And it cannot be assumed that if the mother did not go to work, the child would benefit from the time freed up by streamlined household operations and smaller families. Mothering does not always have a positive effect on the child. In one longitudinal study (Moore, 1975), full-time mothering revealed some vulnerabilities. It was found that boys who experienced full-time mothering during preschool years were more competent intellectually but also more ready to conform, fearful, and inhibited as adolescents. And the educated nonworking mother may overinvest her energies in her children, fostering an excess of worry and discouraging independence. In such situations, the mother may inject more mothering into parent-child relationships than the child can profitably handle (Hoffman, 1974).

In the past, socialization experiences indicated that girls would spend most of their adult life as mothers while boys would spend it as breadwinners. But because there is greater availability of employment for women today and there is a movement toward more equitable wages and opportunities, motherhood now takes up less of a woman's life, and work outside the home takes up more. Although occupation is still a strong component of the male adult's identity, his role as the breadwinner is now more often shared with his partner, and he may be more active in childrearing than his father was.

Infant and Preschool Years   There is no compelling evidence that employment of the mother outside the home has negative effects on infants and preschoolers. In one investigation it was learned that employed mothers actually spend just as much time in one-to-one interaction with their preschool child as do mothers who are homemakers (Goldberg, 1977). In two other studies, no differences in quality of the parenting of women who work at home and those who work outside were found in the first year of the infant's life (Cohen, 1978; Hock, in press). However, one of these investigations did show that during the infant's second year of life, the infants of mothers who were at home did engage in more positive interactions, vocalized more, and performed better on developmental tests (Cohen, 1978).

Father Absence and Family Structure
In previous eras, the majority of families consisted of a man and a woman who were married and who had one or more children living with them—known as a nuclear family. In most of these families the father was employed outside of the home and the mother was not. No longer are the majority of children exposed to this traditional family structure. Children are growing up in a greater variety of family structures than ever before in history (Eiduson & Zimmerman, 1978).

The increase in the number of children growing up in single-parent families is staggering. One estimate indicates that about 25 percent of the children born between 1910 and 1960 lived in a single-parent family sometime during their development. However, 40 to 50 percent of individuals born during the 1970s will spend some part of their childhood in a single-parent home (Bane, 1978). About 11 percent of all American households now are made up of so-called blended families, which include families with stepparents or cohabitating adults. Such families often expose the child to competing bonds of loyalty and changing authority roles.

Effects of Divorce on Children
Divorce is global in magnitude. Its effects on the child are mediated by a host of other factors, including the relationship of the child to the custodial parent; the availability of and reliance on family support systems, such as friends, relatives, and other adults; peer support; whether there is an ongoing, positive relationship with the noncustodial parent; and so forth. Many generalizations about the effects divorced parents have on children are stereotypical and do not take into account the uniqueness of many single-parent family structures.

One study (Santrock & Tracy, 1978) vividly showed that boys from divorced homes are often treated differently from boys from two-parent homes. Thirty teachers were shown a videotape that focused on the social interaction of a boy. Half the teachers were informed that he was from an "intact" home, while the other half were given a background information sheet that indicated the boy had parents who were divorced. The teachers were asked to view the videotape and then to rate the boy on eleven personality traits (e.g., anxiety, social deviance, and happiness) and to predict what his behavior would be like in five different school situations (e.g., ability to cope with stress, popularity). The teachers rated the "divorced" boy more negatively on three counts—in terms of happiness, emotional adjustment, and ability to cope with stress.

There are, of course, stress, conflict, and problems involved in family dynamics that predispose children from homes in which the father is absent to be less competent in social and cognitive development (e.g., Lamb, 1976). Not all the blame, however, should fall on the family per se, as is indicated by the teachers' stereotyped responses toward homes in which the parents were divorced. Many people expect children from these homes to have problems, whether they actually do or not.

Family conflict, the child's relationship with both parents, and the availability of support systems are important aspects of divorce that influence the child's behavior (Hetherington, 1979). Many separations and divorces are highly charged emotional affairs that enmesh the child in conflict.

Conflict is a critical aspect of family functioning, so critical that it appears to outweigh the influence of family structure on the child's behavior. Children in single-parent families function better than those in conflict-ridden nuclear families (Hetherington, Cox, & Cox, 1978; Rutter, 1983; Santrock, Warshak, Lindbergh, & Meadows, 1982). Escape from conflict may be a positive benefit of divorce for children, but unfortunately, in the year immediately following the divorce, conflict does not decline but rather increases (Hetherington et al., 1978). At this time, children—particularly boys—in divorced families show more adjustment problems than do children in homes in which both parents are present.

The child's relationship with both parents after the divorce influences the ability to cope with stress (Hetherington et al., 1978; Kelly, 1978). During the first year after the divorce, the quality of parenting the child experiences is often very poor; parents seem to be preoccupied with their own needs and adjustment, experiencing anger, depression, confusion, and emotional instability, which inhibit their ability to respond sensitively to the child's needs. During this period, parents tend to discipline the child inconsistently, be less affectionate, and be ineffective in controlling the child. But during the second year after the divorce, parents are more effective at these important childrearing duties (Hetherington et al., 1978).

The majority of information we have about divorced families emphasizes the absent father or the relationship between the custodial parent and the child, but child psychologists have become increasingly interested in the role of support systems available to the child and the family. Support systems for divorced families seem more important for low-income than middle-income families (Colletta, 1978). The extended family and community services played a more critical role in family functioning of low-income families in Colletta's investigation. Competent support systems may be particularly important for divorced parents with infant and preschool children because the majority of these parents must work full time to make ends meet.

Another issue involving children of divorce focuses on the age of the child at the time of the divorce. Preschool children are not as accurate as elementary school children and adolescents in evaluating the cause of divorce, their own role in the divorce, and possible outcomes. Consequently, young children may blame themselves more for the divorce and distort the feelings and behavior of their parents, including hopes for their reconciliation. Even adolescents experience a great deal of conflict and pain over their parents' divorce; but after the immediate impact of the divorce, they seem to be better than younger children at assigning responsibility for the divorce, resolving loyalty conflicts, and understanding the divorce process (Wallerstein & Kelly, 1980).

Virtually all of our information about children from divorced families is collected *after* the separation or divorce of parents. It is usually assumed that divorce is a critical life event that induces stress and leads to changes in the interaction of individuals in the family system. But the possibility exists that long before the separation or divorce occurs family members may be interacting with one another in a maladaptive way. If so, then the postdivorce functioning of the family is not discontinuous with family functioning in the years prior to the divorce. In one recent investigation (Morrison, Gjerde, & Block, 1983), the home environments of families were studied as long as six years before divorce—those families that eventually were disrupted by divorce were observed to be less stable, less peaceful, and less child-centered than families that remained intact. In particular, the mothers of boys from divorcing families emphasized strict discipline and the control of feelings, while de-emphasizing warm and intimate interaction with their sons. Thus parental functioning in some families may decline in important ways years before the separation or divorce of the parents occurs. This suggests that in studying and evaluating divorced families we should not only look at postdivorce family functioning but at the unfolding of family drama in years prior to the divorce as well.

The relationship between parent and child is an important influence on the child's social behavior. In the next section we will look more closely at some different dimensions of parenting and discuss the reciprocal nature of parent-child relationships and how the family functions as a system.

Parent-Child Relationships

If I said it to them once I said it a million times. Is it my imagination or have I spent a lifetime shutting refrigerator doors, emptying nose tissue from pants pockets before washing, writing checks for milk, picking up wet towels and finding library books in the clothes hamper?

Mr. Matterling said, "Parenting is loving." (What did he know? He was an old Child Psychology teacher who didn't have any children. He only had twenty-two guppies and two catfish to clean the bowl.) How I wish that for one day I could teach Mr. Matterling's class. How I would like to tell him it's more than loving. More than clean gravel. More than eating the ones you don't like.

Parenting is frustration that you have to see to believe. Would I have ever imagined there would be whole days when I didn't have time to comb my hair? Mornings after a slumber party when I looked like Margaret Mead with a migraine? Could I have ever comprehended that something so simple, so beautiful and so uncomplicated as a child could drive you to shout, "We are a family and you're a part of this family and by God, you're going to spend a Friday night with us having a good time if we have to chain you to the bed!"

And a plaintive voice within me sighed, "Why don't you grow up!" (Bombeck & Keane, 1971, pp. 169–70)

There are many dimensions to parenting, one of which is warmth.

Dimensions of Parenting

As this introduction by Erma Bombeck suggests, parents want their children to grow into socially mature individuals, and they often feel a great deal of frustration in their role as parents. Child psychologists have long searched for ingredients of parenting that will promote competent social development in their children. Recall John Watson's prescription in the 1930s that most parents are too affectionate toward their children. In our discussion of divorce we found that parents often have a great deal of difficulty exercising control over their children in the year following divorce. The dimension of parenting referred to as *control* has been the focus of considerable debate in child psychology. When a wide variety of ways that parents can deal with children are surveyed, the dimensions of **control-autonomy** and **warmth-hostility** frequently appear.

Control-Autonomy The control-autonomy dimension of parenting refers to the parents' establishment and enforcement of rules and to the techniques used to promote or hinder the child's development of independence. Control-autonomy actually can be subdivided

into **psychological control-psychological autonomy** and **firm control-lax control.** Psychological control consists of parental behavior that keeps the child closely tied to the parent, while psychological autonomy refers to parent behavior that allows the child to develop more independently. Firm control occurs when the parent sets rules and regulations and requires the child to abide by them, while lax control results when the parent establishes rules but does not enforce them or does not develop clear-cut standards for the child's behavior.

How do these parenting orientations influence the child's social behavior? A high degree of psychological control promotes dependent, regressive behavior—crying and thumb sucking, for example—and difficulty in establishing peer relationships. Also, extensive control of the child's activities and demands for obedience by parents may result in inhibited, shy behavior in children, while little or no parental control is often related to impulsive behavior in children. Competent parenting is characterized, then, by behavior that is neither excessively high nor low in control. Diana Baumrind's (1971) research supports the belief that parents should be neither punitive toward their children nor aloof from them but rather should develop rules and regulations for their children and enforce them.

Warmth-Hostility   Note that one component of competent parenting in Baumrind's research is warmth and verbal give-and-take between the parent and child. Warmth-hostility (sometimes referred to as acceptance-rejection) in parenting is associated with predictable social behavior in children (McCord, McCord, & Howard, 1961). Overly hostile parents who show little affection toward their children have children who show patterns of hostile and aggressive behavior. Parents who show a high degree of warmth, nurturance, and acceptance toward their children have children who show high self-esteem (Coopersmith, 1967) and altruism (Zahn-Waxler, Radke-Yarrow, & King, 1979). It also should be mentioned that parents who show warmth toward their children are more likely to use reasoning and explanation in dealing with their children's transgressions than parents who are aloof and cold toward their children. The use of reasoning during discipline helps children to internalize rules and regulations and to understand the circumstances in which they can act in particular ways. The parent's nurturant orientation toward the child makes that parent someone the child wants to approach rather than avoid, increasing the likelihood of interaction between them. And parental warmth, rather than hostility and punitiveness, helps to reduce anxiety and make the parent-child relationship less fearful and power-oriented for the child.

Types of Parenting

Diana Baumrind (1971) emphasizes three types of parenting that are associated with different aspects of the child's social behavior: authoritarian, authoritative, and laissez-faire (permissive).

Authoritarian parenting describes parents who are restrictive, have a punitive orientation, exhort the child to follow their directions, respect work and effort, and place limits and controls on the child, with little verbal give-and-take between parent and child. This type of parenting behavior is linked with the following social behaviors of the child: an anxiety about social comparison, failure to initiate activity, and ineffective social interaction.

Authoritative parenting encourages the child to be independent but still places limits, demands, and controls on actions. There is extensive verbal give-and-take, and parents demonstrate a high degree of warmth and nurturance toward the child. This type of parenting behavior is associated with social competency, particularly self-reliance and social responsibility.

Laissez-faire (permissive) parenting places relatively low demands, limits, and controls on the child's behavior. The child is given considerable freedom to regulate his or her own behavior, with parents taking a nonpunitive stance. Parents are not very involved with

Peers are powerful social agents.

their child. This type of parenting behavior is associated with the following social behaviors of the child: immature, regressive behavior, poor self-restraint, and inability to direct and assume leadership.

Perhaps the most significant distinction is between authoritarian and authoritative parenting. For many years arguments have been aired about the best way to rear children. Is an authoritarian style better than a permissive style? Or vice versa? Many parents were not completely satisfied with either approach. The same could be said for teachers. Many teachers were afraid they would be branded "punitive," "harsh," or "cold" if they tried to exert control over the children in their classrooms—particularly where child-centered, affective, and humanistic educational approaches are popular. However, many teachers and parents alike believe that a controlling but warm approach may be best.

Next we see that to understand the nature of social development in early childhood, peer relations as well as parent-child relations need to be considered.

Peers

Children show a heightened interest in peers during early childhood. In this section we consider the main functions of the peer group, one aspect of early childhood that dominates the lives of many young children—play—and the manner in which the family and peers interact.

Functions of the Peer Group

Children spend a great deal of time with their peers; many of their greatest frustrations and happiest moments come when with their peers. The term *peers* usually refers to children who are about the same age, but

Controlling aggression involves analysis of many aspects of social settings.

children often interact with children who are three or four years older or younger. Peers also have been described as children who interact at about the same behavioral level (Lewis & Rosenblum, 1975). Defining peers in terms of behavioral level places more emphasis on the maturity of the children than on their age. For example, consider the precociously developed thirteen-year-old female adolescent who feels very funny around underdeveloped girls her own age. She may well find more satisfaction in time spent with adolescents of seventeen to eighteen years of age than with those her own age.

The influence of children who are the same age may be quite different from that of younger or older peers. For example, mixed-age groups often produce more dominant and altruistic behavior than do groups of children of the same age. Social contacts and aggression, though, are more characteristic of same-age peers. Willard Hartup (1976) has emphasized that same-age peer interaction serves a unique role in our culture:

I am convinced that age grading would occur even if our schools were not age graded and children were left alone to determine the composition of their own societies. After all, one can only learn to be a good fighter among age-mates: the bigger guys will kill you, and the littler ones are no challenge.

Perhaps one of the most important functions of the peer group is to provide a source of information and comparison about the world outside the family. From the peer group the child receives feedback about his or her abilities. The child evaluates what he or she does in terms of whether it is better than,

as good as, or worse than what other children do. It is hard to do this at home because siblings are usually older or younger. (p. 10)

Studies about the necessity of peers for competent social development have been limited primarily to animals. For example, when peer monkeys who have been reared together are separated from each other, indications of depression and less advanced social development are observed (Suomi, Harlow, & Domek, 1970). Attempts to use peer monkeys to counteract the effects of social isolation prove more beneficial when the deprived monkeys are placed with younger peers (Suomi & Harlow, 1972). Willard Hartup (Furman, Rahe, & Hartup, 1979) is trying out the younger-peer therapeutic technique with human peer isolates in a nursery school. Initial reports indicate that the technique is as effective with humans as it has been with monkeys.

In the human development literature there is a classic example of the importance of peers. Anna Freud (Freud & Dann, 1951) studied six children from different families who banded together after their parents were killed in World War II. Intensive peer attachment was observed; the children were a tightly knit group, dependent on one another and aloof with outsiders. Even though deprived of parental care, they became neither delinquent nor psychotic.

The frequency of peer interaction, both positive and negative, continues to increase throughout early childhood (Hartup, 1983). Although aggressive interaction and rough-and-tumble play increase, the *proportion* of aggressive exchanges to friendly interactions decreases, especially among middle-class boys. Children tend to abandon this immature and inefficient social interaction with age and acquire more mature methods of relating to peers.

Nonetheless, in most preschools we find that at least one or two boys engage in aggressive behavior toward their peers that cannot just be allowed to run its course. In application 9.1 we ask you to put yourself in the situation of being a teacher in a preschool with a boy who is showing a lot of aggression toward his peers.

Socialization cannot be described solely in terms of the quality of social activity, however. Evidence suggests that social differentiation is also a major achievement of the maturing child. Children become more adept at using social skills, so that by the end of the preschool years, a rudimentary peer system has emerged.

Play

Perhaps the most elaborate attempt to examine developmental changes in children's social play was conducted many years ago by Mildred Parten (1932). Based on observations of children in free play at nursery schools, she developed the following categories of play.

Unoccupied The child is not engaging in play as it is commonly understood. He or she may stand in one spot, look around the room, or perform random movements that seem to have no goal. In most nursery schools unoccupied play is less frequent than other types of play.

Solitary The child plays independently. The child seems engrossed in what he or she is doing and does not care much about anything else that is going on. Parten found that two- and three-year-olds engage more frequently in solitary play than older preschoolers do.

Onlooker The child watches other children playing. He or she may talk with them or ask questions but does not enter into their play behavior. The child's active interest in other children's play distinguishes this type of play from unoccupied play.

Parallel The child plays alone but with toys like those that other children are using or in a manner that mimics the behavior of other playing children. The older the child, the less frequently he or she engages in this type of play; even older preschool children, however, engage in parallel play relatively often.

Associative Social interaction is involved in associative play but with little or no organization. Children engage in play activities similar to those of other children; however, they appear to be more interested in being associated with each other than in the tasks they are involved with. Borrowing or lending toys and materials and following or leading one another in a line are examples of associative play. The child plays as he or she wishes; there is no effort at placing the group first and himself or herself last.

Cooperative Social interaction in a group characterizes cooperative play. A sense of group identity is present, and activity is organized. Children's formal games, competition aimed at winning something, and groups formed by the teacher for doing things together usually are examples of this type of play. Cooperative play is the prototype for the games of middle childhood; little of it is seen in the preschool years.

Parten's categories are still a relevant and valuable method for observing children.

To see whether Parten's findings were dated, Keith Barnes (1971) observed a group of preschoolers using Parten's categories of play. He watched the children's activities during an hour-long free-play period each schoolday for twelve weeks. He found that children in the 1970s did not engage in as much associative or cooperative play as they did in the 1930s. Several reasons were advanced to explain this difference: (1) children have become more passive because of television viewing; (2) toys today are more abundant and attractive than they were forty years ago, so solitary play may be more natural; and (3) parents today may encourage children to play by themselves more than parents did years ago.

During the preschool years peer interaction may involve highly ritualized social interchanges. A **ritual** is a form of spontaneous play that involves controlled repetition. These interchanges have been referred to as *turns* and *rounds* by Katherine Garvey (1977). The contribution of each child is called a turn, while the total sequence of alternating turns constitutes a round.

Following is an example of a round between two five-year-olds:

Boy	Girl
(1) Can you carry this?	(2) Yeah, if I weighed fifty pounds.
(3) You can't even carry it.	
Ritual	
(4) Can you carry it by the string?	(5) Yeah. Yes, I can (lifts toy fish overhead by string)
(6) Can you carry it by the eye?	(7) (carries it by eye)
(8) Can you carry it by the nose?	(9) Where's the nose?
(10) That yellow one.	(11) This (carries it by nose)
Ritual	
(12) Can you carry it by its tail?	(13) Yeah, (carries it by tail)
(14) Can you carry it by its fur?	(15) (carries it by fur)
(16) Can you carry it by its body?	(17) (carries it by body)
(18) Can you carry it like this? (shows how to carry it by fin)	(19) (carries it by fin)
(20) Right.	(21) I weigh fifty pounds almost, right? (pp. 118–19)

In this ritual between a five-year-old boy and girl, both language and motion were involved. The boy's turns were verbal; the girl's mainly variations of picking up and carrying the fish. There was a tendency for the five-year-old children to engage in more complex rituals than younger children, but three-year-old children were more likely to participate in longer rituals than their older counterparts. For example, a ritual among three-year-olds might involve the sequence "You're a girl," "No, I'm not," repeated for as long as several minutes. As children become older and enter the elementary school years, rituals may become more formal and can be found in games like red rover and London Bridge.

When children are asked what they enjoy most, they invariably say "playing." When children talk with each other, the word *play* is conspicuous: "What can we play?" "Let's play hide-and-seek." "No, let's play outside." "Why don't we play tag?" The major portion of many young children's days is spent in play. In the next section, we look at what could be called the typical play of children, pretend play, and discuss the various functions play can fulfill in the child's development.

Pretend Play

When children engage in pretend play, they have transformed the physical environment into a symbol. Make-believe play appears rather abruptly at about eighteen months of age, continues to develop between ages three and four, peaks between five and six years, and then declines. In the early elementary school years children's interests begin to shift to games.

In pretend play, children try out many different roles—they may be the mother, the father, the teacher, the next-door neighbor, and so forth. Sometimes their pretend play reflects an adult role; at other times it may make fun of it. An example of pretend play follows (Hartley, Frank, & Goldenson, 1952).

Harvey was playing with Karen, his twin sister. Karen began to push the carriage. Harvey said, "Let me be the baby, Karen," and started to talk like a baby. He got into the carriage. Karen pushed him around the room as he squinted his eyes and cried. She stopped the carriage, patted his shoulder, he squinted his eyes and cried. She stopped the carriage, patted his shoulder, saying, "Don't cry baby." He squirmed around, put his thumb in his mouth, and swayed his body.

Josie came to the carriage and wanted to push Harvey. He jumped out and hit her in the face. She walked away almost crying. He went to her, put his arm around her and said, in a sympathetic manner, "Come, you be the baby, I'll push you in the carriage." She climbed in. He ran and got the dog and gave it to her saying, "Here, baby." She smiled and began to play with the dog. He went to the housekeeping corner, got a cup and held it to her mouth. He smacked his lips, looking at her, smiling. He pushed her around in the carriage. Karen ran to him and said, "Harvey, let me push the carriage, I'll be the mamma, you be the daddy." Harvey said "O.K.," and reached his hand in his pocket and gave her money. He said, "Bye, baby," waving his hand. (pp. 70–72)

You probably can remember many episodes of pretend play from your own childhood—playing doctor, teacher, superman, and so on. One of the many functions of play is to maintain affiliation with peers. Play also allows the child to work out anxieties and conflicts, advances cognitive development, and provides an opportunity to practice the roles he or she will assume later in life and to explore the world.

Play is an elusive concept. It can range from an infant's simple exercise of a new-found sensorimotor talent to the preschool child's riding a tricycle to the older child's participation in organized games. One expert on play and games has observed that there is no universally accepted definition of play, probably because it can encompass so many different kinds of activities (Sutton-Smith, 1973).

Next we see that we can benefit by looking at the social worlds of peers and the family simultaneously.

Family and Peers

Peer relations are both similar to and different from parent-child relations. For example, infants touch, smile, and vocalize when they interact with both parents and other children. However, rough-and-tumble play occurs mainly with other children and not with adults. Another difference in children's orientation toward peers and parents is that in times of stress, children usually move toward their parents rather than their peers. Willard Hartup (1979) described some of the most important ideas about the interrelation of the worlds of child-child and parent-child relations.

As children grow older, their interactions with adult associates and with child associates become more extensively differentiated: (a) Different actions are used to express affection to child associates and to adults, and (b) dominance and nurturance are directed from adults to children, but appeals and submissions are directed more frequently by children to adults than vice versa.

The evidence, then, suggests that children live in distinctive, albeit coordinate, social worlds. Family relations and peer relations constitute similar sociobehavioral contexts in some ways and different ones in others. Children may not conceive of separate normative worlds until early adolescence, because child associates are not used extensively as normative models before that time (Emmerich, Goldman, & Shore, 1971). But the family system and the peer system elicit distinctive socioemotional activity many years before these normative distinctions are made. The complex interrelations between the family and peer systems thus work themselves out over long periods of time (Hill, 1980). (pp. 947–48)

More specifically, it has been argued by ethologists that the role of the mother is to provide a "secure" base for the child's early attachment, which in turn reduces the child's fears and promotes exploration of the environment. The reduction in fear and increase in exploratory behavior could be expected to increase the likelihood that the child would seek out age-mates with whom to play. And while parents are not usually as good at playing with their children as children are among themselves, parents, and particularly mothers, often take an active role in monitoring their children's choice of playmates and the form of their play.

Recent research supports the contention that a secure early attachment to the mother promotes positive peer relations (Waters, Wippman, & Sroufe, in press). For example, in one investigation a group of fifteen-month-old infants were observed interacting with their mothers and classified by the observers as "securely" or "anxiously" attached. Later, when the children were three-and-one-half years old, they were observed during peer interaction for a period of five weeks. Compared with their "anxiously" attached age-mates, the "securely" attached children were more socially active, more often sought out by other children, more likely to serve as leaders, and more sympathetic to the distress of their peers.

Further comments by Alan Sroufe (1983) point to the coordinated worlds of children and parents. He points out that children who are "bullies" are more likely to have rejecting, punitive parents while "whipping boys," those who are frequently singled out as targets for aggression in the peer group, are more likely to have overprotective, overinvolved relationships with their parents.

Hartup (1979) cautions, however, that it is risky to conclude that healthy parent-child relations are a prerequisite for healthy peer relations. Nonetheless, the data are consistent with the belief that the child's relations with his or her parents serve as emotional bases for exploring and enjoying positive peer relations.

So far in this chapter we have seen that the social worlds of family and peers play primary roles in the child's social and emotional development. During early childhood, most children are extensively exposed to television—next we explore the effects of television on development.

The Role of Television

Television has been called a lot of things, not all of them good; depending on one's point of view, it may be a window on the world, the one-eyed monster, or the boob tube. Television has been attacked as one of the reasons that scores on national achievement tests in reading and mathematics are lower now than they have been in the past. Television, it is claimed, attracts children away from books and schoolwork. Furthermore, it is argued that television trains the child to become a passive learner; rarely, if ever, does television call for active responses from the observer.

Of particular concern has been the extent to which children are exposed to violence and aggression on television. Up to 80 percent of the prime-time shows include such violent acts as beatings, shootings, or stabbings. And there are usually about five of these violent acts per hour on prime-time shows. The frequency of violence is even greater on the Saturday morning cartoon shows, where there is an average of more than twenty-five violent episodes per hour (Friedrich & Stein, 1973).

Television also is said to deceive; that is, it teaches children that problems are easily resolved and that everything always comes out right in the end. For example, it usually takes only from thirty to ninety minutes for detectives to sort through a complex array of clues and discover the killer—and they always find the killer. Violence is pictured as a way of life in many shows. It is all right for police to use violence and to

break moral codes in their fight against evildoers. And the lasting results of violence are rarely brought home to the viewer. A person who is injured appears to suffer for only a few seconds, even though in real life a person with such an injury may not recover for several weeks or months or perhaps not at all. Yet one out of every two first-grade children says that the adults on television are like adults in real life (Lyle & Hoffman, 1972).

Children watch a lot of television, and they seem to be watching more all the time. In the 1950s three-year-olds watched television for less than one hour a day, and five-year-olds watched for slightly over two hours a day (Schramm, Lyle, & Parker, 1961). But in the 1970s preschool children watched television for an average of four hours a day, and elementary school children watched for as long as six hours each day (Friedrich & Stein, 1973).

Other than television, the only medium reaching large numbers of children in this country is books. Children also read comic books, magazines, and some newspaper comic strips; they go to movies; and they listen to the radio and to their records and tapes. Television, comic books, movies, and comic strips can be thought of as pictorial media; the children who use one of these pictorial media regularly tend to use the others also. But children who frequently use pictorial media are not necessarily frequent consumers of the printed media, such as books and the written, nonpictorial parts of newspapers and magazines (e.g., Greenberg & Domonick, 1969). Their use of the pictorial media increases until they are about twelve, after which time it declines. Children from low-income backgrounds use pictorial media more than children from middle-income homes, and black children are exposed to pictorial media more than white children (Schramm et al., 1961).

Television as a Social Agent

George Comstock (1978) argues that television is such a strong socialization force on the child that it should be given status as a social agent, competing with parents, teachers, and other agents in providing models for emulation and information that influence the child's beliefs, values, and expectations. What social scientists are not sure of is whether television's influence is positive or negative.

Earlier, a number of negative comments were made about the effects of television on children. However, there are some possible positive aspects to its influences on children as well. For one, television presents the child with a world that is often different from the one he or she lives in. This means that through television the child is exposed to a wider variety of views and knowledge than may be the case from parents, teachers, or peers.

Television is also a medium through which the child can learn new behaviors. The modeling theory of Albert Bandura (e.g. Bandura, 1977) has served as a theoretical source for a number of inquiries about observational learning and the effects of television on children.

Television's Influences on Behavior

Television affects children's behavior as well as their values and attitudes. For instance, television violence contributes to antisocial behavior in children, particularly their aggression toward other children. Let's look at one example that demonstrates this fact clearly. One group of children was exposed to cartoons of the violent Saturday morning type; another group was shown the same cartoons with the violence removed. Children who saw the cartoons with the violence later kicked, choked, and pushed their friends more than the children who saw the same cartoons without the violent acts (Steuer, Applefield, & Smith, 1971).

When children watch television, they not only see cartoon shows and adult programs, but they also are exposed to commercials. The average television-viewing child, somewhat amazingly, sees over 20,000 commercials per year. A significant proportion of those commercials involve highly sugared food products (Barcus, 1978). To investigate the effects of television food commercials and pronutritional public service announcements on children's snack choices, Joann Galst (1980) exposed three- to six-year-old children to television cartoons over a four-week period. The advertising content of the shows consisted of either commercials for food products with added sugar content, for food products with no added sugar content, or pronutritional public service announcements. The children were allowed to select a snack each day after the television show. The no-sugar commercial and the pronutritional public service announcement were the most effective in reducing children's selection of sugar-added snacks.

Television can also teach children that it is better to behave in prosocial rather than in antisocial ways. Aimee Leifer (1973) has demonstrated how television can instill prosocial behaviors in young children. From the television show "Sesame Street" she selected a number of episodes that reflected positive social interchanges. She was particularly interested in situations that teach the child how to use social skills. For example, in one exchange two men were fighting over the amount of space available to them; they gradually began to cooperate and to share the space. Children who watched these episodes copied these behaviors and in later social situations applied the lessons they had learned.

Family Environment and Television Watching During the Preschool Years

Recently psychologists have been interested in studying the home environment of children during the preschool years to see how it might influence their television watching. The age period from two and one-half to six seems to be an important formative period for television viewing habits. In one recent investigation (Huston, Seigle, & Bremer, 1983), families kept a one-week diary of television viewing for each family member. A home interview was conducted prior to the diary week to obtain information about various child and family characteristics. Although parents with higher occupational status and more education had children who watched less television than their lower socioeconomic status counterparts, maternal employment was not linked with young children's television watching. Low viewing was characteristic of children who attended preschool and day care. Further, children with younger siblings watched television more than those with older siblings, possibly because they were at home more. Mothers of high viewers reported more arguments about television rules and discussions about television content than did mothers of low viewers. Maternal regulation of television watching was only related to low viewing for the five-year-olds. At age five boys watched more television than girls, and children who used books and the printed media watched less than those who did not. Thus by looking at what goes on within the home environment we are obtaining a clearer picture of children's television viewing habits.

Personality Development

In this section, we describe two of the most important aspects of personality development in early childhood—the self and sex-typed behavior.

The Self

You saw in chapter 2 that the self is the fundamental unit in the humanistic perspective of development. The self also is an important part of the cognitive structural view of Lawrence Kohlberg. Kohlberg (1976) believes that personality develops within the framework of Piaget's stages of cognitive development. The concept of personality structure, then, is a part of rational thinking and the development of cognitive structures. The various strands of personality development (such as sex-role development, morality, identity, and so forth) are wired together by the child's developing sense of self and perceptions of the self in relation to other individuals (particularly in role-taking relationships).

Recently, investigators such as John Flavell (1977) have found that children as young as three years of age have a basic idea that they have a private self to which others do not have access. Flavell reports the following exchange between an experimenter and a three-year-old:

(Can I see you thinking?) "No." (Even if I look in your eyes, do I see you thinking?) "No." (Why not?) "Cause I don't have any big holes." (You mean there would have to be a hole there for me to see you thinking?) Child nods. (p. 16)

Another child said that the experimenter could not see his thinking processes because he had skin over his head.

Young children also distinguish this inner self from their bodily self or outer self, a distinction that seems to emerge sometime between three and four years of age. After they have developed an understanding that they have a private self, children then set about the task of defining the characteristics of their private self. Initially children's self-definition focuses on external characteristics, such as how they look, where they live, and what activities they are involved in, but later—after about the age of six or seven—they begin to describe themselves more in terms of psychological traits (e.g., how they feel, their personality characteristics, and their relationships with others). And with increasing age, group membership assumes a more important status in self-definition.

Sex-Typed Behavior

All of us, particularly young children, are curious about our gender. Do you remember the images you had when you were young of what girls and boys must be like? And the way your parents might have stumbled in trying to answer your questions about sexuality?

In this section we will look in depth at the concept of androgyny. As part of this discussion, definitions of a number of terms related to sex-role development will be given. The roles of biology, cognition, and the developmental course of sex roles will be discussed, and the role of the environment in sex-role development will be explored.

Androgyny and the Components of Sex-Role Development

The label **sex role** has been used to describe the different characteristics children display because of their sex. However, some experts (e.g., Spence & Helmreich, 1978) define sex role as the behaviors that are *expected* of children because they are either male or female.

Another important aspect of the child's sexual makeup is what is referred to as **sexual, or gender, identity.** We can define this as the extent to which individual children actually take on as part of their personalities the behaviors and attitudes associated with either the male or female role. In the United States and in most other countries, the well-adjusted child has traditionally been one who has developed a sex-appropriate sex role. That is, males are supposed to be "masculine" and females are supposed to be "feminine." In past years most research on children's sex roles has been conducted along this line; researchers have assessed the concept of sex roles as a bipolar construct,

"Please don't bring me anything that requires my acting out traditional female roles!"

© 1973 by NEA, Inc.

We live in a society of changing sex roles. Females increasingly are engaging in formerly "masculine" activities.

with masculinity and femininity considered as opposites. Recently, an alternative view of children's sex roles has been developed and is based on the concept of **androgyny.**

The belief that masculinity and femininity are opposites was refuted by psychologists in the mid-1970s when they began to suggest not only that masculinity and femininity are independent of one another but also that the healthiest way to conceive of sex roles may be to view all children as having both masculine and feminine characteristics.

Androgyny has become a byword in research on sex roles in the late 1970s and early 1980s. What does it mean if we say twelve-year-old Bob is androgynous? It means that his psychological makeup includes both masculine and feminine aspects of behavior; sometimes it is said that people like Bob have an androgynous sex-role orientation. Sandra Bem (1977) and Janet Spence (Spence & Helmreich, 1978) pioneered the notion that sex roles should not be looked at as bipolar sexual extremes but rather as dualistic dimensions within each sex. In other words every male child has and should have some feminine attributes, and every female child has and should have some masculine attributes. Furthermore, both Bem and Spence believe that androgyny is not only natural but allows the child to adapt more competently to a wide variety of situations (e.g., Spence, 1982).

Bem created the Bem Sex Role Inventory (BSRI) and Spence developed the Personality Attributes Questionnaire (PAQ), both of which measure androgyny. Spence (Spence & Helmreich, 1978) also developed the Child's Personal Attributes Questionnaire (Children's PAQ) to assess children's androgyny.

The Children's PAQ includes such positively valued "masculine" traits as independence, competitiveness, ability to make decisions easily, unwillingness to give up easily, self-confidence, and a sense of superiority; positive "feminine" characteristics include gentleness, helpfulness, kindness, and awareness of others' feelings. Although androgyny has been scored in different ways by researchers, Spence had her colleagues (Spence, Helmreich, & Stapp, 1975) advocate classifying those who score high on both the feminine and masculine scales as androgynous. Individuals who score low on both the masculine and feminine scales are labeled "undifferentiated"; and the sex role is categorized as "masculine" or "feminine" if the child scores high on one scale and low on the other.

Androgynous children are viewed positively for two reasons. First, the classification of a child as androgynous is based on the appearance of both masculine and feminine characteristics rather than the absence of both. Second, and more importantly, the attributes that comprise androgyny are those aspects of masculinity and femininity that are valued by our culture. The androgynous child is achievement oriented, shows high self-esteem, is a warm individual, and so on (Babladelis, 1979).

Not everyone agrees with Spence and Bem's belief that we ought to be developing androgynous individuals. For example, the culmination of Phyllis Katz's (1979) developmental view is conformity to socially prescribed sex roles. She believes that sex-role socialization is a lifelong process and that socialization agents outside the family play more important roles than was previously thought. The first developmental period in her theory is infancy-puberty, at which time children learn appropriate child sex roles. During adolescence, a second developmental period appears in the form of preparation for adult sex roles. Sexual maturation, heterosexual relationships, and career goals represent areas of sexual change in adolescence. The third developmental level refers to adult sex-role development, involving adjustment to changing family structure and occupational roles. Diana Baumrind (1982), whose parenting styles were discussed earlier, agrees that the most competent parents, adults, and children are traditionally sex-typed. In application 9.2 we look at how easy and how ethical it is to change young children's sex-typed behavior.

Biological Forces and Cognitive Factors and Development

There has been increased interest in the developmental aspects of sex roles in recent years, as witnessed by the number of theoretical views on sex roles that contain developmental components. Most developmental views of sex roles rely heavily on biological and cognitive processes, as will be seen next.

Biological Forces   One of Freud's basic assumptions is that human behavior and history are directly related to reproductive processes. From this assumption arises the belief that sexuality is essentially unlearned and *instinctual.* Erik Erikson (1968) has extended this argument, claiming that psychological differences in males and females stem from anatomical differences between the two groups. Erikson argues that because of genital structure, males are more intrusive and aggressive, while females are more inclusive and passive. Erikson's belief is sometimes referred to as the "anatomy is destiny" doctrine.

One period during which sex hormones are produced extensively is before birth. Anna Ehrhardt has studied the influence of prenatal hormonal changes on sex-role development (Ehrhardt & Baker, 1973). In the 1950s a number of expectant mothers were given doses of androgen (a male sex hormone); these women had a history of miscarriage, and the hormone is believed to ameliorate conditions that cause this problem. Six offspring of these mothers were studied, ranging from four to twenty-six years of age. They were compared with siblings of the same sex whose mothers had not been treated with androgen during the prenatal period.

Results indicate that hormones are an important factor in sex-role development. The girls whose mothers received androgen expended comparatively more energy in their play and seemed to prefer boys over girls as playmates. Instead of dolls they chose male sex-typed toys for play. They displayed little interest in future marriage and did not enjoy taking care of babies. They also preferred functional over attractive clothes and were generally unconcerned with their appearance. The boys whose mothers received androgen engaged in rough-and-tumble play and outdoor sports to a greater extent than their unaffected brothers did.

Ehrhardt's work has been criticized for a number of reasons. For one, the inflated androgen levels require that these individuals be treated with cortisone for the remainder of their lives. One of the side effects of cortisone is a high activity level. The high energy and activity levels of the girls and boys, then, may be due to the cortisone treatment rather than to high levels of androgen (Quadagno, Briscoe, & Quadagno, 1977). Second, "masculinized" girls may be perceived as deviant by their parents, siblings, and peers. Those around them may have thought of them as "boys" and treated them accordingly.

No one argues the existence of genetic, biochemical, and anatomical differences between the sexes. Even environmentally oriented psychologists acknowledge that boys and girls will be treated differently because of their physical differences and their different roles in reproduction. Consequently, the importance of biological factors is not at issue; what is at issue is the directness or indirectness of the effect of biological factors on social behavior.

According to Aletha Huston (1983), if a high androgen level directly influences the central nervous system, which in turn produces a higher activity level, then the effect is reasonably direct. By contrast, if a high level of androgen produces strong muscle development, which in turn causes others to expect the child to be a good athlete and in turn leads her to participate in sports, then the biological effect is more indirect.

Cognitive Factors and Development   In addition to biology and culture, cognitive development is an important aspect of understanding children's sex roles. In order to have an idea of what is masculine or feminine, Kohlberg (1966) asserts, the child has to be able to categorize objects and behaviors into these two groups.

Application 9.2

Changing the Sex-Typed Behavior of Young Children: How Easy, How Ethical?

In a recent review of children's sex-typed behavior, Aletha Huston (1983) concluded that efforts to change children's sex-typed behavior have taken two directions: *gender-deviant* children are trained to show more appropriate sex-typed behavior, and attempts are made to free normal children from rigidly sex-typed patterns. Both types of interventions create ethical concerns; yet both produce valuable information about sex typing, that is, the psychological aspects of being male or female.

Most studies of gender deviance have included only boys who are diagnosed as gender deviant when they play mostly with feminine sex-typed toys, dress up in female clothes, choose girls rather than boys as playmates, engage in female role playing, fantasize about being a girl, and express themselves with feminine gestures (Rekers, 1979). These gender-deviant boys not only preferred feminine activities but also purposely avoided masculine activities. In particular they indicated that the rough-and-tumble play of other boys either disinterested or frightened them (Green, 1974).

Huston pointed out that gender deviance among girls has received less attention, possibly because our society allows girls more flexibility in their dress, play activities, and sex-typed interests than it does boys. The characteristics used to describe gender-deviant girls are similar to those used for boys—preferring masculine activities and boys as playmates, taking male roles in fantasy, fantasizing about being a boy, and dressing in male clothes. While masculine clothing and interests are commonplace among girls, the gender-deviant girls also are characterized by strong avoidance of feminine clothing, activities, and playmates.

Although diagnosis and treatment of gender deviance has occurred, we have little knowledge of the origins of such patterns. One possibility is that many parents are indifferent to the occurrence of gender-deviant patterns of behavior in young children. Some parents think it is cute when little boys continue to dress up as females and play with dolls. Such children often are referred for treatment only after someone outside the family points out the child's effeminate characteristics. Other factors that show up in the case histories of some gender-deviant boys are maternal overprotection of boys and restrictions on rough-and-tumble play, absence of an adult male, weak father-son relationship, physical beauty on the part of the small boy that led to his being treated as a girl, absence of male playmates, and maternal dominance.

Both behavioral and psychoanalytic treatment procedures have been used in attempts to alter the sex-typed behavior of gender-deviant children. These treatment procedures have led to changes in children's play patterns but usually only in the situation where the treatment occurred. Consequently, clinical treatment has been augmented by direct interventions at home and at school.

Are such interventions ethical? Some experts believe that traditional sex roles should not be forced on children who deviate from expected societal patterns (Nordyke, Baer, Etzel, & LeBlanc, 1977). They point out that the individual behavior patterns of children should be respected and that it is the societal norm rather than the behavior that is wrong. The intervention advocates agree that efforts to change societal norms should be made, but they also add that gender-deviant males in particular often show extensive social isolation and unhappiness that lasts for many years. An additional argument for intervention is the belief that parental desires provide ethical grounds for intervening in children's lives. If parents believe their child's behavior is undesirable, then, it is argued, the psychologist should abide by those desires.

In addition to attempting to change the sex-typed behavior of gender-deviant children, another effort focused on teaching children about androgyny. Many feminists have developed programs targeted to reduce traditional sex-typing in children. One such effort is a curriculum that lasted for one year and was implemented in the kindergarten, fifth- and ninth-grade classes. (Guttentag & Bray, 1976). It involved books, discussion materials, and classroom exercises. The program was most successful with the fifth graders and was the least successful with the ninth-graders (who actually displayed a "boomerang effect" that produced even more rigid sex-typed behavior). The program's success varied from class to class, seeming to be most effective when the teacher produced sympathetic reaction in the peer group; however, students in some classes ridiculed and rejected the curriculum.

Ethical concerns are also aroused when the issue is one of teaching children to depart from socially approved behavior patterns, particularly when there is no evidence of extreme sex typing in the groups of children to whom the interventions are applied. The advocates of the androgyny programs believe that traditional sex typing is psychologically harmful for all children and that it has prevented many girls and women from experiencing equal opportunity. Huston concluded that while the research indicates that androgyny is more adaptive than either a traditional masculine or feminine pattern, it is not possible to ignore the imbalance within our culture, which values masculinity more than femininity.

According to Kohlberg, the categories become relatively stable for a child by the age of six; that is, by this age children have a fairly definite idea of which category they belong to. Furthermore, they understand what is entailed by the category and seldom fluctuate in their category judgments. This self-categorization provides the impetus for the unfolding of sex-role development.

Kohlberg reasons that sex-role development proceeds in this sequence: "I am a boy, I want to do boy things, therefore, the opportunity to do boy things is rewarding" (p. 89). The child, having acquired the ability to categorize, strives toward consistency between use of the categories and actual behavior. This striving for consistency forms the basis for the development of sex typing.

A second developmental theory that has received attention in recent years is Jeanne Block's view that sex-role development is a component of a more general personality structure called the ego. According to Block (1973), sex-role development proceeds in the following invariant manner:

Stage 1: Gender identity and self-enhancement

Stage 2: External sex-role standards

Stage 3: Internalized sex-role standards

Stage 4: Androgyny

This type of development follows closely the thinking of Kohlberg (1976), who argues that development proceeds from preconformity, through conformity, to postconformity levels. Block believes that very young children are mainly concerned with assertion, extending their self, and becoming independent of parental restrictions. The second stage is the point at which conformity to rules and roles becomes more apparent. An important sex difference occurs at this stage in that boys are rewarded for controlling and suppressing affection and nurturance, while girls are rewarded for repressing assertiveness and aggressiveness. Block's last two stages occur primarily in adulthood and involve the perception that masculine and feminine elements can be integrated in the form of an androgynous personality.

Environmental Influences
In our culture adults begin to discriminate between sexes shortly after the infant's birth. The "pink and blue treatment" is often applied to girls and boys even before they leave the hospital. Soon afterward the differences in hair styles, clothes, and toys become obvious. Adults and other children reinforce these differences throughout childhood, but boys and girls also learn appropriate role behavior by watching what other people say and do. For example, a seven-year-old boy who knows he is a boy readily labels appropriate objects as male or female, but he has parents who support the feminist movement and stress equality between the sexes. His behavior will be less stereotyped along masculine lines than that of boys reared in more traditional homes.

One considerable change in the role of environmental influences on sex-role development in recent years has resulted in a de-emphasis on parents as the critical socialization agents. There has been a corresponding increase in the belief that schools, peers, media, and other family members should be given more attention when the child's sex-role development is at issue. Parents clearly are only one of many sources through which children learn about sex-role development. Yet it is important to guard against swinging too far in this direction, because particularly in the early years of life, parents do play a very important role in their child's sex-role development.

The Role of Parents   Fathers and mothers both are psychologically important for children even during infancy. Fathers seem to play a particularly important role in the sex typing of both boys and girls. Reviews of sex-typing research indicate that fathers are more likely to act differently toward sons and daughters than mothers are (e.g., Huston, 1983). And most reviews of the father-absence literature (e.g., Lamb, 1981) conclude that boys show a more feminine patterning of behavior in father-absent than in father-present homes; however, close inspection of those studies suggests that this conclusion is more appropriate for young children, while the findings for elementary and secondary school children are mixed. For example, Hetherington, Cox, & Cox (1978) found that children's sex-typed behavior reflected more than the unavailability of a consistent adult male model. While many single-parent mothers were overprotective and apprehensive about their son's independence, when single parents encouraged masculine and exploratory behavior and did not have a negative attitude toward the absent father, disruption in the son's sex-typed behavior did not occur.

Many parents encourage boys and girls to engage in different types of play activities even during infancy. In particular many parents emphasize that doll play is for girls only, while boys are more likely to be rewarded for engaging in gross motor activities. And often parents play more actively with male babies and respond more positively to physical activity by boys. There also is some evidence that parents encourage girls to be more dependent, show affection, and express tender emotions than boys; but there is no indication that parents show different reactions to aggression according to their child's sex. And with increasing age, boys are permitted more freedom by parents. (Huston, 1983).

Teachers and peers, as models and through feedback, influence children's sex-role development.

Thus we can see that parents, by action and example, influence their child's sex-role development. In the psychoanalytic view this influence stems principally from the child's identification with the parent of the same sex. The child develops a sense of likeness to the parent of the same sex and strives to emulate that parent.

Parents provide the earliest discrimination of sex-typed behavior in the child's development, but before long peers and teachers have joined the societal process of providing substantial feedback about masculine and feminine roles.

Teachers and Peers Children have acquired a preference for sex-typed toys and activities before most of them are exposed to school. During the preschool and elementary school years, teachers and peers usually maintain these preferences through feedback.

Actual observations of teacher behavior in both preschool and elementary school classes suggest that boys are given more disapproval, scolding, and other forms of negative attention than girls (Serbin, O'Leary, Kent, & Tonick, 1973). However, the findings for positive teacher behavior are mixed; some investigators find that teachers give more positive attention to girls (Fagot, 1973), while others find that boys get more positive attention (e.g., Serbin et al., 1973). Similarly, there is no consistent evidence that teachers reward sex-typed social behaviors differently for boys and girls (Huston, 1983). Sometimes, however, the fact that boys do not do as well as girls in school early in their development is attributed to the fact that either female teachers treat boys differently from girls or that boys have few male models as teachers.

Female teachers are more likely to reward "feminine" behavior than "masculine" behavior. Fagot (1975) reasoned that teachers would most probably support student behaviors that were a part of their own behavioral system. Because most preschool and elementary school teachers are females, they would be expected to reward behaviors consistent with the feminine, or "good girl," stereotype. As expected, she found that teachers reinforced both boys' and girls' feminine behaviors 83 percent of the time. In a similar study McCandless (1973) found that female teachers rewarded feminine behaviors 51 percent of the time and masculine behaviors 49 percent of the time. Perhaps if more male adults were involved in early education, there would be more support of masculine behavior and activity.

Summary

There has been an increase in child abuse in the United States—psychologists believe that by analyzing cultural, familial, and community influences rather than focusing solely on negative personality traits of parents, child abuse can be better understood. Parents and peers are clearly two of the most important social agents who influence the child's development. Children are exposed to a greater variety of family structures than in any other era of history. The two most profound changes in family structure are the increase in single-parent families and the entrance into the work force of a large number of mothers. Divorce rates are increasing exponentially, often leaving the child with feelings of loss and deprivation. The fact that the child's mother works outside the home does not necessarily lead to incompetent parenting on her part; it likely benefits some aspects of her relationship with her child and harms others. Many complex factors mediate the effects of father absence and the mother's employment outside the home on the child's development.

Psychologists have applied many labels to the socialization techniques parents use to deal with their children. Two dimensions psychologists have used to categorize parenting techniques are control-autonomy and warmth-hostility. In a comparison of authoritarian, authoritative, and laissez-faire parenting styles, only authoritative parenting was associated with social competence in children.

The child's development is also extensively influenced by peers, or age-mates. The peer group provides a unique opportunity for practicing roles and finding out information about the world outside of the family.

During the toddler years toys take on increased importance during peer interaction, and in the preschool years words begin to replace toys as the primary medium of peer interaction. During the early years of the child's life play takes up a large portion of the day. Perhaps the most prolific form of play is pretend play, which allows the child to practice many different roles.

Family relations and peer relations constitute similar social worlds in some ways and different ones in others. For example, infants touch, smile, and vocalize when they interact with both parents and age-mates. Yet rough-and-tumble play occurs mainly with other children, not with adults. Family experiences may serve as a basis for the development of peer relations, positively through the mother's role as a secure attachment for the infant and negatively through the stress of divorce.

Another aspect of our culture that has a pervasive influence on children's development is television. Children often spend more time watching television than they do interacting with peers or parents; for this reason alone television merits consideration as a socializing influence. Television can produce both aggressive and prosocial behaviors. Its programs project many stereotypes of different groups and distorts reality—and the child's perceptions of reality—in its portrayal of events in everyday life. Changes have been observed in children's ability to distinguish between reality and fantasy, to remember what was shown, and to comprehend complex character motivation and behavior on television.

Two important aspects of early childhood are the self and sex-typed behavior. Lawrence Kohlberg believes that self-development is rooted in the development of rational thought. In early childhood, Kohlberg argues, the child is in the concrete-individual stage, a time when he or she becomes preoccupied with the distinctiveness of himself or herself and perceives that the world revolves around him or her. At some point during the preschool years, the child does discover that he or she has a private self to which others do not have access.

Traditionally sex roles have been studied in terms of a bipolar construct of masculinity and femininity. More recently, the concept of androgyny has been introduced. This concept suggests that every child is to some degree androgynous, having both feminine and masculine attributes. Knowledge of sex roles begins very early in development and is influenced by both biology and culture. In the period from eighteen months to three years, children begin to show a great deal of interest in sex-typed play and activities, and from age three to seven, they begin to understand the concept of gender constancy and to enjoy being with same-sex peers. Environmental influences on the child's sex-role development include a host of social agents and other aspects of the culture in which the child grows up, among them, parental standards, teacher-child relations, peer relations, and the media.

Key Terms

androgyny

associative play

authoritarian parenting

authoritative parenting

control-automony

cooperative play

firm control-lax control

laissez-faire (permissive) parenting

onlooker play

parallel play

pretend play

psychological control-psychological autonomy

ritual

sex role

sex-typed behavior

sexual (gender) identity

solitary play

unoccupied play

warmth-hostility

Review Questions

1. Describe how parents should adapt to the developing child and how changes in parents can influence the child.
2. How is the structure of the family changing, and how have these changes influenced children?
3. What are some effective socialization techniques for dealing with children?
4. Discuss some of the positive and negative ways siblings can socialize each other.
5. Describe the development of peer relations in the first six years of life.
6. What function does play serve in the child's development?
7. Discuss the interrelation of the social world of the family and the social world of peers.
8. Describe some aspects of the child's life that are affected by television.
9. Describe some of the different components of sex typing.

Further Readings

Becker, W. *Parents are teachers*. Champaign, Ill.: Research Press, 1971.
Wesley Becker has studied parental influences on children for many years. In his paperback he outlines some principles of behavior modification that can be taught to parents and includes a number of exercises for observing family interaction. Easy to read.

Garvey, C. *Play*. Cambridge, Mass.: Harvard University Press, 1977.
This short book is an excellent overview of the most important aspects of children's play. Many examples reflecting the unique play experiences of children at different developmental levels are given. Medium reading level.

Huston, A. C. Sex-typing. In E. M. Hetherington (ed.), *Carmichael's manual of child psychology* (4th ed.). New York: Wiley, 1983.
A lengthy, up-to-date overview of what we know about the sex typing of children. Includes detailed information about androgyny and biological and cultural influences on sex role development. Moderately difficult reading level.

Journal of Social Issues, 1979, 35 (4). Children of divorce.
The entire issue is devoted to information about children from divorced families. Included is an excellent introduction that summarizes some of the most important issues involved in the study of the effects of divorce on children. Moderately difficult reading.

Lewis, M., & Rosenblum, L. A. (eds.). *The child and its family*. New York: Plenum, 1979.
This volume focuses on the immediate social world into which the child is born and subsequently develops. Various chapters deal with the social network of the family, including parent-infant and sibling relations and the early development of peer relations. Moderately difficult reading level.

Lewis, M., & Rosenblum, L. A. (eds.) *Friendship and peer relations* (vol. 4). New York: Wiley, 1975.
Articles by experts on peer relations representing diverse ideas and including recent theoretical perspectives. Moderately difficult reading.

Liebert, R. M., Neale, J. M., & Davidson, E. S. *The early window: Effects of television on children and youth.* Elmsford, N.Y.: Pergamon Press, 1973.
Excellent overview of the effects of television on youth. Provides ideas about the psychological processes underlying the influence of television as well as critical analysis of whether television has a positive or negative influence on youth. Medium reading difficulty.

Know Yourself

It is time for us to talk again about your understanding of yourself and your development. Think about your early childhood years, from the time you were two years old until the time you entered the first grade. You probably won't remember much about the time when you were two to three years old, but you may have some images and memories of when you were four and five years old. Do you remember any of your possessions from those years—maybe a tricycle, a wagon, a favorite doll, a pet, or the house and neighborhood you lived in? Ask your parents what you were like when you were growing from a toddler into early childhood and what you were like when you were four or five years old. By thinking hard about your early childhood years and by talking with your parents about what you and your life was like then, you should be able to come up with some sense of the importance of the early childhood years in your development.

How did your parents interact with you during your early childhood years? As you continued to explore a wider social world, were they willing to let you do this or did they try to monitor your world perhaps too closely? Did you spend a lot of time playing? Probably so. What were the kids you played with like, and what kind of things did you play? Did you go to kindergarten or a preschool? If so, what was it like? How do you think you were influenced by either going through this type of schooling or not going through it? Let's return to your family life. Was there much conflict between your parents? Did your mother work? Did you grow up in a divorced or an intact family? What socioeconomic class did you grow up in? What was your sex-role orientation like? Did you have any problems in your physical growth, or did you grow within the standard range for children your age?

Now that we have explored your own early childhood years, once again talk with one or two classmates or friends about what their early childhood was like. Did their parents treat them the same way your parents treated you? Did they go to kindergarten or a preschool? If so, what was it like? Were their parents divorced or did they grow up in an intact family? How do they think this might have affected their development? How much time did they spend in play? What were their peer relations like in early childhood? Did their mothers work? What socioeconomic class did they grow up in? How do they think these experiences influenced their development?

Now that you have thought about your own early childhood and talked with others about their early childhood, make every effort to observe some three-, four-, and five-year-old children. Many of you are attending a college or university with a preschool. If so, the task of observing and talking with some preschool children will be made easier. If not, there are probably preschool programs in your community where you are likely to be welcomed as an observer. In either case be sure to contact the program director well ahead of the time you would like to go, telling her or him you would like to learn more about young children and that you have been told the best way to accomplish this is to spend time watching young children. You will also find young children in supermarkets, malls, stores, churches, and many other settings. Next time you are in one of these locations, look to see if there are any preschool children and their parents walking around—don't be snoopy; just casually watch how the child acts, the parent acts, what they are talking about, and how positive or negative you feel the interaction sequences are.

Now that you have spent some time observing preschool children, exploring your own early childhood years, and conversing with others about the nature of their early childhood experiences, think about your own ideas concerning early childhood. If you were to become a parent and your child were now three to five years old, what would be foremost in your mind about how you would want to deal with and interact with her or him? How important do you think it is for your child to grow up in an intact family? If you and your spouse worked full time would you worry about the quality of care your child would be getting at a preschool? If you were to place your young child in a preschool program, what kind of program would you select? How closely would you monitor your child's life? Do you think your child should already be reading by the time she or he enters the first grade, or should this skill be allowed to develop during middle childhood? How structured would you want your child's life to be? Would you want it filled with lots of activities, school, and so forth, or would you want your young child to spend a lot more time in play and more casual peer relations?

By reading the description of early childhood in this section, by observing preschool children, by talking to your parents about your own early childhood years, by conversing with others about their preschool years, and by thinking about what kind of parent you would be with your own preschool child, you should know yourself better.

Profile

Stacy Henson is eight years old and is in the third grade at a suburban elementary school. She is four feet, three inches tall and weighs sixty-five pounds. She often still spends her after-school hours playing with several of her girl friends in the neighborhood, who no longer spend as much time in pretend play. Each week Stacy goes to dance class, takes tennis lessons, and goes to a Girl Scout meeting. As we follow Stacy through her middle and late childhood years, we find that as in early childhood much of her physical growth is gradual. By the age of ten, she is four feet, eight inches tall and weighs seventy-five pounds. Although her legs have become longer, she still looks a little "chubby." Her motor development is much smoother now than it was in the preschool years. For example, her tennis instructor feels that she is doing well in her tennis class.

When Stacy was eight, her mother received a call from her teacher informing Mrs. Henson that Stacy was doing very well in school and that she was being considered for the school's gifted program. One of the criteria for the gifted program is an above average intelligence, so it was necessary for Stacy to take an individually administered intelligence test for admission to the program. Stacy was given the Wechsler Intelligence Scale for Children and scored 126, well above the cutoff for admission to the gifted program.

Although Stacy has advanced cognitively during middle and late childhood—her use of imagery seems to have become a more effective memory tool, her attention to tasks is even better than in early childhood, she is able to solve more complex problems, and she reads much more effectively than she did when she started elementary school—nonetheless, she still seems to need objects and events present in order to think and reason about them.

What about Mark Parke? He and Stacy still live next door to each other, and they still don't care very much for each other. Mark is doing well in school, but not as well as Stacy. His mother did not get a call inviting him to participate in the gifted program, but his attentional skills are better than they were during the early childhood years. Still, Mark has difficulty concentrating on one thing for a prolonged period of time, and his teacher believes that he would be one of her best students if his attention skills and persistence would improve. Nevertheless, many students in Mark's class do much more poorly in school than he does.

Mark has developed a strong interest in basketball. His father put up a backboard and hoop in the driveway, and almost every day Mark and several of his friends shoot baskets and play basketball. Last month, at the age of eight, Mark played in his first organized basketball game as part of a YMCA program. He has turned out to be reasonably tall for his age—four feet, eight inches—and he weighs sixty pounds. His mother doesn't think he eats very well, and she would like for him to gain some weight, but he is not about to eat some of the "stuff" she tries to make him eat. If Mark had his way, he would live on McDonald hamburgers and Pepsi.

Don Mitchell, the boy who moved into the neighborhood is still there. Don and Mark are still good friends. They play a lot of basketball together on weekends and some evenings after school. Last year, when Don was ten, his parents decided that a private school might provide the best education for him. Don's father has moved up to a vice-presidency in the bank where he works so Don's parents can send him to the best private school in the city. Don is not so sure he wants to go, though, because he really has enjoyed the public school he has been attending for the past four years. Nonetheless, his parents convince him that the private school is in his best interest. During his first year in private school Don is not a very happy ten-year-old. He thinks many of the people there are "stuffy," and he has to get up an hour earlier every morning because his mother has to drive him to the school, which is fifteen miles from their house. After one year at the private school, Don's parents agree to let him return to his old elementary school, where he will be in the sixth grade.

Recall Chip—his last name is Martin. He is the boy who lived near Mark and Don during their preschool years. When Chip was in second grade, his parents separated and eventually were divorced. His father moved into an apartment. Later his mother, who has custody of Chip, moved to another city where she got a better job. Now Chip rarely sees his father, who has remarried and has two other children. Chip has not done as well in school as Stacy, Don, or Mark. He has difficulty with reading, and his teachers have commented to his mother on several occasions that he may have a learning disability although they are not certain.

When we ask Mark, Stacy, Don, and Chip to describe themselves when they are ten years old, Mark says, "I am big and tall, and I am good at basketball. I love to play sports, and I have a lot of friends—we play basketball together." Stacy describes herself: "I have blonde hair and blue eyes, and I am pretty smart. I do well in school. I like to be with Barbara and Patty and do things with them after school." Don says about himself, "I am black, tall, very good at sports, quiet around people, and I study hard." And Chip has this to say about himself: "I am kinda short; I like to fool around and play a lot. I don't like school, but I do like to play video games."

For Mark, Stacy, Don, and Chip, more time is spent away from their parents than was the case during early childhood. They have become accustomed to spending long hours at school, although Chip and Mark less so than Stacy and Don. And although they have disagreements with their parents, for the most part they are not involved in much conflict with them. They say that their most enjoyable moments come when they are playing with their peers, but they all agree that life without television and video games would be rough.

10 Physical Development and Intelligence

Imagine . . . *that you are a black parent and your child is being placed in classes for mentally retarded children*

For many years heated debate in psychological and educational circles has focused on whether standard intelligence tests are culturally biased. This controversy has now entered the legal arena and has been the target of a major class action lawsuit challenging the use of standard IQ tests to place black elementary school students in classes for the educable mentally retarded (EMR).

The initial lawsuit, *Larry P.* v. *Riles*, was filed in a federal court in San Francisco. The intent of the suit was to test the plaintiff's claim that standard IQ tests are biased against blacks and that they systematically underestimate the learning ability of black children. The suit asked relief for all black elementary school children in California who have been inappropriately placed in EMR classes on the basis of results from individual IQ tests. The plaintiffs—children and their parents, represented by such groups as the National Association for the Advancement of Colored People, among others—asserted that IQ tests, such as the WISC-R and the Stanford-Binet, improperly evaluate blacks by unduly emphasizing verbal skills and by failing to account for the cultural background of black children. The result, they contended, is that thousands of black children have been incorrectly labeled mentally retarded and are forever saddled with the stigma of mental retardation.

The plaintiffs agree with the conclusions of sociologist Jane Mercer, who wrote in *Sociocultural Factors in Educational Labeling* that "present psychological assessment practices in the public schools violate five rights of children: Their right to be evaluated within a culturally appropriate normative framework; their right to be assessed as a multidimensional human being; their right to be fully educated; their right to be free of stigmatizing labels; and their right to ethnic identity and respect."

In the California case it was ruled that IQ tests are biased and their use is racially discriminatory. The ruling continued the moratorium on the use of IQ tests in decisions about placement of a child in EMR classes. The litigation in California revealed a dramatic racial imbalance in EMR classes. At the onset of the case in 1971, 66 percent of elementary school students in EMR classes in San Francisco were black, while blacks comprised only 28.5 percent of the San Francisco school population. Statewide, the disparity was even greater. Although blacks comprised only 9.1 percent of the school children in California, more than 27 percent of children in programs for the mentally retarded were black. More recent figures reveal no drop in the statewide disproportion of blacks in EMR classes.

In the trial, the plaintiffs argued that this marked imbalance in the composition of EMR classes results from culturally biased testing instruments, and furthermore that this test bias is not accidental but has been built into American IQ tests from the time of their formulation. They were able to convince the court that the perpetuation of racial imbalances as a result of state-required procedures constituted unconstitutional racial discrimination that violates federal laws.

Early in the history of the lengthy court battle, the plaintiffs produced graphic evidence that standard IQ tests do not properly assess the abilities of blacks and that they therefore should not be used to place black children in EMR classes. For example, six black EMR students were independently retested by members of the Bay Area Association of Black Psychologists who were fully qualified to administer such tests. These psychologists used techniques designed to take into account the cultural experiences of the black schoolchildren. The psychologists emphasized the establishment of good rapport with the children and made special efforts to overcome any defeatism or early distraction among the students. Certain items were rewarded in terms more consistent with the children's cultural background and language experience, and recognition was given to nonstandard answers that nevertheless showed an intelligent approach to problems in the context of that background. On retesting, each of the six children scored above the ceiling for placement in EMR classes. The scores ranged from 79 to 104, or 17 to 38 points higher than the scores the students received when tested by school psychologists.

During the long course of litigation, the state did little to explain the racial imbalance in EMR placements. At one point the state suggested that since black people tend to be poor and poor pregnant women tend to suffer from inadequate nutrition, it is possible that the brain development of many black children has been retarded by their mothers' poor diets during pregnancy. However, from the outset of the case, an undercurrent in the state's position was that blacks are genetically inferior to whites. In papers filed with the court, the state defendants suggested that the racial imbalance in EMR placements is caused by differences in the inherited intelligence of the races, presumably meaning that blacks are genetically not as intelligent as whites.

Ernest Brody and Nathan Brody (1976) have recently noted the "cooling out" function of IQ testing: the scores help educators to justify poor academic achievement. Brody and Brody say that the citation of intelligence test scores of black children essentially serves the purpose of absolving schools and teachers for poor academic achievement of blacks.

Their conclusion supports a central premise of the plaintiffs in the *Larry P.* case. California schools segregate pupils they believe are inferior into separate and unequal classes, and such segregation falls most heavily

on blacks. Thus, the IQ test is used to give a seemingly scientific imprimatur to what is in effect institutional racial discrimination. When the asserted scientific basis for isolating black children (the IQ test) has been removed, the disproportion of blacks in EMR classes will be without a legitimate justification (Opton, 1977).

The decision in favor of Larry P. is currently being appealed, and in another court case, *Pase* v. *Hannon* in Illinois, it was ruled that IQ tests are not culturally biased (Armstrong, 1980). Many psychologists continue to take exception to the ruling in the *Larry P.* case, arguing that the required method for determining overrepresentation of minority children in special classes is not flawed, that the evidence does not suggest the tests are biased, and that informed consent procedures and regular review of children's progress in special education would protect rights to equal protection under the law, as well as rights to special education services when needed.

Introduction

You have just read about two of the most important topics of this chapter—intelligence and mental retardation. In this chapter we will survey a number of different intelligence tests, focusing initially on the two most widely used individual tests, the Binet and the WISC. We will attempt to define the elusive concept of intelligence and compare the approach of those who measure intelligence to Piaget's ideas. The extent to which intelligence is stable from one period of development to another will be covered, and a discussion of the genetic basis of intelligence is included. The extremes of intelligence will be discussed toward the end of the chapter with topics on mental retardation and giftedness. The concluding section reveals that children may not only think intelligently, but that they may think creatively as well. To begin the chapter, however, we continue our description of physical development, focusing on the changes that occur during middle and late childhood. And we extensively discuss handicapped children and their special education.

Physical Development

The period of middle and late childhood involves slow, consistent growth—the calm before the rapid growth spurt that will appear in adolescence.

Basic Physical Attributes

During the elementary school years, children grow an average of two to three inches per year until at the age of eleven, the average girl is four feet, ten inches tall and the average boy is four feet, nine and one-half inches tall. Weight increases range from three to five pounds per year until at the age of eleven, the average girl weighs eighty-eight and one-half pounds and the average boy weighs eighty-five and one-half pounds (Krogman, 1970).

During middle and late childhood, children's legs become longer and their trunks slimmer, and they are steadier on their feet. Fat tissue tends to develop more rapidly than muscle tissue (which increases substantially in adolescence). Children who had a rounded, somewhat "chubby" body build (sometimes referred to as **endomorphic**) have noticeably more fat tissue than muscle tissue, while the reverse is true of children with **mesomorphic** body builds (athletic, muscular). **Ectomorphs** (skinny, thin body build) do not have a predominance of fat or muscle, which accounts for their tendency to appear somewhat scrawny (Hurlock, 1980).

During middle and late childhood, the motor development of children becomes much smoother and more coordinated than was the case in early childhood. For example, it is one child in a thousand who can even hit a tennis ball over the net at the age of four, yet by the age of eleven, most children can learn to play this sport. In the early elementary school years, children can become competent at running, climbing, throwing and catching a ball, skipping rope, swimming, bicycle riding, and skating, to name just some of the many physical skills that, when mastered, provide a considerable source of pleasure and accomplishment. Developing competence in these physical skills indicates increases in children's strength, speed, flexibility, and precision, including steadiness, balance, and aiming (Lundsteen & Bernstein-Tarrow, 1981). Recall from our description of physical development in chapter 7 that there usually are marked sex differences in these gross motor skills, with boys outperforming girls rather handily. However, in fine motor skills, girls generally outperform boys.

During middle and late childhood, sensory mechanisms continue to mature. Early farsightedness is overcome, binocular vision becomes well-developed, and hearing acuity increases. Children of this age have fewer illnesses than younger children, particularly fewer respiratory and gastrointestinal problems. Widespread immunization has considerably reduced the incidence of disease, and many illnesses can be prevented by practicing habits of good health, safety, and nutrition (Lundsteen & Bernstein-Tarrow, 1981).

Children's Concept of Health and Their Health Behavior

It is important not only to look at the incidence of children's illnesses but also to investigate children's concept of health and their health behavior. When elementary school children are asked about their health, they seem to understand that it is not just something that will stay positive but rather that good health is something they have to work at almost continually. Children recognize that nutrition and physical fitness are important in maintaining their health. Interestingly, most children do not define health in terms of illness. And as they grow through the middle and late childhood years, boys and girls are likely to define health in more abstract and global terms (O'Conner-Francoeur, 1983).

The Child in Competitive Sports

Competitive sports programs for boys and girls have increased in recent years, and parents often place their children in such programs at very young ages. Anywhere in the United States you are likely to find preschool and elementary school-aged children engaged in competitive sports—in Minnesota it might be hockey, in Texas football, in Florida soccer. While there is surprisingly little empirical information about the effects such competitive activities have on physical and emotional development, some researchers have investigated possible links between physical skills competition

During middle and late childhood, children's legs become longer and their trunks slimmer.

and the child's maturing bone structure, as well as the possible stress of early physical overload on the young child.

Bryant Cratty (1978) concluded that of all competitive sports, there is no team sport anywhere in the world in which the occurrence of injury is greater than in football. Soccer, baseball, and basketball, for example, appear to be far less frought with damage to the child's body. However, bone breaks, if properly set, are likely to heal and not cause growth retardation or malformation.

In addition to information about the effects of competitive sports on bone development, scientists have been interested in the exposure of young children's cardiovascular systems to moderate or severe stress. It appears that vigorous exercise in young children whose cardiovascular systems are sound (tested under exercise stress), if not carried to extremes (exercise that gives the child's system time to recover between "bouts" or sessions not so severe as to produce chronic fatigue), is likely to be beneficial exercise and will probably provide a sound base for later superior endurance performance.

Handicapped Children

Some children have serious handicaps—some are blind, some are deaf, others are speech impaired, yet others have a learning disability, and as we will see later in the chapter, still others are mentally retarded.

The Prevalence of Handicapped Children

How many handicapped children are there? Figure 10.1 reveals the incidence of handicapped children served by education in the late 1970s. It has been estimated that approximately 10 percent of all children are handicapped, although estimates vary mainly because of problems in classification and testing. Experts differ in how they define the various categories of handicapped children. And different tests may be used by different school systems or psychologists to determine whether a child is handicapped. Further, it often is not clear whether the tests or other assessments are always picking up whether the child is handicapped or not. Some teachers have estimated that approximately one fourth of elementary school students require some type of special educational assistance because of some form of handicap (Roberts & Baird, 1972).

All states have now been ordered by the federal government to make every effort to educate handicapped and nonhandicapped children in the same setting (i.e., in the public school classroom). If the child's handicap is too severe, then the state must educate the child in special education classes at no cost to the parents or provide funds for the education of the child at home. Within the last several years, universities and colleges have added to their special education staffs to handle the large numbers of students who are seeking special training in teaching handicapped children. Each handicapped child must have an individually prescribed educational program. This program must meet with the acceptance of the child's parents, counselors,

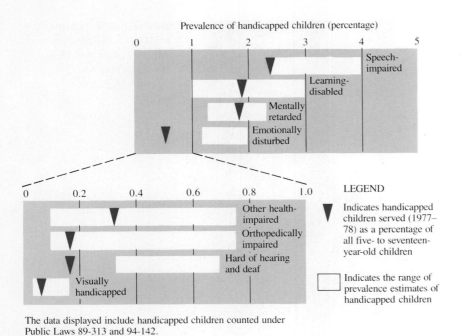

Prevalence of handicapped children (percentage)

Figure 10.1 Percentage of children served relative to various prevalence estimates.
(*Source:* Bureau for the Education of the Handicapped, 1979, p. 16.)

LEGEND

▼ Indicates handicapped children served (1977–78) as a percentage of all five- to seventeen-year-old children

☐ Indicates the range of prevalence estimates of handicapped children

The data displayed include handicapped children counted under Public Laws 89-313 and 94-142.

a local education agency representative, and (when feasible) the child herself. The program must include short- and long-term objectives, and it must be evaluated periodically.

Issues in the Special Education of Handicapped Children: Labeling and Mainstreaming

There are many controversial issues in special education, but two that have had overriding importance in recent years are labeling and mainstreaming. **Labeling** refers to the assignment of a label, or category, to a child and the effects that label or category may then have. (If, for example, a child is labeled "learning disabled" rather than "mentally retarded," will it lead people to treat the child differently?) **Mainstreaming** refers to the process in which children in need of special education are placed in regular classrooms rather than special classrooms.

Labeling

Thomas Szasz (1970) believes that labeling should be abandoned. In *The Manufacture of Madness*, he argues that labeling a person as having a mental problem (such as a behavioral disorder or learning disability) produces a public stigma. Everybody then expects the child with the label to be slow, crazy, strange, or even violent, regardless of whether the child actually behaves this way. The expectations others have for the child's behavior may make the behavior worse than it was before.

Labeling may cause children with problems real harm, but some experts believe that abandoning all attempts at classification would be an overreaction (e.g., Martin, 1977). They argue that the public use of labels should definitely be minimized, but that "judicious and sensitive use of classification categories by researchers and clinicians who are aware of these pitfalls still seems desirable—for the long-term benefit of the [child] as well as for general scientific goals." (Martin, 1977, p. 111)

There is a trend in educational circles no longer to categorize children with special problems as "learning disabled," "behaviorally disordered," and "mentally retarded." Instead, diagnosticians refer to the skills and functioning level of the special education child without attaching a label. Hence, instead of labeling the child who has a learning problem as "LD" or "learning disabled," the child in question might be said to have attentional difficulties and problems in auditorially decoding words.

Mainstreaming

There is a strong trend toward mainstreaming in instructing children who need special education. Most school systems have no choice because federal legislation now requires all states to provide for the education of handicapped children in the regular classroom if at all possible.

Some people believe that mainstreaming means that there will be a number of profoundly retarded, drugged children and adolescents sitting in classrooms in dazed, unresponsive states. Others are concerned that special education students will be given so much attention by the teacher that too much class time will be taken away from "normal" children. Some even believe that special education children will have negative effects on the social interactions of the normal children in the class.

The actual picture is not as bleak as many of these critics suggest. Virtually all profoundly retarded children are institutionalized and will never appear in public school classrooms; those who are being mainstreamed are only mildly retarded. Interestingly, not too long ago there were no elementary and high school special education classes for mildly retarded, learning disabled, and behaviorally disordered children and adolescents. They were mainstreamed, although the label and process of mainstreaming was not an issue then. It only has been in recent years that self-contained classrooms for special education children have been created (Turnbull & Schulz, 1979).

In the 1970s there was a trend toward placing learning disabled, mentally retarded, and behaviorally disordered children into separate special education classes. Now there is a trend toward using one or more special education resource teachers to work with children with any of these problems. The amount of time children with problems spend outside of their regular classroom varies with the severity of their problems and the particular school system.

But should special education children spend most or all of their time in the regular classroom? Some people believe that placing such children in a special class singles them out as "different" and prevents them from having the opportunity to learn from children who are brighter and more competent than they are. Furthermore, the majority of their social interactions will be with other special education children rather than with normal children. Others argue that retarded children who are placed in a classroom with normal children will experience many failures and will constantly engage in negative social comparisons with the other children. In one review of segregated versus integrated classrooms for special education students, it was concluded that segregated classrooms demonstrated no benefits, either academically or socially (Bartel & Guskin, 1971).

The stigma attached to being a member of a special education class is illustrated by the following incident. A seventh grader had been in self-contained special education classes part of each school day for about one year. One of his special education teachers spoke to him in the hall during lunch hour. Later in the day, he called her aside in the special education class and said: "If you ever speak to me again in the hall, I'll kill you! Act like you don't know who I am!" When

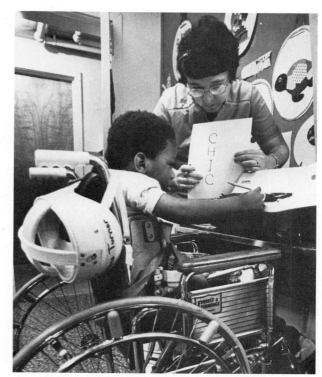

There are a number of different educational programs available for handicapped children.

she asked why, he responded that none of his friends knew he was in the "tard" class, and he wanted to keep it that way. Later in the year this seventh grader broke his leg, and a friend pushed him around in a wheelchair to his various classes. He reported to the special education teacher that "the kids will probably call me a crippled tard now." This case illustrates that children and adolescents do feel defensive and sensitive about being in special education classes—special education carries a label that may embarrass them.

What kinds of educational interventions are possible for handicapped children other than those related to categorization and mainstreaming? Obviously, there are many. In application 10.1 we look at three major types of interventions that are used with handicapped children.

Next we look at two of the most prevalent types of handicaps school-aged children experience—learning disabilities and hyperactivity.

Learning Disabilities

Pediatricians, school psychologists, psychiatrists, and clinical psychologists are being called on more frequently to determine whether a child has a learning

Application 10.1
Educational Intervention Programs for Handicapped Children

The following overview provides a general framework within which the available options for special education children can be discussed (Deshler, 1978; Deshler, Lowrey, & Alley, in press).

First, many special education programs involve remedial attempts to remove academic deficits in areas such as math, reading, spelling, and so on. Programming efforts are oriented toward mastering minimal competence in these areas because the students lack necessary skills. Most programs that follow a **remediation model** try to keep children mainstreamed as much as possible and provide special services out of a resource room.

In a **compensation-based program**, students are encouraged to develop strategies of acquiring information through nontraditional methods. For instance, the child may be taught to compensate for a reading problem by using taped materials, peer tutors, and/or visual aids. As much attention is given to changing instructional techniques as to changing the student. Thus the regular classroom teacher may be requested to change his or her classroom teaching strategies to match the learning orientation of the handicapped child. In this approach to special education, students also are kept in the regular classroom as much as possible—the compensatory program services are provided by a resource model.

In the third type of intervention program, an **alternative curriculum** is developed to expose the handicapped child to a curriculum that is different from the regular one in the school he or she attends. In such cases, the regular curriculum is irrelevant or too difficult for the handicapped child. In most instances, the alternative curriculum stresses the importance of developing functional adjustment skills that will aid the child. This third approach most often operates as a self-contained model in which the handicapped child spends little time in the regular classroom.

The difficulty and complexity of developing appropriate educational curricula for handicapped children should not be underestimated. Teachers and special education resource personnel need to resist the temptation to think that a simple solution is going to work miracles for the handicapped child. There has been a tendency in the special education field to embrace too quickly apparent solutions to educating children only to find out a few years later that the approach is ineffective. Programs available at this time should be thought of as temporary approaches that will need modification as more empirical bases of information about special education develop.

A number of barriers hinder effective delivery of educational services to handicapped children. For one, scheduling conflicts restrict cooperative planning between special education and regular classroom personnel. Second, time restrictions keep classroom teachers from working intensively with handicapped children beause they must spend most of their day on the core curricula for the majority of their students. Consequently, it may be necessary to create alternative educational sequences for handicapped children. Some school days may need to begin earlier or continue later for special education students, and summer programs need to be examined more carefully as a source of more intense training for the special education student.

---

disability. While there seems to be no universal agreement on just what a learning disability is, a child diagnosed as learning-disabled generally has (1) significant deficits in some area of educational achievement, (2) a normal overall score on a standardized intelligence test, (3) no primary emotional-behavioral disturbances, (4) no uncorrected sensory deficits, and (5) no history of severe emotional deprivation (Gearheart, 1973).

This global definition of **learning disabilities** would probably include children diagnosed as dyslexic, children with minimal brain dysfunction, and children who are hyperactive. The following statement by the National Advisory Committee on Handicapped Children (1968) refines the definition further:

Children with special learning disabilities exhibit a disorder in one or more of the basic psychological processes involved in understanding or in using spoken or written languages. These may be manifested in disorders of listening, thinking, talking, reading, writing, spelling, or arithmetic. They include conditions which have been referred to as perceptual handicaps, brain injury, minimal brain dysfunction, dyslexia, developmental aphasia, etc. They do not include learning problems which are due primarily to visual, hearing, or motor handicaps, to mental retardation, to emotional disturbance, or to environmental disadvantage.

Behavioral Characteristics of Learning-Disabled
Children

Although the definition of learning disability is fairly broad, it does allow for reasonably consistent agreement on which children should be diagnosed as learning-disabled. As a result of this very broadness of the defining criteria, however, the children so classified are a heterogeneous group. For example, a checklist completed by the teachers of 284 learning-disabled children reveals an extremely wide range of behavioral characteristics for these children (Meier, 1971). Table 10.1 includes the characteristics that were checked for at least one-third of the children.

Developmental Lag

Many young children in learning disabilities programs experience a **developmental lag**; in other words, they are slow in developing. Lerner (1971) has even gone so far as to say that most children who are labeled learning-disabled early (e.g., in kindergarten) are not very different from normal children. He believes that these children do not have a dysfunction of the central nervous system but are experiencing a developmental, or maturational, lag involving important brain functions. They do not have less ability than others have; their ability is simply developing more slowly. Lauretta Bender (1968) argued that children with reading disabilities usually show immaturity in other areas of development as well. For example, their motor development is usually immature; they appear to be very clumsy, even though they are diagnosed as free of neurological problems. These children more often than not are left-handed, which is one indication of a maturational lag in the development of cortical dominance in the brain. Furthermore, they are often described as having a "less mature" personality than that of their peers, contributing to their learning difficulties.

It is not hard to imagine how damaging it would be for the teacher to think that these children are "dumb," "not trying," "permanently brain-damaged," and the like. Experts suggest that patience and reassuring words from both teachers and parents greatly benefit children with a developmental lag.

Hyperactive Children

Hyperactive children are often viewed as children with learning disabilities (Havighurst, 1976). It has been estimated that as many as 5 percent of American children (about four times as many boys as girls) are diagnosed as hyperactive. In 1971 the Office of Child Development defined the symptoms of **hyperactivity** as "an increase of purposeless physical activity and a significant impaired span of focused attention which may generate other conditions, such as disturbed mood and behavior, within the home, at play with peers, and in the schoolroom." Frequently excessive physical activity and distractibility are believed to interfere with the child's ability to read and to do well in academic settings.

The Use of Drugs

Drugs are increasingly used to control the behavior of hyperactive children. Best guesses by experts on the number of hyperactive children being treated by drugs is about 2 percent of the children in kindergarten and in first through eighth grades (Sprague & Gadow, 1976)—about 500,000 children. The drugs most widely prescribed for hyperactive children are **amphetamines**, particularly the amphetamine Ritalin. For most people amphetamines act as a stimulant, but for the hyperactive child they have a calming effect. Over a period of time their effectiveness is reduced so the dosage must be increased gradually to continue control of the child's behavior.

What are the results of this use of drugs? Do the amphetamines improve school performance? Ritalin does have a calming effect on the hyperactive child; however, sometimes the dosage given is too great, and teachers report that the child goes about as if in a daze. Some studies indicate that Ritalin has a positive effect on classroom performance, while others indicate no positive effect. One study demonstrated that Ritalin had positive effects on hyperactive children's school performance (Sprague & Sleator, 1975), but these effects varied according to the size of the dose administered. A low dose had a more positive effect than a high dose in an assessment of learning performance. However, when social behavior was evaluated, a high dose had a more positive effect. These researchers have found similar results in other investigations.

The effects of Ritalin on the hyperactive child are not always positive, however. It is reported that as many as 20 percent of the hyperactive children treated do not respond to Ritalin. An alternative to drugs in the treatment of hyperactive children is discussed in application 10.2, as we evaluate how impulsive learning can be modified.

This concludes our discussion of handicapped children and physical development. Next we discuss the pervasive topic of intelligence and the controversial topic of intelligence testing. As part of our discussion we will look further at one set of handicapped children, those who are mentally retarded.

Table 10.1

Descriptions of Behavior Most Frequently Checked by Teachers for Second-Grade Children Meeting Diagnostic Guidelines for Learning Disabilities

Description of Behavior	Percentage of Children for Whom Description Was Checked	Description of Behavior	Percentage of Children for Whom Description Was Checked
1. Substitutes words which distort meaning ("when" for "where")	70%	19. Reverses and/or rotates letters and numbers (reads *b* for *d*, *u* for *n*, and 6 for 9) far more than most peers	47%
2. Reads silently or aloud far more slowly than peers (word by word while reading aloud)	68%	20. Difficulty with arithmetic (e.g., can't determine what number follows 8 or 16, may begin to add in the middle of a subtraction problem)	46%
3. Unusually short attention span for daily work	67%	21. Poor drawing of crossing, wavy lines compared with peers' drawing	46%
4. Easily distracted from school work (can't concentrate with even the slightest disturbances from other students' moving around or talking quietly)	66%	22. Omits words while reading grade-level material aloud (omits more than one of every 10)	44%
5. Can't follow written directions, which most peers can follow, when read orally or silently	65%	23. Poor drawing of a man compared with peers' drawings	43%
6. Does very poorly in written spelling tests compared with peers	64%	24. Can read orally but does not comprehend the meaning of written grade-level words (word-caller)	43%
7. Can't sound out or "unlock" words	64%	25. Excessive inconsistency in quality of performance from day to day and even hour to hour	43%
8. Reading ability at least ¾ of a year below most peers	63%	26. Seems quite immature (doesn't act his or her own age)	43%
9. Has trouble telling time	62%	27. Unable to learn the sounds of letters (can't associate appropriate phoneme with its grapheme)	41%
10. Doesn't seem to listen to daily classroom instructions or directions (often asks to have them repeated whereas rest of class goes ahead)	61%	28. Avoids work calling for concentrated visual attention	39%
11. Is slow to finish work (doesn't apply self, daydreams a lot, falls asleep in school)	56%	29. Mistakes own left from right (confuses left-hand side of paper)	39%
12. Repeats the same behavior over and over again	56%	30. Demands unusual amount of attention during regular classroom activities	39%
13. Has trouble organizing written work (seems scatter-brained, confused)	56%	31. Loses place more than once while reading aloud for more than one minute	38%
14. Can't correctly recall oral directions (e.g., item 10 above) when asked to repeat them	54%	32. Cannot apply the classroom or school regulations to own behavior whereas peers can	37%
15. Poor handwriting compared with peers' writing	52%	33. Tense or disturbed (bites lip, needs to go to the bathroom often, twists hair, high-strung)	36%
16. Reverses and/or rotates letters, numbers, or words (writes *p* for *q*, *saw* for *was*, 2 for 7) far more frequently than peers	52%	34. Poor drawing of diamond compared with peers' drawings	36%
17. Seems very bright in many ways but does poorly in school	50%	35. Overactive (can't sit still in class—shakes or swings legs, fidgety)	34%
18. Points at words while reading silently or aloud	49%		

Application 10.2
Modifying Impulsive Learning

In virtually any classroom you might observe a child who has a short attention span, is fidgety, and is constantly moving around. A brief conversation with his teachers will reveal that the child has a problem with learning. He does not concentrate very well, and his classwork is often rushed and full of mistakes. You might also observe a child who attends well, works patiently and quietly at his desk, and rarely moves around in the classroom. His teachers will tell you that he is a model student, concentrates well, and finishes his assignments without errors.

These children represent the extremes on a dimension of learning that Jerome Kagan has called *reflection-impulsivity* (Kagan, 1966; Kagan & Kogan, 1970). The reflective child works patiently at a problem and makes few errors. The impulsive child works quickly and makes many mistakes. Impulsivity has been found to be associated with hyperactivity, reading failure, and other learning disabilities. However, there is also a normal range of impulsivity, that is, a degree of impulsivity that, although interfering with learning, is not associated with behavior problems or school failure.

A child's reflection-impulsivity is measured by means of Matching Familiar Figures task, a procedure developed by Kagan. Children look at a standard geometric form and then try to select an identical form from six figures, five of which are variants of the standard. The child's speed of guessing and the number of errors he makes are used together to identify his style. Children who make few errors and have slow response times are called *reflective*. Those who make many errors and respond quickly are called *impulsive*.

Several attempts have been made to modify impulsive behavior. Donald Meichenbaum has worked out an effective technique based upon teaching children to talk to themselves.

In one study Meichenbaum and Goodman (1971) identified fifteen impulsive children in a second-grade classroom and taught them a strategy of "talking oneself through" an activity. Each child was seen individually in half-hour sessions over a two-week period. In each session the experimenter first performed some task and described each important part of the task. The child was then asked to do what the experimenter had done. The child was encouraged to complete the task a second time, this time whispering the description to himself.

The following is an example of the verbal description that accompanied one of the many different tasks employed in the training sessions. This task called on the child or adult to copy a picture. Others involved reproducing designs, following instructions from the Stanford-Binet intelligence test, and completing picture series.

"Okay, what is it I have to do? You want me to copy the picture with the different lines. I have to go slow and be careful. Okay, draw the line down, down, good; then to the right, that's it; now down some more and to the left. Good, I'm doing fine so far. Remember, go slow. Now back up again. No, I was supposed to go down. That's okay. Just erase the line carefully. . . . Good. Even if I make an error I can go on slowly and carefully. Okay, I have to go down now. Finished. I did it." (page 117)

Compared with groups of impulsive children who did not receive such training, the ability of these second-graders to handle a number of learning problems—a maze task, Kagan's MFF, and several scales on the WISC intelligence test—showed marked improvement. It is significant that this improvement was still evident one month after the training sessions had ended.

Teaching children to talk to themselves to regulate learning and problem solving turns out to have powerful consequences. There is still some disagreement, however, about the most effective way to employ this self-guided language. Should the child talk aloud, whisper, or merely "talk silently" to himself? Research is now underway in several different laboratories to answer this question.

Intelligence

In our discussion of intelligence in chapter 8 we looked at several definitions of intelligence, as well as the role of genetic-environmental influences, and the stability and individual differences apparent in intelligence. Here we look in even greater depth at the concept of **intelligence**, focusing first on the most widely used individually administered intelligence tests.

The Binet Tests

Alfred Binet and Theodore Simon devised the first intelligence test in 1905 to determine which students in the schools of Paris would not benefit from regular classes and consequently should be placed in special classes. Binet and Simon did not work from a basic definition of intelligence but proceeded in a trial-and-error fashion, simply relying on the test's ability to discriminate between children who were successful in school

The Binet test includes verbal and nonverbal responses.

from those who were not. On this basis they found that "higher" mental abilities (memory attention, and comprehension) were better at making this distinction than "lower" mental abilities (reaction time, speed of hand movement in a specified amount of space, and the like). The latter measures had been used by the American psychologist James McKeen Cattell as indicators of intelligence, but Binet found that they were not very good at predicting which children would succeed in French schools.

Although the Binet test was made up of items that tested several different mental capacities (including memory comprehension, attention, moral judgment, and aesthetic appreciation), Binet was primarily concerned with the child's general intelligence, which he noted simply as the letter **g**, rather than the child's specific mental abilities.

Binet developed the concept of **mental age (MA)** to reflect the general level of the child's intellectual functioning. This term was devised to refer to the number of items an individual child answered correctly in relation to the number of items that the average child of a given age answered correctly. For example, if an eight-year-old child had only as many items correct as an average six-year-old, then that child would be said to have the MA of a six-year-old child even though he or she was eight years old chronologically. By comparing

the child's general level of intellectual functioning with that of the average child at that age, Binet had a means of predicting how dull or how bright the child would probably be in the classroom.

Standardization of the Binet

Over the years extensive effort has been expended to standardize the Binet test. The test has been given to many thousands of children and adults of different ages, selected at random from different parts of the United States. By administering the test to large numbers of people and recording the results, it has been found that intelligence, as measured by the Binet, has an almost **normal distribution** (see figure 10.2).

The revisions of the Binet tests have resulted in what are now called the **Stanford-Binet** tests (*Stanford* for Stanford University, where the revisions were done). The Stanford-Binet has a mean of 100 and a standard deviation of 16. The mean is the average score, and the **standard deviation** tells how much the scores vary. As you can see by looking at figure 10.2, about 55 percent of the scores fall within what is called the average range: 88 to 112.

In the 1972 revision of the Stanford-Binet, preschool children scored an average of about 110 on the test, compared with a mean of 100. The 1972 sampling included more children from minority groups than was true of earlier samplings—the revision in the 1930s, for example, included only white children. What could explain the 1972 increase in IQ scores? Well, preschool children today are experiencing more visual and verbal stimulation from books, television, toys, and other educational materials than was true of earlier generations. And their parents average two or three more years of education than in earlier test standardizations.

Historically, labels have been used to reflect how far away from the mean a child scores on the IQ test. A child who scored 102 was labeled "average"; one who scored 60 was labeled "mentally retarded"; and one who scored 156 was labeled "genius." The evaluation of intelligence is rapidly moving away from such categorization. Many experts believe than an intelligence quotient based on the results of a single intelligence test should not be the basis for classifying a child as mentally retarded or, for that matter, as a genius. Such a label has often remained with the child for many years even though circumstances of the testing may have led to inappropriate measurement of intelligence.

The Binet Today

The current Stanford-Binet test can be given to individuals from the age of two years through adulthood. It includes many different types of items, some requiring verbal responses and some calling for nonverbal

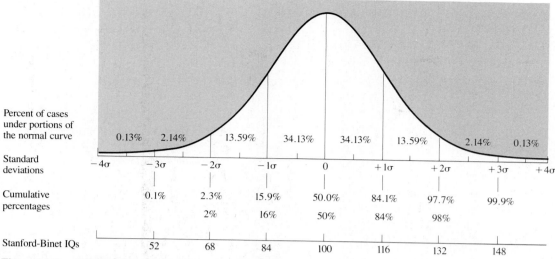

Percent of cases under portions of the normal curve: 0.13% 2.14% 13.59% 34.13% 34.13% 13.59% 2.14% 0.13%

Standard deviations: -4σ -3σ -2σ -1σ 0 $+1\sigma$ $+2\sigma$ $+3\sigma$ $+4\sigma$

Cumulative percentages: 0.1% 2.3% 15.9% 50.0% 84.1% 97.7% 99.9%
2% 16% 50% 84% 98%

Stanford-Binet IQs: 52 68 84 100 116 132 148

Figure 10.2 Relationship of normal curve to scores on the Stanford-Binet Intelligence Test.
(*Source:* Saddler, J. M. *Assessment of childrens' intelligence and special abilities.* Boston: Allyn & Bacon, 1982, p. 16.)

performance. For example, items that characterize the six-year old's performance on the test include the verbal ability to define at least six words, such as orange and envelope, and the nonverbal ability to trace a path through a maze. Although it contains both verbal and nonverbal items and measures of attention, comprehension, memory, and so forth, these components of intelligence are not scored individually. The child is still given an overall score that indicates IQ, or general level of intellectual functioning, on the test.

While the Binet is still widely used as an individual measure of intelligence, another psychologist, David Wechsler, devised several different intelligence tests that are being used just as widely as the Binet.

The Wechsler Scales

The most widely used Wechsler scale for children is the Wechsler Intelligence Scale for Children (WISC), used for children from five to eighteen years of age. An updated and revised version of this test now being used is called the WISC-R. Another Wechsler scale, the Wechsler Preschool and Primary Intelligence Scale (WPPSI), was devised for children from four to six and one-half years of age.

Like the Binet, the Wechsler Scales provide a score that reflects the child's general level of intellectual functioning. By providing a general score for intelligence, the test reflects Wechsler's belief that intelligence is a general capacity of the child. However, one of the main reasons many psychologists prefer the Wechsler Scales over the Binet is the division of the

Table 10.2
Examples of Subtests of the Wechsler Intelligence Scale for Children

Verbal	Performance
Similarities: The child must think abstractly and logically to answer sixteen questions. Example: "How are a skunk and a rabbit the same?"	*Picture Arrangement*: With each of eleven items the child is to rearrange parts of a figure or picture to make it complete or to tell a meaningful story. This test of nonverbal reasoning requires that the child understand how parts of a picture or a story go together. The pictures are shown to the child, who manually arranges the pieces in the right order
Vocabulary: Forty words are used to test word knowledge. This subtest is thought to be an excellent indicator of general intelligence, measuring a variety of cognitive functions including concept formation, memory, and language development. Example: "Tell me what the word *cabinet* means."	*Block Design*: The child must put together a set of different-colored blocks ten times to match each of ten designs the examiner shows. Visual-motor coordination, perceptual organization, and an ability to visualize spatially are among the cognitive functions measured. This subtest is one of the best for measuring general intelligence.

Application 10.3
Clinical Use of the WISC

Question: *What is the value of the WISC?*

Dr. L.: It allows us to pinpoint areas of strength and weakness in a child's mental performance. A child may demonstrate a good vocabulary, for example, but poor visual-motor coordination. Such knowledge is important because it allows us to help him work to improve in areas where he is weak. An overall IQ score hides the peaks and valleys in a child's abilities.

Dr. R.: The Binet doesn't permit us to quantify and compare children's subscales.

Dr. B.: Many clinical psychologists believe valuable information about other aspects of a child's psychological functioning can be gained from the WISC as well.

Question: *Can you give some examples?*

Dr. L.: The testing situation is approached as a structured interaction between the psychologist and the child. It provides an opportunity to sample a child's behavior and from it to develop inferences about the child's thought processes and emotions.

Dr. B.: These inferences are based on observations of the child's behavior in the assessment situation as well as the child's responses to the test items.

Dr. R.: During testing we observe the ease with which rapport is established, the level of energy and enthusiasm the child expresses, and the degree of frustration, tolerance and persistence the child shows in performing difficult tasks. Each of these observations contributes information that can help us understand an individual child.

Question: *Can any of you give an example of an actual case in which you feel the WISC was extremely helpful in providing clinical information about the child?*

Dr. B.: Yes. A nine-year-old boy, Robert, seemed dissatisfied with his responses while taking the WISC—even though later analysis rated his performance as superior. He often asked if his answers were correct, and in the middle of the test he asked whether anyone had ever given correct answers on everything in the test. On the Picture Arrangement subtest Robert put the pictures in the correct order, but for each sequence he described how they could be put in another order to tell a different story. Because he was unable to be satisfied with his work, it took him much longer to commit himself to a solution, and so he lost bonus points for fast work.

Dr. L.: This behavior does seem unusual for a nine-year-old boy in this situation. Most children show anxiety about their test performance, but it usually doesn't interfere with their success. Also, by the middle of the test most children have responded to reassuring and supporting comments and are much more relaxed.

Dr. B.: Since Robert's teacher had reported that he had trouble completing assignments on time and seemed withdrawn in group discussions, I formed a tentative hypothesis. Perhaps Robert's perfectionistic needs and fear of failure affect his classroom performance in the same way they seem to be interfering with his performance on the WISC. I made a mental note to look for

---

Wechsler Scales into a number of different subtests and into verbal and performance categories. The Binet is organized in terms of age levels rather than types of intellectual functioning. While retaining the idea of general intelligence, the Wechsler Scales also approach intelligence as clusters of many different abilities. In table 10.2 some of the various subtests of the WISC are listed, along with examples of items used to measure different types of intellectual functioning.

Because of its organization into various subtests, psychologists feel that the WISC provides a better opportunity than the Binet to analyze the strong and weak components of the child's thought processes. For example, a child may have a good vocabulary but have poor visual-motor coordination. The testing situation involves structured interaction between the psychologist and the child; thus the opportunity to develop inferences about the child is possible. The inferences are based on observation of the child's behavior as well as

other evidence that would confirm or contradict this hypothesis and to try to learn from further interviews and personality tests what was behind Robert's compulsive needs for perfection.

Dr. R.: This case example illustrates several processes involved in the clinical use of the WISC. First, the clinician notes behavior that seems to be affecting the child's adjustment adversely. Next this behavior is compared with a set of internal norms built up over years of testing and may find that it is very different from the way children typically behave in a test situation. This observation is then used to generate a hypothesis that will guide further observations during the evaluation. If other information appears to contradict the hypothesis, the clinician is prepared to reject the original assumption and pursue another explanation for this sample of the child's behavior. For example, if the child reveals that just prior to testing he was told by an older child that poor performance on the test would result in his being sent to a reform school, then the clinician's original assumption would have to be modified. Finally, information about the child's psychological processes is related to the original problems for which that child is being evaluated.

Question: *What about responses to test items—what can these reveal about psychological processes?*

Dr. L.: I'll answer that question by giving an example—one in which the quality of an incorrect answer on the WISC revealed something about a child's psychological difficulties. On the Block Design task a child named Sarah constructed several designs that were rotated 90 degrees from the test stimuli. On the Coding Subtest she copied many of the symbols in reverse and was unable to work fast enough to achieve an average score. Since the rest of her performance was in the IQ range for average, her difficulty on these two subtests raised the possibility of perceptual or visual-motor coordination problems. The psychologist decided to assess this possibility by using additional procedures.

Dr. R.: As you can see from this example, specific items are studied in the context of the entire evaluation. The psychologist doesn't approach the WISC looking for signs that can be translated automatically into an understanding of the child—it's the entire pattern that's studied. The more evidence that points in one direction, the more confident the psychologist can be in drawing conclusions.

Dr. B.: When the psychologist needs more data, additional assessment tools are used. An accurate description of the child depends on the psychologist's ability to combine knowledge of cognitive functioning, emotional development, and psychopathology with behavioral observations and test data.

the responses to test items. Psychologists observe the ease with which rapport is established, the child's level of energy and enthusiasm, and the child's degree of frustration, tolerance, and persistence. Read application 10.3 to see how several experts use the WISC to reveal important information about the child.

Regardless of the type of intelligence test given—whether it is a Binet, WISC, or one of many others—cultural bias may be built into the test. In the next section we will take a closer look at attempts to eliminate or reduce cultural bias in intelligence tests.

Culture-Free and Culture-Fair Intelligence Tests
Cultural bias in intelligence tests has been identified as one of the reasons that children from minority groups and from low-income families do not perform as well on intelligence tests as children from white and higher-income families. In particular it has been emphasized that the language of most intelligence tests reflects a middle-class white society.

Administering the WISC involves observing the child's behavior as well as the child's test responses.

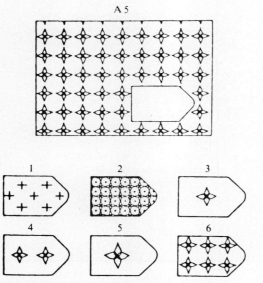

Figure 10.3 Sample item from the Raven Progressive Matrices Test.

Accordingly, many nonverbal performance intelligence tests were constructed. It has been found, however, that subtle cultural biases often enter into performance tests as well (e.g., Vernon, 1965). For example, pictures and nonverbal items may be even more difficult to translate into a different culture than words are.

One of the most widely used **culture-fair tests** is the Raven Progressive Matrices Test. The test consists of sixty designs, each requiring the person to select a missing part from alternatives presented. A sample item is shown in figure 10.3. Although this test was originally designed to be a culture-free test, there is evidence that it is actually not culture free. For example, in a review of research pertaining to the Raven test, Anne Anastasi (1976) concluded that individuals with more education do better on the test than individuals with less education.

Efforts to develop **culture-free tests** for blacks also have been attempted. The Dove Counterbalance General Intelligence Test, sometimes referred to as the Chitling Test, was developed by a black sociologist,

Adrian Dove, as a sarcastic rejoinder to the middle-class bias of most intelligence tests. It should be mentioned that Dove's test was not presented as a serious effort to develop a culture-free test for blacks; it was designed to illustrate how the language used by many blacks differs from that of middle-class whites. The language black children experience as they are growing up is often not reflected in the intelligence test they are given or in the language the tester uses in presenting test items to them. Some items from Dove's Chitling Test are presented in table 10.3. See how well you can do with this "intelligence test."

So far, test makers have not come up with culture-free or culture-fair tests that really are culture-free or culture-fair. Some experts believe that attempts to develop culture-fair tests sometimes focus too heavily on performance and not enough on competence—the Chitling Test is a good example. They point out that the underlying competence of the child's intelligence should always be kept in mind in developing culture-fair tests. What the experts believe is badly needed, then, are culture-fair tests that retain an evaluation of the child's underlying cognitive competence and effectively predict success in the academic and social world. They believe the Raven Progressive Matrices Test is probably the best effort in this direction so far, even though it too falls far short of what is needed.

Some experts believe it is virtually impossible to eliminate cultural bias in testing intelligence, even were it possible to develop a truly culture-free or culture-fair test.

Cultural Expectations in Intelligence Testing

Knowing different facts about a child may influence the way a child is treated. For example, you are a teacher in the teacher's lounge the day after school has started in the fall. You mention a student, Johnny Jones, by name. A fellow teacher remarks that she had Johnny in class last year. She comments that he was a real dunce, that she saw his IQ test scores once—seventy-eight on one test and eighty-one on the other. You cannot help but remember this information, and it may lead to thoughts that children like Johnny Jones just do not have much on the ball and that it is useless to spend much time trying to help them.

Consider another conversation you (a teacher) might have with a well-to-do family in the community during the first PTA meeting of the year. Jimmy Smith's

Table 10.3
The Chitling Intelligence Test

1. A "gas head" is a person who has a:
   (a) fast-moving car
   (b) stable of "lace"
   (c) "process"
   (d) habit of stealing cars
   (e) long jail record for arson
2. "Bo Diddley" is a:
   (a) game for children
   (b) down-home cheap wine
   (c) down-home singer
   (d) new dance
   (e) Moejoe call
3. If a pimp is uptight with a woman who gets state aid, what does he mean when he talks about "Mother's day"?
   (a) second Sunday in May
   (b) third Sunday in June
   (c) first of every month
   (d) none of these
   (e) first and fifteenth of every month
4. A "handkerchief head" is:
   (a) a cool cat
   (b) a porter
   (c) an Uncle Tom
   (d) a hoddi
   (e) a preacher
5. If a man is called a "blood," then he is a:
   (a) fighter
   (b) Mexican-American
   (c) Negro
   (d) Hungry hemophile
   (e) red man, or Indian
6. Cheap chitlings (not the kind you purchase at a frozen-food counter) will taste rubbery unless they are cooked long enough. How soon can you quit cooking them to eat and enjoy them?
   (a) 45 minutes
   (b) two hours
   (c) 24 hours
   (d) one week (on a low flame)
   (e) one hour

Answers
1. c
2. c
3. e
4. c
5. c
6. c

Taking the Chitling Test. *Newsweek*, July 15, 1968, pp. 51–52.

So far test makers have not come up with culture-free or culture-fair intelligence tests.

..BOY, WHEN IT COMES TO A VOCABULARY...IT'S HARD TO TOP THAT GUY WEBSTER...HE HAD A WORD FOR EVERYTHING!!

mother mentions to you that he spent the summer in Paris, where he studied French. At the end of the conversation, she points out that just before school started he was given a battery of tests by a professional testing service, and his IQ was measured at 136. How will this kind of information influence the way you interact with Jimmy in school? Will it lead you to provide him with more challenging work and spend more time with him because you know he is able to learn the material?

Questions like these led Robert Rosenthal and Lenore Jacobsen (1968) to study self-fulfilling prophecies in the classroom. According to the theory of **self-fulfilling prophecy**, once the teacher knows the child's IQ, he or she adjusts teaching to a level best suited to it and the child is thereby influenced to perform at that level, thus "fulfilling" his or her "prophecy."

Because of the effects of self-fulfilling prophecy, which stems from knowledge of a child's IQ, some states (e.g., New York, California, and Wisconsin) have stopped administering IQ tests to students. In these states tests are still given to individual students for special purposes, such as to determine whether or not a child should be placed in a learning disabilities program.

A Final Note about Intelligence Tests

Although intelligence tests have been widely criticized, they are still used pervasively in our society. At some point in your life you have had or may have some experience with intelligence tests, perhaps in elementary

Table 10.4
Classification of Mental Retardation

Level of Mental Retardation	Educational Description	Range in IQ for WISC	Approximate Mental Age at Adulthood	Approximate Percent in Population
Mild	Educable	69–55	8–3 to 10–9	2.7
Moderate	Trainable	54–40	5–7 to 8–2	0.2
Severe	Trainable (dependent)	39–25	3–2 to 5–6	0.1
Profound	Custodial (life support)	less than 25	less than 3–2	0.05

school or as part of a battery of tests for prospective employment. A child of yours may be given some type of intelligence test. If you become a teacher, you may receive reports from school psychologists telling you about your students' performances on the WISC or the Stanford-Binet. As a teacher or counselor, you may even administer intelligence tests.

Because intelligence tests are so widely used and misused, we have chosen to present extensive information about different kinds of intelligence tests. Many other developmental psychology tests prefer to rely almost exclusively on Piaget's theories and the cognitive-developmental emphasis on qualitative changes in intelligence. Indeed, many Piagetians are among the most vocal critics of the use of IQ tests to measure intelligence.

Mental Retardation, Giftedness, and Creativity

In this section we not only will explore extremes in intelligence by evaluating the concepts of mental retardation and giftedness, but we also will explore what we mean by creativity and attempt to distinguish between intelligence and creativity.

Mental Retardation

What is mental retardation? How is it determined that one child is mentally retarded and another is not? Not everyone agrees on this important matter. In 1973 the American Association on Mental Deficiency defined **mental retardation** as "significantly subaverage general intellectual functioning existing concurrently with deficits in adaptive behavior and manifested during the developmental period." (p. 11) Traditionally, IQ has been the primary criterion for identifying a child as mentally retarded. Table 10.4 shows how scores on the WISC are often used to classify individuals at different levels of mental retardation.

However, cultural and socioeconomic differences can influence performance on IQ tests. Such differences may result in the categorization of blacks, Mexican-Americans, and children from non–English-speaking backgrounds, for example, as mentally retarded even though they actually are not. Therefore, assessment for retardation should go beyond standardized IQ tests to include observations of children in everyday circumstances and environments—at home, in the community, in the classroom with an understanding teacher—to reveal whether or not they can follow instructions and handle problems successfully. Aspects of social competence should be considered in addition to intellectual competence.

Mental Retardation: A Label
Mental retardation is not some kind of disease; it is a label that describes the child's position in relation to other children, based on some standard (or standards) of performance. Thus, if a child scores below seventy on the WISC, he or she is demonstrating less efficient performance than that of a large majority of same-age children who have taken the test. The child is likely to be labeled "mentally retarded," generating a number of inferences (Ross, 1974).

For example, the term *trainable* has been applied to children whose scores are between twenty-five and fifty-four, and the term *educable* to those whose scores are between fifty-five and sixty-nine. An educable mentally retarded child is supposed to be able to successfully perform academic work at the third- to the sixth-grade level by the time he or she is sixteen years old. A trainable mentally retarded child is supposed to be unable to perform academic work at all; he or she is generally taught personal care and how to cope with some basic, simple routines in life. These children are not taught to read and write. Thus, a child's score on an IQ test has important implications for the type of treatment program to which he or she is assigned.

Many organic causes of mental retardation are associated with pregnancy and birth.

It is important to remember that an IQ score reflects a child's *current* performance; it does not always indicate academic *potential*. Therefore, the use of diagnostic labels that suggest assumptions about a child's potential can be dangerous. Remarkable strides are sometimes made in teaching retarded children to perform academic tasks that were thought to be impossible. Many experts believe the terms *trainable* and *educable*, as well as *mental retardation*, should always be thought of as labels that index only current performance. Because a child's level of performance may well change later, it may be wise to discard the label.

A score in the mentally retarded range on an IQ test reveals nothing about why the child is retarded. Next we will find that the most widely used classification of the causes of mental retardation distinguishes between organic and cultural-familial causes.

Causes of Retardation

Damage to the central nervous system, particularly to the brain, can produce mental retardation. This damage to the brain may occur during prenatal or postnatal development or as a result of an abnormal chromosome configuration. Down's syndrome is a well-known example of mental retardation that has an organic cause, the presence of an extra chromosome. Another type of organic disturbance that results in severe mental retardation is inadequate production of hormones, as in **cretinism**. Cretinism is caused by a hormone deficiency in the thyroid gland. When this deficiency is untreated, physical and mental development is stunted.

Many organic causes of mental retardation are linked to pregnancy and birth. For example, overdoses of radiation or the contraction of syphilis during pregnancy can cause retardation. Accidental injury to the brain of the fetus, as through a bad fall by the mother or the birth process itself, can cause mental retardation. Furthermore, although no clear link to mental retardation itself has been uncovered, inadequate protein intake on the part of the mother may be a contributing factor for mental retardation.

Most instances of mental retardation do not have a known organic cause. Such retardation is termed **cultural-familial**. For retardation to be considered cultural-familial, the following criteria must be met: there can be no detectable brain abnormality; the retardation must be mild; and at least one of the parents or one of the siblings must also be mentally retarded (Davison & Neale, 1975). It has been estimated that the number of people whose mental retardation is considered cultural-familial represents about 75 percent of the retarded population. Their intelligence test scores generally fall between fifty and seventy, whereas the scores of those with organic retardation are likely to be much lower.

Both genetic and environmental factors contribute to the occurrence of cultural-familial retardation. For instance, parents who have low IQs not only are more likely to transmit genes for a lower intelligence to their offspring but also tend to provide them with a less enriched environment (Ross, 1974).

Some experts believe that replacing the impoverished environment of the cultural-familial retarded child with a more enriched one may stimulate normal or even superior intellectual growth. Even though these

children may make intellectual gains, however, the gains are usually limited. Of course, intensive effort at teaching mentally retarded children should not be abandoned—to the contrary, every effort should be made to encourage retarded children to learn and to achieve to the best of their abilities. However, the process of change is usually an arduous one that requires great patience and commitment on the part of the teacher.

At the other end of the intelligence spectrum are those children with well-above-average intelligence, often referred to as gifted children. In the next section, we will look at what it means for a child to be gifted and the educational programs that have been developed for such children.

Gifted Children

Many years ago the label "gifted" had a single meaning, namely high intelligence (White House Conference on Children, 1931). The **gifted child** still is described as an individual with well-above-average intellectual capacity (an IQ of 120 or more, for example), but he or she may also be a child with a superior talent for something (Owen, Froman, & Moscow, 1981). In their selection of children for gifted programs, most school systems still place the heaviest weight on intellectual superiority and academic aptitude and do not look as carefully at such areas of competence as the visual and performing arts, psychomotor abilities, and other specific aptitudes.

One classic study dominates our knowledge about gifted children, that of Lewis Terman (1925). In the 1920s Terman began to study approximately 1,500 children whose Stanford-Binet IQ scores averaged 150. Terman's research was designed to follow these children through their adulthood—it will not be complete until the year 2010.

The accomplishments of the 1,500 children in Terman's study are remarkable. Of the 800 males, 78 have obtained Ph.D.s, 48 have earned M.D.s, and 85 have been granted law degrees. Nearly all of these figures are ten to thirty times greater than would have been found among 800 men of the same age chosen randomly (Getzels & Dillon, 1973).

Scrutiny of the gifted 1,500 continues. The most recent investigation focused on whether the gifted individuals had been satisfied with their lives (Sears, 1977). When the average age of the Terman gifted population was sixty-two, four target factors were assessed: life-cycle satisfaction with occupation; satisfaction with family life; degree of work persistence into their sixties; and unbroken marriage versus a history of divorce. The recorded events and expressions of feelings have been obtained at decade intervals since 1922. One of the most interesting findings of the study is that in spite of their autonomy and extensive success in their occupations, these men placed more importance on achieving satisfaction in their family life than in their work. Furthermore, the gifted individuals felt that they had found such satisfaction. As Terman suggested, they are not only superior intellectually but are physically, emotionally, morally, and socially more able as well.

Programs for gifted children usually follow one of three paths: **enrichment, grouping,** or **acceleration. Enrichment** focuses on special provisions for gifted children, including college-level courses in high school, advanced classes, independent study, and so forth. **Grouping** occurs when students with similar capacities are placed in a class together. **Acceleration** refers to any strategy that abbreviates the time required for a student to graduate, such as skipping a grade (Owen, Froman, & Moscow, 1981).

Do such programs work? Julian Stanley (1977), widely known for his study of gifted children, has pointed out that most gifted children enrichment programs are comprised of busywork, are irrelevant, and in many instances are just plain boring. Research directed at assessing the impact of acceleration provides a more favorable picture; a summary of the acceleration studies suggests that, from first grade through college, acceleration seems to have a positive intellectual and emotional effect on gifted children (Laycock, 1979).

In the Terman study, for example, the individuals who had been accelerated in school were more successful in their jobs, education, and marriage and

maintained better physical health than those who had not been accelerated (Terman & Oden, 1959). Grouping has been much more controversial than enrichment or acceleration. Research on grouping children into tracks has produced mixed results (Esposito, 1973), and many critics point out that it is unfair to poor children and ethnic minority groups.

Individuals who turn out to have exceptional talents as adults suggest that there is more to becoming a "star" in their respective fields than gifted programs. In one recent inquiry (Bloom, 1983), 120 individuals who had achieved stardom in six different areas—concert pianists and sculptors (Arts), Olympic swimmers and tennis champions (Psychomotor), and research mathematicians and research neurologists (Cognitive) were interviewed to learn what they felt was responsible for their lofty accomplishments. It seems that exceptional accomplishments require particular kinds of environmental support, special experiences, excellent teaching, and motivational encouragement throughout development. Regardless of the quality of their gifts, each of the individuals experienced many years of special attention under the tutelage and supervision of a remarkable series of teachers and coaches. And they also were given considerable support and attention by their parents. All of the "stars" devoted great amounts of time to practice and training, easily outrivaling the amount of time spent in other activities.

Closely related to the study of gifted children is creativity, an important aspect of mental functioning that is not measured by traditional IQ tests, a fact that has triggered considerable criticism of these intelligence tests. As will be seen in the next section, children not only think they think creatively.

Creativity

Most of us would like to be creative, and parents and teachers would like to be able to develop situations that promote creative thinking in children. Why was Thomas Edison able to invent so many things? Was he simply more intelligent than most people? Did he spend long hours toiling away in private? Somewhat surprisingly, when Edison was a young boy his teacher told him he was too dumb to learn anything! And there are other examples of famous individuals whose creative genius went unnoticed when they were younger (Larson, 1973): Walt Disney was fired from a newspaper because he did not have any good ideas; Enrico Caruso's music teacher informed him that he could not sing and that he didn't have any voice at all; Albert Einstein was four years old before he could speak and seven before he could read; and Winston Churchill failed one year of secondary school. Among the reasons such individuals are overlooked as youngsters is the difficulty we have in defining and measuring **creativity**. In this section we also will look at development changes in creativity, the role of imagery in creative thinking, and educational programs developed to promote creativity.

Definition and Measurement

The prevailing belief of experts who study creativity is that intelligence and creativity are not the same (Wallach, 1973). For example, scores on widely used tests of creativity developed by J. P. Guilford and by Michael Wallach and Nathan Kogan are only weakly related to intelligence scores (Richards, 1976). Yet it is as difficult to define creativity as it is to define intelligence. Just as intelligence consists of many disparate elements, so also creativity is a many-faceted phenomenon. An important question is whether measuring general creative functioning is appropriate or even possible.

David Ausubel (1968) emphasized that *creativity* is one of the most ambiguous and confusing terms in psychology and education. He believes that the term *creative* should not be applied to as many people as it is but should be reserved for describing people who make unique and original contributions to society.

The term *creativity* has been used in many ways. Following are the ways that some well-known figures define creativity and attempt to measure it in individuals.

Guilford's Concept of Divergent Thinking   Creative thinking is part of J. P. Guilford's model of intelligence (Guilford, 1967). The aspect of his theory of intelligence that is most closely related to creativity is what he called **divergent thinking**, a type of thinking that produces many different answers to a single question. Divergent thinking is distinguished from **convergent thinking**, a type of thinking that goes toward one correct answer. For example, there is one correct answer to this intellectual problem-solving task: "How many quarters can you get from sixty dimes?" It calls for convergent thinking. But there are many possible answers to this question: "What are some unique things a coat hanger can be used for?" This question requires divergent thinking. Going off in different directions may sometimes lead to more productive answers. Examples of what Guilford means by divergent thinking (his term for creativity) and ways of measuring it follows:

Word fluency: How facile are you with words? For example, name as many words as possible and as fast as possible that contain the letter *z*.

Ideational fluency: Here you have to name words that belong to a particular class. For example, name as many objects as you can that weigh less than one pound.

Adaptive flexibility: In this type of divergent thinking you must be able to vary your ideas widely when this is called for. For example, if you are shown a series of match sticks lined up on a table, you may be asked to put them together to form four triangles.

Originality: This time you would be required to name some unique ways to use an object. For example, what are some unusual ways to use hairpins?

Wallach's and Kogan's Work   Michael Wallach and Nathan Kogan (1965) attempted to refine the ability to separate creativity from intelligence. Their work has included efforts to specify how creative people in the arts and sciences think. People who are rated as highly creative individuals are asked to probe introspectively into what it is that enables them to produce creative pieces of work. Two major factors evolve from this self-analysis by creative people. (1) They have what is called **associative flow**. That is, they can generate large amounts of associative content in their effort to attain novel solutions to problems. (2) They have the freedom to entertain a wide range of possible solutions in a playful manner. These responses led Wallach and Kogan to remove time limits from tests of creativity and to make sure that the tests were given in very relaxed, nonthreatening, informal situations.

Developmental Changes in Creativity
Some commonly held beliefs about developmental changes in creativity are (1) it begins to weaken around the age of five because of the societal pressure to conform; (2) serious drops in creativity occur at the age of nine and at the age of twelve; (3) adults are less creative than children (Dudek, 1974).

These stereotypes are not supported by good research data. Actually, a drop in creativity probably does not occur at the age of nine; what happens instead is that the child's form of expression changes. At about eight or nine years of age the child begins to develop a more differentiated view of reality compared to an earlier, more global view. The child is freer from perceptual dominance and clearly into the concrete operations stage. Consider the child's art, for example. The child now paints as he or she sees, not feels. Feeling does not entirely disappear from art, but it now is less important to the child than realistic detail.

According to Steven Dudek (1974) this change represents increased subtlety in thought and increased imagination, not less. Others may interpret the art as less creative and less imaginative because surprise and vividness are missing. It has lost some of its spontaneity but not its complexity. At this point the child may require time to master the skills of the concrete operational period before he or she can use them spontaneously and freely.

The drop in creativity reported at about the age of twelve also occurs just after the child has entered a new stage in Piaget's theory. In the formal operations stage the child is learning how to develop hypotheses, how to combine ideas in complex ways, and how to think in more imaginative and abstract ways. Piaget has pointed out that when children begin to develop new cognitive skills, egocentrism often results and pressures to conform are very strong. An increase in creativity might be expected during adolescence as the child gradually masters the use of these newly acquired cognitive skills.

Evidence suggests that if repressive forces are not too strong, creativity does seem to increase in adolescence (Greenacre, 1971). Hence, neither adolescents nor adults are necessarily less creative than young children.

Encouraging Creativity

Let's look at ways creativity can be encouraged. You are an elementary school teacher. How might you go about fostering creativity on the part of your students? **Brainstorming** is one technique that has been effective in several programs developed to stimulate creativity in children. In brainstorming sessions a topic is presented for consideration and participants are encouraged to suggest ideas related to it. Criticism of ideas contributed must be withheld initially to prevent stopping the flow of ideas. The more freewheeling the ideas, the better. Participants are also encouraged to combine ideas that have already been suggested. Studies with children in regular classrooms (e.g., Torrance & Torrance, 1972) and in classrooms with educationally handicapped children (e.g., Sharpe, 1976) indicate that brainstorming can be an effective strategy for increasing creative thinking.

Another useful technique is called **playing with improbabilities**. This method forces children to think about the events that might follow an unlikely occurrence. Torrance gave the following examples of questions that can be used to foster classroom discussion:

What could happen if it always rained on Saturday? What could happen if it were against the law to sing? . . . Just suppose you could visit the prehistoric section of the museum and the animals could come alive? Just suppose you could enter into the life of a pond and become whatever you wanted to become? (pp. 436–37)

To answer these questions, the child must break out of conventional modes of thought and wander through fantasyland.

More important perhaps than any specific technique, however, is the need to foster a *creative atmosphere* in the classroom. Children need to feel that they can try out ideas, even if the ideas seem crazy or farfetched, without being criticized by the teacher. The only way to produce a creative environment on a sustained basis is to *do* things creatively on a regular basis.

Creative thinking can be encouraged in any type of curriculum and in any kind of classroom situation; neither an open classroom nor progressive education is required. A word of caution, however: although experts believe that creative thinking exercises should be practiced in every classroom, they caution against spending too much time on creative activities at the expense of other equally important learning activities. Michael Wallach (1973), for one, has commented that many children do not need to read more creatively, they just need to learn how to read.

The discussion of creativity ends our discussion of physical development and intelligence. In the next chapter we continue our evaluation of cognitive development in middle and late childhood, focusing again on Piaget's cognitive-structural theory and the information processing perspective.

Summary

Physical growth slows during the middle and late childhood years. Most children become more proficient at athletic skills in middle and late childhood, and in most areas of motor development, movement is more coordinated and smoother than in early childhood.

Special education for children has received a great deal of attention since the federal ruling that all handicapped children have the right to an education in a regular classroom setting if at all possible. Two major issues in the special education of handicapped children are labeling and mainstreaming. In recent years, the use of labels to categorize special education students has decreased and the inclusion of handicapped children in the mainstream of regular public school classrooms has increased. Learning disabilities and hyperactivity are two prominent aspects of special education. The term *learning disabled* refers to children of normal intelligence who have difficulty in learning one or more academic subjects. A special learning problem is posed by the hyperactive child and by the use of drugs to control hyperactivity.

The definition of intelligence is closely related to the way it is measured. One of the most widely used measures of intelligence, the Stanford-Binet test, was originally developed to determine which students would succeed in school. It focuses on measurement of general intelligence rather than specific mental abilities. The Wechsler Scales (WISC), also widely used, are designed to provide scores for overall intelligence as well as for the individual functions or abilities through which intelligence is revealed and by which it can be measured. Efforts to develop culture-free or culture-fair intelligence tests have been largely unsuccessful; the Raven Progressive Matrices Test is perhaps the best (though far from perfect) culture-fair test.

Piaget's views of intelligence differ substantially from those of the intelligence measurers, the psychometricians. Piaget is concerned with how new cognitive structures emerge and how intelligence changes qualitatively rather than quantitatively. It also is important to remember that intelligence is influenced by the interaction of heredity and environment through the home, school, cultural and social environment, and even nutrition.

Two extremes of intellectual functioning are mental retardation and giftedness. Mental retardation refers to the lower-than-average intelligence of a child as measured by a standardized intelligence test. Some forms of retardation have an organic cause, such as Down's syndrome, while others, particularly the milder forms, stem from cultural-familial causes. The most successful techniques for educating the mentally retarded take into account the fact that the learning process itself is the same for both retarded and normal children, but this process should be enhanced to address the specific problems of retarded children.

The term *gifted* applies to students of well-above-average intelligence. Despite the persistent popular belief that the highly intelligent are likely to be eccentric, longitudinal studies of such individuals suggest the opposite to be true. A group of 1,500 individuals whose IQs average 150 is being followed by Lewis Terman from childhood through adulthood. The individuals are not only superior intellectually but are emotionally and physically more able as well. Programs designed to help the gifted emphasize enrichment, acceleration, and grouping. Studies that focus on the effectiveness of these programs indicate that acceleration may be the best strategy.

An important aspect of mental functioning not usually assessed by intelligence tests is creativity. Extensive efforts have been made to devise definitions and tests of creativity that are not measures of general intellectual functioning. Originality and flexibility are two factors that tests of creativity attempt to measure.

Developmental changes occur in creativity just as they do in general intelligence; these changes seem to coincide with the transitions in Piaget's stage of cognitive development. Although some have argued that creativity falls off as the child grows older, it seems more accurate to say that creativity merely changes form at different points in development. Most experts believe that creativity exercises should be practiced in every classroom but not to the detriment of developing sound academic skills.

Key Terms

acceleration	gifted children
alternative curriculum	grouping
amphetamines	hyperactivity
associative flow	intelligence
brainstorming	labeling
compensation-based program	learning disabilities
convergent thinking	mainstreaming
creativity	mental age (MA)
cretinism	mental retardation
cultural-familial mental retardation	mesomorphic
culture-fair tests	normal distribution
culture-free tests	playing with improbabilities
developmental lag	remediation model
divergent thinking	self-fulfilling prophecy
ectomorphic	standard deviation
endomorphic	Stanford-Binet
enrichment	

Review Questions

1. What is the nature of physical growth during middle and late childhood?
2. Discuss the nature of special education for handicapped children.
3. Describe the nature of learning disabilities and hyperactivity.
4. How did Binet define intelligence? What kind of IQ test did he construct to measure it?
5. What is the Wechsler intelligence test? How is it like and unlike the Binet?
6. What is the purpose of culture-free and culture-fair intelligence tests?
7. How does Piaget's approach to intelligence differ from that of the psychometricians?
8. Describe Terman's study of the gifted. What have been the results of the study?
9. Name three types of programs developed to help gifted children. Describe them and discuss their effectiveness.
10. How does Guilford define and measure creativity?
11. What has Wallach's and Kogan's research revealed about the relationship of creativity and intelligence?
12. How can creativity be promoted in the classroom?

Further Readings

American Psychologist, vol. 36, no. 10, October, 1981.
Special issue testing: concepts, policy, practice, and research.
American Psychologist *is the Journal of the American Psychological Association. This entire issue is devoted to psychological testing and includes articles written by a number of experts. Reading level is moderately difficult.*

Brody, E. G., & Brody, N. *Intelligence: nature, determinants, and consequences.* New York: Academic Press, 1976.
This book is an excellent source of information about the complex factors that affect intelligence. An up-to-date evaluation of the genetic-environmental controversy regarding intelligence.

Cratty, B. *Perceptual and motor development in infants and children.* 2d ed. Englewood Cliffs, N.J.: Prentice-Hall, 1979.
This book provides a detailed description of many different aspects of physical development in middle and late childhood. Extensive information is given about the awkward child and the child in competitive sport. Easy reading.

Davis, G. A., & Scott, J. A. (eds.). *Training creative thinking.* New York: Holt, Rinehart & Winston, 1971.
A collection of articles by several psychologists who study creativity, with practical suggestions on how to stimulate creativity in the classroom. Most of the articles are easy to read.

Gowan, J. C., Khatena, J., & Torrance, E. P. (eds.). *Educating the ablest.* 2d ed. Itasca, Ill.: F. E. Peacock, 1979.
A selected book of readings on a variety of topics that relate to gifted children and the process of creativity. Includes sections on programs and curriculum for gifted and creative children, the role of imagery, and developmental characteristics. Easy to read.

Sattler, J. *Assessment of children's intelligence.* 2d ed. Philadelphia: Saunders, 1980.
The author provides extensive information about the history of intelligence testing, with emphasis on the Binet and WISC tests. Extensive information is given about a variety of intelligence tests currently used with children.

Torrance, E. P., & Myers, R. E. *Creative learning and teaching.* New York: Dodd, 1970.
An easy-to-read introduction to ideas about what creativity is and how to foster it in the classroom. Torrance is one of the leaders in the field.

11 Cognitive Development

Imagine . . . *that you are in elementary school and the teacher asks you to re- member something*

An ancient mnemonic attributed to the Greek poet Si- monides (fifth century B.C.) is the method of places, or "loci." Simonides was able to use this method to identify all the guests who had been at a banquet with him and were then maimed beyond recognition when the building collapsed and crushed them. (Fortu- itously, Simonides was not present when the building collapsed.) He was able to accomplish this great feat by generating vivid images of each individual and men- tally picturing where they had sat at the banquet table.

This is a mnemonic device that you can apply to memory problems of your own. Suppose you have a list of chores to do. To make sure you remember them all, first associate a concrete object with each chore. A trip to the store becomes a dollar bill, a telephone call to a friend becomes a telephone, clean-up duty becomes a broom, and so on. Then create an image for each "ob- ject" so that you imagine it in a particular room or lo- cation in a familiar building, such as your house. You might imagine the dollar bill in the kitchen, the tele- phone in the dining room, and so forth. The vividness of the image and the unique placement of it virtually guarantee recollection. It helps to move mentally through the house in some logical way as the images are "placed."

A very powerful imagery mnemonic first sug- gested by Richard Atkinson (1975) is the **keyword method.** It has been used to great practical advantage by Joel Levin (1980). Professor Levin and his associ- ates have shown the technique to be an efficient pro- cedure for teaching schoolchildren how to rapidly master new information such as foreign vocabulary words, the states and capitals in the United States, and the names of United States presidents.

Here, in Professor Levin's words, is an explanation of how it was applied to teach capitals:

In one study, fourth and fifth graders learned the capital cit- ies of the United States using what we called a *dual keyword approach.* . . . Let me illustrate using one of my favorites, Annapolis, Maryland. In the first of a three-stage process, students were taught keywords for the states, such that when a state was given *(Maryland)* they could supply the keyword *(marry).* Then, since the criterion task required that the stu- dent supply the capital in response to a state name, in the second stage we gave students the reverse type of keyword practice with the capitals. That is, they had to respond with the capital *(Annapolis)* when given a keyword *(apple).* Fi- nally, in the third stage, an illustration . . . was provided. In comparison to a very liberal control condition that allowed unrestricted study and self-testing, keyword subjects were better at remembering the capitals. This was true on an im- mediate test, but especially so on a surprise retest three days later. (p. 20)

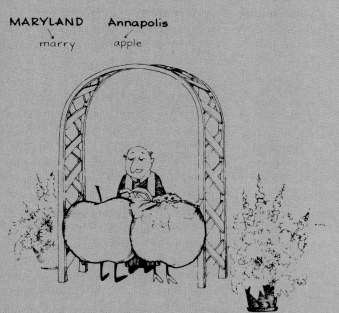

MARYLAND   Annapolis
marry   apple

Dual keyword illustration for learning the states and capitals.

Reprinted from "The Keyword Method in the Classroom: How to Remember the States and Their Capitals" by Joel Levin et al, Elementary School Journal *80* (4), University of Chicago Press © 1980.

The keyword method has been proven effective in the classroom setting.

Introduction

In this chapter we continue our discussion of cognitive development, focusing first on Piaget's stage of concrete operational thought. In the discussion of concrete operational thought we will look further at how children in middle and late childhood use classification to organize their thoughts. In chapter 8 we introduced a view that is competing with Piaget's cognitive-structural perspective to win the plaudits of developmental psychologists—the information processing approach. This approach analyzes the various steps involved in cognitive activity—in chapter 8 we described attention, the step that occurs first in many cognitive activities. In this chapter we explore in greater detail other steps involved in cognitive activity—memory and problem solving—paying particular attention to their role in children's cognition during middle and late childhood.

Piaget's Stage of Concrete Operational Thought

In this section we not only will describe what Piaget means by concrete operational thought, but we will critically evaluate Piaget's theory.

The *concrete operational* stage lasts from about seven to eleven years of age, cutting across the major portion of the elementary school years. During this time the child's thinking crystallizes into more of a system, and the many flaws associated with the preoperational stage completely disappear. The actual system is described by Piaget in terms of relatively complex logic. By way of a simple comparison to the preceding stage, however, the concrete thinker has none of the limitations of the preoperational thinker and is capable of thought in all the respects that the preoperational thinker is not.

This shift to a more perfect system of thinking is brought about by several gradual changes. One of these is the shift from egocentrism to relativism. The child can now decenter, or operate with two or more aspects of a problem simultaneously. For example, Michael Chandler and David Greenspan (1972) told children stories about characters who experience different emotions. In a story one character might feel sad because he lost a toy, and another might feel happy because she received a treat. The children were asked to repeat the stories. The seven-year-olds often confused the emotional perspectives of the characters in the stories. Ten- and eleven-year-olds rarely did.

Another change is reversibility. The child can now mentally pose and operate on a series of actions, for example, perform mental arithmetic, imagine a game of Ping-Pong, mentally pour liquids back and forth, and so on.

One limitation of concrete thinking is its reliance on clearly available perceptual and physical supports. The child needs to have objects and events on hand in order to think about them.

What is a concrete operation? A concrete operation is an idealized version of how a child's thought is structured. It can be described by reference to the different tasks that the child is able to solve, such as conservation or class inclusion, or more formally put in terms of certain properties of sets in modern algebra. That is, Piaget borrows some ideas from modern algebra to describe the logical properties of the child's thought processes, or the way the child is able to think and reason under ideal circumstances.

Many of the concrete operations identified by Piaget concern the manner in which children reason about properties of objects. An important skill of middle and late childhood is to be able to divide things into different sets and subsets and to consider their interrelationships. By describing a simple hierarchy of classes, we can see how one concrete operation is defined.

Let us suppose that a child is to deal with the following hierarchy:

A = class of spaniels

A^1 = all other subclasses within the class of domestic dogs

B = class of domestic dogs

B^1 = all other subclasses within the class of canines

C = class of canines

According to Piaget, the concrete thinker could add these classes together—for example, combining all domestic dogs (B) with all spaniels (A)—subtract one from the next—for example, eliminating all spaniels (A) from the larger class of domestic dogs (B)—and combine them in different ways. While doing so, the child's reasoning would obey the following principles:

1. The subclasses would be *associative;* the order in which they are combined does not matter.
2. The subclasses are a *composition;* if any two classes are combined, the resulting class is also part of the system.

During the concrete operational stage, the child's thinking crystallizes into more of a system.

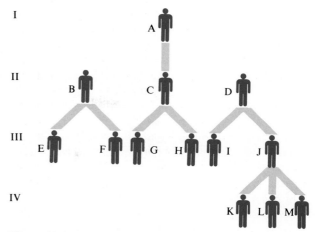

Figure 11.1 A family tree of four generations (I) to (IV).

3. There exists one or more *identity* operations. For example, a class could be spread out physically, but it is still the same class.
4. For every act in which the classes are combined in some way, it is possible to *reverse* the combination.

As we have seen, all classification involves a grouping or sorting of objects into classes according to some rule or principle.

Hans Furth and Harry Wachs (1975) conclude that many classifications occur on a horizontal level; that is, the different dimensions have no intrinsic relation to each other. Hair color, marital status, and education are unrelated characteristics by which people can be classified. However, this horizontal level is only the beginning of classification. Classification becomes more complex when we consider its vertical and hierarchical characteristics as well.

The family tree of four generations shown in figure 11.1 suggests that the grandfather (A) has three children (B, C, D), each of whom has in turn two children (E to J), and finally one of these children (J) has three children (K, L, M). This is an excellent example of hierarchical classification in that all classes stand in necessary relation to each other. The class of sons at level II implies the presence of the class of father at level I and of the classes of children and grandchildren at levels III and IV. A child who comprehends the classification system can mentally move up or down a level (vertically) and across a given level (horizontally) or up and down and across (obliquely) within this system. He or she understands that a person J can be at the same time father, brother, son, and grandson. In addition, I and J are alike in that they are related children of the same parent (D), while H and J are alike in that they are related grandchildren of the same grandparent (A). These relations characterize the respective classes of siblings and cousins and show how the two classes are different, yet alike.

Evaluation of Piaget's Theory

Piaget was a brilliant observer of children. He collected thousands of firsthand observations of what children do and how they seem to think that have withstood the scrutiny of time (in some cases thirty to fifty years). There are many reasons for crediting Piaget with genius, but this accomplishment alone would be sufficient. Piaget's insights are easily and often surprisingly verified. The young infant really does fail to search for an object when it is hidden. The four-year-old who watches a liquid poured from one container into another differently shaped actually says that there is now "more" or "less" liquid than before. The nine-year-old really does get stuck in hypothetical-deductive problem solving. There are literally hundreds of such observations, first made by Piaget, that accurately describe how children generally reason in these situations.

A second contribution is that Piaget has given us many good ideas about what to look for in development. For example, he has shown us that infants are very complex and subtle creatures whose seemingly chaotic patterns of response are actually highly organized and structured. Contemporary experts on infancy have benefited to an extraordinary degree by his suggestions and descriptions of this organization. As another example, he has shown us that the major change from childhood to adolescence involves a shift from the world of concrete and narrow logic to the plane of verbal reasoning and broad generalization. This insight has had a widely felt influence on educators and those who work with adolescents.

A third contribution is Piaget's focus on the qualitative nature of mental life. By always directing us to think of what the child's "mental environment looks like," he has served up a forceful argument for adults to learn how to deal with children on their own intellectual terms. This qualitative focus has also been a refreshing antidote to the behavioral psychologist's lack of concern for the subject's mental life and the psychometric expert's preoccupation with attaching numbers to intellectual performance.

A fourth contribution is the host of imaginative ideas that Piaget has offered about how the child changes. The concepts of *assimilation* and *accommodation,* for example, are now well-rehearsed terms in the vocabulary of most psychologists. The concepts remind us of the double-sided nature of each of our exchanges with the environment. We must make the experience fit our cognitive framework (schemas, operations), yet simultaneously adjust our cognitive framework to the experience. The concept of **equilibration** offers an elegant view of developmental pacing. According to this idea, significant cognitive change comes only when our cognitive frameworks are clearly shown to be inconsistent with each other and the environment. And the change will only be likely if the situation is structured to permit gradual movement to the next higher level of cognition.

A fifth important contribution of Piaget lies in the area of education. Hardly a day passes without the appearance of a new article applying the principles of Piaget's theory of cognitive development to the education of American children. Frank Murray (1978) describes why Americans have moved so swiftly to embrace Piaget. Two social crises, the proliferation of behaviorism and the dominance of the psychometric approach to intelligence (IQ testing), have made the adoption of Piagetian theory inevitable, he says. The first social crisis was the post-Sputnik concern of a country preoccupied with its deteriorating position as

Chess is a thinking game that stimulates logical thinking skills.

the engineering and scientific leader in the world, and the second was the need for compensatory education for minority groups and the poor. Curriculum projects that soon came into being after these social crises include the "new math," Science Curriculum Improvement Study, Project Physics, "discovery learning," and Man: A Course of Study. All of these projects have been based upon Piaget's notion of cognitive developmental changes in thought structure. Piaget's theory contains a great deal of information about the young person's reasoning in the areas of math, science, and logic—material not found anywhere else in the literature of developmental psychology. See application 11.1 for further uses of Piaget's ideas in the education of children.

But what are the major criticisms of the theory that have led to a mood for change? Perhaps the broadest criticism concerns Piaget's claim for stages of development (Brainerd, 1978; Flavell, 1977). To claim that a child is in a particular stage of development is to claim that he or she possesses a universally characteristic prototypical system by which he or she approaches many different tasks. It should be possible to detect many similarities in the quality of thinking in a variety of tasks, and there should be clear links between stages of development such that successful attainment of one conceptual understanding predicts successful attainment of another. For example, we might expect children to learn how to conserve at about the same time that they learn how to cross-classify or seriate items. All three capabilities are supposed to provide evidence of concrete operational thought. As several critics have

Application 11.1
Piaget, Education, and Thinking Games for Children

Piaget is not an educator, nor is he principally concerned with problems of education. However, he has provided a scientifically sound conceptual framework from which to view educational problems. Recall in chapter 8 our discussion of the similarity in the way Piaget and Maria Montessori believe children learn. In summarizing the general principles of education implicit in Piaget's image of the child, David Elkind (1976) concluded:

First of all . . . the foremost problem of education is *communication*. According to the Piaget image, the child's mind is not an empty slate. Quite the contrary, the child has a host of ideas about the physical and natural world, but these ideas differ from those of adults and are expressed in a different linguistic mode. . . . We must learn to comprehend what children are saying and to respond in the same mode of discourse.

A second implication is that the child is always unlearning and relearning as well as acquiring entirely new knowledge. The child comes to school with his own ideas about space, time, causality, quantity, and number. . . .

Still a third implication for educational philosophy . . . is that the child is by nature a knowing creature. If the child has ideas about the world which he has not been taught (because they are foreign to adults) and which he has not inherited (because they change with age) then he must have acquired these notions through his spontaneous interactions with the environment . . . education needs to insure that it does not dull this eagerness to know by overly rigid curricula that disrupt the child's own rhythm and pace of learning. (pp. 108–109)

An application of Piaget's ideas to education that is particularly creative and innovative is the elementary school program of Hans Furth and Harry Wachs (1975, p. 171). They seemed to take the following comment by Piaget seriously:

Whenever anyone can succeed in transforming their first steps in reading, or arithmetic, or spelling into a *game* [em-

phasis added], you will see children become passionately absorbed in those occupations, which are ordinarily presented as dreary chores. (Piaget, 1970, p. 155)

Furth and Wachs developed 179 thinking games that were to be incorporated into the day-to-day learning of children in the primary grades. They tried out this method for two years in an experimental school in Charleston, West Virginia—the Tyler Thinking School.

One of the games they developed is called Overlaps. This game works on several different properties of thought at the same time—ordering things, seeing different perspectives, and working with combinations.

This game demonstrates for children that an outline of overlapping forms does not always make clear which piece has been placed first. It emphasizes the importance of temporal ordering. A series of overlapping forms (triangles, circles, squares) is drawn on a card. Each form bears a number which indicates whether it was drawn first, second, third, and so on. The child is given similar forms cut out of cardboard or plastic. He follows the instruction of the model to discover that the pieces can be arranged in various orders of overlap to create entirely new patterns which retain the original outline [See the figure below].

In a variation, a concrete pattern constructed from the cutout forms becomes the model, and the child selects the proper card to match it. Later the child may construct and draw his own patterns. This can be considered as a permutation-combination task. The game can be varied by asking the child to transpose the parts of the pattern or attempt to think of how it would look from different positions.

Some of the games were specifically directed toward such basic skills as reading and mathematics. Other games were directed to more general knowledge about the world—the typical preoccupation of Piagetians. This general knowledge is a foundation on which school learning builds.

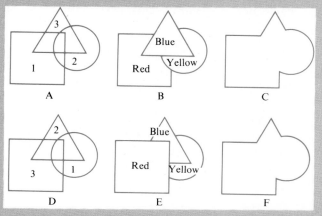

From *Thinking Goes to School: Piaget's Theory in Practice* by Hans G. Farth and Harry Wachs. Copyright © 1975 by Oxford University Press, Inc. Reprinted by permission.

noted, however, lack of similarity, lack of cross-linkages, and lack of predictability seem to be present everywhere (Brainerd & Pressley, in press). According to Kurt Fischer, unevenness seems to be the rule in cognitive development rather than the exception.

Another problem is that the most interesting concepts in the theory—assimilation, accommodation, and equilibration—which are used to explain how progress is made in development, are tricky to pin down operationally, despite their theoretical glitter. That is, unlike concepts like reinforcement and imitation, these Piagetian concepts have very loose ties to experimental procedures and manipulations. Despite work over the years to flesh out these concepts and anchor them in concrete procedures, not much progress had been made.

A final problem to be considered here is the mounting evidence that very few of the cognitive phenomena discovered by Piaget behave in the precise way he claims or really depend upon the particular processes he invokes to explain them. It would take a whole book to list and describe all of this evidence. But a few examples might give you a sense of the difficulty. Helene Borke (1971) has shown, for example, that three- and four-year-old children can identify correctly the emotions experienced by characters in a story (e.g., happiness, sadness, anger, fearfulness); but to do so, children presumably need to understand an emotional point of view that is independent of their own. Marilyn Shatz and Rochel Gelman (1973) and others have shown four-year-olds to be capable of adapting their manner of speech to different listener's perspectives. Both the Borke and Shatz and the Gelman findings fly in the face of egocentrism.

Each one of these examples poses no real threat to Piaget's theory. A theory could be wrong in a few respects but right in most others. But from the vantage point of the 1980s, we now have many "errors" or "exceptions" such as these, and they cannot be dismissed lightly. Taken together all of these concerns suggest a need for change in the theory. The stage concept is questionable, the concepts of change are hard to operationalize, and many of Piaget's explanations are simply wrong.

Next we continue our discussion of another perspective on cognitive development—information processing—and see that it strays from a strict Piagetian interpretation of children's cognitive development.

Information Processing

Piaget's theory focuses on how the child *thinks* and *represents* the world and how these capabilities change with development. There is another perspective, however, from which to view cognitive development. It is dubbed the *information processing approach* (e.g., Klahr & Wallace, 1975; Siegler, 1983). In this view, mental activity is synonymous with the processing of information. To make the exposition smoother, we will occasionally abbreviate the term information processing as *IP*.

Refer to figure 8.5 for an illustration of the general stages of information processing. To further help you understand the IP approach, we are going to describe a precocious eleven-year-old with an IQ of 170, who, unlike most others in late childhood, is capable of solving algebraic equations. Our eleven-year-old (called Allie) is taking an algebra class as part of his individualized instruction in the gifted program at his school. The mathematics teacher puts the following algebraic equation on the chalkboard with the accompanying instruction: "$2x + 10 = 34$; solve for x."

This event contains information that Allie can detect and understand. Success in detecting and making sense of the equation depends on how completely and efficiently Allie processes the information. One possible set of stages of information processing Allie may use in solving the algebraic equation includes attention, perception, memory, thinking, and problem solving. Once Allie's processing is complete, he produces an observable response (R). In this model, then, cognitive activity refers to the flow of information through the different stages of processing.

Consider how the computerlike, advanced mind of eleven-year-old Allie engages in cognition. Allie looks up and notes that something has been written on the board *(attention)*. This "something" is then determined to be a series of numbers, letters, and signs, and—at a higher level of identification—simply two statements: (1) "$2x + 10 = 34$" and (2) "Solve for x" *(perception)*. Allie must preserve the results of this perceptual analysis over a period of time *(memory)*, even if only for the brief interval needed to write the problem on a worksheet.

Allie then begins to elaborate on the product of perception and memory *(thinking)*. This level of analysis can be described best with an imaginary mental soliloquy (do not take the soliloquy literally; in Allie's mind, the thoughts associated with the hypothetical words here may transpire in some nonverbal medium altogether): "Oh! It's an equation—x is the unknown, and I'm supposed to figure out the value of x. Let's see. How do I do that?" And the final level of analysis *(problem solving)* addresses this question: "How do I do that?" Problem solving then takes the following form: "Okay. $2x + 10 = 34$. First I have to collect the unknown on one side of the equation and the known values on the other side. To do this, I'll leave the $2x$ where it is—on the left. Then I'll subtract 10 from each side to remove the 10 from the left. This leaves $2x = 24$. Now I have to express the equation as '$x = $ something,' and it's solved. How do I do this? I know! Divide each side by 2 and that will leave $1x$, or x on the left side. Now I have $x = 12$. That's the answer!"

Most eleven-year-olds would get stuck in rendering a high-level analysis of this information for a variety of reasons. One child may fail at the first stage of information processing by not paying *attention*. A severely mentally retarded eleven-year-old may attend but be unable to decode the writing as letters, numbers, and symbols—a failure in *perception*. A "normal" eleven-year-old may attend, perceive, and remember but fail to comprehend that he or she is examining a mathematical equation with an unknown *(x)* and an implicit goal to find the numerical equivalent of x. A thirteen-year-old just beginning the study of algebra may attend, perceive, remember, and comprehend but not define the answer to the question, How do I do that?—a failure in *problem-solving*.

The minds of children are continually processing information.

Memory

Memory is the retention of information over time. Three general topics are considered in this discussion of the manner in which children remember information. First, what are the different kinds of memory that play an important role in development? Second, what are the basic processes employed in remembering? And third, how do these basic processes change as the child matures?

Kinds of Memory

Although the word *memory* may conjure up an image of a singular, all-or-none process, it is clear that there are actually many kinds of memory, each of which may be somewhat independent of the others (Brown, 1975). One way to describe memory is by the different ways people are called upon to remember and the ways memory may be assessed—recall, recognition, and paired associates.

The most popularly studied kind of memory is **recall.** Recollection of a telephone number you have just heard, a list of items you are to purchase at the store, and a list of dates you learned in history class are all examples of recall.

A second type of memory is **recognition,** which is generally easier than recall. For example, someone lists three grocery items and you are to signal when one is

ZIGGY™

OVERDUE LIBRARY BOOKS

iT'S eMBARRASSiNG PAYiNG AN OVERDUE FiNe FOR A BOOK ON "HOW TO iMPROVe YOUR MEMORY"

Tom Wilson

mentioned that was on your last shopping list; or your history instructor gives four dates and you are to choose the one that goes with a specific historical event. In recall, you try to repeat an experience; in recognition, you simply indicate which of several events was experienced. People often underestimate just how powerful their recognition memory is.

Recall improves substantially across the childhood years, but for many kinds of recognition memory, there is little, if any, change across a wide span of childhood (e.g., Perlmutter, 1980).

Another kind of memory, **paired associates,** has been studied extensively. Examples include remembering an article of clothing someone else was wearing, the color of a car, and the name of a person whose face is familiar.

Memory as the Flow of Information

One prominent view conceives of memory as the flow of information through the human mind. Three broad stages of information processing can be distinguished. First, there is a sensory register, that is, a very short-term sensory memory of the event. At the second level there is a short-term, or working, memory. At the third level there is a long-term memory, where information is held over a long period of time.

Roughly speaking, the *sensory register* concerns memories that last for no more than a second. If a line of print were flashed at you very rapidly—say, for one-tenth of a second—all the letters you can visualize for

a brief moment after that presentation constitute the sensory register. This visualization disappears after one second. The ability to retrieve information from the sensory register does not change much as children mature (Wickens, 1974).

When you are trying to recall a telephone number that you heard a few seconds earlier, the name of a person who has just been introduced, or the substance of the remarks just made by a teacher in class, you are calling on **short-term memory,** or working memory. It lasts from a few seconds to a minute. You need this kind of memory for retaining ideas and thoughts as you work on problems. In writing a letter, for example, you must be able to keep the last sentence in mind as you compose the next. To solve an arithmetic problem like $(3 \times 3) + (4 \times 2)$ in your head, you need to keep the intermediate results in mind (i.e., $3 \times 3 = 9$) to be able to solve the entire problem. This working memory is therefore quite useful.

Operationally, the short-term memory of children may be studied by giving the child a list of items to recall and noting recall of the last few items on the list. These last few items are generally recalled better than the others—a phenomenon known as the recency effect. Memory for these recent items is remarkably similar across a wide spectrum of ages in childhood (Cole, Frankel, & Sharpe, 1971), leading to the conclusion that short-term memory also changes very little throughout childhood.

Long-term memory lasts from a minute or so to weeks or even years. From long-term memory you can call up general information about the world that you learned on previous occasions, memory for specific past experiences, or specific rules previously learned. The most significant changes in memory development are presumed to occur in the long-term storage stage or in the phase of shifting information from short- to long-term storage.

Memory Processes

Among the processes assumed to be responsible for shifting information to long-term storage are rehearsal, elaboration, organization, and various constructive memory processes.

Rehearsal If a response to a stimulus is repeated, either aloud or only in the mind, it is more likely to be remembered than if it is not repeated. This repetition is one form of **rehearsal.**

Repetition is just one way to rehearse a response. Another is to create an image for the response and rehearse the image "in one's head." A third is to employ gestures to repeat an observed response. And a fourth is to create a symbolic code for the response and then to rehearse the code.

There may also be differences in the manner of rehearsal. Given a list of items to remember, some children may rehearse each item in a list once and then stop, others may keep cycling through the list, and yet others may select a small subset of the list and rehearse only the items in the subset. Both the appropriateness of the kind of rehearsal and the manner in which it is used may influence memory (Naus, in press).

Elaboration   When you hear or see something, you may try to remember it by adding to it, or elaborating. By the memory process called **elaboration** you may associate the experience with something familiar to you, generate an image for it, or develop a sentence or short story about it in your mind. Many of these techniques improve retention of the experience (Pressley, Heisel, McCormick, & Nakamura, 1982).

In general, the study of elaboration has focused on the memory abilities of elementary and secondary schoolchildren, while the study of rehearsal has focused on the preschool and elementary school years. It has been suggested that elaboration skills are more advanced than rehearsal skills. However, there is probably a great deal of overlap between the two. And as with rehearsal, there are different kinds of elaboration, each with its own history of development.

Organization   Yet another technique for extending the short-term life of experiences or for moving them into long-term storage is **organization.** George Miller, in a classic article, argued that most human memory is limited. Short-term, or working, memory cannot deal with more than about seven discrete experiences, or bits, of information. When we are confronted with more than this, we lose some of it, finding it difficult to move all the information into our permanent, long-term memory storage (Miller, 1956).

Unwieldy information may be retained by organizing it into smaller units, or **chunks,** as Miller calls them. If the number of chunks is seven or less and each one is well learned, there is a good possibility that all the information will be retained. Chunking is done frequently: we recall ten-digit telephone numbers by segmenting them into a three-digit area code, a three-digit exchange, and a four-digit final sequence. Similar chunking is done with social security numbers, bank numbers, and credit card account numbers.

A more common way to organize information is to place items into meaningful categories (Mandler, 1967). If you are to remember fifteen things to be purchased at the grocery store, your task is made easier if you group them into such categories as meats, vegetables, and fruits. Individuals often recall better when they categorize information in this fashion (Kail, 1979).

If there are too many categories, if the categories are abstract or not obvious, and if there are too many items within categories, categorization may be unable to benefit memory.

A typical finding with children from four to ten years of age is that the younger children engage in very little categorizing; there is a steady increase in categorizing as age increases. However, the pattern of change may not appear with children of this age group if the difficulty of the task is altered. The categories in a list may be made salient and thus easy to notice, or the list may be constructed with obscure or very abstract categories. Saliency markedly increases categorizing activity in the youngest children, while obscuring the categories may decrease it in the oldest.

One demonstration offered startling proof of the power of chunking joined together with meaningful categorization. An average college student was transformed into a virtual wizard at one memory task—recalling long strings of unrelated numbers (e.g., 3, 7, 9, 5, 8 . . .). Ordinarily, most of us can remember strings with only seven or eight digits in them. Over the course of a school year, the student practiced listening to and recalling longer and longer strings of numbers. The numbers were read at about one per second. Using a variety of tricks such as relating groups of numbers to running activities (e.g., imagined rare distances and times, training mileage) and historical events, eventually the student was able to recall number strings of over seventy digits.

A number of devices—called **mnemonics**—can be used to help us remember. Mnemonics were described in the Imagine section at the beginning of the chapter. Remember how imagery helps to remember?

Summarizing the main points we have covered about the nature of memory and retrieval, then, we have said that there are several types of memory, that memory can be conceived of as the flow of information through storage systems lasting for different lengths of time, and that there are important processes that enhance memory including rehearsal, elaboration, organization, and categorization.

The next section considers the way children put to use the information that has been remembered and retrieved. In this section we will discuss how children draw *inferences* with the information they have; or as Jerome Bruner once put it, "how they go beyond the information given."

As they mature, children improve in their ability to make inferences.

Drawing Inferences

An **inference** is a relation noted between one event and another that is not directly stated. Thus far, we have considered three stages in information processing—attending to something, perceiving it, and remembering it. Our world would be a rather simple place, indeed, if our mental activity stopped there. It would consist of unconnected and unrelated events. So what does it mean that the sun rises and soon after people wake up and get on with the day's business? What is the connection between a child's falling off a bicycle one moment and an adult's holding her the next moment while the youngster cries? Throughout our lives, we experience events that are logically or matter-of-factly related to one another. The study of inferencing helps us to understand how people construct these relations.

Sometimes the connection between events is logical. We need not even experience the events directly to understand how they are related to one another. Thus, suppose we hear someone describe a situation as follows:

There was an older man, a man, and a boy.
The older man said to the man, "I'm glad you're my son."
The man said to the boy, "And, I'm glad you're my son."
What is the relation between the older man and the boy?

The answer is based on our logical understanding of family relations and inference—the relationship is one of grandfather and grandson.

Another type of inference is made when we rely on substantial prior knowledge to interpret experiences. Substantial reliance on prior knowledge is required to make an appropriate inference about the following:

Albert spotted a worm in the water. He swam over to the worm and bit into him. Albert was caught and pulled through the water. Who was Albert? Why did he bite the worm? Who caught him and how?

The paragraph provides no clues to answer these questions, but our own experiences and prior knowledge offer some help. Albert is probably a fish who was hungry and was caught on the hook of a fisherman.

Children improve dramatically in their abilities to draw certain types of inferences as they mature. Their understanding of relations in narrative folktales improves across the elementary school years. Children also improve in making a variety of linguistic inferences and analogical inferences (i.e., drawing analogies) across the elementary school years. And they improve in making inferences on a host of traditional reading comprehension and cognitive assessment measures as well (e.g., WISC intelligence test; Yussen, 1982).

Next we look at yet another aspect of the information processing that has been given extensive attention—problem solving.

Problem Solving

The last stage of information processing to be considered here is problem solving. A helpful way to describe problem solving is *processing information to fulfill a major goal.* Attention, perception, remembering, and drawing inferences may all occur rather quickly as the child examines information. And the child may devote little conscious effort or awareness to these former activities. By contrast, problem solving usually occurs over an extended period of time and mobilizes considerable cognitive resources of the child, that is, considerable effort and conscious awareness are involved.

Problem solving may also be thought of as a *regulator of information processing.* It directs us to the particular information we will process and governs the manner in which the information is processed. In this sense, our decision to discuss problem solving as the last stage in information processing may be misleading. We just as easily could have conceptualized problem solving as the first stage. The best solution is to treat problem solving as a regulator or nonworking monitor for the flow of information. It helps decide what other information processing steps take place and in what order of occurrence. Reconceptualizing figure 8.5, then, we have the picture of information processing shown in figure 11.2.

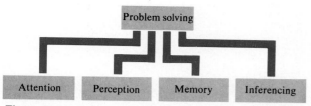

Figure 11.2 Information processing regulated by problem solving.

Problem solving often requires intense concentration.

Examples of Problem Solving

The study of problem solving has a rich and diverse history in psychology. For example, Karl Duncker (1945), a famous Gestalt psychologist, posed the following question:

If a human being has an inoperable stomach tumor, how can the tumor be removed by rays that destroy organic tissue at sufficient intensity without destroying the healthy tissue surrounding it?

The question has been asked of many generations of college students to illustrate how they proceed to think through alternative solutions.

With children, a common tactic has been to formulate a problem that requires them to apply some newly learned academic skills in a practical context. For example, consider young elementary school children's ability to solve "word problems" involving addition and subtraction. Following are four examples:

1. Wally has three pennies. His father gave him six more pennies. How many pennies does Wally have altogether?
2. Patrick has nine fish. His sister Jill has fourteen fish. How many more fish does Jill have than Patrick?
3. Fred has eight M&M's. How many more M&M's does he have to put with them so he has thirteen M&M's altogether?
4. There are five jars of paint. Three jars are red and the rest are blue. How many jars of blue paint are there?

As a final example, consider some of the exercises in creative problem solving suggested by psychologists such as J. P. Guilford (1967), Paul Torrance (1966), and Gary Davis (1981), described in chapter 10. At a conference for talented young writers (children from ages seven to twelve years), a developmental psychologist attended a session where children were asked to imagine *ice cream* and write out all of the different things it reminded them of. This is an example of an exercise in divergent thinking, discussed in some detail in chapter 10 under the topic of *creativity*.

Components of Problem Solving

How do children and adults go about solving problems? What accounts for change, as children mature, in problem-solving ability? There are at least four important components of problem solving.

First, we have to figure out what the problem is, precisely, and set one or more goals. This has sometimes been referred to as *problem finding* and *goal setting* (e.g., Miller, Galanter, & Pribram, 1960; Schank & Abelson, 1977). The previous example problems are all pretty well defined. The creators of the problems have taken pains to set up the context and to tell us what they want us to find. In everyday problem solving, however, we often have to find out what the problem is and what, precisely, we have to do. For example, if a child is asked to clean up her room, she must first figure out what must be done. What must the room look like when she is finished, and what currently is out of order?

Once the problem and goal have been defined, a second step is *plan the approach* to solving the problem. Planning may involve isolating the correct pieces to the puzzle and working out the general pattern to solve the problem with these pieces. For example, in Duncker's "tumor-removal" problem, the student would have to isolate these crucial elements: a tumor is to be destroyed with an intense ray; the tumor is in the stomach; no tissue around the tumor can be destroyed. The problem then is to devise ways to make

Application 11.2
Learning Mathematics the Fun Way

Mary is a second-grade student. It's time for her mathematics lesson. Mr. Jones, her teacher, hands her a booklet and a package of materials, and she begins her lesson.

For the first problem, she selects three pieces of string and a ruler to measure them. She determines that the strings have the following lengths: A = 6 inches, B = 3 inches, C = 9 inches. She writes the following in the answer booklet: "A > B, A < C." Reading further, she is asked how to make strings A and B equal in length. She thinks about this for a moment and then writes: "To make A and B the same, take 3 inches from A." Then Mary measures string A and cuts it in half.

For the next problem, Mary finds twelve identical balls and is asked how many different groups she can make with them. After a preliminary grouping attempt, she arrives at six clusters of two and writes in her booklet: "6 groups." But then she thinks about it some more, divides the group of balls in half, and writes: "2 groups." Still not satisfied, Mary tries several more arrangements, with answers of 1, 3, 4, and 12, respectively.

Mary is in a specially designed mathematics curriculum known as *Developing Mathematical Processes* (DMP), which is part of a larger curriculum effort known as *Individually Guided Education* (IGE). Both were developed at the University of Wisconsin in the late 1960s and early 1970s as part of an effort to maximize each child's learning potential in school. At this writing the DMP program is employed in well over 3,000 elementary schools in the United States and is proving very successful in enhancing learning of mathematics (Klausmeier, Rossmiller, & Saily, 1977).

The principal architect of DMP, Thomas Romberg, describes the program this way:

A sound program for IGE mathematics was developed by using a measurement approach in DMP. In a measurement approach, the children examine the objects in their world and focus on some attribute (length, numerousness, weight, capacity, area, time, etc.). They use various processes (describing, classifying, comparing, ordering, equalizing, joining, separating, grouping, and partitioning) to explore relationships between objects. Once they are familiar with each attribute, they symbolically represent (measure) it. Likewise, they symbolically represent the relationships between objects with mathematical sentences. In turn, they represent mathematical sentences with real objects to check their validity. . . .

A second mathematical emphasis in DMP is problem solving. Not only are problems presented for children to solve, but also a need for a new or a more efficient way to solve the problem is invoked. Two stereotypes of mathematics problems that DMP tries to overcome are that there is always one correct answer and that there is only one way to solve a given problem. To counter the "one correct answer" stereotype, DMP presents problems which have no answers and problems which have many answers. Children are often encouraged to solve problems in their own way. (Romberg, 1977, pp. 81, 82)

Children enjoy DMP. It excites them to learn by involving them actively in the learning process. And it challenges them to think and not be overwhelmed by "mistakes."

Common responses of teachers who have taught DMP and observers who have watched DMP in action are "Children have a positive attitude toward math." "A well-planned program which children enjoy as they learn." "An exciting way to introduce children to mathematics." "They love the manipulative materials and even ask for them in play time." (Romberg, 1977, pp. 84–85)

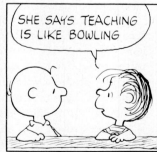

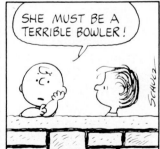

the ray intensely focused on the tumor, but not anywhere else. By brainstorming and calling upon popular knowledge about technology and physics, a number of ideas may be tried out and discarded as impractical, until a single elegant solution suggests itself. With Carpenter's arithmetic word problems, a similar phenomenon of planning may occur for younger children.

A third step is to *monitor the progress* of the problem-solving activity. Basically, this involves taking stock of how the solution process is faring—a kind of self-assessment in midstream. For example, as ideas for solving the tumor problem come forth, the student may stop to ponder whether a given idea is an improvement over the preceding one and whether he or she is still keeping the correct problem elements and goal in mind. As another example, younger children working out the arithmetic problem may wonder if they are proceeding smoothly. There are several common approaches taken by first and second graders to solve these problems. Some count on their fingers; some rely on number facts "in their heads", and some use counting props made available by the experimenter (Carpenter, 1980). The monitoring activity, then, may consist of children's self-assessments of the viability of the counting technique each has chosen.

Based on the results of monitoring activity, problem solvers may go in one of two directions. A sense of smooth progress will support continuation of the approach. By contrast, a sense that progress has been slow or impeded will direct them backwards to reconsider the problem definition or the solution plan. The problem may then become redefined or a new solution plan may be thought up. Negative progress and repeated monitoring efforts signal that the individual is faced with a challenging problem.

The fourth and final step is to *check solutions*. Whereas monitoring focuses on the progress of problem-solving efforts, this final step occurs when individuals feel they have completed their tasks. Simply put, it is to check the solution in whatever way possible. In the tumor problem the student may compare the final solution offered against the initial criteria that had to be met, against the solutions that other classmates have thought up, or against published accounts of its ideal solution. Children solving Carpenter's arithmetic problems may recheck their adding and subtracting. For more information about how problem solving in mathematics can be enjoyable for children, read application 11.2.

This concludes our discussion of cognitive development in middle and late childhood. In the next chapter we look at how children develop socially and emotionally during middle and late childhood.

Summary

During the period of concrete operations, the child moves beyond concentrated thought to *relativism,* is able to mentally reverse and transform observed actions, and develops a network of thought structures called operations. Many of the operations are defined in terms of properties of an algebraic group.

Recently, Piaget's theory has come under increasing criticism. Despite the wealth of penetrating observations he offers, his sound ideas about the qualitative nature of thinking, and his imaginative concepts about cognitive change, critics worry that there is no good evidence for global stages, that his key concepts about changes are hard to operationalize, and that very few of the phenomena he describes behave precisely as he claims they do.

A different starting point for analyzing the mind is the implicit framework of the information processing theory. With its roots in the early development of computers (e.g., Broadbent, 1958; Miller, Galanter, & Pribram, 1960) and recent advances in the software of computing (e.g., Klahr & Wallace, 1975; Simon, 1980), this perspective assumes that for every event experienced in the environment, cognition involves a series of steps to process the event. Many information processing views of cognitive development recognize common, important steps: attending to the event; perceiving it; storing and retrieving representations of it over time (memory); and acting upon the memories of it in some abstract way—that is, drawing some inference about the experience or resolving a problem by virtue of it. Development can be equated with the individual's becoming a more complete and efficient information processing "mechanism."

Two parts in information processing were emphasized in this chapter—memory and problem solving. Memory is the retention of information over time. Often it is studied by assessing *recall,* or *recognition,* of events or the ability to associate pairs of things—referred to as *paired associates.* Memory may be conceived of as the flow of information over time, captured in a fleeting moment in a *sensory register,* slightly longer in a *short-term* or working memory, or finally, in a relatively permanent repository of knowledge called *long-term* memory. The processes that help explain how information is moved through the system include rehearsal, elaboration, and organization.

An inference is a relation noted between one event and another where the relation has not been revealed or identified directly. Some inferences are *logical,* based on our general understanding of how things go together in the world; other inferences are based on our specialized knowledge of persons, places, and things. Successful inferential activity requires knowing when to draw inferences and activating relevant prior knowledge.

Problem solving is processing information to fulfill a major goal. It may also be viewed as a regulatory function of information processing. The important components of problem solving include problem finding and goal setting, planning, monitoring progress, and checking solutions.

Key Terms

chunks	organization
elaboration	paired associates
equilibration	recall
inference	recognition
keyword method	rehearsal
long-term memory	short-term memory
mnemonics	

Review Questions

1. What is concrete operational thought?
2. Critically evaluate Piaget's theory.
3. Discuss the different ways of assessing memory and the different memory storage systems.
4. Discuss the different processes underlying memory.
5. What is an inference? Describe some different types of inferences and the underlying improvement in inferring ability.
6. What is problem solving? What are some key parts of regulating information processing?

Further Readings

Elkind, D. *Children and adolescents.* 2d ed. New York: Oxford, 1974.

An excellent, easy-to-read introduction to Piaget's ideas. Many practical examples are given to help you understand Piaget's theory.

Furth, H. G., & Wachs, H. *Thinking goes to school.* New York: Oxford, 1975.

An easy-to-read application of Piaget's view to education in the middle and late childhood years. Includes 179 thinking games that can be incorporated in the day-to-day teaching of children.

Kail, Robert. *The development of memory in children.* San Francisco: Freeman, 1979.

An easy-to-read survey of ideas and research on children's memory.

Klahr, D., & Wallace, J. G. *Cognitive development: an information processing perspective.* Hillsdale, N.J.: Erlbaum, 1975.

A technical explanation of information processing theory by two leading experts. Moderate to difficult reading.

12 Social Development

Imagine . . . that you could visit China and observe children at home and at school

The following comments about childhood in China are based on the observations of a team of social scientists, including William Kessen, Harold Stevenson, Urie Bronfenbrenner, Eleanor Maccoby, Marian Radke Yarrow, and Martin Whyte (Kessen, 1975).

Frequent communication between schools and parents occurs in Chinese education. These interchanges include formal meetings and notebooks with messages given to students to take home, which are referred to as "communication," or "connection," notebooks. Informal exchanges are also common when students are dropped off at school. The interface of schools and families appears to be much smoother and continuous than in the United States.

At home and at school, the child is exposed to standards that stress the importance of service and self-reliance. School assignments and out-of-school peer group sessions provide opportunities for the Chinese child to practice self-control and social control. Membership in groups like the Little Red Soldiers and the Red Guards serves the same purpose.

Chinese extended family ties are strong. Even though children and family members often have had to spend large chunks of time away from home because of service to the country, the family system in China is a stable one. Grandparents and relatives interact with children more often than in most American families. And if parents or grandparents fail to supervise their children, local committees look into the matter and provide support. Informal support systems of neighbors and retired workers are fairly common. The picture, then, with regard to the ties between schools, home, and community for Chinese children, is one of coherent support directed toward the development of

the nation. Parents and schools preach the same doctrine in China, and local committees, acting as arms of the national government, closely monitor how this doctrine is inculcated in Chinese children.

American observers indicate that they are surprised at the extent to which Chinese children are conforming, dutiful, well organized, and devoted to the values of adults. The students have no choice in the courses they take, and no free exploration of information sources (such as browsing in a library). Children in China clearly are exposed to a body of knowledge that is practical in nature. Compared to typical American schools, then, opportunities for student creativity and problem solving are low. For very talented students, there are opportunities to spend time inventing, creating musical productions, and so forth. But there is little or no creativity in the literature the average students read—most stories focus on the ideological message conveyed in revolutionary army practices.

However, close friendships actually may be more easily developed by Chinese children than American children because the Chinese often stay in the same class with the same students throughout the elementary and secondary school years. In the junior high years, there does seem to be easy, happy social interaction within peer groups, usually involving pairs of boys and girls.

Observers of Chinese children raise important questions about the way Chinese children are socialized—for example, what are the implications of a strong cultural indoctrination that is clearly laid out and closely monitored? What are the effects of the absence of independent decision making on a career? What are the effects of the absence of a distinction between the private and public life of the student and the parents? (Kessen, 1975)

Introduction

In this chapter we explore many aspects of social development in middle and late childhood. In particular we evaluate the important social settings or contexts in which development occurs during middle and late childhood. In the Imagine section you read how schools are an important vehicle for the transmission of cultural standards in China. In this chapter we provide further details about the important role of schools in children's lives during middle and late childhood. Discussion of families and peers continues with further information about the changing nature of families, the influence of siblings, and the powerful role peers play in middle and late childhood.

Families

During middle and late childhood, social agents outside the child's family take on more importance; peers, teachers, and other adults play increasingly important roles in the child's life. By the time children enter elementary school, they are capable of asking complex questions about themselves and their world. A parent needs to change from a model who knows everything to someone who doesn't know all the answers. Two frequent questions parents ask during the middle childhood years are How much do our children need us? and How much can they do without us?

The child entering elementary school can take care of himself or herself for a large part of the day and feels good about being able to do this. Competent parents need to adjust their behavior and let go of children at this time so that they can explore the world more independently. Eight-year-olds don't seek the attention of either parent to the extent that toddlers do. Sometimes this can be disturbing to parents who see their children growing away from their control and influence. Children in middle childhood still are very much dependent on their parents and still require extensive guidance and monitoring, but parents need to operate more in the background at this time. Parents should recognize that while they still are the most important adults in the child's life, they are no longer the only significant adult figures.

Work and achievement are other themes of middle childhood that require adaptation and guidance on the part of parents. During the elementary school years, it is important that parents encourage children to develop a sense of industry and accomplishment, that is, to be able to work and to make things work. In our American culture, parents sometimes push too hard and too early for achievement, shoving their children into tension-provoking comparisons with peers. The opposite extreme, that of lack of involvement and concern for the child's achievement and school success, can lead to difficulties as well. In the latter situation, children may feel that their parents do not value education and achievement and consequently the children will not be motivated to achieve.

The Changing Family

As indicated in chapter 9, children are growing up in a greater variety of family structures than ever before. Information on school-age children suggests that one reason employment of mothers may not have a negative effect is that many mothers compensate for their absence by increasing the amount of direct interaction with their children when they are at home. Such compensation does not always occur, however, and when it does it may be guilt induced and result in overindulgence (Hoffman, 1974).

When children enter elementary school, the problem of child care is reduced considerably since a greater number of socialization agents have an impact on the child—peers, teachers, and significant adults in the community. Children spend less time with their mothers, and even in traditional families, fathers are more often involved in the socialization process than during the child's earlier years.

Elementary school children whose mothers go to work are likely to be encouraged by their mothers to show independent behavior. It has been found that in lower-class and single-parent families employed mothers are more likely to have structured roles for their children (Hoffman, 1974). Both the independent behavior and the rule-governed households are logical adaptations to the working mother's role—they help the household to function more smoothly in her absence. In addition, there are some rather consistent findings in achievement of the daughters of working mothers; for example, compared to daughters whose mothers don't work outside the home, they admire their mothers more and hold the female role in higher esteem (Romer & Cherry, 1978).

In chapter 9 the effects of divorce on children were also explored. One aspect of divorce that is of growing interest concerns whether the custodial parent is the mother or the father. In studies of elementary school children in single-parent families it was found that the custodial parent has a strong influence on the child's behavior. (Santrock & Warshak, 1979; Santrock, Warshak, & Eliot, 1982). The psychological well-being and childrearing capabilities of the father or the mother are central to the child's ability to cope with the stress of divorce. It appears that divorced mothers have more difficulty with sons than they do with daughters. Mavis Hetherington (1979) believes that divorced mothers and their sons often get involved in what she calls a cycle of coercive interaction. But what about boys growing up in homes in which the father has custody—is there the same coercive cycle?

Father Custody and Children's Social Behavior

In 1817 poet Percy Bysshe Shelley was denied custody of his children because of his "vicious and immoral" atheistic beliefs. This was a rare situation at the time because English law granted fathers nearly absolute right to custody of their children. This was a carry-over from Roman law, which protected the father's absolute life-and-death control over his children.

In the United States, the English common law tradition was perpetuated throughout the nineteenth century. Few women were permitted to own property, so few had adequate means to support children. Because the father was responsible for financially supporting the child, it was believed that he should be given custody.

The twentieth century brought forth a new interest in the child's welfare—the importance of maternal care was repeatedly emphasized, partly because of the sweeping impact of psychoanalytic theory. It was presumed that mothers are uniquely suited to care for their young. It became standard fare for judges to award custody to the mother because they thought it was in the best interest of the child, unless the mother was in a mental hospital or judged to have some severe physical handicap.

Until recently, many courts awarded custody of the children to the mother without considering the actual needs of the children and carefully evaluating the psychological climate in which the child would live. However, there is a growing movement toward a genuine commitment to the actual needs of the child without relying on generalizations that give an a priori claim to either parent.

As noted earlier, Mavis Hetherington (1979) has argued that a coercive relationship develops between single mothers and their sons. The mother is overburdened with the responsibility as a single parent, thus reducing the quality of her interaction and increasing the use of coercion with her youth. Boys, because of their relatively greater tendency to engage in aggressive behavior, probably contribute to this coercive cycle.

In one study (Santrock & Warshak, 1979) boys were more demanding and less mature in a mother-custody arrangement than in a father-custody arrangement. While fathers with custody also have many responsibilities as a single parent, their sons may feel more comfortable with them and the fathers themselves may be more accepting or even encouraging toward traditional masculine behaviors, such as aggressive, rough-and-tumble play. A father is more likely than a mother to play football or other sports with his son and often feels more comfortable in discussing sex-related issues with him. Conversely, because he lacks female role experiences, a father may be less sensitive to his daughter's needs and less capable of fulfilling those needs even if he senses them.

Many fathers are proving that they can be just as caring and competent as mothers in child-custody cases.

In the past, erroneous generalizations about the impact of divorce have been made on the basis of research with mother-custody families. Naturally, any application of the father-custody research should be made with due recognition of the various limitations of the study. Results from psychological research imply probabilities rather than absolute generalizations. In making custody and visitation decisions, each case must be decided on its own merits. There may be unique circumstances in an individual family that warrant attention and consideration. Generalizations to children of different socioeconomic statutes or ages may be inappropriate. We need to know more about the interaction between type of custody and developmental status of children. Also, we know little about the long-term effects of different family environments. Future changes, such as the remarriage of one or both parents, will have a definite impact on children's perspectives of their parents' divorce (e.g., reconciliation wishes may diminish following a remarriage), and the pattern of these effects may differ in father-custody and mother-custody families.

It is clear that the effects of divorce on children are determined by a host of complex factors that include custody arrangement, sex of child, aspects of the custodial parent-child relationship, and availability of and reliance on support systems.

Stepparent Families

While research efforts have increased our knowledge about the effects of divorce on children (e.g., Hetherington, Cox, & Cox, 1978; Santrock & Warshak, 1979; Wallerstein & Kelly, 1980), much less is known about what happens to these children when their custodial parent remarries. Over six million children in the United States now live in stepparent homes. These "blended" families represented 11 percent of all American households in 1977 (Eiduson & Zimmerman, 1978). Current research explores the manner in which children are socialized in these stepparent families (Santrock, Warshak, Lindbergh, & Meadows, 1982).

The effects of remarriage on the parent's and the child's social behavior were studied by comparing twelve children whose mothers remarried, with twelve children whose mothers were divorced but had not remarried and twelve children from intact, father-present families. Half of the children were boys and half were girls aged six to eleven years. The children had been living with their mother and stepfather for a minimum of eighteen months. The data consisted of videotaped observations of parent-child interaction, with the parent's and child's behavior coded separately. The most consistent findings suggested that boys in stepfather families showed more competent social behavior than boys in intact families, which corresponded with more competent parenting behavior in those stepfather families. By contrast, girls in stepfather families were observed to be more anxious than girls in intact families. Boys showed more warmth toward their stepfather than did girls, while there was a trend for girls to show more anger toward their mother than boys in stepfather families. Divorced and stepfather children differed only in a trend for boys from stepfather families to show more mature behavior than boys from divorced homes. Mothers of boys in stepfather families did make more meaningful statements to them than the divorced mothers of boys. Few differences were found between divorced and intact families.

The same study also found that the fathers of boys in intact families were contemplating divorce more than the stepfathers of boys, and that the mothers of boys in intact families wished they had married someone else more often than the stepfathers and remarried mothers

of boys. It appears, then, that the boys in stepfather families were experiencing not only more competent parenting but also were living in families with less marital conflict than the intact family boys—two factors that help to explain differences in the social behavior of boys from the two family structures.

By contrast, girls in stepfather families showed more anxiety than girls in intact families, but there was no corresponding link with parenting behavior when the stepfather and intact families were compared. However, the stepfathers of girls said that they were contemplating divorce more than the mothers of intact family girls, suggesting the likelihood of greater marital conflict between the parents of the stepfather girls than the intact family girls. And the possibility that in some families stepparent-child disharmony may contribute to marital conflict also should be considered.

It was concluded that the social behavior of children is not necessarily less competent in stepfather families than in intact or divorced families. The data suggested that such factors as parenting behavior, sex of child, and marital conflict in any type of family structure are implicated as possible explanations of the child's social behavior.

So far in our discussion of families we have paid attention to changing family structures, parent-child relationships, parenting techniques, and the maturation of the child and the parent. Next, we look at yet another important aspect of families—sibling relationships.

Siblings

Probably the least studied aspect of the family system is the nature of sibling interaction. Sibling interaction usually precedes peer interaction and, as such, may serve as a bridge between family relations and the social world of peers.

Competition among siblings—that is, brothers and/or sisters—along with concern about being treated fairly and equally by parents, are among the most pervasive characteristics of sibling relationships (Santrock, Smith, & Bourbeau, 1976).

More than 80 percent of American children have one or more siblings. Because there are so many possible sibling combinations in a family, it is difficult to generalize about sibling influence and conflict. Among a variety of important factors to be considered in studying sibling relationships are the number of siblings and the number of years separating the siblings in age. Despite the complexities of such studies, there has been considerable research on siblings. These studies usually compare firstborn children with their siblings (e.g., Koch, 1956). Most of the studies focus on

two-child families since interpreting data on sibling experiences in larger families is difficult. In keeping with the text's approach to the family as a system of interacting individuals, let's look first at the mother's interaction with siblings.

The Mother's Interaction with Siblings

The influence of the mother's interaction with her children on sibling behavior usually has been studied indirectly; that is, children of a different birth order are compared with each other. As a result of such studies, it is speculated that mothers treat their children differently, presumably causing changes in their behavior and personality.

For example, firstborn children are more achievement-oriented, affiliative (want to be around people), and compliant than children born later (Sutton-Smith & Rosenberg, 1970). It is usually believed that middle children tend to be somewhat neglected by parents. Mothers seem more anxious and solicitous with their firstborn than with children born later, perhaps causing differences in the children's behavior (Schachter, 1959).

In observations of mother-sibling interaction, mothers consistently gave more attention to their firstborn children than to children born later (Rothbart, 1967). This is perhaps explained by the fact that many mothers anxiously await the birth of their first child and that both parents often have high expectations for the child. By the time the second child is born, much of the novelty and intrigue of rearing a child probably has worn off.

A newborn child can influence both the behavior of the mother and the behavior of the sibling. In one study working-class mothers were observed as they interacted with their firstborn children in a playroom situation, both before and shortly after the birth of a sibling. The mothers and the firstborn exchanged less open affection and were more neutral to each other after the sibling was born (Taylor & Kogan, 1973).

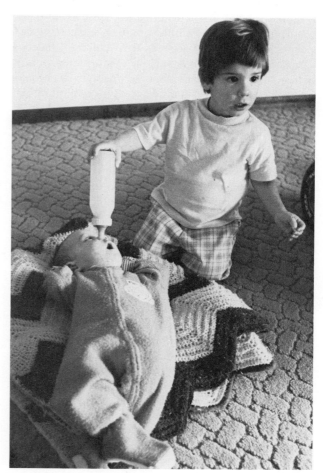

A sibling "helper"?

Siblings' Influences on One Another

A four-year-old child probably feels more threatened by the arrival of a brother or sister than does a child who is one or two years old or a child who is seven or eight. The cognitive development of the very young child is not advanced enough to understand much of what is happening. An older child probably has gained more independence, established stronger ties with peers, and has less fear of the parent's withdrawal of love. There are individual differences, however; an older child who is still tied to his or her mother and does not have many friends may feel just as threatened by the arrival of a younger brother or sister as the preschooler does.

Many parents of siblings express concern about bickering and fighting between their children. Indeed, the process of social comparison is intensified in any sibling relationship. The child has a built-in need to know where he or she stands vis-à-vis his or her brother or sister: Is he or she as strong, as smart, as worthwhile a person? All children are concerned about where they stand in these regards, but a sibling provides a more concrete reminder to the child to question his or her status in the family. Competitive sibling interaction, then, is a fact of sibling life but so, too, are positive and neutral interactions. However, parents may overlook many of the positive and neutral sibling exchanges, responding instead to negative behaviors that require parental intervention.

Is sibling interaction different from parent-child interaction? There is some evidence that it is. Linda Baskett (1974) observed the members of forty-seven families, each with two or three children. The siblings ranged from five to ten years of age. Observations were made for forty-five minutes on five different occasions. The children's observed behaviors included teasing, whining, yelling, commanding, talking, touching, nonverbal interacting, laughing, and complying. The interaction of the children with their parents was far more positive than their interaction with each other. Children and their parents had more varied and positive interchanges—they talked, laughed, and comforted one another more than siblings did. Children also tended to follow the dictates of their parents more than those of their siblings, and they behaved more negatively and punitively during interaction with their siblings than with their parents.

In some instances siblings are a stronger socializing influence on the child than parents are. Victor Cicirelli (1977) believes, in particular, that older siblings teach their younger siblings. Someone close in age to the child may understand his or her problems more readily and be able to communicate more effectively than parents can. In areas such as dealing with peers, coping with difficult teachers, and discussing taboo subjects, siblings often fare better than parents in the socialization process. Older siblings also may serve effectively in teaching younger siblings about identity problems, sexual behavior, and physical appearance—areas in which the parents may be unwilling or incapable of helping a child.

The potential benefits of using siblings as therapists has been demonstrated (Miller & Cantwell, 1976). In families where siblings are involved, therapy is more effective than in families where only the parents and the disturbed child are included. When siblings are not included, they may unknowingly encourage and perpetuate unwanted behaviors in the disturbed child. Instructing the sibling in ways he or she and the parents can more effectively manage the disturbed brother or sister produces more positive outcomes in family therapy.

As mentioned earlier, this sibling interaction may help the child to bridge life in the family with life with peers.

Peers
Peer interaction has been studied in almost as many ways as parent-child interaction. In this section we will see that peers are important models for their age-mates, that in some cases they can serve as effective tutors, and that they can be of great help to age-mates who have social problems. Popularity among peers and how children's groups are formed will also be discussed.

Peer Modeling, Tutoring, and Reinforcement
There has been little effort to use peer modeling in a formal way in our educational system. One technique that is gaining popularity in schools, however, is peer tutoring. When low-achieving fifth-graders were placed in the role of teacher, substantial gains in their reading scores resulted. The reading scores of the tutored third-graders, however, did not increase more than those of a comparable group of children who studied alone. The children may have felt embarrassed about being taught systematically by their own age-mates. Perhaps somewhat older peers should be used for tutoring in school subjects. It may be, however, that the greatest gains will be those made by the tutors themselves (Allen & Feldman, 1976).

Other studies of the relationship between peer models and their observers indicate that a positive relationship with the model (Hartup & Coates, 1967) and a perceived similarity between the model and the observer (Rosenkrans, 1967) enhance modeling. In other words, if the tutor or model has a positive, warm relationship with the observer, or if the observer believes he or she has something in common with the model, modeling will be more effective. In keeping with the idea of perceived similarity, it seems that it would be best to have a middle-class student tutor a middle-class child and lower-class student counsel a lower-class child.

Peer relations are also affected by the extent to which the individuals dispense rewards to each other. The members of a peer group who give out the most reinforcements are the ones most likely to receive the most reinforcements in return (Charlesworth & Hartup, 1967). This indicates the reciprocal nature of peer interaction. In one investigation it was found that training peers to selectively use reinforcement reduced disruptive activity in the classroom (Solomon & Whalen, 1973).

In our educational system teachers and administrators sometimes deliberately have manipulated peer contact. For instance, at the beginning of the school year, students who are less advanced academically (and in some cases, socially) often are placed in classes for so-called slower students. This arrangement is designed to enable the teacher to teach at the cognitive level appropriate for the majority of students in the class (Hartup, 1976). While "tracking" (as it is referred to in educational circles) is usually designed for academic benefits, it may have a considerable effect on social development as well. For example, tracking may break down neighborhood friendships and supplant them with "tracking" friendships although such an influence on friendship patterns is regarded as incidental by school administrators.

As Urie Bronfenbrenner (1970) points out, the educational system in the United States has not systematically called on the peer group to the extent that other countries have. Bronfenbrenner summarized some of the major aspects of socialization practices involving peer relations in the Soviet Union. There, the peer group is assigned important duties in assisting the teacher. Conformity to group norms is stressed through education, and the subordination of the individual to the group is an omnipresent goal. Group competition between grades, schools, rooms, and rows in rooms is emphasized. Although such practices are not foreign to American schools, they are not as systematized as they are in the Soviet Union. In the United States, the peer group may undermine the socialization practices of adults; in the Soviet Union peer-group norms support adult norms.

Probably no other cross-cultural work with children is more widely cited than the work of Beatrice and John Whiting. In 1954 the Whitings and their colleagues began reporting their observations of children in six different cultures. The most recent publication of their work is the book *Children of Six Cultures: A Psychocultural Analysis* (1975). For these observations the Whitings placed six teams of anthropologists in six different cultures, five of which were primarily farming communities: northern India; the Philippines; Okinawa, Japan; Oaxaca, Mexico; and western Kenya. The sixth setting was a small nonfarming town in New England. The teams interviewed the mothers and conducted standardized observations of the children in the six cultures.

Among the most intriguing findings of the project were the consistent differences in adult-child and peer interactions across the cultures. Dependency, nurturance, and intimacy were rarely observed in peer relations but were frequently observed in adult-child interaction. By contrast, aggressiveness, prosocial activity, and sociable behavior were the most frequently occurring behaviors in peer relations across the six cultures. Such findings support the belief that there may be universal differences between adult-child and peer interactions.

In this section we have seen that the relatively straightforward application of the principles of modeling and reinforcement often can be effective in influencing children's peer relations and that there are similarities as well as differences when we study peer relations in different cultures. Next we see that children are increasingly called upon to help their peers with problems.

Peer Sociotherapy

One **conglomerate strategy** (i.e., a series of coordinated strategies) used to help children get along better with their peers is called **coaching,** which combines demonstration (or modeling), rational discussion sessions, and shaping (the use of reinforcement). In one coaching study, students with few friends were selected for a coaching session that focused on how to have fun with your peers (Oden & Asher, 1975). The "unpopular" students were encouraged to participate fully, to show interest in others, to cooperate, and to maintain communication. A control group of students (who also had few friends) were directed in play experiences but were not coached with specific strategies. Later, the coached group showed more sociability with peers than the uncoached group did.

A Peer-Oriented Clinic for Children with Problems

Robert Selman's work has been conducted at the Manville School, a clinic in the Judge Baker Guidance Center in Boston for learning-disabled and emotionally disturbed seven- to fifteen-year-olds. Many of these students have great difficulty in interpersonal relationships, particularly with their peers. The staff at the Manville School has been trained to help peers provide support and encouragement to each other in group settings, a process referred to as **peer sociotherapy.**

Structured programs at the Manville School are designed to help the children assist each other in such areas as cooperation, trust, leadership, and conformity. Four school activities were developed to improve the student's social reasoning skills in these areas.

First, there is a weekly peer problem-solving session in the classroom in which the peers work cooperatively to plan activities and relate problems. At the end of each week the peers evaluate their effectiveness in making improvements in areas like cooperation, conflict resolution, and so forth.

Second, the members of a class, numbering from six to eight students, plan a series of weekly field trips, for example, going to the movies or visiting historical sites. While the counselor provides some assistance, peer decision making dominates. When each activity is completed, the students discuss how things went and what might have been done to improve social relations with each other on the outings.

Third, Selman recognizes that there are times when the student has to get away from a setting where intense frustration occurs. When the student finds himself or herself in a highly frustrating situation (e.g., angry enough to strike out at a classmate), he or she is allowed to leave the room and go to a private "time-out" area of the school to regain composure. In time-out, the student also is given the opportunity to discuss the problems with a counselor who has been trained to help the child or adolescent improve social reasoning skills.

Fourth, during social studies and current events discussion sessions, the students evaluate a number of moral and societal issues that incorporate the thinking of theorists such as Lawrence Kohlberg.

Another example of effective conglomerate strategy in peer therapy is Robert Selman's (Selman, Newberger, & Jacquette, 1977) psychological and educational program, emphasizing the importance of peer relations in classroom settings, group activities, and sports. His work is described in application 12.1.

Popularity

Elementary and secondary school children often think, What can I do to have all of the kids at school like me? How can I be popular with both girls and guys? What's wrong with me? There must be something wrong, or I would be more popular. Sometimes children will go to great lengths to be popular; and in some cases parents go to even greater lengths to try to insulate their offspring from rejection and to increase the likelihood that they will be popular.

What makes a child popular with peers? In one study children who gave the most reinforcements were found to gain popularity among their peers (Hartup, 1970). In the coaching sessions discussed earlier (Oden & Asher, 1975) students were encouraged to overcome their difficulty in interacting with their peers by listening carefully to their peers' conversation and by maintaining open lines of communication with their peers.

In another study (Hartup, 1970) it was found that being yourself, being happy, showing enthusiasm and concern for others, and showing self-confidence but not conceit are among the characteristics that lead to popularity. In many instances the opposites of these behaviors were found to invite rejection from peers (Hollingshead, 1975).

Certain physical and cultural factors also can affect a child's popularity. Some research has shown that children who are physically attractive are more popular than those who are not; and contrary to what some believe, brighter children are more popular than less intelligent ones. Children growing up in middle-class surroundings tend to be more popular than those growing up in lower-class surroundings, presumably in part because they are more in control of establishing standards for popularity (e.g., Hollingshead, 1975). But remember that findings such as these reflect group averages; there are many physically attractive children who are unpopular and physically unattractive children who are very well liked. And with the increased concern for equal treatment of minority groups, lower-class and ethnic group children can be expected to gain more influence in establishing the standards of popularity.

Finally, popularity may fluctuate, and children sense the tenuous nature of popularity; even the child who is very popular with peers may have doubts about his or her ability to maintain popularity.

Children's Groups

So far in our discussion of peer relations, little has been said about how the child functions in groups. In this section we will look at how children's groups are formed, compare children's groups with adolescent groups, and describe social-class variations in children's groups.

The most extensive work conducted on the formation of children's and adolescents' groups is that of Muzafer Sherif and his colleagues (Sherif, 1951; Sherif, 1966; Sherif, Harvey, Hoyt, Hood, & Sherif, 1961). The Sherif naturalistic experiments often proceed according to a particular format. Middle-class white Protestant boys are recruited and moved to a campsite during the summer. There they are exposed to an experiment in the natural setting of the camp. The observers are members of the camp staff.

In the first phase of the experiment, in-group formation is established by placing two groups of boys who don't know one another together for a few days. In the second phase, the two groups are brought together for the intergroup conflict phase. This conflict includes win-lose competition and planned frustration that is expected to increase the tension between the groups. In the third phase, ways to reduce intergroup conflict are explored. The observers use strategies such as experiencing a common enemy or constructing superordinate goals that the two groups can only achieve together to reduce conflict.

Some of the important findings to come out of Sherif's naturalistic experiments are (1) hierarchical structures invariably emerge within the groups. The top and bottom status positions are filled first, then the middle positions. (2) Norms develop in all groups, "We-they" talk is a frequent part of the groups' conversations. The groups often adopt nicknames, like the Bulldogs or the Sorcerers. (3) Frustration and competition contribute to hostility between the groups. (4) Intergroup hostility often can be reduced by setting up a superordinate goal that requires the mutual efforts of both groups. For example, Sherif's camp directors deliberately broke a water line so both groups of boys would have to pitch in together to help fix it. Another time, the camp truck taking the boys to a movie in town was driven into a muddy ditch, requiring considerable team effort to get it out.

Children's Groups Versus Adolescent Groups

Children's groups differ from adolescent groups in several important ways. The members of children's groups are often friends or neighborhood acquaintances. Their groups are usually not as formalized as many adolescent groups. During the adolescent years, groups tend to include a broader array of members—in other words, adolescents other than friends or neighborhood acquaintances are often members of the groups. Try to recall the student council, honor society, or football team at your junior high school. If you were a member of any of these junior high organizations, you likely recall that they were comprised of a number of individuals you had not met before and that they were a more heterogeneous group than your childhood peer groups. Rules and regulations were probably well defined, and captains or leaders were formally elected or appointed. Formalized structure and definition of status positions probably did not characterize many of your childhood peer groups.

In addition to more formalized structure and greater heterogeneity of members, adolescent peer groups are also more often cross-sexed than children's peer groups (Dunphy, 1963). The increased frequency of formal groups in junior high, combined with the psychological changes of puberty, explain to some extent why adolescent groups have mixtures of boys and girls more often than children's groups do.

Social Class Variations in Childhood Peer Groups

Whether a child grows up as part of the peer culture in a ghetto or in a middle-class suburban area influences the nature of the groups he or she belongs to. For example, in a comparison of middle- and lower-class groups, lower-class children displayed more aggression toward the low-status member of the group but showed less aggression toward the president of the group than their middle-class counterparts did (Maas, 1954).

In many schools, peer groups are virtually segregated according to race and social class. Where middle- and lower-class students are both included, the middle-class students often assume the leadership roles in formal organizations such as the student council, the honor society, fraternity-sorority groups, and so forth. Athletic teams represent one type of group where blacks and lower-class students have been able to gain parity with or surpass middle-class students in achieving status.

Black and white (and lower- and middle-class) students have spent more time with each other during the past two decades than in previous eras. But it has been in schools rather than in neighborhoods where the greatest mixture of different backgrounds has occurred. Even when schools are mixed in terms of ethnic and social-class background, it still appears that friendships, cliques, and crowds are more likely to follow social-class and ethnic group lines (Hartup, 1970).

In many schools peer groups are of the same race and social class.

It is usually in formal groups, such as athletic teams and student councils, that the greatest mixture of social class and ethnicity occurs.

This means that family and cultural backgrounds play critical parts in the development of both informal and formal peer groups. As John Hill (1980a) indicates, even though children often spend greater amounts of time with their peers than with their parents, isolation from parental values does not necessarily ensue.

In summarizing the major changes in peer relations from early childhood to middle and late childhood, Willard Hartup (1983) concluded:

Qualitative changes in child-child interaction continue beyond the preschool years. With school entrance, children increase their contacts with other children and begin to recognize that other individuals have ideas and points of view that are different from their own. Peer interaction undoubtedly profits from the decline in egocentrism as well as contributes to it. . . .

Reciprocity is necessary in many situations confronted by the older child—playing games, participating in groups, and friendships. . . . The child's understanding of intentionality and the ability to cope with complex social messages increase in middle childhood and almost certainly underlie changes in social interaction. (pp. 46, 52)

Schools

Not all children attend preschool classes, but virtually every child in the United States does go to elementary school. For those who do not attend preschool classes, entering the first grade can be a shocking experience; the first grade is often the first time these children have been separated from their mothers for long periods of time.

Schools are one of the major institutions by which a culture transmits information and values to its children. By the time children have reached the age of five to six, most in America spend as many of their waking hours in school as at home.

Most children in American society spend twelve or more years in formal schooling. It is not atypical for many individuals to spend up to twenty-three years in school, including one or two years of nursery school, one year of kindergarten, twelve years of elementary and high school, four years of college, and four years of graduate or professional school. It would be surprising, then, if school were anything but a powerful force in the development of children. Indeed, it may be the most influential of society's many institutions.

We will look at the nature of children's schooling, including the different kinds of schools, the organization of schools, the teacher's role in children's social development, and ethnicity and schools.

Schools are important settings for both cognitive and social development. For this reason, in our section on early childhood we placed the discussion of schools under cognitive development. In this section and the following one on adolescence we discuss schools under social development.

The Nature of the Child's Schooling

Educators who stress the importance of humanistic and affective education believe that schools are often inhumane and fail to give adequate consideration to the child's feelings. They believe that educational institutions should be working toward developing the child's self-awareness and self-confidence as much or more than teaching how to write essays or do math problems. Advocates of humanistic and affective education feel that the child should receive more individual attention from the teacher, particularly in regard to problems, conflicts, and anxieties. Furthermore, they say, teachers should be less dictatorial and allow the child freedom to make decisions. Schools that stress these goals are sometimes referred to as providing **progressive education.**

Another view is that schools should be providing a **traditional education.** Traditional schools are preoccupied with transmitting basic academic skills to all children—skills that are seen as necessary for getting along in a complex society. In the early elementary years this concern is seen in the familiar emphasis on reading, writing, and arithmetic.

Progressive schools take a broader view of education. They suppose that basic skills are important but that the child must also learn how to get along with other people, acquire an appreciation of aesthetics and human values, and be exposed to activities that will be a source of pleasure in later life. In progressive education emphasis is on the needs and competencies of the individual child; no activity is so important that every child must be forced into it regardless of ability or motivation for participation.

Open schools, free schools, and *alternative schools* are labels that have been applied to classroom settings and schools that differ from the structured, teacher-centered approach of traditional schools. These *progressive* schools became popular during the late 1960s and early 1970s at a time when educators were seeking new ways to stimulate students and allow for optimum growth. Humanistic and affective education may now be on the wane as advocates of traditional schools have become more vociferous. "Let's get back to the basics in our schools," they say. "Our schools are not teaching children how to write and read correctly." Advocates of the "back to the basics" movement cite declining achievement scores on standardized tests of verbal and mathematics skills as evidence that these basic skills are not being taught effectively (e.g., Forbes, 1976). They want to do away with the new "frills" of moral education, innovative programs, and child-centered curricula and return to reading, writing, and mathematics, and science skills.

There is no easy answer to the question of which type of education, traditional or progressive, is better for children. It is very difficult to obtain empirical information about this matter; both traditional and progressive programs vary among themselves along many different dimensions. Also, different types of programs may have different outcomes for different children. Some education experts believe that the most important facet of education is variety; in others words it is

important to have several education modes to choose from in order to suit the specific needs and abilities of individual children.

One dimension of the traditional versus progressive education issue that has been quite thoroughly studied is control. This dimension is significant in many contexts—with school boards and principals, with reference to how much centralized control there is in a school system and within a school; in the classroom, with reference to how the teacher disciplines students; and in who controls the schools, with reference to how much influence parents have over what their children are taught.

John Hill (1978) suggests that how parents view the control issue depends upon their social class. A rather common prescription for elementary and secondary education is *authoritarian control,* held by school administrators and teachers because it is believed that such power is necessary to repress the rebellious nature of children, particularly boys. Many lower-class parents agree with this strategy because they themselves are more likely to use authoritarian discipline in dealing with their youth. But such a discipline strategy may be viewed skeptically by many middle-class parents who see authoritarian discipline as inhibiting and repressive.

The dimension of control also seems to be linked with the incidence of violence in schools. A report by the National Institute of Education (1978) suggests that violence is less likely to occur in schools where principals firmly enforce rules, where the rules and controls are considered reasonable by students, and where the students perceive that they have at least some control over their own lives. Vandalism also occurs less frequently when rules are fairly and firmly administered than when teachers adopt hostile attitudes and discipline in an authoritarian fashion.

Organization of Schools

There are many ways the child's school years can be organized. Perhaps the most common is to divide the twelve years of schooling into six years at an elementary school, three years at a junior high school, and the final three years at a high school. However, there has been an increase in recent years in the number of school districts that have gone to a middle school organization. In this system, the child goes through first through fifth grades in an elementary school, sixth through eighth grades in a middle school, and ninth through twelfth grades in a high school.

Very little is known about how different forms of school organization affect the child's development. In one review of the education practices of middle schools

We need to know more about how classroom structure and school organization influence children's development.

compared with junior high schools, there were no differences between the two types of schools in teaching strategies, curricula, academic progress, student work load, or extracurricular activities (Gatewood, 1971). But what about the effects of the organization on students? It may be that the physical, social, and cognitive development of children is affected by such factors as whether they are the oldest, largest, and most competent in a group of 300 to 400 young people, or the youngest, smallest, and least competent among such a group. A sixth grader in a middle school is likely to have very different experiences than a sixth grader in an elementary school. This would apply as well to a ninth grader in a junior high school compared with a ninth grader in a senior high school.

In one of the few investigations that has compared sixth graders in a middle school with sixth graders in an elementary school, significant differences in the social development of the two groups were found (Shovlin, 1967). Girls in the middle school showed much greater interest in the opposite sex than girls in the elementary school, while there was little difference for sixth-grade boys in the two schooling structures. On the other hand, boys in the elementary school had higher levels of self-esteem than girls did, but the reverse occurred in middle school.

As John Hill (1978) indicates, these findings are probably due to the fact that more sixth-grade girls than boys have entered the pubertal cycle. The physical maturity of the sixth-grade girls fits better with the role expectations of the adolescents in middle school than with those of the boys and girls in grade school. By contrast, the sixth-grade boys are the biggest and strongest in the elementary school but are not as mature as most of the boys and girls in the middle school. Status in school, particularly for boys, is often influenced by physical size and athletic competence—hence the low self-esteem of sixth-grade boys in middle schools.

In another investigation, when a transition to a new school was combined with the onset of puberty, the child's adjustment was difficult (Blyth, Simmons, & Bush, in press). In a longitudinal investigation, the effects of progressing from sixth to seventh grade in a kindergarten through eighth-grade school were compared with the effects of going from sixth grade in an elementary school to seventh grade in a junior high school. When both types of students were evaluated in the seventh grade, the following differences were found: students in the kindergarten through eighth-grade setting had more positive self-concepts, perceived themselves as better integrated into the school and various peer groups, and were involved in more activities and clubs than were the junior high students.

Application 12.2
Sex Roles in the School Hierarchy

The distribution of males and females in the educational system is well known: most teachers are women, most administrators are men. There are more male teachers in secondary schools than in the early grades, but many teach science and math, whereas female teachers more often teach English and foreign languages (Stockard et al., 1980). Issues about gender imbalance in administration or the rights of pregnant teachers filter through the system but are not directly experienced by the children. On the other hand, distinctions in status between male principals and female teachers and the clustering of female and male teachers in certain subjects are part of the immediate school context. They may have a direct impact on children's identification with teaching adults and on what they learn about the distribution of power in the adult world. We do not know of any research that examines children's perceptions of these phenomena.

Because American education has not been uniform, it would be interesting to know if these biases have been as characteristic of alternative settings as traditional schools. Comparative research reported earlier indicates that sex-role behavior is less stereotyped in open settings, but alternative environments have not been systematically examined from this point of view. A close look at teacher interaction with boys and girls and at curriculum materials in nontraditional settings might well uncover some conventional patterns. Detailed analysis of equity and bias in alternative settings offers an interesting arena for investigation.

In considering the research on bias in the schools, it is important to regard the children themselves as part of a self-perpetuating system because they have internalized the same assumptions as those appearing in school material and held by school personnel. Children have clear images of gender-associated occupations, reinforce each other for sex-typed behavior, and may resist possibilities for new directions and nonstereotyped careers (e.g., Weinraub & Brown, in press). Efforts to change materials, opportunities, and relationships in the school setting are essential if equity is desired, but it is simplistic to postulate immediate modifications in children's behavior and development. (Minuchin & Shapiro, 1983, pp. 134–36)

Yet another way to look at how schools are organized is to consider sex roles in the school hierarchy. Think about your school years. Were most of your teachers in elementary school females? Were more of your teachers in high school males? Read application 12.2 to discover the different roles males and females perform in the school hierarchy.

Aptitude × Treatment Interaction

Some children may benefit more from structure than others, and some teachers may be able to handle a flexible curriculum better than others. As a result, a whole field of educational research has sprung up and is referred to as **Aptitude × Treatment Interaction, or (ATI).** The term *aptitude* refers to academic potential and personality dimensions in which students differ; *treatment* refers to the educational technique (e.g., structured class or flexible class) adopted in the classroom. Lee Cronbach and Richard Snow (1977), as well as other education experts, argue that ATI is the best way to study teaching effectiveness.

A child's achievement level (aptitude) may interact directly with classroom structure (treatment) to produce the best learning and the most enjoyable learning environment (Peterson, 1977). That is, students with high-achievement orientation often do well

in a flexible classroom and enjoy it; students with low-achievement orientation do not usually do as well and dislike the flexibility. The reverse is true in a structured classroom. There are many other ATI factors operating in the classroom. Education experts are just beginning to pin some of these down; further clarification of aptitude × treatment interaction should lead to useful information about how children can be taught more effectively.

To fully realize the importance of considering aptitude × treatment interaction, it is necessary only to look at information about teaching strategies. Two ways the teacher's orientation can be classified are as challenging and demanding, or as encouraging good performance. Jere Brophy (1979) reviewed several studies that focused on these types of teacher orientation. Teachers who work with high-socioeconomic status/high-ability students usually are more successful if they move at a quick pace, frequently communicating high expectations and enforcing high standards. These teachers try to keep students challenged, will not accept inferior work, and occasionally criticize the students' work when it does not meet their standards.

Teachers who generally are successful with low-socioeconomic status/low-ability students also are interested in getting the most out of their students, but they usually do so by being warm and encouraging rather than demanding. They are friendly with their students, take more time out from academic subject matter to motivate the children, praise and encourage more often, rarely criticize poor work, and move the curriculum along at a slower pace. When they call on individual students, they allow more time for the student to respond; they may provide hints to help the student get the correct answer (Brophy & Evertson, 1974, 1976). As can be readily seen in this example, successful teaching varies according to the type of student being taught—one teaching strategy is superior with lower-ability students, another with higher-ability students.

Next we see that it often seems as though one of the major functions of schools in this country is to train children to function in and contribute to middle-class society, because politicians who vote on school funding are usually middle class, school-board members are predominantly middle class, and principals and teachers are often middle class. In fact, it has been stated many times that schools function in a middle-class society, and critics believe they have not done a good job in educating lower-class children to overcome the cultural barriers that make it difficult to enhance their social position.

Social Class and Schools

In *Dark Ghetto* Kenneth Clark (1965) described some of the ways lower- and middle-class children are treated differently in school. Teachers in the middle-class school spend more time in teaching their students and evaluate their work more than twice as often as do teachers in the low-income school. And teachers in the low-income school make three times as many negative comments to students as do teachers in the middle-class school; the latter make more positive than negative comments to their students.

Alexander Moore (1967) vividly describes an elementary class comprised of lower-class students in a large urban slum area.

The class is one that the principal himself warned visitors, with a kind of negative pride, to be one of the "wild" classes. He was not at all reluctant that visitors should witness the problems his school faced. The class is in ill repute throughout the school: several teachers commented on it, one calling it a "zoo." There are twenty-four students on the roll, fifteen boys and nine girls. They are all in the reading readiness stage (kindergarten level). On this day there are only eighteen present.

The song is over and the teacher, attempting to drill them on the days of the week, asks them, "What is today? What day will tomorrow be?" As the children call out the names of the various days, she stops to correct them: "Give me your answers in sentences!"

Meanwhile several children are noisily running around the room and hitting one another. Others sit in a stupor, apparently unaware of their surroundings. In the space of the first ten minutes, the teacher has used physical force and actually hurts the children in an attempt to control them. Yet she has not achieved control of the class, nor does she at any time during the morning. She frequently addresses her noisy restless class, saying, "When I have everyone's attention and your hands are folded, then I will listen to what you're really trying to say." Since this never really happens, she never really listens to any of the children during the morning, yet many of them seem to want to say something to her. (p. 26)

School situations like these are described in Charles Silberman's *Crisis in the Classroom* (1970) and John Holt's *How Children Fail* (1964).

Educational Aspirations

Perhaps the most interesting information about children's educational aspirations is the relation between what they would like to do and what they expect to do. For instance, the discrepancy between job aspirations and job expectations is greater for lower-class adolescents than for middle-class adolescents (Gribbons & Lohnes, 1964). The aspirations of lower-class students are as high as those of middle-class students; however, when asked which occupation they actually expected to enter, lower-class adolescents mentioned occupations no more prestigious than those of their parents.

Parents can have a significant impact on their children's aspirations. Lower-class high-school boys whose parents encouraged them to advance their educational and occupational level revealed higher aspirations than did boys whose parents did not (Kandel & Lesser, 1969).

Teachers' Attitudes

Teachers have lower expectations for children from low-income families than for children from middle-income families. A teacher who knows that a child comes from a lower-class background may spend less time trying to help him or her solve a problem and may anticipate that the child will frequently get into trouble. The teacher may also perceive a gap between his or her own middle-class position and the lower-class status of the child's parents; as a result the teacher may believe that the parents are not interested in helping the child and may make fewer efforts to communicate with them.

The environmental experiences of teachers with a middle-class background are quite different from those of children or teachers with a lower-class background.

Historically, schools have catered to the middle-class segments of society at the expense of those students who attend schools in low-income areas.

A teacher from the middle class has probably not gone hungry for weeks at a time or experienced the conditions of an overcrowded apartment, perhaps without electricity or plumbing, where several children may sleep with one or two adults in one small room.

There is evidence from at least one study that teachers with lower-class origins may have different attitudes toward lower-class students than middle-class teachers have (Gottlieb, 1966). Perhaps because they have experienced many inequities themselves, they tend to be empathetic to the problems that lower-class children encounter. In this study, for example, the teachers were asked to indicate the most outstanding characteristics of their lower-class students. The middle-class teachers checked adjectives like "lazy," "rebellious," and "fun-loving"; the lower-class teachers, however, checked such adjectives as "happy," "cooperative," "energetic," and "ambitious." The teachers with lower-class backgrounds perceived the behaviors of the lower-class children as adaptive, whereas the middle-class teachers viewed the same behavior as falling short of middle-class standards.

Not only do students from lower-class backgrounds often experience discrimination in our schools but so do children from many different ethnic backgrounds, as we see next.

Ethnicity and Schools

Black, Mexican-American, Puerto Rican, Native American, Japanese, and Asian Indian children are minorities. Teachers have often been ignorant of different cultural meanings that non-Anglo children have learned in their communities. The problems that boys and girls from non-Anglo backgrounds have had in conventional schools is well-documented (e.g., Casteñada, Ramirez, Cortes, & Barrera, 1971; Minuchin & Shapiro, 1983).

The social and academic development of children from minority groups depends on such factors as teacher expectations; the teacher's preparation for working with children from different backgrounds; the white middle-class nature of the curriculum; the presence of role models in the school for minority students; the quality of relations between school personnel and parents from different ethnic, economic, and educational backgrounds; and the relation between the school and the community (Minuchin & Shapiro, 1983).

By far the largest effort to study the role of ethnicity in schools has focused on desegregation (e.g., Bell, 1980). The focus of desegregation has been on improving the ratio of black to white children and adolescents attending the same school. Efforts to improve

Factors outside of the school influence interracial relationships at school.

this ratio have typically involved busing students, usually the minority individuals, from local neighborhoods to more distant schools. An underlying belief has been that bringing different groups together will reduce stereotyped attitudes and improve intergroup relationships. But busing tells us nothing about what is going on inside of the school. Black children bused to a predominantly white school are usually resegregated in the classroom. Segregation is frequently reinstituted by seating patterns, ability grouping, and tracking systems (e.g., Epstein, 1980).

One attempt to improve intergroup relations among black and white children has been the development of structured cooperative learning situations. In one investigation (Weigel, Wiser, & Cook, 1975), mixed groups of white, black, and Mexican-American students in newly integrated schools were placed in cooperative learning programs. The members of each group divided their labor and helped one another achieve common goals and rewards as they competed against other groups. The results suggested that harmonious relationships within a group developed across racial lines, as evidenced by more cross-racial helping and less interracial conflict.

Of course, there certainly are factors outside of the school that influence interracial relationships. Most research on desegregation treats the school in an environmental vacuum in the sense that community and family influences are rarely studied in combination with what is going on within the school (Minuchin & Shapiro, 1983). One relevant investigation (Stephan & Rosenfield, 1978 a, b) focused on the relation between family influences and the attitudes of children and adolescents in a multiethnic school situation. A questionnaire was given to mothers of fifth- and sixth-grade students, eliciting information about authoritarian attitudes, punitiveness, and attitudes toward integration. Two years later the investigators continued to evaluate a number of students who had been in either segregated schools or triethnic schools. Increased ethnic contact was related to the self-esteem of the adolescents, and both were found to be negatively related to parental punitiveness and authoritarian parenting. Such investigations that attempt to link school and family settings over time are far too rare in our attempts to understand children's development.

As Patricia Minuchin and Edna Shapiro (1983) conclude, there has been an assumption in desegregating schools that it will be unmitigatingly good. But contact between different ethnic groups can produce hostility and intensify stereotypes unless such contact is long term, institutionally sanctioned, and organized between groups of equal status striving for shared goals. Such conditions are very difficult to meet. For many minority students, the school may be the first social institution in which they experience the values of a dominant white society. It has been found that black students in desegregated schools frequently experience racial prejudice, conflicting values, and difficult academic competition (Rosenberg & Simmons, 1971).

Although our culture has been more cordial toward minority groups than many cultures have, as we have seen, there still is a tremendous amount of progress to be made. We have seen that schools may be the part of our culture that represents a particularly important opportunity to improve the development of children from minority-group backgrounds. Through school personnel who support the advancement of minority students, curricula that acknowledges pluralism, and the participation of students in cooperative learning situations, greater success and happiness for minority group children can be achieved.

In the next chapter, we look at personality development during middle and late childhood, focusing on the self, sex-role development, and moral development.

Summary

In middle and late childhood, the child's family continues to be an important socializing influence. To help children develop social competence parents need to adjust to the developmental changes that distinguish early childhood from middle and late childhood. Among the changes that parents need to adapt to are the child's increasing cognitive capabilities, heightened interest in peers, and schooling. In this chapter we continued our discussion of the changing family structure, which focused on custody decisions and stepparent families. While there is some evidence that boys seem to be better adjusted in father-custody families and girls better adjusted in mother-custody families, many factors mediate the effects of family structure and divorce on children—among those discussed are parenting behavior, marital conflict, and the availability of support systems.

The majority of children grow up in a family in which one or more siblings are present. Sibling relations often are characterized by competitiveness and the concern to be treated fairly by parents. In some instances, though, older siblings may be as effective, or more effective, than their parents in socializing their younger brothers and sisters. Competitiveness among siblings seems to be greatest when they are close in age.

With school entrance, children increase their contacts with other children and begin to recognize that other individuals have ideas and points of view that are different from their own. The child's development in middle and late childhood is extensively influenced by peers, or age-mates. The peer group provides a unique opportunity for practicing roles and finding out information about the world outside of the family. The socialization processes of reinforcement and modeling are important in peer relations as well as parent-child relations. In some instances these processes, as well as others, have been combined to develop programs in peer sociotherapy. Another aspect of social relations in the peer group that is important to the child is popularity. Children participate in groups as well as peer relations. There are more formal groups in adolescence than in childhood, and there is a greater mixture of males and females in adolescent than in childhood groups. Status positions and norms develop in virtually all groups, but the nature of children's peer groups may vary according to social class.

Among the socializing institutions that directly or indirectly influence development are the schools. During middle and late childhood, education is usually provided by the public school system. The organization of schools may influence the child's social development and may affect boys and girls differently. Advocates of alternative educational movements share some of the concerns of progressive and humanistic education; one of the primary functions of school, they assert, should be to teach children skills for adjustment to life, not merely mastery of basic academic subjects. And it is important to consider sex roles in the school hierarchy.

Schools represent a very important social setting for children from lower-class and ethnic group backgrounds. Although schools can be an important avenue for such children to advance their cognitive and social development, the schools have not been very responsive to the needs of these children. Schools are basically white middle-class institutions. Desegregation of schools represents the most pervasive effort to improve the cognitive and social skills of black children. However, desegregation per se has not been very successful. Nonetheless, several admiral desegregation programs that focus on important aspects of the school and community setting do seem beneficial for minority-group children.

Key Terms

Aptitude × Treatment
   Interaction (ATI)
coaching
conglomerate strategy

peer sociotherapy
progressive education
traditional education

Review Questions

1. Describe how parents should adapt to the developing child as he or she grows from early childhood into middle and late childhood.
2. What do we know about the effects of father custody on the child's social development? How is the child influenced by growing up in a stepparent family?
3. Discuss some of the positive and negative ways siblings can socialize each other.
4. Describe the development of peer relations during middle and late childhood.
5. What are some of the functions of the peer group in the socialization of the child?
6. How are children's groups in middle and late childhood different from adolescent groups?
7. How are children's schools organized, and what effects can organization have on their development?
8. What is meant by aptitude treatment interaction? How can ATI be applied to teaching children?

Further Readings

Brophy, J., and Good, T. *Teacher-student relationship: Causes and consequences.* New York: Holt, Rinehart & Winston, 1974.
An excellent book for understanding the social interaction of teachers with children. Includes many examples of teacher-student interaction and teaching strategies that can be used to modify student behavior. Level of reading is similar to that of this text.

Hartup, W. W. The peer system. In P. H. Mussen (ed.-in-chief) and E. M. Hetherington (ed.), *Carmichael's manual of child psychology,* 4th ed. (vol. 4). New York: Wiley, 1982.
Willard Hartup, a respected authority on peer relations, provides an up-to-date description of research and ideas about peer relations. Reading level is medium to difficult.

Harvard education review.
Go to the library and leaf through the issues of the last three to four years. You'll find a number of articles that address the issues raised in this chapter about schools. Moderately difficult reading.

Lewis, M., & Rosenblum, L. A. (eds.). *Friendship and peer relations,* vol. 4. New York: Wiley, 1975.
Articles by experts on peer relations representing diverse ideas and including recent theoretical perspectives. Moderately difficult reading.

Roman, M., & Haddad, W. *The disposable parent.* New York: Holt, Rinehart & Winston, 1978.
This book, by a prominent clinical psychologist, explores the case for joint custody. The stress of divorce and custody decisions on children is described. Easy to read.

Sutton-Smith, B., & Rosenberg, B. G. *The sibling.* New York: Holt, Rinehart & Winston, 1970.
Complete survey of theory and research pertaining to the sibling's role in the child's development. Extensive coverage of the impact of sibling order and age spacing. Easy to medium reading level.

13 Emotional and Personality Development

Imagine . . . that you are faced with the task of developing a moral education curriculum

What would you put in the curriculum? What would you have students do? What would you have them think about? Should schools even be in the business of moral education?

The most widely discussed contemporary view of moral development has been developed by Lawrence Kohlberg (1976). Cornel Hamm (1977) believes that Kohlberg (1976) is incorrect in claiming that his theory is devoid of virtues. Hamm argues that Kohlberg's view emphasizes that moral education ought to include emphasis on virtues such as honesty, loyalty, courage, and fair play.

Hamm goes on to say that parents, teachers, and peers "teach" moral values by establishing rules and regulations and by rewarding and punishing behavior. Parents and teachers have not always effectively taught moral values to their children, but Hamm believes they are capable of doing so. There are some socialization techniques that are better than others for developing moral values in children. Sensible youth who have a feeling for fairness and respect for others usually come from social environments in which adult social agents show a warm acceptance towards them, combined with a firm and consistent enforcement of rules.

Hamm also believes that children need to be reminded consistently of why actions *a* and *b* and *c* are required, and why *x* and *y* and *z* are prohibited. This allows the child to call these rules and reasons to mind when moral decisions have to be made.

Furthermore, through social experiences with parents, teachers, peers, and other social agents, Hamm believes, moral virtues can be learned. But exactly what virtues should be taught? At a general level most people agree that we should teach children to be honest, fair, and impartial; to consider other people's rights and avoid interfering with their freedom; to refrain from killing or injuring others; to keep promises and abide by contracts; and to make no discriminations against others on the basis of irrelevant differences such as color, sex, or ethnic origin.

Some of Hamm's critics think that these moral virtues are too heavily laden with middle-class values, but Hamm (1977) insists that most people would agree that they are universal values rather than old-fashioned, middle-class standards.

Other educational theorists believe that, while it is difficult to specify the appropriate moral virtues to instill in children, it is possible to identify generally accepted moral virtues and to inform students about them (Hamm, 1977).

Yet other theorists believe that there are no universally agreed upon moral virtues and therefore that subjective "virtues" should not be taught to children. Led by Lawrence Kohlberg, this group of educational theorists stresses that it is the moral reasoning skills of children—not an adherence to any particular value system—that should be developed. In Kohlberg's view absolute rights and wrongs do not exist; what is important is to create settings that allow children to think about alternative, logical solutions to moral dilemmas. Many of the environmental experiences that Kohlberg feels are best suited to stimulate advanced moral thinking focus on democratic peer rule and discussion.

Not everyone agrees that Kohlberg's approach to moral development is the best one, but there has been an absence of alternative approaches to moral education (Aron, 1977). As we will see later in this chapter, even Kohlberg has changed his thinking about moral education.

In most schools morality is approached either through a dogmatic statement of authority or by a complete avoidance of moral issues. Next to Kohlberg's theory, the two most widely practiced systematic programs of moral education are behavior modification and values clarification. Recall that behavior modification involves rewarding positive behavior and taking varied approaches toward negative behavior. **Values clarification** emphasizes that students need to have the opportunity to air their value judgments in group discussion. By being exposed to the value judgments of others, children may see the relative nature of values.

Introduction

In keeping with the theme that schools represent a very important socializing influence in middle and late childhood, the Imagine section describes some of the issues involved in moral education. In this chapter we will evaluate the child's attributions about self and others and the development of sex differences and sex-role stereotypes; discuss Piaget's view of moral reasoning, Lawrence Kohlberg's cognitive structural theory, the social learning perspective of moral development, moral feelings and guilt, and altruism; and outline some of the most common problems and disturbances in middle and late childhood. First, we begin with some introductory comments about how the self changes in middle and late childhood.

The Self

An important part of the development of a self-concept is the child's increasing ability to understand how he or she is viewed by others. Very young children have difficulty in understanding others' perspective of them, and they often are not aware of the impressions their behavior makes on others. But gradually children begin to understand that their behavior will trigger reactions from others, and they begin to monitor their actions, acting differently depending on whom they are with and which aspect of their social self they want to be seen. This represents a time at which children are more cautious about revealing themselves to others.

Developmental changes in self-concept seem to occur as children go through early childhood, middle and late childhood, and adolescence. First, children develop a differentiated view of themselves as they grow older. As young children they may simply have perceived themselves as "good" or "bad." By late childhood and adolescence, they are likely to perceive themselves in more detailed ways, such as "I am a good person most of the time, except when my older sister bugs me, or when my father won't let me have the car, or when I have to study for an exam."

Second, older children develop a more individuated view of themselves than they had as young children. This indicates that older children have a more distinct view of themselves as unique persons and more readily differentiate themselves from others than do young children. As young children, they may have labeled themselves in terms of how they were similar to their peers, but as they approach adolescence they tend to describe themselves more in terms of how they are different from their peers.

Third, the older child's self-concept is likely to be more stable than the young child's. But in an extreme form, stability can lead to rigidity and unrealistic self-appraisals. Even though we say that the self-concept of the child becomes more stable, this does not imply that self-concept does not change. It clearly does change, but as children and adolescents mature cognitively, they become more capable of integrating incoming information into a stable sense of who they are and where they are going.

Another recent developmental approach to self-concept formation has been based on cognitive-developmental theory. Piaget's theory of cognitive development stresses that the adolescent's cognitions are more abstract and less concrete than the child's. To test this idea about the development of self-concepts, Raymond Montemayor and Marvin Eisen (1977) studied 136 males and 126 females in grades four, six, eight, ten, and twelve. The students were given the Twenty Statements Test (Bugental & Zelen, 1950) in which twenty spaces are available to write responses to the question, "Who am I?" The responses were coded according to thirty different categories, such as sex, age, religion, occupational role, social status, intellectual interests, career, physical self and body image, sense of unity, and situational references.

The results suggested that children do evaluate themselves in more concrete and less abstract ways than adolescents do. The children were more likely to describe themselves in terms of their address, physical appearance, possessions, and play activities. By contrast, adolescents relied more on personal beliefs, motivations, and interpersonal characteristics to describe what they were like. Montemayor and Eisen (1977) provided the following quotations from a nine-year-old, an eleven-and-one-half-year-old, and a seventeen-year-old that reflect developmental changes in self-conception:

Nine-year-old boy: (concrete descriptions) My name is Bruce C. I have brown eyes. I have brown hair. I have brown eyebrows. I'm nine years old. I love! sports. I have seven people in my family. I have great! eye site. I have lots! of friends. I live on 1923 Pinecrest Drive. I'm going on ten in September. I'm a boy. I have an uncle that is almost seven feet tall. My school is Pinecrest. My teacher is Mrs. V. I play hockey! I'm almost the smartest boy in the class. I love food! I love fresh air. I love school.

Eleven-and-one-half-year-old girl: (increase in interpersonal descriptions) My name is A. I'm a human being. I'm a girl. I'm a truthful person. I'm not pretty. I do so-so in my studies. I'm a very good cellist. I'm a very good pianist. I'm a little bit tall for my age. I like several boys. I like several girls. I'm old fashioned. I play tennis. I am a very good musician. I try to be helpful. I'm always ready to be friends with anybody. Mostly I'm good, but I lose my temper. I'm not well liked by some girls and boys. I don't know if boys like me or not.

Seventeen-year-old girl: (increase in interpersonal descriptions, characteristic mood states, and ideological and belief statements) I am a human being. I am a girl. I am an individual. I don't know who I am. I am Pisces. I am a moody person. I am an indecisive person. I am an ambitious person.

I am a big curious person. I am not an individual. I am lonely. I am an American (God help me). I am a Democrat. I am a liberal person. I am a radical. I am conservative. I am a pseudoliberal. I am an atheist. I am not a classifiable person (i.e., I don't want to be). (pp. 317–18)

Recently there has been considerable interest in a view of the self referred to as *attribution theory*. Next we see how this perspective can be used to explain children's perceptions of their self and of others.

Children's Attributions about Their Self and Others

Some developmental psychologists explain social phenomena in childhood by referring to the attributions children make about others. In the simplest sense **attribution theory** encompasses how the child makes intellectual sense of the actions of others as well as of his or her own actions.

In their everyday perceptions children try to simplify their understanding of people by pinpointing singular causes for behavior. A boy complains because a sport is too difficult for him, the athlete competes because he is motivated to achieve, the girl fails a math test because she was unlucky that day, the singer excels because she has extraordinary musical talent, and so on. Fritz Heider believes that these are naive analyses of action. Such analyses take one of two forms: the child attributes the action either to some personal force within the person or to some environmental force that impinges on the person from without. Within each category, two further subdivisions can be made. The child may presume that a personal force is a relatively permanent, long-lasting phenomenon; that is, he or she may believe some ability or predilection exists (for example, the singer's talent). Or, the child may view the personal force as a temporary state that fluctuates widely (for example, the athlete's motivation). Similarly, the child may perceive an environmental force as stable (such as the sport that is too difficult for a certain child) or unstable (such as the "bad luck" that caused a student to fail a test).

Personality descriptions children make in regard to themselves and others also follow patterns similar to those of their attributions. Of course, generalized personality descriptions can be very helpful when the child needs to describe broad, dominant personality characteristics of different persons. Such generalizations help children to organize and to make sense of human behavior. But such attributions do not tell us very much about variability in behavior and the specific conditions under which this variability occurs. It is in this sense, just as Heider argued, that children's attributions are often naive or simplistic. Not only may these attributions be ineffective predictors of behavior, but they may actually be misleading at times.

Children who view themselves in positive ways could be expected to make attributions that are different from those of children who perceive themselves in negative ways. That is, differences in children's self-concepts should be reflected in the way they categorize incoming information and interpret their own or others' behavior. To investigate this idea, Carol Ames and Donald Felker (in press) studied 150 boys and girls by first rating them on the Piers-Harris self-concept scale. Those who either scored quite high or quite low were then given an achievement task on which they either succeeded or failed. Each child was asked to interpret his or her performance on the task, attributing success or failure to either skill or to luck (or the lack of them). Success was more often attributed to skill by the high self-concept boys and girls. Thus, the self-perceptions of children influence the way they interpret behavior.

One aspect of the child's self-evaluation that is closely linked with self-concept is self-esteem, which is discussed next.

Self-Esteem

Many theorists and researchers use the labels self-concept and self-esteem interchangeably. For example, one definition of self-esteem is the value children place on themselves and their behavior, which would be evaluated by finding out whether the children feel good or bad about themselves (McCandless & Evans, 1973). Other definitions of self-esteem embrace only the positive parts of self-concept, such as feeling proud of oneself or evaluating one's attributes highly (Wylie, 1974).

There is a positive relation between children's self-esteem and their school performance.

Stanley Coopersmith (1967) has developed a personality scale that attempts to measure boys' and girls' self-esteem. Like other measures of self-concept, Coopersmith's inventory (called the Self-Esteem Inventory, or SEI) asks the child to read a number of statements and check whether each of these is "like me" or "unlike me." The statements include the extent to which the youth worry about themselves, the degree to which they are proud of their school performances, how popular they are with peers, how happy they are, and so on.

In one investigation, the Self-Esteem Inventory was administered to a large group of elementary school boys. In addition, the boys, their mothers, and the boys' teachers at school were interviewed about various matters relating to the social experiences and self-perceptions of the boys. The following parental attributes were linked with the development of high self-esteem in the boys:

1. Expression of affection
2. Concern about the youth's problems
3. Harmony in the home
4. Participation in friendly joint activities
5. Availability to give competent, organized help to the boys when they need it
6. Setting clear and fair rules
7. Abiding by these rules
8. Allowing the youth freedom within well-prescribed limits

Self-Esteem and School Performance

Many studies indicate a positive correlation between the child's self-concept and different measures of achievement and school performance (e.g., Taylor, Winne, & Marx, 1975). These studies seem to show that a student with a good self-concept excels in school. But what is the nature of this relationship? Does the child do well in school because of a positive self-concept? Or is a positive self-concept the result of doing well in school? There is evidence that the latter is closer to the truth. A teacher or counselor will apparently be more successful in changing a student's behavior (elevating achievement level), and thereby improving the student's self-image, than in changing the self-image and, as a result, improving achievement (Bandura, 1969).

It may even be hazardous to use techniques that give a child a falsely inflated view of his or her ability. Suppose, for example, that a child does not read well, and the teacher decides that the child's major problem is a negative self-concept. The teacher attempts to foster a positive self-image and some confidence in the child. After some progress, the teacher asks the child to read in front of the class. With newfound confidence the child begins to read, but as he or she stumbles and mumbles through several sentences, and the other students begin to laugh, he or she is emotionally shattered. In this case it was not enough for the teacher to instill self-confidence in the child; working on the child's reading skills also was necessary.

Measuring Self-Concept and Self-Esteem

Although it is generally accepted that each child has a self-esteem and that self-evaluation is an important aspect of personality, psychologists, counselors, and educators have had a difficult time trying to measure self-esteem. One method that has been used frequently is the Piers-Harris Scale (Piers & Harris, 1964), which consists of eighty items designed to measure the child's overall self-esteem. School psychologists often use the scale with boys and girls who have been referred to them for evaluation. By responding yes or no to such items as "I have good ideas," children reveal how they view themselves. The Piers-Harris Scale requires about fifteen to twenty minutes for completion and can be administered to groups as well as to individuals.

Children's self-perception often changes according to the situation, although self-concept measures like the Piers-Harris Scale are designed to measure a stable, consistent aspect of personality. Also, with self-reporting, it is difficult to determine whether children are telling about the way they really are or the way they want someone else to think they are. Even though the instructions on the Piers-Harris Scale and other measures of self-concept direct youth to respond as they really are, there is no assurance that they will do so (Wylie, 1974).

A promising measure of self-concept has been developed by Susan Harter (1982). Her scale is called the Perceived Competence Scale for Children. Emphasis is placed on assessing the child's sense of competence across different domains rather than viewing perceived competence as a unitary concept. Three types of skills are assessed on separate subscales: cognitive (good at schoolwork; remember things easily); social (have a lot of friends; most kids like me); and physical (do well at sports; first chosen for games). A fourth subscale measures general self-worth (sure of myself; happy the way I am) independent of any particular skill domain. The importance of Harter's measure is that prior measures of self-concept, such as the Piers-Harris, lump together the child's perceptions of his or her competencies in a variety of domains in an effort to come up with an overall measure of the child's self-concept. Harter's scale does an excellent job of separating the child's self-perceptions of his or her abilities in different skill areas; and when general self-worth is assessed, questions that focus on overall perceptions of the self are used rather than questions that are directed at specific skill domains.

To conclude our discussion of the self in the middle and late childhood years, we present an overview of the developmental changes that occur in the self-system. In our discussion of the self we have seen that children's self-descriptions change from concrete, observable components, such as physical attributes and behaviors, to personality traits as they grow into middle and late childhood. And in adolescence there is a further shift toward self-descriptions that are more abstract, such as thoughts, attitudes, and emotions.

In chapter 15 we will continue our discussion of the development of the self—we will discover that the governing theme of self-evaluation in adolescence is identity. Next we look at one aspect of the self that takes on increasing importance in middle and late childhood, sex-role development.

Sex-Role Development

In the middle childhood years, two divergent trends in sex typing occur. Children increase their understanding of culturally defined expectations for males and females, and simultaneously the behavior and attitude of boys increasingly reflect masculine sex typing. However, during the middle years of childhood girls do not show an increased interest in feminine activities. Actually, many girls begin to show a stronger preference for masculine interests and activities, a finding that has appeared in research studies conducted from the 1920s to the present. But, on the other hand, boys and girls begin to show more flexibility in their understanding of sex-role stereotypes; they see that stereotypes are not absolute and that alternatives are feasible (Huston, 1983).

Sex-role stereotypes are rampant in our culture, not just on television but in the beliefs held by parents, teachers, and peers. In the United States, as in most industrialized countries in the world, stereotyped sex roles are gradually being eliminated and women are engaging in activities previously viewed as available only to men. As a result, research data about sex differences in children is often dated. This further substantiates the role of cultural values and societal standards in determining sex-role behavior.

Sex Differences and Stereotypes

Walter Mischel (1970) defines sex-role stereotypes as broad categories that reflect our impressions about people, events, and ourselves. The world is extremely complex; every day we are confronted with thousands of different stimuli. The use of stereotypes is one way we simplify this complexity. If we simply assign a label (e.g., the quality of "softness" in women) to someone, we then have much less to consider when we think about the person. However, once these labels have been assigned, we find it remarkably difficult to abandon them, even in the face of contradictory evidence. Do you think you have a repertory of sex-role stereotypes? Table 13.1 provides a brief exercise in understanding sex-role behavior.

Table 13.1
Knowing the Sexes

How well do you know the sexes? For each of the adjectives listed below, indicate whether you think it *best* describes women or men—or neither—in our society. Be honest with yourself, and follow your first impulse in responding.

a. verbal
b. sensitive
c. active
d. competitive
e. compliant
f. dominant
g. mathematical
h. suggestible
i. analytic
j. social
k. aggressive

After recording your answers, continue reading this chapter for an interpretation of your responses.

Boys are increasingly engaging in what once were thought to be traditional "feminine" activities.

How Stereotypes Operate

Many stereotypes are extremely ambiguous. The stereotypes "masculine" and "feminine," for example, call up very diverse behaviors to support the stereotype. The stereotype, of course, may also be modified in the face of cultural change; whereas at one time muscular development might be thought masculine, at another time masculinity may be typified by a lithe, slender physique. Furthermore, the behaviors popularly agreed upon as reflecting the stereotype may fluctuate according to subculture.

Mischel (1970) comments that even though the behaviors that are supposed to fit the stereotype often do not, the label itself may have significant consequences for the individual. Labeling a person "homosexual," "queer," or "sissy" can produce dire social consequences in terms of status and acceptance in groups, even when the person is none of these. Regardless of their accuracy, stereotypes can cause tremendous emotional upheaval in an individual.

Sex Differences

How well did you do with the adjectives in table 13.1? According to Eleanor Maccoby and Carol Nagy Jacklin (1974), females are more verbal, males are more mathematical and aggressive, and all the other adjectives are really characteristic of neither.

With regard to verbal ability, girls tend to understand and produce language more competently than boys. Girls are superior to boys in higher-order verbal tasks, such as making analogies, understanding difficult written material, and writing creatively, as well as in lower-order verbal tasks, such as spelling. Maccoby

and Jacklin speculated that girls probably get an early start in the use of language, but studies indicate that differences in the verbal abilities of boys and girls are not consistent until about the age of eleven.

A similar developmental trend can be seen for mathematical skills, but this time in favor of boys. Boys' superiority in math skills does not usually appear until the age of twelve or thirteen and does not seem to be entirely influenced by the fact that boys take more math courses. Likewise, male superiority on visual-spatial tasks does not consistently appear until adolescence. However, sex differences in aggression appear early, by the age of two or three, and continue through adolescence. The differences are not confined to physical aggression—boys also show more verbal aggression as well as more fantasy aggression (imagining harm to someone or to some object rather than actually performing an aggressive act).

Not everyone agrees with all of the conclusions of Maccoby's and Jacklin's widely quoted work on sex differences. Jeanne Block (1976) acknowledges that Maccoby and Jacklin have made an important contribution to information about sex roles, but she also believes that some of their conclusions, and some of the data on which the conclusions are based, are shakier than Maccoby and Jacklin lead readers to believe. Block argues that Maccoby and Jacklin did not differentiate between those studies that were methodologically sound and those that were not. She further criticizes the decisions they made about what kinds of studies should go into a particular category. For example, Maccoby and Jacklin lumped together many measures of parental pressure on achievement motivation including the following: amount of praise or criticism for intellectual performance; parental standards for intellectual performance as expressed on a questionnaire item; expectations of household help from the youth; the ages at which parents feel it is appropriate to teach a boy or girl more mature behaviors; the number of anxious intrusions in the youth's task performance; and pressure for success on memory tasks. While many of the measures are clearly linked with the achievement dimension, others may be more peripheral.

Next we look at a controversial aspect of sex differences in contemporary society—sex differences in achievement.

Achievement

Few topics have generated more controversy in the last decade than the belief that many women have been socialized to assume roles of incompetency rather than competency. Diana Baumrind (1972) has distinguished between **instrumental competence** and incompetence. Boys, she says, are trained to become instrumentally competent, while girls learn how to become instrumentally incompetent. By instrumental competence, Baumrind means behavior that is socially responsible and purposeful. Instrumental incompetence is generally aimless behavior.

The following evidence is offered by Baumrind in support of her argument: (1) few women obtain jobs in science, and of those who do, few achieve high positions; (2) being a female is devalued by society; (3) being independent and achieving intellectual status causes the female to lose her "femininity" in society's eyes—both men and women devalue such behaviors in women; (4) parents usually have lower achievement aspirations for girls than boys (for example, parents expect their sons to become doctors and their daughters to become nurses); and (5) girls and women are more oriented toward expressive behavior than boys and men are.

Aletha Huston-Stein and Ann Higgens-Trenk (1978) have discussed the developmental precursors of sex differences in achievement orientation. Women who as adults are career and achievement oriented usually show the signs of this orientation early in their childhood years. Adult women who are attracted to traditionally feminine activities were likely attracted to such activities during middle childhood and adolescence (Kagan & Moss, 1962).

Achievement behavior was more consistent over the childhood, adolescent, and young adult years than any other personality attribute studied in these longitudinal investigations. Interest in "masculine" play activities in childhood and in "masculine" subject matter is linked with achievement orientation in females during adolescence and young adulthood. In sum, childhood

"Don't be too rough with Dolly! Remember—she's just a little GIRL!"

The Family Circus. Reprinted courtesy the Register and Tribune Syndicate, Inc.

socialization experiences seem to be critical in influencing the achievement orientation of females during adolescence and even into young adulthood.

A great deal of attention has been focused on expectancy for success, which seems to cross many areas of achievement. In general, girls tend to have lower expectancies for success, lower levels of aspiration, more anxiety about failing, a stronger tendency to avoid risking failure, and to be more likely to accept failure than boys (Parsons, Ruble, Hodges, & Small, 1976). And girls are more likely to attribute failure to their own inability and success to external causes, while boys are more likely to assign success to ability and failure to external causes.

Findings such as these have led researchers such as Carol Dweck (1983) to introduce the concept of **learned helplessness** as one explanation of the comparatively low achievement orientation of females. Basically, learned helplessness develops when the child believes that the rewards he or she receives are beyond personal control.

Two major systems of learned helplessness are a lack of motivation and negative affect. If the child in a failure situation sees her behavior as irrelevant to the outcome, she is displaying learned helplessness. Such perceptions lead to attributions that are seen as uncontrollable or unchangeable, such as lack of ability, difficulty of the task, or presumably fixed attitudes of other people. In addition, attributions of failure to these factors are often linked with deterioration of performance

Girls may develop a sense of learned helplessness in achievement settings.

in the face of failure. Individuals who attribute their failure to controllable or changeable factors, such as effort or luck, are more likely to show improvement in their performance (Dweck, 1975). Girls are more likely to attribute failure to uncontrollable factors, like lack of ability, than boys are, to display disrupted performance or decreased effort under the pressure of impending failure or evaluation, and to avoid situations in which failure is likely (Dweck, 1983).

When the total picture is considered, it does seem that girls have been socialized into roles of instrumental incompetence. There is reason to believe that differences in the achievement orientations of boys and girls are learned—not innately determined by sex.

Aletha Stein and Margaret Bailey (1973) have listed several parental characteristics or attributes that are associated with the development of achievement orientation in girls. For example, achievement orientation can be encouraged through the modeling of a mother who has a career. In some instances, particularly when the mother assumes a traditional female role, the social interaction of the father takes on greater importance. Stein and Bailey also point out that socialization practices fostering so-called femininity in girls often run counter to those practices producing achievement orientation. Moderate parental permissiveness,

coupled with attempts to accelerate achievement, is related to achievement orientation in girls. This kind of parenting is not compatible with what is usually prescribed for rearing a young woman.

There is evidence that achievement settings entail many moral decisions. For example, in one investigation individuals were asked: "What might cause you to feel guilty?" A frequent response was "a failure to expend sufficient effort to accomplish one's aim" (Leedham, Signori, & Sampson, 1967, p. 918). And individuals seem inclined to be punitive toward others who are able but fail because of a lack of effort (Weiner & Kukla, 1970). Children, then, often feel guilty and are judged harshly for failing to use their capabilities.

The crime and violence that seem increasingly to characterize our society call attention to moral development, which involves an understanding of how children come to handle the inevitable conflict between personal needs and social obligations (Hoffman, 1979). Next we look in greater detail at the moral development of children.

Moral Development

In one sense moral development has a longer history than virtually any aspect of development we will discuss in this text. As you may recall reading in chapter 1, in prescientific periods philosophers and theologians heatedly debated the child's moral status at birth, which they felt had important implications for how the child was to be reared. Today people are hardly neutral about moral development; most have very strong opinions about acceptable and unacceptable behavior, ethical and unethical conduct, and the ways that acceptable and ethical behaviors are to be fostered in children.

Moral development concerns rules and conventions about what people should do in their interactions with other people. In studying these rules, psychologists examine three different domains of moral development. First, how do children reason or think about rules for ethical conduct? For example, cheating is generally considered unacceptable. The child can be presented with a story in which someone has a conflict about whether or not to cheat in a specific situation. The child is asked to decide what is appropriate for the character to do and why. The focus is thereby placed on the rationale, the type of reasoning the child uses to justify his or her moral decision.

A second domain concerns how children actually behave in the face of rules for ethical conduct. Here, for example, the concern is whether the child actually cheats in different situations and what factors influence this behavior.

A third domain concerns how the child feels after making a moral decision. There has been more interest in a child's feelings after doing something wrong than after doing something right. Here the concern is whether a child feels guilty as the result of having cheated. In the remainder of this section, attention will be directed at these three facets of moral development—thought, action, and feeling.

Moral Reasoning: Piaget's View

Jean Piaget is best known for his general theory of cognitive development. His greatest contribution to understanding socialization has been his thoughts and observations about moral development. Piaget conducted extensive observations and interviews with children from four to twelve years of age. He watched them in natural play with marbles, trying to understand the manner in which they used and thought about the rules of the game. Later he asked them several questions about ethical concepts (e.g., theft, lies, punishment, justice) in order to arrive at a similar understanding of how children think about ethical rules.

Piaget concluded that there are two different modes (or stages) of moral thought. The more primitive one, **moral realism** is associated with younger children (from four to seven years old); the more advanced one, **moral autonomy,** is associated with older children (ten years old and older). Children from seven to ten years old are in a transition period between the two stages, evidencing some features of each.

What are some of the characteristics of these two stages? The *moral realist* judges the rightness or goodness of behavior by considering the consequences of the behavior, not the intentions of the actor. For example, a realist would say that breaking twelve cups accidentally is worse than breaking one cup intentionally while trying to steal a cookie. For the *moral autonomist,* the reverse is true; the intention of the actor becomes more important.

The *moral realist* believes that all rules are unchangeable and are handed down by all-powerful authorities. When Piaget suggested that new rules be introduced into the game of marbles, the young children became troubled; they insisted that the rules had always existed as they were and could not be changed. The *moral autonomist,* by contrast, accepts change and recognizes that rules are merely convenient, socially agreed-upon conventions, subject to change by consensus.

A third characteristic is the *moral realist's* belief in imminent justice—if a rule is broken, punishment will be meted out immediately. The realist believes that the violation is connected in some mechanical or reflexlike way to the punishment. Thus, young children often look around worriedly after committing a transgression, expecting inevitable punishment. The *moral autonomist* recognizes that punishment is a socially mediated event that occurs only if a relevant person witnesses the wrongdoing and even then punishment is not inevitable.

Kohlberg

Lawrence Kohlberg elaborated upon Piaget's two stages and characterized moral thought as developing in six distinct stages. The stages are associated with changes in thought structures that begin around the age of six and may continue well into adulthood (the late twenties). Not everyone reaches Kohlberg's final stage of moral thought.

Kohlberg (1976) arrived at this view after some twenty years of interviewing children, adolescents, and adults, using a unique procedure. In the interview the individual is first presented with a series of stories in which characters face moral dilemmas. The following is one of the more popular Kohlberg dilemmas:

In Europe a woman was near death from a special kind of cancer. There was one drug that the doctors thought might save her. It was a form of radium that a druggist in the same town had recently discovered. The drug was expensive to make, but the druggist was charging ten times what the drug cost him to make. He paid $200 for the radium and charged $2,000 for a small dose of the drug. The sick woman's husband, Heinz, went to everyone he knew to borrow the money, but he could only get together $1,000 which is half of what it cost. He told the druggist that his wife was dying and asked him to sell it cheaper or let him pay later. But the druggist said, "No, I discovered the drug, and I am going to make money from it." So Heinz got desperate and broke into the man's store to steal the drug for his wife. (p. 379)

The interviewee is then asked a series of questions about each dilemma. For the Heinz dilemma, for example, Kohlberg asks such questions as these: Should Heinz have done that? Was it actually wrong or right? Why? Is it a husband's duty to steal the drug for his wife if he can get it no other way? Would a good husband do it? Did the druggist have the right to charge that much when there was no law actually setting a limit to the price? Why?

Based upon the types of reasons given to this and to other moral problems, Kohlberg arrived at the six stages of moral development described in table 13.2.

Kohlberg (1976) believes that most children under age nine are at the **preconventional level of moral development** (stages 1 and 2). Interestingly, some adolescents, particularly those who are delinquent, also score at this level. It is not until the adolescent years that most individuals think at the **conventional level** (stages 3 and 4) when they are faced with moral dilemmas.

Table 13.2
Kohlberg's Six Moral Stages

Level and Stage	What Is Right	Reasons for Doing Right	Social Perspective of Stage
Level I: *Preconventional* Stage 1: Heteronomous morality	To avoid breaking rules backed by punishment, obedience for its own sake, and avoiding physical damage to persons and property.	Avoidance of punishment, and the superior power of authorities.	Egocentric point of view. Doesn't consider the interests of others or recognize that they differ from the actor's; doesn't relate two points of view. Actions are considered physically rather than in terms of psychological interests of others. Confusion of authority's perspective with one's own.
Stage 2: Individualism, instrumental purpose, and exchange	Following rules only when it is to someone's immediate interest; acting to meet one's own interests and needs and letting others do the same. Right is also what's fair, what's an equal exchange, a deal, an agreement.	To serve one's own needs or interests in a world where you have to recognize that other people have their interests, too.	Concrete individualistic perspective. Aware that everybody has his or her own interest to pursue and that these interests conflict, so that right is relative (in the concrete individualistic sense).
Level II: Conventional Stage 3: Mutual interpersonal expectations, relationships and interpersonal conformity	Living up to what is expected by people close to you or what people generally expect of your role as son, brother, friend, etc. "Being good" is important and means having good motives, showing concern about others. It also means keeping mutual relationships, such as trust, loyalty, respect, and gratitude.	The need to be a good person in your own eyes and those of others. Your caring for others. Belief in the Golden Rule. Desire to maintain rules and authority which support stereotypical good behavior.	Perspective of the individual in relationships with other individuals. Aware of shared feelings, agreements, and expectations, which take primacy over individual interests. Relates points of view through the concrete Golden Rule, putting oneself in the other guy's shoes. Does not yet consider generalized system perspective.
Stage 4: Social system and conscience	Fulfilling the actual duties to which you have agreed. Laws are to be upheld except in extreme cases where they conflict with other fixed social duties. Right is also contributing to society, the group, or institution.	To keep the institution going as a whole, to avoid the breakdown in the system "if everyone did it," or the imperative of conscience to meet one's defined obligations (easily confused with stage 3 belief in rules and authority).	Differentiates societal points of view from interpersonal agreement or motives. Takes the point of view of the system that defines roles and rules. Considers individual relations in terms of place in the system.

Level and Stage	What Is Right	Reasons for Doing Right	Social Perspective of Stage
Level III: *Postconventional, or* *Principled* Stage 5: Social contract or utility and individual rights	Being aware that people hold a variety of values and opinions, that most values and rules are relative to your group. These relative rules should usually be upheld, however, in the interest of impartiality and because they are the social contract. Some nonrelative values and rights like *life* and *liberty,* however, must be upheld in any society and regardless of majority opinion.	A sense of obligation to law because of one's social contract to make and abide by laws for the welfare of all and for the protection of all people's rights. A feeling of contractual commitment, freely entered upon, to family, friendship, trust, and work obligations. Concern that laws and duties be based on rational calculation of overall utility, "the greatest good for the greatest number."	Prior-to-society perspective. Perspective of a rational individual aware of values and rights prior to social attachments and contracts. Integrates perspectives by formal mechanisms of agreement, contract, objective impartiality, and due process. Considers moral and legal points of view; recognizes that they sometimes conflict and finds it difficult to integrate them.
Stage 6: Universal ethical principles	Following self-chosen ethical principles. Particular laws or social agreements are usually valid because they rest on such principles. When laws violate these principles, one acts in accordance with the principle. Principles are universal principles of justice: the equality of human rights and respect for the dignity of human beings as individual persons.	The belief as a rational person in the validity of universal moral principles, and a sense of personal commitment to them.	Perspective of a moral point of view from which social arrangements derive. Perspective is that of any rational individual recognizing the nature of morality or the fact that persons are ends in themselves and must be treated as such.

Source: Kohlberg, 1976, pp. 34–35.

Only a small percentage of adolescents reach the **post-conventional level** (stages 5 and 6), but usually this is not attained until after the age of twenty. Even then, only a minority of individuals reach the postconventional level.

The label *conventional* means that children conform to and uphold the laws and conventions of society simply because they are the laws and conventions of the society. The individual who reaches postconventional thinking understands, and for the most part accepts, the society's rules and regulations, but his or her reasoning goes deeper than that of the person who thinks in a conventional manner. For an individual at the postconventional level, the rules of the society have to mesh with underlying moral principles. In cases where the rules of the society come into conflict with the individual's principles, the individual will follow his or her own principles rather than the conventions of the society.

Kohlberg's Studies
In his original work, Kohlberg (1958) found that as the age of the child increases, moral judgments become more advanced. He also reported that age changes in children's responses to moral judgment items have been found in most industrialized Western countries, such as the United States, France, and Great Britain. And these changes occur regardless of the child's sex or social class. The stages are also significantly related to intelligence (Kohlberg, 1969). Kohlberg (1958) also found support for his belief that social participation in groups is one way to advance the moral judgment of children.

As further support for his cognitive-developmental theory of morality, Kohlberg and his colleagues (Colby, Kohlberg, Gibbs, & Lieberman, 1980) reported data from a twenty-year longitudinal study of moral judgment. The subjects were fifty-three boys aged ten, thirteen, and sixteen at the first time of assessment. In

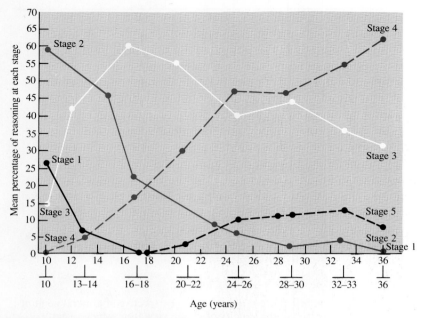

Figure 13.1 Kohlberg's longitudinal study of moral reasoning.
(*Source:* Colby, Kohlberg, Gibbs, and Lieberman, 1980).

addition to the original moral judgment interview, the boys were studied five more times at intervals of three to four years. The boys did proceed through the Kohlberg developmental stages in the predicted order, with no one skipping any stage and only 4 percent showing any backsliding within a stage from one testing time to the next. As with his earlier data, Kohlberg found that again moral judgment was significantly linked with age, sociometric status, IQ, and education. Note in figure 13.1 that in Kohlberg's recent work a majority of the individuals in late childhood were stage 2 moral thinkers and a majority of adolescents were in stage 2 and stage 3 and that not until the beginning of early adulthood did even stage 4 become a dominant mode of moral thinking for most individuals.

Evaluating Kohlberg's Contributions
Although stimulating a great deal of interest, Kohlberg's theory has not been without its share of criticism. Kohlberg has been attacked for his ideas about the cultural universality of morality, problems in the way he collects information about moral judgments, and his failure to incorporate the needs and feelings of the

individual into his theory. Elizabeth Simpson (1976) and Urie Bronfenbrenner (Bronfenbrenner & Garbarino, 1976) believe that Kohlberg's theory is ethnocentric and culturally biased. In other words, analysis of cross-cultural information about morality indicates that individuals around the world do not think as consistently at particular stages of morality as Kohlberg believes they do.

Bronfenbrenner (1970) argued that children in the American culture are taught to think in individualistic terms. To assess this belief, Soviet and American children were asked to respond to a situation in which they observed a classmate cheating on an exam. The Soviet children indicated that the cheating would be wrong because it violates a group rule, and they said that they felt it was their obligation to talk to the child who cheated and express the reasons why he or she should not cheat. The American children were much more concerned about getting caught and were three times as likely as the Soviet children to say that they would tell on the cheater by informing an adult about the deviation. Bronfenbrenner believes that the emphasis on individualism is largely responsible for the breakdown of moral responsibility in our culture.

Bronfenbrenner (Bronfenbrenner & Garbarino, 1976) points out that, except for the incest taboo, which is virtually universal, the substance of moral prohibition varies greatly across cultures and is deeply embedded in the values of each individual culture. This view corresponds to the beliefs of many anthropologists and sociologists (e.g., Benedict, 1958; Murdock, 1949).

Elizabeth Simpson (1976) also faults Kohlberg's idea that getting individuals to reason at a more advanced level will result in corresponding positive changes in their moral behavior. Reasons can be a shelter, as we all know, especially when they are developed after the fact and are applied to our own behavior or to that of someone in whom we have an ego investment. Passionate irrationality in the name of impassioned reason occurs in the market, the classroom, and in science, as well as elsewhere, and often unconsciously.

Sex Differences in Moral Reasoning

According to Kohlberg, most American males eventually reach the fifth stage of his theory, at which point their sense of justice is based on recognition of the rights of others. From Kohlberg's perspective, the guiding standard in a male's moral system is what rational men can agree is fair and equitable. This system is built on the Golden Rule, namely the idea that individuals have the right to do as they want as long as they don't interfere with the rights of others.

Carol Gilligan (1977) believes Kohlberg's view is not as applicable to the lives of females as it is to those of males. She points out that females are more oriented toward relationships of interdependence than males are.

In her research, Gilligan has found such a concern for interdependence in the moral systems of females. The female system is based on what women see as their responsibilities to themselves, families, friends, and the world in general. Women often make moral decisions on the basis of how they will influence their network of relationships and often put aside their own interests in favor of a decision that will strengthen the social network.

This overview of Gilligan's findings about the moral systems of females suggests that stage three in Kohlberg's theory (which he sees as primarily occurring in early adolescence) may be the highest level of thinking for females. It follows that Gilligan believes the ordering of Kohlberg's stages is inaccurate for females. She rejects Kohlberg's theory because it is primarily based on observations of males.

Before we leave our discussion of Kohlberg's provocative views on moral development, more needs to be said about how his views on moral education have changed in the 1980s. Recall our initial discussion of various approaches to moral education in Imagine; for further details about how Kohlberg has changed his views on moral education, read application 13.1.

It is important to learn how individuals think when presented with a moral dilemma, but to fully understand development we must attempt to learn how they behave as well. Ultimately, it is behavior we seek to influence. No one wants a nation of minds reasoning at Kohlberg's stage 5 or 6, but when behavior is observed we find that cheating, lying, and stealing are prevalent.

Application 13.1
Kohlberg's Revisionist Thinking about Moral Education

Although moral education programs embodying Kohlberg's beliefs vary from school to school, most have emphasized the role of the teacher as a facilitator rather than a lecturer, the importance of discussing moral dilemmas, and the belief that moral advancement comes through give-and-take peer group discussion. However, in somewhat of an about-face, in 1974 Kohlberg established the "Just Community," a small school for black and white students from different socioeconomic backgrounds (Recall our description of the Just Community in chapter 2). In the Just Community emphasis was placed on considering realistic issues that arise in school, the nature of moral behavior as well as moral thought, and an active role for teachers as moral advocates.

The Just Community shared with other alternative schools a belief in self-governance, mutual caring, and group solidarity. The goal for moral development was geared toward increasing students' responsibility to the community (stage 4 in Kohlberg's theory) rather than self-principled reasoning. In a recent investigation of the effectiveness of the Just Community—actually named the Cluster School—(Power, 1979), it was found that a more positive orientation toward the community did develop and that students were likely to adhere to the rules they had established. However, although the moral reasoning of the students at the Cluster School did advance, students who simply participated in moral discussion programs advanced their moral reasoning just as much as the students in the Cluster School.

The manner in which Kohlberg set up the Cluster School brings him closer to educators who are concerned with the moral "givens" in life, such as those described by Cornell Hamm in our Imagine section. However, as indicated before, most programs that have included Kohlberg's ideas emphasize the process of moral reasoning rather than a specific moral content (e.g., Adams, 1977). The effectiveness of the programs often varies from school to school and from student to student. Success is usually better at the lower stages (2, 3, and 4) than at postconventional levels (5, 6) (Minuchin & Shapiro, 1983), and in open schools rather than traditional schools (e.g., Sullivan, 1975). There is also some question about the persistence of the effects—how long lasting are the effects of such moral education programs? Usually, assessment takes place immediately after the semester in which moral education is taught, and rarely are there long-term follow-ups.

With the development of the Cluster School in the middle 1970s Kohlberg himself seemed to change his ideas about moral education. Kohlberg (1980) reported that he was not satisfied with the discussion approach to moral education. He realized that attempts to instill principled reasoning about morality in adolescents may be unrealistic because most people do not reach this level of cognitive maturity even in adulthood. And he began to believe that the moral climate of the country was shifting to an emphasis on the self and away from a concern for others in the 1970s. As a consequence, Kohlberg began to show a stronger interest in the school as a social system and in creating moral school communities (Minuchin & Shapiro, 1983).

As a further indication of Kohlberg's belief in the importance of the moral atmosphere of the school, he has developed the Moral Atmosphere Interview. This interview poses dilemmas that deal with typically occurring problems in high schools, problems that are likely to involve social responsibility. In a recent investigation (Higgins, Power, & Kohlberg, 1983), the Moral Atmosphere Interview was administered to samples of approximately twenty students from three democratic alternative high schools and three more traditional, authoritarian high schools. Students in the democratic schools perceived the rules of their schools to be more collective and described themselves and their peers as more willing to act responsibly than did students from the traditional schools.

Moral Behavior

In everyday life, laws and conventions are compromised by people who allow themselves to act in accordance with a lax interpretation of them. A boy takes a test in school with the understanding that his activity should be confined to his own work; instead, he decides to cheat and peeks at a classmate's answers. A woman files her federal tax return with the understanding that she can deduct only those business expenses for which she has a record or an accurate recollection; instead, she cheats by padding her deductions with fictitious expenses so that her tax bill will be smaller.

It has been found that students cheat more when they are informed that their scores will be posted outside the classroom, when they are told that other students have always scored just beyond what the student is capable of scoring, and when students are not monitored by adults (e.g., Hill, 1980). Such findings provide strong support for the view that the actual moral behavior of the child is heavily influenced by the pressures of the situation—rather than consistently showing honesty, children may cheat in one situation but not in others (e.g., Hartshorne & May, 1928–1930). In one investigation, lower-class boys cheated more on tests of physical strength than on vocabulary tests (Santrock, 1975).

Some Conclusions about the Behavioral Social Learning View of Morality

In the behavioral social learning view, each child has a unique learning history. Therefore, it is to be expected that his or her pattern of moral behavior will be different from that of every other child. There is no reason to expect, however, that a child will act in the same way in every realm of moral behavior. The socialization forces that contribute to one behavioral domain may have no effect on another. For this reason, a slightly different pattern of moral development emerges in each area, and any attempt to summarize findings must be approached cautiously. Still, there are some broad conclusions that seem applicable to the moral behavior of children and the social learning view.

There is little evidence of consistency in the moral behavior of an individual child. What children do in one behavioral realm is only weakly correlated with what they do in another. The evidence also suggests that this lack of moral unity may be reflected in smaller behavioral patterns as well. For example, children do not seem to have a consistent trait for cheating (Hartshorne & May, 1928–1930) or for behaving in an altruistic manner (Staub, 1974). Although they will cheat in one situation, they may scrupulously avoid doing so in another. In other words, moral behavior is situation

specific. The characteristics of the situation and the person's learning history (rather than some general trait) determine how the individual will behave.

Combining elements of the cognitive development process with elements of the behavioral learning process highlights the cognitive social learning view of Walter and Harriet Mischel (1975). They distinguish between the child's **moral competence,** or ability to produce moral behaviors, and **moral performance** of those behaviors in specific situations. In their view, competence depends primarily on cognitive-sensory processes; it is an outgrowth of these processes. The competencies include the child's abilities, knowledge, skills, awareness of moral rules and regulations, and cognitive ability to construct behaviors. Moral performance, or behavior, however, is determined by motivation and the rewards and incentives to act in a specific moral way.

In general, social learning theorists have been critical of Kohlberg's view. Among other reasons, they believe he places too little emphasis on moral behavior and the situational determinants of morality. However, while Kohlberg argues that moral judgment is an important determinant of moral behavior, he, like the Mischels, stresses that the individual's interpretation of both the moral and factual aspects of a situation lead to a moral decision (Kohlberg & Candee, 1979). For example, Kohlberg mentions that "extramoral" factors, like the desire to avoid embarrassment, may cause the child to avoid doing what he or she believes to be morally right. In sum, both the Mischels and Kohlberg believe that moral action is influenced by a complex number of factors.

Moral Feelings and Guilt

Moral feelings have traditionally been thought of in terms of guilt, but recently there has been a great deal of interest in the role of empathy. **Empathy** is the ability to understand the feelings or ideas of another person. Emphasizing empathic response stresses the positive side of moral development more than its negative side.

In psychoanalytic accounts the development of **guilt** occurs in the following way. Through identification with parents and their use of love-withdrawal for disciplinary purposes, the child turns his or her hostility inward and experiences guilt. This guilt is primarily unconscious and reflects the structure of the personality known as the *superego* (recall the discussion in chapter 2). It is assumed that guilt-prone individuals avoid transgressing in order to avoid *anxiety;* on the other hand, the person with little guilt has little reason to resist temptation. Thus, in this view, guilt is responsible for harnessing the evil drives of the *id* and for maintaining the world as a safe place in which to live. In the psychoanalytic perspective early childhood is a particularly important period for the child's moral development. Recall that Erik Erikson even refers to early childhood as the initiative versus guilt stage.

Guilt and Empathy   Children as well as adults often try to make sense out of their world by attributing causes to their behavior and the events around them. For example, when someone is in distress it would be expected that the child would make inferences about the cause of the victim's distress. The child's ideas about the cause of the victim's distress likely combine with empathic feelings that are aroused because of the victim's suffering to produce a feeling of guilt.

The positive side of moral development can be evaluated by examining a trait such as **altruism** (or the selfless concern for the welfare of others). Altruism has been given a phenomenal amount of attention in recent years—so much that the study of altruism is competing with Kohlberg's theory as the aspect of moral development receiving the greatest amount of research interest.

Altruism

Altruistic behaviors include sharing possessions, contributing to worthy causes, and helping people in distress. In general, altruism increases as children develop (e.g., Underwood & Moore, 1980): older children usually are more likely to be helpful or to share than are younger children, and older children show a greater variety of prosocial behaviors.

Role-Taking and Perspective-Taking Skills   **Role-taking** and **perspective-taking skills** refer to the understanding that other people have feelings and perceptions different from one's own. By seven or eight years of age, the child has mastered complex role-taking skills (Selman, 1971), but there are others mastered as early as the age of two or three (Flavell, 1977). The elementary school child's empathy is directed toward helping the other person, but he or she seeks to find the true source of the other person's distress. The child is also likely to discover the tentative and hypothetical nature of inferences. Thus motivation to relieve the other's distress is less egocentric and based to a greater degree on the accurate assessment of the other's needs, trial and error, and response to corrective feedback (Hoffman, 1975).

Sometimes development does not proceed smoothly—next we will look at the most common problems and disturbances that surface during middle and late childhood.

Problems and Disturbances

Entering school means conformity to routines for long hours and expectations of the child's productive performance. Children may develop *school phobia,* the inability to attend school because of the fears associated with being there. School phobia is but one of the many neurotic disturbances that may surface at this time. Neurotic disturbances refer to nonpsychotic disorders that involve a variety of symptoms such as anxiety, depression, obsessions, or compulsions. Considerable space will be devoted to anxiety. But first let's look at the range of problems elementary school children experience, as described by Thomas Achenbach (1978).

Frequent Problems Reported by Elementary School Children

Possibly because of the need for increased conformity to routines and the more noticeable comparisons of children's social and intellectual development, the rate of referrals to mental health clinics increases rapidly in the elementary school years. Referral rates for elementary school children are three times what they are for preschool children, and at all ages boys are referred more frequently than girls (Rosen, Bahn, & Kramer, 1964).

In table 13.3, the most common problems reported by parents who have taken their six- to eleven-year-old children to mental health clinics are numerically compared to similar problems reported by parents who did not refer their children to such clinics. (The latter group is labeled "normal" in the table.) The most noticeable difference between the two sets of boys is in the area of poor schoolwork, whereas for the girls the largest differences were unhappiness and nervousness. And girls seem to show more internalized problems than boys, for example, showing off less, exhibiting fewer temper tantrums, and acting less impulsively. Achenbach (1978) concluded that the greatest increase in mental health referrals in the elementary school years is, indeed, school related.

In a more recent analysis of behavioral problems and competencies, Achenbach and Edelbrock (1981) found that parents of lower-class children reported their children had more problems and fewer competencies than the parents of middle-class children reported. Most of the problems reported more frequently for lower-class children and for boys were undercontrolled, externalizing behaviors, while the problems reported more frequently for middle-class children and for girls tended to be either overcontrolled, internalizing behaviors or not clearly classifiable as undercontrolled or overcontrolled. Certain problems that have been the subject of a great deal of clinical literature did not distinguish between clinical and nonclinical children. These included

Table 13.3
Percentage Comparison of Problem Frequency between Children Referred to Clinics and "Normal" Children

Problem	Boys		Girls	
	Clinic	Normal	Clinic	Normal
Acts too young for age	65	34	66	24
Argues a lot	88	64	83	58
Attention demanding	83	33	80	40
Bragging, boasting	67	57	42	40
Can't concentrate	87	44	72	29
Can't sit still, restless, hyperactive	84	38	61	32
Disobedient at home	83	40	75	37
Disobedient at school	73	20	43	10
Easily jealous	67	36	73	42
Feels that no one loves him/her	53	21	64	31
Gets teased a lot	72	36	62	32
Impulsive	78	38	63	28
Nervous, highstrung, tense	73	24	77	22
Poor schoolwork	71	17	55	7
Self-conscious	65	43	71	48
Showing off, clowning	80	57	54	44
Sudden changes of mood	62	20	65	21
Sullen, stubborn, irritable	79	45	76	37
Temper tantrums	69	31	57	21
Unhappy, sad, depressed	58	8	66	9

fears of certain animals, situations, or places and bed-wetting. Indications of unhappiness and poor school-work, however, clearly characterized the clinical group of children more than the nonclinical group.

Neurotic Disturbances

Anxieties, phobias, obsessions, compulsions, and depression are the most common neurotic disturbances experienced by children. **Anxiety** can have either a debilitating or a positive effect on the child's behavior. In this section we will look at situations in which anxiety produces problems and disturbances for the child. In its milder forms anxiety is experienced as a feeling of apprehension often accompanied by restlessness, fatigue, and some visceral reaction such as a headache, an empty feeling in the stomach, or a heaviness in the chest. During acute anxiety attacks, the child's apprehension is intensified. He or she may believe that something horrible is about to happen and may complain

about an inability to breathe or a racing heart. An extremely anxious child may blame anxiety on others. He or she may be hostile and violent toward another person one moment, and cling to the person as a source of security the next. Following the anxiety attack, the child may be as puzzled about the behavior as others.

Anxiety is one of the most difficult psychological terms to define; yet it is one of the most widely employed. Most people agree that anxiety is an unpleasant state, that it is linked to the physiological arousal of the child, and that it involves the anticipation of something uncomfortable or painful (e.g., Sarason & Spielberger, 1975). Anxiety is usually described as a diffuse state; that is, the child cannot pin down the specific reasons for nervousness. Fear also involves discomfort and pain, but the child knows what it is that is frightening. This is the most common distinction made between anxiety and fear.

A term closely related to fear is **phobia**—a strong, often unreasonable fear of certain people, objects, or situations. Children may develop many different types of phobias; one type of phobic reaction is fear of school. School phobia in childhood may be traced to worries about exams, peer problems, teacher problems, and real or imagined fear of parental desertion. In one investigation, it was reported that school phobia usually peaks

Anxiety is an unpleasant state that involves the anticipation of something uncomfortable.

around age eleven or twelve and occurs in as many as 2 to 8 percent of the children referred to child guidance clinics (Kahn & Nursten, 1962).

Chess and Hassibi (1978) paint the following clinical picture of a child suffering from school phobia. The child often begins to complain in a vague way at about breakfast time. He or she may feel nauseated, have a headache, or say his or her stomach feels funny. If forced to go to school, the child may not be willing to enter the classroom or may feel sick while in class. The child often worries about what is going on at home while at school and may even call home to see if everything is all right. At bedtime, he or she may begin to worry about the next morning.

In the majority of cases, the school-phobic child eventually refuses to go to school. The child may offer to study at home. However, if allowed to remain homebound, the child will isolate himself or herself more and more from the outside world. Parents may become angry about this behavior in such situations and openly display hostility. When such children appear at a guidance clinic or in a psychiatrist's office, they usually appear anxious, depressed, angry, and lacking in self-esteem.

Sometimes a high level of anxiety is associated with obsessive-compulsive behavior in childhood. **Obsessions** are usually unwarranted ideas or fears that continue or intrude into the child's thoughts without any noticeable external cause. **Compulsions** refer to repetitive, stereotyped actions called into play to ward off some imaginary threat. When the child has an obsessive-compulsive personality problem, it means that he or she has a tendency to be rigid, excessively concerned about orderliness, and very much a perfectionist. This problem rarely occurs in early childhood; it is most likely to appear at about six to ten years of age. The compulsive child may feel a great deal of anxiety if he or she doesn't carry out the compulsion. Such children often experience a great deal of guilt and fear of failure as well. Parental expectations of perfect behavior represent one likely cause of compulsive behavior.

The causes of anxiety reactions during childhood are varied. They may range from biological changes to shifting relationships with family, peers, and teachers. The majority of children are capable of handling everyday problems without developing acute anxiety reactions or phobias. The moderate degree of stress encountered by most children may even serve as a motivating force to energize efforts to cope with the world. Those children with consistently high levels of anxiety, however, may need professional help. In application 13.2 ways to help children with high anxiety levels are discussed.

Application 13.2
Helping Children Cope with Anxiety

If children are experiencing a high level of anxiety, how can they best cope with it, or how can others help them cope? Lois Murphy (1962) has described the complex nature of the coping process.

> The child may attempt to reduce the threat, postpone it, bypass it, create distance between himself and the threat, divide his attention, and the like. He may attempt to control it by setting limits, or by changing or transforming the situation. He might even try to eliminate or destroy the threat. Or he may balance the threat with security measures, changing the relation of himself to the threat or to the environment which contains it, but which also includes sources of reassurance. Instead of dealing with the actual threat itself, he may deal primarily with the tension aroused by the threat: discharging tension by action, or by affect release displacement into fantasy, dramatizing activities or creative work. Or he may attempt to contain the tension via insight, conscious formulation of the nature of the threat, defense maneuvers such as being brave, reassuring himself that he would be able to deal with it. (p. 277)

Donald Meichenbaum (1975) believes that developing coping skills to help the child deal more effectively with achievement situations is a complex process. For example, a coping skill that works for one child may not work with another. Successful coping skills entail strategies that focus on challenging the child's interaction with his or her environment. These include cognitive plans for dealing with the anxiety in the world. Cognitive rehearsal is an important part of these cognitive plans. When children are being trained to reduce their anxiety in achievement situations, exposure to less threatening events may be helpful.

Cognitive rehearsal can be a valuable technique for decreasing anxiety. For instance, children who continue saying to themselves that they are afraid of college, that they cannot go to class anymore because it is too scary, or that they don't have enough talent to do well in school will probably not reduce their anxiety in such situations. The following examples of mind-set rehearsal statements (Meichenbaum, Turk, & Burstein, 1975) have been used successfully to reduce stress and anxiety at different times in anxiety-provoking achievement situations.

Preparing for anxiety or stress:

> What do I have to do?
>
> I'm going to map out a plan to deal with it.
>
> I'll just think about what I have to do.
>
> I won't worry; worry doesn't help anything.
>
> I have a lot of different strategies to call on.

Confronting and handling the pain:

> I can meet the challenge.
>
> I'll keep on taking just one step at a time; I can handle it.
>
> I'll just relax, breathe deeply, and use one of the strategies.
>
> I won't think about the pain. I'll think about what I have to do.

Coping with feelings at critical moments:

> What is it I have to do?
>
> I was supposed to expect the pain to increase; I just have to keep myself in control.
>
> When the pain comes, I'll just pause and keep focusing on what I have to do.

Reinforcing statements:

> Good, I did it.
>
> I handled it well.
>
> I knew I could do it.
>
> Wait until I tell other people how I did it!

As can be seen, these statements focus on specific ways of coping with anxiety rather than on thinking general good thoughts about oneself. By following these guidelines and procedures, children can prepare more efficiently for anxiety and cope more effectively with it when it arrives.

Summary

In this chapter we focused on three important aspects of personality development—the self, sex-role development, and moral development—and described the most common problems of middle and late childhood.

An important aspect of self-development involves the increasing ability with age to take the perspective of others—elementary school children are better at this than preschool children. Elementary school children also are more likely to describe themselves in terms of traits, whereas preschoolers are more likely to refer to themselves in terms of physical attributes. Compared to elementary school children, adolescents engage in more abstract self-perceptions. As children grow older their self-perceptions become more differentiated, individuated, and stable. Psychologists also have studied children's self-esteem, although self-esteem is generally described so broadly in terms of the child's either having a positive or negative self-concept that it is difficult to measure.

In the most extensive review of sex differences, it is indicated that many of the stereotypes about differences between the sexes are unsupported by the facts. However, girls do have more verbal ability than boys, boys surpass girls in math and visual-spatial reasoning, and boys are more aggressive than girls are. Some experts believe there are many more psychological differences between the sexes than the four just mentioned. One possible sex difference that has stirred a great deal of controversy involves achievement. Ours is an achievement-oriented society; we rear children to be competitive, to be the best, to win. It appears, though, that females have traditionally been socialized differently from males in regard to achievement. It seems that girls, even as early as kindergarten, have been trained to become instrumentally incompetent, whereas males have been oriented toward instrumental competence.

Our discussion of moral development focused heavily on Kohlberg's cognitive structural stage theory. Most children in middle and late childhood are in stage 2 of Kohlberg's six-stage theory, suggesting they reason about moral dilemmas in predominantly premoral ways. Some experts believe that there is more cultural variation in moral development than Kohlberg suggests, that there are problems in measuring the stages, and that reasons sometimes can be a shelter for immoral conduct. The behavioral social learning perspective of moral development emphasizes the importance of the child's moral actions. One of these moral actions—cheating—becomes more important during middle and late childhood as the child enters formal schooling. The behavioral social learning perspective emphasizes that morality often varies substantially from one situation to another, while the cognitive social learning view stresses a distinction between competence and performance. The content of moral education has been a value-laden issue for many years and still is comprised of many different approaches. Recently, Kohlberg has changed his perspective on moral education, believing that the school needs to be viewed as a moral system rather than merely getting children to reason at higher moral levels.

Entry into school brings with it problems related to demands for conformity to routines for long periods and increased expectations of the child's performance. There is an increase in referrals to mental health clinics during the elementary school years, and at all ages referrals for boys outnumber those for girls. Poor schoolwork is a major problem for boys in this age period, while girls tend to be characterized more by unhappiness and nervousness. Anxieties, phobias, obsessions, and compulsions are among the most common neurotic disturbances of children. All children experience anxiety and fear, but some encounter such high levels of anxiety that their competence is impaired. Anxiety is a diffuse state, whereas fear is related to a specific situation, person, or object. A phobia is viewed as an unreasonable fear, and one of the most common phobias among children is school phobia.

Key Terms

altruism
anxiety
attribution theory
compulsions
conventional level of
  moral development
empathy
guilt
instrumental competence
learned helplessness
moral autonomy
moral competence
moral development
moral performance

moral realism
obsessions
perspective-taking skills
phobia
postconventional level of
  moral development
preconventional level of
  moral development
role-taking skills
values clarification

Review Questions

1. Discuss the changes in self-perception that occur during middle and late childhood.
2. Evaluate the labels of self-esteem and self-concept and describe why they are so difficult to measure.
3. What are some real and mythical differences between the sexes?
4. Discuss the role of learned helplessness in the development of achievement orientation in females.
5. Outline Kohlberg's theory of moral development. How has it been criticized?
6. Evaluate the behavioral social learning view of moral development.
7. Discuss the nature of moral education. Should moral education be a part of schooling?
8. What are some of the common problems and disturbances in the elementary school years?

Further Readings

Achenbach, T. A. Developmental aspects of psychopathology in children and adolescents. In M. Lamb (ed.), *Social and personality development.* New York: Holt, Rinehart & Winston, 1978.
An excellent chapter on the developmental aspects of problems and disturbances in infancy, childhood, and adolescence. Includes information on hyperactivity and the treatment of children with problems and disturbances. Medium reading difficulty.

Coopersmith, S. *The antecedent of self-esteem.* San Francisco: Freeman, 1967.
A study of parental characteristics that are associated with children's low, medium, and high self-esteem in middle and late childhood. Includes a self-esteem measure that can be given to children, and an interview for parents. Easy to read.

Huston-Stein, A., & Higgens-Trenk, A. Development of females from childhood through adulthood: Career and feminine orientations. In P. Baltes (ed.), *Life-span development and behavior* (vol. 4). New York: Academic Press, 1978.
An excellent overview of achievement and career orientation in girls and women, with particular attention being given to the socializing influences that have led to different achievement and career paths for girls and boys. Reasonably easy reading.

Knopf, I. J. *Childhood psychopathology.* Englewood Cliffs, N.J.: Prentice-Hall, 1979.
A thorough overview of the major disturbances in children. Includes information on conceptual models of psychopathology, the nature of psychopathology, the assessment of children with problems, and treatment approaches. Reasonably easy reading.

Lickona, T. (ed.). *Moral development and behavior.* New York: Holt, Rinehart & Winston, 1976.
Contemporary essays outline the major theories, research findings, and educational implications of moral development. Included are essays by Kohlberg, Hoffman, Mischel, Bronfenbrenner, and Rest. Moderately difficult.

Know Yourself

Let's discuss your own development through childhood some more. Think about your life from the time you were six years old through the end of your elementary school years. The chances are good that you will remember more about this period of time than about what went on during early childhood. Still, it would be helpful for you to talk with your parents about your middle and late childhood years. Think first about your intelligence and your school experiences. Did you ever take an intelligence test? If so, do you know how well you did on the test? Were you above average, average, or below average during elementary school? Were you attentive in class, and did you get along well with your teachers? Or was elementary school a pain in the neck? Did you hate having to sit in your seat most of the day? Or wasn't your school as authoritarian as many schools? Think about your teachers in grades one through six. Try to remember their names, their dominant characteristics, and how much you feel you learned from them.

What about your peers and friends—did you spend even more time with them as you grew through middle and late childhood? Think about who your best friends were and the kinds of things you did together. Think also about your life at home and in your neighborhood—what was your relationship with your parents like during middle and late childhood? Do you have any brothers and sisters? If so, what was your relationship with them like? How did they influence your development? And think about your neighborhood and the socioeconomic atmosphere you grew up in. Did you live in the inner city in an area where there were a lot of other children who came from poor families, did you live in the suburbs in a middle-class family, or did you grow up in a rural area? Are you from a white family or from an ethnic minority family? How do you think these cultural factors influenced your development?

Now that you have thought about your own development during the elementary school years, talk with one or two classmates or friends about what their middle and late childhood years were like. Did they ever take an intelligence test? If so, how well did they do?

Do you think they are telling the truth? What was elementary school like for them—what were their teachers like? What were their friends like? What kind of things did they play? What kind of neighborhood did they grow up in? How do you think these factors influenced their development?

Now that you have thought about your own elementary school years and talked with others about their middle and late childhood, try to spend some time observing and talking with some children between six and eleven years old. You probably won't be able to go into an elementary school as easily as into a preschool. Nonetheless, you might be able to watch and listen as these children play at recess. You can also find children of this age at YMCAs and YWCAs, clubs, shopping malls, parks, and so forth. Listen to their conversations and find out what kinds of things they talk about and what interests them. If possible, notice if they behave differently when they are with their parents as compared to when they are with their peers.

Now think about what your own ideas are about middle and late childhood. Put yourself in the role of a parent with an eight-year-old child. What would be your most important concerns? Chances are you would be concerned about the quality of education your child is receiving, whether you are effectively rearing your child to be a competent, caring individual, how well your child gets along with other children and adults, whether your child is developing one or more competencies and skills that will make him feel good about himself, and about how much time and money it takes to be a parent.

By reading our description of middle and late childhood in this section, by thinking about your own middle and late childhood years and talking with your parents about them, by conversing with others, by observing elementary school children, and by thinking about what kind of parent you would be with your own school-aged child, you should know yourself better.

In This Section You Will Learn About

Introduction and Physical and Cognitive Development

Whether puberty can come any earlier

The historical background of the study of adolescence, including G. Stanley Hall's storm and stress view

How easy it is to stereotype adolescents

The nature of the pubertal process

Physical changes in height, weight, and sexual maturation

The considerable degree of individual variation in puberty

Contemporary sexual attitudes and behavior

Sex education in the schools

Psychological adaptation to changes in physical development, including early and late maturation

Formal operational thought

Piaget and adolescent education

Individual variation in cognitive development

Social cognition

Social Development

Parents and peers—conflict and conformity

The nature of increased conflict between parents and adolescents

Strategies for reducing parent-adolescent conflict

The effects of divorce on adolescents

Adolescents who become parents

The nature of friendship in adolescence

Adolescent groups—cliques and crowds

Dating

Cross-cultural comparisons of adolescents, including rites of passage

The nature of adolescent schooling

Social interaction at school

Positive characteristics of junior high school teachers

Strategies for teaching low- and high-ability students

Emotional and Personality Development

Erik Erikson's analysis of the identity development of famous people

The development of the self

The nature of identity development, including the four statuses of identity

Drug use by adolescents

School policy and drug use

Alcohol use

Juvenile delinquency

Intervention programs designed to help delinquents

School-related problems

Eating disorders, including anorexia nervosa

Schizophrenia

Profile

Mark Parke is now thirteen years old and in the eighth grade. Gradually over the last year, Mark has entered puberty. He has some pubic hair, his voice is getting deeper, and he is five feet, seven inches tall and weighs 110 pounds. (He is still not eating what his mother wants him to.) Last week he woke up somewhat surprised, surprised because he had his first wet dream. Last week he also went to an eighth-grade party at the home of one of his friends. Mark showed a strong interest in girls. Unfortunately, the girl he likes doesn't seem to like him as much as he likes her. Every time he tries to talk to her she abruptly walks away—maybe it is because he is so thin, he thinks.

Stacy Henson also is thirteen years old now and in the eighth grade. Stacy is much further into puberty than Mark. She had her first period sixteen months ago, and her breasts are almost fully developed. She is trying to get the captain of the junior high football team, a ninth grader, to ask her to the homecoming dance. So far, she hasn't been successful, but she is working on it. Last night, for example, one of her girl friends called the captain on the phone and told him how much Stacy likes him.

Don Mitchell at the age of fourteen is in the ninth grade of his junior high school. He is an excellent basketball player and is the leading scorer on his school team. He is one of the most popular boys in junior high school. Don's parents still monitor his academic and social world closely—"sometimes too closely," as Don puts it. His mother recently got a transfer to his school, where she is teaching eighth-grade English. Don frankly would rather have had his mother stay at the school where she was teaching.

Remember Chip Martin, who was not doing very well in school during middle and late childhood? At the age of thirteen, Chip still is not making good grades. Furthermore, his mother is worried because he seems to have gotten into a clique that rides motorcycles. Recently, she received a call from the school counselor, who told her that Chip had been skipping a lot of classes and yesterday "smarted off" to his math teacher and got into a yelling bout with her.

Cognitively, several changes seem to have just begun for Mark, Stacy, Don, and Chip. All four have started to think in more abstract ways, not always relying on concrete experiences for generating thoughts, and they are more organized problem solvers than they were when we last visited them in the fifth grade. They seem to show a sort of egocentric pattern in which they think that people are always looking at them. The other day, for example, Stacy walked into a restaurant with her parents and said, "Oh, no, I can't believe it. What can I do?" When her parents asked her what was the matter, she replied, "Everybody is looking at me—look at this hair, it just won't stay down." (Stacy had just walked by a mirror at the entrance of the restaurant and checked her appearance.)

When we question the four adolescents and their parents, they all agree that parent-adolescent conflict seems to be greater now than it was when Mark, Stacy, Don, and Chip were in the fifth grade. Mark's parents say that he just doesn't seem to want to listen to their rules anymore. Stacy's mother says that she has a hard time taking the catty comments Stacy makes about her. The young adolescents are pushing more for independence from their parents than they did three years ago, and their parents seem to be having a bit of a tough time accepting this. Mark and Stacy's parents seem to want Mark and Stacy to conform to their adult standards. Even though the parent-adolescent conflict between Mark, Stacy, and Don and their parents has increased in the last year or so, it has not even come close to the point at which we could say that the conflict is pathological. However, the conflict between Chip and his mother is at an intense level.

Although Mark, Stacy, Don, and Chip began to show increased interest in peers during the latter part of the elementary school years, as young adolescents they seem to want to spend just about all of their free time with their peers. Indeed, they spend a lot of time during the week thinking about what they can do with their friends on the weekend.

At the age of seventeen, Mark, Stacy, and Don are seniors. All three have already sent their applications to several colleges and universities. Mark is now six feet, three inches tall and weighs 170 pounds. Stacy is still five feet, one inch tall, but now weighs 115 pounds. Both Mark and Stacy think about their body image a good deal, but it doesn't preoccupy their thoughts as much as was true when they were in the eighth grade. Mark is much more muscular than he was in the eighth grade, and his body image has improved. Mark and Stacy have come very close to having sexual intercourse with the people they are going steady with, but so far they have not gone all the way. Stacy says that it is getting harder and harder not to have sexual intercourse with Robert, whom she has been dating for about fourteen months.

Don is the leading scorer on his high school basketball team. College coaches already are talking with him about a possible college scholarship. Don's parents are very proud of him; he has successfully managed to juggle the demands of sports and a rigorous set of classes in school. He has an A- average. Don's parents intelligently have recognized that he now is capable of making more mature decisions on his own so they feel more comfortable in "letting him loose" than they did in the junior high school years. Not that Don has not done some things they consider wrong. Last summer he and several of his friends went on a drinking binge. At 3:00 A.M. they didn't know where he was, and they were frantic. At 3:30 A.M. Don and his friends finally realized they had better go home, even if they weren't very sober. His parents were not very understanding. Don wishes they would recognize that a person doesn't become an adult overnight, that going from childhood to adulthood is a very long, very gradual process that takes some ten to fifteen years, and that adolescents are going to fall on their faces more than once during this time. Still, Don says he doesn't think he is going to stay out until 3:30 A.M. anymore, and when he drinks he is going to do it more moderately and be very careful that his parents do not find out.

At the age of seventeen, Chip also is a senior, but he is not planning to go to college. He has taken a vocational curriculum during the last few years, and he works at a fast-food restaurant about twenty-five hours a week. Almost two years ago his mother remarried. Chip likes his stepfather now although initially he wasn't so sure about him. Chip is very proud of the car he drives; he is paying for it with the money he earns at his job.

Cognitively, at the age of seventeen, all four adolescents are more advanced thinkers than they were in the junior high school years. Their thoughts have become even more abstract, and they engage more frequently in extended speculation about what their lives are going to be like, what the possibilities are for them, and what an ideal world would be like. As part of their concern about their future, they have begun to think much more seriously about the kind of occupation they are going to pursue. Indeed, a dilemma for Stacy is whether she will get married after high school or pursue a college degree. Recently, she has entertained the possibility of doing both. Mark is not sure what he wants to do with his life, but it's not because he hasn't thought about it a lot. He has continued to do reasonably well in school and has thought about becoming a stock broker or an accountant. During the coming summer he plans to work in either an accounting firm or a stock brokerage office as a "gopher," running errands but also being able to find out what life in such a job would be like.

Relationships between parents and offspring have cooled down somewhat. Both Mark and Stacy seem to think more independently from both their parents and their peers now. Still, they retain close ties to their parents and peers, spending more and more time with their friends but still being monitored and influenced by the values of their parents. Nonetheless, an overriding concern of both Mark and Stacy, as well as Don and Chip, seems to be the development of an identity, a sense of who they are, what they are all about, and what they are going to do with their lives.

14 Introduction and Physical and Cognitive Development

*I*magine . . . puberty's beginning at a much earlier age

Imagine a toddler displaying all the features of **puberty**—a three-year-old girl with fully developed breasts, or a boy just slightly older with a deep male voice. That is what we will see by the year 2250 if the age at which puberty arrives keeps getting younger at its current pace.

In Norway, the average girl begins to menstruate at just over 13 years of age, as opposed to 17 years in the 1840s. In the United States—where children mature up to a year earlier than in European countries— the average age at first menstruation has declined from 14.2 in 1900 to about 12.45 today. According to British pediatrician J. M. Tanner, who has compiled statistics on the subject, the age at menarche (first menstruation) has declined an average of four months per decade for the past century.

Fortunately, perhaps, we are unlikely to see pubescent toddlers, since what has happened during this century may be quite special. Tanner has noted that an extrapolation of the recent trend backward to medieval times would have the average woman beginning to menstruate in her early thirties, an age not much younger than the life expectancy in those times. Had this been the case, our species would have become extinct, or at least "endangered," because women's reproductive years would have been comparatively few. Writers from this period make references to **menarche** typically occurring somewhere between the fifteenth and twentieth year of life: the historian Quarinonium, writing in 1610, says that Austrian peasant girls seldom menstruate before their seventeenth, eighteenth, or even twentieth years.

If teenage puberty was a fact of life even in medieval times, something must have happened more recently to decrease the age of onset. The best guess is that "that something" is a higher level of nutrition and health. The available data show that the age of menarche began to get earlier at about the time of the Industrial Revolution, a period associated with an increasing standard of living and advances in medical science.

Cross-cultural data also suggest that better nutrition is related to earlier maturation. Girls growing up in countries or regions with adequate diets tend to begin menstruating earlier than those with less nutritious diets. Similarly, earlier menarche has been associated with higher social class, fewer children in the family, and living in urban rather than rural areas—all of which may reflect nutritional status.

If improved nutrition and the corresponding decrease in illness and disease are responsible for the trend toward earlier puberty in the past century, the trend should level off when people are nourished at an optimal level. There is some evidence that this is occurring in industrialized countries. The average age of menarche is becoming more similar from country to country. Where major variations exist, there also appear to be large differences in nutrition and the general level of health care. In New Guinea, for example, two highland tribes show ages at menarche of 17.6 and 18.1 years.

Does this mean that in the future all youth will begin puberty at the same age? It's unlikely. There are other sources of variation that appear to be unrelated to nutrition and health. For example, girls living at lower elevations menstruate earlier than those of similar socioeconomic status living at higher elevations.

Genetic factors also play a role. By comparing identical and fraternal twins, we see the impact of heredity when diet is presumably controlled. Identical twins typically differ in age at menarche by about two months (a minimal difference, attributable to slight differences in birth weight), while fraternal twins differ by about eight months. In addition, girls in countries

with differing economic levels sometimes show the reverse of what we would expect if nutrition alone determined the age at menarche. One study found that Chinese girls, even those who were very poor, menstruated earlier than several different groups of much wealthier Europeans. Genetic factors currently account for only about 10 to 15 percent of the variation in age at menarche, a proportion that is increasing as growing uniformity of nutrition and health eliminates other variations.

What initiates the onset of puberty? Rose Frisch and Roger Revelle at Harvard have found that menarche occurs at a relatively constant weight in girls. Similarly, they have found that the adolescent growth spurt begins at relatively constant weights for boys and girls. Though the spurt occurs two years later in boys than in girls, and at a higher weight, it begins at a similar metabolic level for both groups. Frisch and Revelle speculate that attainment of a critical metabolic rate triggers the physiological processes of puberty. New data from Frisch suggest that for menarche to begin and to continue, fat must make up about 17 percent of body weight. Thus, both teenage anorexics (loss of appetite) whose weight drops precipitously and female athletes in certain sports may become **amenorrheic** (abnormal absence of suppression of menstrual discharge).

The Frisch and Revelle explanation is intriguing and does fit much of the existing information. Some researchers, however, remain skeptical; they note that causality has not been shown and that alternative explanations are possible.

Defining what puberty is has complicated the search for its "trigger." Puberty is not a single, sudden event, but part of a slowly unfolding process beginning at conception. We know when a young person is going through puberty, but pinpointing the onset and cessation of the process is more difficult. Except for menarche, which occurs relatively late in the process, there is no single event heralding puberty. In boys, the first seminal emission ("wet dream") and the first whiskers are events that could be used to mark its arrival. Both may go unnoticed.

Pubertal changes, however, are well defined: there is a spurt in growth as well as clear changes in secondary sex characteristics, endocrine levels and processes, and other physiological factors. But these are all gradual processes. The gradual nature of puberty has made it difficult to study its causes.

Further complicating the study of what initiates puberty is that several different characteristics are changing and they do not all change together. For example, the development of reproductive capacities and the adolescent growth spurt have slightly different hormonal determinants, and may proceed at different rates, but are both components of the pubertal process.

Perhaps the most accurate way of thinking about puberty is that it is a phase in the maturational process over the life span from conception to death. It signals the beginning of reproductive capacity, a capacity that diminishes later in life. In general, reproduction requires a minimal level of nutritional adequacy and general health status; it is the first system to shut down when the body is poorly nourished or diseased.

Our improved health has led to a lengthening of the reproductive years; puberty is coming earlier, and, at the same time, the age when fertility ends is getting later and later. The longer period of reproduction has implications not only for biological processes but also for social and psychological development.

Information on the social and psychological correlates of puberty is surprisingly meager. In our own research with adolescents, we have begun to examine the impact of pubertal development as a psychological experience, observing the way it affects relationships with peers and parents. When our research is completed, we may know what "growing up faster" really means."

Source: Petersen, January 1979, pp. 45–56. Reprinted by permission.

Introduction

In this chapter you are introduced to the period of development known as adolescence, which is entered roughly between the ages of ten and thirteen and exited approximately between the ages of eighteen and twenty-two. You will read about the beginning of the scientific study of adolescence, how easy it is to stereotype adolescents, the tremendous physical changes that characterize the pubertal process, and the psychological accompaniments of those changes. You also will read about the nature of cognitive development in adolescence, including Piaget's stage of formal operational thought and social cognition, or reasoning about social matters.

Historical Background of Adolescence

Most historians label G. Stanley Hall the father of the scientific study of adolescence. Hall's ideas were published in the two-volume set, *Adolescence,* in 1904. Hall's work included the following chapters:

Volume I

Hall's strong emphasis on the biological basis of adolescence can be seen in the large number of chapters on physical growth, instincts, evolution, and periodicity. His concern for education also is evident, as is

G. Stanley Hall.

his interest in religion. Further insight into Hall's concept of adolescence can be gleaned from his preface to the volumes:

Development (in adolescence) is less gradual and more saltatory, suggestive of some ancient period of storm and stress when old moorings were broken and a higher level attained. . . .

Nature arms youth for conflict with all the resources at her command—speed, power of shoulder, biceps, back, leg, jaw—strengthens and enlarges skull, thorax, hips, makes man aggressive and prepares woman's frame for maternity. . . .

Sex asserts its mastery in field after field, and works its havoc in the form of secret vice, debauch, disease, and enfeebled heredity, cadences the soul to both its normal and abnormal rhythms, and sends many thousand youth a year to quacks, because neither parents, teachers, preachers, or physicians know how to deal with its problems. . . . The social instincts undergo sudden unfoldment and the new life of love awakens. . . Youth awakes to a new world and understands neither it nor himself. . . .

Never has youth been exposed to such dangers of both perversion and arrest as in our land and day. Urban life has increased temptations, prematurities, sedentary occupations, and passive stimuli, just when an active, objective life is most needed. Adolescents' lives today lack some of the regulations they still have in older lands with more conservative traditions. . . (Volume I, pp. xi, xiii, xv)

Hall's preoccupation with the evils of adolescence are threaded throughout the texts. This is nowhere more clear than in his comments about masturbation:

One of the very saddest of all the aspects of human weakness and sin is [masturbation] . . . Tissot, in 1759, found every pupil guilty. . . Dr. G. Bachin (1895) argued that growth, especially in the moral and intellectual regions, is dwarfed and stunted [by masturbation]. Bachin also felt that masturbation caused gray hairs, and especially baldness, a stooping and enfeebled gait. . . .

Perhaps masturbation is the most perfect type of individual vice and sin . . . it is the acme of selfishness.

Prominent among predisposing causes are often placed erotic reading, pictures, and theatrical presentations. . . Schiller protests against trouser pockets for boys, as do others against feather beds, while even horseback riding and the bicycle have been placed under the ban by a few extremist writers.

. . . The Medical cures of masturbation that have been prescribed are almost without number: bromide, ergot, lupin, blistering, clitoridectomy, section of certain nerves, small mechanical appliances, of which the Patent Office at Washington has quite a collection. Regimen rather than special treatment must, however, be chiefly relied on. Work reduces temptation, and so does early rising . . . Good music is a moral tonic . . . (Volume I, pp. 411–471)

Clearly, our current beliefs about masturbation differ substantially from those of Hall's time. As indicated in the overview of chapters in Hall's volumes, he wrote about many other aspects of adolescence in addition to sex and masturbation. His books are entertaining as well as informative. You are encouraged to look up his original work in your library and compare his comments with those made about adolescence in this text.

Charles Darwin, the famous evolutionary theorist, had a tremendous impact on Hall's thinking. Hall applied the scientific, biological aspects of Darwin's views to the study of adolescent development. He believed that all development is controlled by genetically determined physiological factors. Environmental influences on development were minimized, particularly in infancy and childhood. Hall did acknowledge that, during adolescence, the environment accounts for more change in development than in earlier age periods. Thus, Hall believed—as we do today—that at least during adolescence, heredity interacts with environmental influences to determine the individual's development.

Hall subscribed to a four-stage approach to development: infancy, childhood, youth, and adolescence. Adolescence is the period of time from about twelve to about twenty-three years of age, or when adulthood is achieved. Hall saw adolescence as the period of **sturm und drang,** which means storm and stress. This label was borrowed from the German writings of Goethe and Schiller, who wrote novels full of idealism, commitments to goals, revolution, passion, and feeling. Hall sensed there was a parallel between the themes of the German authors and the psychological development of adolescents.

According to Hall, the adolescent period of storm and stress is full of contradictions and wide swings in mood and emotion. Thoughts, feelings, and actions oscillate between conceit and humility, goodness and temptation, and happiness and sadness. One moment the adolescent may be nasty to a peer, yet in the next moment be extremely nice. At one time the adolescent may want to be left alone, but shortly thereafter desire to cling to somebody. In sum, G. Stanley Hall views adolescence as a turbulent time charged with conflict (Ross, 1972).

Studies in different cultures indicate that stress and conflict are not inevitable during adolescent development. Anthropologist Margaret Mead found that in some societies adolescence is a pleasant period of development (Mead, 1930).

The Period of Adolescence: 1900 to the Present

Between 1890 and 1920 a cadre of psychologists, urban reformers, educators, youth workers, and counselors began to mold the concept of adolescence. At this time, young people, especially boys, no longer were viewed as decadent problem causers, but instead were seen as increasingly passive and vulnerable—qualities previously associated only with the adolescent female. When Hall's book on adolescence was published in 1904, it played a major role in restructuring thinking about adolescents. Hall was saying that while many adolescents appear to be passive, they are experiencing considerable turmoil within.

By 1950, the developmental period we refer to as adolescence had come of age—not only did it possess physical and social identity, but legal attention was paid to it as well. Every state by 1950 had developed special laws for youth between the ages of sixteen and eighteen or twenty. Adolescents in the 1950s have been described as the silent generation (Lee, 1970). Life was much better for adolescents in the 1950s than it had been in the 1930s and 1940s. The government was paying for many adolescents' college educations through the GI bill, and television was beginning to become a convenience in most homes. Getting a college degree, the key to a good job, was on the minds of many adolescents during the 1950s—so were getting married, having a family, and settling down to the life of luxury displayed in television commercials.

In the 1920s, the Roaring Twenties atmosphere rubbed off on the behavior of adolescents.

While the persuit of higher education persisted among adolescents in the 1960s, it became painfully apparent that many black adolescents not only were being denied a college education, but were receiving an inferior secondary education as well. Racial conflicts in the form of riots and "sit-ins" were pervasive, with college-age adolescents among the most vocal participants.

The political protests of adolescents reached a peak in the late 1960s and early 1970s, when millions of adolescents violently reacted to what they saw as unreasonable American participation in the Vietnam war. As parents watched the 1968 Democratic presidential convention, they not only saw political speeches in support of candidates but also their adolescents fighting with the police, yelling obscenities at adults, and staging sit-ins.

Parents became more concerned in the 1960s about teenage drug use and abuse than in past eras. Sexual permissiveness in the form of premarital sex, cohabitation, and endorsement of previously prohibited sexual conduct also increased.

Stereotypes of Adolescents

There is complexity and diversity in the thoughts, feelings, and actions of adolescents in any era. Unfortunately, many negative **stereotypes** of adolescents have developed, even in the face of contradictory evidence (Hill, 1983).

A study by Daniel Yankelovich (1974) indicates that many such stereotypes about youth are false. Yankelovich compared the attitudes of adolescents with those of their parents about different values, life styles, and codes of personal conduct. There was little or no difference in the attitudes of the adolescents and their parents toward self-control, hard work, saving money, competition, compromise, legal authority, and private property. There was a substantial difference between the adolescents and their parents when their attitudes toward religion were sampled (89 percent of the parents said that religion was important to them, compared to only 66 percent of the adolescents). But note that even a majority of the adolescents subscribed to the belief that religion is important.

Next we outline the important physical changes that occur during adolescent development. Although physical development slows during middle and late childhood, early adolescence is a time of tremendous growth and biological change.

Physical Development

Many biological changes characterize the period of adolescence. Some of the most important ones involve height, weight, and sexual characteristics. Before we describe such changes, let's look at the nature of the pubertal process itself.

The Pubertal Process

Recall from the Imagine section that puberty is not a single, sudden event but part of a slowly unfolding process that begins at conception. Although we know when a young person is going through puberty, we have difficulty pinpointing the onset and end of the process.

At the outset it is important to note that puberty can be distinguished from the phase of development referred to as adolescence. Generally, puberty has ended long before the individual has left adolescence. However, puberty often is thought of as the most important marker for the beginning of adolescence. For the most part, then, puberty coincides with early adolescence rather than late adolescence.

Puberty is usually defined as the period of rapid change to maturation. First, we discuss physical changes in height and weight and then describe the many sexual changes that occur during puberty.

Adolescents grow in varying degrees.

"Why don't you grow up?"

Illustration by Bil Keane from *Just Wait 'Till You Have Children of Your Own.* Copyright © 1971 by Erma Bombeck and Bil Keane. Reprinted by permission of Doubleday & Company, Inc.

Height and Weight Changes

As individuals undergo the adolescent growth spurt, they make rapid gains in height and weight. But as indicated in figure 14.1, the growth spurt for girls occurs approximately two years earlier than for boys. The growth spurt in girls begins at approximately age ten and one-half and lasts for about two years. During this time period, girls increase in height by about three and one-half inches per year. The growth spurt for boys usually begins at about twelve and one-half years of age and also lasts for approximately two years. Boys usually grow about four inches per year in height during this growth spurt (Tanner, 1970). These averages do not reflect the fairly wide range of time within which the adolescent growth spurt begins. Girls may start the growth spurt as early as age seven and one-half or as late as age eleven and one-half, while boys may begin as early as age ten and one-half or as late as age sixteen (Faust, 1977).

Boys and girls who are shorter or taller than their peers before adolescence are likely to remain so during adolescence (e.g., Tanner, 1970). In our society, there is a stigma attached to short boys and tall girls. At the beginning of the adolescent period, girls tend to be as tall or taller than boys their age, but by the end of the junior high years most boys have caught up or, in many cases, even surpassed girls in height. And even though height in the elementary school years is a good predictor of height later in adolescence, there is still room for the individual's height to change in relation to the

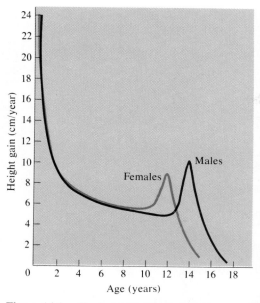

Figure 14.1 Typical individual growth curves for height in boys and girls. These curves represent the height of the typical boy and girl at any given age.

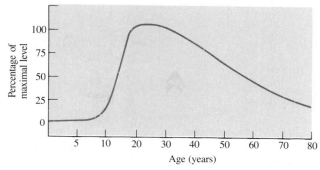

Figure 14.2 Hypothetical representation of sexual development in terms of sex hormone levels.
(*Source:* Petersen, A. C. & Taylor, B. *The biological approach to adolescence: biological change and physiological adaptation.* In J. Adelson (ed.) *Handbook of Adolescent Psychology.* New York: John Wiley, 1980.)

height of his or her peers. As much as 30 percent of the height of late adolescents is unexplained by height in the elementary school years (Tanner, 1970).

The rate at which adolescents gain weight follows approximately the same developmental timetable as the rate at which they gain height. Marked weight gains coincide with the onset of puberty. During early adolescence, girls tend to outweigh boys, but by about age fourteen, just as with height, boys begin to surpass girls (e.g., Faust, 1977; Tanner, 1970).

It is important to remember that these growth curves represent averages. The wide age range during which the features of the adolescent growth spurt appear suggests the importance of considering both individual and cultural differences in physical development.

Sexual Maturation

Think back to your last few years of childhood and then to your first few years of adolescence. Probably nothing comes to mind more clearly than the fact that during the last few years of childhood you were not maturing sexually, whereas during the first few years of adolescence you were indeed maturing sexually. Similarly, you probably recall that during your last few years of childhood your interest in sexual activity and sexual relationships was nowhere near the level they reached during your first few years of adolescence. Few aspects of our development throughout the life cycle bring about more curiosity and mystery than the onset of our sexual maturation during early adolescence. Sexual maturation is one of the most prominent aspects of the

pubertal process. In figure 14.2, a rough representation of sexual maturation and decline is presented in terms of our knowledge about sex-hormone levels (Petersen & Taylor, 1980).

Three of the most noticeable changes in the sexual maturation of boys are penis elongation, testes development, and the growth of pubic hair. The normal range and average age of development of these sexual characteristics, as well as height spurt, are shown in figure 14.3.

Two of the most noticeable aspects of the female's sexual maturation are pubic hair and breast development. Figure 14.4 illustrates the normal range and average age of development of these sexual characteristics, as well as information about menarche and height gain.

For the most part we have described the average time at which sexual maturation occurs in boys and girls. Although we have called attention to the tremendous individual variation in the onset of pubertal events, such variation merits further attention.

Individual Variation

For most boys, the pubertal sequence may begin as early as ten and as late as thirteen and one-half years, at which time there is an acceleration in the growth of the testes. If this sequence ends at the time of the first ejaculation, the average age at termination is thirteen and one-half to fourteen (although ejaculation could happen much earlier or later, depending upon when the process started). Among the most remarkable normal variations is the fact that two boys may be the same chronological age, and yet one may complete the pubertal sequence before the other has begun it. For most girls, the first menstrual period may occur at the age of ten or it may not happen until the age of fifteen and one-half (Hill, 1980).

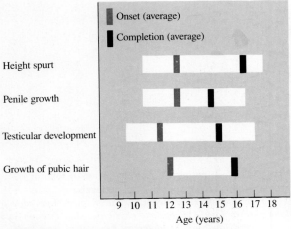

Figure 14.3 Normal range and average age of development of sexual characteristics in males.
(Data from "Growing Up," by J. M. Tanner, *Scientific American,* 1973, 229, 35–42. Reprinted by permission of W. H. Freeman and Company, Publishers.)

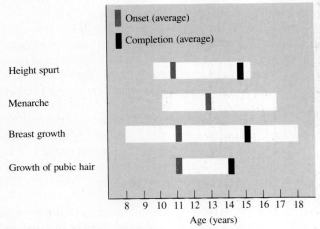

Figure 14.4 Normal range and average age of development of sexual characteristics in females.
(Data from "Growing Up," by J. M. Tanner, *Scientific American,* 1973, 229, 35–42. Reprinted by permission of W. H. Freeman and Company, Publishers.)

Sexual maturation characterizes the onset of puberty.

Contemporary Sexual Attitudes and Behavior in Adolescence

Not only does puberty involve marked changes in height, weight, and the physical nature of sexual characteristics, but substantial changes in sexual attitudes and behavior appear as well. First, we look at a light, entertaining introduction to how many parents fail to do a very good job of sex education; then we survey contemporary trends in self-stimulation, homosexual behavior, and heterosexual behavior.

"There is no need for you to be embarrassed about S-E-X," I told my daughter. "Sit down and I will tell you all I know about it. First, Lassie is a girl. Second, I lied. Sensuous lips do not mean fever blisters. Third, I did not conceive you by drinking the blood of an owl and spitting three times at a full moon. Here is the bra and girdle section from the Sears catalogue. If you have any questions, keep them to yourself."

I don't suppose that was too technical, but a friend of mine overdid it. She bought books and charts depicting the reproduction cycles of chickens. Together they studied mating, fertilization, and a racy chapter on chromosomes. Her daughter knew more about chickens than any young girl has a right to know.

One day, her mother walked out on the front porch and saw a rooster perched on the porch swing and liked to have had a heart attack. (Bombeck & Keane, 1971, p. 99)

Adolescence is a time when exploratory and experimental sex play turns into more purposeful sexual behavior. However, many adolescents, because of social and religious standards, stop short of sexual intercourse. Even when they find a partner they would sincerely like to have sexual intercourse with, they often restrict themselves to "petting." For the majority of adolescents, the main sexual outlet is masturbation.

As a rule, adolescent females are more sexually inhibited than adolescent males are. Most adolescent girls are not encouraged to acknowledge their sexual needs. Although they are taught to make themselves attractive, their own sexual feelings often go undiscussed. Thus the sexual drive of adolescent girls often tends toward fantasies about the future—becoming a bride, a lover, and so forth.

By contrast, the sexual fantasies of adolescent boys focus more specifically on sexual activity itself. Some experts suggest that it is only toward the end of adolescence that males begin to see sex as an important component of human communication and that females discover the robust potential of their bodies (Haeberle, 1978). Let's look more closely at various aspects of adolescent attitudes and behavior that are involved in self-stimulation, homosexual relationships, and heterosexual relationships.

Self-Stimulation
The most extensive data collected about adolescent sexual behavior are those reported by Alfred Kinsey (1948). A rapid increase in the incidence of masturbation occurs for boys between the ages of thirteen and fifteen. By age fifteen, for example, 82 percent of all boys interviewed had masturbated. Girls tend to begin masturbating later, and do not do so as often as boys. For example, by the age of fifteen, only 25 percent of all girls have masturbated to orgasm. Another investigation (Hass, 1979) also reveals that masturbation is very common among adolescents. For example, among sixteen- to nineteen-year-olds more than two-thirds of the boys and half of the girls masturbate once or more a week. Sexually active adolescents tend to masturbate more than those who are less sexually active. However, boys involved in sexual relationships tend not to masturbate as much, whereas the opposite is true for girls— apparently to release sexual tensions that result from failure to achieve orgasm.

Homosexuality
There are three consistent findings in regard to homosexuality during adolescence (Dreyer, 1982). First, homosexual contacts occur more frequently before the age of fifteen and involve boys more than girls (Hass, 1979).

Second, acceptance of homosexuality is widespread. Nearly 70 percent of sixteen- to nineteen-year-olds accept sexual relationships between two girls and only slightly fewer adolescents accept such contacts between boys. As a rule, boys accept female homosexuality more than male homosexuality, whereas girls accept both about equally (Hass, 1979). Third, in spite of liberal attitudes about homosexuality, less than 15 percent of boys and 10 percent of girls report that they have ever had even one homosexual contact during adolescence. Only 3 percent of the boys and 2 percent of the girls report participating in an ongoing homosexual relationship (Chilman, 1979; Hass, 1979). Although many other types of sexual behavior in adolescence seem to have increased during recent years, participation in homosexual relationships appears to have remained the same or possibly even declined (Chilman, 1979).

Heterosexual Attitudes and Behavior
Attitudes about sexual behavior have changed toward greater acceptance of sexual expression for adolescent males and females. However, one clear finding is that sexual behavior by adolescents is linked to the degree of personal involvement they have with the other individual (see table 14.1). Similarly, although the overwhelming majority of adolescents approve of premarital sexual intercourse, such approval is not indiscriminate. The new norm suggests that sex is acceptable within the boundary of a loving and affectionate relationship. By contrast, promiscuity, exploitation, and unprotected sexual intercourse are perceived as unacceptable and are not usually sanctioned by adolescents (Dreyer, 1982).

From the middle to the end of the adolescent years, heterosexual behavior increases rapidly. Boys and girls, becoming young men and young women, are not as likely to be satisfied with petting as they were earlier. Instead, they are more inclined to engage in sexual intercourse. In one investigation of when adolescents first had sexual intercourse, the majority reported that they had experienced sexual intercourse by the time they were eighteen years of age (see table 14.2). In another investigation (Sorensen, 1973), 44 percent of the boys and 30 percent of the girls reported having had sexual intercourse prior to age sixteen.

Table 14.1
Approval of Petting and Full Sexual Relations by Stage of Relationship

	Adults		Students	
	Percent		Percent	
	For men	For women	For men	For women
Petting:				
When engaged	60.8	56.1	85.0	81.8
In love	59.4	52.6	80.4	75.2
Strong affection	54.3	45.6	67.0	56.7
No affection	28.6	20.3	34.3	18.0
Full Sex Relations:				
When engaged	19.5	16.9	52.2	44.0
In love	17.6	14.2	47.6	38.7
Strong affection	16.3	12.5	36.9	27.2
No affection	11.9	7.4	20.8	10.8
N	1390	1411	811	806

Source: Data from Reiss, I. *The social contexts of sexual permissiveness.* New York: Holt, Rinehart & Winston, 1967.

Table 14.2
Age at First Intercourse By Age Group

	Females		Males	
Age Group	15–16	17–18	15–16	17–18
Age of first intercourse				
13	7	3	18	7
16	31	41	43	42

Hass, 1979—nonrandom sample of 625 teenagers, 15 to 19 years old (307 boys, 318 girls); 90% from high schools in southern California, 10% from schools in Michigan, New York, New Jersey, and Texas; 12% minority (black, Hispanic, Asian-American); no data reported as to socioeconomic level of subjects. Self-administered paper and pencil questionnaires; 10% of subjects interviewed by same sex interviewer. Data reported as percentages responding to various statements and categories.

Source: Adapted from Chilman, C. S. *Adolescent sexuality in a changing American society. Social and psychological perspectives.* Washington, D.C.: Public Health Service, National Institute of Public Health, 1979.

Overall, it appears that adolescents are engaging in more different forms of sexual behavior and at younger ages than in the past. Although boys still usually start practicing sexual behavior at an earlier age than girls do, differences between male and female sexual practices are narrowing. Further, adolescents' knowledge about contraception is terribly inadequate as indicated by the fact that whereas the birthrate among women over twenty has been declining since 1960, the birthrate among young teenagers, particularly girls thirteen to fifteen years of age, has increased substantially.

One of the most intriguing aspects of sexuality in adolescence is the degree to which attitudes about sexual matters correspond to actual sexual behavior. Currently, there is a trend for attitudinal acceptance of sex to exceed participation in sexual activity. For example, in one investigation of fifteen- to nineteen-year-olds, (Hass, 1979), 95 percent of the boys and 83 percent of the girls approved of genital touching, whereas only 55 percent of the boys and 43 percent of the girls had experienced this kind of heavy petting. The same trend was true for oral sex; 90 percent of the boys and 70 percent of the girls approved of it, but only about one-third had actually engaged in oral sex.

Sex Education
Hershel Thornburg has been surveying adolescents' sources of sex information for a number of years (e.g., Thornburg, 1968, 1981). He recently asked all 1152 students in a midwestern high school where they first learned about a number of aspects of sex, including sexually transmitted diseases, seminal emissions, prostitution, petting, menstruation, masturbation, intercourse, homosexuality, ejaculation, contraception,

During adolescence sexual interests increase dramatically.

"That's not the way we learned it in Sex Ed, Dad. Mrs. Thompson said that . . ."

The Family Circus. Reprinted courtesy the Register and Tribune Syndicate, Inc.

conception, and abortion. Students were asked which of the following sources they got their information from: mother, father, peers, literature (including media), school, physician, minister, experience. As in other investigations, peers were the most cited source of information (more than 37 percent of sex information came from peers), followed by literature, mother, and school. Experience was the adolescents' teacher more often than father, physician, and minister. It is important to note that although the school is often thought to be the primary source of sex information for adolescents, in the recent survey by Thornburg (1981) the school was not the main source.

Because sexuality is wrapped up in individual values, it also seems logical to look for sexual guidance from various religious organizations. But religious organizations typically do not reach the adolescents who could benefit the most from instruction (and this is not necessarily because of a lack of effort on the organizations' part).

Although schools may not be the most appropriate or logical alternative, in the long run they may be the most effective and best equipped to handle sex education. Schools reach the greatest number of adolescents

of all ages, and the teachers responsible for sex education are usually knowledgeable in many different aspects of adolescent development, family studies, biological development, and psychology. In application 14.1 you can read about sex education in the schools.

Psychological Adaptation to Changes in Physical Development

A host of psychological characteristics and social consequences accompany changes in the adolescent's physical development. Think once again about your own changing body as you began puberty. Not only did you probably begin to think in different ways about yourself, but important individuals in your life, such as peers and parents, probably began acting differently toward you as well. Maybe you were proud of your changing body, even though you may have been perplexed about what was going on. Or maybe you felt embarrassed about the changes that were taking place and experienced a lot of anxiety. Perhaps you looked in the mirror on a daily or sometimes even on an hourly basis to see if you were maturing physically and to see if you could detect anything different about your changing body.

Sex Education in the Schools

Clearly, whether sex education should be a part of the curriculum of secondary schools has been one of the most heated issues in education in recent years. In particular, the anti-sex education movement began to heat up in the late 1960s. Although the issue has not been settled, the controversy has declined in recent years. One point is clear, however: Adolescents do not get a very large percentage of their sex education from schools. In Thornburg's surveys, adolescents consistently were getting about 16 percent of their sex information from schools.

What is the nature of sex education in the schools? One recent survey of ninety-nine secondary schools in the United States provides information about what is being taught in sex education classes at the ninth, tenth, eleventh, and twelfth grades (Newton, 1982). As shown in the table, sex education is most likely to be taught in the tenth grade. And sex education programs are much more likely to appear in grades nine through twelve than grades seven and eight. The emphasis in sex education classes is on biological topics such as anatomy and physiology, reproduction, pregnancy and childbirth, and venereal disease. These topics are twice as likely to be discussed as social topics like homosexuality, variations in sexuality, and prostitution. However, an exception to this rule focuses on topics such as love, marriage, and sex roles, all of which receive relatively high attention in grades nine through twelve.

Sex education programs vary extensively from school to school. Many schools have no sex education programs, for example. A sex education program can refer to a well-developed, full semester course on human sexuality or a two-week unit on anatomy and physiology in a biology course. Indeed, biology at the tenth grade level is the most likely place adolescents will be exposed to at least a small dose of sex education.

Another concern for a quality sex education program is the teacher—the qualifications and talents of the person who handles the curriculum. Most instructors have majored in biology, health education, home economics, or physical education. Few have majored in human sexuality per se (Newton, 1982). The teacher doesn't have to have a Ph.D. in human sexuality to impart adequate and useful information about sexual matters to adolescents, but he or she should be reasonably well trained and knowledgeable about sexuality. Among other characteristics that may help the sex education instructor in secondary schools is the willingness to admit when he or she doesn't know an answer and to look things up in reference books for or with the students. The sex education teacher also should be skilled in handling adolescent emotions. In a class of twenty to thirty junior high school students, at least half of them will probably be embarrassed or uncomfortable discussing sex-related topics. The teacher's ability to make the students feel at ease in discussing sexual matters can be a key ingredient in helping adolescents learn about sexuality in a competent and healthy manner.

Inset Table
Topics and Grade Levels for Most Popular Topics in Sex Education Programs

Topic/Grade Level	Number of Cases*
Anatomy and Physiology (10)	41/20 = 61
Reproduction (10)	32/26 = 58
Venereal Disease (10)	28/28 = 56
Pregnancy and Childbirth (10)	36/19 = 55
Contraception (10)	13/36 = 49
Sex Roles (10)	22/25 = 47
Anatomy and Physiology (9)	30/16 = 46
Pregnancy and Childbirth (12)	32/14 = 46
Love (10)	23/33 = 46
Abortion (12)	14/30 = 44
Reproduction (9)	20/25 = 45
Sex Roles (12)	27/17 = 44
Love (12)	26/18 = 44

Topics mentioned by more than 40 respondents: Sexual Intercourse (10); Anatomy and Physiology (11); Marriage and Nonmarriage (11 and 12); Venereal Disease (10, 11, 12); Reproduction (12); Contraception (12); and Pregnancy and Childbirth (9).

*Shown are the numbers giving "heavy"/"moderate" emphasis and then total of these two. That is, for anatomy and physiology, grade 10, 41 respondents report giving "heavy" emphasis to this topic, and 20 a "moderate" emphasis, for a total of 61 respondents on this topic and grade level.

Source: Newton, 1982.

Early maturation has more consistent positive effects for boys than for girls.

Possibly you were no longer treated as the "little boy" or the "little girl" and instead were perceived by peers in terms of your sexual attractiveness. Perhaps your parents no longer perceived you as someone they could sit in bed and watch television with or as someone who should be kissed good night. One of the major ways in which psychological aspects of pubertal change have been investigated is to study adolescents who are early or late maturers.

Social and Psychological Consequences of Early and Late Maturation
The majority of research that has addressed the issue of early and late maturation in adolescence has been collected as part of a longitudinal growth study at the University of California.

In most instances, early or late maturation has a significant influence on the personality and social behavior of adolescents (Mussen & Jones, 1958). The upshot of the California investigations concerning early and late maturation is that boys who mature early in adolescence (as measured by their skeletal growth) perceive themselves more positively and are more successful in peer relations than their late-maturing counterparts. Both peers and adults rated the early-maturing

boys as physically more attractive, more composed, and more socially sophisticated than the late-maturing boys. Most of these investigations focused on the self-perceptions of boys in early and middle adolescence (about twelve to seventeen years of age). Also, the Berkeley longitudinal study found that some of the psychological characteristics associated with early maturation (such as dominance, independence, and self-control) were still apparent even when the individuals were in their thirties (Jones & Mussen, 1958).

A few years ago another longitudinal investigation of early and late maturation was conducted (Blyth, Bulcroft, & Simmons, 1981). Rather than skeletal development, the presence or absence of menstruation and relative onset of menses were used to classify girls as early, middle, and late maturers. For boys, the classification was made on the basis of the peak rate of height growth. More than 450 individuals were followed for five years beginning in the sixth grade and continuing through the tenth grade in Milwaukee, Wisconsin, from 1974 to 1979. Students were individually interviewed, and achievement test scores and grade-point averages were obtained.

"Notice anything different about my face?"
"Yeah. Your acne stands out more."

Illustration by Bil Keane from *Just Wait 'Till You Have Children of Your Own.* Copyright © 1971 by Erma Bombeck and Bil Keane. Reprinted by permission of Doubleday & Company, Inc.

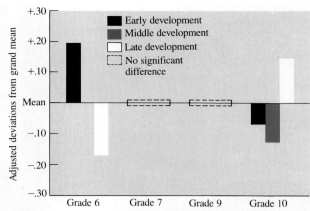

Figure 14.5 Pubertal development and satisfaction with figure.
(*Source:* Blyth, D. A. Bulcroft, R. & Simmons, R. G. *The impact of puberty on adolescents: A logitudinal study.* Paper presented at the American Psychological Association meeting. Los Angeles, August, 1981.)

Somewhat surprisingly, there were fewer significant relationships between pubertal development and psychological and social development than was anticipated. However, the significant findings that did occur reveal some interesting patterns, particularly those pertaining to body image, which we discuss next.

The Body Images of Early and Late Maturing Adolescent Girls   One of the most important tasks of adolescence is to incorporate dramatic physical changes into a positive body image. Students in the Milwaukee study were asked to report how satisfied they were with their height, weight, and figure development (if a girl) or muscular development (if a boy). Early maturers were less satisfied with their bodies than were later maturers. And early maturers were less satisfied with their weight at all grade levels. When actual weight was controlled, the significant difference between early and late maturers disappeared, suggesting that weight was the culprit, not early maturation.

With regard to the girls' satisfaction with their figures, a complex pattern developed (see figure 14.5). More developed, menstruating girls showed greater satisfaction with their figures in the sixth grade than did late maturing girls. But by the ninth and tenth grades, the pattern was reversed. When all girls were developed, it was the late maturers who were the most satisfied with their figures. So by the ninth and tenth

grades early maturers were less satisfied with their height, weight, and figures than were late maturers. One reason for this pattern of findings is that by the ninth and tenth grades early maturers usually are shorter and stockier and late maturers are often taller and thinner. Possibly the late maturing female in the ninth and tenth grades more closely approximates the American ideal of feminine beauty—tall and with a slim figure.

In summary, in the recent longitudinal investigation by Dale Blyth and his colleagues, early maturation for girls seemed to have mixed effects, whereas early maturation for boys seemed to have an overall positive effect. However, it is important to examine the particular dimension of psychological and social development in question. For example, in this investigation, although early maturation seemed to be disadvantageous for a girl's body image, school performance, and school behavior, it appeared to be an advantage in opposite-sex relationships and independence. Nonetheless, when we piece together the many findings of the California longitudinal study and the Milwaukee project, early maturation favors boys but has mixed blessings for girls.

This concludes our discussion of physical development. In the next section, we look at another aspect of adolescent development that has close ties to physical development, the cognitive changes that unfold as individuals grow from the end of childhood to adulthood.

Cognitive Development

In this section we look more closely at Piaget's stage of formal operational thought and describe the important emerging field of social cognition.

Formal Operational Thought

The formal operational stage comes into play between the ages of eleven and fourteen. By the time the child reaches adolescence, he or she has reached the most advanced stage of thinking possible. Some may argue that reaching adulthood entails many significant cognitive changes. For Piaget, however, these changes are no more than window dressing. A nuclear physicist may engage in a kind of thinking that cannot be matched by the adolescent, but the adolescent and the nuclear physicist differ only in their familiarity with an academic field of inquiry—in the *content* of thought, not in the operations that are brought to bear upon that content (Piaget, 1970). Most cognitive psychologists now recognize that the onset of adolescence does not necessarily mean that formal operational thought will appear. It even has been demonstrated that significant proportions of college- and middle-aged adults do not use formal operational thought when asked to solve problems (Keating, 1980).

What is formal operational thinking like? Most significantly, it is abstract. The adolescent is no longer limited to actual, concrete experience as an anchor for thought. Instead, he or she may conjure make-believe situations, events that are strictly hypothetical possibilities, or purely abstract propositions and proceed to reason logically with them.

The abstract quality of thought at the formal operational stage is evidenced primarily in the adolescent's verbal problem solving. While the concrete thinker would need to *see* the concrete elements A, B, and C to be able to make the logical inference that if A>B and B>C, then A>C, the formal operational thinker can solve this problem merely through verbal presentation.

On the social plane, one important implication of this theory is that the formal thinker no longer need rely on concrete experiences with people to form complex judgments about them. The formal thinker may make such judgments largely on the basis of verbal description, speculation, or gossip.

The make-believe nature of thought can be seen in the adolescent's ability to propose and work with **contrary-to-fact reasoning.** Suppose, for example, that the adolescent is asked to imagine that the room in which she is sitting suddenly has no walls and to describe what she now sees. The adolescent can easily perform such mental gymnastics (e.g., Elkind, 1976). The important point is that this mental feat involves representing an imaginary event that counters the concrete reality of the moment.

There are many examples that demonstrate how this thought influences the individual in his social sphere. The adolescent for the first time engages in extended speculation about ideal characteristics of people, himself as well as others. Ideals, which are contrary-to-fact representations, often preoccupy the adolescent. He may become impatient with his inability to make reality conform to these newfound ideals, and he is perplexed over which of the many available ideal selves to adopt.

Adolescents' ability to work with conjured-up possibilities is easily seen in the way they approach problem solving. The style of problem solving used has often been referred to as **deductive hypothesis testing.** Consider a modification of the familiar game Twenty Questions that Jerome Bruner (1966) and his associates used in extensive research with children of varying ages. The person is shown a set of forty-two colorful pictures displayed in a rectangular array (six rows of seven pictures each) and is asked to determine which picture the experimenter has in mind (that is, which is "correct"). The person is allowed to ask only questions to which the experimenter can reply yes or no. The object of the game is to select the correct picture by asking as few questions as possible. The person who is a deductive hypothesis tester formulates a plan to propose and test a series of hypotheses, each of which narrows the field of choices considerably. The most effective plan consists in a "halving" strategy. (*Q:* Is it in the right half of the array? *A:* No. *Q:* Okay; is it in the top half? And so on.) Used correctly, the halving strategy guarantees the questioner the correct solution in seven questions or less, no matter where the correct picture is located in the array. Even if he or she is using a less elegant strategy than the optimal "halving" one, the deductive hypothesis tester understands that when the experimenter answers no to one of his or her guesses, several possibilities are immediately eliminated.

By contrast, the concrete thinker may persist with questions that continue to test some of the same possibilities that previous questions should have eliminated. For example, the child may have asked whether the correct picture was in row 1 and received the answer no but later asks whether the correct picture is *x*, which is in row 1.

Thus, the formal operational thinker tests his or her hypotheses with judiciously chosen questions and tests. Often a single question or test will help him or her to eliminate an untenable hypothesis. By contrast, the concrete thinker often fails to understand the relation between a hypothesis and a well-chosen test of

Adolescents spend a lot of time monitoring their social world.

it—stubbornly clinging to the idea despite clear, logical disconfirmation of it. The social implications of this cognitive difference are quite instructive and amusing.

When adolescents meet people, their abstract hypotheses about what others are like are more amenable to practical verification based upon the actions and attitudes the people convey. An adolescent boy's belief in the goodness and beauty of a female may be quickly dispelled if he observes her being nasty to a friend. A concrete thinker would be less open to disenchantment from such practical experience.

Finally, we consider one last property of formal thinking, the ability of the adolescent to appreciate metaphorical meaning. A metaphor is a contrast or implied comparison between two ideas that is conveyed by the abstract meanings contained in the words used to make the comparison. A person's faith and a piece of glass may be alike in that both can be shattered easily. A runner's performance and a politician's speech may be alike in that both are predictable. Concrete thinkers find it difficult to understand such metaphorical relations. Consequently, many elementary school children are puzzled by the meanings of parables and fables (Elkind, 1976).

The social implication of the use of metaphor is obvious. Metaphor greatly extends the network of symbols and meaning that the adolescent is able to use in thinking about people. It makes possible a host of abstract comparisons between people and nonliving things, people and animals, and people and plants, among others. Metaphorical thinking has received a great deal of attention in recent years.

Individual Variation in Adolescent Cognitive Development

For the most part, Piaget emphasizes universal and consistent patterns of formal operational thought. Piaget's theory does not adequately account for the unique, individual differences that characterize the cognitive development of adolescents. These differences have been documented in a far-ranging set of studies, meaning that certain modifications in Piaget's theory of formal operational thought need to be pursued (Neimark, 1982). The studies suggest that formal operational thought does develop during early adolescence for many boys and girls but that this stage of thinking is far from pervasive. Instead, early adolescence is more likely to be characterized by a consolidation of concrete operational thought (Hill, 1983).

Piaget and Adolescent Education

When Piaget's ideas have been applied to adolescent education, the focus has been on the single underlying theme that many adolescents are still concrete thinkers and are not as yet formal operational thinkers (see chapters 2 and 11 for a discussion of concrete operational thought). Therefore, the curricula many adolescents are exposed to may be too complex and abstract for them to comprehend. Many adolescents are likely to benefit from instruction based on concrete explanations of different phenomena.

Consider a curriculum area that virtually every adolescent is exposed to during the junior high and high school years—biology. Most biology courses (or at least the majority of the units taught in each of them) are taught in a reasonably formal, straight-lecture format. Classifications of animals and plants are memorized through exposure to the teacher's lectures and the text. Some educational experts believe that such a procedure is not a good approach to teaching the scientific method or to promoting learning among many adolescents who have not yet reached the stage of formal operational thought. Instead, they believe that improved learning will occur if the adolescents observe and collect organisms from their natural habitats and then relate them to various subjects covered in the course. Through this method, often referred to as **discovery learning,** the adolescent is forced to restructure his or her concrete way of thinking about the world and to logically categorize events and objects in more formal logical ways (Renner & Stafford, 1972).

Some researchers have compared biology students who learn about animals and plants in this manner with those who learn in the more traditional lecture-text format (e.g., Lawson & Wollman, 1975). By participating in laboratory experiments, collecting data, discussing ideas, and testing out hypotheses, the discovery-learning students far outdistanced their counterparts who learned in more traditional ways.

Recently, Piaget's theory has even provided the conceptual framework for a revision of curriculum at the university level. At the University of Nebraska at Lincoln, a Piagetian-based program labeled ADAPT has been developed for freshman students taking courses in economics, math, history, physics, anthropology, and writing. The basic assumption underlying the program is that many student failures are due to the fact that many younger college students still function at the concrete level of thinking, while the curriculum they are exposed to is geared to formal operational thinking. The freshmen are introduced to a learning cycle in which basic information about the discipline is given to the students to whet their appetites for more information and increase their motivation to pursue solutions to problems. In this way, it is hoped that the students will develop, on their own, hypotheses and ideas about the subject matter—hypotheses and ideas that normally are presented by a lecturer.

Before we leave Piaget's ideas about adolescent thought we evaluate the application of his views to adolescent education. Interestingly, as suggested in application 14.2, the most frequent applications have involved the belief that the majority of adolescents are concrete rather than formal operational thinkers.

Social Cognition

Cognitive developmental theorists have begun to study how children and adolescents reason about social matters rather than confining their study to impersonal objects like numbers, space, and time. The subdiscipline of cognitive developmental theory devoted to social reasoning is called **social cognition.** How do children and adolescents conceptualize and reason about their social world—the people they watch, the relationships between people, and the groups in which they participate? What are the developmental changes in such concepts and reasoning? And how is social cognitive

functioning linked with social behavior? These are some of the central questions of social cognition (Shantz, 1983).

Let's look at an example of how social cognition might work during adolescence. Bob, a sixteen-year-old, feels that he does not know as much as he wants or needs to know about Sally, another sixteen-year-old; he also wants and needs to know more about Sally's relationship with Brian, a seventeen-year-old. Let's also assume that Bob wants to know more about the groups that Sally belongs to—her student council friends, the clique she belongs to, and so forth. Bob thinks about these things and decides that he is not sure how close he is to understanding them. He decides to find out how close he is to his goals of discovering this information by taking some appropriate feedback-producing action. What he finds out by taking that action will generate information about his social cognitive progress and how difficult his social cognitive task is. Notice that the immediate aim of this feedback-producing action is not to make progress toward the main goal but to monitor that progress.

Adolescents engage in a number of cognitive monitorings on a daily basis. A student may meet someone new and make a quick appraisal to obtain a preview of how hard it is going to be to learn whatever she thinks she needs to learn about the person. Another adolescent may check incoming impressions about an organization (school, club, gang) to determine if they are consistent with his or her impressions of the school, club, or gang. Yet another adolescent may question someone or paraphrase what she has just said about her feelings to ensure that she has understood that person correctly.

Now that you have been introduced to an overview of the field of social cognition and read about one of its latest developments—cognitive monitoring of social matters—let's look in a more detailed way at another area that has given attention to this field of inquiry, that of egocentrism.

Adolescent Egocentrism
David Elkind (1978) believes that the onset of formal operational thought in adolescence brings with it a unique sort of egocentrism. In this type of egocentric thought, the adolescent acts as if others are as preoccupied with his behavior, feelings, and thoughts as he himself is (self-consciousness). Elkind believes that such **adolescent egocentrism** accounts for much of the boorishness and preoccupation with the body that young adolescents seem to have. Adolescent egocentrism often leads to more preoccupation with the adolescent's own body than the attention given to it by others. Most early adolescents are not aware of such egocentrism. Some individuals with physical deformities may seem to be happy and well adjusted as children, but upon entering adolescence, they may begin to show the first signs of depression about their handicap, possibly because they are beginning to reflect about what others are thinking about them.

There are also other possible connections of adolescent characteristics to adolescent egocentrism (Elkind, 1978). Attention-getting behavior may reflect egocentrism—that is, the desire to be noticed, visible, and "on stage." Short-lived romantic affairs, conformity to the influence of the peer group, and even friendships may serve an egocentric need. Egocentric adolescents often feel that others are as concerned, critical, and admiring of them as they themselves are. As a result, many adolescents construct an imaginary audience. An adolescent boy may think that others are aware of the small spot or wrinkle in his trousers, or even that he has masturbated. An adolescent girl, walking into a restaurant, may think that all eyes are riveted on the one hair that is out of place or the one small blemish on her face.

This concludes our discussion of social cognition. Note how different strands—in this case cognitive and social—have been woven together to provide a more complete picture of development.

Moving from this chapter on physical and cognitive development in adolescence, in the next chapter we explore a number of important aspects of social development in adolescence, focusing heavily on families and peers. We also will discuss two important aspects of the lives of many adolescents that have close ties to cognitive development—school and work.

Summary

It was not until the turn of the century that the scientific study of the period now known as adolescence began. Adolescents in different periods of time have been characterized by certain labels, such as the "rebellious" adolescents of the late 1960s and early 1970s. However, it is easy to fall into the trap of stereotyping the adolescents of any generation on the basis of media portrayal.

Physical development during the period known as adolescence is distinct from physical development during other periods. The most important physical changes in the adolescent are increased height and weight and the maturation of sexual characteristics. These facets of development are involved in the growth spurt at the onset of adolescence, which begins, on the average, at about ten or eleven years of age in girls and a year or two later in boys.

Puberty is a shorter time period than adolescence, corresponding more closely with the phase we call early adolescence than with late adolescence. Puberty is not a single, sudden event, but a complex set of events that actually begins at conception. Determining when puberty begins and ends has not been an easy task, although we can usually detect when an individual is in puberty. There are remarkable normal variations in the onset of puberty; some boys will end puberty before others begin it, and a girl's menarche may occur as early as ten or as late as fifteen and one-half years of age.

Not only does puberty consist of physical changes in sexual maturation but of the accompanying changes in sexual attitudes and behavior as well. Masturbation is the most frequent sexual outlet for adolescents. Although adolescents have accepting attitudes toward homosexuality, a very small percentage have ever engaged in homosexual behavior. Every indication is that adolescents now are engaging in sexual intercourse more frequently and at earlier ages than in the past. By the end of adolescence, a majority of individuals have had sexual intercourse. However, most adolescents want sexual intercourse to happen in the context of a loving, caring relationship. Peers are the most frequent source of sex education. Little sex education comes from parents, and most school systems don't do a very thorough job of sex education.

Longitudinal studies of early and late maturation suggest that early maturation is likely to benefit boys but provide mixed possibilities for girls. In particular, early maturation seems to be disadvantageous for a girl's body image, school performance, and school behavior, although it seems to have positive consequences for relationships with boys and for independence. Preoccupation with a changing body seems to be pervasive in adolescence.

The ideas of Jean Piaget form the cornerstone for modern work in adolescent cognitive development. His theory proposes a series of stages of development from infancy through adolescence. Most adolescents are usually in the stage of concrete operations or formal operations.

Formal operational thought differs from concrete operational thought in that it is more abstract and more organized. The formal operational thinker can reason with contrary-to-fact realities and engages in scientific-like thinking, deductive hypothesis testing, and the use of metaphor. However, most cognitive developmentalists believe that the onset of adolescence does not signal the appearance of full-blown formal operational thought. One alternative view emphasizes that the dominant path of adolescent thought is formal operational in nature but that other routes are possible as well. The majority of applications of Piaget's ideas to adolescent education have been based on the belief that most adolescents are concrete operational thinkers.

Piaget's theory has stimulated a great deal of current interest in extending thought to social matters as well as nonsocial matters; this part of cognitive development is called social cognition. Social cognition focuses on how individuals reason about their social world—about the people they watch, relationships between people, and the groups in which they participate. John Flavell believes that an important aspect of social cognition is cognitive monitoring, a process that enables adolescents to make more logical and detailed sense of their social world than children do. At the same time, many adolescents develop a peculiar sort of egocentrism, in which they show a strong preoccupation with their bodies and see themselves as actors who are "on stage" and others as their audience.

Key Terms

adolescent egocentrism

amenorrheic

contrary-to-fact reasoning

deductive hypothesis testing

discovery learning

menarche

puberty

social cognition

stereotypes

sturm und drang

Review Questions

1. Describe the beginning of the scientific study of adolescence.
2. Discuss why it is easy to stereotype adolescents.
3. Describe the components and sequencing of the adolescent growth spurt, first for boys and then for girls.
4. How does sexual maturation influence sexual attitudes and behavior?
5. What is the nature of sex education?
6. How do scientists study early versus late maturation during adolescence? What are the conclusions reached from research on this important topic?
7. Outline Piaget's ideas on formal operational thought.
8. Discuss the application of Piaget's ideas to adolescent education.
9. What is social cognition? Describe John Flavell's ideas about cognitive monitoring of social matters.
10. What do we know about egocentrism in adolescence?

Further Readings

Brooks-Gunn, J., & Petersen, A. C. (eds.). *Girls at puberty: Biological and psychological perspectives.* New York: Plenum, 1982.
A series of articles by leading scholars that represent up-to-date information about how females experience puberty. Reading level moderately difficult.

Elkind, D. *Child development and education.* New York: Oxford University Press, 1976.
An excellent, easy-to-read introduction to the implications of Piaget's ideas for educators. Practical examples are given for approaching classroom teaching from the Piagetian perspective.

Hyde, J. S. *Understanding human sexuality.* New York: McGraw-Hill, 1979.
A scholarly but entertaining look at the physical aspects of sexual development, including much material focused on understanding our sexuality. Easy to read.

Netter, F. H. *Reproductive system. The Ciba Collection of Medical Illustrations* (vol. 2). Summit, N.J.: Ciba, 1965.
A book filled with what is generally considered the best set of illustrations on sexual anatomy available.

Ross, D. G. *Stanley Hall: The psychologist as prophet.* Chicago: University of Chicago Press, 1972.
An intriguing biographical sketch of the father of adolescent psychology, G. Stanley Hall. Reasonably easy to read.

Shantz, C. U. *Social cognition.* In J. H. Flavell & E. M. Markman (eds.), *Carmichael's manual of child psychology,* 4th ed. New York: John Wiley, 1983.
Carolyn Shantz, one of the pioneers of research on contemporary issues in social cognition, provides a very detailed and critical appraisal of information about social-cognitive development. Moderately difficult reading level.

15 Social Development

Imagine . . . what happens when parental and peer pressures are at odds

Parents and **peers** are the two most important social agents that influence children and adolescents. Although toddlers, and even infants, engage in peer relations more today than in the past, primarily because of their attendance at day-care centers, conflict between the influence of parents and peers does not surface during young childhood.

When children enter elementary school, they spend more and more time with peers, and by the seventh grade, boys and girls characteristically spend as much, or more, time interacting with peers as with their parents. In an investigation of 766 students in the sixth grade, it was found that children spent more than twice as much time over the course of a weekend with peers as with parents (Condry, Simon, & Bronfenbrenner, 1968).

Because they spend more time with peers, do children conform more to the ideas and behaviors of their peers than to those advocated by parents? There are several ways to look at peer conformity. First, the influences that are exerted by parents and peers may be contradictory, and children may choose to conform to the perspectives of those they are with the most; or they may simply choose to rebel against parental authority. Second, children may become more responsible for themselves, seeing themselves as more independent of their parents and capable of making their own decisions. A third possibility is that a combination of both these perspectives may come into play.

In an effort to explore the developmental patterns of parental and peer conformity, Thomas Berndt (1978) studied 273 third-through-twelfth-grade students. Hypothetical dilemmas were presented to the students, requiring them to make choices about conformity with friends on prosocial and antisocial behavior and conformity with parents on neutral and prosocial behaviors. For example, one prosocial item questioned whether students relied on their parents' advice in such situations as deciding about helping at the library or instructing another child to swim. An antisocial question asked a boy what he would do if one of his peers wanted him to help steal some candy. A neutral question asked a girl if she would follow peer suggestions to engage in an activity she wasn't interested in—for example, going to a movie she didn't want to see.

Some interesting developmental patterns were found in this investigation. In the third grade, parent and peer influences often directly contradicted each other. Because parent conformity is much greater for third-grade children, children of this age are probably still closely tied to and dependent on their parents. However by the sixth grade, parent and peer influences were found to be no longer in direct opposition. Peer conformity had increased, but parent and peer influences were operating in different situations—parents had more impact in some situations, whereas peers had more clout in others. For example, it was found that parents were more influential in a discussion of political parties but peers seemed to have more say when sexual behavior and attitudes were at issue (Hyman, 1959; Vandiver, 1972).

By the ninth grade, parent and peer influences were once again in strong opposition to one another, probably because the increased conformity of **adolescents** to the social behavior of peers is much stronger at this grade level than at any other. At this time adolescent adoption of antisocial standards endorsed by the peer group inevitably leads to conflict between adolescents and parents. The adolescent's attempt to gain independence meets with more parental opposition around the

ninth grade than at any other time (Douvan & Adelson, 1966; Kandel & Lesser, 1969). As an indication of the importance of peers, consider the comments of one youth:

I feel a lot of pressure from my friends to smoke and steal and things like that. My parents do not allow me to smoke, but my best friends are really pushing me to do it. They call me a pansy and a momma's boy if I don't. I really don't like the idea of smoking, but my good friend Steve told me in front of some of our friends, "Kevin, you are an idiot and a chicken all wrapped up in one little body." I couldn't stand it any more, so I smoked with them. I was coughing and humped over, but I still said, "This is really fun—yeah, I like it." I felt like I was part of the group.

Youths engage in all sorts of negative conformity behavior. They may go places in cars with people they are afraid of, use vulgar language, steal, vandalize, and make fun of their parents and teachers. But many conformity behaviors are also positive. The majority of youth go to school and do not cause trouble for teachers; they may belong to clubs or groups that have pro-social functions; and they may belong to cliques that engage in constructive rather than destructive behaviors.

A stereotypical view of parent-child relationships suggests that parent-peer opposition continues into the late high school and college years. But Berndt (1978) found that adolescent conformity to antisocial, peer-endorsed behavior decreases in the late high school years, and greater agreement between parents and peers begins to occur in some areas. In addition, by the eleventh and twelfth grades, students show signs of developing a decision-making style more independent of peer and parent influence.

Introduction

This chapter focuses on social development during adolescence. As suggested by the Imagine section, the worlds of parents and peers are important social systems in the adolescent's development. Adolescents do not just move away from and diametrically oppose parental dictates in a single step. Instead, as we will discover in this chapter, the development of autonomy and social maturity depends on the complex interaction of the youth's maturing cognitive skills and ongoing relationships with both parents and peers. We discuss a number of aspects of family and peer influences on the adolescent and explore the impact of schools and work on the adolescent.

Family

Although peer relationships become increasingly important during adolescence, family relationships are also still central to understanding the adolescent's development. In this section, we will explore the adolescent's push for independence from parents, the extent to which conflict characterizes parent-adolescent relationships, and how a change in family structure—divorce—influences the adolescent's development. Then we will examine the circumstances when adolescents become parents themselves.

Adolescent Autonomy

The adolescent's quest for autonomy and a sense of responsibility creates puzzlement and conflict for many parents. Parents begin to see their teenager slipping away from their grasp. Often the urge is to take stronger control as the adolescent seeks autonomy and responsibility for himself or herself. Heated emotional exchanges may ensue, with either side calling names, making threats, and doing whatever seems necessary to gain control. Often, parents are frustrated because they expected their teenager to heed their advice, to want to spend time with his or her family, and to grow up to do what is right. To be sure, they anticipated that their teenager would have some difficulty adjusting to the changes adolescence brings, but few parents are able to accurately imagine and predict just how strong the adolescent's desire will be to be with peers, and how much the adolescent will want to show that it is he or she, not they, who is responsible for his or her success or failure.

Adolescents do not just simply move from parental influence into a decision-making process all their own. At the same time they are beginning to show signs of independence from parental influence, they rapidly come under more intense peer influence. But it is incorrect to think that adolescent autonomy from parents is synonymous with the adolescent's total conformity to his or her peer culture. Instead, the adolescent's autonomy is influenced by a variety of social agents, the two most important sets being parents and peers.

In one investigation, the continuing influence of parents on adolescents was evident even when the adolescents were also influenced considerably by peers (Brittain, 1963). Adolescents were queried about whether they are influenced more by their peers or their parents in a variety of contexts, such as taking different classes at school, selecting different styles of clothing, or choosing to decline or accept a part-time job offer. As you might anticipate, in some situations the adolescents chose to adhere to the wishes of their friends while in other contexts they chose to rely on their parents' advice. For example, when decisions involved basic values and vocation orientations, they were more likely to listen to their parents; but when peer activities were involved, they were more likely to accede to the influence of their friends.

In a cross-cultural study of adolescents and their families, authoritarian parenting was related to a lack of autonomy in adolescents (Kandel & Lesser, 1969). The structure of the average American family is much more authoritarian than the structure of a typical family in Denmark. This difference in family structure should indicate that Danish adolescents are generally more autonomous than their American counterparts.

Although there is agreement that an authoritarian family structure restricts the adolescent's development of autonomy, there is not as much consistency in pinpointing the parenting practices that increase autonomy. Sometimes a permissive parenting strategy is associated with the adolescent's becoming more independent (Elder, 1968), whereas at other times a democratic parenting strategy seems more facilitative (Kandel & Lesser, 1969). Although investigators vary in how they define permissive and democratic parenting techniques, in most instances a permissive strategy generally entails little parental involvement and fewer parental standards. By contrast, a democratic strategy usually consists of equal involvement on the part of parents and adolescents, with the parents having the final authority to set limits on their teenagers. When the overall competence and adjustment of the adolescent is evaluated (rather than just autonomy) an even more clearcut advantage can be attributed to democratic over permissive strategies of parenting.

One recent investigation indicated that going away to college may not only benefit the adolescent's development of autonomy but also lead to a more positive relationship with his or her parents (Sullivan & Sullivan, 1980). Two groups of parents and their sons were

Few parents realize how strong their adolescents' push for independence will be.

evaluated; one group of sons left home to board at school, while the other group remained at home and commuted daily to college. The youth were studied both before they finished high school and after they had attended college. The adolescents who boarded at college showed more affection toward their parents, better communication and more satisfaction with them, and greater independence from them.

Adolescence is a period of development in which the individual pushes for autonomy (or the perception that he or she has control over his or her behavior) and gradually develops the ability to take that control. This ability may be acquired through appropriate adult reactions to the adolescent's desire for control. At the onset of adolescence, the average person does not have the knowledge to make appropriate or mature decisions in all areas of life. As he or she pushes for autonomy, the wise adult will relinquish control in areas where the adolescent can make mature decisions and help the adolescent to make reasonable decisions in areas where his or her knowledge is more limited. Gradually, the adolescent will acquire the ability to make mature decisions on his or her own.

Parent-Adolescent Conflict

There appears to be some increase in conflict between parents and adolescents during early adolescence, although the degree of this conflict often is not as severe

"A SCARF? Nobody wears a SCARF!"

"Mom, have you seen my scarf?"

Illustration by Bil Keane from *Just Wait 'Till You Have Children of Your Own.* Copyright © 1971 by Erma Bombeck and Bil Keane. Reprinted by permission of Doubleday & Company, Inc.

Illustration by Bil Keane from *Just Wait 'Till You Have Children of Your Own.* Copyright © 1971 by Erma Bombeck and Bil Keane. Reprinted by permission of Doubleday & Company, Inc.

A moderate amount of parent-adolescent conflict may help the adolescent develop independence and a sense of identity.

as many parents expect it to be and not as intense and pervasive as the media often picture it. Many different reasons have been given as to why there is an increase in parent-adolescent conflict during early adolescence; these ideas include biological changes in levels of aggression, the appearance of adult sexuality, the push for independence, and the quest for identity. Other explanations focus on the difficulties parents may have as they enter mid-life and the mother's unwillingness to let her adolescent loose from the family circle. Still other explanations emphasize the disequilibrium that erupts in the family social system with the onset of adolescence, an upheaval that replaces the relatively smoothly functioning family system that existed during childhood.

In reviewing the existing research on parent-adolescent conflict, Raymond Montemayor (1982a) concluded that conflict increases during **early adolescence,** is reasonably stable during **middle adolescence,** and declines in **late adolescence,** when the adolescent moves away from home.

Most arguments between parents and their adolescents focus on normal, everyday goings on, such as schoolwork, social life, peers, home chores, disobedience, sibling fights, and personal hygiene (Montemayor, 1982b). Although many of these conflicts are a result of the adolescent's push for independence, they often are also a product of parents' continuing efforts to teach their offspring to delay gratification and conform to a set of societal and family rules and regulations.

There seems to be an increasing consensus that parent-adolescent conflict does not reach the proportions suggested by G. Stanley Hall's concept of storm and stress. But as Montemayor suggests, it would be a mistake to go too far in the direction of thinking that parent-adolescent conflict does not exist. Indeed, the conflict that seems to characterize parent-adolescent relationships, particularly during early adolescence, is seen by many theorists as an important part of normal development. Indeed, in one recent investigation (Cooper, Grotevant, Moore, & Condon, 1982), adolescent identity exploration was positively related to frequency of expression of disagreement with parents during a family discussion task. Within some normal range, then, conflict with parents may be psychologically healthy for the adolescent's development. A virtually conflict-free relationship may suggest that an adolescent has a fear of separation, exploration, and independence.

There have been a number of suggestions as to how parents should deal with adolescents. In application 15.1 we look at several ideas that may help to keep parent-adolescent conflicts from becoming too intense.

Application 15.1
Between Parent and Teenager *and* Man the Manipulator

In his best-selling book, *Between Parent and Teenager,* Haim Ginott (1969) details a number of common-sense solutions and strategies for coping with the everyday problems of adolescents. Ginott, in the humanistic tradition, stresses above all else that the key to peaceful co-existence between parents and adolescents is for parents to let go. He says that the adolescent's need is to *not* need parents, and that the parent should resist the need to hold on, even when it seems the most necessary. This attitude, says Ginott, is what parental love for an adolescent is all about.

Relying on catchy phrases like "don't collect thorns" and "don't step on corns," Ginott describes how to let the adolescent become a mature person. Ginott's phrase "don't collect thorns" refers to his belief that parents who constantly detect imperfections in themselves often expect perfection from adolescents. "Don't step on corns" indicates that although all teenagers have a lot of imperfections they are sensitive about (ranging from zits to dimples), they don't need parents to make them acutely aware of such imperfections. Other "Ginottisms" that make sense include the following: "Don't talk in chapters" refers to lecturing rather than sensitive communication; "don't futurize" captures the frequent parental habit of telling the adolescent he or she won't ever amount to anything in the future; "don't violate his privacy" reminds parents that teens need their own territory to develop their sense of autonomy and identity; "don't emulate his language and conduct" warns parents not to use teenage slang—because most teens resent it; and "accept his restlessness and discontent" reminds parents that adolescence is a period of uncertainty and difficulty. Parents can help by not prying into many of their teenagers' affairs.

Other strategies Ginott recommends for parents of adolescents also focus on the parent's struggle to let go of the adolescent. For example, Ginott advises: "Don't push them into popularity battles," "don't push them into early dating," "consider the feelings of the adolescent," and "don't put down their wishes and fantasies." In regard to the first two suggestions, Ginott describes a young girl whose mother constantly prods her to be the most popular girl in school, and another girl whose mother set up a party for boy-girl pairs of twelve-year-olds. This same mother purchased a padded bra for her daughter when the girl was only eleven.

Ginott talks intelligently and simply about many different situations that result in conflict between parents and teenagers—driving, drinking, drugs, sex, and values are but a few of the many topics for which he suggests coping strategies. His descriptions of conversations between adolescents and parents can provide a useful source of information about the real world of parents and teenagers—take a look at some of them and think about whether you would handle them in the way Ginott suggests.

Everett Shostrum, author of *Man, the Manipulator: The Inner Journey from Manipulation to Actualization* (1967), believes that to help teenagers become competent adults, parents have to "let go" when they most want to hold on. Shostrum details conversations between parents and teenagers to illustrate how most parents are not self-actualized in the way they communicate with their teenagers.

Shostrum describes the ways teenagers manipulate their parents and vice versa. Teens say, "You don't love me or you would———," "Everybody else is going," and "I'm going to quit school if you don't———." They play one parent against the other, blackmail, and mope to get what they want from their parents. Parents manipulate by making threats and comparisons: "Bob does better in school than you do," "If you loved me you wouldn't do that," "I'll tell your father when he gets home." Teenagers see interaction with parents as a competition. The game is between the "top dog" (the parent) and the "underdog" (the adolescent). Many encounters with parents end up as minor skirmishes.

Shostrum mentions several specific examples of competitive parent-teen encounters. Steve doesn't want to wear a particular coat his mother tells him he has to wear, and Mary tries to coerce her parents into letting her go out on a date Saturday night. In most cases like these, the parents and the teenagers assume an "I win-you lose" strategy. Shostrum says that the key for parents is to turn such battles into mutual win-win experiences—sharing love and respect for each other's feelings.

The primary goal of the self-actualized parent is to assist rather than inhibit the adolescent in channeling his or her feelings into competent behavior. Parents must recognize that their teenagers are going to try to battle with them and realize that this is the teens' way of trying to adapt to a frustrating world. As part of the actualizing process, parents should create an atmosphere in which teenagers feel comfortable about discussing their true feelings, and in which the parents feel secure about telling the teenager their own feelings as well.

Shostrum goes on to say that teenagers are not as bad as many parents think they are. And, he says, if parents will stay out of the picture, most teenagers will turn into mature, competent young adults. Above all else, Shostrum says, parents must recognize and accept that the teenager is a manipulating individual trying to become a self-actualizing one.

It is possible that intense, prolonged parent-adolescent conflict causes some adolescent problems, but it also is possible that many of these problems had their origins before the onset of adolescence. It is the belief of Albert Bandura and Richard Walters (1959) that most serious adolescent problems can be traced to circumstances that existed before adolescence. Simply because the child is much smaller than the parents, the parents may be able to suppress oppositional behavior. But by adolescence, some individuals have grown as large or larger than their parents—and with increased size and strength comes an increase in indifference to parental dictates. Consider the following case example:

Interviewer What sort of things does your mother object to your doing when you are out with your friends?

Boy She don't know what I do.

Interviewer What about staying out late at night?

Boy She says, "Be home at 11 o'clock." I'll come home at one.

Interviewer How about using the family car?

Boy No. I wrecked mine, and my father wrecked his a month before I wrecked mine, and I can't even get near his. And I got a license and everything. I'm going to hot wire it some night and cut out.

Interviewer How honest do you feel you can be to your mother about where you've been and what things you have done?

Boy I tell her where I've been, period.

Interviewer How about what you've done?

Boy No. I won't tell her what I've done. If we're going to have a beer bust, I'm not going to tell her. I'll tell her I've been to a show or something.

Interviewer How about your father?

Boy I'll tell him where I've been, period.

Thus, although we believe that intense parent-adolescent conflict is not characteristic of the majority of parent-adolescent relationships, a moderate degree of conflict is characteristic, particularly in early adolescence. The moderate degree of conflict actually seems to serve an important developmental function in allowing the young adolescent to increase his or her independence and identity. However, in the minority of parent-adolescent relationships that are characterized by intense, prolonged parent-adolescent conflict, there is a link with adolescent problems and disturbances. One estimate of the percentage of adolescents who experience intense, prolonged conflict with their parents is between 15 and 20 percent (Montemayor, 1982a).

Although this figure represents a minority of adolescents and their parents, it suggests that between four and five million American families are involved in serious, stressful parent-adolescent conflict.

Effects of Divorce on Adolescents

An increasing number of studies have focused on the effects of divorce on adolescents (e.g., Adams, 1982; Hetherington, 1972; Parish & Taylor, 1978; Santrock, in press; Wallerstein & Kelly, 1980). You may recall our description of the work of Judith Wallerstein and Joan Kelly (1974), which represents an important body of information about how divorce influences children and adolescents of different ages. Wallerstein and Kelly studied 131 children and adolescents from divorced homes. Each member of the family was seen by a clinical psychologist in four to six counseling sessions over a six-week span, beginning an average of five months after the separation of the parents. Of the 131 youth, twenty-one were thirteen years old or older at the time of the divorce decision.

Almost without exception, the twenty-one adolescents perceived their parents' divorce as a painful family event. In some instances, the pain was very intense and extremely difficult for the adolescents to cope with. For example, one fourteen-year old said that he felt the rug had been pulled out from under him when he learned that his parents were going to get a divorce. He begged and pleaded with them to settle things and get back together. He even stressed to the parents that their reconciliation would be financially beneficial. During counseling, he sadly reported his helplessness in getting his parents back together but asked the therapist to try one more time.

Some of the adolescents said that the divorce was not a very painful or disruptive event in their lives. However, some of the adolescents who initially distanced themselves from their parents' divorce reported one to two years later that things would have been much better if their parents had not divorced.

The most intense conflict for adolescents occurred during the year following their parents' announcement that they were getting a divorce. One to two years later, most of the adolescents were able to restabilize their lives and proceed toward young adulthood at a reasonable pace. The adolescents who had the most difficult time coping with divorce had histories of long-standing difficulties in their families. These difficulties became even more exacerbated by the problems of their parents during the divorce proceedings.

The adolescents who seemed to be coping more effectively than others with the trauma of divorce had distanced themselves from the parental crisis. In many instances, their parents kept them as uninvolved as possible in the divorce proceedings. The parents of these adolescents also had allowed them to maintain strong ties with their peers. Keeping a certain distance from the center of the divorce and establishing strong peer and friendship relations seemed to produce better adjustment on the part of the adolescents. At first, these youth seemed insensitive and even somewhat self-centered to their counselors, but over time they were better able than any other adolescents to realistically assess their family situations.

It is clear that the effects of divorce on youth are determined by a host of complex factors that include custody arrangement, sex of the youth, aspects of the custodial parent-youth relationship, and the availability of and reliance on support systems. In one of the most thorough investigations of the effects of divorce on adolescents, Mavis Hetherington (1972, 1977) studied the heterosexual behavior of adolescent girls.

The Heterosexual Behavior of Adolescent Daughters of Divorced Parents

Mavis Hetherington (1972) has shown that the heterosexual behavior of adolescent girls from father-absent and father-present homes is different. The adolescent girls with absent fathers acted in one of two extreme ways. They were either very withdrawn, passive, and subdued around boys or were overly active, aggressive, and flirtatious. The girls who were inhibited, rigid, and restrained around males were more likely to have come from widowed homes. Those who sought the attention of males, who showed early heterosexual behavior, and who seemed more open and uninhibited were more likely to have come from homes in which the parents were divorced. In addition, separation from fathers usually was associated with more profound effects, and the mothers' attitudes toward themselves and marriage differed from that of widows and divorcees. Divorced women were more anxious, unhappy, hostile toward males, and more negative about marriage than were the widows. And perhaps not surprisingly, daughters of divorcees had more negative attitudes about men than did the daughters of widows.

Several examples of the actual behavior of the girls should provide a clearer picture of the study. One technique used to investigate the girls' behavior was to interview them sometimes with a male interviewer and sometimes with a female interviewer. Four chairs were placed in the room, including one for the interviewer. Daughters of widows most frequently chose the chair farthest from the male interviewer, while daughters of divorcees generally selected the chair closest to him. There were no differences when the interviewer was a female. The interviewer also observed the girls at a dance and during activities at the recreational center.

At the dance the daughters of widows often refused to dance when asked. One widow's daughter even spent the entire evening in the restroom. The daughters of the divorcees were more likely to accept the boys' invitations to dance. At school, the daughters of divorcees were more frequently observed outside the gym where boys were playing, while the daughters of the widows more often engaged in traditional "female" activities, like sewing and cooking.

Hetherington (1977) is continuing to study these girls, following them into young adulthood to determine their sexual behavior, marital choices, and marital behavior. The daughters of divorcees tend to marry younger (eight of the daughters of widowed mothers still were not married at the time of the report), and tend to select marital partners who more frequently have drug problems and inconsistent work histories. In contrast, daughters of widows tend to marry men with a more puritanical makeup. In addition, both the daughters of the widows and the divorcees report more sexual adjustment problems than the daughters from intact homes; for example, the daughters from homes where the father is absent generally experienced fewer orgasms than daughters from intact homes. The daughters from intact homes also showed more variation in their sex-role behavior and marital adjustment. They seemed to be more relaxed and dealt more competently with their roles as wives, suggesting that they have worked through their relationships with their fathers and are more psychologically free to deal successfully in their relationships with other males. On the other hand, the daughters of the divorcees and widows appear to be marrying images of their fathers.

It should be recognized that findings such as Hetherington's (1972) may not hold as the woman's role in society continues to change. Also the findings are from a restricted sample of middle-class families living in one city—hence, the results may not be as clear when adolescents from other subcultures are studied. Nonetheless, Hetherington's results do point to some likely vulnerabilities of adolescent girls growing up in divorced and widowed families.

To conclude our discussion of families, we focus on a very different aspect than has been discussed so far. There is increasing interest in adolescents who become parents themselves. As we see next, comparisons are being made between adolescents as parents and adults as parents.

Adolescent Parents

Popular wisdom suggests that childbearing should occur between the ages of twenty-two and thirty-one. At earlier ages it is believed that biomedical risks increase, child behavioral outcomes are less positive, and/or maternal attitudes are less competent. In some cases, though, research has not supported such beliefs. For example, recent reviews of biomedical outcomes have minimized the risk due to early childbearing (Baldwin & Cain, 1980).

However, studies of subsequent child behavioral outcomes do show substantive relationships between maternal age and children's intellectual development. Children born to adolescent mothers do not perform as well on intelligence tests as those born to mothers in their twenties. (Broman, 1981). Furthermore, teenage mothers express less desirable childrearing attitudes and have less realistic expectations for infants' development than do older mothers (Epstein, 1980).

It may be that such negative effects of adolescent parenting are better explained in terms of the postnatal environment of offspring of younger and older mothers in terms of biological consequences of adolescent pregnancy. Stress that is associated with adolescent pregnancy, emotional immaturity, and egocentrism are likely candidates for explaining differences in adolescent and adult parenting.

It is well documented that divorce rates among adolescent parents are much higher than those in the general population (Furstenburg, 1976). In addition, teenage mothers frequently harbor unrealistic expectations about the father's marriage plans. In one investigation (Lorenzi, Klerman, & Jekel, 1977), of the 47 percent of the mothers who expected to marry the father, only 36 percent had married him by the second birthday of the baby. However, Ross Parke and his colleagues (1980) believe that such figures have been overemphasized in the literature of adolescent parenting and may in part be responsible for the predominantly negative perception of the adolescent father. Parke recommends the development of cultural support systems that recognize the full range of needs of adolescent fathers, both as individuals and as parents. Providing such supportive interventions may produce positive consequences for the father, mother, and child. Parke calls for programs that teach adolescent fathers parenting skills and for school districts to provide infant care services in locations near high school facilities that would permit both the mother and the father to continue their education.

This ends our discussion of the role of the family in the adolescent's development. Next we look in greater detail at the adolescent's peer system, including information about the pervasiveness of group activities.

Competent adolescent fathering can have a positive impact on the psychological well-being of the infant.

Peers and Group Behavior

Adolescents spend a great deal of time with their peers; many of their greatest frustrations and happiest moments come when they are with their peers. To many adolescents, how they are seen by peers is the most important aspect of their lives. Some adolescents will go along with anything just to be included as a member of the group. To them, being excluded means stress, frustration, and sadness. Think about Bob, who has no close friends to speak of, in contrast to Steve, who has three close buddies he pals around with all of the time . . . Sally, who was turned down by the club at school she was working to get into for six months, in contrast to Sandra, who is a member of the club and who frequently is told by her peers how "super" her personality is.

Some friends of mine have a daughter who is thirteen years old. Last year, she had a number of girl-friends—she spent a lot of time on the phone talking with them and they frequently visited each other's homes. Then her family moved and this thirteen-year-old girl had to attend a school with a lower socioeconomic mix of students than at her previous school. Many of the girls at the new school feel my friends' daughter is "too good" for them, and the young adolescent is having difficulty making friends this year. One of her most frequent complaints is, "I don't have any friends. . . . None of the kids at school ever call me. And none of them ever ask me over to their houses. What can I do?"

Friendships are an important aspect of adolescent peer relationships. In this section, we evaluate a number of factors associated with the development of friendships in adolescence. We also examine adolescent groups, including crowds and cliques, and the nature of dating.

Friendship

My best friend is nice. She's honest, and I can trust her. I can tell her my innermost secrets and know that nobody else will find out about them. I have other friends, too, but she is my best friend. We consider each other's feelings and don't want to hurt each other. We help each other out when we have problems. We make up funny names for people and laugh ourselves silly. We make lists of which boys are the sexiest and which are the ugliest, which are the biggest jerks, and so on. Some of these things we share with other friends, but some we don't.

Although all adolescents want to be popular with large segments of their age group, they also want to have one or two "best friends." Unfortunately, however, many adolescents do not have a best friend, or even a circle of friends, in whom they can confide. A certain school psychologist always made a practice of asking children and adolescents about their friends. One twelve-year-old boy, when asked who his best friend was, replied, "My kite." Further discussion revealed that his parents had insulated him from the society of neighborhood peers. Similarly, in one investigation of college-age youth, as many as one out of every three students surveyed said that they had not found, or were not sure whether they had found, a close, meaningful relationship with a same-sex peer (Katz, 1968). There are several explanations for why many adolescents have difficulty establishing close friendships. While many adolescents indicate that meaningful friendships are high on their list of needs, they may lack the skills necessary to get and retain friends (for example, the ability to consistently demonstrate active listening and open communication styles). It also may be that adolescents have a more stringent definition of "meaningful" friendship than other age segments in the population. And although many adolescents stress that they have a strong need for close friends, they may be suspicious of what such a commitment will mean in terms of reciprocation— "Can I really trust her? Does she really like me for me, or is she just using me?" In sum, while friendship is considered a strong need by adolescents, many lack the skills to initiate and maintain friendships, and others are wary of the commitments such friendship brings.

"Kathy?"

Illustration by Bil Keane from *Just Wait 'Till You Have Children of Your Own.* Copyright © 1971 by Erma Bombeck and Bil Keane. Reprinted by permission of Doubleday & Company, Inc.

There recently has been an increasing interest in the nature and development of friendships. Two aspects of this interest focus on the intimacy of friends' conversations and their knowledge of each other, and the degree of similarity or complementarity between friends.

Intimacy in Friendships
Although intimate relationships with a best friend seem to have their onset in early adolescence, this period does not appear to be the time when adolescents rate their intimate friendships as the most positive. Why might early adolescence be a time of less positive intimate relationships in friendship than late adolescence? The decline in positive ratings of friendship that seem to appear around the age of thirteen may be explained by the temporary period of conflict that may be generated because of an adolescent's cross-sex interests, or it may be due to the changes in friendships that accompany the transition to junior high school.

It has been argued that girls have more intimate friendships during adolescence than boys do (Douvan & Adelson, 1966). Emphasis is placed on sex-role differences that suggest that girls are more oriented toward interpersonal relationships whereas boys are interested in assertiveness and achievement rather than warmth and empathy. Furthermore, intimacy among boys may be discouraged because of the fear that it may lead to homosexuality. When adolescents are asked to describe their best friends, girls more than boys refer to intimate conversations and intimate knowledge and show more concern about faithfulness and rejection (Berndt, 1982).

Similarity Between Friends
The extent to which there is similarity between friends on a variety of characteristics has been of interest to psychologists for many years. Throughout the childhood and adolescent years, friends are similar in terms of age, sex, and race (Hallinan, 1979). Friends also usually have similar attitudes toward school, similar educational aspirations, and closely aligned achievement orientations (Epstein, in press). Such findings reveal the importance of schooling in adolescents' lives and the need for agreement between friends on its importance. If friends have different attitudes about school, one of them may want to play basketball or go shopping rather than do homework. If one friend insists on completing his homework and the other insists on playing basketball, over time such conflicts are likely to weaken the friendship.

Friends also are similar in their orientation toward the teenage or youth culture. Friends like the same kind of music, like the same kinds of clothes, and like to engage in the same kind of leisure activities. Some friendships are based on even more specific interests, such as horseback riding, playing in golf tournaments, or working crossword puzzles together.

So far in our discussion of peer relations, little has been said about how the adolescent functions in groups. Next we look extensively at a number of aspects of adolescent groups.

Adolescent Groups
Think back to your junior high and high school years once again. This time think about the groups you were involved in. It is likely that you were a member of both formal and informal groups. In regard to formal groups, you might have been a member of the student council, Girl Scouts, a football team, a debating team, or a math club. In terms of informal groups, most of you were part of some clique. In this section, we explore the nature of adolescent groups, first focusing on the type of adolescent groups that exist. We also evaluate differences in children's and adolescents' groups and discuss how adolescent groups vary from culture to culture.

Crowds and Cliques
Most peer group relationships in adolescence can be categorized in one of three ways: the **crowd,** the **clique,** or individual friendships. The largest and least personal of these groups is the crowd. The members of the crowd meet because of their mutual interest in activities, not because they are mutually attracted to each other. By contrast, the members of cliques and friendships are attracted to each other on the basis of similar interests and social ideals. Cliques are smaller in size, involve greater intimacy among members, and have more group cohesion than crowds.

One of the most widely quoted studies of adolescent crowds and cliques is that of James Coleman (1961). Students in ten different high schools were asked to identify the leading crowds in their schools. They also were asked to name the students who were the most outstanding in athletics, popularity, and different activities in the school. Regardless of the school sampled, the leading crowds were likely to be composed of athletes and popular girls. Much less power in the leading crowd was attributed to the bright student. Coleman's finding that being an athlete contributes to popularity for boys was reconfirmed more recently (Eitzen, 1975).

The exact nature of crowds and cliques depends on the geographical region of the country in which adolescents live. For instance, in towns and cities in Texas, the "kickers" and the "potheads" often create the most controversy. This dichotomy (as well as the dichotomy between groups in most areas) is due to the mixing of cultures—urban and rural, Northern and Southern. The term "kicker" originates from cowboy boots, which were worn mostly by working cowboys. The term has been modified to either "chip kickers" or "cowboys," depending on the purposes of the adolescent using the label. Observers say the kickers may or may not have anything to do with agriculture, but they usually wear cowboy boots and western shirts and jeans, listen to country-and-western music, often drive pickups, and carry around tins of snuff in their hip pockets. The other side of the dichotomy has a wider variety of names, depending on the locale: freaks, potheads, slickers, or thugs. Freaks supposedly prefer rock music, dress like hippies, and drive hyped-up cars.

In one investigation (Riester & Zucker 1968), students described six distinct groups in their high school. One clearly defined group, called the "collegiates," was comprised of establishment-oriented, socially active, "all-American" students. Another group was called the "leathers." They were described as rough and tough— "hoods" was another label applied to them. A third group was called "the true individuals." Their most distinct feature was their clothing; over the years, they

The crowd is one form of adolescent group.

have been called "beatniks," "hippies," and "freaks." Three other more or less distinct groups were identified: the "quiet kids," who were independent, did their own thing, and sometimes belonged to more identifiable groups outside of school; the "intellectuals," who studied a lot and were usually very serious about some particular area of academic work; and "the kids going steady," who spent considerable lengths of time with each other and sometimes with other couples.

Although the labels for groups and cliques change over time and from one geographical area to another, we could go to any high school in the United States and discover three to six well-defined crowds or cliques.

Allegiance to groups exerts powerful control over the lives of many adolescents. Group identity often overrides personal identity. The leader of a group may place a member in a position of considerable moral conflict, asking in effect, "What's more important, our code or your parents'?" or "Are you looking out for yourself or for the members of the group?" Labels like "brother" and "sister" sometimes are adopted and used in group members' conversations with one another. These labels symbolize the intensity of the bond between the members and suggest the high status of membership in the group.

In recent investigations (Brown & Lohr, 1983; Lohr & Brown, 1983), the relationship between being associated with the major crowds (jocks, socies, druggies, etc.) in grades nine through twelve and the student's self-esteem was evaluated. As expected, self-esteem was higher among members of high-status crowds and lower among "neglected" students, classmates who were relatively unknown to the crowd members.

Cliques often provide a more intense camaraderie than membership in more formal adolescent organizations, such as an honor society, the student council, and so forth. However, intense feelings of group cohesion and brotherhood or sisterhood also may be felt by the members of athletic teams or political groups as well. For many adolescents, many hours of the day are spent performing the roles ascribed to them in these cliques and groups.

Cross-Cultural Variations in Adolescent Groups
In some cultures, children are placed in peer groups for much greater lengths of time and at an earlier age than they are in the United States. For example, in the Murian culture of eastern India, both male and female

children live in a dormitory from the age of six until they get married. The dormitory is seen as a religious haven where members are devoted to work and spiritual harmony. Children work for their parents, and the parents arrange the children's marriages. When the children wed, they must leave the dormitory.

The development of independence is even more extreme for children living in the Nyakyusan culture in East Africa. Children leave home with their peers when they are ten years old to develop a new village. They build huts, get married and have children, and cultivate fields. Many of the adolescents, then, in the cultures of the Muria and the Nyakyusa are given the chance to become autonomous and perform adult roles long before they reach adulthood.

Marriage and parenthood for adolescents is not nearly as rigidly defined in our present-day American culture as it is in the Murian and Nyakyusan cultures. Instead, most adolescents go through an extensive period of dating, and many individuals do not marry until well after adolescence.

Dating

I met this really neat, good-looking guy, Frank—a college senior. He seemed to like me, but why would a college guy be interested in me, a high school junior, anyway? . . . That guy, Frank, asked me out. I think he is pretty nice, but I'm not sure I want the kind of experience he wants to show me! . . . At any rate, I said he could pick me up after school. I thought he might not show up because he would be too embarrassed to be seen at the high school. . . . But he came, and we went out for some pizza and talked. He wanted me to go out with him that night, but I told him I had to study, and he should take me home. He did. He keeps calling all the time, and my mother always is saying to me, "Who is that guy that keeps calling you all the time?" (I don't want her to know I'm going out with somebody as old as Frank is.) . . . Frank sure is persistent. I finally agreed to go out with him again. And then I went out with him again, and again. Now, I think I'm falling in love with him. . . . I'm starting to get jealous when he doesn't call me every evening—I think maybe he is out with some girl who is older and a lot more experienced than I am. I sure hope not. . . . Frank is so neat—he is so much more mature than most of the guys in our high school. He is sensitive to my feelings, and doesn't smart off to get attention. . . . But I'm still not sure why he likes me.

The adolescent girl in this situation is far along in the social institution our society calls dating. While many adolescent boys and girls have social interchanges through formal and informal peer groups, it is through dating that more serious contacts between the sexes occur. Many agonizing moments are spent by young male adolescents worrying about whether they should call a certain girl and ask her out— "Will she turn me down?" "What if she says yes; what do I say next?" "How am I going to get her to the dance? I don't want my mother to take us!" "I want to kiss her, but what if she pushes me away?" "How can I get to be alone with her?" And on the other side of the coin: "He's not the best-looking guy in the world, but I want to go to the dance." "Maybe this is a good opportunity to see what a date is like." Or, "I really don't want to go with him. Maybe I should wait two more days and see if Bill will call me." Think about your junior high, high school, and early college years. You probably spent a lot of time thinking about how you were going to get a particular girl or boy to go out with you. And many of your weekend evenings were likely spent on dates, or on envying others who had dates. Some of you went steady, perhaps even during junior high school—others of you may have been engaged to be married by the end of high school.

Dating is a relatively recent phenomenon. It wasn't until the 1920s that dating as we know it became a reality, and even then, its primary role was still for the purpose of selecting and winning a mate. Prior to this period, mate selection was the *sole* purpose of dating, and "dates" were carefully monitored by parents, who completely controlled the nature of any heterosexual companionship. Often, parents bargained with each other about the merits of their adolescents as potential marriage partners and even chose mates for their children. In recent times, of course, adolescents themselves have gained much more control over the dating process; today's adolescents are not as much at the whims of their parents in regard to whom they go out with. Furthermore, dating has evolved into something more than just courtship for marriage. Dating today serves four main functions for adolescents (Skipper & Nass, 1966):

1. Dating can be a form of recreation. Adolescents who date seem to have fun and see dating as a source of enjoyment and recreation.
2. Dating is a source of status and achievement. Part of the social comparison process in adolescence involves evaluating the status of dates—are they the best looking, the most popular, and so forth.
3. Dating is part of the socialization process in adolescence—it helps adolescents learn how to get along with others and assists them in learning to be mannerly and sociable.
4. Dating can be a means of mate sorting and selection—it retains its original courtship function.

In addition to these four functions, dating also can serve as a testing ground for sexual behavior and as a means of learning about intimacy. Dating today, then, has gone far beyond the single purpose of courtship it once served some sixty years ago.

Our discussion of the social development of adolescents would not be complete without considering the vast cultural differences in how adolescents are socialized.

Cross-Cultural Comparisons of Adolescents

Ideas about the nature of adolescence and the techniques used to raise adolescents may differ from culture to culture and within the same culture over different time periods. The cultural beliefs that leaders within a society share about adolescents have important implications for how adolescents are dealt with. Governments and political bodies can exert strong influences on the lives of adolescents through such decision making. Consider the different experiences adolescents will have if leaders of a country decide to wage war against another country (as in the case of Vietnam) and many adolescents are forced to make critical decisions about whether to follow or confront and resist the adult decision makers. Further, consider the experiences of those youth who do go to war compared to youth who grow up in an era when there is a nonaggressive political orientation. In ways such as these, government and political structures in a culture can exert a strong influence on youth.

There are many other aspects of the cultural milieu to consider in addition to political structure. We already have analyzed the effects of several important aspects of the cultural milieu—namely, the institutions of family and peers. Later in the chapter we will look at another important aspect of the culture in which the adolescent grows up—schools. In addition to analyzing various aspects of the culture in which the adolescent grows up, it is helpful to compare the experiences of adolescents in different cultures.

When anthropologists and psychologists study adolescents in different cultures, one aspect of development that they study extensively is sexuality.

Sexual Behavior

Cross-cultural studies of adolescent sexual behavior indicate that culture and learning play a major role in shaping sexual conduct. Such studies indicate that sexual behavior is not totally under the control of biological influences. For example, women who live in the Ines Beag culture off the coast of Ireland never have orgasms. But every woman who lives in the Mangaia culture in the South Pacific achieves an orgasm. The two sets of women have similarly constructed vaginas and clitorises that are approximately the same size and that have virtually the same nerve supply. The reason for the difference, then, must be learned. Let's look more

closely to see if the experience of adolescents in the two cultures has anything to do with the differences in sexual behavior.

John Messinger (1971) describes life in Ines Beag. The inhabitants of Ines Beag are among the most sexually repressed in the world. They know nothing about French kissing, breast kissing, or hand stimulation of the penis. Sex education is nonexistent. They believe that after marriage, nature will take its course.

The men believe that intercourse is bad for their health. And they detest nudity—only babies can bathe nude. Adults wash only the parts of their body that extend beyond their clothing. Premarital sex is totally taboo, and after marriage, the sexual partners keep their underwear on during intercourse. It is not too difficult to understand why females in the Ines Beag culture never achieve orgasm.

In contrast, in the Mangaian culture, boys learn about masturbation as early as age six or seven; by age eight or nine, they usually have started to masturbate. When a boy is thirteen, he undergoes a ritual in which a long incision is made in his penis, a custom designed to introduce him into manhood. The person who conducts the ritual provides the boy with information about sexual strategies—how to kiss and suck a woman's breasts and how to help his partner achieve an orgasm before he does. Two weeks after the incision ceremony, the thirteen-year-old boy has intercourse with an experienced woman, which causes the scab from his penis to be removed. The woman trains the boy in various sexual techniques and helps him to learn how to hold back ejaculation so she can achieve orgasm with him. Soon after, the boy looks for girls with whom to try out his techniques—or they search for him, knowing that he is now a "man." Adolescent girls expect him to have intercourse with them—if he does not, it is a sign that he does not like them. By late adolescence, Mangaian boys and girls have sex every night and average three orgasms per night. It is thus easy to see how cultural experiences influence the Mangaian woman's ability to achieve orgasm.

Before we end our description of cross-cultural comparisons of adolescent sexuality, something more should be said about the rites of passage that punctuate the lives of adolescents in many primitive cultures.

Rites of Passage: Boys and Girls in Primitive Cultures

Barbara Sommer (1978) has provided a thorough overview of ceremonies and activities associated with **rites of passage** in a number of primitive cultures. Sometimes the ceremonies are referred to as puberty

Many rites of passage for adolescents have occurred in African cultures.

rites, being defined as the avenue through which adolescents gain access to sacred adult practices, to knowledge, and to sexuality. These rites often involve very dramatic practices intended to enhance separation of the adolescent from the immediate family, particularly the mother. The transformation usually is characterized by some form of ritual death and rebirth or by means of contact with the spiritual world. And by means of shared ritual, hazards, and secrets, bonds between the adolescent and his or her adult instructors are forged and these bonds allow him or her to enter into the adult world, particularly the world of the adult of the same sex. Such rituals stimulate a forceful and discontinuous entry into the adult world at a time when the youth is ready for change.

According to Sommer, rites of transition reveal more of a direct relation to the specific events of puberty for females than for males. That there is a more direct link for females is probably a consequence of the single marker of menarche, whereas no such clear marker for puberty is available for males. In addition, for boys, initiation reflects an introduction to a world that is not immediate, the world of spirit and culture, whereas for girls more emphasis is placed on the secrets of such natural phenomena as menstruation and childbirth.

Africa has been the location of many rites of passage for adolescents, particularly the area known as Sub-Saharan Africa. Under the influence of Western culture, many of the rites are disappearing today. However, vestiges of these rites still remain, and in some locations where education has not been prevalent, rites of passage during early adolescence are still prominent.

Separation, transition, and incorporation seem to be three themes that characterize puberty initiation rites. An underlying belief in such rites of passage is recognition that puberty brings with it changes in sexual maturation and intellectual prowess. In the culture of the United States, we clearly do not have such elaborate initiation rites, and passage into adolescence and into adulthood is much more continuous.

Thus, we see that findings from cross-cultural studies of adolescence are useful in confirming or disconfirming ideas about generalized principles that have been based primarily on observations in only one culture. Both variation and congruence have been noted across cultures in adolescent development.

This concludes our discussion of cultural comparisons of adolescents. Next we look at two very important aspects of culture that most adolescents experience—schools and work.

Adolescents spend years in school as members of a small society.

Schools and Work

The United States is an achievement-oriented culture. We rear our adolescents to be competitive, to do well in whatever they attempt, to win. Comparisons of adolescents in the United States with adolescents in other cultures document that in our culture adolescents are more self-oriented than family oriented (Holtzmann, 1982) and are socialized to be more competitive than cooperative (Barry, Child, & Bacon, 1959). Indeed, many psychologists believe we are producing a nation of "hurried youth" who are pushed to achieve beyond what is optimally healthy (Elkind, 1979). As part of the achievement orientation in our culture, virtually all adolescents go to secondary schools, and increasingly adolescents are working at part-time jobs. We explore each of these important aspects of the adolescent's world—schools and work—in turn.

Schools

Concern about the impact of schools is justified because of the scale of influence. By the time an individual has graduated from high school, he or she will have spent 10,000 hours in the classroom. At any one time, approximately 16 million adolescents are in high school alone. Such numbers and the breadth of the school's influence are more important today than in past generations because more adolescents are in school longer.

For example, in 1900, 11.4 percent of fourteen- to seventeen-year-olds were in school, whereas currently 94 percent of the same age group are in school.

Adolescents spend years in schools as members of a small society in which there are tasks to be accomplished, people to be socialized and to be socialized by, and many rules that define the possibilities for behavior, feelings, and attitudes. Such experiences are likely to have a strong influence on the adolescent in areas such as the development of an identity, the belief in one's competence, images of life possibilities as a male or female, social relationships, views of standards of right and wrong, and conceptions of how a social system beyond the family functions (Minuchin & Shapiro, 1983).

Let's look at two important aspects of the adolescent's schooling experiences: patterns of social interaction in secondary schools and desirable characteristics of junior high school teachers.

Patterns of Social Interaction among Peers in Schools
In this section, we look more closely at the patterns of social interaction among adolescents themselves in the school setting. In secondary schools, the entire school is more likely to be used as a social context than in elementary schools, where students are more likely to be

confined to one or two classrooms for most of the school day. In secondary schools, adolescents come in contact with a variety of teachers and peers and are given the choice of a number of different activities outside the classroom. Social behavior is often oriented toward peers, toward extracurricular activities, and toward the community. In adolescence, the individual becomes more aware of the school as a social system and organization than in the elementary school years, and he or she may either adapt and participate in the social system or attempt to challenge the system (Minuchin & Shapiro, 1983).

There are few times in life when friendships and bonds between peers are stronger than in adolescence. Adolescence is a transitional period bridging the life of the child and the young adult. Because adolescents are gaining independence from the family of their childhood, but have not yet become a part of the family they will be in as an adult, their peers have an especially strong impact on their life. James Coleman (1961) believes that high schools are partly responsible for such strong peer ties. At school, adolescents are with each other for at least six hours every day. The school also provides the locus for many of the adolescents' activities after school and on weekends.

Coleman (1961) analyzed the peer associations of boys and girls separately in small schools. Boys achieved status within their schools in a variety of ways. In some schools, the "all-around boy"—athlete, ladies' man, and to some extent, scholar—achieved status, while in other schools, being either an athlete or a scholar was enough to assure high status.

There was a considerable amount of variation in the association patterns of the girls in small schools as well. Elmtown had the largest number of girl cliques, the largest percentage of girls in cliques, and the smallest average clique size. Marketville was the opposite in each of these respects. In Marketville and Maple Grove, middle-class girls from well-educated families formed cliques that dominated social activities, school activities, and adolescent attention. Teachers perceived these cliques as being in control of the student body and as the girls most encouraged by the adults in the community.

Athletic achievement played an important role in the status systems of boys in all ten schools Coleman studied. Why are athletics so important in the status systems of American high schools? Adolescents identify strongly with their schools and communities. The identification, in part at least, is due to the fact that the school and the community of adolescents are virtually synonymous. They compete as a school against other schools in athletic contests. So the heroes of the system, those with high status, are the boys who win for the school and the community of adolescents. When they win, the entire school and the entire community of adolescents feel better about themselves.

Because boys have had greater opportunity to participate in interscholastic athletics than girls have, they have been more likely to attain high-status positions in schools. However, in the 1970s the federal government took a big step toward reducing this form of discrimination against female adolescents. Title IX of the 1972 Educational Amendments Act prohibits any educational program from receiving federal funds if sex discrimination is practiced. So far this act has not produced parity for girls and boys in interscholastic athletics, but girls have made greater strides than ever before in participating in interscholastic events. Also since the passage of Title IX, female enrollments in previously male-dominated fields such as engineering, medicine, law, and business have more than doubled, and reams have been written about sexism in the language, policies, and practices of education.

But even though some progress has been made for adolescent females in regard to their participation in athletics, differential access to sports activities still is widely practiced. Sports for boys are more varied and extensive than for girls and have much larger budgets. Girls do not have the same opportunities for physical training, for developing competitive skills, or for the experience of team camaraderie as boys do. However, many adolescent boys may suffer from excessive emphasis on competition rather than the pleasures of participation and mastery (Minuchin & Shapiro, 1983).

Participation in school activities is likely to be an important ingredient of the adolescent's identity with the school and the development of his or her own identity. Remember our comments earlier about small and large schools, namely, that in smaller schools adolescents have a greater chance of participating in school activities, such that even marginal students (those not usually thought of as socially facile) have a greater opportunity to participate in activities and may develop a stronger sense of identity with the school. In large schools the same students may be thought of as "tribe members" rather than "citizens"; citizens are described as being involved in activities and satisfied with the school, whereas tribe members are inactive and alienated or opposed (Todd, 1979).

Not only is peer interaction an important aspect of school for adolescents, but so, too, is the nature of teacher-student interaction. Next we look at some desirable characteristics of junior high school teachers.

Teaching Strategies with Low- and High-Ability Students

Two ways in which the teacher's orientation can be classified are as (1) challenging and demanding good performance and (2) encouraging good performance. Jere Brophy (1979) reviewed several studies focused on these types of teacher orientation. Teachers who work with high-socioeconomic status/high-ability students usually are more successful if they move at a quick pace, frequently communicating high expectations and enforcing high standards. These teachers try to keep students challenged, will not accept inferior work, and occasionally criticize the students' work when it does not meet their standards.

Teachers who generally are successful with low-socioeconomic status/low-ability students also are inter-ested in getting the most out of their students, but they usually do so by being warm and encouraging rather than demanding. They are friendly with their students, take more time out from academic subject matter to motivate the youth, praise and encourage more often, rarely criticize poor work, and move the curriculum along at a slower pace. When they call on individual students, they allow more time for the student to respond; they may provide hints to help the student get the correct answer (Brophy & Evertson, 1974, 1976).

As can be readily seen in this example successful teaching varies according to the type of student being taught—one teaching strategy is superior with high-ability students, another with low-ability students.

Some Desirable Characteristics of Junior High School Teachers

Early childhood educators believe that meaningful learning takes place in a setting where developmental characteristics of the age group are understood, where basic trust has been established, and where children feel free to explore, to experiment, and to make mistakes. The personal qualities of the teacher are essential, for the teacher creates the setting in which children can direct their own growth and learning within the context of supportive, nurturing, and respectful relationships.

Adults who work with the young adolescent age group would do well to have some of the same characteristics possessed by good teachers of young children. The variability of young adolescent students can make them a difficult age group to teach, but knowledge of their developmental characteristics could help middle-grade teachers respond as rationally to their students' behavior and idiosyncrasies as early childhood educators respond to theirs.

Because early adolescence is a time of transition, it is often characterized by restlessness, ambivalence, and rebelliousness. The student who leans on the teacher one day may be striving for independence the next. Teachers who enjoy working with the age group remember well and have mastered the developmental tasks of their own teenage years. Able to recall their youthful vulnerability, they understand and respect their students' sensitivity to criticism, desire for group acceptance, and feelings of being acutely conspicuous. Such teachers, who are secure in their adult identity and comfortable with their sexuality, are capable of supporting children's good feelings about themselves. Possessing clear values, these teachers are aware of the necessity of using power and authority wisely and are sensitive to their own feelings as well as the feelings of their students.

Young adolescents respond best to adults who exercise natural authority—based on greater age, experience, and wisdom—rather than arbitrary authority or abdication of authority by adults who try to be "just pals." Young people need adults who are trustworthy, who are fair and consistent, who set reasonable limits, and who realize that adolescents need to have someone to push against while testing those limits. Teachers who know themselves and who understand adolescence can help teenagers learn about themselves and learn to cope with their feelings, their peers, and their families (Feeny, 1980, pp. 15–16).

In addition to the personal qualities of teachers, recall from chapter 12 that we also need to look at the teaching strategies they use. In application 15.2, you will find information about how it may be beneficial for teachers to use different strategies with low- and high-ability students.

Teaching strategies that are effective with high-ability students may not be as effective with low-ability students.

To conclude our discussion of the various social contexts and settings in which adolescent development occurs, we look at the world of work, which is becoming an increasingly common area of experience for adolescent students in the United States.

The Role of Work During Adolescence

In 1974, the government Panel on Youth, headed by James Coleman, concluded that work has a positive influence on adolescents. According to Coleman and his colleagues, a job during adolescence creates a positive attitude toward work, allows students to learn from adults other than teachers or parents, and may help keep them out of trouble. The Panel on Youth recommended that more youth should be included in the work force of our country. To accomplish this goal, the panel suggested that more work/study programs be developed, that the minimum wage be lowered, and that more flexible school/work schedules be allowed.

Over the past hundred years, the percentage of youth who work full time as opposed to those who are in school has decreased dramatically. During the last half of the 1800s, fewer than one of every twenty high school-aged adolescents were in school, whereas more than nine of every ten adolescents receive high school diplomas today. In the nineteenth century, many adolescents learned a trade from their father or some other adult member of the community. Now a much more prolonged period of educational training has kept most adolescents out of the full-time work force.

Part-Time Work and Its Relation to School
Most high school seniors already have had some experience in the world of work. In a recent national survey of 17,000 high school seniors (Bachman, 1982), three out of four reported that they have some job income during the average school week. For 41 percent of the males and 30 percent of the females this income exceeded fifty dollars a week. The typical part-time job for high school seniors is sixteen to twenty hours a week, although 10 percent work thirty or more hours a week.

Clearly, more adolescent students are working today than in past years. For example, in 1940 only one out of twenty-five tenth-grade males attended school and simultaneously worked part-time, whereas in 1970 the number had increased to more than one out of every four. More recent estimates suggest that one out of every three ninth and tenth graders are combining school and work (Cole, 1981).

Adolescents also are working longer hours now than in the past. For instance, the number of fourteen- and fifteen-year olds who work more than fourteen hours per week has increased substantially in the last twenty years. A similar picture emerges for sixteen-year-olds. In 1960, 44 percent of the sixteen-year old males who attended school worked more than fourteen hours a week, but by 1970, the figure had increased to 56 percent.

Does this increase in work have a positive influence on adolescents? In some cases yes, in others no. Ellen Greenberger and Laurence Steinberg (1980, 1981) gave a questionnaire focusing on work experiences to students in four California high schools. Their findings disproved some common myths. For example, it generally is assumed that youth get extensive on-the-job training when they are hired for work—the reality is that they get little training at all, according to the researchers. Also, it is assumed that youth, through work experiences, learn to get along better with adults. However, adolescents reported that they rarely feel close to the adults they work with. The work experiences of the adolescents did help them understand how the business world works, how to get and keep a job, and how to manage money. Working also helped the youth to learn to budget their time, to take pride in their accomplishments, and to evaluate their goals. Working adolescents often have to give up sports, social affairs with peers, and sometimes sleep. And the youth have to balance the demands of work, school, and family.

In their investigation, Greenberger and Steinberg asked adolescents about their grade-point averages, school attendance, satisfaction from school, and the number of hours spent studying and in extracurricular activities since they began working. The findings: working adolescents had lower grade-point averages than nonworkers. More than one of every four students reported that their grades dropped when they began working; whereas only one of nine said their grades improved. But it wasn't just working that affected the adolescents' grades—more importantly, it was the number of hours worked. Tenth graders who worked more than fourteen hours a week suffered a drop in grades; whereas eleventh graders worked up to twenty hours a week before their grades began to drop. When adolescents are spending more than twenty hours a week working, there is little time to study for tests and do homework assignments.

In addition to the effect of work on grades, working adolescents also felt less involved in school, were absent more, and said they didn't enjoy school as much (compared to their nonworking peers). Adolescents who worked also spent less time with their families—but just as much time with their peers—as their nonworking counterparts.

In weighing the benefits and pitfalls of work during adolescence, Sheila Cole (1980) concluded:

Working is a part of growing up. Like other aspects of growing up, it brings young people independence and freedom. And, like growing up, it introduces teenagers to the limitations of their own lives.

Adolescents do not like to have to ask for money each time they want to go somewhere or buy something. Having their own money makes them free to act and brings a wonderful, powerful feeling that, at least initially, outweighs all but the most serious annoyances of work.

It is natural for young people to grow impatient with the sheltered circle of family, school, and friends and to want to test themselves in the wider world. Work gives adolescents an opportunity to do just that. It also requires them to get along with others and to adjust their behavior so that a job gets done. And it gives them a chance to learn about money and the general aspects of working that they will need to know as adults.

Families also benefit, at least financially, when a teenager works. Many families can no longer afford to give their children enough pocket money to go out with their friends, to learn skills such as playing the guitar or skiing, to buy the

Working too many hours a week during adolescence may have a negative influence on grades.

materials for hobbies and projects, or to run a car—the only means of access to social life in some parts of the country. Few would argue that activities of this sort are unnecessary. But having to pay for them is a strain that may cause resentment. Adolescents who take some of the burden on themselves earn parental respect and often reduce household tensions.

The benefits to society also seem apparent. Working teenagers participate in society and contribute to it by being productive. High schoolers working part-time do not take jobs away from adults; students work in the service and retail sectors of the economy at jobs that adults cannot generally afford to take because the pay is too low and fringe benefits and job protection are lacking. Many companies that employ teenagers would not survive without a ready supply of part-time labor willing to work under such conditions. Adolescent workers also contribute to the economy as consumers. On the average, working high school students in the Greenberger-Steinberg study earned more than two hundred dollars a month.

But there are negative aspects of work that make me a cautious advocate—especially for those who have a choice. While working helps a high school student pay for social activities, it also takes time away from these activities. Teenage jobholders often complain about how little time they have left just to daydream and fool around. Yet daydreaming and fooling around without responsibility to anyone or anything are essential to exploring oneself and one's interests and relations to others. Adolescence is one of the few times in our lives when we have the freedom to make these explorations. Do we really want a society of teenagers who only work and go to school and go to school and work, who are closed in by organized activity and commitments?

Most of the work that young people are paid to do is not very interesting, enriching, or worthwhile in a broad social sense. Adolescent workers learn that sorry fact early, so money becomes the motivating force in their work. This is natural enough, but is it desirable? Do we want money to assume that kind of importance so early?

Cynicism and apathy are some of the inevitable by-products of jobs that exploit and abuse. Such attitudes cloak feelings of powerlessness and helplessness, but do not assuage them. Do we want our kids to be "broken in" to these attitudes at an early age?

All these are questions of values. In some families, teenage work is a necessity. But for many families, there is a choice. Few American households are so affluent that a little extra income would not be welcome, or so poor that full-time adolescent labor is necessary. For such families there is no formula that will yield a "correct" decision in all cases.

Perhaps the most useful contribution of recent research is the estimate it gives us of how many hours a young person can profitably work. It is helpful to know that, on the average, the benefits of work can be acquired in about fourteen hours of work a week, and that after twenty hours negative consequences begin to outweigh the positive ones. Those ball-park figures, plus common sense, represent our best resources for making decisions about kids and work. (Cole, 1980, p. 68)

We are at the end of the discussion of the social development of the adolescent. In the next chapter, we explore the nature of the adolescent's personality development, focusing initially on self and identity development and then on the various problems and disturbances adolescents experience.

Summary

The roles of the family and peers are crucial in adolescent development. An important aspect of the adolescent's relationship with his or her family focuses on his or her push for independence. The adolescent's development of independence is a gradual process, and the wise parent will relinquish control in areas where the adolescent can make mature decisions and will help the adolescent make mature decisions in areas where his or her knowledge is more limited. Parent-adolescent conflict is a pervasive concern of parents. It appears that this conflict peaks around the end of the junior high school years and coincides with the conformity of the adolescent to antisocial peer norms. Although there is a consensus that parent-adolescent conflict does not reach the proportions suggested by G. Stanley Hall's storm-and-stress view of adolescence, there does appear to be a moderate increase in conflict between parents and their offspring during early adolescence. However, such conflict is usually not intense and prolonged and consists mainly of minor arguments. Nonetheless, a minority of adolescents do experience intense, prolonged conflict with their parents, and such conflict is associated with a number of problems in adolescent development. In many cases, though, the adolescent problems and parent-adolescent conflict originated not in adolescence but in childhood.

An increasing number of adolescents grow up in divorced homes. Divorce is a stressful experience for adolescents as well as for children. Evidence suggests that adolescents who distance themselves from their parents' problems and immerse themselves in peer relations are likely to experience the least amount of stress.

In the matter of adolescent parents, there does not appear to be as much biomedical risk to the offspring of adolescent parents as has often been portrayed, although the cognitive development of their children seems to be hampered. The findings are mixed in regard to the childrearing capabilities of adolescent mothers. Although the adolescent father often does not provide very strong support for the adolescent mother, there frequently is more social interaction between the adolescent mother and father than has commonly been thought.

In regard to peer relations in adolescence, friendships are very important. It seems that intimate interaction characterizes the friendships of girls more than boys and that friendships are typified by similarities among the two individuals. Participation in crowds and cliques is important to most adolescents. Although male and female adolescents mix with each other in school classes, organizations, and informal peer groups, the most serious encounters between them occur through a system called dating. At one time dating served only as a form of mate selection, but now dating provides a number of other socialization functions as well, including recreation, status sorting, and a testing ground for sexual behavior and social skills.

In addition to the contexts of family and peers, the adolescent's development is influenced by the culture in which he or she grows up. Cross-cultural comparisons of adolescents suggest that there are cultures that are both sexually more permissive and restrictive than the sexual standards that American adolescents are exposed to. Some cultures, particularly primitive ones in Sub-Saharan Africa, engage in elaborate initiation rites or rites of passage at the onset of puberty. Such ceremonies provide a much more discontinuous entry into adolescence or adulthood than we find in the American culture.

Schools and work are two other important contexts for adolescent development. Adolescents spend a large portion of the school day with their peers. These school associations carry over to serve as the focal point of many peer contacts outside of school. Peer associations may vary according to the social structure of the school and the community. Adolescents from a middle-class background, males who are athletes, and girls who are attractive seem to have advantages in the hierarchy of school power. Compared to elementary schools, where the majority of social interaction among peers occurs within the classroom, in secondary schools the entire school is the social arena for students. Attempts have been made to define the characteristics of good teachers in secondary schools; in regard to junior high school teachers, these include knowledge about the nature of adolescence and enjoyment in working with adolescents; being trustworthy, fair, and consistent; setting reasonable limits; and recognizing that early adolescents need to have someone to push against while testing such limits. Neither overcontrolling and restrictive teaching nor permissive, uninvolved teaching is the best strategy.

By the time adolescents are seniors in high school, 75 percent engage in some form of work that earns them money. There can be both advantages and disadvantages to adolescents' working. Working aids the adolescent's desire for independence, and making money provides him or her with a sense of power. Work allows adolescents to test their skills in the wider world beyond their family, peer, and school worlds. Further, adolescents learn about general aspects of work that they will need to know as adults. On the other hand, work takes adolescents away from the mainstream of school life and activities and allows them too little leisure time; the jobs most adolescents work at are not very interesting, worthwhile, or enriching; and when students work long hours, their grades often fall.

Key Terms

clique	late adolescence
crowd	middle adolescence
early adolescence	rites of passage

Review Questions

1. What is the nature of parent-adolescent conflict? How pervasive is intense, prolonged parent-adolescent conflict? Describe the developmental course of parent-adolescent conflict and conformity to peer norms.
2. What is the effect of divorce on adolescents?
3. How competent are adolescent parents? Discuss the effects of adolescent parenting in the biomedical, cognitive, and childrearing domains.
4. What is the nature of adolescent friendships?
5. Describe what adolescent crowds and cliques are like.
6. What is the function of dating in adolescence?
7. Describe cross-cultural comparisons of adolescent sexuality and the role of rites of passage in primitive cultures.
8. What is the nature of social interaction among peers in the school setting during adolescence?
9. What are some desirable characteristics of junior high teachers? Should low- and high-ability students be taught differently? Explain.
10. What is the role of work during adolescence? Discuss both the positive and negative aspects of working and going to school at the same time.

Further Readings

Berndt, T. J. The features and effects of friendship in early adolescence. *Child Development,* 1982, *53,* 1447–1460.
An up-to-date, authoritative overview of what we know about the nature of friendships in adolescence. Reading level: medium difficulty.

Feeney, S. *Schools for young adolescents: Adapting the early childhood model.* Carrboro, N.C.: Center for Early Adolescence, 1980.
A superlative examination of the role of the teacher in the lives of early adolescents. Includes valuable information for teachers who plan to work in secondary schools. Easy to read.

Hill, J. P. *Understanding early adolescence: A framework.* Carrboro, N.C.: Center for Early Adolescence, 1980.
An excellent portrayal of how settings such as the family, school, culture, and peer group influence the adolescent's development. Includes other valuable information for understanding the nature of adolescent development; provides a discussion of the simultaneous maturation of adolescents and parents. Reading level: medium difficulty.

Sommer, B. B. *Puberty and adolescence.* New York: Oxford University Press, 1978.
An easy-to-read overview of many aspects of puberty, including extensive information on rites of passage in primitive cultures.

Steinberg, L. D. *Understanding families with young adolescents.* Carrboro, N.C.: Center for Early Adolescence, 1980.
Provides an excellent discussion of the particular issues germaine to parent-adolescent relationships. Also includes information about how to better understand family dynamics when adolescents have a problem or disturbance. Easy reading.

Steinberg, L. D. Jumping off the work experience bandwagon. *Journal of Youth and Adolescence,* 1982, *11,* 183–205.
An up-to-date, competent overview of what we know about the role of work in adolescence. Includes information about part-time jobs of adolescents and also about the outcome of career education and training programs. Easy to read.

16 Emotional and Personality Development

Imagine . . . what the adolescence of Adolf Hitler, Martin Luther, and Mahatma Gandhi was like

Erik Erikson is a master at using the psychoanalytic method to uncover historical clues about identity formation. Erikson has used the psychoanalytic method both with the youth he treats in psychotherapy sessions and in the analysis of the lives of famous individuals. Erikson (1963) believes that the psychoanalytic technique sheds light on human psychological evolution. He also believes that the history of the world is a composite of individual life cycles.

In the following excerpts from Erikson's writings, the psychoanalytic method is used to analyze the youths of Adolf Hitler, Martin Luther, and Mahatma Gandhi.

I will not go into the symbolism of Hitler's urge to build except to say that his shiftless and brutal father had consistently denied the mother a steady residence; one must read how Adolf took care of his mother when she wasted away from breast cancer to get an inkling of this young man's desperate urge to cure. But it would take a very extensive analysis, indeed, to indicate in what way a single boy can daydream his way into history and emerge a sinister genius, and how a whole nation becomes ready to accept the emotive power of that genius as a hope of fulfillment for its national aspirations and as a warrant for national criminality. . . .

The memoirs of young Hitler's friend indicate an almost pitiful fear on the part of the future dictator that he might be nothing. He had to challenge this possibility by being deliberately and totally anonymous; and only out of this self-chosen nothingness could he become everything. (Erikson, 1962, pp. 108–9)

But while the identity crisis of Adolf Hitler led him to turn toward politics in a pathological effort to create a world order, the identity crisis of Martin Luther in a different era led him to turn toward theology in an attempt to deal systematically with human nothingness or lack of identity:

In confession, for example, he was so meticulous in the attempt to be truthful that he spelled out every intention as well as every deed; he splintered relatively acceptable purities into smaller and smaller impurities; he reported temptations in historical sequence, starting back in childhood; and after having confessed for hours, would ask for special appointments in order to correct previous statements. In doing this he was obviously both exceedingly compulsive and, at least unconsciously, rebellious. . . .

At this point we must note a characteristic of great young rebels: their inner split between the temptation to surrender and the need to dominate. A great young rebel is torn between, on the one hand, tendencies to give in and fantasies of defeat (Luther used to resign himself to an early death at times of impending success), and the absolute need, on the other hand, to take the lead, not only over himself but over all the forces and people who impinge on him. (Erikson, 1968, pp. 155, 157)

And in his Pulitzer Prize winning novel on Mahatma Gandhi's life, Erikson (1969) describes the personality formation of Gandhi during his youth:

Straight and yet not stiff; shy and yet not withdrawn; intelligent and yet not bookish; willful and yet not stubborn; sensual and yet not soft. . . . We must try to reflect on the relation of such a youth to his father, because the Mahatma places service to the father and the crushing guilt of failing in such service in the center of his adolescent turbulence. Some

historians and political scientists seem to find it easy to interpret this account in psychoanalytic terms; I do not. For the question is not how a particular version of the Oedipal Complex "causes" a man to be both great and neurotic in a particular way, but rather how such a young person . . . manages the complexes which constrict other men. (Erikson, 1969, p. 113)

In these passages, the workings of an insightful, sensitive mind is shown looking for a historical perspective on matters. Through analysis of the lives of famous individuals such as Hitler, Luther, and Gandhi, and through the thousands of youth he has talked with in person, Erikson has pieced together a descriptive picture of identity development.

Introduction

In this chapter we first explore the development of the self during adolescence, focusing extensively on the hallmark of self development in adolescence—identity. Then we present an overview of the problems and disturbances that adolescents experience. Among these are drug and alcohol use, juvenile delinquency, school-related problems, suicide, eating disorders, and schizophrenia.

The Self and Identity Development

In this section we explore the development of the adolescent's self and present a detailed analysis of the development of the adolescent's identity. First, we discuss the increase in the adolescent's self-awareness and self-consciousness and then provide a picture of the adolescent's self as being more stable than sometimes has been suggested by theorists who view adolescence as a period of crisis.

The Self

Self-awareness, in the form of self-consciousness, becomes particularly acute during adolescence, in contrast with late childhood when the self-concept seems to be more stable (Rosenberg, 1979). It is sometimes argued that unreflective self-acceptance begins to disappear during early adolescence and the self becomes more volatile and evanescent. What had once been unquestioned self-truths now are problematic self-hypotheses, and the search for truth about one's self is on.

Erikson also pictures the adolescent's tortuous self-consciousness. He believes that in their effort to find a coherent, unified self adolescents are often preoccupied with what they appear to be in the eyes of other people and with the question of how to connect earlier roles and skills developed in childhood with their new sense of ideal characteristics for themselves and others. Most theorists believe that preoccupation with the self begins to dissipate toward the end of adolescence and the beginning of early adulthood.

According to both Rosenberg and Erikson, then, we have to pay particular attention to adolescents with low self-esteem because they are likely to experience considerable anxiety and have difficulty in interpersonal relationships. In Rosenberg's (1965) view, low self-esteem is linked with internal distress in several ways. Putting on a front produces anxiety. Adolescents with low self-esteem have a less stable idea of their identity and do not have an adequate frame of reference for self and others. They are often lonely and vulnerable; they are likely to be sensitive to criticism and to be bothered if others have a poor opinion of them; and they often become upset when they sense that they have some inadequacy. Adolescents with low self-esteem are often awkward in social relationships, frequently assume that others do not like them, and infrequently participate in extracurricular activities, class discussions, and informal conversations.

The governing theme of self-evaluation during adolescence is identity—Who am I? Where am I going? What kind of career will I pursue? How well do I relate to females, to males? Am I able to make it on my own? These are questions that clamor for solutions in the adolescent years and that revolve around identity.

Identity

A term that is virtually inseparable from the self is **identity.** Identity is an integrative concept that is used to capture the diverse, complex components of the adolescent's personality development. The description of identity development in the adolescent can be traced directly to the thinking and writing of Erik Erikson (1963, 1968). As you may recall, identity development represents the fifth stage in Erikson's model of development, occurring at about the same time as adolescence. If postadolescents have not developed a positive sense of identity, they are described as having *identity diffusion* or *confusion.*

Certainly the idea of the **identity crisis** has permeated our society. The term is applied to practically anyone of any age who feels a loss of identification or self-image—teenagers who cannot "find" themselves; teachers who have lost their jobs; the newly divorced; business executives who are questioning their values. The term has even been applied to companies and institutions. For example, the federal government might be undergoing an "identity crisis" when it has been rocked by scandal, or a school system may be having an identity crisis when it must choose between a traditional and an innovative curriculum. In fact, the use of the term *identity crisis* has become so pervasive that defining it is difficult.

These general applications have gone far beyond Erikson's original use of the term; for Erikson (1968), identity is primarily the property of an individual person, not a group or an institution. According to Erikson, although identity is important throughout a person's life, it is only in adolescence that identity development reaches crisis proportions. A positive or negative identity is being developed throughout childhood as a result of the way various crises have been handled. The positive resolution of earlier crises, such as trust versus mistrust and industry versus inferiority, helps the individual cope positively with the identity crisis that, Erikson believes, occurs in adolescence.

Self-awareness becomes particularly acute in adolescence.

During adolescence, world views become important to an individual, who enters what Erikson terms a "psychological moratorium"—a gap between the security of childhood and the new autonomy of approaching adulthood. Numerous identities can be drawn from the surrounding culture. Adolescents can experiment with different roles, trying them out and seeing which ones they like. The youth who successfully copes with these conflicting identities during adolescence emerges with a new sense of self that is both refreshing and acceptable. The adolescent who is not successful in resolving this identity crisis becomes confused, suffering what Erikson refers to as identity confusion. This confusion may take one of two courses: the individual may withdraw, isolating herself from peers and family, or she may lose her own identity in that of the crowd.

Adolescents want to be able to decide freely for themselves such matters as what careers they will pursue, whether they will go to college or into military service, and whether or not they will marry. In other words, they want to free themselves from the shackles of their parents and other adults and make their own choices. At the same time, however, many adolescents have a deep fear of making the wrong decisions and of failing.

The choice of an occupation is particularly important in identity development. Erikson (1968) remarks that in a highly technological society like that of the United States, students who have been well trained to

"Gosh, Mom, nobody's PERFECT!"

Illustration by Bil Keane from *Just Wait 'Till You Have Children of Your Own.* Copyright © 1971 by Erma Bombeck and Bil Keane. Reprinted by permission of Doubleday & Company, Inc.

enter a work force that offers the potential of reasonably high self-esteem will experience the least stress during the development of identity. Some students have rejected jobs offering good pay and traditionally high social status, choosing instead to work in situations that allow them to be more genuinely helpful to their fellow humans, such as in the Peace Corps, in mental health clinics, or in schools for children from low-income backgrounds. Some adolescents prefer unemployment to the prospect of working at a job they would be unable to perform well or at which they would feel useless. To Erikson, this attitude reflects the desire to achieve a meaningful identity through being true to oneself (rather than burying one's identity in that of society at large).

Identity confusion may account for the large number of adolescents who run away from home, drop out of school, quit their jobs, stay out all night, or assume bizarre moods. Before Erikson's ideas became popular, these adolescents were often labeled delinquents and looked at with a disapproving eye. As a result of Erikson's writings and analyses, the problems these youth encounter are now viewed in a more positive light. Not only do runaways, school dropouts, and job quitters struggle with identity—virtually all adolescents go through an identity crisis, and some are simply able to resolve the crisis more easily than others.

Thus, the development of an integrated sense of identity is a complex and difficult task. Adolescents are expected to master many different roles in our culture. It is the rare, perhaps even nonexistent, adolescent who doesn't experience serious doubts about his or her capabilities in handling at least some of these roles competently. One psychologist, James Marcia, believes that adolescents wear four different faces in their efforts to achieve occupational and ideological identity.

Marcia's View on the Four Identity Statuses
James Marcia (1966, 1980) has analyzed Erikson's identity theory of adolescence and concluded that four identity statuses, or *modes of resolution,* appear in the theory—identity diffusion, foreclosure, moratorium, and identity achievement. The extent of an adolescent's commitment and crisis is used to classify him or her as having one of the four identity statuses. Marcia (1966) defines crisis as a period during which the adolescent is choosing among meaningful alternatives. He defines commitment as the extent to which an adolescent shows a personal investment in what he or she is doing or is going to do.

Adolescents classified as **identity diffused** (or **confused**) have not experienced any crisis (that is, they haven't explored meaningful alternatives) or made any commitments. Not only are they undecided upon occupational or ideological choices, they also are likely to show little or no interest in such matters.

The adolescent experiencing identity **foreclosure** has made a commitment but has not experienced a crisis. This occurs most often when parents simply hand down commitments to their adolescents, more often than not in an authoritarian manner. In such circumstances, adolescents may not have had enough opportunities to explore different approaches, ideologies, and vocations on their own. Some experts on adolescence, such as Kenneth Kenniston (1971), believe that experiencing a crisis is necessary for the development of a mature and self-integrated identity.

Marcia (1966) states that adolescents in the **moratorium** status are in the midst of a crisis but that their commitments are either absent or only vaguely defined. Such adolescents are searching for commitments by actively questioning alternatives.

Adolescents who have undergone a crisis and made a commitment are referred to as **identity achieved.** In other words, to reach the identity-achievement status, it is necessary for the adolescent to first experience a psychological moratorium, then make an enduring commitment.

According to Erikson the failure to explore a variety of roles in adolescence is likely to produce some type of problem in development. In the remainder of this chapter, we look at a number of problems and disturbances adolescents experience.

Problems and Disturbances
What are the major problems and disturbances of adolescents? One of the most pervasive problems that affects adolescents as opposed to children is the use of drugs.

Drugs
What kinds of drugs do adolescents take? And how prevalent is their use of drugs?

Drug Use at Any Time During Adolescence
Table 16.1 reveals the prevalence of drug use by the 1981 national sample of 17,500 seniors studied by Lloyd Johnson, Jerald Bachman, and Patrick O'Malley (1981). Two thirds of all seniors reported that they had used an illicit drug. It should be pointed out, however, that a substantial portion of these students used *only*

Most studies indicate that marijuana interferes with short-term memory and intellectual performance.

Table 16.1

Prevalence (Percent Ever Used) of Sixteen Types of Drugs: Observed Estimates (1981)

	Lower limit	Observed estimate	Upper limit
(Approx. N = 17,500)			
Marijuana/Hashish	57.3	59.5	61.7
Inhalants	11.5	12.3	13.2
Inhalants Adjusted[a]	16.4	17.4	18.4
Amyl & Butyl Nitrites[b]	8.7	10.1	11.7
Hallucinogens	12.1	13.3	14.6
Hallucinogens Adjusted[c]	14.5	15.7	17.0
LSD	8.8	9.8	10.9
PCP[b]	6.4	7.8	9.4
Cocaine	15.3	16.5	17.8
Heroin	0.9	1.1	1.4
Other opiates[d]	9.3	10.1	11.0
Stimulants[d]	30.6	32.2	33.9
Sedatives[d]	14.8	16.0	17.3
Barbiturates[d]	10.3	11.3	12.4
Methaqualone[d]	9.6	10.6	11.7
Tranquilizers[d]	13.5	14.7	16.0
Alcohol	91.4	92.6	93.6
Cigarettes	69.3	71.0	72.6

[a]Adjusted for underreporting of amyl and butyl nitrites.

[b]Data based on a single questionnaire form. N is one-fifth of N indicated.

[c]Adjusted for underreporting of PCP.

[d]Only drug use which was not under a doctor's orders is included here.

Source: National Institute on Drug Abuse. Student Drug Abuse in America 1975–1981. U.S. Department of Health and Human Services Public Health Service. By Johnston, L. D., Bachman, J. G. & O'Malley, P. M. p. 16.

marijuana (23 percent). Nevertheless, approximately, four in every ten seniors (43 percent), reported using an illicit drug other than marijuana at some point in their lives.

Marijuana is by far the most widely used illicit drug, with 60 percent reporting some use in their lifetime, 45 percent indicating some use in the last year, and 32 percent indicating some use in the last month. The most widely used class of other illicit drugs is stimulants, with a 32 percent lifetime prevalence. Next come inhalants and cocaine, both with a 17 percent incidence of use at least once. These are closely followed by sedatives (16 percent), hallucinogens (16 percent), and tranquilizers (15 percent).

The drug classes with the highest rate of discontinuation (adolescent stops using them) are heroin (35 percent of the users had not taken it within the last twelve months), the hallucinogen PCP (59 percent of the users had not taken it in the last twelve months), and inhalants (66 percent of the users had not taken them in the last twelve months).

The use of the two major licit drugs, alcohol and cigarettes, is still more widespread than the use of any of the illicit drugs. Virtually all students had tried alcohol (93 percent) and a large majority had used it in the last month (71 percent). Approximately 71 percent of all high school seniors surveyed had tried cigarettes at some point in their lives, and 29 percent reported smoking at least some in the last month.

Drug Use on a Daily Basis

Of particular concern in the abuse of drugs is their daily use by adolescents. Figure 16.1 shows the prevalence of daily or near daily use of the various classes of drugs by the national sample of 17,500 seniors in 1981. For all drugs except cigarettes, students were considered daily users if they said they had used the drug on twenty or more occasions in the last thirty days. For cigarettes, they stated whether they had smoked one or more cigarettes per day during the last thirty days. As indicated

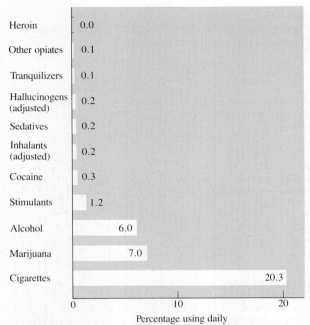

Heroin	0.0
Other opiates	0.1
Tranquilizers	0.1
Hallucinogens (adjusted)	0.2
Sedatives	0.2
Inhalants (adjusted)	0.2
Cocaine	0.3
Stimulants	1.2
Alcohol	6.0
Marijuana	7.0
Cigarettes	20.3

Percentage using daily

Figure 16.1 Thirty-day prevalence of daily use of eleven types of drugs, class of 1981.

by the figure, cigarettes are used by more than 20 percent of high school seniors on a daily basis. In fact, 13.5 percent said they smoke half a pack or more per day. Marijuana was used on a daily basis by a substantial percentage of the adolescents—7 percent. And 6 percent of high school seniors reported using alcohol this often. A very small percentage of the high school seniors took illicit drugs other than marijuana on a daily basis—less than 1.3 percent. It should be mentioned that although alcohol use on a daily basis was reported by only 6 percent of the sample, a much greater proportion said that they occasionally drink heavily. A full 41 percent said that on at least one occasion in the last two weeks they had had five or more drinks in a row!

Sex Differences in Drug Use
Overall, adolescent males are involved in drug use more than their female counterparts are, but the picture for sex differences is complicated. In the national survey by Johnston, Bachman, and O'Malley (1981), marijuana use at some point in life was only somewhat higher for males than females, but on a daily basis, adolescent males used marijuana about twice as much as females did (9.6 versus 4.2 percent). Adolescent males

Adolescent males are more likely to drink on a daily basis than their female counterparts.

also took most other illicit drugs—inhalents, hallucinogens, heroin, cocaine, and barbituates, for example—more often than females did. But in the case of stimulants, the annual prevalence rates as well as frequent usage patterns were higher for females than for males (27 compared to 25 percent). However, this finding may be inaccurate because a much greater proportion of adolescent females take over-the-counter diet preparations and may have mistakenly believed that these are illicit drugs. Males also used alcohol more on a daily basis than females did (8.4 versus 3.4 percent). There was only a very slight difference in the prevalence of smoking a half a pack or more cigarettes daily, with females doing this more often than males (13.8 versus 12.8 percent). When questioned about smoking during the past month, 32 percent of the girls said they had as compared with 27 percent of the males.

The Institute for Social Research at the University of Michigan has been charting drug use of high school seniors for a number of years, beginning with the graduating class of 1975. In this section, we look at the trends in drug use that were found between 1975 and 1981 (Johnston, Bachman, & O'Malley, 1981).

Apparently, 1978 and 1979 represented the crest in a long, dramatic rise in marijuana use by high school students. For example, the annual and thirty day prevalence of marijuana use hardly changed at all between 1978 and 1979, after a steady rise in prior years. Both are now 5 percent below their all-time highs. There has been an even sharper downward trend in daily marijuana use. Daily marijuana use by high school seniors dropped from 10.7 percent in 1978 to 7.0 percent in 1981. Much of this reversal is probably due to increased concern about the possible adverse effects of regular use of marijuana and the perception that peers are now more disapproving of regular marijuana use than in the past.

The use of cocaine and inhalants, on the other hand, increased dramatically. In just three years, 1976 to 1979, the use of cocaine by high school seniors at least once during the year went from 6 percent to 12 percent. However, the use of cocaine by high school students has now leveled off. Like cocaine, inhalent use by adolescents rose steadily in the mid-1970s. Since 1979, however, there has been a decline in annual use from 6.5 percent of high school seniors in 1979 to 3.7 percent in 1981.

Stimulant use, which remained relatively unchanged between 1975 and 1978, began to gradually increase in 1979 and continued to increase in 1980 and 1981. Daily use tripled between 1976 and 1981 (0.4 percent to 1.2 percent). For sedatives, the gradual decline between 1975 and 1979 seems to have stopped and possibly begun to reverse. In particular, methaqualone (Quaaludes) use has risen sharply since 1976. Hallucinogen use declined gradually from 1975 to 1978, but the decline has now leveled out. The specific hallucinogen PCP showed a sizeable decrease in use in both 1980 and 1981.

In summary, it should be pointed out that the overall proportion of seniors using any illicit drugs other than marijuana or amphetamines has not changed a great deal since the mid-1970s. But the mix of drugs adolescents are now using has changed.

In terms of licit drugs, between 1975 and 1978 there was a small increase in alcohol use among seniors. Since 1978, the alcohol prevalence figures have remained nearly constant. For cigarette use, 1976 and 1977 appear to have been peak years. Important is the

It is not unusual for adolescents to mix school and drug use.

fact that daily cigarette use dropped from 29 percent (1977) to 20 percent (1981) of students, and daily use of a half a pack or more dropped from 19.4 to 13.5 percent in the same period.

The school is one important setting where drugs are used by adolescents. In application 16.1, the role of schools in the prevention and intervention of drug abuse is described.

As was indicated earlier, alcohol is a drug. However, because its use has become so widespread among adolescents, we give special, separate attention to it in the next section.

Alcohol

Some mornings the fifteen-year-old cheerleader was too drunk to go to school. Other days, she'd stop for a couple of beers or a screwdriver on the way to school. She is tall, blonde, and good-looking, and no one who sold her liquor, even at 8 o'clock in the morning, questioned how old she was. Where did she get her money? Babysitting and what her mother gave her to buy lunch

Application 16.1
School Policy and Drug Use

Patricia Minuchin and Edna Shapiro (1983) recently reviewed the nature of drug prevention and intervention programs in schools. Beyond policies about substance use on the school premises, many schools have developed or housed drug prevention and intervention programs. During the 1970s, the nature of these programs changed. Earlier programs emphasized detection, discipline, and scare tactics; like similar approaches to sexually transmitted diseases and smoking, they were not successful. Subsequent programs have focused on relevant information and frequently have dealt with psychological issues, such as self-awareness, values clarification, communication skills, decision making, and peer relationships. These programs often have used effective experiential techniques and worked with students in small groups, using medical and psychological experts, ex-addicts, school counselors, teachers, and students as leaders. Most of the programs have been relatively short term, ranging from one or two days to a semester (Volpe, 1977).

It has been argued that as long as people seek pleasure and pleasure-producing substances are available, adolescents will continue to take drugs (Randall & Wong, 1976). Given the likelihood that schools will continue to prohibit the use of drugs on the premises and the generation gap in attitudes (Johnston et al., 1981), many secondary school students probably will continue to see the use of alcohol and drugs as a source of pleasure and a means of challenging authority. School programs designed to prevent or intervene in the use of illicit drugs have, by and large, been only marginally successful. The most promising programs have involved a comprehensive, long-term approach, not only providing specific information and services but dealing in the social organization of the school as a whole as well.

paid for it all. She no longer is a cheerleader, having been kicked off the squad for missing practice frequently. Eventually, her advisor found out about her drinking problem. As the fifteen-year-old reflected on her behavior, she commented how she and several of her peers got high almost every morning. Not infrequently, they drank during and after school too. And sometimes they skipped school and went to the woods to drink. The girl's whole life began to revolve around her drinking. It went on for two years, and during last summer, anytime anybody saw her she was drunk.

Unfortunately, there are hundreds of thousands of adolescents just like the fifteen-year-old cheerleader. They live in both wealthy suburbs and inner-city housing projects. The cheerleader grew up in a Chicago suburb and said she started drinking when she was ten because her older brothers always looked like they were having fun when they were doing it. She said it made her feel good and peaceful. She commented that drinking made her feel more sociable to the point that she felt confident she could talk to anybody about anything. After a while, her parents began to detect what was going on. But even when they punished her, she didn't stop drinking. Finally, this year, she started dating a boy whom she really likes who wouldn't put up with her drinking. She agreed to go to Alcoholics Anonymous and has just completed treatment. She hasn't had a drink for four months now; it is to be hoped that her abstinence will continue.

The Prevalence of Drinking among Adolescents

Alcohol is the most widely used of all drugs by adolescents, according to the national surveys conducted by the Institute of Social Research at the University of Michigan (Johnston, Bachman, & O'Malley, 1981). To summarize some of the recent data: More than half of all adolescents have tried alcohol before entering the tenth grade. Nearly all adolescents have tried alcohol by the time they are seniors in high school (93 percent), with a large majority having used it during the last year (87 percent). Half report using it on at least a weekly basis, and daily use occurs among 6 percent of all seniors. Just as important is information suggesting that 41 percent said that they consumed five or more drinks at least once during the previous two weeks. With regard to recent trends, there was a slight increase in alcohol use by adolescents between 1975 and 1978, but since 1978 such use has remained relatively stable.

Physical, Mental, and Behavioral Effects of Drinking

Alcohol is a depressant that primarily affects the central nervous system. It is popularly believed that alcohol increases arousal and excitement, but in reality it slows down or depresses many of the brain's activities. After a certain level of alcohol accumulates in the bloodstream, the familiar pattern of drunkenness ensues, usually involving a loss of mental and physical alertness and coordination. After prolonged consumption, unconsciousness may result.

Too many adolescents mix heavy drinking and driving.

The use of alcohol in large quantities can have a variety of negative consequences for the physical development of the adolescent. For one, he or she may develop a chronic irritation of the stomach lining, leading to an ulcer. In addition, fat may accumulate in the liver and impair its functioning. And irreparable damage to the central nervous system may eventuate after excessive, prolonged use of alcohol.

The most dramatic consequences of alcohol use pertain to mood and behavior modification. Such alterations of feelings and conduct are due to the action of alcohol on the central nervous system, specifically the brain, and are in direct proportion to the blood-alcohol level or blood-alcohol concentration.

The startling statistic mentioned earlier, that in the last two weeks 41 percent of the seniors in the United States had five or more drinks on at least one occasion, combined with the increasing number of adolescents who drive can only lead to one conclusion—too many alcohol-related adolescent driving accidents and deaths. In 1976 alone, for example, 8,000 adolescents died in alcohol-related car accidents, and most of the drunk drivers who caused those accidents were under twenty-five years of age (Martin, 1977).

Delinquents may drink for reasons different from those of nondelinquents—more for the effect than nondelinquents, who are more likely to drink to help them socialize, celebrate, or simply "to have fun" (Barnes, 1977). At any rate, the relation between drinking and delinquency merits further study. Next, we look in greater detail at the prevalent problem of juvenile delinquency in our society.

Juvenile Delinquency
The label "juvenile delinquent" is applied to an adolescent who breaks the law or engages in behavior that is considered illegal. Like other categories of disturbance, juvenile delinquency is a broad concept; legal infractions may range from littering to murder. Because the youth technically becomes a juvenile delinquent only after judged guilty of a crime by a court of law, official records do not accurately reflect the number of illegal acts committed. Nevertheless, there is still every indication that in the last ten or fifteen years, juvenile delinquency has increased in relation to the number of crimes committed by adults.

Estimates regarding the number of juvenile delinquents in the United States are sketchy, although FBI statistics suggest that at least 2 percent of all youths are involved in juvenile court cases. The number of girls found guilty of juvenile delinquency has increased significantly in recent years. Delinquency rates among blacks, other minority groups, and the lower class are particularly high in relation to the overall populations of these groups. However, such groups have less influence than others over the judicial decision-making process in the United States and thus may be judged delinquent more readily than their white, middle-class counterparts.

The National Survey of Youth (Gold & Reimer, 1975) asked 1,395 adolescents about their delinquent behavior. As indicated in figure 16.2, the incidence of nontrivial delinquent acts rose from the early part of adolescence to the later part. For example, eighteen-year-olds confessed to about five times more nontrivial delinquent behavior than did eleven-year-olds. Note that there is an acceleration of delinquent acts around the age of fifteen.

In application 16.2, another, very important aspect of delinquency is discussed: What is the best way to intervene and help adolescents who frequently commit delinquent acts?

School-Related Problems

Difficulties in school achievement, whether secondary to other kinds of disturbance or primary in their own right, seem to account for more referrals of adolescents for clinical treatment than any other problem (Weiner, 1980). One pervasive aspect of school-related problems and disturbances is underachievement.

School underachievement refers to the student's failure to receive grades commensurate with his or her intellectual abilities. Unexpected poor school performance has been estimated to occur in 25 percent of schoolchildren. And it appears that approximately one third of adolescents seen in psychiatric clinics are referred because of school learning problems (Gardner & Speery, 1974). Furthermore, more than 50 percent of college students who request counseling and psychotherapy do so because of worries about studying and grades (Blaine & McArthur, 1971).

School underachievement may occur because of sociocultural factors such as family and neighborhood value systems that minimize the importance of education and peer group attitudes that stamp academic success as unmanly for boys and unfeminine for girls. From Weiner's perspective, this type of underachievement does not constitute a psychological disturbance. Rather, school problems that involve psychological disturbances can be traced to two circumstances: The first is attention, concentration, and specific learning handicap, often associated with neurological problems, which are usually detected in the elementary school years. Second, neurotic patterns of family interaction may produce a pattern of passive-aggressive underachievement. It is the second pattern of underachievement that is more characteristic of a majority of adolescents with achievement problems, and the one we will focus on here.

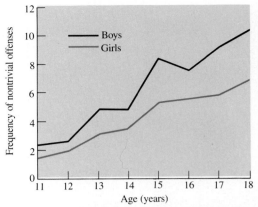

Figure 16.2 Mean frequency of nontrivial incidents committed by adolescents.
(*Source:* Gold, M. & Petronio, R. J. *Delinquint behavior in adolescence.* In J. Adelson (ed.), *Handbook of Adolescent Psychology.* New York: John Wiley, 1980.)

From Weiner's perspective, there are three factors that usually contribute to the development of passive-aggressive underachievement:

1. Extensive hostility, usually toward parents, that cannot be expressed directly.
2. Worry about rivalry with parents and siblings that produces fear of failure or fear of success.
3. Adoption of a passive-aggressive pattern of behavior in coping with difficult, stressful situations.

The underlying anger of passive-aggressive underachieving adolescents and their anxiety about rivalry may not be obvious. Such anxiety often is not detected until the adolescent undergoes therapy. However, such behavior is often easy to detect from the adolescent's obvious passive-aggressive style of coping with academic matters. What does it mean when we say the achievement behavior of certain adolescents is **passive-aggressive**? It means that they are purposely inactive. They work hard at making sure nothing happens that will raise their grades up to their ability. Passive-aggressive underachieving adolescents may turn their energy to extracurricular activities or work to the point at which they have little time for studying. Compared to their achieving peers, these adolescents are just as energetic and hard working, but when confronted with having to do schoolwork, they study less and often do not hand in assignments on time.

Think about your own secondary school years or about adolescents you know today. Chances are you will be able to pick out a number of people you knew or know now whose behavior follows the underachieving patterns we have described here.

Next we look at a serious disturbance that has been increasing in recent years—adolescent suicide.

Application 16.2
Intervention Programs Designed to Help Delinquents

As Martin Gold and Richard Petronio (1980) comment, a large book could be filled with brief descriptions of the varied attempts to reduce delinquency—these include individual and group psychotherapy, family therapy, behavior modification, recreation, vocational training, alternative schools, survival camping and wilderness canoeing, incarceration and probation, "big brothers" and "big sisters," community organization, and Bible reading, to name some of the more popular suggestions. However, we actually know surprisingly little about what actually does work, and it appears, for the most part, that most programs have not been very successful. If they were very successful, we should be seeing a reduction in delinquency rates, but we are not.

In a review of intervention programs designed to help delinquents (Gold & Petronio, 1980), it was concluded that the major treatment of delinquency has been housed in the juvenile justice system. Since about 1900, juveniles have been treated differently from adults by the court system. The underlying belief is that the antisocial behavior of children and adolescents, who still are in their formative years, should be viewed more as mental illness than criminal behavior. From this perspective, guilt for the offense should not be laid on the individual adolescent, and treatment should be more curative than punitive.

Arguments for change in the juvenile delinquency system are rooted in the belief that a system that was created to promote child and adolescent development has had the opposite effect, namely to harm growth and development. The charges include arguments that the freedom of too many adolescents has been restricted on the basis of insufficient evidence and for insufficient reasons, that treatment has been more punitive than curative, and that the overall effect of the judicial system has been to increase rather than decrease juvenile delinquency. There is actually good reason to believe that the judicial system for handling delinquency does need to be overhauled, although there is not agreement on what should be done. For example, investigations usually show that the judicial system is either ineffective (Gold & Williams, 1969) or the evidence is not clear one way or the other (Gold & Petronio, 1980).

In addition to the judicial system, there are many other attempts to curb delinquent behavior, as was mentioned at the beginning of this section. Even though most programs do not seem to work very effectively, it would be wrong to conclude that nothing works.

One intervention program that was effective in reducing the delinquency rate focused on an alternative school in Quincy, Illinois (Bowman, 1959). Sixty boys in the ninth grade with below average ability who were not doing well in school were selected for the study and randomly assigned to one of three groups. Forty of the boys experienced a curriculum different from the conventional one at the school, whereas the remaining twenty boys continued to attend the conventional classes. The teachers of the two experimental classes were chosen because they seemed to have an interest in and sympathy for adolescents who get in trouble. The classes were small, and the delinquents were given considerable individual attention. Student-teacher interaction was informal and friendly. Formal grading was abandoned, each student instead being evaluated on the basis of his own progress. Discipline was firm but not punitive and focused on problem solving. At the end of the school term, the students were given the choice of returning to conventional classrooms, but only two chose to do so.

Compared to the control group of delinquents who remained in a conventional classroom, those in the experimental classrooms showed marked improvement. Although they did not do better on standardized achievement tests, they perceived that they were doing better academically and said they now liked school more. Their school attendance improved, whereas the attendance of those in the control group declined. School and police records documented that the antisocial and delinquency behavior of the delinquents in the experimental group decreased by one-third, whereas the record for the control group tripled. Finally, a follow-up of these boys suggested that those in the experimental group made a better transition to the world of work than their control counterparts did.

Another attempt to reduce delinquency (Gold & Mattick, 1974) focused on street gangs in Chicago. Boys clubs assigned street workers and community organizers to specific inner-city locations, and nearby neighborhoods were studied as controls. Although there was little reduction in the delinquency rate of the adolescents in the targeted neighborhoods, the workers were successful in helping boys find jobs or return to school.

Indeed, in their review of intervention programs for delinquents, Gold and Petronio (1980) concluded that although the source and style of successful programs often vary, two themes seem to be dominant: (1) the support of warm, accepting relationships with adults, and (2) the enhancement of the adolescent's self-image as an autonomous and effective individual.

A host of intervention strategies have been used to try to curb delinquency.

Suicide

Nationally, the suicide rate for adolescents suggests that suicide is the third major cause of death, after accidents and murder. And the suicide rate for adolescents has increased 300 percent since 1950. Further, on the average, each minute of the day an adolescent attempts suicide somewhere in the United States. Every day about fourteen succeed. (See figure 16.3.) The typical adolescent suicide victim is white, male, and from the middle class. Guns are the means most often used, and the most common reason is depression over the loss of loved ones or status.

Some experts predict that the adolescent suicide rate will go down in the 1980s as the population of the adolescent age group declines. From this perspective, it is suggested that lessening competition for such important matters as jobs and college admission will mean that more adolescents will achieve their goals, and thus fewer will be pressured to commit suicide. But other experts believe that the adolescent suicide rate will not decline until the incidence of violence and the pace of family disintegration in our culture slows down. From this perspective, it is predicted that by the year 2000 the suicide rate for adolescent males will increase 120 percent, and the rate for adolescent females will rise to 114 percent of its current level (Austin & Little, 1982).

A conversation between a young boy and his therapist indicates how a suicide attempt may develop:

Therapist Tell me, what went wrong?

Boy When?

Therapist I want to know why you have come to see me.

Boy O.K. You might as well know. I tried to kill myself.

Therapist Why?

Boy Things are horrible at home. My mother bitches at me all the time and my father is an alcoholic. I can't do anything right in their eyes. They never help me with anything, and they always are cutting me down. I don't have any friends either. I'm doing poorly in school, and my parents have gotten on me more and more about that. I just decided that the only way out was to kill myself.

In one comprehensive study of adolescent suicide, fifty adolescents who had attempted suicide were interviewed about their lives (Jacobs, 1971). These adolescents were then compared with a group of adolescents who had not attempted suicide in order to discover how their lives differed. The parents of the adolescents who attempted suicide were much more likely than the other parents to state that their youth were

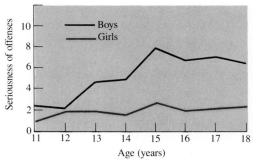

Figure 16.3 Suicide rates for persons ten to nineteen years old in the ten largest cities in 1981. (*Source:* U.S. Bureau of the Census, 1981.)

There have been dramatic increases in adolescent suicides in recent years.

gloomy, silent, and withdrawn and had run away from home. The suicidal youth also were considered more disobedient and defiant. The adolescents who had attempted suicide said that their parents were much more likely to nag at them, criticize them, and withhold affection from them than did the nonsuicidal group. Fifty-eight percent of the suicidal youth reported that their parents had divorced, separated, or remarried within the five years preceding the suicide attempt, compared to only 10 percent of the nonsuicidal group. The alienation of the adolescent from his or her family appears to be associated with suicide attempts. Excessive criticism, little positive feedback, arguing, divorce, and other stressful family events may be the context and trigger for suicide attempts during adolescence. The more such negative experiences and events that pile up in the adolescent's life, the more likely the adolescent is to consider taking his or her own life.

In other research, it has been indicated that a broken home in itself is no more likely to appear in the backgrounds of adolescent suicide attempters than in those of nonattempters (Stanley & Barter, 1970). However, this same investigation did find that the parents of youth who attempted suicide talked about and threatened divorce more than the parents of the nonsuicidal group did. Some of the youths in this study attempted suicide again after they had been hospitalized for their first suicide attempt. Those who attempted suicide again were more likely to have poor relations with peers than those who did not attempt it again. Thus, in some instances parental problems may be the main factor in the suicide attempt, whereas in others peer problems may be at the root of the disturbance. When the adolescent has few positive experiences in either of these spheres, depression and suicidal tendencies are likely to become even more pronounced.

Can we predict whether an adolescent will attempt to commit suicide? It isn't easy, but there are some signs that might serve as clues. For example, the adolescent who talks about committing suicide often is serious. And adolescents who attempt suicide once are likely to try it again. Severe family problems, the loss of a loved one, and other highly stressful events can signal an approaching suicide attempt.

As part of the effort to provide mental health services to those individuals in acute need of psychological help, a number of community mental health services have set up crisis intervention centers. Trained volunteers monitor incoming calls and try to comfort, reason with, and dissuade the callers from acting rashly. Some of these centers focus exclusively on suicide prevention and are appropriately called suicide prevention centers. Although such centers are a positive step in helping adolescents cope with severe depression, there is some indication that suicide prevention centers in their present form cannot always do the job. For example, in one investigation (Wilkins, 1970), it was estimated that 98 percent of the individuals who commit suicide never call such centers.

The increase in adolescent suicide during the last twenty-five years is a symptom of the stress that many adolescents now experience as they try to grow from dependent children to independent adults. But remember that while suicide attempts have increased, suicidal adolescents represent a very small minority of the adolescents in our culture. The large majority of adolescents learn to deal effectively with stress and tension and never become so immersed in depression that they would consider taking their own lives.

Next we look at another problem that has increased in adolescence—eating disorders.

Eating Disorders

The ideal female in our culture today is characterized by a thin, "perfect" body more than in past years, when a more shapely, robust body was the ideal. As part of this search for the ideal female figure, many girls and women constantly worry about their weight. Kim Chernin (1981) has described two facts that make the current obsession with weight loss unusual. One is the scope of it. Throughout history there have been dieters, including Roman matrons who were willing to starve themselves. But there never has been a period as now when such large numbers of adolescents and adults have spent so much money, time, and energy on their weight. The second unusual aspect of the current concern about weight loss is the degree to which it involves females rather than males. Although our nation has its share of adolescent and adult males who want to lose weight, the truly excessively obsessive dieter is almost inevitably female. Females make up more than 90 percent of the people who suffer from **anorexia nervosa,** a personality disorder that leads to self-starvation. Similarly, **bulimia,** a condition in which periods of heavy eating are followed by self-induced vomiting, is almost exclusively a female phenomenon. Along with obesity, anorexia nervosa and bulimia are the major eating disorders in adolescence. Let's look in more detail at the disturbance of anorexia nervosa.

Anorexia Nervosa

Several physical and psychosocial features characterize anorexia in adolescence (Bruch, 1973). Severe malnutrition and emaciation are accompanied by amenorrhea (no menstrual periods occur as a result of a decrease in body fat). Often anorexic adolescents show an obsession with activity that they feel will peel off fat. Although anorexic adolescents avoid eating, the term *anorexia* is somewhat misleading. Actually, such adolescents have an intense interest in food, cook for others, talk about food, and insist on watching others eat. Usually when they begin dieting they are of average weight. However, many anorexic adolescents do not feel in control of their lives or useful. Many anorexics experience their bodies as something extra—not part of themselves. They complain of feeling full after a few bites of food, which symbolizes a sense of control. (By contrast, the obese adolescent feels empty after a full meal and does not feel that he or she can control food). The anorexic adolescent also is excessively preoccupied with body size. A close look at the anorexic adolescent's family often reveals serious problems. The case study presented in application 16.3 reflects some of the family dynamics that often characterize the anorexic adolescent.

As anorexia progresses, abstinence of food alternates with uncontrollable eating binges during which the adolescent doesn't feel hungry. Many adolescents try to remove the food by forced vomiting, enemas, laxatives, or fasting.

Next we look at a disturbance that does not occur very frequently. This is fortunate because schizophrenia is a very serious, debilitating disturbance.

Schizophrenia

Schizophrenia, a form of psychosis characterized by illogical thought, hallucinations, and erratic behavior, is one of the most severe forms of disturbance in adolescence. Fortunately, a very small percentage of adolescents are schizophrenic. Although approximately 1 percent of the adult population is considered schizophrenic, only about 4 percent of this group (or 0.04 percent of the total adult population) became schizophrenic during childhood. The majority of schizophrenic adults first showed signs of schizophrenia in late adolescence or young adulthood (Erikson, 1978).

In discussing the nature of schizophrenia, Irving Weiner (1980) concludes that when its onset occurs in adolescence three characteristics distinguish it from schizophrenia initially occurring in adulthood:

1. Schizophrenia that begins in adolescence is more likely to present a mixed disturbance in which identifying features of the schizophrenia are obscured by other symptoms. For example, the schizophrenic adolescent initially may complain

Application 16.3
Jane: A Sixteen-Year-Old Anorexic

Sixteen-year-old Jane is the second of three children from a warm, middle-class, Irish Catholic family. She was an "easy" baby who never demanded cuddling. She was a helpful toddler who learned how to fold clothes at two, but she felt her siblings deserved more attention. In family snapshots she often stood off to the side like a spectator observing the rest of the family. Her parents were doting but preoccupied with their own troubles—Mr. Denton was just starting a new business, and Mrs. Denton was trying to cope with the death of her father. The Denton household was well stocked with food, but both parents in different ways, broadcast clear messages that thinness was desirable. When Jane was fifteen, she felt that she had an ugly face and a dull personality and that she was too fat (five feet, eight inches; 135 pounds). She didn't know how to change her looks or personality, but she could lose weight. She felt very threatened by the pressure of school, both academically and socially. Gradually, she began eliminating foods until she subsisted *only* on applesauce and eggnog. Jane spent many hours observing her body; she often would wrap her fingers around her wrist to see if it was getting thinner. At the same time she fantasized that she was going to become a beautiful blond who would wear designer bathing suits. But even when she reached ninety pounds, she perceived that she was still fat!

She had disowned her body and spoke in a whisper so she would be inaudible as well as invisible. The thought of meeting a boy terrified her. Feelings of incompetence and loss of control overwhelmed Jane. Her parents begged and then nagged her to eat. Clinical help was not sought by her parents, however, until she totally isolated and emaciated herself.

Jane's case involved three areas of disordered psychological functions that often characterize anorexic adolescents. First, there was a disturbance of delusional proportion in body concept; second, there was a disturbance in the accuracy or cognitive interpretation of stimuli arising in the body, with failure to recognize hunger or nutritional needs; and third, there was a paralyzing sense of ineffectiveness that pervaded virtually all thinking and activities (Deutsch, 1982).

The ideal female in our culture today is thin.

primarily about depressive symptoms or show sociopathic tendencies, such as running away and truancy. The initial onset of schizophrenia, therefore, is often more difficult to detect in adolescence than in adulthood. Sometimes only the persistence of schizophrenic characteristics, such as incoherent thinking, inaccurate perceptions, and inappropriate affect, after the other symptoms have lessened, allow the disorder to be diagnosed as schizophrenia.

2. Certain aspects of social and personality development during childhood and adolescence can be identified as having a relatively high risk for the subsequent appearance of schizophrenia. Poor peer group relationships, having very few friends or infrequently interacting with friends, and sociopathic behavior within the home itself rather than outside of the home increase the likelihood that adolescents will become schizophrenic.

3. The long-term prognosis for the successful treatment of adolescents who develop schizophrenia is not as good as when the disorder first appears in adulthood.

Our discussion of the factors that distinguish adolescent schizophrenia from adult schizophrenia concludes our overview of the types of problems and disturbances adolescents experience.

Although we are at the end of our discussion of development from conception through adolescence and there are no more chapters to read, the epilogue that follows this chapter describes the nature of the transition from adolescence to adulthood.

Summary

Most psychologists agree that the self is an important aspect of adolescent development. There has been considerable interest in the extent to which the self remains stable or changes a great deal during adolescence. Most experts argue that the changes are not as stressful as some once envisioned but that in response to changes in physical development, cognitive development, and social relationships, the self gradually changes.

The hallmark of development of self in adolescence is identity. Erik Erikson's construct of identity is recognized by many psychologists as the most important integrative concept in the study of adolescence. Erikson believes that the onset of adolescence is associated with the beginning of the fifth stage of development, which he calls identity versus identity diffusion or confusion. Identity development requires adolescents to piece together information about themselves in a meaningful way.

Erikson has relied upon the methods of psychoanalysis to gain knowledge about identity development. As part of his attempt to understand the identity-formation process, he has analyzed the life histories of many famous individuals, including Adolf Hitler, Martin Luther, and Mahatma Gandhi. Erikson believes that as part of identity development the adolescent must experiment with a variety of roles and personalities. In particular, exposure to vocational and ideological alternatives stimulates the achievement of a stable identity.

James Marcia has refined Erikson's concept of identity development into four different statuses that capture the essence of Erikson's ideas. The four statuses are identity diffusion or confusion, foreclosure, moratorium, and identity achievement.

Adolescents encounter a variety of problems and disturbances as they grow from childhood to adulthood, but most teenagers are able to overcome these problems.

Among the problems and disturbances in adolescence are drug use, juvenile delinquency, poor schoolwork, and feelings of unhappiness or depression.

Although the overall rate of drug use by adolescence does not seem to be increasing, there has been a change in the mix of drugs adolescents have been using in recent years. For example, marijuana use has decreased, but inhalent use has increased since the mid-1970s. Adolescents are smoking less now than they were in the mid-1970s. Although the number of adolescents who drink does not seem to be increasing, many adolescents still often go on drinking binges. Even though adolescent males are much more likely to use illicit drugs than females are, in the licit drug category of nicotine, girls now smoke more frequently than males do. Among adolescents, alcohol is the most widely used drug, and marijuana is the most widely used illicit drug.

Juvenile delinquency represents another pervasive problem in adolescence. It is important to recognize that most estimates of the incidence of delinquency are underreported because technically to become a juvenile you have to be judged as such by the legal system. Clearly, the majority of delinquent acts by adolescents go undetected. The juvenile justice system does not seem to be effective in curbing delinquency. Good evidence suggests that when we consider all delinquent acts, there is an increase in such acts from the beginning of adolescence to the end, although the peak time of serious delinquent acts occurs at about the age of fifteen. A host of intervention programs have been designed to help delinquents. Although most intervention programs are not successful, those that are seem to involve warm, supportive adults and to increase the adolescent's sense of effectiveness and autonomy.

Some adolescent problems originate with the school setting, whereas many other problems are in some way linked with the school setting even though they may not have originated because of school. Neurotic patterns of family interaction that are likely to promote underachievement in school include direct hostility toward parents that cannot be expressed; family rivalry that produces fear of failure or fear of success; development of a passive-aggressive style of coping with stress. Suicide is the third leading cause of death in adolescence, having tripled since 1950. It often occurs when adolescents lose someone they love and feel helpless in being able to control that aspect of their lives.

There seems to be an increase in adolescent eating disorders. One major reason for the increase in adolescent female eating disorders focuses on the cultural standard of the ideal female, which has changed from a more full, shapely figure to a thinner body. In anorexia nervosa, the adolescent virtually starves herself to the point where she becomes emaciated. In bulimia, the adolescent pursues a diet-binge-purge sequence. These two eating disorders are almost exclusively female.

Some experts believe it is important to distinguish between schizophrenia that has its onset in adolescence as opposed to adulthood. In this regard, adolescent schizophrenia is more debilitating because in its earliest form it is obscured by other symptoms, it is more likely to be characterized by poor peer group and friendship relations, and it has a poorer prognosis for successful treatment.

Key Terms

anorexia nervosa
bulimia
foreclosure
identity
identity achieved
identity crisis
identity diffused (confused)
moratorium
passive-aggressive behavior
schizophrenia

Review Questions

1. What is the nature of the development of the self in adolescence? To what extent is the development of the self stable or changing during adolescence?
2. Discuss Erik Erikson's theory of identity development. Also describe James Marcia's four identity statuses.
3. Describe the drugs that adolescents have taken most and those they have taken least during their adolescent years.
4. Describe the extent to which adolescents take different drugs on a daily basis. Also discuss recent trends in drug use by adolescents.
5. Evaluate the role of the school in the prevention and intervention of drug use by adolescents.
6. Describe the developmental course of delinquency from late childhood through adolescence.
7. Narrate the effectiveness of various intervention programs designed to reduce delinquency.
8. Discuss the reasons why many adolescents underachieve in school.
9. Why do adolescents commit suicide?
10. Describe the nature of anorexia nervosa, including in your answer information about the psychological and family characteristics related to this disorder.
11. What is the nature of schizophrenia? How can the onset of schizophrenia in adolescence be differentiated from schizophrenia that begins in adulthood?

Further Readings

Achenbach, T. M., & Edelbrock, C. S. Behavioral problems and competencies reported by parents of normal and disturbed children aged four through sixteen. *Monographs of the Society for Research in Child Development,* serial no. 188, vol. 46, no. 1. *The complete data collected by Achenbach and Edelbrock are presented, including graphs of all 118 items on the Child Behavioral Checklist. Tells how to differentiate adolescents referred for clinical treatment from those who are not. Medium reading difficulty.*

Bruch, H. *Eating disorders.* New York: Basic Books, 1973. *An excellent source of information about obese, bulimic, and anorexic adolescents. Reasonably easy reading.*

Engs, R. C. *Responsible drug and alcohol use.* New York: Macmillan, 1979. *Contains valuable information about intelligent, responsible choices related to drug and alcohol use. Includes many studies about the effects of various drugs on the human body, including possible harmful effects. Reasonably easy to read.*

Gold M., & Petronio, R. J. Delinquent behavior in adolscence. In J. Adelson (ed.), *Handbook of Adolescent Psychology.* New York: John Wiley, 1980. *An excellent overview of the nature of delinquency, developmental factors involved in delinquency, and intervention programs. Reading level: medium difficulty.*

Jacobs, J. *Adolescent suicide.* New York: John Wiley, 1971. *An easy-to-read comprehensive study of a number of youth who have attempted suicide.*

Johnston, L. D., Bachman, J. G., & O'Malley, P. M. *Student drug use in America 1975–1981.* Rockville, Md.: National Institute on Drug Abuse, 1981. *A massive 433-page document that presents the findings of a longitudinal study of drugs used by adolescents; filled with charts and tables on the use of various drugs by adolescents. Reasonably easy reading.*

Weiner, I. B. Psychopathology in adolescence. In J. Adelson (ed.), *Handbook of adolescent psychology.* New York: John Wiley, 1980. *Weiner's chapter represents an excellent analysis of some of the major disturbances in adolescence. Included is information about school-related problems, schizophrenia, depression, and suicide.*

Know Yourself

You probably will remember more about your adolescent years than any other period of development that we have discussed. For many of you it wasn't very long ago that you graduated from high school. Think first about your early adolescent years. When did you start puberty? How much concern did you show about your changing body? Did you spend long hours in front of the mirror? How moody were you? When you were in junior high school what kind of career did you want to pursue? Has it changed? What were your relationships with your parents like? Did conflict with your parents increase during the junior high school years? What kinds of things did you and your parents agree and disagree about? Were you able to think more abstractly? Did you question your parents' reasoning and logic a lot more? Did you show an increased interest in religion? Did you get into any trouble or commit any delinquent acts while you were in junior high school? Did you want to spend as much time with your friends and peers as possible? How much did you conform to your peers' standards? What were the "in" things in your clique? Remember your first date. What was it like?

Now let's turn the clock ahead to the late adolescent years. Think about what you were like as a senior in high school. Making it through that algebra class was a long time ago, and much happened to you between early and later adolescence. When you were a senior in high school did you show as much interest in your body image as you did a few years earlier? Had your plans for college crytallized? Did you have a better idea of the type of career you wanted to follow? Did you have some work experiences by the time you were a senior? Did you have your driver's licence? Although you probably still had conflicts with your parents, were such conflicts as frequent as they were in junior high?

Did your parents allow you to do more things on your own when you were a senior? During your last few years of high school did you engage in speculation about different possibilities in your life—when you would get married or if you would get married? What about your present drinking habits? Your sexual experiences? Have these changed now that you are in college, or are they about the same as in your high school years? What do you want to do with your life?

Once again you should enjoy discussing some of these experiences with one or two friends or classmates. Ask them about their early- and late-adolescent experiences. What were their peer group experiences like? What was their puberty like? Were they early or late maturers, or did they mature on a regular schedule? How egocentric were they? How much time did they spend thinking about their body? What was their relationship with their parents like? Did they get into trouble?

You also should enjoy spending some time talking with some junior high and high school students at this point in your life. You probably know some students who are still in high school—talk with them and see if they are psychologically different from you. And try to talk with some junior high school students. Video stores, malls, athletic fields, and parks are public places where you are likely to find plenty of early adolescents. Listen to their conversations and watch their behavior—how well do they fit the image of early adolescence we have portrayed?

Now think about what you would be like as the parent of an adolescent. Would you deal with your own adolescent in the same way your parents handled you? If not, what would you do differently? What would you do if your son or daughter came in drunk or stole something from a store? What would you do if she or he started hanging around with peers you thought were undesirable? How closely would you monitor your adolescent's life?

What would you do if your sixteen-year-old said she was seriously thinking about getting married? And how would you handle the situation if your seventeen-year-old announced that he was quitting school to work in a garage because he wanted to make more money right now? Think also about what life would be like with one or two adolescents in your family compared to life without adolescents.

By reading our description of adolescence in this section, by thinking about your own adolescence, by conversing with other students, by observing adolescents, and by thinking about what kind of parent you would be with your own adolescents, you should know yourself better.

Epilogue: The Transition from Adolescence to Adulthood

We have talked about how it is difficult to tell when adolescence is entered and when it is exited. Many psychologists believe that the task of determining the beginning of adolescence is easier than pinpointing its end. One reason given by some scholars is that adolescence begins in biology and ends in culture. In concluding this book, it seems appropriate to think about what constitutes the end of adolescence and the beginning of adulthood. Although there is no consensus about when adolescence is left behind and adulthood is entered, the following description provides some ideas that should be considered as we attempt to understand this transition in the life cycle.

Faced with a complex world of work, with highly specialized tasks, many postteenagers must spend an extended period of time being trained in technical institutes, colleges, and postgraduate centers to acquire specialized skills, educational experiences, and professional training. For many of them, this creates an extended period of economic and personal "temporariness." Earning levels are low and sporadic and established residences may change frequently. Marriage and a family often are shunned. In many instances this period lasts from two to four years, although it is not unusual for it to last more than eight years.

This stage, phase, or transition in development has been called *youth* by some social scientists. Kenneth Kenniston (1970) suggests that youth have not settled the questions whose answers once defined adulthood—questions of their relationship to the existing society, of vocation, and of social roles and life styles. Youth differs from adolescence in the sense that there is a struggle between developing an autonomous sense of self and becoming socially involved in the case of youth, whereas a struggle for self-definition represents the core conflict of adolescence. Kenniston also believes that adolescents are trying to develop toward an end point—an identity of self-definition, wheras youth already have such a sense of self and continually show an interest in change and development. Youth do not like being in a rut or getting nowhere in life but rather see themselves as on the move.

Two criteria that may signal the end of youth and the beginning of early adulthood are *economic independence* and *autonomous decision making*. Probably the most widely recognized marker of entrance into adulthood is the occasion when the young individual takes a more-or-less permanent full-time job. It usually happens when we finish school—high school for some, college for others, and graduate school for still others.

The stage of youth may represent a transition between adolescence and adulthood.

For those who finish high school, move away from home, and assume a career, the transition to adulthood seems to have occurred. However, such a clear-cut pattern is the exception rather than the rule. One of every four adolescents does not complete high school, and many students who finish college cannot find a job. Furthermore, only a small percentage of graduates settle into jobs that will remain permanent throughout their adult years. We also need to consider that attaining economic independence from parents usually is a gradual rather than an abrupt process. It is not unusual to find many college graduates getting a job and continuing to live, or returning to live, with their parents, particularly in the economic climate in which we live today.

The ability to make decisions is another characteristic of early adulthood that does not seem to be fully developed in youth. We refer broadly here to decision making about a career, values, family and relationships, and life style. During youth, the individual may still be trying out many different roles, exploring alternative careers, thinking about a variety of life styles, and considering the plurality of relationships available.

Although decisions about some or all of these alternatives may still not be made in early adulthood, and may reemerge in middle and late adulthood, the individual who enters early adulthood usually has made some decisions about a career, life style, and marriage.

Even though there seems to be a great deal of change going on during late adolescence, youth, and the beginning of early adulthood, several recent investigations have clearly shown the continuity that exists between adolescence and adulthood. First, we describe the well-known national survey of adolescent life styles conducted by Jerald Bachman and his associates. Next, the relationship of attachment patterns in adolescence to interpersonal relations in young adulthood evaluated by Toni Antonucci is outlined. And we conclude with a brief overview of some important findings from a longitudinal study at the University of California that has spanned nearly fifty years.

In *Youth in Transition: Adolescence to Adulthood—Change and Stability in the Lives of Men,* Jerald Bachman, Patrick O'Malley, and Jerome Johnston (1978) reported longitudinal data collected on a national sample of more than 2,000 boys. They initially studied the boys when they were in the tenth grade in 1968 and then collected information on them for a period of eight years, following their movements along several paths—dropout or graduation, military service or civilian life, college or labor market, employment or unemployment. By individually interviewing the boys and having them respond to questionnaires during the eight years (measurement occurred five times—in the tenth grade, eleventh grade, twelfth grade, one year after the twelfth grade, and five years after the twelfth grade), the researchers were able to determine the impact of various post-high school environments and experiences (educational, occupational, military, marital, and parental) on values, attitudes, and behaviors.

The dominant picture of the individuals as they went through eight years of their lives was stability rather than change. Although there were a number of differences between the groups of young men studied—such as between high school dropouts and graduates and between those who were delinquents and drug abusers and those who were not—these differences seemed to remain remarkably stable over the course of the eight years the young men were studied. For instance, the tenth graders who showed the highest self-esteem also were the ones most likely to show the highest self-esteem five years after high school. The same kind of patterning was found for achievement orientation. However, there were some changes. For example, data on illegal drug use suggested the effects of two different environments—marriage tended to reduce drug use, whereas unemployment tended to elevate it.

Long-range occupational aspirations were influenced by post-high school experiences: individuals who were successful in school and in a career sustained their high achievement aspirations, whereas many of those with less educational and occupational success showed a decline in achievement orientation.

In a second investigation that reveals a link between adolescence and adulthood, Toni Antonucci (1981) studied the social interactive/social supportive behaviors of adolescents and considered them in relation to the adolescents' own attitudes about future social interaction (specifically, age at marriage) and their own actual behaviors (reported eleven years after high school graduation). The data used in this investigation came from Project Talent, an enormous effort to study the personal, educational, and experiential factors that promote or inhibit the development of human talent. Of the original sample of 400,000 students in grades nine through twelve in Project Talent, 4,000 subjects were selected for study by Antonucci. High school students were asked several questions that could be considered to reflect attachment to family and peers. The high school attachment measures included discussion of future plans with father and with mother; age at which marriage is intended; and activity level in affiliative high school activities, such as groups and clubs. The age at which the respondent first married was assessed. In adulthood, questions focused on such factors as marital satisfaction, parenting satisfaction, and happiness in social life.

What were labeled attachment behaviors in adolescence were linked with social behavior and interaction in adulthood. Some of the findings indicate that what has been described as insecure attachment in infancy may have some applicability to later social interactions as well. For example, adolescents who date very early and often marry early may be showing a form of insecure attachment, according to Antonucci. Adolescents who engage in appropriate and varied sex-typed behaviors, such as affiliative behaviors for boys and achievement/vocational related behaviors for girls may be expressing a more secure attachment. Indeed, these latter adolescents were more likely to report high levels of marital satisfaction, life satisfaction, and a happier social life some eleven years after their high school graduation.

A third research project that documents the continuity between adolescence and adulthood also is a longitudinal study of enormous proportions that spans nearly a half a century. Perhaps the most important data that bear on the issue of stability and change from the childhood and adolescent years through the middle adulthood years have been collected as part of the California Longitudinal Study. The data actually represent three longitudinal studies, two of which were begun in 1928–1929 (MacFarlane's Guidance Study and Bayley's Berkeley Growth Study), the other in 1931 (Stolz and Jones's Oakland Growth Study). Although the three projects initially had different intents, they subsequently were merged into a single sample with two cohorts that differ by approximately eight years.

Many, but by no means all, of the methods and procedures used with the groups were the same. Initially, the total of the three samples reached 521 subjects, but because of death, withdrawal, or the lack of comparable measures among the groups, the data analyses often are conducted on fewer adults. Most of the analyses are on subgroups of fewer than one hundred subjects of each sex. The data reported in *Present and Past in Middle Life* (Eichorn et al., 1981), the most recent profile of information, traces the lives of these individuals from early adolescence to mid-life. Q-sorts were used in this investigation. The *Q-sort technique* is a method of obtaining trait ratings that consist of many cards, on each of which is printed a trait description. The rater groups the cards in a series of piles ranging from those that are least characteristic to those that are most characteristic of the rated person.

In commenting on issues of consistency, stability, discontinuity, and change, Dorothy Eichorn and her colleagues (1981) concluded that their results from early adolesence to mid-life on a host of personality characteristics and life styles do not support either extreme in the debate over whether adult personality development is characterized by stability or change. Personologists—traditional personality trait theorists—argue for stability, whereas behavioral, contextual, social learning theorists emphasize the contextual, situational, changing nature of adult personality development. In all domains of personality assessed in the California Longitudinal Study, some evidence for individual consistency was found, but as would be expected, some characteristics were more stable across time than others, and some individuals changed markedly even on characteristics for which the group as a whole was consistent.

Dimensions more directly concerned with the self (cognitively invested, self-confident, and open/closed self) showed greater consistency from early adolescence to mid-life than dimensions more reflective of the quality of interpersonal interactions (nurturant/hostile, undercontrolled/overcontrolled, and heterosexual/homosexual). Possibly the latter group of personality characteristics is more influenced by actual changes and demands of interpersonal relationships.

The architects of *Present and Past Middle Life* (Eichorn et al., 1981) concluded that the pervasive influence of personality was evident in every domain of life examined. Two of the most influential personality dimensions were cognitive investment and emotional control, as reflected on both the Q-sort and the California Psychological Personality Inventory measures. Emotional control, for instance, appears to influence the overall course of lives, for it predicts adult health status, early death, problem drinking, and even IQ. People with poor impulse control may take more risks in their lives and may find it more difficult to break maladaptive habits.

To see why it is important to look at childhood and adolescent antecedents of personality in early adulthood, consider a twenty-five-year-old woman who has just completed law school and has just accepted a job with a law firm. During childhood her parents encouraged her to do well in school and emphasized that a career was as important as, or more important than, marriage and a family. During childhood and adolescence her peers shared many of her achievement-oriented goals. One of her girl friends just completed four years of medical school, for example. Both girls' parents paid for all of their undergraduate as well as graduate education. The law school graduate is a very competitive and extroverted person but has a reasonably high level of anxiety. She has dated different people, but she never has developed what could be called a serious relationship. Clearly, by looking only at the woman's adult life and experiences, we would get an incomplete picture of her development and what contributed to her personality development. So too would we be far off target if we only began searching through a thirty-three-year-old's first five to ten years of life in trying to predict why he is having difficulty coping with a problem in the latter part of early adulthood.

We have described some of the continuities in the California studies, but stability and continuity were not universal by any means. For example, marital status at age forty was not a good predictor of marital status at age fifty, and personality dimensions of individuals involved in good and bad marriages were not very clear-cut. Psychological health at mid-life was even more complex, both in terms of its antecedents in adolescence and its continuity from adolescence to mid-life. The truth about personality, then, lies somewhere between the infant determinism of Freud and a contextual approach that ignores the antecedents of the adult years completely.

Many of you reading this book are in your early twenties; some of you may still be nineteen; others of you are at a later point in life. Think back to your early adolescence. Either jot down on paper or go over in your mind what you were like when you were ten to fifteen years old. Was what you were like then predictive of what you are like now? Or are you a very different person now, and was your early adolescence not a very good marker for charting your psychological health now that you are entering or have lived through some of your adult life?

Some of you will agree that information about your early adolescence was a good indicator of what you are like now. You may have remembered that when you were twelve you were extroverted, got along well with people, got As in school, had parents who cared a lot about you and looked after your best interests, and you had a lot of friends. You still are extroverted and get along well with people, make As, are dating a really terrific person, and still get along well with your parents. Yes, you would have to say that your early adolescence was a good source for predicting what you are like now.

By contrast, you may remember that your early adolescence was a mess—you were very shy, you did not have very many friends, you felt alienated from your parents, and you did not do well in school. But now you get along well with people, you are happily married, have a five-year-old child whom you enjoy a great deal, work at a part-time job, and go to school part-time. You are busy but happy, and you like your life. In your case, early adolescence was not a very good index of what your adult life was going to be like.

We could go on and give a virtually endless number of examples of different types of individuals experiencing different events in their lives that led or did not lead to particular adult outcomes. Even though we are beginning to chart some of the characteristics of adolescence that allow us to make some predictions about how psychologically healthy individuals will be in adulthood, the complex nature of adolescence, the many changes that take place throughout the life cycle, and the difficulty in obtaining valid information make the task very difficult.

In summary, during the transition from adolescence to adulthood there is constancy as well as change. The tendency on the part of many scholars has been to emphasize the tremendous upheaval and change that occur during adolescence and youth, but data such as those reported in the three longitudinal investigations discussed here remind us that there is continuity as well in the lives of individuals as they grow from adolescence to adulthood.

You have come to the end of this book. We hope you have learned a lot and *enjoyed* the book as well. We also hope that we have motivated you to think about your infant, childhood, and adolescent years and how they contributed to what you are like as a person today. And we hope that those of you who become the parents of infants, children, and adolescents or work with infants, children, and adolescents in some capacity, such as a teacher, counselor, or community leader, feel that you now have a better grasp of what their development is all about.

Glossary

a

acceleration
One aspect of normal approaches to gifted children in school; involves any strategy that shortens the time necessary for a student to graduate.

accommodation
In visual perception, a property of focusing in which the lens of each eye flattens or becomes more spherical.

accommodation
In Piaget's theory, the act of modifying a current mode or structure of thought to deal with new features of the environment; the converse of *assimilation*.

adaptation
The process of altering one's own behavior to interact effectively with the environment.

adolescence
The period between childhood and adulthood. In contemporary Western society, adolescence starts at about age twelve and ends somewhere between seventeen and twenty.

adolescent egocentrism
A unique form of egocentrism, which has its onset in adolescence. The adolescent acts as if others are as preoccupied with his behavior, feelings, and thoughts as he himself is (self-consciousness).

albinism
Genetically determined condition characterized by lack of skin pigment.

alternative curriculum
A special education intervention program that stresses the importance of developing functional adjustment skills to aid the special educational student, particularly in the post-school years.

altruism
The act of doing something with the intention of helping other people without consideration for personal gain.

amenorrheic
Abnormal absence or suppression of menstrual discharge.

amniocentesis
A procedure for withdrawing and examining amniotic fluid from the uterus to check on the health of a developing fetus.

amphetamines
Synthetic stimulants that are usually available in the form of pills. Amphetamines are often used by students to maintain high levels of performance for short periods of time.

anal stage
In Freud's theory, the period during which the child seeks pleasure through exercising the anus and eliminating waste; this stage occurs during the second year of life and is the second Freudian stage.

androgyny
A sex-role orientation in which the person incorporates both masculine and feminine aspects into behaviors.

animism
A characteristic of preoperational thought in which human qualities are inappropriately attributed to inanimate objects.

anorexia nervosa
A severe diminishment of appetite, particularly among adolescent females. The adolescent girl has an intense fear of becoming obese, even when emaciated.

anthropological or sociological perspective
Developmental theory that maintains that by analyzing societal structures and individuals' roles in society, one can understand life-span development.

411

anxiety
A general feeling of psychological discomfort without a well-defined cause.

Apgar Scale
A method used to evaluate the health of a child at birth. Heart rate, respiratory effect, reflex irritability, muscle tone, and body color are each rated between one and ten, the high score being the most favorable.

Aptitude $\times$ Treatment Interaction (ATI)
A crossing of the necessary ingredients for student success; any of several teaching methods (treatments) that may be best for an individual student, depending on ability or learning style (aptitude).

assimilation
In Piaget's theory, the act of incorporating a feature of the environment into an existing mode or structure of thought; the converse of *accommodation*. Also, a synonym for acculturation.

association areas of the cortex
Portions of the cortex responsible for integrating and coordinating sensation and action pathways, storing memories, and allowing us to perform a number of intellectual operations.

associative flow
The production of many ideas and combinations from a starting idea.

associative play
A type of play in which the child plays in a group and is more concerned with association with the group than with the group's activity.

asynchrony
Situation in which the parent is slow to notice and respond to the needs of the infant. A lack of proper timing between a change in the individual and a change in his or her environment.

attachment
A strong and important relationship between two people, characterized by affection and high mutual responsiveness.

attention
In discussions of information processing, the point at which a stimulus is noticed or encoded. Also, the process of noticing this stimulus in the environment.

attribution theory
An approach to describing an individual's social perceptions and self-concept. It is concerned with how the child makes intellectual sense of the actions of others as well as the self. The origins of the approach are traced to Fritz Heider. Two elements of his theory are the naive analysis of action and levels of social responsibility.

authoritarian parenting
A style of childrearing that focuses on parental power and strict obedience to rules.

authoritative parenting
A childrearing pattern that places moderate restrictions on the range of acceptable behaviors but also incorporates nurturance and sensitivity to the child's needs.

autonomy versus shame and doubt
The second stage in Erikson's eight-stage theory of development. At this stage, the child may develop the healthy attitude that he or she is capable of independent control of actions or may develop an unhealthy attitude of shame or doubt that he or she is incapable of such control.

behavioral social learning perspective
Developmental theory emphasizing that an individual's actions are influenced by encounters with rewarding and punishing situations.

behavior modification
A method of changing behavior, based on principles of association, operant conditioning, and imitation.

bereavement
The process through which we review our memories of loss.

biological environment
The individual's set of experiences with regard to nutrition, medical care, drugs, physical accidents, and similar situations.

brainstorming
A method of stimulating the formulation of ideas by a group; any and all notions are encouraged, with analysis and criticism initially withheld.

bulimia
A disorder in which the individual indulges in secret and episodic eating binges, which usually end in self-induced vomiting.

cause-and-effect
Relationships between factors in an experiment suggest a correlation; association between elements in an experiment in which one factor leads to the other.

centration
A tendency to focus exclusively on one aspect of a situation, at the expense of others.

cephalo-caudal pattern
A general pattern of physical growth. The greatest growth in anatomical differentiation occurs first in the region of the head and later in lower regions in turn.

channel
In the communications field, the medium over which a message is transmitted. A message is sent over a particular channel of communication to a specific receiver.

child-centered

An extremely broad term used to describe a wide range of goals and curriculum in nursery schools.

chromosomes

Rod-shaped structures carrying genes and hereditary information; each normal infant inherits forty-six chromosomes, twenty-three from each parent.

chunks

Bits of information organized into larger single units.

classical conditioning

A form of learning in which a previously neutral stimulus (CS) elicits a response (CR) by being consistently paired with a stimulus (UCS) that automatically elicits the response (UCR).

clique

A group smaller in size, more cohesive, and having greater intimacy among members than a crowd does.

coaching

Providing didactic instruction.

cognitive development

Age-related changes that occur with regard to mental activity; for example, thought, memory, perception, attention, and language.

cognitive social learning theory

A theory that combines what is known about learning processes and thinking patterns to explain social behavior.

cognitive structural perspective

The theoretical paradigm stressing the organization and stages of thought as the primary force behind development.

cohort

A group of subjects of the same age, born at approximately the same time (for example, the same year).

combined longitudinal cross-sectional method

A complex design in which age changes are examined by drawing cross-sections of children at different ages, and at the same time, testing some of the children longitudinally.

communications

A field that seeks to develop a general model of the process of sending a message across a channel to a receiver. Communications is an important influence on the development of information processing.

compensation-based program

A special education intervention program in which the student is encouraged to develop strategies for acquiring new information through nontraditional methods, such as taped materials, peer tutors, and/or visual aids.

compensatory education

Special school programs for children in poverty areas, designed to raise their level of educational readiness.

compulsions

Repetitive, stereotyped actions called into play to ward off some imaginary threat.

conception

The movement at which a male sperm cell joins or fertilizes a female ovum, marking the beginning of prenatal development.

concrete operational stage

In Piagetian theory, the stage of thought that follows preoperations, lasting from about seven to eleven years of age; marked primarily by a need to anchor thought to concrete events.

conditioned response (CR)

The learned response to a conditioned stimulus.

conditioned stimulus (CS)

An environmental event that elicits a response (CR) by being associated repeatedly with an unconditioned stimulus (UCS).

conditioning

Providing situations designed to establish a response in a subject.

conglomerate strategy

A series of coordinated strategies.

conservation

The understanding that basic properties of objects (for example, weight, volume, number, area) remain unchanged when the superficial appearance of the objects is altered.

consolidation of individuality

A stage in Mahler's theory of the development of achievement occurring between twenty-four and thirty months. The child gradually accepts, once again, separation from the mother and seems to prefer staying in a familiar playroom without the mother.

consonants

In standard English, one of two basic phonemic classes; formed by interrupting the flow of air in the oral cavity and then releasing it.

continuum of indirectness

A concept developed by Anne Anastasi to determine the degree to which various traits are determined by genetic influences.

contrary-to-fact reasoning

Representing an imaginary event that counters the concrete reality of the moment.

control-autonomy

A dimension along which parents can be discriminated in how they interact with their children. At one extreme (control), parents exhibit considerable interest in dictating what and how a child shall act. At the other extreme (autonomy), the child is given considerable freedom and choice over a variety of his or her decisions and actions.

conventional level of moral development
A term applied to the middle two stages in Kohlberg's theory of moral development. Moral thought is based on the desire to preserve good interpersonal relations and maintain good interpersonal concordance (stage 3) or to comply with formalized rules, laws, and customs that exist in society (stage 4).

convergence
The turning inward of the eyes to view an object close at hand; important also to depth perception.

convergent thinking
A type of thought wherein attention is directed toward finding a single solution from a given set of circumstances; contrast with *divergent thinking*.

cooing
Vowellike sounds; after crying, this sound is among the first made by an infant.

cooperative play
A type of play that involves group social interaction. The child is conscious of the activity, the others in the group, and his or her position in the group; characteristic of older children, seldom of preschoolers.

correlation
Measure of degree of relationship between two distributions (samples). The correlation coefficient ranges from + 1.00 to − 1.00. A *positive* coefficient means that the distributions increase together; a *negative* coefficient means that as one increases the other decreases; and a *zero* coefficient means no correlation.

creativity
An important aspect of mental functioning, not usually considered in intelligence testing; originality and flexibility are two of the creativity factors measured.

cretinism
Condition caused by a hormone deficiency in the thyroid gland; results in severe mental retardation and dwarfism.

critical period
A point or stage in early development when a person is unusually receptive to environmental events; learning during critical periods can be the basis of certain behavior patterns that persist throughout life.

cross-sectional method
A procedure for establishing age changes by testing independent groups of children of different ages.

crowd
The crowd is the largest and least personal of the three ways to characterize relations. The members of a crowd meet because of a mutual interest in some activity, not because they are mutually attracted to one another.

cultural-familial mental retardation
The most prevalent form of mental retardation in which there is no known organic cause. Retardation is mild, and at least one of the parents or siblings must be retarded.

cultural or social evolution
The manner in which behavior is modified through cultural transmissions; for example, customs and practices of a group.

culture
The environment in which a child grows up—the groups, institutions and values that hold the greatest influence.

culture-fair tests
Intelligence tests in which one cultural background is not favored over another through factors that should be irrelevant.

culture-free tests
Intelligence tests in which all reference to cultural forms or contact has been excluded.

d

deductive hypothesis testing
The ability of adolescents to work with conjured-up possibilities that help them to solve problems. Hypotheses are tested with carefully chosen questions and tests.

deep structure
The basic idea underlying a sentence. *See also* **surface structure.**

defense mechanisms
Techniques used by the ego to prevent feared impulses of the id from becoming conscious.

dependent variable
Some facet of a child's functioning that is measured in an experiment and presumed to be under the control of one or more manipulated factors. *See also* **independent variable.**

deprivation dwarfism
Retardation in a child's physical growth resulting from emotional factors, such as parental rejection or an overload of stress.

development
Progression of movement or change that begins its pattern at conception and continues throughout life; complex pattern of movement that is the product of many processes; processes and events that contribute to lifelong change.

developmental functions
Basis for study of nature of the species investigations; general statements about behavior, mental phenomena, or developmental changes, summarizing what is typical of the species.

developmental lag
A theory that traces learning disabilities to slow, but not necessarily permanently impaired, maturational processes.

developmental scales
Standardized tests created to measure an infant's or child's normative progress in areas of social, motor, language, and intellectual growth.

differentiation

The process by which global experience or thought is separated into distinct parts.

discovery learning

A method of instruction in which the adolescent is required to go beyond concrete thought and to view events and objects in logical ways. The student does not depend solely on lectures, but must explore and categorize as well.

distinctive features theory

A theory of learning based on recognizing differences; the child learns more basic differences among objects and events as he or she explores the world. Repeated exploration leads to the child's developing more variation in responses and ability to distinguish events.

divergence

The turning outward of the eye to focus and view an object far away; important also to depth perception.

divergent thinking

A kind of creative thought process exercised when a person's imagination provides many different answers to a single question; contrast with *convergent thinking*.

DNA (deoxyribonucleic acid)

A complex molecule that forms the basis for genetic structure in man.

dominant gene

A gene that exerts its full characteristic effect regardless of its gene partner. For example, if one parent gives a gene signaling brown eyes (dominant) and the other gives the "blue-eyed" gene (recessive), the offspring will have brown eyes.

double helix

Term used to describe the physical structure of a DNA molecule; two long strands are connected by several short strands, giving an arrangement resembling a spiral staircase.

Down's syndrome

A form of mental retardation caused by an extra chromosome; its physical characteristics include a flattened skull, an extra fold of skin over the eyelid, and a protruding tongue.

 e

early adolescence

The period of adolescence that roughly corresponds to the junior high school years. Often ranges from ten or twelve to fourteen or fifteen years of age. The period of adolescence in which puberty occurs and in which maturation is greatest.

early childhood

Period extending from infancy to five or six years; characterized by development of personal care, self-sufficiency, and readiness for school-related tasks.

echoing

A strategy used by adults to influence children's language development: the adult tries to clarify an unintelligible part of the child's message by repeating the intelligible portion in question form.

echolalia

A speech pattern in which the child repeats rather than responds to spoken communications; characteristic of autistic children.

eclectic orientation

Taking information from various sources; position designed to present more than one perspective.

ecological structure

According to sociologist Alex Inkeles, one of the cultural structures influencing development; involving the size, density, and physical distribution of the individual family and the society as a whole.

economic structure

A concept of the sociologist's view of life-span development that emphasizes the material resources of a society. The occupational opportunities that a society provides influence the child's development.

ectomorphic

Type of body build without predominant fat or muscle; thin, skinny.

ego

According to Freud, the part of the personality that copes with the real world in a rational manner.

egocentrism

Failure to appreciate that another person's perceptions of a situation may differ from one's own; a characteristic of preoperational thought.

ego integrity versus despair

The final conflict in Erikson's theory of development. This stage involves retrospective glances at and evaluations of life.

Eight Ages of Man

Term used to describe Erikson's eight-stage theory of development.

elaboration

A memory process in which an individual tries to improve retention of information by adding something to it.

Electra complex

A Freudian conflict involving young girls that is parallel to the Oedipus conflict in boys. There is sexual desire of the girl for her father accompanied by hostility toward her mother.

embryonic period

The period of prenatal growth that follows the germinal period, lasting from the second to the eighth week after conception; marked by development of a primitive human form and life-support system.

emotional development
Consideration of development that stresses the individual's feelings and affective reactions to situations.

empathy
Experiencing the same feelings and psychological state of mind that someone else has.

enculturation
The process of becoming socialized and assimilating the lessons of one's culture.

endomorphic
Rounded body build, evidenced by more fat tissue than muscle tissue.

enrichment
Programs for gifted children aimed at providing special opportunities such as college classes in high school, independent study, and so forth.

equilibration
In Piaget's theory, the mechanism by which the child resolves cognitive conflict and reaches a balance in thought.

erogenous zones
Parts of the body stimulated or exercised to produce pleasurable feelings.

ethological or evolutionary perspective
Developmental theory stressing the individual's biological heritage and adaptation to the environment.

ethology
School of thought that views development as heavily influenced by biologically inherited response tendencies.

evolution
Any change in organisms from generation to generation. Biological evolution deals specifically with genetic transmission of such changing characteristics.

expansion
A technique used by adults to influence children's language development. The adult provides a more complete and grammatically correct adaptation of what the child says.

experiences
The process or fact of personally observing, encountering, or undergoing something; a key to development.

experiment
A technique used to study the impact of one or more kinds of events (independent variables) on some facet of children's functioning (dependent variable); the independent variable is carefully controlled, and the dependent variable is measured.

expressive movement
An aspect of the child's physical movement in which the body is used to express ideas and feelings.

family system
The network of the family; the interaction of the individual members and the working of these individuals as a group.

fetal period
The period of prenatal growth lasting from about the eighth week until birth.

fine motor skills
Physical activities requiring finer dexterity; for example, turning the pages of a book or coordination of alternating between one hand and the other.

firm control—lax control
An aspect of the control-autonomy relationship between parent and child. Firm control involves the setting of firm rules by the parent and insistence that the child comply. With lax control, the rules are set, but the parent is not firm about compliance.

fixation
In Freudian theory, the act of getting "stuck," or "fixed," in an early psychosexual stage.

foreclosure
Marcia's category of identity development in which the adolescent has made a commitment but has not experienced a crisis.

formal operational stage
In Piaget's model, the most advanced stage of thinking possible; it emerges between eleven and fourteen years of age and is characterized by abstract thought.

g
A factor of general or nonspecific intelligence, the measurement of which is the aim of most standardized IQ tests.

gene
A small biochemical substance composed of DNA and believed to be a basic building block in hereditary transmission of information; thousands of genes are present in each chromosome.

generativity versus stagnation
The seventh conflict in Erikson's theory of development. This stage is positively resolved if an adult assists the younger generation in developing and leading useful lives.

genetic-environmental interaction
Reciprocal influence between the child's genetic inheritance and the environmental conditions.

genital stage
In Freud's theory, the period during which sexual conflicts are resolved, a stable identity is reached, and personality reaches its highest form of organization; this stage is associated with adolescence and is the last Freudian stage.

genotype
The unique constellation of genes in an individual; the person's genetic makeup.

germinal period
The first two weeks of prenatal growth after fertilization, during which rapid cell division takes place.

Gestalt view
Concepts about the way people organize their perceptions.

gifted children
Children with well-above-average intellectual capacity or with an outstanding talent in a particular area.

grammar
A formal, systematic description of the syntax of a language.

gross motor skills
Activities such as walking, running, and jumping; the child makes great advancements in mastery of these skills during the second year.

grouping
Placement of children with similar levels of ability in the same class; program used often with gifted children.

guilt
The affective state of psychological discomfort arising from a person's feeling of having done something morally wrong.

h

handedness
An important aspect of motor development referring to which hand we prefer to use.

hardware
In computers, the physical equipment employed (the storage unit, the logic unit, the printer, and so forth); by analogy, in human intelligence, the physical equipment for thinking (the brain and central nervous system); contrast with *software*.

harmful genes
Genes that produce undesirable traits in individuals. Such recessive genes may cause diabetes, heart disease, muscular dystrophy, or other disorders.

heritability
Degree to which a particular characteristic is genetically determined; expressed as a mathematical estimate.

high-risk infant
Term used to describe babies whose histories contain factors related to psychological or educational handicaps; for example, problems related to the parents' genetic makeup, the mother's pregnancy, or the birth process.

historical time
According to Neugarten and Datan, the life cycle aspect that controls the social system; this in turn changes norms and ultimately, the individual's life cycle. It can refer to long-term processes (industrialization) or to individual social events.

holophrase
The single-word utterance of a child who is just learning to talk; from the child's point of view, the single word may be an entire phrase or message.

humanistic perspective
Views development as an open-ended, creative process in which the child acquires a unique self-identity and creative skills.

hyperactivity
A state of excessive activity, usually accompanied by an inability to concentrate.

i

id
According to Freud, the instinctual part of the personality, which operates unconsciously and irrationally.

identification
In Freudian theory, a defense mechanism in which the values, attitudes, and behavior of another person are assumed.

identity
Erikson's term for a person's sense of who he or she is as a unique individual; for Erikson, this is the main task of adolescence, in which the teenager establishes vocational, sexual, political, and moral identities.

identity achieved
Marcia's concept involving the weathering of an identity crisis and the formation of a commitment.

identity crisis
The time during which the individual examines who he or she is and considers alternative ways to achieve an identity.

identity diffused (or confused)
According to James Marcia, an adolescent at this stage of identity development has made no ideological or occupational choices and has no interest in doing so.

identity versus role confusion
Erikson's fifth crisis of psychological development; the adolescent may become confident and purposeful, or may develop an ill-defined identity.

imaginary audience
The adolescent's sense that his or her feelings and beliefs are transparent to others.

imitation
A form of learning in which new behaviors are acquired by observing others performing the behaviors.

imprinting
A rapid form of learned attachment observed in many animals and believed to serve as a good role model of the ethological or instinctual root of many social attachments formed by humans as well.

incentive conditions
The contexts and expectations that motivate a person to acquire a behavior.

independent variable
An event or factor that is manipulated in an experiment to determine its impact on a child's functioning (dependent variable). *See also* **dependent variable.**

individual differences
Variations in behavior attributed to the distinct characteristics of the particular child; thus, developmental concepts apply to most infants or children, but not necessarily to all.

industry versus inferiority
Erikson's fourth crisis of psychological development; the school-aged child may develop a capacity for work and task-directedness, or he may view himself as inadequate.

infancy
Life-span phase extending from birth until eighteen to twenty-four months of age; characterized by almost total dependence and the beginnings of physiological and psychological activities.

infantile autism
A condition characterized by withdrawal from reality and inability to relate to others, long periods of inaction, and extremely immature speech patterns.

inference
Drawing a conclusion from the information available.

information processing approach
A theoretical view of cognition that analyzes cognitive activity in terms of successive stages of information processing such as attention, perception, memory, thinking, and problem solving.

initiative versus guilt
Erikson's third crisis of psychological development, occurring during the preschool years; the child may develop a desire for achievement, or he or she may be held back by self-criticism.

innate knowledge
Knowledge that exists in the child's mind at birth; a predisposition to learn and think.

insecurely attached—avoidance
According to Ainsworth, a mother-infant bond that is insecure and distinguished by the child's avoiding the mother and failing to seek closeness.

insecurely attached—resistant
An insecure mother-infant bond marked by the child's reaching for the mother, but then showing ambivalence or hitting and pushing.

instinct
An innate biological force that motivates a response.

institutionalization
The rearing of children in an environment other than the normal family setting, such as an orphanage.

instrumental competence
Effectiveness in dealing with other people and the environment, particularly exhibiting independence, self-initiated activities, and self-esteem about one's intellectual and physical abilities.

instrumental conditioning
A type of learning advocated by Skinner in which the individual operates or acts on his environment, and what happens to him, in turn, controls his behavior. In other words, the individual's behavior is controlled by its consequences. Also referred to as operant conditioning.

intelligence
The individual's capacity to think and act; the definition of intelligence is closely related to the way it is measured.

intentionality
The separation of means and goals in accomplishing simple tasks; involves more deliberate coordination on the part of the infant.

interview
A method of study in which children are asked questions and the investigator jots down their answers.

intimacy versus isolation
Erikson's sixth crisis of psychosocial development: the young adult may achieve a capacity for honest, close relationships, or be unable to form these ties.

in vitro fertilization
Fertilization of an ovum in a laboratory setting, outside the woman's body. The egg is later implanted in the woman's uterus. Commonly referred to as "test-tube" fertilization.

irreversibility
The inability to undo or reverse an action or an imagined action in thought.

keyword method
Richard Atkinson's technique to improve memory using powerful images related to key words.

labeling
The assignment of a label or category to an individual and the effects the label or category may have on that person.

laissez-faire (permissive) parenting
Childrearing style distinguished by its lack of parental restriction, control, or involvement.

language
A system of rules for speaking, listening, and writing; recognized by adult members of the language community.

Language Acquisition Device (LAD)
An imaginary machine that processes language rules as output; a metaphor that describes how the child acquires language.

language universals
Aspects of language and the capacity for language that are innate and thus common to all children at birth.

late adolescence
The period of adolescence that begins around the age of fifteen to sixteen and lasts until twenty to twenty-two years of age. Roughly corresponds to the high school years and sometimes the several years after high school.

late childhood
Life-span phase extending until approximately eleven years of age; noted for concrete thought processes, mastery of basic school skills, and greater exposure to cultural subjects.

latency stage
In Freud's theory, the period during which the child's anxious feelings and thoughts about sexual conflicts are actively repressed; this stage is associated with the elementary school years and is the fourth Freudian stage.

learned helplessness
Attitude of an individual who believes that rewards are beyond personal control and that personal behavior will not affect the outcome of a situation.

learning
A relatively permanent change in behavior due to experience or practice, as opposed to natural biological processes.

learning disabilities
Specific deficits in a child's sensory, learning, or language abilities that are not seen as part of an overall pattern of low intelligence or retardation.

Leboyer method
A method of childbirth proposed by a French physician, Leboyer. The newborn is not spanked or held by the feet after birth but is placed on the abdomen of the mother, and a peaceful and calm postdelivery environment is maintained to minimize the shock of childbirth for the infant.

life time
An aspect of the life cycle, according to Neugarten and Datan; expressed as a biological (that is, chronological) age. Must be accompanied by knowledge of the particular society to be useful.

longitudinal method (comparison)
Repeated testing of the same subject or group of subjects over a significant period of time.

long-term memory
A third level of memory storage, where processes such as rehearsal, elaboration, and organization are assumed to transform information from short-term to long-term storage.

looming
A technique for gauging depth sensitivity in infants; the researcher creates the illusion of an object being hurled at the child.

m

mainstreaming
The inclusion of learning disabled or handicapped children in classes with normal children rather than in special classes.

maturation
Physical growth of the body and central nervous system.

mean length of utterance (MLU)
The average number of words per sentence spoken by a child, calculated from a substantial sample of the child's speech (fifty to one-hundred sentences); a reliable and convenient measure of language maturity.

"mechanical mirror" theory
According to social learning theorists, the concept that the individual does not control his own development, but mirrors his environment in a purely mechanical fashion. The behavior of the individual, then, is not his own to control; he is manipulated by his environment.

menarche
A girl's first menstrual period.

mental age (MA)
A level of reasoning skill attained by a child, expressed in terms of the age group whose average test scores most closely resemble his or her own.

mental retardation
A condition of slow intellectual development and below-normal intelligence; may be inherited or caused by environmental circumstances.

mesomorphic
Athletic, muscular body build characterized by proportionately more muscle tissue than fat tissue.

middle adolescence
When adolescence is subdivided into three periods, middle adolescence corresponds to the high school years, roughly 15–18 years of age.

middle childhood
Phase in the life cycle beginning at about six years of age; notable by the child's increased ability in reading, writing, and similar school skills; concrete thought processes are most dominant.

mitosis
The cell division process that produces the germ cells, each having twenty-three single chromosomes instead of pairs.

mnemonics
Techniques to improve memory.

modeling
A form of social learning in which an individual acquires a behavior by imitating the actions of another person.

moral autonomy
The second stage of moral development in Piaget's theory; the child becomes aware that rules and laws are created by people, relative to social systems, and that in judging an action one should consider the actor's intentions as well as the act's consequences.

moral competence
Knowledge of moral rules indicating that the person is capable of acting in appropriate moral ways.

moral development
The acquisition of feelings, thoughts, and actions with regard to standards of right and wrong.

moral performance
The carrying out of a particular moral behavior, dependent on factors of motivation as well as of moral understanding.

moral realism
The first stage of moral development in Piaget's theory; justice and rules are conceived of as unchangeable properties of the world, removed from the control of people.

moratorium
Adolescents who are suffering an identity crisis and whose commitments are either vaguely defined or absent are, in James Marcia's terms, in the midst of a moratorium.

morpheme
The basic unit of a language that is meaningful; these include prefixes, suffixes, and verb-tense markers.

morphology
Study of the basic units of language that are meaningful, including prefixes, suffixes, and verb-tense markers.

motor cortex
Portions of the cortex primarily responsible for sending signals down through the spinal cord to different muscle groups.

motoric reproduction
The ability of a person to perform an observed behavior, based on nerve-muscle development; a prerequisite for learning the behavior through modeling (for example, limitations in eye-hand coordination may make it impossible for a preschooler to stay within the lines when coloring a picture).

n

nativism
The belief that a number of psychological characteristics are inherited or essentially present at birth.

naturalistic observation
A method of studying children in which they are observed in realistic, everyday situations.

negative reinforcement
The repeated removal of some stimulus following a response causes the response to increase over trials.

neonate
A newborn child.

normal distribution
Symmetrical mathematical curve (usually called a bell curve because of its shape) that describes the variability of a measurable characteristic in a sample. Most scores fall near the mean (forming the highest point of the bell), with relatively few high or low scores.

o

objective movement
An aspect of a child's physical activity in which the purpose is to develop the power of the body.

object permanence
The understanding that an object exists independent of the self and continues to exist even when it cannot be immediately perceived.

obsessions
Unwarranted ideas or fears that continue to intrude into the child's thoughts without any noticeable external cause.

Oedipus complex
A Freudian conflict beginning in early childhood in which the boy exhibits sexual desire for the mother and hostility and fear of the father, and eventually renounces the mother and identifies with the father.

onlooker play
A type of play characterized by the child watching other children playing, but not joining with them in the activities.

operant conditioning
A form of learning in which the strength of a behavior is increased or decreased as a result of its consequences.

operations
Internalized sets of actions that allow the child to do mentally what has been done before physically. Operations are not fully formed in the preoperational stage, are formed in the operational stage, and are more advanced in the formal-operational stage of Piaget's perspective.

oral stage
In Freud's theory, the period during which the child seeks pleasure by stimulating the mouth, lips, tongue, and gums; the first psychoanalytic stage.

organization
The continuous process of combining and integrating subskills to form a more perfect way of thinking.

original sin
The state of sin into which all human beings are born (according to Christian theology) and as a result of which are considered to be "bad" at birth.

paired associates
A kind of memory that involves recalling that two items are associated with one another.

parallel play
Activities that are characterized by the child playing separately from others, but with the same type of toys or the same type of activities as the others.

Parent Effectiveness Training (P.E.T.)
Program developed by Thomas Gordon; designed to help parents learn to interact more effectively with their children.

passive-aggressive behavior
Purposely inactive behavior; a person who exhibits this behavior works hard at making sure nothing happens.

peer
A person in an individual's environment that is of about the same age, grade, and status.

peer sociotherapy
Using peer interaction as a means to correct a social problem in a child, such as isolation, aggressiveness, or inappropriate social interactions.

perception
Product of sensation; the act of interpreting a sensory event or making it meaningful.

perceptual-motor training program
Program designed to promote physical development, emphasizing input or reception and how the child's ultimate performance is affected. Performance alone is not the emphasis of this type of program.

personality development
Developmental focus that emphasizes the individual's self-perception, sex role, and moral development.

perspective-taking skills
The understanding, by a child, that others have perspectives that are different from his own.

phallic stage
In Freud's theory, the period during which the child's genital area is the chief source of pleasure; this stage lasts from about four to five years of age and is the third Freudian stage.

phenotype
The unique constellation of measurable characteristics in a person—height, weight, IQ, and so forth.

phenylketonuria (PKU)
A genetically based form of retardation caused by the failure of the body to produce an enzyme to break down an amino acid, thus interfering with metabolism and poisoning the nervous system.

phobia
An unusually strong fear or apprehension associated with things or situations that most people perceive as nonthreatening, such as heights, crowds, or school.

phoneme
Basic unit of the sound system in language. A class of sounds perceived as identical by speakers of a given language.

phonology
The study of the sound system; concerned with the rules used to combine sounds. All languages employ such rules, although the rules vary from one language to another.

physical development
Growth and change in physical and anatomical features.

playing with improbabilities
A technique employed to increase creative thinking; children are forced to think about events that might happen after an unlikely situation.

pleasure principle
According to Freud, the early basis of behavior; the infant searches for an object to satisfy a need without regard for its need-reducing value.

political structure
A concept of the sociologist's view of development, emphasizing the importance of power structures in a society. Youth who participate in the political structure will be socialized differently than those who are subordinate to the system.

polygenically
Characteristics determined by the interaction of many different genes.

postconventional level of moral development
A term applied to the final two stages of Kohlberg's theory of moral development. Moral thought is based upon the application of laws and rules through appeal to their purposes, their democratic origin, and the social contexts within which they operate (stage 5), or by appeal to universal principles of ethics (stage 6).

practice
The repetition of behavior that is being learned.

practicing
A term used by Mahler to describe a stage in the formation of independence of the child. Between eight and fifteen months of age, the infant shows a steadily increasing interest in practicing motor skills and exploring and expanding the environment.

pragmatics
Rules concerned with the appropriate use of language in social contexts.

pragnanz
German, meaning "good form"; principles of perceptual organization in the Gestalt view.

preconventional level of moral development
A term applied to the first two stages of Kohlberg's theory of moral development. Moral thought is based on fear of punishment and authority (stage 1) or naive instrumental hedonism (stage 2).

premature birth
The birth of a baby significantly before completion of the expected nine months, or with a very low body weight (less than four pounds).

prenatal period
The period of development between conception and birth.

preoperational stage
In Piagetian theory, the stage of thought that lasts from about two to seven years of age and follows the sensorimotor period; although logical thought is present, there are several "flaws," such as egocentrism, that limit its possibilities.

pretend play
Play in which the child takes on different roles; make-believe activities in which the child may pretend to be an adult or may make fun of adults.

primary circular reactions
A reaction, generally occurring between one and four months of age, in which the infant attempts to repeat a pleasurable event that first happened by chance; for example, sucking the fingers when they accidentally come close to the mouth.

progressive education
A broad classification of teaching perspectives and styles that share a common goal; the total social and intellectual development of the child in a nonauthoritarian setting; compared with traditional education, the classroom is usually less structured and the students have more say in decision making.

Project Follow Through
A program instituted in 1967 as an adjunct to Project Head Start under which children from low-income families would receive additional compensatory education through early elementary school years.

Project Head Start
A preschool program started in 1965 to help children from low-income families acquire the skills and experiences considered prerequisite for success in school.

projection
In Freudian theory, a defense mechanism by which a person attributes his own undesirable traits to others; this mechanism prevents the person from dealing with anxiety.

prompting
A strategy used by adults to influence language development in children.

proximo-distal development
Growth starting at the center of the body and moving toward the extremities.

psychoanalytic perspective
View based on Freud's model of development, or any of the modern-day offshoots from it (for example, Erikson's perspective).

psycholinguistics
The study of language development from a dual perspective, combining the approaches of psychology and linguistics.

psychological control-psychological autonomy
An aspect of the control-autonomy relationship between parent and child. Psychological control is parental behavior that keeps the child dependent on the parent. Psychological autonomy involves parental behavior that encourages independent development by the child.

psychometric approach
A measurement approach to understanding such traits as intelligence and personality, with emphasis on how individuals differ.

psychosis
A severe pathological condition in which the personality is seriously disorganized and there is loss of contact with reality.

puberty
The stage of development at which the individual becomes capable of reproduction; in many cases, this stage is linked with the onset of adolescence.

punishment
The presentation of an unpleasant event following a behavior, decreasing the probability that the behavior will be repeated.

q

quasi experiment
An approximation to an experiment in which there is some loss of control over the independent variables due to the real-life manner in which they are defined.

questionnaire
A method used to obtain information from people that is similar to a highly structured interview, except the subject reads the questions and marks their answers on a sheet of paper rather than verbally responding to the interviewer.

r

randomization
In an experiment, the assignment of children or other subjects to groups on a random, or nondirected, basis.

rapprochement
A stage in Mahler's theory of the formation of independence. It lasts from about fifteen to twenty-four months and roughly coincides with the period of development we refer to as toddlerhood. As the child becomes aware of physical separateness and ability to move away from the mother, he or she experiences a new need for the mother to share in every new acquisition of skill and experience.

reaction formation
In Freudian theory, a defense mechanism in which a person conceals an undesirable motive by expending a great deal of energy in expressing the opposite view.

reality principle
According to Freud, an acquired manner of responding that follows and contrasts with the pleasure principle; the child channels energy onto objects that realistically reduce need states.

recall
A kind of memory that involves recollecting an experience.

receiver
In the field of communications, the specific point at which the transmitted information is picked up. A message is sent over a particular channel of communication to a specific receiver.

recessive gene
A gene whose code will be masked by a dominant gene and will only be expressed when paired with another recessive gene. A gene code for blue eyes will only be manifested if coupled with another recessive code.

reciprocal determinism
The belief that the agency that shapes change in someone is also influenced by the person it shapes. Thus mothers teach their children, and the act of teaching alters the mothers' behavior as well.

reciprocal socialization
A view of the socialization process that considers the interaction of the child and his or her parents and other adults, rather than viewing socialization as a process performed by adults in regard to their children.

reflexes
Involuntary responses to particular stimuli; for example, stroking a newborn's foot causes the whole leg to be withdrawn and the foot to flex.

regression
In Freudian theory, a defense mechanism in which a person returns to an earlier stage of development.

rehearsal
A process of memory in which the items to be recalled are repeated by the memorizer.

reinforcement
The presentation of a pleasant event following a behavior, increasing the probability that the behavior will be repeated.

reliability
Degree to which statistical measurements are consistent on repeated trials.

remediation model
The dominant special education model in which children are mainstreamed as much as possible while still receiving services from a resource teacher.

repression
Driving thoughts and feelings from conscious awareness and locking them away in the unconscious.

retention
Stage in Bandura's model of learning; synonymous with remembering or retrieving information.

rites of passage
Rituals usually involving ceremonies in which adolescents gain access to sacred adult practices, knowledge, and sexuality.

ritual
A form of spontaneous play that involves controlled repetition.

roles
The different patterns of social behavior that a person takes on in different situations.

role-taking skills
The ability, first developed in the young child, to understand the feelings and cognitions that other people are experiencing.

S

scheme (schema)
The basic unit for an organized pattern of functioning; for example, sucking, rooting, and blinking.

schizophrenia
A severe form of mental disturbance that is characterized by disorganized, illogical thought and speech, hallucinations, erratic behavior, and delusions.

scientific theory
An organized and logical set of statements, laws, and axioms; designed to describe, explain, and predict some particular observable event.

secondary circular reactions
Between four and eight months of age, actions that the infant attempts for more than personal need satisfaction; for example, shaking a rattle, or imitating baby talk or physical gestures for the objective result.

securely attached
An infant-mother bond distinguished by consistent positive emotional responses; this bond allows for the gradual growth of infant independence.

self
The hypothetical core of personality in many theories; what distinguishes the phenomenal experiences of one person from another.

self-fulfilling prophecy (sometimes referred to as the Rosenthal Effect)
The idea that once someone knows something about an individual, he or she often develops expectations for that person's behavior; in turn, those expectations may change the way the individual treats the other person and the way the person actually performs.

semantics
The expressed meanings of words and sentences.

sensation
The process of reacting to stimulation as it reaches sensory receptors, for example, the eyes, ears, nose, tongue, and skin.

sensorimotor stage
The earliest stage of thought in Piaget's model of cognitive development, comprising six substages through which an infant progresses; this stage extends from simple reflexes through the use of primitive symbols as the means of coordinating sensation and action.

sensory cortex
Portions of the cortex primarily responsible for receiving signals transmitted from the different senses.

separation-individuation
Terms used by Mahler to describe the process by which the young child acquires independence. During the first three years of life, the child emerges from the symbiotic relationship with the mother (separation) and acquires a number of individual characteristics (individuation).

sex role
A culturally defined pattern for maleness or femaleness.

sex-typed behavior
Actions and responses that fit a culturally predicted picture of typical male and female patterns.

sexual (gender) identity
The extent to which individual children actually take on as part of their personalities the behaviors and attitudes associated with either the male or female role.

short-term memory
The second level of memory storage, where stimuli are stored and retrievable for up to about a minute; also called working memory.

situational variability
Effects of the circumstances on the expression of a particular behavior; for example, a child reacts to a stranger according to the particular situation in which the stranger is encountered.

social cognition
A subfield of cognitive developmental theory emphasizing that the individual thinks about social matters as well as nonsocial ones; includes research on moral development, role taking, and impression formation.

social desirability
A strategy for answering interview questions in which the person responds in terms of what he or she thinks society sees as most desirable, not what the person actually thinks.

social development
Aspect of development focusing on the individual's encounters with and reactions to others.

social environment
The individual's experiences with family, schools, community, peers, and the media.

socialization
The process whereby people influence other people, usually through interaction with them; socialization has been traditionally defined as the transmission of the rules and knowledge of the adult culture to children, but the process is broader than that, entailing the child's socialization of adults as well.

social structure
An important construct in the sociologist's analysis of culture and society; a component of society such as ecological structure, economic structure, political structure, or value structure.

social time
The aspect of the life cycle that depends upon the age-grade system of the individual society. For example, a girl may be thought ready for marriage when she reaches puberty in one society but not in another.

sociolinguistics
The study of language and language functioning within the context of interacting with other people.

software
In computers, the programs that make the physical equipment operate; by analogy, in human intelligence, the routines that make the brain and central nervous system work (plans, intentions, strategies, and goals); contrast with *hardware.*

solitary play
Category of play in which the child plays alone and is not concerned with those around him or her.

speech perception
Ability to perceive and distinguish speech sounds; one aspect of authority perception in the infant.

stages (stage theories)
Sequential phases of development. Psychoanalytic and cognitive-structural views suggest the existence of such age-related periods of development.

standard deviation
The average difference between individual scores and the mean score in a distribution; obtained by squaring the deviation scores, summing these, dividing by one less than the number of scores, and taking the square root of the result.

standardized testing (standardization)
The use of tests to assess human characteristics and individual differences. The tests are developed on large samples and have established norms, reliability, and evidence of validity.

Stanford-Binet
A general, individually administered test of intelligence based on items originally devised by French psychologist Alfred Binet (ca. 1900) to predict children's ability to succeed in school.

stereotype
A broad category that reflects our impressions about people, including ourselves.

stimuli
Observable events that are associated with a response.

sturm und drang
G. Stanley Hall's term for the storm and stress he believed all adolescents experience.

sudden infant death syndrome (SIDS)
Sometimes referred to as crib death, this term refers to the unexplained death of a child in the first year of life, usually between the ages of two and five months. Although the cause is not well understood, recent speculation is that some newborns may have insufficiently built-in defense responses to respiratory threats.

superego
According to Freud, the moral part of the personality where each person has internalized dos and don'ts.

surface structure
The actual sentence, spoken or heard, that is meant to convey a particular deep structure; many surface forms may reflect the same deep structural idea. *See also* **deep structure.**

symbiotic infantile psychosis
A condition in which a child has intense anxiety and panic about being separated from the mother. It usually is manifested between the ages of two and one-half and five years and often is preceded by normal development.

symbol
An abstract event (for example, image or word) that represents a concrete experience or object.

synchrony
The ability of some parents to quickly sense and fulfill their infant's needs.

syntax
The rules used in a particular language to form acceptable phrases and sentences.

t

tabula rasa
Literally, a "blank tablet"; phrase used to describe the child's mind at birth as empty of all knowledge until acquired through experience.

temperament
The individual's personal nature or attitudes; it can be argued that the infant's nature is dependent on the mother, or that the mother learns to adapt to the temperament of the individual child.

tension reduction
Release of stored psychological energy. In psychoanalytic theory, it is the release of instinctual energy (libido) from the id.

teratogen
Any agent that causes birth defects.

teratology
A field of study that focuses on birth defects.

tertiary circular reactions
Schemes in which the infant (between ages twelve to eighteen months) explores new possibilities with the same object, changing what is done and examining the results. This is the first reaction that is not imitation; marking the beginnings of curiosity.

time sampling
A method of recording observations in limited frames of time, which are interspersed with rest or with nonobservation segments.

traditional education
The teaching philosophy of most American public schools, which focuses on learning basic academic skills at a common pace in group settings, under the firm direction of a single teacher.

transformations (transformational rules)
Syntactical rules that explain how a common deep structure can assume alternative surface forms, such as active and passive, positive and negative, statement and question.

trust versus mistrust
The first stage in Erikson's eight-stage theory of development, in which the infant develops either the comfortable feeling that those around him care for his needs or the worry that his needs will not be taken care of.

u

unconditioned response (UCR)
A reflex; an automatic response to an unconditioned stimulus.

unconditioned stimulus (UCS)
An environmental event that automatically triggers a response (UCR), without learning having to take place.

unoccupied play
Type of play in which the child is not engaged in activities that are normally regarded as play.

V

validity
The extent to which a measure of test evaluates what it purports to.

values clarification
An approach to moral education in which students are given the opportunity to air their opinions and value judgments in a group setting. By being exposed to the value judgments of others, students come to appreciate the relative nature of values.

value structure
According to the sociologist's view of development, this involves cultural ethics and rules of right and wrong. The value structure of a society is transmitted to the child through moral education.

vergence
The property of visual focusing in which the lens of each eye turns inward or outward to establish the proper focal length between the retina and the object being seen.

vicarious learning
The strengthening of a behavior in a person through his observation of someone else's being rewarded for that behavior; learning that occurs through modeling or imitation.

visual acuity
The ability of the eyes to resolve an image or see fine detail.

visual cliff technique
A visual situation designed to give the illusion of a steep cliff; used with infants to test development of depth perception and to note sensitivity to a steep drop.

voiced consonant
When pluralizing English words, if the final consonant is *voiced (m, n, g)*, the plural is voiced; for example, dogs.

voiceless consonant
When pluralizing English words, if the final consonant is *voiceless (k, f, t, b)*, the plural is also voiceless; for example, cats.

vowels
In standard English, one of two basic phoneme classes; formed by passing air over the vocal cords and allowing it to flow unimpeded through the oral cavity.

W

warmth-hostility
A dimension along which parents can be discriminated in how they interact with their children. At one extreme (warmth), parents exhibit considerable affection, love, and reinforcement toward their children. At the other extreme (hostility), the child is treated harshly, is the subject of repeated anger, and may be punished but not reinforced very often.

Whorf/Sapir hypothesis
The idea that people who speak different languages also experience the world differently, with each language creating unique perceptual and intellectual biases.

References

a

Achenbach, T. M. Developmental aspects of psychopathology in children and adolescents. In M. E. Lamb (ed.), *Social and personality development*. New York: John Wiley, 1978.

Achenbach, T. M., & Edelbrock, C. S. Behavioral problems and competencies reported by parents of normal and disturbed children aged four through sixteen. *Monographs of the Society for Research in Child Development*, 1981, serial no. 188, vol. 46, no. 1.

Adams, B. N. Interaction theory and the social network. *Sociometry*, 1967, *30*, 64–78.

Adams, D. Building moral dilemma activities. *Learning*, 1977, *5*, 44–46.

Adams, G. M., & deVries, H. A. Physiological effects of an exercise training regimen among women aged 52 to 79. *Journal of Gerontology*, 1973, *28*, 50–55.

Adams, G. R. The effects of divorce on adolescents. *The High School Journal*, March 1982, pp. 205–11.

Adams, R. S., & Biddle, B.J. *Realities of teaching*. New York: Holt, Rinehart & Winston, 1970.

Adelson, J. Adolescence and the generalization gap. *Psychology Today*, 1979, pp. 33–37.

Adelson, J., & Doehman, M. J. The psychodynamic approach to adolescence. In J. Adelson (ed.), *Handbook of adolescent psychology*. New York: John Wiley, January 1980.

Ainsworth, M. D. *Infancy in Uganda: Infant care and the growth of love*. Baltimore: Johns Hopkins Press, 1967.

Ainsworth, M. D. S., Bell, S. M., & Stayton, D. J. Individual differences in strange-situation behavior of one-year olds. In H. R. Schaffer (ed.), *The origins of human social relations*. London: Academic Press, 1971, p. 17–52.

Allen, V. L., & Feldman, R. S. Studies on the role of tutor. In V. L. Allen (ed.), *Children as teachers: Theory and research on tutoring*. New York: Academic Press, 1976.

Ames, C., & Felker, D. W. Effects of self-concept on children's causal attributions and self-reinforcement. *Journal of Educational Psychology*, in press.

Anastasi, A. Heredity, environment, and the question "how." *Psychological Review*, 1958, *65*, 197–208.

Anastasi, A. *Psychological testing*, 2d ed. New York: Macmillan, 1976.

Anderson, D. R., & Levin, S. R. Young children's attention to "Sesame Street." *Child Development*, 1976, *47*, 806–11.

Andrews, S. R., Blumenthal, J. M., Bache, W. L., & Weiner, G. *The New Orleans model: Parents as early childhood educators*. Paper presented at the meeting of the Society for Research in Child Development, Denver, April 1975.

Anthony, E. J. An experimental approach to the psychopathology of childhood: Encopresis. *British Journal of Medical Psychology*, 1957, *30*, 146–75.

Antonucci, T. *Attachment from adolescence to adulthood*. Paper presented at the meeting of the American Psychological Association, Los Angeles, August 1981.

Apgar, V. A. A proposal for a new method of evaluation of a newborn infant. *Anesthesia and Analgesia: Current Research*, 1953, *32*, 260–67.

Aries, P. *Centuries of childhood* (R.Baldick, Trans.). New York: Knopf, 1962.

Armstrong, B. Illinois judge upholds IQ test use: Departs from *Larry P. APA Monitor*, November 1980, pp. 6–7.

Aron, I. E. Moral philosophy and moral education: A critique of Kohlberg's theory. *School Review*, 1977, *85*, 197–217.

Atkinson, R., & Low, B. *The usefulness of evolutionary theory for studies of child development*. Paper presented at the biennial meeting of the Society for Research in Child Development, Detroit, April 1983.

Atkinson, R. C. Mnemotechnics in second-language learning. *American Psychologist*, 1975, *30*, 821–28.

Austin L., & Little, L. Teenage suicide: Dallas' growing tragedy. *Dallas Times Herald,* Section A, April 18, 1982, pp. 21–23.

Ausubel, D. P. *Educational psychology.* New York: Holt, Rinehart & Winston, 1968.

Ausubel, D. P., Sullivan, E. V., & Ives, S. W. *Theory and problems of child development* (3d ed.). New York: Grune & Stratton, 1980.

b

Babladelis, G. Accentuate the positive. *Contemporary Psychology,* 1979, *24,* 3–4.

Bachman, J. G. *The American high school student: A profile based on national survey data.* Paper presented at the conference, "The American High School Today and Tomorrow," Berkeley, Calif., June 28, 1982.

Bachman, J., O'Malley, P., & Johnston, L. D. *Youth in transition* (vol. VI). *Adolescence to adulthood—change and stability of the lives of young men.* Ann Arbor. Institute for Social Research: University of Michigan, 1978.

Bailey, K. V. A study of human growth in the framework of applied nutrition and public health nutrition programs in the Western Pacific region. In J. Brozek (ed.), *Monographs of the Society for Research in Child Development,* 1970, *35,* Serial No. 140.

Baldwin, A. L. Differences in parent behavior toward three- and nine-year-old children. *Journal of Personality,* 1946, *15,* 143–65.

Baldwin, W. & Cain, V. S. The children of teenage parents. *Family Planning Perspectives,* 1980, *12,* 34–43.

Ball, S., & Bogatz, G. A. *The first year of "Sesame Street": An evaluation.* Princeton: Educational Testing Service, 1970.

Bandura, A. *Principles of behavior modification.* New York: Holt, Rinehart & Winston, 1969.

Bandura, A. *Social learning theory.* New York: General Learning Press, 1971.

Bandura, A. *Social learning theory.* Englewood Cliffs, N.J.: Prentice-Hall, 1977.

Bandura, A., & MacDonald, F. J. Influence of social reinforcement and the behavior of models in shaping children's moral judgments. *Journal of Abnormal and Social Psychology,* 1963, *67,* 274–81.

Bandura, A., & Walters, R. M. *Adolescent aggression.* New York: Ronald, 1959.

Bane, M. J. HEW policy toward children, youth, and families. Discussion paper prepared under Order #SA-8139–77 for the Office of the Assistant Secretary for Planning and Evaluation. Cambridge, Mass., 1978.

Banks, M., & Salapatek, P. Infant pattern vision: A new approach based on the contrast sensitivity function. *Journal of Experimental Child Psychology,* 1981, *31*(1), 1–45.

Barcus, F. E. *Commercial children's television on weekends and weekday afternoons.* Newtonville, Mass.: Action for Children's Television, 1978.

Barker, R. G. *Ecological psychology,* Stanford, Calif.: Stanford University Press, 1968.

Barker, R. G., & Gump, P. V. *Big school, small school: High school size and student behavior.* Stanford, Calif.: Stanford University Press, 1964.

Barnes, G. M. The development of adolescent drinking behavior: An evaluative review of the impact of the socialization process within the family. *Adolescence,* 1977, *13,* 571–91.

Barnes, K. E. Preschool play norms: A replication. *Developmental Psychology,* 1971, *5,* 99–103.

Barrett, D. E., & Radke-Yarrow, M. Chronic malnutrition and child behavior: Effects of early calorie supplementation on social-emotional functioning at school age. *Developmental Psychology,* 1982, *18,* 541–56.

Barrett, D. E., & Radke-Yarrow, M. *Effects of nutritional supplement on children's responses to novel, frustrating, and competitive situations.* Paper presented at the biennial meeting of the Society for Research in Child Development, Detroit, April 1983.

Barry, H., Child, I. L., & Bacon, M. K. Relation of child training to subsistence economy. *American Anthropologist,* 1959, *61,* 51–63.

Bartel, N. R., & Guskin, S. L. A handicap as a social phenomena. In W. M. Cruikshank (ed.), *Psychology of exceptional children and youth.* Englewood Cliffs, N.J.: Prentice-Hall, 1971.

Baskett, L. *The young child's interactions with parents and siblings: A behavioral analysis.* Unpublished doctoral dissertation, University of Oregon, 1974.

Baumrind, D. Current patterns of parental authority. *Developmental Psychology Monographs,* 1971, *4* (1, pt. 2).

Baumrind, D. From each according to her ability. *School Review,* 1972, *80,* 161–97.

Baumrind, D. Socialization and instrumental competence in young children. In W. W. Hartup (ed.), *The young child* (vol. 2). Washington, D. C.: National Association for the Education of Young Children, 1972.

Baumrind, D. Are androgynous individuals more effective persons and parents? *Child Psychology,* 1982, *53,* 44–75.

Bayley, N. Research in child development: A longitudinal perspective. *Merrill Palmer Quarterly,* 1965, *11,* 183–208.

Bayley, N. Development of mental abilities. In P. H. Mussen (ed.), *Carmichael's manual of child psychology,* 3d ed. (vol. 1). New York: John Wiley, 1970.

Belkin, G. S., & Gray, J. L. *Educational psychology: An introduction.* Dubuque, Iowa: Wm. C. Brown Co., 1977. Reprinted by permission.

Bell, D. (ed.). *Shades of brown: New perspectives on school desegregation.* New York: Teachers College Press, 1980.

Bell, R. Q. A reinterpretation of the direction of effects in studies of socialization. *Psychological Review,* 1968, *75,* 81–85.

Bell, R. Q. Parent, child, and reciprocal influences. *American Psychologist,* 1979, *34,* 821–26.

Bell, R. Q., & Costello, N. S. Three tests for sex differences in tactile sensitivity in the newborn. *Biologia Neonat.,* 1964, *7,* 335–47.

Beloff, H. The structure and origin of the anal character. *Genetic Psychology Monographs,* 1962, *55,* 275–78.

Belsky, J. Early human experience: A family perspective. *Developmental Psychology,* 1981, *17,* 3–23.

Belsky, J., & Steinberg, L. D. The effects of day care: A critical review. *Child Development,* 1978, *49,* 929–49.

Bem, S. L. On the utility of alternative procedures for assessing psychological androgyny. *Journal of Consulting and Clinical Psychology,* 1977, *45,* 196–205.

Bender, L. Neuropsychiatric disturbance in dyslexia. In A. H. Keeney & V. J. Keeney (eds.), *Dyslexia,* St. Louis: Mosby, 1968.

Benedict, R. *Patterns of culture.* New York: New American Library, 1958. (Originally published, 1934.)

Benet, S. *How to live to be 100.* New York: The Dial Press, 1976.

Benson, *Texas Monthly,* 1981.

Berndt, T. J. *Developmental changes in conformity to peers and parents.* Paper presented at the Annual Meeting of the American Psychological Association, Toronto, Canada, August 1978.

Berndt, T. J. The features and effects of friendship in early adolescence. *Child Development,* 1982, *53,* 1447–60.

Bernstein, B. A sociolinguistic approach to socialization: With some reference to educability. In F. Williams (ed.), *Language and poverty.* Chicago: Markham, 1970.

Bertenthal, B. I., & Fischer, K. W. Development of self-recognition in the infant. *Developmental Psychology,* 1978, *14,* 44–50.

Berzonsky, M. Formal reasoning in adolescence: An alternative view. *Adolescence,* 1978, *13,* 280–90.

Bijou, S. W. *The basic stage of early childhood development.* Englewood Cliffs, N.J.: Prentice-Hall, 1976.

Birrell, R. G., & Birrell, J. M. W. The maltreatment syndrome in children: A hospital survey. *Medical Journal of Australia,* 1968, *3,* 1023–29.

Bjorklid-Chu, P. A survey of children's outdoor activities in two modern housing areas in Sweden. In B. Tizard & D. Harvey (eds.), *The biology of play.* Philadelphia: Lippincott, 1977.

Blaine, G. B., & McArthur, C. C. Problems connected with studying. In G. B. Blaine, & C. C. McArthur (eds.), *Emotional problems of the student,* 2d ed. New York: Appleton-Century-Crofts, 1971.

Block, J. Conception of sex role: Some cross-cultural and longitudinal perspectives. *American Psychologist,* 1973, *28,* 512–26.

Block, J. Issues, problems, and pitfalls in assessing sex differences: A critical review of the psychology of sex differences. *Merrill-Palmer Quarterly,* 1976, *22,* 283–308.

Block, J. The many faces of continuity. *Contemporary Psychology,* 1981, *26,* 748–50.

Block, M. R., Davidson, J. L., & Grambs, J. D. *Women over forty.* New York: Springer, 1981.

Blom, G. E., Waite, R. R., & Zimet, S. G. A motivational content analysis of children's printers. In P. M. Mussen, J. J. Conger, & J. Kagan (eds.), *Readings in child development and personality.* New York: Harper & Row, 1970.

Bloom, B. S. *The development of exceptional talent.* Paper presented at the biennial meeting of the Society for Research in Child Development, Detroit, April 1983.

Blos, P. *On adolescence.* New York: Free Press, 1962.

Blumberg, M. L. Psychopathology of the abusing parent. *American Journal of Psychotherapy,* 1974, *28,* 1121–29.

Blyth, D. A., Bulcroft, R., & Simmons, R. G. *The impact of puberty on adolescents: A longitudinal study.* Paper presented at the annual meeting of the American Psychological Association, Los Angeles, August 1981.

Blyth, D. A., Simmons, R. G., & Bush, D. The transition into early adolescence: A longitudinal comparison of youth in two educational contexts. *Sociology of Education,* in press.

Bombeck, E., & Keane, B. *Just wait till you have children of your own.* Copyright © 1971 by Erma Bombeck and Bil Keane. Reprinted by permission of Doubleday & Company, Inc.

Boring, E. G. Intelligence as the tests test it. *New Republic,* 1923, *35,* 35–37.

Borke, H. Interpersonal perception of young children: Egocentrism or empathy? *Developmental Psychology,* 1971, *5,* 263–69.

Bower, T. G. R. *Development in infancy.* San Francisco: W. H. Freeman, 1974.

Bowlby, J. The nature of the child's tie to his mother. *International Journal of Psychoanalysis,* 1958, *39,* 350–73.

Bowlby, J. *Attachment and loss,* vol. 1. London: Hogarth (New York: Basic Books), 1969.

Bowman, P. H. Effects of a revised school program on potential delinquents. *Annals,* 1959, *322,* 53–62.

Brackbill, Y. *Research and clinical work with children.* Washington, D. C.: American Psychological Association, 1962.

Brainerd, C. J. The state question in cognitive-developmental theory. *The Behavioral and Brain Sciences,* 1978, *1,* 173–82.

Brainerd, C. J., & Pressley, M. *Progress in cognitive development research* (vol. 2), *Verbal processes in children.* New York: Springer-Verlag, in press.

Brazelton, T. B. *Neonatal behavioral assessment scale.* Philadelphia, Pa.: International Ideas, 1974.

Brecher, M. *Licit and illicit drugs.* Boston: Little, Brown, 1972.

Breitmeyer, B. J., & Ramey, C. T. *Biological vulnerability and quality of postnatal environment as co-determinants of intellectual development.* Paper presented at the biennial meeting of the Society for Research in Child Development, Detroit, April 1983.

Brim, O. G., & Kagan, J. (eds.). *Constancy and change in human development*. Cambridge, Mass.: Harvard University Press, 1980.

Brittain, C. V. Adolescent choices and parent-peer cross pressures. *American Sociological Review*, 1963, *13*, 59–68.

Broadbent, D. E. *Perception and communication*. London: Pergamon Press, 1958.

Broca, P. Remarques sur le siege de Faculte du langage articule suivies d'une observation d'aphemie. *Bulletin de la Societe Anatomique de Paris*, 1861, *6*, 330–57.

Brody, E. B., & Brody, N. *Intelligence: Nature, determinants, and consequences*. New York: Academic Press, 1976.

Broman, S. Longterm development of children born to teenagers. In K. G. Scott, T. Field, & E. Robertson (eds.), *Teenage parents and their offspring*. New York: Grune & Stratton, 1981.

Bronfenbrenner, U. *Two worlds of childhood: U. S. and U.S.S.R.* New York: Russell Sage Foundation, 1970.

Bronfenbrenner, U. Is 80% of intelligence genetically determined? In U. Bronfenbrenner (ed.), *Influences on human development*. Hinsdale, Ill.: Dryden Press, 1972.

Bronfenbrenner, U., & Garbarino, J. The socialization of moral judgment and behavior in cross-cultural perspective. In T. Lickona (ed.), *Moral development and behavior*. New York: Holt, Rinehart & Winston, 1976.

Brooks-Gunn, J., & Ruble, D. N. The development of menstrual-related beliefs and behavior during adolescence. *Child Development*, 1982, *53*, 1567–77.

Brophy, J. Teacher behavior and its effects. *Journal of Educational Psychology*, 1979, *71*, 733–50.

Brophy, J., & Evertson, C. *The Texas teacher effectiveness project: Presentation of nonlinear relationships and summary discussion* (report no. 74–6). Austin: University of Texas Research and Development Center for Teacher Education, 1974.

Brophy, J., & Evertson, C. *Learning from teaching: A developmental perspective*. Boston: Allyn & Bacon, 1976.

Brown, A. L. The development of memory: Knowing, knowing about knowing, and knowing how to know. In H. W. Reese (ed.), *Advances in child development and behavior* (vol. 10). New York: Academic Press, 1975.

Brown, B. B., & Lohr, M. J. *Adolescent peer group stereotypes, member conformity, and identity development*. Paper presented at the biennial meeting of the Society for Research in Child Development, Detroit, April 1983.

Brown, R. *A first language: The early stages*. Cambridge, Mass.: Harvard University Press, 1973.

Bruch, H. *Eating disorders: Obesity, anorexia nervosa, and the person within*. New York: Basic Books, 1973.

Bruner, J. S. The course of cognitive growth. *American Psychologist*, 1964, *19*, 1–15.

Bruner, J. S. *Toward a theory of instruction*. Cambridge, Mass.: Harvard University Press, 1966.

Bruner, J. S. *Beyond the information given*. New York: Norton, 1973.

Bugental, J. F. T., & Zelen, S. L. Investigation into "self-concept": The W-A-Y technique. *Journal of Personality*, 1950, *18*, 483–98.

Buim, N., Rynders, J., & Turnure, J. Early maternal linguistic environment of normal and Down's Syndrome language learning children. *American Journal of Mental Deficiency*, 1974, *79*, 752–58.

Burt, C. The evidence for the concept of intelligence. *British Journal of Educational Psychology*, 1955, *25*, 158–77.

C

Cairns, R. B. *Social development: The origins and plasticity of interchanges*. San Francisco: W. H. Freeman, 1979.

Caplan, F. *The first twelve months of life*. The Princeton Center for Infancy and Early Childhood, Frank Caplan, General Editor. Copyright © 1971, 1972, 1973 by Edcom Systems, Inc. Used by permission of Bantam Books, Inc. All rights reserved. 1981.

Caplan, F., & Caplan, T. Motor development in the twenty-fourth month. *The second twelve months of life*. Copyright © 1977 by Frank Caplan. Reprinted by permission of Grossett & Dunlap, Inc.

Caplan, F., & Caplan, T. *The second twelve months of life*. New York: Bantam, 1981.

Carpenter, T. P. Cognitive development and mathematics learning. In R. Shumway (ed.), *Research in mathematics education*. Reston, Va.: National Council of Teachers of Mathematics, 1980.

Casteñeda, A., Ramirez, M., Cortes, C. E., & Barrera, M. (eds.). *Mexican Americans and educational change*. A symposium at the University of California, Riverside, 1971. (mimeo)

Cattell, R. B. Confirmation and clarification of primary personality factors. *Psychometrika*, 1947, *12*, 197–220.

Cazden, C. *Child language and education*. New York: Holt, Rinehart & Winston, 1972.

Chandler, M. J. Egocentrism and antisocial behavior: The assessment and training of social perspective taking skills. *Developmental Psychology*, 1973, *9*, 326–32.

Chandler, M.J., & Greenspan, D. Ersatz egocentrism: A reply to H. Borke. *Developmental Psychology*, 1972, *7*, 104–6.

Chapman, R. S. Issues in child language acquisition. In L. Lass, N. Northern, D. Yoder, & L. McReynolds (eds.), *Speech, language, and hearing*. Philadelphia: Saunders, 1981.

Charlesworth, R., & Hartup, W. W. Positive social reinforcement in the nursery school peer group. *Child Development*, 1967, *38*, 993–1002.

Chernin, K. Women and weight consciousness. *New York Times News Service*, November 22, 1981. © 1981 by The New York Times Company. Reprinted by permission.

Chess, S., & Hassibi, M. *Principles and practice of child psychiatry*. New York: Plenum, 1978.

Chess, S., & Thomas, A. Temperamental individuality from childhood to adolescence. *Journal of Child Psychiatry,* 1977, *16,* 218–26.

Chilman, C. *Adolescent sexuality in a changing American society: Social and psychological perspectives.* Washington, D.C.: U.S. Government Printing Office, 1979.

Chomsky, C. S. *The acquisition of syntax in children from 5 to 10.* Cambridge, Mass.: MIT Press, 1969.

Chomsky, N. *Syntactic structures.* The Hague: Mouton, 1957.

Chomsky, N. *Aspects of the theory of syntax.* Cambridge, Mass.: MIT Press, 1965.

Chomsky, N. *Language and mind* (2d ed.). New York: Harcourt, 1972.

Cicirelli, V. Family structure and interaction: Sibling effects on socialization. In M. McMillan & M. Sergio (eds.), *Child psychiatry: Treatment and research.* New York: Brunner/Mazel, 1977.

Clark, K. *Dark ghetto.* New York: Harper & Row, 1965.

Clarke-Stewart, K. A. Interactions between mothers and their young children: Characteristics and consequences. *Monographs of the Society for Research in Child Development,* 1973, *38* (6–7, serial no. 153).

Clarke-Stewart, K. A. Recasting the lone stranger. In J. Glick & K. A. Clarke-Stewart (eds.), *The development of social understanding.* New York: Gardner Press, 1978.

Cohen, L. J. Our developing knowledge of infant perception and cognition. *American Psychologist,* 1979, *34,* 894–99.

Cohen, S. E. Maternal employment and mother-child interaction. *Merrill-Palmer Quarterly,* 1978, *24,* 189–97.

Colby, A., Kohlberg, L., Gibbs, J., & Lieberman, M. *A longitudinal study of moral judgment.* Unpublished manuscript, Harvard University, 1980.

Cole, M., Frankel, F., & Sharpe, D. Development of free recall learning in children. *Developmental Psychology,* 1971, *4,* 109–23.

Cole, S. Send our children to work? *Psychology Today,* July 1980, pp. 44–68.

Cole, S. *Working kids on working.* New York: Lothrop, Lee, & Shephard, 1981.

Coleman, J. S. *The adolescent society.* New York: Free Press, 1961.

Coles, R. *Erik Erikson: The growth of his work.* Boston: Little, Brown, 1970.

Colletta, N. D. *Divorced mothers at two income levels: Stress, support, and child-rearing practices.* Unpublished thesis, Cornell University, 1978.

Comstock, G. A. The impact of television on American institutions. *Journal of Communication.* Spring 1978, 12–28.

Condry, J. C., Simon, M. L., & Bronfenbrenner, U. *Characteristics of peer- and adult-oriented children.* Unpublished manuscript, Cornell University, Ithaca, New York, 1968.

Cooper, R., Grotevant, H. D., Moore, M. S., & Condon, S. M. *Family support and conflict: Both foster adolescent identity and role taking.* Paper presented at the annual meeting of the American Psychological Association, August 1982.

Coopersmith, S. *The antecedents of self-esteem.* San Francisco: W. H. Freeman, 1967.

Corrigan, R. The effects of task and practice on search for invisibly displaced objects. *Developmental Review,* 1981, *1,* 1–17.

Cowen, P. A., Langer, J., Heavenrich, J., & Nathanson, M. Social learning of Piaget's cognitive theory of moral development. *Journal of Personality and Social Psychology,* 1969, *11,* 211–74.

Cratty, B. *Psycho-motor behavior in education and sport.* Springfield, Ill.: Charles C. Thomas, 1974.

Cratty, B. *Perceptual and motor development in infants and children,* 2d ed. Englewood Cliffs, N.J.: Prentice-Hall, 1978.

Crick, M. *Explorations in language and meaning: Toward a semantic anthropology.* New York: Halsted Press, 1977.

Cronbach, L. J., & Snow, R. E. *Aptitudes and instructional methods.* New York: Irvington Books, 1977.

Cross, T. G. Mothers' speech and its association with rate of syntactic acquisition in young children. In N. Waterson & C. Snow (eds.), *The development of communication.* New York: John Wiley, 1978.

Cruikshank, W. *The brain-injured child in the home, the school, and the community.* Syracuse, N.Y.: Syracuse University Press, 1967.

d

Dale, P. *Language development: Structure and function,* 2d ed. New York: Holt, Rinehart & Winston, 1976.

Damon, W. *The social world of the child.* San Francisco: Jossey-Bass, 1977.

Davids, A., & Hainsworth, P. K. Maternal attitudes about family life and childrearing as avowed by mothers and perceived by their underachieving and high-achieving sons. *Journal of Consulting Psychology,* 1967, *31,* 29–37.

Davis, G. A. *Creativity is forever.* Cross Plains, Wisc.: Badger Press, 1981.

Davison, G. C., & Neale, J. M. *Abnormal psychology.* New York: John Wiley, 1975.

Day, P. S., & Ulatowska, H. K. Perceptual, cognitive, and linguistic development after early hemispherectomy: Two case studies. *Brain and Language,* 1979, *1,* 17–33.

DeOreo, K. L. Unpublished current work on the assessment of the development of gross motor skills. Kent State University, Kent, Ohio, 1976.

Deshler, D. D. Issues related to the education of learning disabled adolescents. *Learning Disability Quarterly,* 1978, *1,* 2–11.

Deshler, D. D., Lowrey, N., & Alley, G. R. Programming alternatives for learning disabled adolescents: A nationwide survey. *Academic Therapy,* in press.

Deutsch, G. *Eating disorders in adolescence.* Unpublished manuscript, University of Texas at Dallas, Richardson, Texas, 1982.

Dickson, P. D. *Children's oral communication skills.* New York: Academic Press, 1981.

Dion, K. K. Children's physical attractiveness and sex as determinants of adults' punitiveness. *Developmental Psychology,* 1974, *10,* 772–78.

Donovan, W. A., Leavitt, L. A., & Balling, J. D. Maternal physiological response to infant signals. *Psychopsio,* 1978, *15,* 68–74.

Douvan, E., & Adelson, J. *The adolescent experience.* New York: John Wiley, 1966.

Dove, A. Taking the chitling test. *Newsweek,* July 15, 1968, pp. 51–52.

Dreyer, P. H. Sexuality during adolescence. In B. J. Wolman (ed.), *Handbook of Developmental Psychology.* Englewood Cliffs, N.J.: Prentice-Hall, 1982.

Drillien, C. M. *The growth and development of the prematurely born infant.* Baltimore, Md.: Williams & Wilkins, 1964.

Dudek, S. Z. Creativity in young children—Attitude or ability? *Journal of Creative Behavior,* 1974, *8*(4), 282–92.

Duncker, K. On problem solving. *Psychological Monographs,* 1945, *58*(5, Whole No. 270).

Dunphy, D. C. The social structure of urban adolescent peer groups. *Society,* 1963, *26,* 230–46.

Durio, H. F. Mental imagery and creativity. *Journal of Creative Behavior,* 1975, *9*(4), 233–44.

Dusek, J. B., & Flaherty, F. The development of the self-concept during the adolescent years. *Monographs of the Society for Research in Child Development,* 1981, serial no. 191 (vol. 46, no. 4).

Dweck, C. S. The role of expectations and attributions in the alleviation of learned helplessness. *Journal of Personality and Social Psychology,* 1975, *31,* 674–85.

Dweck, C. S. Achievement. In E. M. Hetherington (ed.), *Carmichael's manual of child psychology,* 4th ed. New York: John Wiley, 1983.

e

Eckerman, C. O., Whatley, J. L., & Kutz, S. L. The growth of social play with peers during the second year of life. *Developmental Psychology,* 1975, *11,* 42–49.

Ehrhardt, A., & Baker, S. W. *Hormonal aberrations and their implications for the understanding of normal sex differentiation.* Paper presented at the meeting of the Society for Research in Child Development, Philadelphia, March 1973.

Eichorn, D. Physiological development. In P. H. Mussen (ed.), *Carmichael's Manual of Child Psychology.* New York: John Wiley, 1970.

Eichorn, D. H., Clausen, J. A., Haan, N., Honzik, M. P., & Mussen, P. H., (eds.) *Present and Past in Middle Life.* New York: Academic Press, 1981.

Eiduson, G. T., & Zimmerman, I. L. *Implications of research on the family for policy.* Paper presented at the American Psychological Association Convention, 1978.

Eimas, P. D. Speech perception in early infancy. In L. B. Cohen & P. Salapatek (eds.), *Infant perception: From sensation to cognition* (vol. 2). New York: Academic Press, 1975.

Eitzen, D. S. Athletics in the status system of male adolescents: A replication of Coleman's *The Adolescent Society. Adolescence,* 1975, *10,* 267–76.

Elder, G. H. Democratic parent-youth relationships in cross-national perspective. *Social Science Quarterly,* 1968, *40,* 216–28.

Elkind, D. Piagetian and psychometric conceptions of intelligence. *Harvard Educational Review,* 1969, *39,* 319–37.

Elkind, D. *Child development and education: A Piagetian perspective.* New York: Oxford University Press, 1976.

Elkind, D. *The child's reality: Three developmental themes.* Hillsdale, N.J.: Erlbaum, 1978.

Elkind, D. Understanding the young adolescent. *Adolescence,* 1978, *13,* 127–34.

Elkind, D. Hurried children. *Psychology Today,* January 1979, pp. 38–43.

Emmerich, W., Goldman, K. S., Kirsh, B., & Sharabany, R. Evidence for a transitional phase in the development of gender constancy. *Developmental Psychology,* in press.

Emmerich, W., Goldman, K. S., & Shore, R. E. Differentiation and development of social norms. *Journal of Personality and Social Psychology,* 1971, *18,* 323–53.

Engelmann, S. How to construct effective language programs for the poverty child. In F. Williams (ed.), *Language and poverty.* Chicago: Markham, 1970.

Engen, T., Lipsitt, L. P., & Kaye, H. Olfactory responses and adaptation in the human neonate. *Journal of Comparative and Physiological Psychology,* 1963, *56,* 73–77.

Epstein, H. T. Phrenoblysis: Special brain and mind growth spurt periods: I, Human brain and skull development; II, Human mental skill development. *Developmental Psychobiology,* 1974, *3.*

Epstein, H. T. A biologically based framework for intervention projects. *Mental Retardation,* 1976, *5.*

Epstein, J. L. *After the bus arrives: Resegregation in desegregated schools.* Paper presented at the meeting of the American Educational Research Association, Boston, 1980.

Epstein, J. L. Selecting friends in contrasting secondary school environments. In J. L. Epstein & N. L. Karweit (eds.), *Friends in School.* New York: Academic Press, in press.

Erickson, K. A., & Simon, H. A. *Retrospective verbal reports as data.* Unpublished manuscript. Carnegie-Mellon University, Pittsburgh, 1978.

Erickson, M. T. *Child psychopathology.* Englewood Cliffs, N.J.: Prentice-Hall, 1978.

Erikson, E. H. *Young man Luther.* New York: Norton, 1962.

Erikson, E. H. *Childhood and society.* New York: Norton, 1963.

Erikson, E. H. *Identity: Youth and crisis.* New York: Norton, 1968.

Erikson, E. H. *Gandhi's truth.* New York: Norton, 1969.

Erikson, E. H. Once more the inner space: Letter to a former student. In J. Strouse (ed.), *Women and analysis.* New York: Dell, 1974.

Esposito, D. Homogeneous and heterogeneous ability grouping: Principal findings and implications for evaluating and designing more effective educational environments. *Review of Educational Research,* 1973, *43,* 163–79.

f

Fagen, J. W. Stimulus preference, reinforcer effectiveness, and relational responding in infants. *Child Development,* 1980, *51,* 372–78.

Fagot, B. I. Influence of teacher behavior in the preschool. *Developmental Psychology,* 1973, *9,* 198–206.

Fantz, R. L., Fagan, J. F., & Miranda, S. B. Early visual acuity. In L. B. Cohen & P. Salapatek (eds.), *Infant perception: From sensation to cognition* (vol. 2). New York: Academic Press, 1975.

Fantz, R. L., & Nevis, S. Pattern preferences and perceptual-cognitive development in early infancy. *Merrill-Palmer Quarterly,* 1967, *13,* 77–108.

Faust, M. Somatic development of adolescent girls. *Monographs of the Society for Research in Child Development,* 1977, serial no. 169, vol. 42, no. 1.

Faust, M. S. Developmental maturity as a determinant in prestige of adolescent girls. *Child Development,* 1960, *31,* 173–84.

Feeney, S. *Schools for young adolescents: Adapting the early childhood model.* Carrboro, N.C.: Center for Early Adolescence, 1980.

Feiring, C., & Lewis, M. The child as a member of the family system. *Behavioral Science,* 1978, *23,* 225–33.

Field, T. The three Rs of infant-adult interactions: Rhythms, repertoires, and responsivity. *Journal of Pediatric Psychology,* 1978, *3,* 131–36.

Fischer, K. W., & Jennings, S. The emergence of representation in search: Understanding the hider as an independent agent. *Quarterly Review of Development,* 1981, *1,* 18–30.

Flavell, J. H. An analysis of cognitive-developmental sequences. *Genetic Psychology Monographs,* 1972, *86,* 279–350.

Flavell, J. H. *Cognitive development.* Englewood Cliffs, N.J.: Prentice-Hall, 1977.

Flavell, J. H. Metacognition and cognitive monitoring: A new area of psychological inquiry. *American Psychologist,* 1979, *34,* 906–11.

Flavell, J. H. A tribute to Piaget. *Society for Research in Child Development Newsletter,* Fall 1980.

Flavell, J. H. Cognitive monitoring. In W. P. Dickson (ed.), *Children's oral communication skills.* New York: Academic Press, 1981.

Forbes, R. H. *National assessment change data: Science, writing, and functional illiteracy.* Paper presented at the meeting of the American Educational Research Association, San Francisco, 1976.

Forehand, G., Ragosta, J., & Rock, D. *Conditions and processes of effective school desegregation.* Final Report, U. S. Office of Education, Department of Health, Education & Welfare. Princeton, N.J.: Educational Testing Service, 1976.

Fraiberg, S. *Every child's birthright: In defense of mothering.* New York: Basic Books, 1977.

Fraiberg, S. *Insights from the blind: Comparative studies of blind and sighted infants.* New York: Basic Books, 1977.

Frankenburg, W. K., Dodds, J. B., & Cohrs, M. *Denver Developmental Screening Test* (Rev. ed.). Denver: Ladoca Project and Publishing Foundation, 1975.

Freud, A. Adolescence. In R. S. Eissler (ed.), *Psychoanalytic study of the child* (vol. 13). New York: International Universities Press, 1958.

Freud, A. Instinctual anxiety during puberty. In *The writings of Anna Freud: The ego and the mechanisms of defense.* New York: International Universities Press, 1966.

Freud, A., & Dann, S. An experiment in group upbringing. In R. S. Eisler, A. Freud, H. Hartmann, & E. Kris (eds.), *The psychoanalytic study of the child* (vol. 6). New York: International Universities Press, 1951.

Freud, S. *An outline of psychoanalysis.* New York: Norton, 1949.

Freud, S. *Collected papers,* vols. I, II, III, IV. New York: Basic Books, 1959.

Friedlander, B. Receptive language development in infancy. *Merrill-Palmer Quarterly,* 1970, *16,* 7–51.

Friedrich, L. K., & Stein, A. H. Aggressive and prosocial TV programs and the natural behavior of preschool children. *Monograph of the Society for Research in Child Development,* 1973, *38* (4, serial no. 151).

Furman, W., Rahe, D. F., & Hartup, W. W. Rehabilitation of socially withdrawn preschool children through mixed-age and same-age socialization. *Child Development,* 1979, *50,* 915–22.

Furrow, D., Nelson, K., & Benedict, H. Mothers' speech to children and syntactic development: Some simple relationships. *Journal of Child Language,* 1979, *6,* 423–42.

Furstenberg, F. F. *Unplanned parenthood.* New York: Free Press, 1976.

Furth, H. G. Linguistic deficiency and thinking: Research with deaf subjects, 1964–69. *Psychological Bulletin,* 1971, *75,* 58–72.

Furth, H. G., & Wachs, H. *Thinking goes to school.* New York: Oxford University Press, 1975.

g

Gage, N. L. Desirable behaviors of teachers. *Urban Education,* 1965, *1,* 85–95.

Gagné, R. M. *The conditions of learning* (3d ed.). New York: Holt, Rinehart & Winston, 1977.

Gallup, G. Self-recognition in primates. A comparative approach to the bidirectional properties of consciousness. *American Psychologist,* 1977, *32,* 329–38.

Galst, J. Q. Television food commercials and pro-nutritional public service announcements as determinants of young children's snack choices. *Child Development,* 1980, *51,* 935–38.

Garbarino, J. The ecological correlates of child abuse: The impact of socioeconomic stress on mothers. *Child Development,* 1976, *47,* 178–85.

Gardner, B. T., & Gardner, R. A. Two-way communication with an infant chimpanzee. In A. Schrier & F. Stollnitz (eds.), *Behavior of nonhuman primates* (vol. 4). New York: Academic Press, 1971.

Gardner, G. E., & Speery, B. M. School problems: Learning disabilities and school phobia. In S. Arieti (ed.), *American handbook of psychiatry* (vol. 2). New York: Basic Books, 1974.

Gardner, L. I. Deprivation dwarfism. *Scientific American,* 1972, *227,* 76–82.

Garmezy, N. Intervention with children at risk for behavior pathology. *Clinical Psychologist,* 1975, *28,* 12–14.

Garmezy, N., & Rutter, M. Stress and coping in children. In E. M. Hetherington (ed.), *Carmichael's manual of child psychology,* 4th ed. New York: John Wiley, 1983.

Garvey, C. *Play.* Cambridge, Mass.: Harvard University Press, 1977.

Gatewood, T. E. What research says about the junior high versus the middle school. *North Central Association Quarterly,* 1971, *46,* 264–76.

Gay, J., & Tweney, R. D. Comprehension and production of standard and black English by lower-class black children. *Developmental Psychology,* 1976, *12,* 262–68.

Gearheart, B. R. *Learning disabilities: Educational strategies.* St. Louis: Mosby, 1973.

Geis, G., & Monahan, J. The social ecology of violence. In T. Lickona (ed.), *Moral development and behavior.* New York: Holt, Rinehart & Winston, 1976.

Gesell, A. The ontogenesis of infant behavior. In L. Carmichael (ed.), *Manual of child psychology.* New York: John Wiley, 1954.

Getman, G. N. *How to develop your child's intelligence.* Luverne, A research publication, G. N. Getman, 1952.

Getzels, J. W., & Dillon, T. J. The nature of giftedness and the education of the gifted. In R. M. W. Travers (ed.), *Second handbook of research on teaching.* Chicago: Rand McNally, 1973.

Gewirtz, J. L. Attachment and dependence, and a distinction in terms of stimulus control. In J. L. Gewirtz (ed.), *Attachment and dependency.* Washington, D. C.: V. H. Winston & Sons, 1972, 139–77.

Gibson, E. J. *Principles of perceptual learning and development.* New York: Appleton-Century-Crofts, 1969.

Gibson, E. J. *The ecological approach to visual perception.* Boston: Houghton-Mifflin, 1979.

Gibson, E. J., & Levin, H. *The psychology of reading.* Cambridge, Mass.: MIT Press, 1975.

Gilligan, C. In a different voice: Women's conceptions of self and of morality. *Harvard Educational Review,* 1977, *47,* 481–517.

Girott, H. *Between parent and teenager.* New York: Avon Books, 1969.

Glucksberg, S., & Krauss, R. M. What do people say after they have learned to talk? *Merrill-Palmer Quarterly,* 1967, *13,* 309–16.

Gold, D., Andres, D., & Glorieux, J. The development of Francophone nursery school children with employed and nonemployed mothers. *Canadian Journal of Behavioral Science,* 1979, *11,* 169–73.

Gold, M., & Mattick, H. W. *Experiment in the streets: The Chicago Youth Development Project.* Ann Arbor, Mich.: Institute for Social Research, 1974.

Gold, M., & Petronio, R. J. Delinquent behavior in adolescence. In J. Adelson (ed.), *Handbook of adolescent psychology,* New York: John Wiley, 1980.

Gold, M., & Reimer, D. J. Changing patterns of delinquent behavior among Americans 13 through 16 years old: 1967–72. *Crime and Delinquency Literature,* 1975, *7,* 483–517.

Gold, M., & Williams, J. R. The effect of "getting caught"; Apprehension of the juvenile offender as a cause of subsequent delinquencies. *Prospectus,* 1969, *3,* 1–12.

Goldberg, R. J. *Maternal time use and preschool performance.* Paper presented at the meeting of the Society for Research in Child Development, New Orleans, March 1977.

Goldberg, S. Prematurity: Effects on parent-infant interaction. *Merrill-Palmer Quarterly,* 1977, *23,* 163–77.

Goldberg, S., Brachfeld, S., & DiVitto, B. Feeding, fussing, and play. In T. M. Field, S. Goldberg, D. Stern, & A. M. Sostek (eds.), *High-risk infants and children: Adult and peer interactions.* New York: Academic Press, 1980.

Gollin, E. S. Factors affecting the visual recognition of incomplete objects: A comparative investigation of children and adults. *Perceptual Motor Skills,* 1962, *15,* 583–90.

Good, T. L., Biddle, B., & Brophy, J. E. *Teachers make a difference.* New York: Holt, Rinehart & Winston, 1975.

Good, T. L., & Brophy, J. E. Changing teacher and student behavior: An empirical investigation. *Journal of Educational Psychology,* 1974, *66,* 390–405.

Gordon, D. C. *Overcoming the fear of death.* New York: Macmillan, 1970.

Gordon, T. *Parent effectiveness training.* New York: New American Library, 1970.

Gottlieb, D. Teaching and students: The views of Negro and white teachers. *Sociology of Education,* 1966, *37,* 345–53.

Gratch, G. A study of the relative dominance of vision and touch in six-month-old infants. *Child Development,* 1972, *43,* 615–23.

Gratch, G. Review of Piagetian infancy research: Object concept development. In W. F. Overton & J. M. Gallagher (eds.), *Knowledge and development* (vol. 1). New York: Plenum, 1977.

Green, R. One-hundred-ten feminine and masculine boys: Behavioral contrasts and demographic similarities. *Archives of Sexual Behavior*, 1974, *5*, 425–46.

Greenacre, P. The childhood of the artist. In P. Greenacre (ed.), *Emotional growth*. New York: International Universities Press, 1971.

Greenberg, B. S., & Domonick, J. R. *Television behavior among disadvantaged children*. Unpublished manuscript, Michigan State University, East Lansing, Michigan, 1969.

Greenberger, E., & Steinberg, L. *Project for the study of adolescent work: Final report*. Prepared for the National Institute of Education, U. S. Department of Education, Washington, D. C., 1981.

Greenfield, J. *A child called Noah*. New York: Holt, Rinehart & Winston, 1972. From *A Child Called Noah* by Josh Greenfield. Copyright © 1970, 1971, 1972 by Josh Greenfield. Reprinted by permission of Holt, Rinehart and Winston, Publishers.

Gribbons, W. D., & Lohnes, P. R. Relationships among measures of readiness for vocational planning. *Journal of Counseling Psychology*, 1964, *11*, 13–19.

Grimes, J. W., & Allinsmith, W. Compulsivity, anxiety, and school achievement. *Merrill-Palmer Quarterly*, 1961, *7*, 247–69.

Grotevant, M. D., Scarr, S., & Weinberg, R. A. *Intellectual development in family constellations with adopted and natural children: A test of the Zajonc and Markus model*. Paper presented at the meeting of the Society for Research in Child Development, New Orleans, March 1975.

Guilford, J. P. *The nature of human intelligence*. New York: McGraw-Hill, 1967.

Guthrie, G. M., Masangkay, Z., & Guthrie, H. A. Behavior, malnutrition, and mental development. *Journal of Cross-cultural Psychology*, 1976, *7*, 169–80.

Guttentag, M., & Bray, H. *Undoing sex stereotypes, research and resources for educators*. New York: McGraw-Hill, 1976.

h

Haeberle, E. *The sex atlas*. New York: Seaburg Press, 1978.

Hall, C. S., & Lindzey, G. *Theories of personality*. New York: John Wiley, 1978.

Hall, G. S. *Adolescence: Its psychology and its relations to physiology, anthropology, sociology, sex, crime, religion, and education* (vol. 1). Englewood Cliffs, N.J.: Prentice-Hall, 1904–5.

Hallinan, M. T. Structural effects on children's friendships and cliques. *Social Psychology Quarterly*, 1979, *42*, 43–54.

Halverson, L. E. Development of motor patterns in young children. *Quest*, Monograph 6, 1966, 44–53.

Halwes, T., & Jenkins, J. J. Problem of serial order in behavior is not resolved by context-associative memory models. *Psychological Review*, 1971, *78*, 122–29.

Hamm, C. M. The content of moral education, or in defense of the "bag of virtues." *School Review*, 1977, *85*, 218–28.

Hardyck, C., & Petronovich, L. F. Left-handedness. *Psychological Bulletin*, 1977, *84*, 385–404.

Harter, S. The perceived competence scale for children. *Child Development*, 1982, *53*, 87–97.

Harter, S. Developmental perspectives on the self-system. In E. M. Hetherington (ed.), *Carmichael's manual of child psychology*, 4th ed. (vol. IV). New York: John Wiley, 1983.

Hartley, R. E., Frank, L. K., & Goldenson, R. M. *Understanding children's play*. New York: Columbia University Press, 1952.

Hartshorne, H., & May, M. S. *Studies in the nature of character. Studies in deceit* (vol. 1). *Studies in self-control* (vol. 2). *Studies in the organization of character* (vol. 3). New York: Macmillan, 1928–30.

Hartup, W. W. Peer interaction and social organization. In P. H. Mussen (ed.), *Carmichael's manual of child psychology*, 3d ed. (vol. 2). New York: John Wiley, 1970.

Hartup, W. W. Peer interaction and the development of the individual child. In E. Schopler & R. J. Reichler (eds.), *Psychopathology and child development*. New York: Plenum, 1976.

Hartup, W. W. The social worlds of childhood. *American Psychologist*, 1979, *34*, 944–50.

Hartup, W. W. Peers as a context for social development. In E. M. Hetherington (ed.), *Carmichael's manual of child psychology*, 4th ed., (vol. IV). New York: John Wiley, 1983.

Hartup, W. W., & Coates, B. Imitation of a peer as a function of reinforcement from the peer group and rewardingness of the model. *Child Development*, 1967, *38*, 1003–16.

Hass, A. *Teenage sexuality of a survey of teenage sexual behavior*. New York: Macmillan, 1979.

Havighurst, R. J. *Developmental tasks and education*. New York: McKay, 1972.

Havighurst, R. J. Choosing a middle path for the use of drugs with hyperactive children. *School Review*, 1976, *85*, 61–77.

Havighurst, R. J., & Neugarten, B. L. *American Indian and white children*. Chicago: University of Chicago Press, 1955.

Hay, D. F. Multiple functions of proximity seeking in infancy. *Child Development*, 1980, *51*, 636–45.

Hayes, K. J., & Hayes, C. Picture perception in a home-raised chimpanzee. *Journal of Comparative and Physiological Psychology*, 1951, *46*, 470–74.

Hebb, D. O. *Organization of behavior*. New York: John Wiley, 1949.

Heber, R. (ed.). A manual on terminology and classification in mental retardation (2d ed.). *American Journal of Mental Deficiency Monograph Supplement,* 1961.

Helms, D., & Turner, J. *Exploring child behavior.* New York: Holt, Rinehart & Winston, 1981.

Henderson, N. D. Human behavior genetics. *Annual Review of Psychology,* 1982, *33,* 403–40.

Herkowitz, J. Assessing the motor development of children: Presentation and critique of tests. In M. V. Ridenour et al. (eds.), *Motor Development,* 1978.

Hess, R. D., & Shipman, V. C. Early experience and the socialization of cognitive modes in children. *Child Development,* 1965, *36,* 869–86.

Hess, R. D., & Shipman, V. C. Maternal influences upon early learning: The cognitive environments of urban preschool children. In R. D. Hess & R. M. Bear (eds.), *Early education.* Chicago: Aldine, 1968.

Hetherington, E. M. Effects of father absence on personality development in adolescent daughters. *Developmental Psychology,* 1972, *7,* 313–26.

Hetherington, E. M. *My heart belongs to daddy: A study of the marriages of daughters of divorcees and widows.* Unpublished manuscript, University of Virginia, 1977.

Hetherington, E. M. Divorce: A child's perspective. *American Psychologist,* 1979, *34,* 851–58.

Hetherington, E. M., Cox, M., & Cox, R. The aftermath of divorce. In J. H. Stevens & M. Mathews (eds.), *Mother-child/father-child relations.* Washington, D.C.: National Association for the Education of Young Children, 1978.

Higgins, A., Power, C., & Kohlberg, L. Moral atmosphere and moral judgment. Paper presented at the biennial meeting of the Society for Research in Child Development, Detroit, April 1983.

Hill, J. P. *Secondary schools, socialization, and social development during adolescence.* Position paper prepared for the National Institute of Education, U.S. Department of Health, Education, and Welfare, June 1978.

Hill, J. P. The early adolescent and the family. In *The seventy-ninth yearbook of the national society for the study of education.* Chicago: University of Chicago Press, 1980. (a)

Hill, J. P. *Understanding Adolescence: A Framework.* Carrboro, N.C.: Center for Early Adolescence, 1980. (b)

Hill, J. P. Adolescent Development. Invited lecture at the biennial meeting of the Society for Research in Child Development, Detroit, April 1983. (a)

Hill, J. P. Commentary. *Monographs of the Society for Research in Child Development,* 1981, *46,* No. 4. (b)

Hinde, R. A. Influence of social companions and of temporary separation on mother-infant relations in rhesus monkeys. In B. M. Foss (ed.), *Determinants of infant behavior IV.* London: Methuen (New York: John Wiley), 1969.

Hinde, R. A. Can an evolutionary approach help the study of child development? Invited symposium at the biennial meeting of the Society for Research in Child Development, Detroit, April 1983.

Hock, E. Working and nonworking mothers and their infants: A comparative study of maternal caregiving characteristics and infant social behavior. *Merrill-Palmer Quarterly,* in press.

Hockett, C. F. Logical considerations in the study of animal communication. In W. E. Lanyon & W. M. Taudga (eds.), *Animal sounds and animal communication.* Washington, D.C.: American Institute of Biological Sciences, 1960.

Hoffman, L. W. Effects of maternal employment on the child: A review of the research. *Developmental Psychology,* 1974, *10,* 204–28.

Hoffman, M. L. Moral development. In P. H. Mussen (ed.), *Carmichael's manual of child psychology,* 3d ed., (vol. 2). New York: John Wiley, 1970.

Hoffman, M. L. Developmental synthesis of affect and cognition and its implications for altruistic motivation. *Developmental Psychology,* 1975, *11,* 607–22.

Hoffman, M. L. Development of moral thought, feeling, and behavior. *American Psychologist,* 1979, *34,* 958–66.

Hoffman, M. L. Empathy, guilt, and social cognition. In W. Overton (ed.), *Relation between social and cognitive development.* Hillsdale, N.J.: Erlbaum, in press.

Hollingshead, A. B. *Elmtown's youth and Elmtown revisited.* New York: John Wiley, 1975.

Holmberg, M. C. The development of social interchange patterns from 12 to 42 months. *Child Development,* 1980, *51,* 448–56.

Holt, J. *How children fail.* Belmont, Calif.: Pitman, 1964.

Holtzmann, W. Cross-cultural comparisons of personality development in Mexico and the United States. In D. Wagner & H. Stevenson (eds.), *Cultural perspectives on child development.* San Francisco: W. H. Freeman, 1982.

Homme, L., Csanyi, A., Gonzales, M. A., & Rechs, J. *How to use contingency contracting in the classroom.* Champaign, Ill.: Research Press, 1970.

Horney, K. *Neurosis and human growth.* New York: Norton, 1950.

Hubbard, R. Test-tube babies: Solution or problem. *Technology Review,* 1980, *85.*

Hudson, W. Pictorial depth perception in subcultural groups in Africa. *Journal of Social Psychology,* 1960, *52,* 183–208.

Hudson, W. The study of pictorial perception among unacculturated groups. *International Journal of Psychology,* 1967, *2,* 90–107.

Hultch, D. F., & Plemons, J. K. Life events and life-span development. In P. B. Baltes & O. G. Brim, Jr. (eds.), *Life-span development and behavior* (vol.2). New York: Academic Press, 1979.

Hurlock, E. B. *Developmental psychology,* 5th ed. New York: McGraw-Hill, 1980.

Huston, A. C. Sex-typing. In E. M. Hetherington (ed.), *Carmichael's manual of child psychology,* 4th ed. (vol. IV). New York: John Wiley, 1983.

Huston, A. C., Seigle, J., & Bremer, M. *Family environment and television use by preschool children.* Paper presented at the biennial meeting of the Society for Research in Child Development, Detroit, April 1983.

Huston-Stein, A., & Higgins-Trenk, A. Development of females from childhood through adulthood: Career and feminine role orientations. In P. Baltes (ed.), *Life-span development and behavior* (vol. 1). New York: Academic Press, 1978.

Hyde, J. S. *Understanding human sexuality.* New York: McGraw-Hill, 1979.

Hyman, H. M. *Political socialization.* New York: Free Press, 1959.

i

Inkeles, A. Social structure and socialization. In D. Goslind (ed.), *Handbook of socialization theory and research.* Chicago: Rand McNally, 1969.

j

Jacobs, J. *Adolescent suicide.* New York: Wiley, 1971.

Jacobson, S. W. Maternal caffeine consumption prior to pregnancy: Effects on the newborn. Paper presented at the biennial meeting of the Society for Research in Child Development, Detroit, April 1983.

James, W. *The principles of psychology* (vol. 1). New York: Holt, Rinehart & Winston, 1890.

Jenkins, J. J. Language and thought. In J. F. Voss (ed.), *Approaches to thought.* Columbus: Merrill, 1969.

Jensen, A. R. How much can we boost IQ and scholastic achievement? *Harvard Educational Review,* 1969, *39,* 1–123.

Johnson, R. C. A study of children's moral judgments. *Child Development,* 1962, *33,* 603–5.

Johnston, L. D., Bachman, J. G., & O'Malley, P. M. *Student drug use in America 1975–1981.* Rockville, Md.: National Institute of Drug Abuse, 1981.

Jones, M. C. A laboratory study of fear: The case of Peter. *Pedagogical Seminary,* 1924, *31,* 308–15.

Jones, M. C. Psychological correlates of somatic development. *Child Development,* 1965, *36,* 899–911.

Jones, M. C., & Mussen, P. H. Self-conceptions, motivations, and interpersonal attitudes of early- and late-maturing girls. *Child Development,* 1958, *29,* 491–501.

Jones, R. R., Reid, J. B., & Patterson, G. R. Naturalistic observation in clinical assessment. In P. McReynolds (ed.), *Advances in psychological assessment* (vol. 3). San Francisco: Jossey-Bass, 1974.

k

Kagan, J. Reflection-impulsivity: The generality and dynamics of conceptual tempo. *Journal of Abnormal Psychology,* 1966, *71,* 17–24.

Kagan, J. *Change and continuity in infancy.* New York: John Wiley, 1971.

Kagan, J. Emergent themes in human development. *American Scientist,* 1976, *64,* 186–96.

Kagan, J. Family experience and the child's development. *American Psychologist,* 1979, *34,* 886–91.

Kagan, J., Kearsley, R. B., & Zelazo, P. R. *Infancy.* Cambridge, Mass.: Harvard University Press, 1978.

Kagan, J., & Kogan, N. Individual variation in cognitive processes. In P. H. Mussen (ed.), *Carmichael's manual of child psychology,* 3d ed. (vol. 1). New York: John Wiley, 1970.

Kagan, J., & Moss, H. A. *Birth to maturity.* New York: John Wiley, 1962.

Kahn, J. H., & Nursten, J. P. School phobias: Refusal, a comprehensive view of school phobia, and other failures of school attendance. *American Journal of Orthopsychiatry,* 1962, *32,* 707–18.

Kail, R. V. *Memory development in children.* San Francisco: Freeman, 1979.

Kamin, L. J. *The science and politics of IQ.* New York: Halsted Press, 1974.

Kandel, D., & Lesser, G. S. Parent-adolescent relationships and adolescent independence in the United States and Denmark. *Journal of Marriage and the Family,* 1969, *31,* 348–58.

Katz, J. *No time for youth: Growth and constraint in college.* San Francisco: Jossey-Bass, 1968.

Katz, P. A. The development of female identity. *Sex Roles,* 1979, *5,* 155–78.

Kaye, K., & Fogel, A. The temporal structure of face-to-face communication between mothers and infants. *Developmental Psychology,* 1980, *16*(5), 454–64.

Keating, D. P. Thinking processes in adolescence. In J. Adelson (ed.), *Handbook of Adolescent Psychology.* New York: Wiley—Interscience, 1980.

Kellogg, R. *Analyzing children's art.* Palo Alto, Calif.: Mayfield, 1970. By permission of Mayfield Publishing Company. Copyright © 1969, 1970 by Rhonda Kellogg.

Kellogg, W. N., & Kellogg, L. A. *The ape and the child.* New York: McGraw-Hill, 1933.

Kelly, J. B. *Children and parents in the midst of divorce: Major factors contributing to differential response.* Paper presented at the National Institute of Mental Health Conference on Divorce, Washington, D. C., February 1978.

Kenniston, K. Youth: A "new" stage of life. *The American Scholar,* 1970, *39,* 631–54.

Kenniston, K. The tasks of adolescence. *Developmental Psychology Today.* Del Mar, Calif.: CRM Books, 1971.

Kephart, N. *The slow learner in the classroom.* Columbus: Charles F. Merrill, 1971.

Kessen, W. *Childhood in China.* New Haven, Conn.: Yale University Press, 1975.

Kessen, W., Haith, M. H., & Salapatek, P. H. Infancy. In P. H. Mussen (ed.), *Carmichael's manual of child psychology,* 3d ed. (vol. 1). New York: John Wiley, 1970.

Khatena, J. Creativity imagination imagery: Where is it going? *Journal of Creative Behavior,* 1976, *10*(3), 189–92.

Khatena, J., & Torrance, E. P. *Thinking creatively with sounds and words.* Lexington, Mass.: Personnel Press, 1973.

Kinsey, A. C., Pomeroy, W. B., & Martin, C. E. *Sexual behavior in the human male.* Philadelphia: Saunders, 1948.

Kintsch, W. Text representation. In W. Otto & S. White (eds.), *Reading expository text.* New York: Academic Press, 1982.

Klahr, D., & Wallace, J. G. *Cognitive development: An information processing view.* Hillsdale, N.J.: Erlbaum, 1975.

Klaus, M., & Kennell, J. *Maternal-infant bonding,* 2d ed. St. Louis: Mosby, 1982.

Klausmeier, Herbert S. Educational experience and cognitive development. *Educational Psychologist,* 1977, Vol. 12(2), pp. 179–96.

Klein, N. C., Alexander, J. F., & Parsons, B. V. Impact of family systems intervention on recidivism and sibling delinquency: A model of primary prevention and program evaluation. *Journal of Consulting and Clinical Psychology,* 1977, *45*, 469–74.

Klein, R. F., Freeman, H. F., & Yarborough, C. Effect of protein calorie malnutrition on mental development. *Advances in Pediatrics,* 1971, *18*, 75–91.

Koch, H. Some emotional attitudes of the young child in relation to characteristics of his sibling. *Child Development,* 1956, *27*, 393–426.

Koffka, K. *Principles of Gestalt psychology.* New York: Harcourt, 1935.

Kohlberg, L. *The development of modes of moral thinking and choice in the years 10 to 16.* Unpublished doctoral dissertation, University of Chicago, 1958.

Kohlberg, L. A cognitive-developmental analysis of children's sex-role concepts and attitudes. In E. E. Maccoby (ed.), *The development of sex differences.* Stanford, Calif.: Stanford University Press, 1966.

Kohlberg, L. Stage and sequence: The cognitive-developmental approach to socialization. In D. A. Goslin (ed.), *Handbook of socialization theory and research.* Chicago: Rand McNally, 1969. Copyright © 1969 by Houghton-Mifflin Company. Used by permission.

Kohlberg, L. Moral stages and moralization. The cognitive-developmental approach. In T. Lickona (ed.), *Moral development and behavior.* New York: Holt, Rinehart & Winston, 1976. Reprinted by permission.

Kohlberg, L., & Candee, D. *Relationships between moral judgment and moral action.* Unpublished manuscript, Harvard University, 1979.

Kohlberg, L. (ed.). *Recent research in moral development.* New York: Holt, Rinehart & Winston, 1980.

Kohler, W. *Gestalt psychology.* New York: New American Library, Mentor Books, 1959. (Originally published, 1947.)

Kravitz, H., & Boehm, J. Rhythmic habit patterns in infancy: Their sequences, age of onset, and frequency. *Child Development,* 1971, *42*, 399–413.

Krogman, W. M. Growth of head, face, trunk, and limbs in Philadelphia white and negro children of elementary and high school age. *Monographs of the Society for Research in Child Development,* 1970, serial no. 136, vol. *35,* no.3.

l

Labov, W. The logic of nonstandard English. In F. Williams (ed.), *Language and poverty.* Chicago: Markham, 1970.

Labov, W. Systematically misleading data from test questions. *The Urban Review,* 1976, *9*, 146–69.

Lahey, B. B. Behavior modification with learning disabilities and related problems. In M. Hersen, R. Eisler, & P. Miller (eds.), *Progress in behavior modification.* New York: Academic Press, 1975.

Lamb, M. E. (ed.). *The role of the father in child development.* New York: John Wiley, 1976.

Lamb, M. E. Father-infant and mother-infant interaction in the first year of life. *Child Development,* 1977, *48,* 167–81.

Lamb, M. E. Fathers and child development: An integrative overview. In M. E. Lamb (ed.), *The father's role in child development,* 2d ed. New York: John Wiley, 1981.

Lamb, M. E., & Sherrod, L. R. (eds.). *Infant social cognition: Empirical and theoretical considerations.* Hillsdale, N.J.: Erlbaum, 1981.

Landesman-Dwyer, S., & Sackett, G. P. *Prenatal nicotine exposure and sleep-wake patterns in infancy.* Paper presented at the biennial meeting of the Society for Research in Child Development, Detroit, April 1983.

Langer, J. *Theories of development.* New York: Holt, Rinehart & Winston, 1969.

Larson, M. E. Humbling cases for career counselors. *Phi Delta Kappan,* 1973, *54,* 374.

Lasater, T. M., Briggs, J., Malone, P., Gilliom, C. F., & Weisburg, P. *The Birmingham model for parent education.* Paper presented at the meeting of the Society for Research in Child Development, Denver, April 1975.

Lasko, J. K. Parent behavior toward first-born and second-born children. *Genetic Psychology Monographs,* 1954, *4a.*

Lasky, R. E., & Klein, R. E. The reactions of five-month-old infants to eye contact of the mother and of a stranger. *Merrill-Palmer Quarterly,* 1979, *25*, 163–70.

Lavine, L. O. *The development of perception of writing in prereading children: A cross-cultural study.* Unpublished doctoral dissertation, Cornell University, Ithaca, New York, 1972.

Lawson, A. E., & Wollman, W. T. *Encouraging the transition from concrete to abstract cognitive functioning: An experiment.* Unpublished manuscript, University of California at Berkeley, 1975.

Laxalt, P. *The family protection act.* A legislative bill introduced in the United States Senate, Congressional Record, 1980.

Laycock, F. *Gifted children.* Glenview, Ill.: Scott, Foresman, 1979.

Leboyer, F. *Birth without violence.* New York: Knopf, 1975.

Lee, C. B. T. *The campus scene: 1900–1970.* New York: McKay, 1970.

Lee, L. C. *Social encounters of infants: The beginnings of popularity.* Paper presented at the meeting of the International Society for the Study of Behavioral Development, Ann Arbor, Michigan, August 1973.

Lee, T. Perceived distance as a function of direction in the city. *Environment & Behavior,* 1970, *2,* 40–51.

Leedham, L. R., Signori, E. I., & Sampson, D. L. G. Survey of areas of moral awareness and formation of principles basic to the construction of a scale to measure conscience. *Psychological Reports,* 1967, *21,* 913–19.

LeFurgy, W. G., & Woloshin, G. W. Immediate and long-term effects of experimentally induced social influence in the modification of adolescents' moral judgments. *Journal of Abnormal and Social Psychology,* 1969, *12,* 104–10.

Leifer, A. D. *Television and the development of social behavior.* Paper presented at the meeting of the International Society for the Study of Behavioral Development, Ann Arbor, Michigan, 1973.

Leler, H., Johnson, D. L., Kahn, A. J., Hines, R. P., & Torres, M. *The Houston model for parent education.* Paper presented at the meeting of the Society for Research in Child Development, Denver, April 1975.

Lenneberg, E. H. *Biological foundation of language.* New York: John Wiley, 1967.

Leona, M. H. An examination of adolescent clique language in a suburban secondary school. *Adolescence,* 1978, *51,* 496–502.

Lerner, J. W. *Children with learning disabilities: Theories, diagnosis, and teaching strategies.* Boston: Houghton Mifflin, 1971.

Lesser, G. Learning, teaching, and television production for children: The experience of Sesame Street. *Harvard Education Review,* 1972, *42,* 232–72.

Levin, J. R. *The mnemonic '80s: Keywords in the classroom.* Theoretical Paper No. 86, Wisconsin Research and Development Center for Individualized Schooling, Madison, 1980.

LeVine, R. A. *Culture, behavior, and personality.* Chicago: Aldine, 1973.

Levinson, D. J. *The seasons of a man's life.* New York: Knopf, 1978.

Lewis, M., & Brooks-Gunn, J. *Social cognition and the acquisition of the self.* New York: Plenum, 1979.

Lewis, M., & Cherry, L. Social behavior and language acquisition. In M. Lewis & L. Rosenblum (eds.), *Interaction conversation and the development of language: The origins of behavior* (vol. 5). New York: John Wiley, 1977.

Lewis, M., & Rosenblum, L. A. (eds.). *Friendship and peer relations* (vol. 4). New York: John Wiley, 1975.

Lipsitt, L. P. Learning in the human infant. In H. W. Stevenson, E. H. Hess, & H. L. Rheingold (eds.), *Early behavior: Comparative and developmental approaches.* New York: John Wiley, 1967.

Lipsitt, L. P. Learning capacities in the human infant. In R. J. Robinson (ed.), *Brain and early behavior.* New York: Academic Press, 1969.

Lipsitt, L. P. Critical conditions in infancy: A psychological perspective. *American Psychologist,* 1979, *34,* 973–80.

Lipsitt, L. P., & Levy, N. Electroactual threshold in the neonate. *Child Development,* 1959, *30,* 547–54.

Lohr, M. J., & Brown, B. B. *"Neglected" adolescents: The affects of peer group membership on self-esteem.* Paper presented at the biennial meeting of the Society for Research in Child Development, Detroit, April 1983.

Lorenz, K. Z. *Evolution and modification of behavior.* Chicago: University of Chicago Press, 1965.

Lorenzi, M. E., Klerman, L. V., & Jekel, J. F. School-age parents: How permanent a relationship? *Adolescence,* 1977, *45,* 13–22.

Lowrey, G. H. *Growth and development of children,* 7th ed. Chicago: Year Book Medical Publishers, 1978.

Lundsteen, S. W., & Bernstein-Tarrow, N. B. *Guiding young children's learning.* New York: McGraw-Hill, 1981.

Lyle, J., & Hoffman, H. R. Children's use of television and other media. In E. A. Rubenstein, G. A. Comstock, & J. P. Murray (eds.), *Television and social behavior* (vol. 4). Washington, D. C.: U.S. Government Printing Office, 1972.

m

Maas, H. S. The role of members in clubs of lower-class and middle-class adolescents. *Child Development,* 1954, *25,* 241–51.

McCall, R. B. Nature-nurture and the two realms of development: A proposed integration with respect to mental development. *Child Development,* 1981, *52,* 1–12.

McCandless, B. R. *Male caregivers in day care: Demonstration project* (Family Research and Development Foundation report). Atlanta, Ga.: Emory University, 1973.

McCandless, B. R., & Evans, E. *Children and youth: Psychosocial development.* Hillsdale, Ill.: Dryden Press, 1973.

Maccoby, E. E. *Social development.* New York: Harcourt, 1980.

Maccoby, E. E. *Socialization and developmental change.* Presidential address, biennial meeting of the Society for Research in Child Development, Detroit, April 1983.

Maccoby, E. E., & Jacklin, C. N. *The psychology of sex differences.* Stanford, Calif.: Stanford University Press, 1974.

Maccoby, E. E., & Jacklin, C. N. Sex differences in aggression: A rejoinder and reprise. *Child Development,* 1980, *51,* 964–80.

McCord, W., McCord, J., & Howard, A. Familial correlates of aggression in nondelinquent male children. *Journal of Abnormal and Social Psychology,* 1961, *62,* 79–83.

MacFarlane, A. What a baby knows. *Human Nature,* February 1978.

McNeill, D. The development of language. In P. H. Mussen (ed.), *Carmichael's manual of child psychology,* 3d ed. (vol. 1). New York: John Wiley, 1970.

Mahler, M. S. *Infantile psychosis and early contributions,* vol. 1. London: Jason Aronson, 1979. (a)

Mahler, M. S. *Separation-individuation,* vol. II. London: Jason Aronson, 1979. (b)

Main, M. *Exploration, play and cognitive functioning as related to child-mother attachment.* Unpublished doctoral dissertation, Johns Hopkins University, 1973.

Mandler, G. Organization and memory. In K. W. Spence and J. T. Spence (eds.), *The psychology of learning and motivation, 1.* New York: Academic Press, 1967.

Mannarino, A. P. The relationship between friendship and altruism in preadolescent girls. *Psychiatry,* 1979, *42,* 280–84.

Marcia, J. Development and validation of ego-identity status. *Journal of Personality and Social Psychology,* 1966, *3,* 551–58.

Marcia, J. *Identity in adolescence.* In J. Adelson (ed.), *Handbook of Adolescent Psychology.* New York: Wiley-Interscience, 1980.

Marjoribanks, K., Walberg, H. S., & Bargen, M. Mental abilities: Sibling constellations and social class correlates. *British Journal of Social and Clinical Psychology,* 1975, *14,* 104–16.

Markman, E. Comprehension monitoring. In W. P. Dickson (ed.), *Children's oral communication skills.* New York: Academic Press, 1981.

Marshall, N. R., Hegrenes, J. R., & Goldstein, S. Verbal interactions: Mothers and their retarded children vs. mothers and their nonretarded children. *Journal of Mental Deficiency,* 1974, *79,* 241–61.

Martin. B. *Abnormal psychology.* New York: Holt, Rinehart & Winston, 1977.

Maurer, D., & Salapatek, P. Developmental changes in the scanning of faces by young infants. *Child Development,* 1976, *47,* 523–27.

Mead, M. Adolescence in primitive and in modern society. In V. F. Calverton and S. D. Schmalhausen (eds.), *The New Generation.* New York: MacAuley, 1930.

Meichenbaum, D. A. A self-instructional approach to stress management: A proposal for stress inoculation training. In C. Spielberger & I. Sarason (eds.), *Stress and anxiety* (vol. 1). Washington, D.C.: Hemisphere Publishing, 1975.

Meichenbaum, D., & Goodman, J. Training impulsive children to talk to themselves. A means of developing self-control. *Journal of Abnormal Psychology,* 1971, *77,* 115–26.

Meichenbaum, D., Turk, D., & Burstein, S. The nature of coping with stress. In I. Sarason & C. Spielberger (eds.), *Stress and anxiety* (vol. 1). Washington, D.C.: Hemisphere Publishing, 1975.

Meier, J. H. Prevalence and characteristics of learning disabilities found in second-grade children. *Journal of Learning Disabilities,* 1971, *4,* 1–16.

Menzel, E. W. A group of young chimpanzees in a one-acre field. In A. M. Schrier & F. Stollnitz (eds.), *Behavior of nonhuman primates.* New York: Academic Press, 1974.

Meredith, H. V. Research between 1960 and 1970 on the standing height of young children in different parts of the world. In H. W. Reese & L. P. Lipsitt (eds.), *Advances in child development and behavior* (vol. 12). New York: Academic Press, 1978.

Merton, R. K. *Social theory and social structure.* Glencoe, Ill.: The Free Press, 1957.

Messinger, J. C. Sex and repression in an Irish folk community. In D. S. Marshall & R.C. Suggs (eds.), *Human sexual behavior: Variations in the ethnographic spectrum.* New York: Basic Books, 1971.

Milham, J., Widmayer, S., Bauer, C. R., & Peterson, L. *Predicting cognitive deficits for preterm, low birthweight infants.* Paper presented at the biennial meeting of the Society for Research in Child Development, Detroit, April 1983.

Miller, G. A. The magical number seven, plus or minus two: Some limits on our capacity for processing information. *Psychological Review,* 1956, *63,* 81–97.

Miller, G. A., Galanter, E., & Pribram, K. H. *Plans and the structure of behavior.* New York: Holt, Rinehart & Winston, 1960.

Miller, N. B., & Cantwell, D. P. Siblings as therapists. *American Journal of Psychiatry,* 1976, *133,* 447–50.

Minuchin, P. *Differential use of the open classroom: A study of exploratory and cautious children.* Final report to the National Institute of Education, 1976.

Minuchin, P. P., & Shapiro, E. K. The school as a context for social development. In P. H. Mussen (ed.), *Carmichael's manual of child psychology,* 4th ed. New York: John Wiley, 1983.

Minuchin, S. Families and family therapy. Cambridge Mass.: Harvard University Press, 1974.

Mischel, W. Sex-typing and socialization. In P. H. Mussen (ed.), *Carmichael's manual of child psychology,* 3d ed. (vol. 2). New York: John Wiley, 1970.

Mischel, W. On the future of personality measurement. *American Psychologist,* 1977, *32,* 246–64.

Mischel, W., & Mischel, H. *A cognitive social learning analysis of moral development.* Paper presented at the meeting of the Society for Research in Child Development, Denver, April 1975.

Montemayor, R. *Parent-adolescent conflict: A critical review of the literature.* Paper presented at the first biennial conference on adolescent research. Tuscon, Arizona, October 1982. (a)

Montemayor, R. The relationship between parent-adolescent conflict and the amount of time adolescents spend with parents, peers, and alone. *Child Development,* 1982, *53,* 1512–19. (b)

Montemayor, R., & Eisen, M. The development of self-conceptions from childhood to adolescence. *Developmental Psychology,* 1977, *13,* 314–19.

Montesorri, M. *Discovery of the Child.* M. J. Costelloe, S. J., Trans. Notre Dame, Ind.: Fides, 1967. Reprinted by permission of Fides/Claretian, 221 West Madison, Chicago, Ill. 60606.

Moore, G. A. *Realities of the urban classroom*. Garden City, N.Y.: Doubleday, Anchor Books, 1967.

Moore, T. W. Exclusive early mothering and its alternatives. *Scandinavian Journal of Psychology*, 1975, *16*, 256–72.

Moos, R. H., & Moos, B. S. Classroom social climate and student absences and grades. *Journal of Educational Psychology*, 1978, *70*, 263–69.

Morgan, G. A., & Ricciuti, H. N. Infants' responses to strangers during the first year. In B. M. Foss (ed.), *Determinants of Infant Behavior* (vol. 4). London: Methuen, 1969, pp. 253–72.

Morrison, A., Gjerde, P., & Block, J. H. *A prospective study of divorce and its relation to family functioning*. Paper presented at the biennial meeting of the Society for Research in Child Development, Detroit, April 1983.

Morsbach, G. and Murphy, M. C. Recognition of individual neonates' cries by experienced and inexperienced adults. *Journal of Child Language*, 1979, *6*.

Mueller, E., & Brenner, J. The origins of social skills and interaction among playgroup toddlers. *Child Development*, 1977, *48*, 854–61.

Mundy-Castle, A. C. Pictorial depth perception in Ghanian children. *International Journal of Psychology*, 1966, *1*, 290–300.

Murdock, G. *Social structure*. New York: Macmillan, 1949.

Murphy, L. D. *The widening world of childhood*. New York: Basic Books, 1962.

Murray, F. B. *Generation of educational practice from developmental theory*. Paper presented at the meeting of the American Psychological Association, Toronto, Canada, August 1978.

Mussen, P. H., & Eisenberg-Berg, N. *Roots of caring, sharing, and helping*. San Francisco: W. H. Freeman, 1977.

Mussen, P. H., & Jones, M. C. The behavior-inferred motivations of late- and early-maturing boys. *Child Development*, 1958, *29*, 61–67.

Mussen, P. H. (ed.). *Carmichael's manual of child psychology*, 3d ed. (vol. 1). New York: John Wiley, 1970.

Mussen, P. H. (ed.). *Carmichael's manual of child psychology*, 4th ed. New York: John Wiley, 1983.

n

Napier, A., & Whitaker, C. *The family crucible*. New York: Harper & Row, 1980.

National Advisory Committee on Handicapped Children. *Special education for handicapped children, first annual report*. Washington, D.C.: U.S. Dept. of Health, Education, and Welfare, 1968. (Conference)

National Institute of Education. *Report on crime and violence in schools*. Washington, D.C., 1978.

Naus, M.J. Memory development in the young reader: The combined effects of knowledge base and memory processing. In W. Otto & S. White (eds.), *Reading expository text*. New York: Academic Press, in press.

Neimark, E. D. Adolescent thought: Transition to formal operations. In B. J. Wolman (ed.), *Handbook of developmental psychology*. Englewood Cliffs, N.J.: Prentice-Hall, 1982.

Nelson, K. Structure and strategy in learning to talk. *Monographs of the Society for Research in Child Development*, 1973, *38*, no. 149.

Nelson, K. E. *Children's language* (vol. 1). New York: Gardner Press, 1978.

Nesselroade, J. R., & Baltes, P. B. Adolescent personality development and historical change: 1970, 1972. *Monographs of the Society for Research in Child Development*, 1974, *39*(1, Serial No. 154).

Nettleton, C. A., & Cline, D. W. Dating patterns, sexual relationships, and use of contraceptives of 700 unwed mothers during a two year period following delivery. *Adolescence*, 1975, *37*, 45–57.

Neugarten, B. L. The future and the young—old. *Gerontologist*, 1975, *15*, 4–9.

Neugarten, B. L. Must everything be a midlife crisis? *Prime Time*, February 1980.

Neugarten, B. L., & Datan, N. Sociological perspectives on the life cycle. In P. B. Baltes & K. W. Schaie (eds.), *Life-span developmental psychology*. New York: Academic Press, 1973.

Newell, A., & Simon, H. A. *Human problem solving*. Englewood Cliffs, N.J.: Prentice-Hall, 1972.

Newton, D. E. The status of programs in human sexuality: A preliminary study. *The High School Journal*, 1982, 232–39.

Ninio, A., & Bruner, J. The achievement and antecedents of labelling. *Journal of Child Language*, 1978, *5*, 1–15.

Nordyke, N. S., Baer, D. M., Etzel, B. C., & LeBlanc, J. M. Implications of the stereotyping and modification of sex role. *Journal of Applied Behavior Analysis*, 1977, *10*, 553–57.

O

O'Conner-Francoeur, P. Children's concepts of health and their health behavior. Paper presented at the Society for Research in Child Development meeting, Detroit, April 1983.

Oden, S. L., & Asher, S. R. *Coaching children in social skills for friendship making*. Paper presented at the biannual meeting of the Society for Research in Child Development, Denver, April 1975.

O'Malley, P. M., Bachman, J. G., & Johnston, J. *Youth in Transition. Final Report: Five years beyond high school: Causes and consequences of educational attainment*. Ann Arbor, Mich.: Institute for Social Research, 1977.

Osofsky, J. D. *Neonatal characteristics and directional effect in mother-infant interaction*. Paper presented at the meeting of the Society for Research in Child Development, Denver, April 1975.

Ottinger, D. R., & Simmons, J. E. Behavior of human neonates and prenatal maternal anxiety. *Psychological Reports*, 1964, *14*, 391–94.

Owen, S. V., Froman, R. D., & Moscow, H. *Educational Psychology*. Boston: Little, Brown, 1981.

p

Parish, T. S., & Taylor, J. C. The impact of divorce and subsequent father absense in children's and adolescent's self-concepts. *Journal of Youth and Adolescence*, 1978, *8*, 427–32.

Parke, R. D., & Collmer, C. W. Child abuse: An interdisciplinary analysis. In E. M. Hetherington (ed.), *Review of child development research* (vol. 5). Chicago: University of Chicago Press, 1976.

Parke, R. D., & Lewis, N. G. The family in context: A multilevel interactional analysis of child abuse. In R. W. Henderson (ed.), *Parent-child interaction: Theory, research, and prospect*. New York: Academic Press, 1980.

Parke, R. D., Power, T. G., & Fisher, T. The adolescent father's impact on the mother and the child. *Journal of Social Issues*, 1980, *36*, 88–106.

Parmelee, A. J., Jr. Development of visual behavior and neurological organization in preterm and full-term infants. In A. Pick (ed.). *Minnesota Symposia on Child Psychology* (vol. 10). Minneapolis: University of Minnesota Press, 1976.

Parsons, J. E., Ruble, D. N., Hodges, K. L., & Small, A. W. Cognitive-developmental factors in emerging sex differences in achievement-related expectancies. *Journal of Social Issues*, 1976, *32*(3), 47–61.

Parten, M. Social play among preschool children. *Journal of Abnormal and Social Psychology*, 1932, *27*, 243–69.

Pascual-Leone, J. Constructive problems for constructive theories: The current relevance of Piaget's work and a critique of information-processing simulation psychology. In R. H. Kluwe & H. Spada (eds.), *Developmental models of thinking*. New York: Academic Press, 1980.

Patterson, G. R. A performance theory for coercive family interaction. In R. B. Cairns (ed.), Social interaction: Methods, analysis, and illustrations. *Monographs of the Society for Research in Child Development*, in press.

Patterson, G. R., Cobb, J. A., & Ray, R. S. Direct intervention in the classroom. In F. W. Clark, D. R. Evans, & L. A. Hamerlynck (eds.). *Implementing behavioral programs for schools and clinics*. Champaign, Ill.: Research Press, 1972.

Pavlov, I. P. *Conditioned reflexes* (G. V. Anrep, trans. and ed.). New York: Dover, 1927.

Pearce, J., & Garrett, H. D. A comparison of the drinking behavior of delinquent youth versus nondelinquent youth in the states of Idaho and Utah. *Journal of School Health*, 1970, *40*, 131–35.

Pearson, P. D. A psycholinguistic model of reading. *Language Arts*, 1976, *53*, 309–14.

Pedersen, F. A., Anderson, B. J., & Cain, R. L. *An approach to understanding linkages between the parent-infant and spouse relationships*. Paper presented to the meeting of the Society for Research in Child Development, New Orleans, Louisiana, March 1977.

Perlmutter, M. Development of memory in the preschool years. In R. Green & T. D. Yawkey (eds.), *Early and middle childhood: Growth, abuse, and delinquency and its effects on individual, family, and community*. Westport, Conn.: Technomic, 1980.

Petersen, A. C. Can puberty come any faster? *Psychology Today*, February 1979. Reprinted from *Psychology Today* magazine. Copyright 1979 Ziff-Davis Publishing Company.

Petersen, A. C., & Taylor, B. The biological approach to adolescence: Biological change and psychological adaptation. In J. Adelson (ed.), *Handbook of Adolescent Psychology*. New York: John Wiley, 1980.

Peterson, C. L., Danner, F. W., & Flavell, J. H. Developmental changes in children's response to three indications of communicative failure. *Child Development*, 1972, *43*, 1463–68.

Peterson, P. L. Interactive effects of student anxiety, achievement orientation, and teacher behavior on student achievement and attitude. *Journal of Educational Psychology*, 1977, *69*, 779–92.

Phillips, J. L., Jr. *The Origins of Intellect: Piaget's Theory*, 2d ed. New York: W. H. Freeman, 1975.

Piaget, J. *The origins of intelligence in children* (M. Cook, Trans.). New York: International Universities Press, 1952.

Piaget, J. *The construction of reality in the child*. New York: Basic Books, 1954.

Piaget, J. *Six psychological studies* (A. Tenzer, trans., & D. Elkind, ed.). New York: Random House, Vintage Books, 1968.

Piaget, J. Piaget's theory. In P. H. Mussen (ed.), *Carmichael's manual of child psychology*, 3d ed. (vol. 1). New York: John Wiley, 1970.

Piaget, J. Intellectual evolution from adolescence to adulthood. *Human Development*, 1972, *15*, 1–12.

Piaget, J. *L'equilibration des structures cognitives (probleme central du developpement). Etudes d'epistemologie genetique*. (vol. 33). Paris: P.U.F., 1975.

Piaget, J. The role of action in the development of thinking. In W. F. Overton & J. M. Gallagher (eds.), *Knowledge and development* (vol. I). New York: Plenum, 1977.

Pick, A. D. Improvement of visual and tactual form discrimination. *Journal of Experimental Psychology*, 1965, *69*, 331–39.

Pick, H. L. Research on taste in the Soviet Union. In M. R. Kare & B. P. Halpern (eds.), *Physiological and behavioral aspects of taste*. Chicago: University of Chicago Press, 1961.

Piers, E. V., & Harris, D. B. Age and other correlates of self-concept in children. *Journal of Educational Psychology,* 1964, *55,* 91–95.

Pines, M. "Genie." *Dallas Morning News,* September/ October, 1981.

Plato [The Republic] (B. Jowett, Trans.). Bridgeport, Conn.: Airmont, 1968.

Plutarch. *The lives of the noble Grecians and Romans.* New York: Modern Library, 1932.

Poppen, P. J., Wandersman, A., & Wandersman, L. P. What are humanism and behaviorism and what can they say to each other? In A. Wandersman, P. Poppen, & D. Ricks (eds.), *Humanism and behaviorism: Dialogue and growth.* Oxford, England: Pergamon Press, 1976.

Power, C. *The moral atmosphere of a just community high school: A four-year longitudinal study.* Unpublished doctoral dissertation, Harvard University, 1979.

Premack, D. *Intelligence in ape and man.* New York: Halsted Press, 1976.

Pressley, M., Heisel, B. E., McCormick, C. B., & Nakamura, G. U. Memory strategy instruction with children. In C. J. Brainerd & M. Pressley (eds.), *Progress in cognitive development research (vol. 2), Verbal processes in children.* New York: Springer-Verlag, 1982.

Pribram, K. *Languages of the brain: Experimental paradoxes and principles in neuropsychology.* Englewood Cliffs, N.J.: Prentice-Hall, 1971.

q

Quadagno, D. M., Briscoe, R., & Quadagno, J. S. Effect of perinatal gonadal hormones on selected nonsexual behavior patterns: A critical assessment of the nonhuman and human literature. *Psychological Bulletin,* 1977, *84,* 62–80.

r

Randall, D., & Wong, M. R. Drug education to date: A review. *Journal of Drug Education,* 1976, *60,* 1–21.

Reese, H. W. Cohort, age, and imagery in children's paired associate learning. *Child Development,* 1974, *45,* 1176–78.

Regan, J. W. Guilt, perceived injustice, and altruistic behavior. *Journal of Personality and Social Psychology,* 1971, *18,* 124–32.

Reiss, I. *The social context of sexual permissiveness.* New York: Holt, Rinehart & Winston, 1967.

Rekers, G. A. Psychosexual and gender problems. In E. J. Mash & L. G. Terdal (eds.), *Behavioral assessment of childhood disorders.* New York: Guilford Press, 1979.

Renner, J. W., & Stafford, D. B. *Teaching science in the secondary school.* New York: Harper & Row, 1972.

Rheingold, H. L. The social and socializing infant. In D. A. Goslin (ed.), *Handbook of socialization theory and research.* Chicago: Rand McNally, 1969.

Rheingold, H. L. Independent behavior of the human infant. In A. Pick (ed.), *Minnesota Symposium of Child Psychology,* vol. 7. Minneapolis: University of Minnesota Press, 1973.

Rheingold, H. L., & Adams, J. L. The significance of speech to newborns. *Developmental Psychology,* 1980, *16*(5), 397–403.

Rheingold, H. L., & Eckerman, C. O. The infant's free entry into a new environment. *Journal of Experimental Child Psychology,* 1969, *8,* 271–83.

Rheingold, H. L., & Eckerman, C. O. The infant separates himself from his mother. *Science,* 1970, *168,* 78–83.

Rheingold, H. L., Gewirtz, J. L., & Ross, H. W. Social conditioning of vocalizations in the infant. *Journal of Comparative and Physiological Psychology,* 1959, *52,* 68–73.

Rheingold, H. L., & Samuels, H. R. Maintaining the positive behavior of infants by increased stimulation. *Developmental Psychology,* 1969, *1,* 520–27.

Richards, R. A. A comparison of selected Guilford and Wallach-Kogan creative thinking tests in conjunction with measures of intelligence. *Journal of Creative Behavior,* 1976, *10*(3), 151–64.

Riester, A. E., & Zucker, R. H. Adolescent social structure and drinking behavior. *Personnel and Guidance Journal,* 1968, *46,* 304–12.

Ringness, T. A. *The affective domain in education.* Boston: Little, Brown, 1975.

Roberts, J., & Baird, J. T. National Center for Health Statistics. *Parental ratings of behavioral patterns for children.* Series 11–#108, DHEW Publication, No. 72–1010, 1971.

Robinson, H. B., & Robinson, N. M. Mental retardation. In P. H. Mussen (ed.), *Carmichael's manual of child psychology,* 3d ed. (vol. 2). New York: John Wiley, 1970.

Robinson, H. F. *Exploring teaching in early childhood education.* Boston: Allyn & Bacon, 1977.

Rogers, C. R. A theory of therapy, personality, and interpersonal relationships as developed in the client-centered framework. In S. Koch (ed.), *Psychology: A study of science* (vol. 3). New York: McGraw-Hill, 1959, 184–256.

Rogers, C. R. Carl R. Rogers. In E. G. Boring & G. Lindzey (eds.), *A history of psychology in autobiography* (vol. V). New York: Appleton-Century-Crofts, 1967.

Rogers, C. R. In retrospect: Forty-six years. *American Psychologist,* 1974, *29,* 115–23.

Romberg, T. A. Developing mathematical processes: The elementary mathematics program for individually guided education. In H. J. Klausmeier, R. A. Rossmiller, and M. Saily (eds.), *Individually guided elementary education: Concepts and practices.* New York: Academic Press, 1977.

Romer, N., & Cherry, D. *Developmental effects of preschool and school age maternal employment on children's sex role concepts.* Unpublished manuscript, Brooklyn College of the City University of New York, 1978.

Rosen, B. M., Bahn, A. K., & Kramer, M. Demographic and diagnostic characteristics of psychiatric outpatients in the U.S.A., 1961, *American Journal of Orthopsychiatry,* 1964, *34,* 455–68.

Rosenbaum, A. L., Churchill, J. A., Shakhashiri, Z. A., & Moody, R. L. Neurophysiologic outcome of children whose mothers had proteinuria during pregnancy: A report from the collaborative study of cerebral palsy. *Obstetrics and Gynecology,* 1969, *33,* 118–23.

Rosenberg, M. Society and the adolescent self-image. Princeton, N.J.: Princeton University Press, 1965.

Rosenberg, M. *Conceiving the self.* New York: Basic Books, 1979.

Rosenberg, M., & Simmons, R.G. *Black and white self-esteem: The urban school child.* Rose Monograph Series, American Sociological Association, Washington, D.C., 1971.

Rosenfield, A. Visiting in the intensive care nursery. *Child Development,* 1980, *51*(3), 939–41.

Rosenkrans, M. A. Imitation in children as a function of perceived similarity to a social model and vicarious reinforcement. *Journal of Personality and Social Psychology,* 1967, *7,* 307–15.

Rosenthal, R., & Jacobsen, L. *Pygmalion in the classroom.* New York: Holt, Rinehart & Winston, 1968.

Ross, A. O. *Psychological disorders of children: A behavioral approach to theory, research, and therapy.* New York: McGraw-Hill, 1974.

Ross, D. G. *Stanley Hall: The psychologist as prophet.* Chicago: University of Chicago Press, 1972.

Rothbart, M. L. K. Birth order and mother-child interaction. *Dissertation Abstracts,* 1967, *27,* 45–57.

Rutter, M. *Influences from family and school.* Invited lecture presented at the biennial meeting of the Society for Research in Child Development, Detroit, April 1983.

S

Saltz, R. Effects of part-time "mothering" on IQ and SQ of young institutionalized children. *Child Development,* 1973, *9,* 166–70.

Samuels, H. R. The effect of an older sibling on infant locomotor exploration of a new environment. *Child Development,* 1980, *51,* 607–9.

Sander, L. W. Infant and caretaking environment: Investigation and conceptualization of adaptive behavior in a system of increasing complexity. In J. Anthony (ed.), *Explorations in child psychiatry,* 1975.

Santrock, J. W. The relations of onset and type of father absence to cognitive development. *Child Development,* 1972, *43,* 455–69.

Santrock, J. W. Moral structure: Interrelations of moral judgment, affect, and behavior. *Journal of Genetic Psychology,* 1975, *127,* 210–13.

Santrock, J. W. Effects of divorce on adolescents: Needed research perspectives. *Adolescence,* in press.

Santrock, J. W. *Adult development and aging.* Dubuque, Iowa: Wm. C. Brown, in press.

Santrock, J. W., Smith, P. C., & Bourbeau, P. Effects of group social comparison upon aggressive and regressive behavior in children. *Child Development,* 1976, *47,* 831–37.

Santrock, J. W., & Tracy, R. L. The effects of children's family structure status on the development of stereotypes by teachers. *Journal of Educational Psychology,* 1978, *70,* 754–57.

Santrock, J. W., & Warshak, R. A. Father custody and social development in boys and girls. *Journal of Social Issues,* 1979, *35,* 112–25.

Santrock, J. W., Warshak, R. A., & Eliot, G. Social development and parent-child interaction in father custody and stepmother families. In M. E. Lamb (ed.), *Nontraditional families.* Hillsdale, N.J.: Erlbaum, 1982.

Santrock, J. W., Warshak, R., Lindbergh, C., & Meadows, L. Children's and parents' observed social behavior in stepfather families. *Child Development,* 1982, *53,* 472–80.

Sapir, E. Language and environment. In D. G. Mandelbaum (ed.), *Selected writings of Edward Sapir in language, culture, and personality.* Berkeley: University of California Press, 1958.

Sarason, I. G., & Spielberger, C. D. (eds.). *Stress and anxiety.* Washington, D.C.: Hemisphere Publishing, 1975.

Scarr, S., & Weinberg, R. A. IQ test performance of black children adopted by white families. *American Psychologist,* 1976, *31,* 726–39.

Scarr-Salapatek, S. Genetics and the development of intelligence. In F. D. Horowitz (ed.), *Review of child development research* (vol. 4). Chicago: University of Chicago Press, 1975.

Schacter, S. *The psychology of affiliation.* Stanford, Calif.: Stanford University Press, 1959.

Schaeffer, H. R. *Mothering.* Cambridge, Mass.: Harvard University Press, 1977.

Schaeffer, H. R., & Emerson, P. E. The development of social attachments in infancy. *Monographs of the Society for Research in Child Development,* 1964, *29.*

Schank, R. C., & Abelson, R. P. *Scripts, plans, goals, and understanding.* Hillsdale, N.J.: Erlbaum, 1977.

Schramm, W., Lyle, J., & Parker, E. B. *Television in the lives of children.* Stanford, Calif.: Stanford University Press, 1961.

Schwartz, K. Proximity to mother and wariness in infants association with exploration of an unfamiliar object. *Dissertation Abstracts International,* 1978, *38,* 12B, 6204–5.

Sears, R. R. Sources of life satisfactions of the Terman gifted men. *American Psychologist,* 1977, *32,* 119–28.

Seay, B., & Gottfried, N. *The development of behavior: A synthesis of developmental and comparative psychology.* Boston: Houghton-Mifflin, 1978.

Selman, R. L. The relation of role-taking ability to the development of moral judgment in children. *Child Development,* 1971, *42,* 79–91.

Selman, R. L., Newberger, C. M., & Jacquette, D. *Observing interpersonal reasoning in a clinic/educational setting: Toward the integration of development and clinical-child psychology.* Paper presented at the meeting for the Society for Research in Child Development, New Orleans, 1977.

Senn, M. J. E. Insights on the child development movement in the United States. *Monographs of the Society for Research in Child Development,* 1975, *40*(3–4, Serial No. 161).

Serbin, L. A., O'Leary, K. D., Kent, R. N., & Tonick, I. J. A comparison of teacher response to the preacademic and problem behavior of boys and girls. *Child Development,* 1973, *44.*

Shantz, C. U. Psychological cognition—Social cognition. In J. H. Flavell, & E. Markman (eds.), *Carmichael's manual of child psychology* (vol. III). 4th ed., New York: John Wiley, 1983.

Sharpe, L. W. The effects of a creative thinking program on intermediate-grade educationally handicapped children. *Journal of Creative Behavior,* 1976, *10*(2), 138–45.

Shatz, M., & Gelman, R. The development of communication skills: Modifications in the speech of young children as a function of listener. *Monographs of the Society for Research in Child Development,* 1973, *38*(5, serial no. 152).

Sherif, M. Experimental study of intergroup relations. In J. H. Rohrer & M. Sherif (eds.), *Social psychology at the crossroads.* New York: Harper & Row, 1951.

Sherif, M. *In common predicament: Social psychology of intergroup conflict and cooperation.* Boston: Houghton-Mifflin, 1966.

Sherif, M., Harvey, O. J., Hoyt, B. J., Hood, W. R., & Sherif, C. W. *Intergroup conflict and cooperation: The robbers cave experiment.* Norman: University of Oklahoma Book Exchange, 1961.

Shostrum, E. L. *Man, the manipulator.* New York: Bantam, 1972.

Shovlin, D. W. *The effect of the middle school environment and the elementary school environment upon sixth-grade students.* Unpublished doctoral dissertation, University of Washington, 1967.

Siegler, R. S. The origins of scientific reasoning. In R. S. Siegler (ed.), *Children's thinking: What develops?* Hillsdale, N.J.: Erlbaum, 1978.

Siegler, R. S. Information processing approaches to development. In W. Kessen (ed.), *Carmichael's manual of child psychology,* 4th ed. (vol. I). New York: John Wiley, 1983.

Siegler, R. S., Liebert, D. C., & Liebert, R. M. Inhelder and Piaget's pendulum problem: Teaching preadolescents to act as scientists. *Developmental Psychology,* 1973, *9,* 97–101.

Silberman, C. E. *Crisis in the classroom: The remaking of American education.* New York: Random House, 1970.

Simon, H. A. Information-processing explanations of understanding. In T. W. Jusczyk & R. M. Klein (eds.), *The nature of thought: Essays in honor of D. O. Hebb.* Hillsdale, N.J.: Erlbaum, 1980.

Simpson, E. L. A holistic approach to moral development and behavior. In T. Lickona (ed.), *Moral development and behavior.* New York: Holt, Rinehart & Winston, 1976.

Sinclair-DeZwart, H. Developmental psycholinguistics. In D. Elkind & J. H. Flavell (eds.), *Studies in cognitive development: Essays in honor of Jean Piaget.* New York: Oxford University Press, 1969.

Skeels, H. Adult status of children with contrasting early life experiences. *Monographs of the Society for Research in Child Development,* 1966, *31*(3, Serial No. 105).

Skinner, B. F. *Walden two.* New York: Macmillan, 1948.

Skinner, B. F. *Science and human behavior.* New York: Macmillan, 1953.

Skinner, B. F. In E. G. Boring & G. Lindzey (eds.). *A history of psychology in autobiography.* New York: Appleton-Century-Crofts, 1967.

Skinner, B. F. *Beyond freedom and dignity.* New York: Knopf, 1971.

Skinner, B. F. *About behaviorism.* New York: Knopf, 1974.

Skinner, B. F. *A conversation between B. F. Skinner and H. Eysenck.* A symposium presented at the annual meeting of the American Psychological Association, Montreal, 1980.

Skipper, J. K., & Nass, G. Dating behavior: A framework for analysis and an illustration. *Journal of Marriage and the Family,* 1966, *28,* 412–20.

Smith, F. Learning to read by reading. *Language Arts,* 1976, *53,* 297–99.

Smock, C. D. *Piaget and Project Follow Through.* Lecture given at the University of Georgia, 1975.

Snow, C. Mother's speech to children learning language. *Child Development,* 1972, *43,* 549–65.

Snow, R. E. Individual differences and instructional theory. *Educational Researcher,* 1977, *6,* 11–15.

Solomon, R. W., & Wahlen, R. G. Peer reinforcement control of classroom problem behavior. *Journal of Applied Behavior Analysis,* 1973, *6,* 49–56.

Sommer, B. B. *Puberty and adolescence.* New York: Oxford University Press, 1978.

Sorensen, R. C. *Adolescent sexuality in contemporary America.* New York: World, 1973.

Spence, J. T. Comments on Baumrind's, Are androgynous individuals more effective persons and parents? *Child Psychology,* 1982, *53,* 76–80.

Spence, J. T., & Helmreich, R. L. *Masculinity and femininity: Their psychological dimensions.* Austin, Texas: University of Texas Press, 1978.

Spence, J. T., Helmreich, R., & Stapp, J. Ratings of self and peers on sex-role attributes and their relation to self-esteem and conceptions of masculinity and femininity. *Journal of Personality and Social Psychology,* 1975, *32,* 29–39.

Spitz, R. A. Hospitalism: An inquiry into the genesis of psychiatric conditions in early childhood. *Psychoanalytic Study of the Child,* 1945, *1,* 53–74.

Sprague, R. L., & Gadow, K. D. The role of the teacher in drug treatment. *School Review,* 1976, *85,* 109–40.

Sprague, R. L., & Sleator, E. K. What is the proper dosage of stimulant drugs in children? *International Journal of Mental Health,* 1975, *4,* 75–104.

Sroufe, L. A. *Conceptual and methodological issues in the study of relationships.* Presentation at the biennial meeting of the Society for Research in Child Development, Detroit, April 1983.

Stallings, J. Implementation and child effects of teaching practices in follow through classrooms. *Monographs of the Society for Research in Child Development,* 1975, *40* (serial no. 163).

Stanley, E. J., & Barter, J. T. Adolescent suicidal behavior. *American Journal of Orthopsychiatry,* 1970, *40,* 87–96.

Stanley, J. C. Rationale of the study of mathematically precocious youth (SMPY) during its first five years of promoting educational acceleration. In Stanley, J. C., George, W. C., & Solano, C. H. (eds.), *The gifted and creative: A fifty-year perspective.* Baltimore: The Johns Hopkins University Press, 1977.

Starr, R. H. Child abuse. *American Psychologist,* 1979, *34,* 886–91.

Staub, E. Helping a distressed person. In L. Berkowitz (ed.), *Advances in experimental social psychology* (vol. 7). New York: Academic Press, 1974.

Stein, A. H., & Bailey, M. M. The socialization of achievement orientation in females. *Psychological Bulletin,* 1973, *80,* 345–65.

Steinberg, L. D. *Understanding families with young adolescents.* Carrboro, N.C.: Center for Early Adolescence, 1980.

Stephan, W. G., & Rosenfield, D. Effects of desegregation on racial attitudes. *Journal of Personality and Social Psychology,* 1978, *36,* 795–804. (a)

Stephan, W. G., & Rosenfield, D. Effects of desegregation on race relations and self-esteem. *Journal of Educational Psychology,* 1978, *70,* 670–79. (b)

Steuer, F. B., Applefield, J. M., & Smith, R. Televised aggression and interpersonal aggression of preschool children. *Journal of Experimental Child Psychology,* 1971, *11,* 442–47.

Stevenson, H. W. *Children's learning.* New York: Appleton-Century-Crofts, 1972.

Stevenson, H. W. Reflections on the China visit. *Society for Research in Child Development Newsletter,* Fall, 1974, *3.*

Stockard, J., Schmuck, P., Kempner, K., Williams, P., Edson, S., & Smith, M. A. *Sex equity in education.* New York: Academic Press, 1980.

Strauss, A. A., & Lehtinen, L. E. *Psychopathology and the education of the brain-injured child,* (vol. I). *Fundamentals and treatment.* New York: Grune, 1947.

Strauss, M. S., & Curtis, L. E. Infant perception of numerosity. *Child Development,* 1982.

Streissguth, A. P., Martin D. C., Barr, H. M., Sandman, B. M., Kirchner, G. L., & Darby, B. L. *Intra-uterine alcohol exposure and a Hentional decrements in 4-year-old children.* Paper presented at the biennial meeting of the Society for Research in Child Development, Detroit, April 1983.

Stuart, R. B. Teaching facts about drugs: Pushing or preventing. *Journal of Educational Psychology,* 1973, *66,* 189–201.

Sullivan, K., & Sullivan, A. Adolescent-parent separation. *Developmental Psychology,* 1980, *16,* 93–99.

Sullivan, P. *A curriculum for stimulating moral reasoning and ego development in adolescence.* Unpublished doctoral dissertation, Boston University, 1975.

Suomi, S. J. Development of attachment and other social behaviors in rhesus monkeys. In T. Alloway, P. Pliner, & L. Drames (eds.), *Attachment behavior.* New York: Plenum, 1977.

Suomi, S. J., & Harlow, H. F. Social rehabilitation of isolate-reared monkeys. *Developmental Psychology,* 1972, *6,* 487–96.

Suomi, S. J., Harlow, H. F., & Domek, C. J. Effect of repetitive infant-infant separations of young monkeys. *Journal of Abnormal Psychology,* 1970, *76,* 161–72.

Sutton-Smith, B. *Child Psychology.* New York: Appleton-Century-Crofts, 1973.

Sutton-Smith, B., & Rosenberg, B. G. *The sibling.* New York: Holt, Rinehart & Winston, 1970.

Swisher, J. D., Warner, R., & Herr, E. An experimental comparison of four approaches to drug education. *Journal of Counseling Psychology,* 1972, *19,* 328–32.

Szasz, T. *The manufacture of madness.* New York: Harper & Row, 1970.

t

Tanner, J. M. Physical growth. In P. H. Mussen (ed.), *Carmichael's manual of child psychology* (vol. 1). New York: John Wiley, 1970.

Taylor, M. K., & Kogan, K. L. Effects of birth of a sibling on mother-child interactions. *Child Psychiatry and Human Development,* 1973, *4,* 53–58.

Taylor, T. D., Winne, P. H., & Marx, R. W. *Sample specificity of self-concept instruments.* Paper presented at the meeting of the Society for Research in Child Development, Denver, April 1975.

Terman, L. M. *Genetic studies of genius: Mental and physical traits of a thousand gifted children* (vol. 1). Stanford, Calif.: Stanford University Press, 1925.

Terman, L. M., & Oden, M.H. *Genetic studies of genius. The gifted at mid-life: Thirty-five years' follow-up of the superior child* (vol. 5). Stanford, Calif.: Stanford University Press, 1959.

Terr, L. C. A family study of child abuse. *Journal of Psychiatry,* 1970, *223, 102–9.*

Terrace, H. *Nim.* New York: Knopf, 1979.

Thelen, E. Rhythmical behavior in infancy: An ethological perspective. *Developmental Psychology,* 1981, *17,* 237–57.

Thompson, R., & Hoffman, M. L. Empathetic arousal and guilt feelings in children. *Developmental Psychology,* in press.

Thornburg, H. D. Evaluating the sex education program. *Arizona Teacher,* 1968, *57,* 18–20.

Thornburg, H. D. Sources of sex education among early adolescents. *Journal of Early Adolescence,* 1981, *1,* 171–84.

Tieger, T. On the biological basis of sex differences in aggression. *Child Development,* 1980, *51,* 943–63.

Tinbergen, N. *The study of instinct.* New York: Oxford University Press, 1969. (Originally published, 1951.)

Todd, D. M. Contrasting adaptations to the social environment of a high school: Implications of a case study of helping behavior in two adolescent subcultures. In J. G. Kelly (ed.), *Adolescent boys in high school.* Hillsdale, N.J.: Erlbaum, 1979.

Toepfer, C. F. Brain growth periodization data: Some suggestions for rethinking middle grades education. *The High School Journal,* 1980, 222–27.

Torrance, E. P. *Torrance tests of creative thinking.* Lexington, Mass.: Personnel Press, 1966.

Torrance, E. P. The Minnesota studies of creative behavior: National and international extensions. *Journal of Creative Behavior,* 1967, *1,* 137–54.

Torrance, E. P., & Torrance, P. Combining creative problem solving with creative expressive activities in the education of disadvantaged young people. *Journal of Creative Behavior,* 1972, 6(1), 1–10.

Trotter, R. Head Start children in young adulthood. *APA Monitor,* 1981, 15, 37.

Tuchmann-Duplessis, H. Drug effects on the fetus. *Monographs on drugs* (vol. 2). Sydney: ADIS Press, 1975.

Tuckman, B., & Oliver, W. Effectiveness of feedback to teachers as a function of source. *Journal of Educational Psychology,* 1968, *59,* 297–301.

Turbull, A. P., & Schulz, J. B. *Mainstreaming handicapped students.* Boston: Allyn & Bacon, 1979.

Turiel, E. An experimental test of the sequentiality of developmental stages in the child's moral judgments. *Journal of Personality and Social Psychology,* 1966, *3,* 611–18.

Turnbull, C. M. *The mountain people.* New York: Simon & Schuster, 1972.

Turnure, C. *Response to voice of mother and stranger by babies in the first year.* Paper presented at the meeting of the Society for Research in Child Development, Santa Monica, March 1969.

u

Underwood, B., & Moore, B. *Perspective-taking and altruism.* Unpublished manuscript, University of Texas, 1980.

U.S. Bureau of Census: Population Statistics. Washington, D.C., 1981.

U.S. Department of Commerce, Bureau of the Census. Population profile of the United States: 1978, population characteristics (Current Population Reports, Series P-20, No. 336). Washington, D.C.: U.S. Government Printing Office, April 1979.

U.S. Government Accounting Office. Report HRD–80–66. Washington, D.C.: U.S. Government Printing Office, 1980.

U.S. Office of Education. *National evaluation of Project Follow Through.* Washington, D.C.: U.S. Government Printing Office, 1974.

U.S. Supreme Court. *In re Gault,* 387 US 1, 1967.

Uzgiris, I. C., & Hunt, J. M. *Assessment in infancy: Ordinal scales of psychological development.* Champaign, Ill.: University of Illinois Press, 1975.

v

Vandell, D. L., Wilson, K. S., & Buchanan, N. R. Peer interaction in the first year of life: An examination of its structure, content, and sensitivity of toys. *Child Development,* 1980, *51,* 481–88.

Vandiver, R. Sources and interrelation of premarital sexual standards and general liberality conservatism. Unpublished doctoral dissertation, Southern Illinois University, 1972.

Van Gennep, A. *The rites of passage.* Chicago: University of Chicago Press, 1960.

Vaughn, B. E., Gove, F. L., & Egeland, B. The relationship between out-of-home care and the quality of infant-mother attachment in an economically disadvantaged population. *Child Development,* 1980, *51,* 1203–14.

Venezky, R. L., & Pittelman, S. D. PRS: A prereading skills program for individually guided education. In H. J. Klausmeier, R. A. Rossmiller, M. Saily (eds.), *Individually guided elementary education: Concepts and practices.* New York: Academic Press, 1977.

Vernon, P. E. Ability factors and environmental influences. *American Psychologist,* 1965, *20,* 723–33.

Volpe, R. Feedback-facilitated relaxation training as primary prevention of drug abuse in early adolescence. *Journal of Drug Education,* 1977, 7, 179–94.

Volterra, V., & Taeschner, T. The acquisition and development of language by bilingual children. *Journal of Child Language,* 1978, *5,* 311–26.

Vygotsky, L.S. *Thought and language* (E. Hanfman & G. Vakar, eds.). Cambridge, Mass.: MIT Press, 1962.

W

Wahler, R. B., House, A. E., & Stambaugh, E. E. *Ecological assessment of child problem behavior: A clinical package for home, school, and institutional settings.* New York: Pergamon Press, 1976.

Waite, R. R. Further attempts to integrate and urbanize first-grade reading textbooks: A research study. *Journal of Negro Education,* 1968, *37,* 62–69.

Walk, R. D. The development of depth perception in animals and human infants. In H. W. Stevenson (ed.), Concept of development. *Monographs of the Society for Research in Child Development,* 1966, 31 (5, serial no. 107).

Walk, R. D., & Gibson, E. J. A comparative and analytic study of visual depth perception. *Psychological Monographs,* 1961, *75* (15, Whole No. 519).

Walkup, L. E. Creativity in science through visualization. *Perceptual and Motor Skills,* 1965, *21,* 35–41.

Wallach, M. A. Creativity. In P. H. Mussen (ed.), *Carmichael's manual of child psychology,* 3d ed. (vol. 1). New York: John Wiley, 1970.

Wallach, M. A. Ideology, evidence, and creative research. *Contemporary Psychology,* 1973, *18,* 162–64.

Wallach, M. A., & Kogan, N. *Modes of thinking in young children.* New York: Holt, Rinehart & Winston, 1965.

Wallach, M. A., & Kogan, N. Creativity and intelligence in children's thinking. *Transaction,* 1967, *4,* 38–43.

Wallerstein, J. S., & Kelly, J. B. The effects of parental divorce: The adolescent experience. In E. J. Anthony & C. Koupernik (eds.), *The child in his family: Children of psychiatric risk* (vol. 3). New York: John Wiley, 1974.

Wallerstein, J. S., & Kelly, J. B. *Surviving the break-up: How children actually cope with divorce.* New York: Basic Books, 1980.

Waters, E., Wippman, J., & Sroufe, L.A. Social competence in preschool children as a function of the security of earlier attachment to the mother. *Child Development,* in press.

Watson, J. B. *Behaviorism.* New York: Norton, 1924.

Watson, J. B., & Rayner, R. Conditioned emotional reactions. *Journal of Experimental Psychology,* 1920, *3,* 1–4.

Watson, J. D. *The double helix.* New York: New American Library, 1968.

Watson, J. D., & Crick, F. H. C. Molecular structure of nucleic acids: A structure for deoxyribonucleic acid. *Nature,* 1953, *171,* 737–38.

Wechsler, D. *The measurement and appraisal of adult intelligence,* 4th ed. Baltimore: Williams & Wilkins, 1958.

Weigel, R. H., Wiser, P. L., & Cook, S. W. The impact of cooperative learning experiences on cross-ethnic relations and attitudes. *Journal of Social Issues,* 1975, *31,* 219–45.

Weiner, B., & Kukla, A. An attributional analysis of achievement motivation. *Journal of Personality and Social Psychology,* 1970, *15,* 1–20.

Weiner, I. B. *Psychopathology in adolescence.* In J. Adelson (ed.), *Handbook of Adolescent Psychology.* New York: John Wiley, 1980.

Weinraub, M., & Brown, L. M. The development of sex role stereotypes in children: Crushing realities. In V. Franks & E. Rothblum (eds.), *Sex role stereotypes and clinical issues: Lessons from the past and implications for the future.* New York: Springer, in press.

Wellman, M., Ritter, K., & Flavell, J. H. Deliberate memory behavior in the delayed reactions of very young children. *Developmental Psychology,* 1975, *11,* 780–87.

Wertheimer, M. *Productive thinking.* New York: Harper & Row, 1945.

White, B. I., & Watts, J. C. *Experience and environment.* Englewood Cliffs, N.J.: Prentice-Hall, 1973.

White House Conference on Children. Report of the committee on special classes. Gifted children. In *Special education: The Handicapped and the gifted. Education and training. Section 3.* New York: Century, 1931, 537–50.

White, S. The idea of development in developmental psychology. In R. M. Leaner (Chair), *Developmental psychology: History of philosophy and philosophy of history.* Symposium presented at the meeting of the American Psychological Association, Montreal, September 1980.

Whiting, B. B., & Whiting, J. W. M. *Children of six cultures: A psychocultural analysis.* Cambridge, Mass.: Harvard University Press, 1975.

Whorf, B. L. *Language, thought, and reality.* New York: John Wiley, 1956; also Cambridge, Mass.: MIT Press, 1956.

Wickens, C. D. Limits of human information processing: A developmental study. *Psychological Bulletin,* 1974, *81,* 739–55.

Widseth, J. C., & Mayer, J. Drinking behavior and attitudes toward alcohol in delinquent girls. *The International Journal of the Addictions,* 1971, *6,* 453–61.

Wilkins, J. A follow-up study of those who called a suicide prevention center. *American Journal of Psychiatry,* 1970, *127,* 155–61.

Willemsen, E. *Understanding Infancy.* San Francisco: W. H. Freeman, 1979.

Williams, F. Some preliminaries and prospects. In F. Williams (ed.), *Language and poverty.* Chicago: Markham, 1970.

Winer, G. A. Class inclusion reasoning in children: A review of the empirical literature. *Child Development,* 1980, *51,* 309–28.

Wing, J. W. *Early childhood autism.* Elmsford, N.Y.: Pergamon Press, 1977.

Witherspoon, R. Birth defects: A risk even before conception. *Dallas Morning News,* November 22, 1980, Section C, p. 1.

Wood, B. (ed.). *A pediatric vade-mecum,* 8th ed. London: Lloyd-Luke, 1974.

Wylie, R. C. *The self-concept.* Lincoln: University of Nebraska Press, 1974.

y

Yakovlev, P. I., & Lecours, A. The myclogenetic cycles of regional maturation of the brain. In A. Minkowski (ed.), *Regional development of the brain in early life.* Oxford: Blackwell Scientific, 1967.

Yankelovich, D. *The new morality: A profile of American youth in the 1970s.* New York: McGraw-Hill, 1974.

Yarrow, L. J. Separation from parents during early childhood. In L. W. Hoffman & M. L. Hoffman (eds.), *Review of child development research* (vol. 1). New York: Russell Sage Foundation, 1964.

Yonas, A. Depth perception. In L. Cohen & P. Salapatek (eds.), *Infant perception: from sensation to cognition* (vol. 1). New York: Academic Press, 1975.

Yussen, S. R. Characteristics of moral dilemmas written by adolescents. *Developmental Psychology,* 1977, *13,* 162–63.

Yussen, S. R., Hiebert, E., & Enright, R. *Cohort effects in adults' moral reasoning.* Unpublished paper, University of Wisconsin, Madison, 1981.

Yussen, S. R., Mathews, S. R., & Hiebert, E. Metacognitive aspects of reading. In N. R. Otto & S. White (eds.). *Reading expository text.* New York: Academic Press, 1982.

z

Zahn-Waxler, C., Radke-Yarrow, M., & King, R. M. Childrearing and children's prosocial initiations toward victims of distress. *Child Development,* 1979, *50,* 319–30.

Zajonc, R. B., & Markus, G. B. Birth order and intellectual development. *Psychological Review,* 1975, *82,* 74–88.

Zamanhof, S., van Marthens, E., & Margolis, F. L. DNA (cell number) and protein in neonatal brain: Alteration by maternal dietary protein restriction. *Science,* 1968, *160,* 322–23.

Zelnick, M., & Kantner, J. F. Sexual and contraceptive experience of young unmarried women in the United States, 1976 and 1971. *Family Planning Perspectives,* 1977, *9*(2) 55–71.

Zigler, E. The retarded child as a whole person. In H. E. Adams & W. K. Boardman (eds.), *Advances in experimental clinical psychology.* Elmsford, N.Y.: Pergamon Press, 1971.

Credits

Table of Contents
Bettmann Archives, Inc.: ix (left); M. P. Allen/Peter Arnold, Inc: ix (center); Jean-Claude Lejeune: ix (right), xi (left, center, right), xiii (center), xiv (right), xv (center, right), xvi (left), xvii (right); Children's Television Workshop: x (left); Rick Smolan: x (center); Steve Takatsuno: x (right); Rohn Engh: xii (left); Bob Coyle: xii (center); Robert Eckert/EKM-Nepenthe: xii (right), xvii (center); Mark Boisclair: xiii (left); © 1974 Joel Gordon: xiii (right), xiv (center), xvii (left); © 1981 Susan Lapides/ Design Conceptions: xvi (left), xvi (right); Peter Karas: xv (left); Allen Ruid: xvi (center).

Section 1
Eli Heller/Picture Group: 2–3.

Chapter 1
Richard Choy/Peter Arnold, Inc.: 6; Jim Shaffer: 8; Bettmann Archives, Inc.: 11; © 1979 Joel Gordon: 13; Peter Karas: 17 (bottom right); Peter Simon/Picture Group: 17 (bottom left); M. P. Allen/Peter Arnold, Inc.: 17 (top); Bob Combs/Free Vision: 19; Jean-Claude Lejeune: 22; Children's Television Workshop: 27.

Chapter 2
Rick Smolan: 30; United Press International: 32 (left), 53; Bettmann Archives, Inc.: 32 (right); Used with permission of B. F. Skinner: 33; National Library of Medicine: 34; Jean-Claude Lejeune: 37, 38; Robert Eckert/EKM-Nepenthe: 40; Marilyn Saunders/Peter Arnold, Inc.: 44; Bryce Flynn/Picture Group: 45; Neena Leen/Time-Life Books: 51; David Strickler: 54.

Section 2
Jack Spratt/Picture Group: 60–61.

Chapter 3
Dennis Cox: 64; Robert Eckert/EKM-Nepenthe: 67, 72, 86 (bottom); Jean Wentworth/Picture Cube: 69; Jill Cannefax/EKM-Nepenthe: 74; United Press International: 75; Donald Yaeger/Camera M.D. Studios: 76–77, courtesy of The Cleveland Health Museum: 82; © 1983 Joel Gordon: 86 (top).

Chapter 4
Pamela Price/Picture Group: 90; © 1983 Joel Gordon: 93; Robert Eckert/EKM-Nepenthe: 95, 101; William Vandivert: 97; Jean-Claude Lejeune: 99; © 1981 Susan Lapides/Design Conceptions: 102; Louis N. Psihoyos: 103; Dr. James Bartlett: 105; used with permission of Albert Bandura: 109; © 1979 Joel Gordon: 110.

Chapter 5
Jean-Claude Lejeune: 112, 115, 119, 120, 132; MIT Museum and Historical Collections: 116; Steve Takatsuno: 126; Hörst Schafer/Peter Arnold, Inc.: 127; Jean-Claude Lejeune/EKM-Nepenthe: 130 (top); © Joel Gordon: 130 (bottom).

Chapter 6
Jean-Claude Lejeune: 136; © 1974 Joel Gordon: 139; Rohn Engh: 141; Bob Coyle: 142, 151; Robert Eckert/EKM-Nepenthe: 143; Dennis Cox: 146, 155; courtesy of Basic Books, Inc.: 145; John Maher/EKM-Nepenthe: 149.

Section 3
Dennis Cox: 160–161.

Chapter 7
Jean-Claude Lejeune: 164, 175 (top left, bottom); Robert Eckert/EKM-Nepenthe: 166, 176; Bob Coyle: 169; Rohn Engh: 173; Hörst Schafer/Peter Arnold, Inc.: 175 (top right).

Chapter 8
Robert Eckert/EKM-Nepenthe: 180, 198, 199; Jean-Claude Lejeune: 183, 185, 189; © 1979 Joel Gordon: 194 (left); Frank Siteman/EKM-Nepenthe: 194 (right); Children's Television Workshop: 202.

Chapter 9
Jean-Claude Lejeune: 206, 209; Sharon Bazarian/Picture Cube: 211; Erika Stone/Peter Arnold: 214; Mark Boisclair: 215; David Strickler: 216; Stuart Rossner/Picture Group: 221; Dan Brinzac/Peter Arnold, Inc.: 223; John Maher/EKM-Nepenthe: 227.

Section 4
Jim Shaffer: 232–233.

Chapter 10
Mary Murphy/Picture Group: 236; Robert Eckert/EKM-Nepenthe: 239; Jean-Claude Lejeune: 241, 254; Peter Karas: 243; Nancy Hayes/Monkmeyer Press Photo Service: 248, 252; © 1981 Susan Lapides/Design Conceptions: 256; James H. Karales/Peter Arnold: 258.

Chapter 11
Bob Coyle: 264; Erika Stone/Peter Arnold, Inc.: 267, 273; Robert Eckert/EKM-Nepenthe: 269, 276, 277; David Strickler: 270.

Chapter 12
Bob Coyle: 282; Al Flory: 285; © 1981 Joel Gordon: 287; Robert Eckert/EKM-Nepenthe: 289; Mark Boisclair: 294; Brent Jones: 296; Jean-Claude Lejeune: 299; Sybil Shelton/Peter Arnold, Inc.: 300.

Chapter 13
Jean-Claude Lejeune: 304, 307, 310, 312, 314; © 1982 Susan Lapides/Design Conceptions: 319; Rick Smolan: 324.

Section 5
John Maher/EKM-Nepenthe: 330–331.

Chapter 14
Bob Coyle: 334, 342; Robert Eckert/EKM-Nepenthe: 337, 349; Historical Pictures Service, Chicago: 339, 341; John Maher/EKM-Nepenthe: 344; Jim Shaffer: 347; David Strickler/Picture Cube: 352.

Chapter 15
Jean-Claude Lejeune: 358, 361, 371, 378; Erika Stone/Peter Arnold: 363; © 1983 Joel Gordon: 364; Robert Eckert/EKM-Nepenthe: 368; Malcolm Kirk/Peter Arnold, Inc.: 374; Allen Ruid: 375; © 1981 Susan Lapides/Design Conceptions: 379.

Chapter 16
Allen Ruid: 384, 398; Bettmann Archives, Inc.: 387; Jean-Claude Lejeune: 389; Bob Combs/Free Vision: 391, 393; © 1981 Susan Lapides/Design Conceptions: 392; Jim Shaffer: 395, 401; Dennis Cox: 399.

Epilogue: Jim Shaffer: 407.

Name Index

Friedrich, L. K., 220
Frisch, R., 337, 338
Froman, R. D., 257
Fromkin, V., 197
Furman, W., 216
Furrow, D., 123
Furstenburg, F. F., 368
Furth, H. G., 131, 269, 271, 281

G

Gadow, K. D., 245
Gagné, R. M., 106
Galanter, E., 277, 279
Gallup, G., 155
Galst, J. Q., 221
Galton, F., 189
Gandhi, M., xxiii, 385, 386, 387, 402
Garbarino, J., 209, 318, 319
Gardner, B. T., 123
Gardner, G. E., 396
Gardner, L., 169
Gardner, R. A., 123
Garvey, C., 218, 229
Gatewood, T. E., 296
Gearheart, B. R., 244
Geis, G., 208
Gelman, R., 125, 272
Getman, G. N., 173
Getzels, J. W., 261
Gibbs, J., 317, 318
Gibson, E. J., 96, 97, 98, 110, 195, 196
Gilligan, C., 319
Ginott, H., 365
Gjerde, P., 213
Glucksberg, S., 132
Gold, M., 396, 397, 404
Goldberg, R. J., 212
Goldenson, R. M., 219
Goldman, K. S., 185, 219
Gonzales, M. A., (46)
Good, T., 302
Goodman, J., 247
Gordon, I., 200
Gordon, T., 48, 49
Gottfried, N., 50
Gottlieb, D., 299
Gove, F. L., 139
Gowan, J. C., 262
Grallo, R., 199
Gratch, G., 101
Gray, J. L., 100
Green, R., 225
Greenacre, P., 260
Greenberg, B. S., 220
Greenberger, E., 378, 379
Greenfield, J., 153

Greenspan, D., 268
Gribbons, W. D., 298
Grotevant, H. D., 364
Guilford, J. P., 258, 259, 261, 277
Guskin, S. L., 243
Guttentag, M., 225

H

Haan, N., (409)
Haddad, W., 302
Haeberle, E., 345
Hall, C. S., 49, 50
Hall, G. S., 331, 339, 340, 364, 380
Hallinan, M. T., 370
Halverson, L. E., 174
Halwes, T., 119
Hamm, C. M., 306, 320
Hardyck, C., 169
Harlow, H. F., 216
Harmon, R., 157
Harris, D. B., 311
Harter, S., 152, 153, 311
Hartley, R. E., 219
Hartshorne, H., 321
Hartup, W. W., 216, 219, 220, 290, 291, 292, 293, 294, 302
Harvey, O. J., 293
Hass, A., 345, 346
Hassibi, M., 324
Hayes, C., 123
Hayes, K. J., 123
Hebb, D. O., 98
Heber, R., 191
Heider, F., 309
Heisel, B. E., 273
Helmreich, R. L., 225
Helms, D., 85
Henderson, N. D., 74, 190
Herkowitz, J., 174
Hetherington, E. M., 212, 213, 226, 286, 287, 288, 302, 366, 367
Higgens-Trenk, A., 313, 327
Higgins, A., 320
Hill, J. P., 219, 294, 295, 296, 321, 341, 343, 352, 382
Hinde, R. A., 51
Hitler, A., xxiii, 385, 386, 387, 402
Hockett, C. F., 123
Hodges, K. L., 313
Hoffman, H. R., 220
Hoffman, L. W., 212, 286
Hoffman, M. L., 314, 322
Hollingshead, A. B., 292
Holt, J., 298
Holtzmann, W., 375
Homme, L., 46
Honzik, M. P., 409
Hood, W. R., 293
Horney, K., 36

House, A. E., 19
Howard, A., 215
Hoyt, B. J., 293
Hubbard, R., 75
Hunt, J. M., 140
Hurlock, E. B., 240
Huston, A. C., 221, 226, 227, 229, 311
Huston-Stein, A., 224, 225, 313, 327
Hyde, J. S., 52, 357
Hyman, H. M., 360

I

Inkeles, A., 53, 54
Ives, S. W., 20

J

Jacklin, C. N., 312
Jacobs, J., 398, 404
Jacobsen, L., 254
Jacobson, S. W., 80
Jacquette, D., 292
James, W., 188
Jekel, J. F., 368
Jenkins, J. J., 119, 130
Jennings, S., 102, 103
Jensen, A. R., 190
Johnston, J., 408
Johnston, L. D., 390, 392, 393, 404
Jones, M. C., 107, 349
Jones, R. R., 19
Jordan, T., 199

K

Kagan, J., 29, 138, 142, 211, 247, 313
Kahn, J. H., 324
Kail, R. V., 275, 281
Kamin, L. J., 190
Kandel, D., 298, 361, 362
Katz, J., 369
Katz, P. A., 224
Kaye, H., (95)
Keane, B., 213, 345
Kearsley, R. B., 138
Keat, R. N., 227
Keating, D. P., 351
Kellogg, L. A., 123
Kellogg, R., 171
Kellogg, W. N., 123
Kelly, J. B., 213, 288, 366
Kempner, K., (297)
Kenniston, K., 390, 407
Kephart, N., 173, 174
Kessen, W., 284
Khatena, J., 262

P

Parish, T. S., 366
Parke, R. D., 157, 208, 368
Parker, E. B., 220
Parmalee, A. J., Jr., 83
Parsons, J. E., 313
Parten, M., 217, 218
Patterson, G. R., 19, 45, 46, 58
Pavlov, I. P., 106
Pederson, F. A., 143
Perlmutter, M., 188, 274
Petersen, A. C., 338, 343, 357
Peterson, L., (83)
Peterson, P. L., 297
Petronio, R. J., 396, 397, 404
Petronovich, L. F., 169
Piaget, J., 3, 31, 32, 33, 35, 41, 42,
    43, 44, 56, 61, 81, 85, 91, 93,
    95, 99, 100, 101, 102, 103, 104,
    109, 110, 111, 131, 140, 142,
    161, 184, 187, 192, 200, 203,
    204, 233, 240, 255, 259, 260,
    261, 265, 268, 269, 270, 271,
    272, 279, 280, 305, 308, 315,
    335, 339, 350, 351, 352, 353,
    355, 356
Pick, A. D., 98
Pick, H. L., 94
Piers, E. V., 311
Pines, M., 196
Pittelman, S. D., 194
Plato, 12
Plutarch, 11
Poppen, P. J., 48
Power, C., 320
Premack, D., 123
Pressley, M., 272, 275
Pribram, K., 122, 277, 279

Q

Quadagno, D. M., 224
Quadagno, J. S., 224
Quarinonium, 336

R

Radke-Yarrow, M., 141, 215, 284
Rahe, D. F., 216
Ramey, C. T., 191
Ramirez, M., 299
Randall, D., 394
Rash, B., 92
Ray, R. S., (46)
Rayner, R., 107

Rechs, J., (46)
Reese, H. W., 26
Reid, J. B., 19
Reimer, D. J., 396
Reiss, I., 346
Rekers, G. A., 225
Renner, J. W., 353
Revelle, R., 337, 338
Rheingold, H. L., 94, 150, 154, 157
Ricciuti, H. N., 150
Richards, R. A., 261
Ridenour, M. C., 179
Riester, A. E., 370
Ringness, T. A., 107, 108
Ritter, K., 188
Roberts, J., 241
Robinson, H. F., 169
Rogers, C. R., 31, 34, 35, 48, 49, 50,
    56
Roman, M., 302
Romberg, T. A., 278
Romer, N., 286
Rosen, B. M., 322
Rosenbaum, A. L., 79
Rosenberg, B. G., 289, 302
Rosenberg, M., 301, 388
Rosenblum, L. A., 216, 229, 302
Rosenfield, D., 300
Rosenkrans, M. A., 291
Rosenthal, R., 254
Ross, A. O., 255, 256
Ross, D. G., 340, 357
Rothbart, M. L. K., 289
Ruble, D. N., 313
Rutter, M., 213

S

Sackett, G. P., 79
Salapatek, P., 95, 96
Saltz, R., 192
Sampson, D. L. G., 314
Samuels, H. R., 150
Sandman, B. M., (80)
Santrock, J. W., 212, 213, 286, 288,
    321, 366
Sapir, E., 129
Sarason, I. G., 323
Sattler, J., 262
Scarr, S., 190
Scarr-Salapatek, S., 74, 189
Schachter, S., 289
Schaeffer, H. R., 124, 140, 144, 147,
    148
Schank, R. C., 188, 277

Schmuck, P., (297)
Schramm, W., 220
Schulz, J. B., 243
Schwartz, K., 150
Scott, J. A., 262
Sears, R. R., 29, 261
Seay, B., 50
Seigle, J., 221
Selman, R. L., 292, 322
Serbin, L. A., 227
Shantz, C. U., 184, 353, 357
Shapiro, E. K., 297, 299, 300, 320,
    375, 376, 394
Sharabany, R., 185
Sharpe, D., 274
Sharpe, L. W., 260
Shatz, M., 125, 272
Shelley, P. B., 287
Sherif, C. W., 293
Sherif, M., 293
Sherrod, L. R., 107
Shore, R. E., 219
Shostrum, E. V., 58, 365
Shovlin, D. W., 296
Siegler, R. S., 43, 187, 205, 272
Signori, E. I., 314
Silberman, C. E., 198, 298
Simmons, J. E., 80
Simmons, R. G., 296, 301, 349, 350
Simon, H. A., 20, 187, 188, 279
Simon, M. L., 360
Simon, T., 247
Simonides, 266
Simpson, E. L., 318, 319
Sinclair-DeZwart, H., 131
Skeels, H., 191
Skinner, B. F., 3, 31, 32, 33, 34, 35,
    44, 45, 47, 48, 56, 104, 107,
    109, 118
Skipper, J. K., 372
Sleator, E. K., 245
Slobin, S. I., 135
Small, A., 313
Smith, F., 194
Smith, M. A., (297)
Smith, P. C., 288
Smith, R., 221
Snow, R. E., 114, 123, 297
Solomon, R. W., 291
Sommer, B. B., 373, 374, 382
Sorensen, R. C., 345
Speery, B. M., 396
Spence, J. T., 223, 224
Spielberger, C. D., 323
Sprague, R. L., 245
Sroufe, L. A., 219, 220

Subject Index

Change vs. stability in adult
personality development, 409
Channel, in communications theory,
187
Cheating, inconsistency of in
children, 321
Child abuse. *See also* Violence;
Aggression
and community support systems,
209
contributing factors, 208–9
incidence in U.S.A. vs. China, 208
prevalence, 11
socialization against, 11
A Child Called Noah, 153
Child-centered nursery schools, 198
Child-centered school curricula vs.
"back-to-basics," 295
Child-freedom parenting, 210
Childhood
as a contemporary concept, 12
emergence of concept in 17th
century, 55
historical realities of, 11
in historical view, 10
phase of child development, 15
and self-perception, 49
Child labor laws, 11, 12
Child psychology
methods of data collection, 18–21
as a science vs. historical views, 18
Children in ancient and medieval art,
84
Children's Personal Attributes
Questionnaire (Children's PAQ),
23
Children's Television Workshop, 202
China doll reflex, 67
Chinese education, 284
Chitling Test (Dove Counterbalance
General Intelligence Test),
252–53
Christian view of child as "sinful,"
12
Chromosomes
number of, 69
in Down's syndrome, 74
pairing in germinal period, 76
splitting, 70
Chunking as memory process, 275
Cigarettes
effect on prenatal development,
79–80
maternal use, and height of
children, 168
use by adolescents, 391–92, 393
Classical conditioning
as basis of learning, 106–7
and language acquisition in
children, 119
toilet training example, 108

Cliques
in schools, 376
and self-esteem, 371
Clumsy children and motor training
programs, 173
Cluster School, in Kohlberg's "Just
Community," 320
Coaching in peer sociotherapy, 291
Cocaine use by adolescents, 391
Cognitive development
of adolescents, 352
in Bandura's social learning theory,
104
and deaf children, 131
defined, 16
in information processing theory,
187–89, 272–73
in middle and late childhood,
268–79
in preoperational thought, 184–87
and psychometric approach,
188–89
and self, 222
in Skinner's operant conditioning
theory, 104
stages of in Piaget's theory, 99–103
Cognitive investment, from
adolescence to mid-life, 409
Cognitive social learning theory of
development, 45, 47–48
Cognitive structural theory of
development, 35, 41–44, 55
Cohorts in "Sesame Street" study, 26
College and adolescent's quest for
autonomy, 362–63
Color blindness and genetic
transmission, 71
Communication
of animals vs. human language, 123
and egocentrism in early childhood,
193
and listening skills, 194
purposes of in infancy, 131–32
Communications theory and
information-processing theory of
cognitive development, 187
Compensatory education, 198–201
for handicapped children, 244
and Piaget's cognitive theories, 270
Competence. *See also*
Comprehension of speech vs.
production
and achievement orientation,
313–14
children's sense of, 311
vs. performance in culture-fair
tests, 253
social vs. intellectual, 255
Competition emphasis in schools, 376
Competitive sports and injuries, 240

Complex behaviors and operant
conditioning, 109
Comprehension of speech vs.
production, 128
Compulsions in children, 323, 324
Conception stage of prenatal
development, 74
Concrete operational thought,
268–72
Concrete operations stage (in
Piaget's theory), 42, 100
Conditioned response (CR), 106
Conditioned stimulus (CS), 106
Congenital defects. *See* Genetic
abnormalities
Conglomerate strategy in peer
sociotherapy, 291
Conscious vs. subconscious mental
processes, 48
Conservation, absence of in
preoperational thought, 184–85
Continuum of indirectness of
hereditary influences, 73
Contraception, adolescents'
knowledge about, 346
Contrary-to-fact reasoning, 351
Control-autonomy dimension of
parenting, 214
Conventional level of moral
development, 315, 316
Convergence of eyes and depth
perception, 95
Cooing, role in language acquisition
of children, 126
Cooperative play, 218
Coordination, sensorimotor, 84–88
Coordination of secondary reactions
(in Piaget's theory), 101
Correlation strategy for scientific
inquiry, 23–24
Cortisone, 224
Creativity, 258–60
and divergent thinking, 277
Cretinism, 256
Crib death, 84
Crisis, identity, 388–90
Crisis intervention centers, 400
and reduction of child abuse, 209
Crisis in the Classroom, 298
Critical period
for imprinting, 50
and irreversibility, 140
for language acquisition, 196–97
for object permanence, language,
and attachment in infancy, 140
Cross-classification, absence of in
preoperational thought, 186

Growth, 84
  pace, 86
  problems, 168–69
  spurts, 13
Guilt feelings
  and achievement orientation, 314
  and anxiety, 321–22
  and moral development, 315

H

Habit (in Piaget's theory), 100–101
Hallucinogens, 391
Handedness, 169–70
Handicapped children, 241–45
Happiness and self-concept, 16
Hardware, as computer machinery
    compared to human brain and
    sensory systems, 187
Head Start programs. See Project
    Head Start
Head turning as conditioned
    response, 67
Health
  children's concept of, 240
  and influence of personality, 409
Hearing
  of infants, newborn, and fetus, 94
  of two-year-old, 88
Heart disease, 71
Height and weight and sociometric
    variables, 168
Hemophilia, 72
Heredity-environment interaction,
    51, 71–74
  and individual differences, 104
  and intelligence, 189, 192
Heritability. See also Genetic
    transmission; Genetic
    abnormalities
  and mental retardation, 73–74
  quotient
    extroversion/introversion, 73
    of intelligence, 74
    of mental retardation, 73
    of physical attributes, 73
    of schizophrenia, 73–74
    of temperament, 73–74
  and twins, 73
Heroin
  effect on newborn, 80
  use by adolescents, 391
Heterosexuality, attitudes and
    behavior of adolescents, 345–46
Hierarchical and cross-classification,
    185–86
High-risk infant, 83
High/Scope: Cognitively Oriented
    Curriculum Model, 200
Historical beliefs about children,
    11–12

Historical time effects on social
    systems, 55
Holophrase, 128
Homosexuality and attitudes and
    behavior of adolescents, 345
How Children Fail, 298
Humanistic theory of development,
    35, 47–50, 55
Hyperactivity, 245, 247

I

Id, defined, 36
Ideals of adolescents, 351
Ideational fluency (creativity), 259
Identification (in Freudian theory),
    37–38
Identity development in adolescence,
    388–90
Identity vs. role confusion, 40
Imagery as mnemonic device, 266,
    267
Imitation, 44, 47
  as basis of learning, 106, 109–10
Imprinting, 50
Impulsivity, 247
Incentive conditions as
    reinforcement, 110
Income maintenance for parents, 11
Independence in young children, 154
Independence theories of
    development
  Erikson's ideas, 153–54
  Mahler's ideas, 150–53
Independent variables, 21, 22
Individual differences
  in adolescent cognitive
    development, 352
  defined, 189
  vs. developmental functions, 104
  in growth patterns, 168
  and infant attachment, 148, 150
  in sexual maturation, 343
Individualism and moral
    responsibility, 318
Individually Guided Education
    (IGE), 278
Industry vs. inferiority, 39–40, 388
Infancy
  importance in life-span
    development, 80–81
  phase of child development, 15
Infant behavior and situational
    variability, 148–50
Infant development and learning
    theory view, 104–10
Infanticide, 11
Infantile autism, 152
Inferences in information processing
    theory of cognitive development,
    276

Information processing theory of
    cognitive development, 43–44,
    272–73
  and computer modeling, 187–88
Informed consent for research with
    children, 25
Inhalants, 391
Initiative vs. guilt, 39
Injuries and immature tissues, 168
Innate knowledge philosophical
    belief, 12
Instinct, 36
Instinctual energy, 36–37
Institute for Developmental Studies
    at New York University, 199
Institutionalization
  and effects of foster grandparents,
    192
  influence on children's intelligence,
    191, 192
Instrumental competence vs.
    incompetence, 313–14
Instrumental conditioning. See
    Operant conditioning
Intelligence. See also IQ
  vs. creativity, 258–59
  definitions, 41, 189
  and environmental influences,
    190–92
  and genetic-environmental factors,
    189, 192
  heritability, 73, 190
  and interaction of biological,
    environmental, and genetic
    influences, 192
  and moral judgment, 318
  and motor training theory, 173
  normal distribution, as measured by
    Binet test, 248
  and popularity, 292
  and role of language development,
    192–93
Intelligence tests. See also IQ tests
  contrasted with Piaget's view, 41
  first developed by Binet, 33
  for infants, 104–5, 170
Intentionality (in Piaget's theory),
    101
Interaction of environment and
    heredity, 71–74
Interaction in family and effect on
    infants, 143–46
  as basis for child's exploration of
    environment, 144
  in family systems approach to
    therapy, 146
  between parents
    and child abuse, 209
    and father's response to infant,
    144

Internalization of schemes in Piaget's theory, 102
Internal vs. external determinants of behavior, 44, 45
International Sign Language, 123
Interpersonal relations, adult compared to adolescent, 408
Intervention programs for juvenile delinquents, 397
Interview and questionnaire, 19–20
Intimacy vs. isolation, 40
IP (information processing) theory of cognitive development, 272–73
IQ. *See also* Intelligence
 defined, 189, 190
 and identical twins, 70
 heritability, 73
 influence of environmental and hereditary similarities, 190
 influence of personality, 409
 and malnutrition in South African studies, 177
IQ tests
 and academic achievement of blacks, 239
 administration of, 254
 Binet tests, 247–49, 250, 255
 criticism of, 251–55
  and Piaget's theories, 255
 and Francis Galton, 189
 and labeling, 248
 in *Larry P.* v. *Riles,* 238
 and placement in EMR classes, 238
 problems of, 21
 and racial-cultural bias, 238, 239, 251–53
 Raven Progressive Matrices as culture-fair test, 252, 253
 Stanford-Binet, 238
 teacher or counselor use, 255
 verbal and performance assessments, 192
 WISC-R, 238
 WISC (Wechsler Scales), 247, 249–51, 255
Irreversibility in preoperational thought, 187

J

"Just Community," 320
Juvenile delinquency, 395–97
Juvenile justice system, 12, 397

K

Knowledge about development, explosion of, 80–81

L

Labeling
 based on IQ tests, 248
 of handicapped children, 242
Labeling activity patterns in mother-child speech interaction, 114
Laissez-faire parenting vs. authoritarian or authoritative, 215
Language
 and animal experiments, 123
 characteristics of, 123
  deep structure vs. surface structure, 117, 125, 193
  and insights of Chomsky, 116
 functions of, 116, 129–32
 fundamental units, 116–18
 influence on memory, 129
 and pragmatics, 118
 and semantics, 117–18
 as symbolic system, 130
 uniqueness of, 116
 universals, 125
Language acquisition by children
 and adult strategies, 123–24
 biological basis of, 121
 and brain, 122
 and classical conditioning theory, 119
 comprehension vs. production, 128
 course of development, 126–29
 critical period for, 140, 196–97
 in Montessori theory, 182
 and morphology, 128–29
 and motivation, 120, 121
 one-word phrase (holophrase) stage, 128
 and operant conditioning theory, 109
 phonology, 126, 128–29, 192–93
 role of environment, 123–24
 and sensorimotor development, 131
 speed of, 116
 stages, according to Brown, 128–29
 syntax and semantics, 126, 128–29
 theory of Chomsky, 197
 theory of Lenneberg, 197
 transformational rules, 193
 universal capacity for, 125
 universality of sequential patterns, 119–20
Language Acquisition Device (LAD), 124–25
Language models and information processing, 188
Language origins and evolution, 121
Larry P. v. *Riles,* 238, 239

Late childhood, defined, 15
Latency stage, 37
Laws of organization (good form; pragnanz), 98
Learned helplessness, 313–14
Learning
 by classical conditioning, 106–7
 by imitation, 109–10
 by operant conditioning, 107–9
Learning difficulties and perceptual motor training programs, 174
Learning disabilities, 243–45
Learning theory view of infant development, 104–10
Leboyer method of delivery, 81–83
Left-handedness, 169
 and writing, 170
Life-span frame of reference, 38
Life styles, adolescent, survey, 408
Life time (chronological age), 54–55
Linguistic competence vs. performance in children, 118
Linguistic model of Chomsky and information processing theory of cognition, 188
Listening
 and egocentrism in children's communication, 193
 in humanistic therapy, 48
The Lives of the Noble Grecians and Romans, 11
Logical skills vs. learned behaviors, 106
Longevity and effect on American life, 53
Longitudinal studies, 24–26
Long-term memory, 274
Looming experimental technique, 97
Los Angeles Children's Hospital, 197–98
Los Angeles Times, 198

M

Mainstreaming, 242–43
Malnutrition. *See also* Diet; Nutrition
 and cultural factors, 176–77
 deficiencies in impoverished areas, 167
 and intellectual development, 177
 in Philippines, 166
 and physical development, 176
Man, the Manipulator: The Inner Journey from Manipulation to Actualization, 365
Mangaian culture and sexual behavior, 52, 373
Manville School, 292

O

Objective movement, 174
Object permanence in Piaget's theory
    and attachment of infants, 148
    critical period, 140
    substages described, 102–3
Observation, as tool for data
    collection, 18–19
Obsessions in children, 323, 324
Occupation choice and identity
    development in adolescence,
    389–90
Oedipus complex, 37
Office of Child Development, 245
Onlooker play, 218
Operant conditioning, 44–45, 107–9
Operations (in Piaget's theory), 184
Oral stage (in Freudian theory), 36
Order, awareness of (in Montessori
    theory), 182
Organization (in Piaget's theory), 43
    as memory process, 275
Originality, 259
Original sin, as basis of moral status
    of children, 12

P

Paired associates memory, 274
Panel on Youth recommendations,
    378
Parables and fables, 352
Parallel play, 218
Parent-child relationships, 210–15,
    286–88, 289–90, 360–68. See
    also Family; Fathers; Mothers;
    Parenting style
    during adolescence, 363–64,
      366–67
    when adolescents are parents,
      367–68
    and autonomy vs. shame and doubt,
      153–54
    in "blended" families, 288
    and children's attitudes toward
      integration, 300
    and children's understanding of
      authority, 210
    after divorce, 213, 286–88, 366–67
    influence of parents vs. peers,
      360–61
Parent Effectiveness Training
    (P.E.T.), 48–49
Parenting style
    and age of child, 210
    of Everett Shostrum, 365
    of Haim Ginott, 365
    and maturing of parents, 211
    types of, 210, 214–15, 362

Parents' influence
    on achievement orientation, 314
    vs. peers', 360
    on sex-role development, 224–27
Pase v. Hannon, 239
Passive-aggressive behavior, 396
PCP (hallucinogen), 391
Peace Corps, 390
Peer interaction. *See also* Peers
    in adolescence, 368–73
    and aggressiveness, 216–17
    in animal studies, 216
    in childhood, 293–94
    compared with family interaction,
      219–20
    defined, 215–16
    in preschool ages, 216–19
    in schools, 290–91, 375–76
    and sex-role development, 227
Peers. *See also* Peer interaction
    and modeling, tutoring, and
      reinforcement in schools,
      290–91
    and popularity, 292–93
    and sociotherapy, 291–92
Perceived Competence Scale for
    Children (of Harter), 311
Perception, 94–99
    defined, 94
    Gestalt view vs. distinctive features
      theory, 97–99
    in information-processing theory of
      cognitive development, 273
    and role of language in Whorf-
      Sapir hypothesis, 129
    visual, by infants, 96–99
Perceptual-motor training programs,
    174, 175. *See also* Motor
    training theory
Performance
    vs. competence in culture-fair tests,
      253
    deterioration of and learned
      helplessness, 313–14
    emphasis in school physical
      education programs, 174
Personal identity, 81
Personality Attributes Questionnaire
    (PAQ), 223
Personality development, 16
    and later life, 409
    and self in childhood, 222
Perspective-taking skills, 322
Phallic stage (in Freudian theory),
    37
Phenotype, 70
Phenylketonuria (PKU), 71, 73–74
Philosophical beliefs
    about children's moral status,
      11–12
    about origin of knowledge, 11–12

Phobias in children, 323–24
Phonemes of English, 126. *See also*
    Speech sounds
    phonology as fundamental language
      elements, 116–17
Phonology, 117, 126
    and transformations in English, 193
Physical attributes, heritability of, 73
Physical development. *See also*
    Height; Weight; Growth
    problems
    defined, 15
    of early childhood, 168
      training programs to improve,
      173–76
    of infant, 84–88
    of middle and late childhood,
      240–41
Physical growth patterns as
    diagnostic tool, 13
Physical punishment, use of in
    U.S.A. vs. China, and child
    abuse, 208
Piaget's theory of development
    (cognitive-structural), 41–44
    application to education, 271
    concrete operational state, 42,
      268–69
    evaluation, 269–70, 272
    formal operational stage, 42, 100,
      184, 259–60, 351–53
    object permanence, 102–3
    preoperational stage, 41, 100,
      184–87
    processes of, 42–44
    sensorimotor stage, 41, 100–103
    stages of, 41–42, 99–103
Pictorial vs. print media, children's
    use of, 220
Piers-Harris Self-Concept Scale, 309,
    311
PKU. *See* Phenylketonuria
Play, 217–19. *See also* Games
    appearance of "make believe," 219
    and effect of television viewing, 218
    functions of, 219
    rituals, 218
Playing with probabilities to
    encourage creativity, 260
Play spaces for children
    guidelines for, 174, 176
    limitations of equipment, 174
Pleasure principle as primary process
    thinking, 36
Political structure, 54
Polygenically determined traits, 71
Popularity, 292–93
Postconventional level of moral
    development, 317
Practice and learning, 106

Repression
  as defense mechanism, 38
  as onset of latency stage, 37
Reproductive period, increasing
    length of, 338
The Republic, 12
Responses in behavioral social
    learning theory, 44, 106–9
Retention and imitation, 109
Reversibility in concrete operational
    thought, 268
Rigidity of learning environment,
    140
Ritalin, 245
Rites of passage in primitive cultures,
    373–74
Ritual social interchanges, 218
Role play in humanistic theory, 48
Roles, distinguished from the
    individual, 54
Role-taking skills, 322
Rooting reflex, 66, 67, 94

S

Salk Institute, 197
Scheme/schema (in Piaget's theory),
    100
Schizophrenia, 73, 400, 402
School hierarchy and sex roles, 297
School phobia, 322
Schools
  discrimination in, 298–301
  in early childhood, 182–83,
    198–201
  impact of on adolescents, 375–76
  in middle and late childhood,
    294–301
  as most influential social institution,
    294
  open, free, alternative, defined, 295
  organization into middle vs.
    elementary-junior high, 295–97
  and peer modeling, teaching,
    reinforcement, 290–91
  progressive vs. traditional, 294–95
  and sex education, 347, 348
  size and students' identification
    with, 376
  as a social system, 320
  and violence and vandalism, 295
Science of child development, 12
Scientific inquiry strategies
  correlational, 23–24
  experimental, 21–22
  multimethod and multisource, 21
  quasi-experimental, 21
  tools, 19–20
Scientific theory, 35

Scribbling and drawing, children's,
    171–72
The Seasons of a Man's Life, 211
Secondary circular reactions in
    Piaget's theory, 101
Secondary process thinking as reality
    principle, 36
Sedatives, use of by adolescents, 391
Self-concept. *See also* Self-esteem
  in adolescence, 388
  and childhood experiences, 49–50
  developmental changes in, 308–9
  in early childhood, 222
  in infancy, development of, 154–56
  measuring, 310, 311
  and personality development, 222
  in Rogers' theory, 49
Self-esteem
  in adolescence, 371, 388
  in childhood
    measuring, 310, 311
    and parental attributes, 310
    and school performance, 310
    vs. self-concept, 309, 311
Self-Esteem Inventory (SEI), 310
Self-fulfilling prophecy, 254
Self-reinforcement, 45
Self-reports, limitations of, 21
Self-stimulation. *See* Masturbation
Semantic knowledge of child, 128
Semantics, 117–18
Sensation, defined, 94
Senses, development of, 94–96
Sensorimotor coordination. *See also*
    Brain
  in first year, 85–86
  milestones in, 87
  in second year, 86–88
Sensorimotor development and
    language acquisition in children,
    131
Sensorimotor stage in Piaget's theory,
    41, 100–103
Sensory abilities, in Montessori
    theory, 182
Sensory and perceptual development,
    94–99
Sentences, grammaticalness vs.
    sensibleness, 118
Separation-individuation (in
    Mahler's theory of
    independence), 150–53
Serialization, absence of in
    preoperational thought, 185
"Sesame Street"
  effects on children, 26
  impact on child's cognitive
    development, 202
  and study of attention of two-to-
    four-year-olds, 188

Sex differences
  in access to sports activities in
    schools, 376
  in cross-cultural rites of passage to
    adulthood, 374
  in drug use, 392–93
  and eating disorders, 400
  and friendships of adolescents,
    369–70
  in gross and fine motor skills, 240
  in instrumental competence and
    achievement, 313–14
  in moral reasoning, 319
  verbal, mathematical, and
    aggressiveness, 312
Sex education
  of adolescents, 346–47
  biological vs. social information
    emphasis, 348
  source of, 347, 348
Sex linkage of genetically
    transmitted traits, 71
Sex-role development
  and biological forces, 224
  cognitive factors, 224, 226
  environmental influences, 226
  in middle childhood, 311
  parents' influence, 226–27
  stages in maturation, 224
  teachers' and peers' influence, 227
Sex roles
  and concept of androgyny, 222–23,
    225
  in school hierarchy, 297
  and stereotyping, 311–12
Sex-typed behavior, ease and ethics
    of changing, 225
Sexual attitudes of adolescents,
    344–47
Sexual behavior of adolescents,
    344–47
  cultural differences, 52, 373–74
  daughters of divorced parents, 367
  in 1960s, 341
Sexual identity, 222–23
Sexual maturation, 343–44
  and hormone levels, 343
  individual differences, 343
  and psychological adaptation, 347,
    349–50
Short-term memory, 274
Siblings
  interaction of, 288–89, 290
  and interaction with mother, 289
  used as therapists, 290
Sickle-cell anemia, 71
Single-parent family structure
  fathers as head, 287
  mothers as head, 287
  prevalence of, 212, 213

Work, part-time, of high school
students
effects on school work and
activities, 378–79
as exploitation of youth, 380
negative aspects of 378, 379–80
Work force, full-time, percentage of
youth in, 378
Working mothers
and attitude of daughters, 286
and quality of parenting, 212
and time with children, 211

World Health Organization, 141
World Student Christian Federation
conference in Peking, 34
Writing vs. nonwriting and children's
ability to recognize, 195–96

X

X (female) chromosome, 71

Y

Y (male) chromosome, 71
*Youth in Transition: Adolescence to
Adulthood—Change and
Stability in the Lives of Men,*
408

Z

Zurich, University of, and Piaget, 33